Pathbreakers

Margrit Müller
Timo Myllyntaus
(eds.)

Pathbreakers

Small European Countries Responding to Globalisation and Deglobalisation

PETER LANG
Bern · Berlin · Bruxelles · Frankfurt am Main · New York · Oxford · Wien

Bibliographic information published by Die Deutsche Bibliothek
Die Deutsche Bibliothek lists this publication in the Deutsche Nationalbibliografie; detailed bibliographic data is available on the Internet at‹http://dnb.ddb.de›.

British Library Cataloguing-in-Publication Data:
A catalogue record for this book is available from The British Library,Great Britain

Library of Congress Cataloging-in-Publication Data

International Economic History Congress (13th : 2002 : Buenos Aires, Argentina)
Pathbreakers : small European countries responding to globalisation and deglobalisation / Margrit Müller, Timo Myllyntaus (eds.).
p. cm.
Papers presented at the Thirteenth Congress of the International Economic History Association (IEHA) in Buenos Aires, Argentina, 22-26 July 2002. 1. States, Small–Economic conditions–Congresses. 2. Europe–Economic conditions–20th century–Congresses. I. Müller, Margrit - II. Myllyntaus, Timo. III. Title.
HC59.15.I575 2002
337.4–dc22

2007032762

Supported by the Swiss Academy
of Humanities and Social Sciences
www.sagw.ch

Cover Design: Thomas Jaberg, Peter Lang Bern

ISBN 978-3-03911-214-2

Hochfeldstrasse 32, Postfach 746, CH-3000 Bern 9, Switzerland
info@peterlang.com, www.peterlang.com, www.peterlang.net

Contents

Preface

The chapters that make up this volume were first written for a session of the Thirteenth Congress of the International Economic History Association (IEHA) in Buenos Aires, Argentina, 22–26 July 2002. This session – 'International Integration and Globalisation: Governance Strategies of Small Countries since the Late XIXth Century' – was organised by Timo Myllyntaus in collaboration with Hein Klemann and Margrit Müller. The aim of the session was to deepen reflection and discussion on an important but rarely raised topic within the general discourse on globalisation, namely the specific constraints and opportunities faced by small countries.

The organisers were able to turn to a network of researchers studying the economic history of small countries which has been operating since the early 1990s. Several members of this network and quite a number of new colleagues attended the pre-conference 'Globalisation vs. Deglobalisation: The Impact on the Economic Policy and Performance of Small European Countries' in Zurich on 15–18 March 2001. We thank especially Peter Solar, participating as expert and main discussant, for his thoughtful comments and suggestions, and we are grateful to Bruno Fritzsche, professor emeritus for economic and social history at the University of Zurich, at the time head of the 'Forschungsstelle für Wirtschafts- und Sozialgeschichte' and co-organiser with Margrit Müller and Timo Myllyntaus of the pre-conference in Zurich. Unfortunately, a few participants did not continue to work on this project for various reasons, but most contributions were presented to a broader audience at the Buenos Aires congress mentioned above. Plans for having the papers published quickly were delayed: we thank the authors for their patience and their readiness to revise and update their contributions, and we are especially grateful for the financial support provided by the scientific and private organisations listed below for initiating this project with the conference in Zurich and for concluding it with the publication of this book.

The general topic – globalisation – is still 'in the news', and the consequences of globalisation, its advantages and disadvantages, are matters of major concern. Globalisation has also become a significant topic in economic history, and publications are plentiful, but most comparative approaches have dealt with large countries. With its focus on the historical experience of small countries this volume certainly adds a new aspect to research and current debates on globalisation. The number of small countries has increased considerably during the last fifty years, and it is important that their historical experience is given due weight not only in research but also in the teaching of economic history.

The small countries dealt with in this volume differ in many ways, both with regard to economic and political conditions. The authors and editors have not been aiming at sweeping generalisations: our main objective has been to gain some new insights on the impact of globalisation by studying processes of internationalisation with a focus on small countries. We hope that this book will broaden the historical perspective on a controversial topic and encourage further research on the economic and social history of small countries, not only in Europe but also in other continents.

Margrit Müller and Timo Myllyntaus

The research project has received financial support from:

NOVARTIS Novartis International AG, Basel
MIGROS kulturprozent Migros-Genossenschafts-Bund, Zürich
Bildungsdirektion, Universität Zürich, Zürich
Joh. Jacob Rieter Stiftung, Winterthur
Swiss Academy of Humanities and Social Sciences, Bern
Schweizerische Nationalbank, Zürich
Swiss National Science Foundation, Bern

Margrit Müller

Introduction

The topic of this volume is the room for manoeuvre available to small European countries within changing world economic regimes from the late nineteenth century to the present. Our aim is to analyse the means that have historically been available for responding to the challenges of the international system, to describe the policies and strategies pursued by governments, industries and firms, to highlight similarities and particularities and to trace the reasons for and the consequences of these choices.

It is widely acknowledged among economic historians that globalisation (defined as the progressive integration of national economies) is not unprecedented. During the period dealt with in this volume it was a discontinuous and uneven process: an earlier period of globalisation started in the middle of the nineteenth century and ended abruptly with the First World War.[1] Post-war attempts at restoring the international economy were not successful, and with the onset of the Great Depression protectionism and isolationism became pervasive. Globalisation returned after the Second World War, but only slowly, especially in factor markets. In the last two or three decades the integration of markets for goods, services and capital – and, to a much lesser extent, for labour – has accelerated, and the 'global economy' has expanded considerably. In the earlier period, globalisation was largely limited to the industrialised European and North American nations, while other world regions were linked only marginally to these core economies.[2]

Economic integration and disintegration affected both large and small countries, but due to their high dependence on foreign markets small countries were clearly more vulnerable to international forces, which in turn exerted a stronger influence upon their economic policy-making. The current discourse on globalisation largely disregards past experience of the phenomenon and particularly the experience of small countries. The focus tends to be on the impact of the current process of globalisation on large countries, where – it is argued – economic dependence upon foreign markets has increased to the extent that the near coincidence of 'nation space' with 'market space' has been lost sight of. For the small European countries such a divergence is hardly a new phenomenon. Governments of large countries have been in the comfortable position of choosing between greater or lesser international economic integration, whilst small countries were forced to seek larger markets via exports and to rely upon imports to a considerable extent, because resources within their borders were limited and the domestic market was too small for production to be efficient. Consequently, the problems their governments and firms had to deal with differed considerably from those of large countries. In order to develop and prosper, small countries had to adapt flexibly to the changing situation outside their borders. They had to find ways of maintaining their political autonomy despite their economic dependence. In the last decades of the twentieth century, the international economic involvement of large states has increased considerably. They have become more dependent on international forces and in this respect more similar to small countries: they are 'growing smaller'.[3] Studying the ways in which small countries have dealt with international economic integration and disintegration will contribute to a better understanding of current developments both in small and in large states.

Definitions of small countries are numerous, and may differ in different fields of research, but primarily small countries are distinguished by their population size, which, taken together with their per-capita GDP, can serve as a measure for the size of their domestic market. In terms of population the countries studied in this volume were in this period all much smaller than the large western European countries France, Germany, Italy, Spain and the UK; but they have differed considerably among themselves. In the interwar period Czechoslovakia was – with about 15 million inhabitants – by far the largest of them, but at the end of the twentieth century the Netherlands ranked first, with over 16 million inhabitants. The other countries have around 9–10 million (Belgium, Portugal and Sweden) and 5 million (Finland, Norway, Slovakia) inhabitants; Switzerland is in a middle position with over 7 million.[4] With a population of 130,000 in the 1940s and less than 300,000 at the end of the century, Iceland may stand as a paradigm for the considerable number of very small states in Europe; about half the European countries have a population of between about 10 and 1 million inhabitants, and over a third have less than a million.

If results are to be meaningful, definitional issues have to be resolved in light of the problems approached and the central research questions. For the theme of this book, the relevant common characteristic of small countries and the critical distinguishing feature between small and large countries is their higher dependence on foreign markets. Although size need not be a significant variable affecting the prosperity and wealth-creating capacity of a country, it does affect the extent to which that prosperity is dependent on international economic transactions.[5] A second characteristic feature – which is related to the first one – is the dual structure of the economy of small countries: some sectors and firms are highly export-oriented and have to compete internationally, while others concentrate mainly on the small domestic market. Focusing on the dual structure of their economy calls attention to the divergent economic interests which governments have had to take into account when trying to simultaneously protect specific sectors of the economy and promote exports. The dual structure restricted the room for manoeuvre, both in the domestic and in the international sphere. The 'economic integration trilemma' (reconciling the three goals of greater economic integration, proper public economic management and national sovereignty) had to be confronted in a context of less national autonomy and stronger internal conflicts of interest than was the case for large countries.[6]

Disadvantages related to the small size of a country are themselves dependent upon the trade regime: in a free-trade environment, and as world markets become larger, country size matters less.[7] During the first half of the twentieth century the economic performance of the small countries dealt with in this volume – measured by their per-capita GDP – differed considerably (Figure 1).

In the second half of the twentieth century we can observe a remarkable convergence, with some exceptions (such as Norway) sprinting ahead or (as Portugal) lagging behind: the other countries have all been approaching similar income levels (Figure 2).[8] The

Figure 1: GDP per capita – SEC 1900–1949 (1990 International Geary-Khamis dollars)

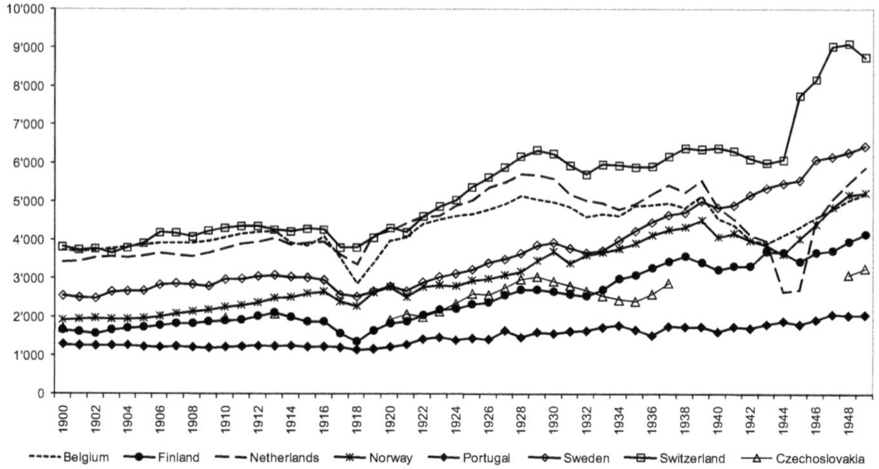

Source: The Conference Board and Groningen Growth and Development Centre, Total Economy Database, September 2006, http://www.ggdc.net.

Figure 2: GDP per capita – SEC 1950–2000 (1990 International Geary-Khamis dollars)

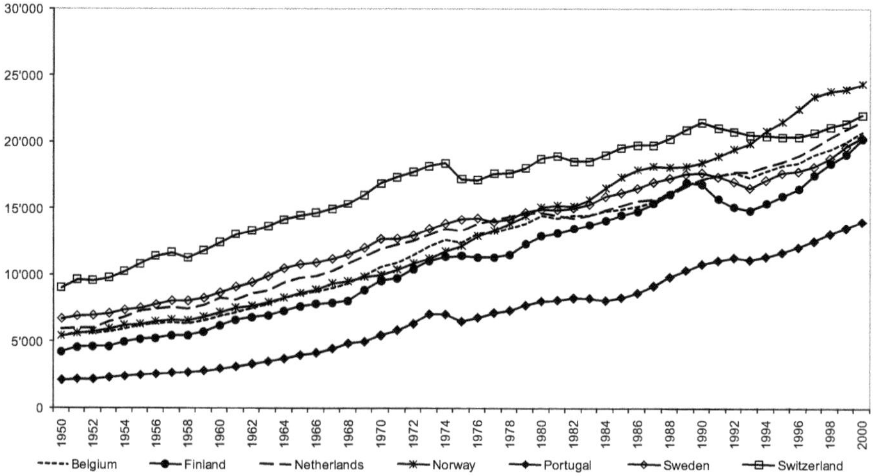

Source: The Conference Board and Groningen Growth and Development Centre, Total Economy Database, September 2006, http://www.ggdc.net.

Figure 3: Average GDP per capita (1990 International Geary-Khamis dollars)

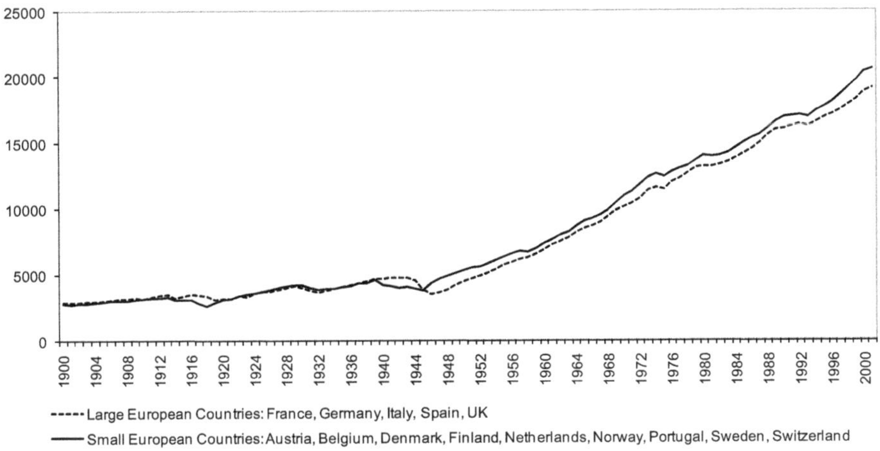

Source: The Conference Board and Groningen Growth and Development Centre, Total Economy Database, September 2006, http://www.ggdc.net.

coincidence of the latest wave of globalisation with the creation of the European Single Market and the breakdown of the Soviet Union caused some serious economic downturns in the 1990s, but these have been followed by rapid growth and rising per-capita GDPs.

If the average economic performance of the small European countries for which GDP data is available for the whole twentieth century is compared with that of the large ones, there is hardly any deviation between the two groups in the first half of the century, except during the two wars when average per-capita GDP of the small countries was lower. In the second half of the century, small countries outperformed the large ones, especially in the last decade (Figure 3). The good economic performance of small countries is noteworthy, because in a world where national borders matter the economic growth potential of the large countries – and, consequently, their per-capita GDP – should have been higher: clearly, the small European countries have been able to compensate for the disadvantages deriving from their size.

Good economic performance has not been limited to the small states of Europe: in other world regions small countries have done so well that some authors have even stressed their advantages in coping with globalisation.[9] However, good economic performance should not be attributed to country size per se, but to the ability of small countries to somehow cope with economic dependence. Peter J. Katzenstein attributed the successful adjustment of small European states in the post-war decades to institutional change, namely the evolution of a 'democratic corporatism' resulting from the experience of dependence upon international forces during the 1930s. But, of course, small states have not automatically created such political systems; and when the context changes, established modes of coping with economic dependence may become obsolete.[10] How small countries learnt to meet the changing demands of the international marketplace while maintaining a high degree of political and cultural autonomy may offer pointers to the larger countries now confronted with similar problems.[11]

Overview of the content of this volume

In this book twenty-four economic historians deal with several small European countries: Belgium, Czechoslovakia, Finland, Iceland, Norway, Portugal, Slovakia, Sweden, Switzerland and the Netherlands. The chapters address shared themes: What was the impact of the major changes in the international economic order upon the economic development of small countries? How much strategic freedom remained for small states highly dependent on foreign markets, and how did their governments resolve the internal conflicts resulting from the dual structure of their economies? Have international agreements and organisations restricted or enhanced the small state's freedom of action? How did firms and industries cope with the consequences of international economic integration or disintegration? While on the political level the room for manoeuvre of small countries is clearly restricted in comparison with larger states, the effect of economic integration or disintegration at company level is less predictable: firms may have overcome trade restrictions, or may have been able to derive advantage from an early enforced multinationalisation. In what way did the strategies pursued by firms and industries interact with the economic policies and institutional changes implemented at the political level?

The impact of globalisation and deglobalisation is analysed at different levels of the economy: the national economy, particular markets (goods and services, capital, labour), economic sectors (competitive or sheltered), industries and firms. Some authors take a broad perspective and emphasise the interplay between the economic and political spheres, while others focus on specific periods, economic sectors or policy areas. The studies covering the whole twentieth century are presented in section 1 below, those focusing on the pre-World War I and the interwar period in section 2, and those concentrating on the post-World War II period in section 3.

Section 1: Coping with different regimes for international trade and changing competitiveness

The common theme of the chapters in this section is the impact of globalisation and deglobalisation upon small European countries' economic development and their room for manoeuvre. How flexible were their governments and firms in responding to the constraints and opportunities imposed by the international economic order? The authors underline path-dependence by tracing the persistent influence of choices made under transitory conditions, and highlight major discontinuities.

OLLE KRANTZ focuses on the economic growth pattern in Sweden in comparison with other industrialised countries (including most of the countries dealt with in this volume) and analyses the influence of Sweden's small-country status upon economic policies and their effects on economic growth. Sweden's economic growth has usually been described as having been impressive from the late nineteenth century up to the early 1970s, but here these 'stylised facts' of Swedish economic history are brought under question. The periods during which Sweden was outperforming and underperforming are identified by comparing Sweden's growth rates with the average growth rates of a set of comparable countries. The result is a clear shift backwards – from 1970 to 1950 – of the point in time that marks the divide between the two periods. Sweden's internal economic and social policies are presumed to be the most likely causes for her economic underperformance in the second half of the twentieth century. The 'Swedish model' – a specific version of 'democratic corporatism' – entailed rigidities and incentive structures which hampered change and adaptation to the ongoing process of globalisation.

In his chapter on the development of labour-market institutions in Sweden from the late nineteenth century to the 1980s LARS SVENSSON gives further support to the suggested periodisation. He analyses the different conditions of labour in the competitive outward-oriented and sheltered domestic sectors of the economy, describes the institutional framework determining wage formation within the 'Swedish model' and traces the structural and institutional changes which brought about its transformation. Conditions in the competitive sector have determined the development of labour-market institutions since the beginning of the twentieth century, but the small open-economy constraints shaping these conditions varied over time. The Swedish concept of 'wage solidarity' was reformulated in the 1950s and in this form it began to influence wage-setting policies in the 1960s, although the 'Swedish Model' as such had been developed in the 1930s and its roots can even be traced back to the early twentieth century. By changing the meaning of 'solidarity' the conflict between the outward- and inward-oriented sectors was transformed into a broadly shared consensus to keep wage levels low. This low-wage policy was intended to favour the export industries, increase average productivity and promote growth, but in effect it resulted in a general levelling of wages between and within sectors and inhibited structural change. The concept of 'wage solidarity' was increasingly contested in the 1970s and 1980s and the conflict was finally resolved in a way that facilitated the transformation and renewal of Swedish industry, especially with regard to 'the new economy'. In the 1990s Sweden seems to have once again become a fast grower (see Krantz's chapter above).

In their chapter on the changing competitiveness of the Dutch economy HERMAN DE JONG and JAN PIETER SMITS explore how economic agents and institutions in the Netherlands reacted to international economic circumstances during the twentieth century, especially with the problems of protectionism in the interwar period and the gradual liberalisation of the international economy after World War II. Competitiveness on an international scale is usually linked with the capability of firms and industries to keep up with technical progress both in terms of new products and of reducing production costs. In this chapter, the long-term change in competitiveness is measured by the share of Dutch exports in international trade and by identifying those industrial sectors where revealed comparative advantage has been above or below average. The results obtained are then linked with broad economic policies affecting all industries and with the role of multinational companies in promoting technological progress. A major discontinuity is identified between the interwar period, when high exchange rates forced companies to rationalise production and increase productivity, and the second half of the century, when a policy focusing on low labour and energy prices reduced incentives to innovate and invest in high-technology sectors. Also in Sweden the pressure for structural change, transformation and innovation was stronger in the 1930s than in the post-war decades, when the country pursued a policy of low wages in order to stimulate exports (see Svensson's chapter above). In contrast with Sweden, wage-moderation policies in the Netherlands were reactivated in the 1980s, and continued to favour the traditional export industries. Foreign direct investments and R&D expenditures of the large multinational companies declined, and the Dutch economy lost some of its competitive strength.

MARGRIT MÜLLER's chapter focuses on the main export-oriented industries in Switzerland and analyses the interactions between the strategies adopted at company and industry level and the rules and policies implemented on the political level. The overall context of protectionism during the interwar period accelerated the ongoing structural change from labour-intensive to technology-intensive industries, which was largely accepted as inevitable and only marginally impeded by government interventions. Swiss companies reacted by rationalising production, expanding exports to new markets and focusing on technological competence and innovation. The strategies pursued in order to adapt to the international reallocation of activities was influenced by sector-specific attitudes, rules and shared visions of competitive advantage in the future. In some sectors globalising the firm by expanding direct investments abroad was a means of countering the disadvantages caused by the disintegration of the world economy, and this strategy was continued in the second half of the twentieth century. Tensions resulting from the coexistence of an important outward-oriented sector with a sheltered, highly regulated domestic sector became a matter of concern only in the 1990s when the country experienced a major economic downturn and lost some of its long-established lead with regard to per-capita GDP (Figure 2 above).

The difficult task of a small country's political authorities in balancing the desire to profit from an open world market with the demand for protection of a small domestic market from foreign competition is described in the chapter of EVEN LANGE and HELGE PHARO. In Norway the mainstream liberal trend was founded on strong economic interests, due to a considerable dependence by the late nineteenth century on foreign trade and capital imports. This policy was challenged by the nationalist impulse which sought economic independence after Norway left the union with Sweden in 1906, increased trade barriers in the interwar period and the need to cushion the impact of liberalisation after World War II for the sheltered domestic industries. The mix of policies pursued enabled the simultaneous promotion and control of capital inflows, and the increase of exports whilst shielding and restructuring weaker industries and protecting the agrarian sector from import competition. In the period of liberalisation after World War II the domestic forces in Norway favouring a greater degree of self-sufficiency gained strength and the tensions with the outward-oriented sectors increased, but the need to participate in the process of liberalisation within the framework of the OEEC prevailed. The considerable freedom of manoeuvre of this small state throughout the twentieth century is related partly to external conditions (stable relations with her main trading partners), partly to sheer luck (the increasing oil revenues in the 1970s), but mainly to the fact that the policies pursued allowed to cope with the dual structure of the economy while taking into account not only the economic importance of the weak sectors of the economy, but also the fact that these sectors represented crucial political constituencies.

Section 2: From an open world economy to economic disintegration and protectionism

The first two chapters of this section reach back to the nineteenth century and emphasize the change from the liberal economic order prevailing up until the First World War to the protectionism and isolationism of the interwar period.

In Portugal, as in other European countries, the liberal corporation laws introduced in the 1860s removed many obstacles to foreign-company formation. MARIA EUGÉNIA MATA highlights the importance of the open capital market for financing the public debt and for the inflow of foreign direct investments into a broad range of business activities. Although a small and less developed country, Portugal was quite an attractive location for foreign firms before 1914. These companies made a major contribution to the modernisation of the Portuguese economy by their introduction to the local communities of achievement-oriented attitudes, new visions and a fascination with modernity. Since the firms were of mixed national origin domestic companies were able to interact with a wide range of European business cultures. The Portuguese economy was insulated from the outside world in the interwar period, but after the Second World War a new process of globalisation set in following Portugal's decision to join the OEEC, EFTA and EC. The historical perspective shows that Portugal's participation in this new process of international integration had its roots in the pre-First World War period.

ANNE-LISE HEAD-KÖNIG's chapter on Switzerland focuses on the labour market and distinguishes between a period of globalisation up to 1913 – characterised by a considerable increase of the foreign workforce and an extensive cross-border trade in semi-finished products – and the interwar period marked by the deterioration of the economic situation, restrictive governmental legislation on foreign labour and the feminisation of factory work. The analysis concentrates on the traditional labour-intensive export industries of embroidery and watches, traces the options of the workforce in these sectors and the different practices applied by the Swiss firms having to compete with cheaper foreign labour in both periods. The state-backed employment policies introduced during the economic depressions of the early 1920s and especially the 1930s form a major topic: they were concentrated on assuring the survival of the watch industry, giving support to the new leading sector (the machine and metallurgy industry) and facilitating the downsizing of capacities in the textile industries, which had largely lost their international competitiveness.

The other four chapters in this section focus on the interwar period, especially on the Great Depression of the 1930s. After the post-war crisis in the early 1920s, the small European countries aimed at restoring a liberal economic regime and continued to support any initiative taken by international organisations for liberalising trade. But governments in small countries also had to take into account political challenges at home, and increasingly turned to the selective protection of politically influential domestic sectors, especially agriculture.

The main question of the chapter on the monetary policies pursued in Switzerland during the interwar period by PATRICK HALBEISEN is why it was possible for a small country, largely dependent on foreign trade, to preserve a considerable autonomy with regard to exchange rates and capital flows and stick to the gold-parity of its currency as late as autumn 1936. Similar questions are raised in the chapter of HEIN A.M. KLEMANN on the Netherlands, while the chapter of OLA HONNINGDAL GRYTTEN examining the effects of the disintegration of the world economy on Norway in comparison with other small European countries highlights the considerable advantage of not having such a choice. In IVAN JAKUBEC'S chapter on Czechoslovakia monetary policy is again treated, but the main topic is how Czechoslovakia managed to cope simultaneously with economic disintegration and reintegration. With the breakup of the Austro-Hungarian Empire domestic markets were transformed into foreign markets, and long-established competitive advantages in the former national context were lost. Restructuring the economy under such circumstances was especially difficult, and the extreme disparities within the country itself, poor transport facilities and high transport costs made the task even more difficult.

Due to its balanced current account, Switzerland was one of the first countries able to return to the pre-war gold parity in 1924; Sweden also returned formally to gold that year,[12] and Czechoslovakia had been able to stabilise its currency as early as 1923: these three countries experienced considerable growth rates up to 1929. That was also the case for the Netherlands, but in Norway the economic situation and the results gained from the implementation of a deflationary monetarist policy in the 1920s were different. The return to pre-war parity was achieved only in 1928 and at the cost of an economic downturn in the middle of the 1920s.

During the depression of the 1930s national and international cartels, import restrictions and subsidies were introduced (see the chapters of Grytten, Head-König, Jakubec and Müller); cartelisation was perceived as a means to stop the downward spiral of prices and regulate competition in narrowing domestic and foreign markets. Cartels were an alternative to raising tariffs on imported goods, a policy that small states highly dependent on foreign markets and anxious about retaliation tried to avoid. But it is often overlooked that small countries not only needed foreign markets for their exports but themselves offered attractive export outlets for their trading partners and were therefore able to negotiate trade agreements which safeguarded to some extent their vital export interests (see Klemann, Lange/Pharo and Müller).

With regard to the range of initiative open to small countries the important point is that they responded quite differently to the depression of the 1930s. In Switzerland the monetary policy of the National Bank was mainly focused on balancing capital accounts and maintaining gold parity, and this policy was not contested. Not even devaluation in autumn 1936 changed the dominant liberal orientation: capital movements remained essentially free, and the Swiss franc continued to be convertible and firmly pegged to gold. In Norway the change from a liberal and deflationary to a protectionist and inflationary policy occurred as early as 1930: in contrast with the Netherlands and Switzerland, there was no attempt to stick to the gold parity after Great Britain had left gold. The decision to leave the gold standard and devalue the krone was made to benefit the export industries (and was beneficial also for the domestic industries), but in effect the Bank of Norway had no choice because of the threat of large-scale speculative capital outflows.

The view that no country left gold except under the pressure of a financial or banking crisis is underlined in the chapter of HEIN

A.M. KLEMANN on the economic and political development of the Netherlands in the 1930s. Like Switzerland, the Netherlands possessed ample reserves and was able to choose between devaluation and sticking to gold parity. Despite the country's enormous interests in international trade, national economic policy was not based on rational economic analysis but emerged as a by-product of internal political constellations and power struggles among politicians.

In Czechoslovakia the first devaluation in spring 1934, mainly the result of a struggle among competing political and business interests, was not very effective (Jakubec). Only the second devaluation in October 1936 resulted in a considerable economic recovery. In Switzerland and in the Netherlands there were no strong interest groups pressing for devaluation, neither from the export-oriented industries nor from any of the major political parties (Halbeisen, Klemann). In the case of Switzerland, the strategies pursued by the export-oriented firms (Müller) offer some explanation for their lack of interest in devaluation. In the Netherlands the politically important agricultural interest groups wanted protection against foreign food imports and government subsidies to promote exports: an alternative policy would have been to limit agricultural protection and instead protect and promote the small-scale inward-oriented industries, but those groups had little political influence and were unable to push their interests through (Klemann). The figures given in the chapter of HERMAN DE JONG and JAN-PIETER SMITS on the revealed comparative advantage of the Netherlands in food processing show that such a reorientation towards the domestic market must have appeared extremely costly. Coping with the depression by concentrating on the domestic market – a popular demand at that time in all countries – was no option for the export industries and the multinational companies in small countries like Switzerland, the Netherlands and Czechoslovakia simply because the home market was too small.

Notwithstanding the difficulties encountered, significant growth took place in all countries during the interwar period as a whole, which implies that the period was not as inimical to trade-dependent small countries as has often been stated. But success or failure is usually assessed with regard to quick or slow recovery from the Great Depression in the 1930s. A quantitative analysis in OLA

HONNINGDAL GRYTTEN'S chapter shows that those countries which left gold early, like Sweden and Norway, had a milder recession and a more rapid recovery than those that remained on gold. However, if we consider the longer-term impact of late devaluation, the results are more ambiguous. In those countries where devaluation was delayed the international competitiveness of their export industries was enhanced because firms were forced to search for new markets, to invest abroad and to innovate and rationalise production processes (de Jong/Smits, Müller). Early devaluation facilitated protectionism and the growth of low-wage, labour intensive and internationally non-competitive industries that in the case of Norway delayed participation in the various trade liberalisation schemes of the 1950s and 1960s (Lange/Pharo, Frøland).

Section 3: Trade liberalisation, European integration and deregulation

The institutional changes and economic policies adopted during the depression of the 1930s continued to mark the economic development of Norway (Lange/Pharo, Frøland) and Switzerland (Halbeisen, Müller) during the post-war decades. Discontinuities were more pronounced in the Netherlands (de Jong/Smits), in Sweden (Krantz, Svensson) and especially in Belgium (Cassiers/Ledent). Such ruptures were related to changes on the political front, while path-dependence was most pronounced where the political power structures established in the 1930s remained intact. In most countries some version of 'democratic corporatism' has been identified, but the type of policy pursued depended on the dominant political parties.[13] Discontinuities must have been most pronounced in the case of Czechoslovakia. The development of this and other central European countries in the transition period of the 1990s in comparison with the interwar period is subject of the last chapter in this section.

During the interwar period the small European countries had pursued policies of protectionism which differed from those of large countries: they tended to apply relatively low tariffs and they were interested in supporting free-trade policies on an international level. They were dependent on foreign markets for exports and therefore constrained to open their domestic market to their trading partners. Furthermore their exports were often based on imports of raw material or semi-finished products. Political dilemmas arose when the protection of domestic sectors increased the costs of imports needed for the export industries or when liberal import regulations disturbed domestic socioeconomic structures: since the late nineteenth century the general solution to this dilemma had been a policy of moderate and selective protectionism. The chapter of HANS OTTO FRØLAND describes how a low-tariff country like Norway was able to continue protecting its inward-oriented, labour-intensive and internationally non-competitive manufacturing industries – introduced in the 1920s and reinforced during the area of protectionism in the 1930s – well into the post-war period. Norway, basically in favour of open markets and multilateralism, continued to protect specific sectors of its economy from rapid and possibly detrimental liberalisation within the OEEC and the GATT by delaying the removal of quota restrictions and reintroducing selective tariff protection. Import quotas were important for the small European states because of their traditionally low tariffs on imported goods, and the different attitudes of small low-tariff and large high-tariff countries resulted in considerable intergovernmental tensions on the international level. Slow and selective liberalisation in Norway was in the end successful, because it was conceived as a temporary measure enabling labour-intensive industries, especially textiles, to become internationally more competitive.

Iceland is another example of a small country which shifted from a traditionally outward-oriented trade regime to protectionism in the 1930s and remained protectionist up until the 1960s, while other European countries had from the 1950s turned to greater openness and increased economic integration. The main question raised in the chapter of GUDMUNDUR JONSSON and SIGURDUR SNAEVARR is why Iceland clung to protectionism so long after World War II. Iceland was in several aspects a special case: the outstanding economic prosperity experienced during World War II continued to influence the country's post-war problems and policies, and possibilities for participation in the process of trade liberalisation were limited by the fact that Iceland's main export product – fish – was considered an agricultural product. In several other countries (for example in Norway and Switzerland) there was a conflict between protecting the agrarian sector and participating in trade liberalisation, but in the case of Iceland it was particularly pronounced. The government adopted an increasingly interventionist economic policy in order to reduce balance-of-payments deficits, and shifted trade relations in the direction of Eastern Europe and the Soviet Union. Only in the 1960s was Iceland able to break out of the deadlock of low growth and balance-of-payments restraints. The authors stress that in addition to the external period- and context-specific constraints and opportunities, internal political conditions were largely responsible for the way in which the government responded to the challenges of the outer world. The return to freer trade in Iceland in the 1960s demonstrates the crucial dependence of a small country on a balanced external economy.

In their chapter on monetary policies in Belgium in the 1950s and 1960s ISABELLE CASSIERS and PHILIPPE LEDENT also focus on the lengthy and complex process of returning to currency convertibility and free trade after the war. They highlight the limitations imposed by the combination of a liberal capital market and regulated international trade. In a clear break with its pre-war policies and in contrast with its neighbouring countries France and the Netherlands and with all the Nordic countries, the government adopted a market-oriented approach and pursued a strictly stability-oriented monetary policy. Belgium's early choices with regard to monetary and exchange-rate policies were in line with the principles laid down at Bretton Woods in 1944, but due to the complex interaction of external and internal pressures and constraints – especially the intricate institutional systems set up in order to balance trade and capital movements – putting them into practice proved rather difficult. The restrictive monetary policies pursued in the 1950s had a negative impact on growth, but the return to full convertibility in 1958 and the creation of the Common Market were much to Belgium's advantage. The choices made in the 1950s encouraged both the outflow and the inflow of direct investments, restricted exports and domestic investments and had a considerable impact on the further course of the economy. It seems that the new wave of globalisation by international mergers and acquisitions reached Belgium earlier and more intensively than the other small western European countries.

The monetary and financial policies pursued by the small European countries in the early post-World War II decades – and consequently the impact of the breakdown of Bretton Woods and the subsequent deregulation of capital markets in the 1970s – differed considerably. In Switzerland, which had had a liberal capital market throughout the twentieth century, the impact was rather moderate (Halbeisen). In countries with a regulated financial sector like Norway, Finland and Sweden the liberalisation of national capital markets in the 1980s had a strong impact on the process of economic internationalisation and thoroughly changed the prerequisites for economic policy. In his contribution on the deregulation of capital movements and Finnish monetary policy TIMO MYLLYNTAUS places the financial policies pursued in Finland into a comparative perspective. Finland belonged – like Sweden and Norway – to the late liberalisers. Due to her special bilateral relations with the Soviet Union, liberalising foreign trade was more complicated for Finland than for the other Nordic countries, but in effect up to the 1980s regulating financial markets and liberalising the other economic sectors had been possible. Regulation fitted well with social corporatism, an instrument applied in all these countries to adjust their economies to external changes. Only in the 1980s did pressures from business interests become strong enough to overcome internal opposition to the liberalisation of capital markets and initiate the removal of currency regulation, allowing Finnish firms to invest in foreign countries and raise loans on foreign capital markets. The Finnish economy adapted quickly to free financial markets during the 1980s, a period of strong economic growth which was followed in the 1990s by the deepest depression of the twentieth century. Still, this drastic economic downturn, made even more incisive by the Soviet collapse, did not shake confidence in the benefits of internationalisation. The process of globalisation and European integration continued, and at the threshold of the new millennium the economies of both Finland and Sweden are among the world's most globally oriented.

The dualism between the domestic sector and the export-oriented sector, between open and regulated markets became less pronounced in the last decades of the twentieth century. Under the continuous pressure from international organisations aimed at liberalising the international economic exchange of goods, services and capital, and from technological change expanding the boundaries of tradability, the means available for protecting and controlling specific economic sectors changed considerably.

The still-significant domestic sector of small-state economies – agriculture, inward-oriented industries, public services – was progressively exposed to international competition, but deregulation and privatisation were adopted selectively. Some countries joined the new wave of globalisation early on, others were forced into adopting reforms as member states of the European Community or when joining the European Common Market, while Switzerland clearly lagged behind. Having been more liberal than other small European countries up to the 1970s with regard to capital markets and trade, it became a latecomer with regard to deregulation and privatisation. Major changes occurred only in the last decade of the twentieth century, and their impact is still difficult to assess. THOMAS DAVID, ANDRÉ MACH and TOBIAS STRAUMANN analyse why and under what circumstances established and broadly accepted mechanisms of 'selective protectionism' were questioned and to some extent repealed. They concentrate on the impact of globalisation on cartelisation and on those institutions which allowed Swiss corporations to protect themselves from foreign takeovers, and identify the external and internal forces leading to the reform of the law on cartels and on new rules for corporate governance. These reforms were strongly influenced by institutional changes within the European Union, and can be understood as a process of Europeanisation. International mergers and acquisitions increased, the large Swiss multinationals began to adapt their corporate governance structures in order to attract foreign investors and to introduce – to some extent – Anglo-Saxon criteria of good management into the traditional Swiss system of ownership control.

KERSTI ULLENHAG's chapter investigates management education in Sweden over the last three decades of the twentieth century and gives some answers to the question of the interplay between economic forces and the role of large multinational corporations as channels for management ideas. An important aspect is that the transfer of American management models has been shaped by the culture of the recipient firms. There was some 'cultural room for manoeuvre' in Swedish multinationals, and this national influence has continued even if, in the course of globalisation, the international connections were expanded and intensified, the Swedish framework changed and the strong links of the multinational firms with Swedish society loosened. As is also underlined in other chapters in this book, reactions on the political level are influenced by the strategies pursued by economic actors and constrained by economic conditions. But these parameters and the opportunities to act within them are perceived and interpreted in different ways. If we wish to gain a clearer picture of the room for manoeuvre both at the political level and at the level of companies, business associations and other interest groups, more attention has to be given to ideas, how they are formed, to what extent they are shared and why they change.

The significant influence of multinational companies – of domestic and foreign origin – on the economy of a small country is underlined in several chapters in this volume. In less developed economies the impact of foreign firms as investors and promoters of organisational, technical and institutional change can hardly be overstated. The important role of foreign direct investments for less developed countries, a topic raised by Maria Eugénia Mata in her chapter on Portugal, is a central theme in the chapter of L'UDOVÍT HALLON on the transition of Czechoslovakia (later Slovakia and the Czech Republic) and other central European states – Poland, Hungary and Slovenia – after 1989. The situation is compared with that after the collapse of the Austro-Hungarian monarchy in 1918, but was more complex since the transformation of external economic relations – the breakup of Soviet economic affiliations and the integration of the central European states into the rapidly expanding world economy – was coupled with the internal transformation of centrally planned into free-market economies. Furthermore, in the early 1990s Slovakia was a newly formed country, the result of the disintegration of Czechoslovakia into two autonomous states. Economic policies were of vital importance and played a leading role in speeding up or forestalling the complex process of transition in post-Communist states. Within a mere dozen years, Slovakia had to adapt to several fundamental changes of external and internal conditions and somehow find its own path between suppressing surging nationalistic tendencies and opening up its economy in order to participate in the ongoing process of globalisation and become a member state of the European Union. The result is quite impressive: after a serious setback in the mid 1990s the country was able to catch up and in some respects even overtake other transition countries.

Conclusion

Notwithstanding their strong economic dependence on external conditions, small countries enjoyed significant freedom of initiative throughout the twentieth century. This was exploited in partly similar, partly different ways, and the differences were more pronounced for the periods of protectionism and gradual liberalisation after World War II than for the last decades of the twentieth century.

In the early period of globalisation up to the First World War small countries tried to maintain low tariffs and open markets in face of the increasing protectionism of their main trading partners and challenges at home. Import and export shares in GDP remained high up to 1913, reaching levels which were in most cases never attained again, or only in the last quarter of the twentieth century. Migration flows continued and the rapid spread of multinational firms serves as an an indicator of considerable outbound and inbound direct investment during this period.

All the countries were seriously affected by the collapse of the international monetary system at the outbreak of the First World War and the widely spread protectionism of the interwar period. The 1920s were marked by a policy aimed at re-establishing the pre-war liberal trade regime by a return to the pre-war gold parity. Some countries achieved this aim quite early; others had difficulties in regaining monetary stability, and missed the opportunities for economic growth in the 1920s. During the Great Depression of the 1930s the duality of the economic structure became more pronounced and the demands of the political pressure groups which governments had to take into account while simultaneously protecting specific sectors of the economy and promoting exports were a major impediment to the adoption of appropriate economic policies, especially in those countries which were not forced into leaving the gold standard and devaluing their currencies. But even under these difficult conditions trade and capital flows were to some extent sustained, since small countries were not only dependent on foreign markets for exports, they were also attractive markets for their trading partners. Furthermore, the outward-oriented firms pursued strategies allowing them to overcome barriers to trade and to compensate location-specific disadvantages.

In the period of liberalisation after World War II the tension between the outward and the inward-oriented sectors as well as the need for political consensus influenced the extent a country was able to participate in the different schemes for trade liberalisation and regional integration. Although small states had little influence on the international level, their room for manoeuvre becomes visible when we turn to the process of policy implementation. A remarkable path-dependence has been identified in strategies and policies introduced in the 1930s and pursued after World War II. Where discontinuities have been stressed, they were mainly due to changes of internal economic policies and not of external economic conditions. The gradual liberalisation of world markets for goods and capital after World War II gave small countries ample room to pursue 'their own way'. It was 'the age of the nation states' (Krantz), when even small countries enjoyed a remarkable degree of economic independence. But this economic autonomy revealed itself as rather costly later on, because protecting small domestic markets entailed considerable inefficiencies.

A lack of adaptability and flexibility seems to have prevailed until the 1970s (another period of economic crisis – and in this respect comparable to the 1930s, but in a completely different international context). The new wave of globalisation and its main driving forces – the demise of Bretton Woods and the liberalisation of capital markets, deregulation and privatisation of public services, the new communication technologies, European integration – exposed formerly sheltered domestic sectors to international competition and increased the possibilities of domestic firms' expanding their activities to foreign markets. Market forces, unleashed by economic liberalisation and enforced by European integration, did stimulate institutional change; but to a large extent this was the deliberate response of governments to inefficiencies in their national economies.

In the last decades of the twentieth century small nations have become integrated into the international economy to a very large extent. Does this imply that their room for manoeuvre has narrowed and that the small countries are less able to go 'their own way'? Major adaptations had become inevitable, and they have been perceived as a loss of economic autonomy. But in the long-term perspective it is not very convincing to link globalisation with a shrinking freedom of initiative for small countries. Of course, the protectionist policies enforced by large states have also widened the possibilities for small states to protect their domestic markets, but to a much lesser extent and at higher costs. It is important to remember that the disintegration of the world economy during the inter-war period forced governments of small countries to turn to selective protectionism and bilateral agreements which were against their primary interests in free trade and multilateralism. In the post-World War II decades the small states' adaptive flexibility was reduced as a result of their dual economic structure and the state-specific versions of 'democratic corporatism' developed to cope with conflicting interests. Selective protectionism may have fuelled a general feeling of economic autonomy – of a coincidence between the 'nation space' and the 'market space' unusual for small countries – up to the 1970s, and in some cases even longer. But in effect these were policy legacies of the past, especially of the Great Depression of the 1930s, limiting the chances to benefit from the opportunities for growth in an increasingly open world.

The impact of globalisation on the autonomy of the nation state is a matter of considerable concern. The increasing influence of international organisations on the rules governing the international movements of goods, services, capital and labour is often interpreted as having restricted the autonomy of the nation state. In fact, however, these rules have considerably increased the costs to large countries of any return to economic protectionism and isolationism. By restricting policy options available principally to large countries, they have secured the 'economic space' of small countries, which lies to a considerable extent outside their borders, allowing them to reap to a much larger extent the advantages of the international division of labour and reduce the costs of being limited to a small domestic market. However, the risk of a return to protectionism has only been reduced rather than eliminated; firms have to compete in the global market, where competition has become more intense; and governments have to preserve the competitiveness of their economies in a world where established comparative advantages have become highly unstable. On the basis of the chapters dealing with the recent decades the conclusion may be drawn that small countries' experience of economic dependence has enabled them to cope with these new global challenges quite easily: they possess the necessary adaptive flexibility because their firms and governments – with the necessary support of their electorates – were able to learn and adjust and seize the opportunities available in an increasingly integrated and rapidly expanding world economy.

Throughout the twentieth century small countries have chosen different paths, and this implies that there has been considerable scope for state autonomy. The most important lesson that can be drawn from the studies presented in this volume is that – notwithstanding the undisputable importance of the international economic regime – coping with externally imposed constraints or taking advantage of economic liberalisation depends first of all on decisions taken by economic actors and governments within the countries themselves.

1 See for example Kevin H. O'Rourke and Jeffrey G. Williamson, 'When did globalisation begin?' *European Review of Economic History*, 1 (2002), 23–50. An overview on globalisation in the late nineteenth century focusing on the European countries and some countries of the New World is given in Jeffrey G. Williamson, 'Globalization, Labor Markets and Policy Backlash in the Past', *Journal of Economic Perspectives*, 12/4 (1998), 51–72.

2 Kevin H. O'Rourke and Jeffrey G. Williamson, *Globalization and History: The Evolution of a Nineteenth Century Atlantic Economy* (Cambridge, MA: MIT Press, 1999).

3 Peter J. Katzenstein, 'Small States and Small States Revisited', *New Political Economy*, 8/1 (2003), 9–30, p. 27. For large countries like the US the current process of globalisation differs considerably from the pre-1914 period: Michael D. Bordo, Barry Eichengreen and Douglas A. Irwin, *Is Globalization Today Really Different than Globalization a Hundred Years Ago?*, NBER Working Paper No.

7195 (June 1999), point to the higher shares of trade and direct investments in GDP as indicators for the loss of economic autonomy. In comparison with small countries these shares are still very low.

4 http:www.nationmaster.com, 19.3.2007, 13:56.

5 John H. Dunning, 'Resolving some Paradoxes of the Emerging Global Economy: Small Nations as Trailblazers', in Van Den Bulcke and Alain Verbeke (eds.), *Globalization and the Small Open Economy* (Cheltenham, UK and Northampton, MA: Edward Elgar, 2001), pp. 14ff.

6 Lawrence H. Summers, Distinguished Lecture on Economics in Government, 'Reflections on Managing Global Integration', *Journal of Economic Perspectives*, 13/2 (1999), 3–18, p. 10.

7 See for example Alberto Alesina and Enrico Spolare, *The Size of Nations* (Cambridge, MA and London: MIT Press, 2003), especially pp. 155–173.

8 Of the central European countries dealt with in the chapter of L'udovít Hallon, only Slovenia with 14,000 international Geary-Khamis dollars approached income levels similar to Portugal in 2000; the Czech Republic, Slovakia and Hungary reached levels between about 7,000 and 9,000.

9 See for example Dunning, 'Resolving some Paradoxes'.

10 Peter J. Katzenstein, *Small States in World Markets. Industrial Policy in Europe* (Ithaca, NY and London: Cornell University Press, 1985).

11 Dunning, 'Resolving some Paradoxes', p. 31.

12 Jan T. Klovland, 'Monetary policy and business cycles in the interwar years: The Scandinavian experience', *European Review of Economic History*, 2 (1998), 309–344.

13 Katzenstein (*Small States in World Markets*, pp. 80ff.) distinguishes between two forms of 'democratic corporatism': liberal and social.

Section I

Coping with Different Regimes for International Trade and Changing Competitiveness

Olle Krantz

Economic Growth and Economic Policy in Sweden in the Twentieth Century: A Comparative Perspective

Two 'stylised facts' about Swedish economic growth are nowadays part of economists' conventional wisdom. One is that Sweden's economy grew at an impressive rate compared to other countries between 1870 and 1970. Only Japan had a better performance.[1] The other stylised fact is that after 1970 Sweden lost its leading place in the growth-rate league and fell back to a position among the OECD countries with the lowest income per capita. While the first 'fact' has practically not been questioned the second one has received more scrutiny, and the reasons given for the slowdown, viz. rigid economic policy and a huge public sector,[2] have become topics for debate.

These two 'stylised facts' will be addressed in this paper. Thus, one question is whether and to what extent Sweden's economic growth has differed from that of other countries since the 1970s, and whether, and if so in what way, the Swedish economic policy contributed to this performance. Then it is also of interest to get a long-term perspective on the Swedish comparative growth performance, which enables us to judge whether it is sufficient only to consider the time after 1970 in this context or if that forms part of a longer course of events. Thereby the other question becomes relevant, namely whether Swedish growth 1870–1970 really was unique or whether some other periodisation would be better. In other words, how impressive was the Swedish growth performance when set in a long-term international perspective?

Another question is whether Sweden's status as a small country was of any importance in this scenario. To what extent can a small State pursue its own economic policy without negative effects on its economic growth? By 'own' in this case is meant that a policy is pursued without considering the international economic situation at all or with only slight regard to it. In other words, how great is the 'international space' for an 'own' policy, or what is the small State's room for manoeuvre? Does this change over time? To analyse these problems we should employ the economic small-State theory or in other words a formal description of the special characteristics of small countries which has evolved in the literature.[3] Of particular importance is how the relevance of this theory has changed over time.

All factors behind economic growth, for instance capital formation, labour-force changes, education and technical change, can not, for obvious reasons, be discussed here, but something will be said about the last of these. In the last 200 years different technological bases or paradigms have dominated. In the early nineteenth century, steam power was the most significant technological base. The steam engine achieved increasing importance in industry, and facilitated the development of the railway system. Towards the end of the century, electricity and the combustion engine gained prominence, and in most of the twentieth century they formed the dominating technological base. Then, in the very last part of that century, ICT has grown in importance and is now probably forming a new technological base. The utilisation of technology could, however, differ between different countries, and how it was utilised depended on the institutional and political environment. Institutions and policies could be favourable to certain uses of technology and to economic growth, but they could also hamper growth; and, as already mentioned, for a small country the effects of various measures could be greatly dependent on the international environment. Thus, growth possibilities could be different in different periods.

A long-term view

Long historical series for GDP and other important macroeconomic variables are nowadays available for a large number of countries. They have been constructed by individual researchers and groups of scholars, but seldom by official authorities. Various scholars have then collected these series, the best known today being perhaps Angus Maddison,[4] who has published his collections and studied international economic growth and change. He maintains that a number of phases are clearly discernible in the long-term development, and they are delimited by external shocks: W.W.I and W.W.II and the oil crises of the 1970s. In Table 1 growth figures for these phases are displayed.

According to Table 1 the annual rate of growth for the sixteen countries 1870–1973 is 1.9 per cent. Japan had the highest rate, and this can be regarded as pretty certain. It is also highly probable that Australia and the early industrialisers, the UK and Belgium, had very low growth rates. With regard to the uncertainty or shakiness of the rates given in Table 1 it is not quite certain that Sweden had the highest growth rate except for Japan in this period. Rather, a group of countries seems to have had fairly similar rates. For 1973–1992 the average growth for all countries was 1.8 per cent: Sweden and Switzerland were far below this figure while Norway and Japan were much higher than the average. The fact that the margins of error in the national accounts are more narrow in recent periods than earlier makes it probable that Sweden and Switzerland were comparatively slow growers during the last decades.

Since there are weaknesses in the data in Table 1, the 'stylised facts' – or, rather, the hypotheses – cannot be accepted or rejected on this basis, and complementary calculations are badly needed. It would then be preferable when making the comparisons to take into consideration data for all the years in question and not only for some benchmark years. There are various ways to do this, for instance by comparing the countries' GDP per capita expressed in the same currency, meaning that levels for each year are compared. Then we need Purchasing Power Parities (PPP) to convert national currencies, but for historical series such data are largely missing. Furthermore, official exchange rates are not suitable as converters because they do not accurately show relations between the internal purchasing power of the countries. Besides, the not uncommon method of using PPPs for one year, for example 1995, and varying them backward with implicit deflator ratios leads to very uncertain results. Therefore, the idea of making comparisons of levels was abandoned in favour of comparing yearly changes in original GDP per capita. Index series for GDP per capita form the basis for the comparison. When these series for different countries or averages for groups of countries are related to each other, the results are new index series showing the changes in the ratios between the original data. If such a ratio series shows a rise/decline, the country or group of countries constituting the nominator has a higher/lower rate of growth than the one constituting the denominator. In the following, such comparisons are made, which, as mentioned, are comparisons of growth and not comparisons of income levels.

When one country, in this case Sweden, is to be compared with a group of countries, it could be a matter of dispute what countries should be included in the comparison group. For modern times, it is common to use the OECD countries, but these are rather disparate. They have for instance very different income levels, and very small countries are included such as Luxembourg and Iceland together with very large countries such as the USA. Therefore, a smaller and more homogeneous group should be used, and the highly industrialised countries – that is, those included in Table 1 – is a more appropriate comparison group, which could also be divided into subgroups.

One subgroup is a number of countries that are similar to Sweden with regard to income level at some point of time. Walter Korpi, the leading proponent of the view that the Swedish growth has not been lagging from the 1970s onwards if appropriate comparisons are made, used such a group when he argued his case. This group consists of countries that around 1970 were roughly on the same income level as Sweden, and includes Denmark, France, Germany, the Netherlands, Switzerland and Britain.[5] Since their income per capita was roughly the same, the catch-up factor should not influence the comparison in the last decades of the century. If a larger group had been chosen, for instance the OECD countries, countries with low income in the beginning of the comparison period could raise the average rate of growth due to the catch-up factor, which means that high-income countries, for instance Sweden, would seem to lag behind.

A third group of countries will also be used as a comparison group, namely the small European countries – smallness in this case

Table 1: Annual percentage growth in GDP per capita 1870–1992 in industrialised countries. Constant prices

	1870–1913	1913–1950	1950–1973	1973–1992	1870–1973
Australia	0.9	0.7	2.4	1.4	1.2
Austria	1.5	0.2	4.9	2.2	1.8
Belgium	1.0	0.7	3.5	1.9	1.4
Canada	2.2	1.4	2.9	1.5	2.1
Denmark	1.6	1.6	3.1	1.6	1.9
Finland	1.4	1.9	4.3	1.6	2.2
France	1.5	1.1	4.0	1.7	1.9
Germany	1.6	0.3	5.0	2.1	1.9
Italy	1.3	0.8	5.0	2.4	1.9
Japan	1.4	0.9	8.0	3.0	2.7
Netherlands	0.9	1.1	3.4	1.4	1.5
Norway	1.3	2.1	3.2	2.9	2.0
Sweden	2.0	2.3	3.0	1.1	2.3
Switzerland	1.2	2.1	3.1	0.8	2.0
UK	1.0	0.8	2.5	1.4	1.3
USA	1.8	1.6	2.4	1.4	1.9
Arithmetic average	1.4	1.2	3.8	1.8	1.9

Source: Angus Maddison, *Dynamic Forces in Capitalist Development: A Long-Run Comparative View* (Oxford: Oxford University Press, 1991) and Angus Maddison, *Monitoring the World Economy 1820–1992* (Paris: Development Centre of the Organisation for Economic Co-operation and Development, 1995), and Olle Krantz, *Swedish Historical National Accounts 1800–1990 – Aggregated Output Series* (Umeå: Mimeo, 2001).

Note: 1. The GDP series are constructed with different methods for different countries and the sources are of different quality, which means that there are margins of error. 2. In Maddison, *Monitoring the World Economy*, p. 62, incorrect growth rates for Switzerland are given. The figures in this table are therefore taken from Maddison, *Dynamic Forces*, p. 49. 3. The data for Sweden provided by Maddison is wholly incorrect. Here figures based on Krantz, *Swedish Historical National Accounts* are used instead. 4. Maddison gives growth rates calculated between the figures for the first and last year in the period only. That this method could lead to uncertain results is well known.

being defined by population size. These countries are Austria, Belgium, Denmark, Finland, The Netherlands, Norway, and Switzerland. However, in a long-term perspective it is difficult to opt for and apply a criterion based on size. Austria for instance was not a small country before W.W.I. Sweden and Norway were united in a union before 1905, and Finland was part of the Russian empire up to 1917, albeit an autonomous part. Belgium and the Netherlands were colonial powers for a long time. And today one could question whether the Netherlands with 16 million inhabitants is a small country. However, in a certain sense, these countries have been economic units during all or most of the period under review.

Furthermore, the effects on the country's economic growth of what is – mostly by Swedish patriots – called 'the Swedish Model' are to be discussed. By this is meant the societal arrangements and policies that evolved from the 1930s. In this comparison the small-State group is appropriate since all these countries have their 'models' as well. It could even be questioned whether there ever was a particular 'Swedish model'. Probably it would be better to talk about a 'Scandinavian' model or a 'Nordic' or even a 'small-State model'; and even then there could of course be individual variants.[6] A principal element in such a model is democratic corporatism, which is essential also in Katzenstein's analysis of European small countries.[7] In summary, the features characterising Sweden fit well into the framework of a 'small-State model'.

Figures 1–3 show Sweden's GDP per capita in relation to the averages for the three comparison groups. The ratio series have 1913 as reference year (1913 = 1), and as mentioned it is only a question of growth comparisons, not comparisons of income levels. The three curves have a similar profile, which is further illustrated in Table 2.

As to economic growth, Sweden did not stand out during the first twenty years of the period; its pace coincided with the average for the industrialised (or industrialising) countries. Then, however, from around 1890 up to around 1950 Sweden grew considerably faster than the comparison groups.[8] In the middle of the twentieth century there was a conspicuous break and a downward tendency set in, which differed only slightly between the three curves. In relation to the six richest countries there was a distinct decrease to around 1960 and then a smaller one up to the crisis of the 1990s.

Figure 1: GDP per capita, Sweden in relation to the average for sixteen industrialised countries 1870–1997. Constant prices. Index 1913=1

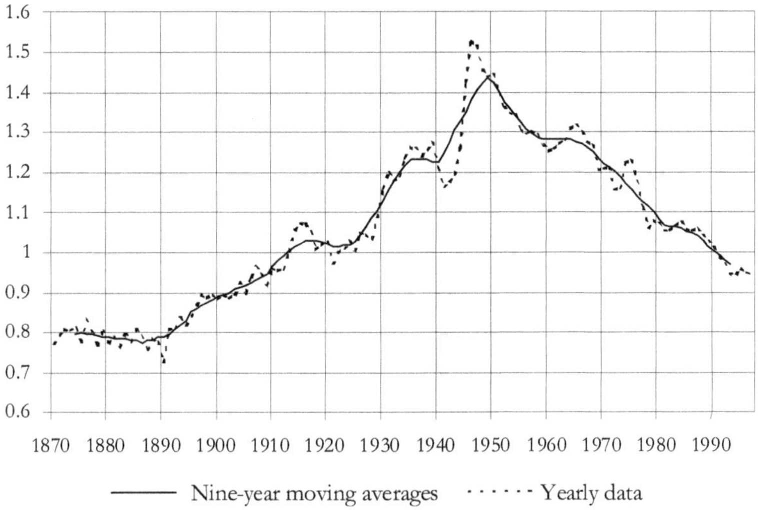

Source: See Table 1.

Figure 2: GDP per capita, Sweden in relation to the average for six rich industrialised countries 1870–1997. Constant prices. Index 1913=1

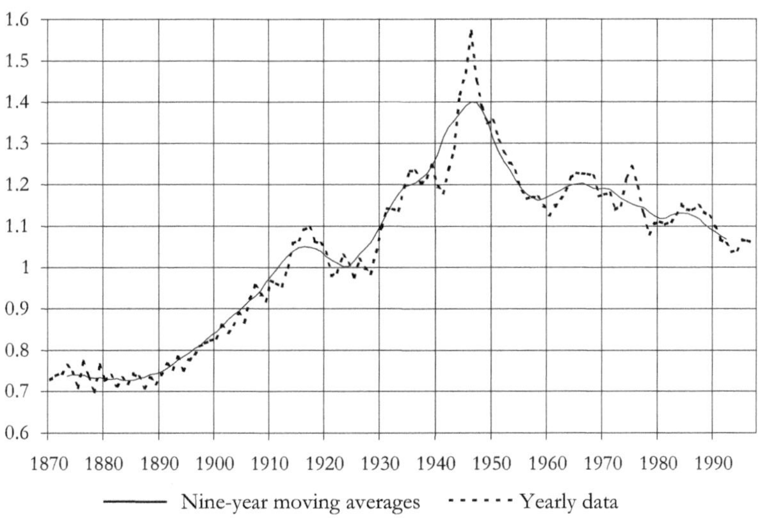

Source: See Table 1.

Figure 3: GDP per capita, Sweden in relation to the average for small European countries 1870–1997. Constant prices. Index 1913=1

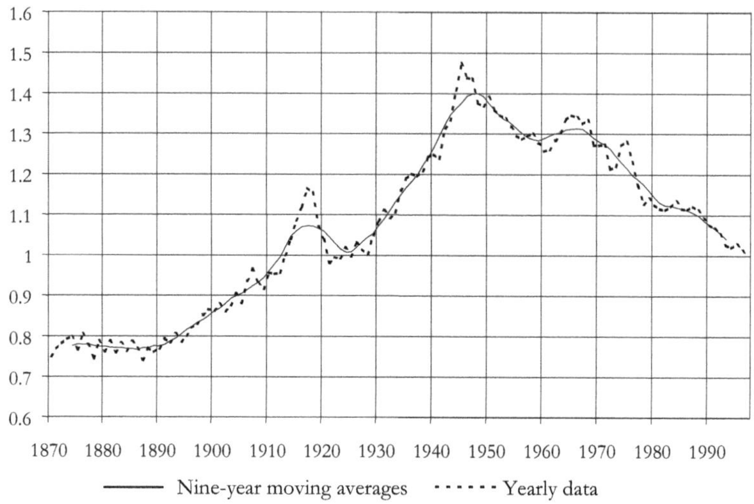

Source: See Table 1.

This tendency was more marked in the other two curves. Thus, there were slightly more similarities between the six and Sweden than between the other groups and Sweden. However, even compared to the six-country group, Sweden had a lower growth.

Thus, there is not only a slowdown of the economic growth relatively seen but also a relative retardation for Sweden in the second half of the twentieth century. However, for the sake of greater certainty another data set will also be examined. It is extracted from the Penn World Table,[9] and in Table 3 ratio figures from this data set are presented. The data set covers the period 1950–1992, i.e. the period of Sweden's relative slowdown and falling behind according to the GDP series used above.

The relative slowdown for Sweden is clear also in Table 3; and, as in the other comparison, the Swedish performance is more similar to the six-country group than to the other groups. It is also clear that the later part of the period (from the late 1960s) showed a greater retardation than the first part.

Thus, the 'stylized facts' that Swedish growth was internationally unique 1870–1970 and that it became very slow in an international comparison from 1970 should be modified.

Table 2: Change in per cent between five-year averages for the relation between Sweden's GDP per capita and the averages for three country groups 1870–1990. Constant prices

	Sweden in relation to		
	Sixteen industrial countries	*The six richest 1970*	*Small European Industrial countries*
1875–1885	–2.5	–2.3	–2.4
1885–1895	8.4	7.5	5.2
1895–1905	8.5	15.0	12.8
1905–1915	13.7	18.1	18.6
1915–1925	–2.2	–5.3	–6.6
1925–1935	20.5	19.2	15.8
1935–1945	11.9	19.9	21.2
1945–1955	–4.7	–16.5	–7.9
1955–1965	–1.8	1.3	1.8
1965–1975	–9.0	–2.5	–7.1
1975–1985	–10.0	–3.8	–9.3
1985–1995	–10.8	–7.7	–9.2

Source: See Table 1.

Note: The years in the first column represent five-year averages.

Table 3: Change in per cent between five-year averages for the relation between Sweden's GDP per capita and the mean for three country groups 1950–1992. Constant prices

	Sweden in relation to		
	Sixteen industrial countries	*The six richest 1970*	*Small European Industrial countries*
1955–1965	0.7	-0.5	–1.0
1965–1975	–8.3	–3.9	–7.0
1975–1985	–5.6	–1.2	–4.2
1985–1990	–3.2	–3.4	–2.3

Source: Penn World Table (Mark 5.6).

Note: 1. The periods in this table are not the same as in table 1 because the data exists only for the period 1950–1992. 2. The years in the first column represent five-year averages.

Sweden's relative growth performance: A divide around 1950

The data reveal that there were two distinctly different periods in Sweden's relative economic growth in the twentieth century, and that they coincided roughly with the first and the second half of the century. In the first period – actually starting c. 1890 – Sweden stands out as a distinct fast-grower and in the second one, there was a clear relative retardation. How are these periods to be analysed in an international and a small-State perspective? It should be said immediately that the following analysis is preliminary and that further research is needed before firm conclusions can be drawn.

In the twenty-odd years around 1900 there was a distinct acceleration of the Swedish growth rate, and if any period in Swedish economic history is to be called the industrial break-through of the country it is this one. There had been 'preparations' for this acceleration in the preceding decades such as intensive railway construction and expansion of the iron and steel industries and of forest industries. These developments formed a point of departure for expansion and consolidation of the whole industrial base, where engineering soon became very important. Thereby, and with the help of an expanding international economy, economic growth could be rapid in the breakthrough decades. During this period a number of new firms were established which quickly became major players: one might mention LM Ericsson (later Ericsson), ASEA (later part of Asea Brown Boveri, ABB) and SKF. This entrepreneurial activity effected a profound transformation of the economy and also set a development pattern that continued up to around the middle of the century. After the transformation in the breakthrough period, the 'new' industrial sector was rationalised in the first decade of the twentieth century and to an even greater extent in the 1920s. The following two decades saw a new transformation similar to that of the earlier breakthrough. The new transformation took its start from the engineering industry, and especially from those firms that had been founded around the turn of the century. In the 1930s the expansion focused upon consumer durables such as cars, refrigerators and other electrical equipment, for instance vacuum cleaners. Thereafter this internal pattern of transformation–rationalisation–transformation became weaker and disappeared in the 1950s and 1960s.

Another factor of great importance for the rapid growth during the first half of the twentieth century was that Sweden was a non-combatant in the two world wars: as a result its productive capacity remained intact during the war periods and exports could expand rapidly immediately afterwards, in particular after W.W. II. Besides, during W.W. I Sweden could pay back a great deal of its international debt due to the wartime inflation which greatly strengthened the country's financial position.

The period of relative slowdown in the second half of the twentieth century meant that a number of countries came closer to Sweden in terms of level of income per capita, which to a certain extent can be ascribed to the so called catching-up factor. A special case is that some countries started from a low production level because of the demolition of the production apparatus during W.W. II, the most conspicuous example being Germany. Other fast-growers – for instance Finland – had not reached the same income level as Sweden at around 1950. But irrespective of which one of the three country groups described above is chosen for comparison, a Swedish slowdown is apparent, and this means that the catch-up factor can not be the only explanation. Hence there is reason to believe that internal Swedish factors affected the rate of growth. However, the relative decrease was not noticed during the era of 'golden growth' when, historically seen, economic growth was very rapid. Instead, it was only from the 1970s that the problems slowly became apparent.

It is not astonishing that a relative Swedish slowdown occurred in the second half of the twentieth century. A continued relative growth rate of the same magnitude as in the first half of the century would have meant that the country sooner or later had reached the highest income level per head in the world. Such a position would have demanded a lead technologically and institutionally in important areas which would certainly have been difficult for a small country.[10] The important thing here is rather that the slowdown was so severe: why did a turn occur from a relative economic growth distinctly above the average of the industrialised countries to one as distinctly below this average? It can be assumed that domestic institutional factors hampered the change and adaptation necessary for a higher relative growth in the period under review. The mechanisms became apparent from the 1970s, but it also makes sense to suppose that they started to work earlier.

An adaptable small State?

In an analysis of the issues presented here the economic small-State model – that is, the description of the special characteristics of small countries – can be of some help. In general a small State is anxious to keep its economy open and hence to abolish trade barriers. Furthermore, there is a specialisation of production to those segments of the country's economy that are the most productive or, in other words, that generate rapid economic growth. At the core is the issue of economies of scale or, rather, that small countries are said to suffer diseconomies of scale. They are then regarded as separate economic units, and the standard economic theory states that production requires a certain size to be efficient. It is a question of the extent of the market, and when the market is seen as synonymous with the domestic market, a small country has too small a market for most of its production to be efficient. Consequently, if there were no remedy, the growth possibilities would be smaller than for a large country with a big home market. To overcome the drawbacks, the small country has to seek larger markets via foreign trade. A large part of what is needed within the country has to be imported while much of what the country is good at producing is exported. The result is that the small country has a larger foreign trade relative to its production than the large one.

The issues touched upon make it necessary for the small country to be highly adaptive to different situations created outside its borders. The performance of the country is of course dependent on the success of this adaptation process. If it is not successful, the country risks doing less well economically. However, the adaptation processes could be of different types during different periods due to varying historical conditions. Thus, this theory and the predictions derived from it are not equally important over the whole modern era (that is, roughly the last four hundred years). Furthermore, different groups of characteristics have been at the fore during different parts of this long period.

In an earlier paper[11] a general chronological framework for this change in small States was traced. The point of departure was the economic characterisation of small States: international dependence mirrored in a relatively large foreign trade; a striving for openness; activities in international organisations; and cooperation with other small States. However, the impact of these small-State characteristics has differed. International economic dependence was a minor factor up to the middle of the nineteenth century: then it grew substantially during the industrialisation period up to W.W. I, which meant that the special economic advantages and disadvantages of smallness of States became successively more evident. There was a growing dependence on the surrounding world, and certain flexibility had evolved which helped coping with this dependence. Judging from the foreign-trade ratios, dependence did not change much in the period from W.W. I up to the 1970s,[12] even if the ratios varied considerably in the short run. In the analysis of the performance in this era, Katzenstein's theory[13] is relevant, especially from the late 1940s. This states that to overcome the disadvantages of being small and of being heavily exposed to the international market, the small countries developed special institutions and arrangements. Democratic corporatism became characteristic and was flourishing up to the 1970s; and as mentioned above it was a constituent part of the Swedish/Scandinavian/Nordic small-State model.

From the late 1940s tendencies towards free trade prevailed, but it was only from the 1970s that foreign-trade ratios rose, seen in a long-term perspective. At the same time, internationalisation – or, as it is also called, globalisation – with its rapid international financial flows, expansion of international companies etc. fundamentally shook the democratic corporate system.

This periodisation can be compared with that obtained from the discussion above on the Swedish growth rate in an international perspective. The turning point of the relative growth curves occurred at the same time as the heyday of democratic corporatism in the Katzensteinian sense commenced, which is around 1950. However, coincidence in time does not mean causality; but it is possible that there is a connection.

Here the hypothesis will be discussed that there was a connection between on the one hand the general societal model (the welfare State and 'the Swedish model' based on democratic corporatism) and the attempts to maintain this or some of its important elements and on the other the relative growth performance of Sweden in the second half of the twentieth century. The assumption is that this model caused an increasing lack of adaptation and flexibility of the kind needed for the economy to work well in a small country according to the small-State theory, and that this affected growth negatively. An underlying assumption is that the forms of democratic corporatism could vary between countries and that this could affect their relative growth rates in different ways. This hypothesis implies that institutional factors of the kind described did not exist at all or did not affect the economic changes negatively in the first part of the century when, instead, the positive impact of entrepreneurship and technical change could work more freely.

A nation-state in the era of globalisation

The first decades after W.W. II saw rapid economic growth all over the industrialised world, but with varying rates between countries. These decades can be conceived as concluding an era of dominance or real – not only formal – economic independence of national industrial societies, even small ones. After this a new phase in capitalist development began.

> The postwar era until 1980 was the age of the *nation state*. Despite significant expansion of international trade, economic modernization in that period predominantly implied the conquest of mass markets delineated by national borders. Besides higher living standards, citizens also gained rights – to welfare benefit, education, health care, codetermination in worklife, etc. – that were essentially guaranteed by each nation state. The debate on the impact of globalization concerns the 1990s, not the decades preceding 1980.[14]

Exactly where the boundaries between economic phases should be located is open to debate, and it could even be claimed that there are no clear-cut boundaries. Conventionally, the end of the golden growth period and the start of a new economic phase are set at 1973, and the first oil crisis is often seen as a crucial factor in – or at least as symbolising – this change.[15] The important thing here is, though, that there was a period boundary in the 1970s.

However, economic internationalisation had commenced earlier: one could even say that it was a companion of capitalism, since this is *per se* an international system. In the period from the 1910s to the 1940s, though, there was a backlash with a return to nationalism – especially in the 1930s – but after W.W. II and particularly from the 1970s the international characteristics have become manifest and clearly dominant: a large and growing part of production emanates from international or transnational firms, and international capital flows have skyrocketed. International trade has grown rapidly, not only in absolute terms but also in relation to production; the export share increasing to values distinctly above those of the period before 1910. The fact that small countries in particular have become globalised is illustrated in Table 4, where a so-called globalisation index is shown – with all the problems connected with such a construction kept in mind. The globalisation index is said to indicate in descending order which countries are the most globalised.[16]

Table 4: The 25 most globalised countries ranked according to a globalisation index

1 Singapore	9 Norway	17 Hungary
2 Netherlands	10 Canada	18 Spain
3 Sweden	11 Denmark	19 Israel
4 Switzerland	12 United States	20 Malaysia
5 Finland	13 Italy	21 New Zealand
6 Ireland	14 Germany	22 Czech Republic
7 Austria	15 Portugal	23 Australia
8 United Kingdom	16 France	24 Greece
		25 Poland

Source: Measuring Globalization, *Foreign Policy*, January/February 2001.

The total list comprises 50 countries, but since the ranking reveals that the most globalised countries are those with the highest GDP per capita only the first 25 are listed here. As to country size, it is evident that the countries at the top of the list are mostly small. The small and wealthy European countries that formed a group in the comparison above – Netherlands, Sweden, Switzerland, Finland, Austria, Norway and Denmark – are all highly ranked.[17]

Globalisation has had a number of important effects on the State. The 'scope for state autonomy is certainly reduced since its control of economic and social processes within its territory has become less exclusive, and its ability to maintain national distinctiveness and cultural homogeneity has been curtailed.'[18] It has also meant that the internal balance of power that was characteristic of democratic corporatism, and which characterised the majority of the small countries, has become clearly weaker. The character of the industrial organisations has changed as the big companies have grown truly international or multinational, and they dominate the economic scene of the small countries with an entirely different authority than in previous periods. Then cooperation with other bodies was in these companies' interest, but now things have changed. This is also true for their employees, since the old type of 'industrial' wage policy was weakened by the growth of new groups, mainly central and local public employees, whose wages and salaries were financed through taxation. In this case, it meant a continuous conflict between what one wants to pay for the services via taxes and what one wants to get back in the form of services from the public authorities. Thus, new or highly altered institutions and organisations were needed in this era, and they are slowly developing.[19]

Small nations have become highly dependent on and to a very large extent integrated into the international economy, which means that their economic autonomy has been circumscribed and in practice, there is little room left for individual economic manoeuvring. In such a course of events it is very important for these countries to be as adaptive as possible and not rigid.

National policy out of step with the world around

Did Sweden act in an adaptive way in the second half of the twentieth century, that is, in the period when the relative growth of the country had switched to a downward tendency?[20] The 1950s and 1960s were as mentioned the heyday of democratic corporatism, which was central to the so-called 'Swedish model'. There was a consensus between capitalist interests represented by the industrial employers' association, the government and the trade unions. However, there were conspicuous exceptions from this consensus in the economic policy in Sweden and as time went by the exceptions increasingly tended to become the rule.[21]

Sweden started early to conduct an economic policy directed towards 'full employment'. A lot of measures were taken in order to keep unemployment low, and these increased from the 1950s. Support to those relocating is one example, and another is retraining of workers. This active employment policy together with other welfare measures led to high taxes and probably to inflationary tendencies, giving them a negative impact on economic growth.

One greatly debated issue in the 1950s was the question of general supplementary pensions for all employees. Should they be compulsory or voluntary? The social democrats argued for compulsory pensions, while the bourgeois parties were in favour of a voluntary scheme. In either case a consequence was that vast capital funds would be built up which in social-democratic opinion should be publicly administered while for the bourgeois parties they would be privately administered. The outcome of the pension issue was a victory for the social-democratic proposal and great publicly administered funds began to be built up. That these funds had an impact on capital formation in the country is very likely, and it is also probable that the flexibility of capital provision in general in the economy was negatively affected. However, more research is needed before definite conclusions can be drawn about this question and how it affected economic growth.

It was not only political measures that affected growth in the 1950s and 1960s. Industrial investments were not very progressive. The economic expansion took place in traditional trajectories, which meant that capacity in existing production units was expanded and the industrial structure did not change much. Besides, the level of investment was relatively low.[22]

The problems that commenced in the 1950s grew more serious later. The one-sidedness of investments towards old lines of production became evident in the 1960s: then industry went through an intensive rationalisation, which in the short run gave great increases in productivity and output. In the long run, however, it led to overcapacity and profitability problems. What can be expected in such a situation is a restructuring or a closedown. There should be 'creative destruction', but this did not happen. Industrial interests – certainly not all – in cooperation with trade union interests – even here not all – cooperated with the government irrespective of its political colour, social democratic or bourgeois. The cooperation resulted in vast government subsidies in the second half of the 1970s and the early 1980s, and here the shipbuilding industry provides a good example. The subsidies made it possible to build ships without making any real profits – and the fact that the large Swedish shipyards were highly advanced technically did not change this. When production in the shipbuilding industry could no longer be maintained, huge subsidies were paid out to establish other industries as compensation to the cities and municipalities that had lost their shipyards. This demonstrates another factor of Swedish political life: the strong connection between central and local government and the pervasive influence of the latter. The compensation industries, however, did not belong to the technologically most advanced segments of industry and they were generally not competitive or profitable. Thus the renewal of industrial production in Sweden was hampered, which in turn had adverse effects on economic growth. It should be added here that it was not only the shipbuilding industry that was heavily subsidised: firms in other industries also enjoyed substantial financial assistance.

The labour market also suffered from politically-motivated legislation at this time. Laws making it extremely difficult to change the composition of the labour force and/or to reduce it are an example, and the law on safety of employment (LAS) is typical. Another example is union representation in the corporate boards of directors and codetermination in all questions at all places of work

(MBL). In practice, however, this did not mean codetermination but obligatory information only. However, it took a long time and a lot of resources for firms to adjust to these measures.

LAS and MBL as well as other measures of a similar kind generated a deep mistrust between the trade unions and Social Democrats on the one hand and the industrial employers on the other. The so-called 'wage-earners' funds' were even more controversial. In the first half of the 1970s, a proposal came from LO, the central trade union that a fraction of a firm's profits should be paid to a central fund which would thereby become a company shareholder. Furthermore, these funds should be managed by the trade unions. As a consequence, after a certain time these funds would be majority owners of the companies. It goes without saying that the industry owners did not like this proposal, and the debate was intensive and disruptive. In the early 1980s a social-democratic government carried through a diluted variant of wage earners' funds; but when the bourgeois parties came into office some years later the funds were abolished. These events left a lasting legacy of distrust between the former constituting parties of democratic corporatism. Furthermore, it is probable that the propensity to invest or to undertake new entrepreneurial ventures were negatively affected, and this could not have been advantageous to economic growth.

Another ingredient in the 'Swedish model' was the so-called solidaristic wage policy, which originally meant equal pay for equal work. Later on, however, the meaning changed to equal pay. It was launched early in the post-war period and together with a highly progressive tax system it had the effect of successively making the income differences smaller. This policy became more and more pronounced during the second half of the twentieth century, and it probably influenced the economy and its growth in a negative way, among other things through changed preference and incentive structures.

The policy also made government expenditure and taxes rise. Around 1960 the numerically visible effects were small and compared to GDP Swedish expenditures did not differ much from those of other countries, as seen in Table 5. Thereafter Sweden definitely took the lead and in 1995 its government expenditure was internationally very high.[23]

Table 5. Government expenditure in a number of countries expressed as percentage of GDP 1960–1995

	1960	1980	1990	1995
Australia	21	32	35	37
Austria	36	48	49	53
Belgium	30	59	55	55
Canada	29	39	46	46
France	35	46	50	54
Germany	32	49	45	50
Ireland	28	49	41	42
Italy	30	42	53	52
Japan	18	32	32	36
Netherlands	34	55	54	51
New Zealand	27	38	41	35
Norway	30	38	54	49
Spain	19	32	42	44
Sweden	31	60	59	66
Switzerland	17	33	34	39
UK	32	43	40	43
USA	27	32	33	33
Arithmetic average	28	43	45	46

Source: Vito Tanzi and Ludger Schuknecht, 'Reforming Government: An Overview of Recent Experience', *European Journal of Political Economy* 3 (1997), p. 397.

Three general comments will be made in connection to this sketch of the Swedish development. Firstly, economic growth, here defined as a long-term increase of GDP or of GDP per capita, does not measure welfare, although it is an important component. A policy of the kind mentioned above could increase welfare, for example through safety at work and an even income distribution. Low unemployment is of course also important for people's welfare. Thus if an index of welfare could be used in the international comparisons it is possible that Sweden's downward tendency in the period following W.W. II would not be as clear as in the case of GDP per capita: it would even be possible that relative welfare did not go down at all. Secondly, international comparisons of growth-promoting or growth-hampering policies are not made to such an extent that it is beyond doubt that the Swedish political measures had the negative effects assumed here. However, there are indications. In a recently published study, research on the effects of government size on growth was made. A conclusion is that

> government size is a negative and statistically significant determinant of the economic growth rate. Moreover, the magnitude implies that a 1 percentage point increase in government size leads to a 0.23 percentage point decline in the growth rate, which translates to an elasticity of –2.4 at the means.[24]

Other investigations indicating the same thing were also referred to in the study. Thus, what is discussed here can be regarded as a set of hypotheses in need of further study – particularly when it comes to historical change. Thirdly, even if the welfare performance is not mirrored in the GDP per capita series in a short period of time, it is possible that over a longer period there would be negative effects if a country has a comparatively low growth: it can end up with problems of foreign trade balance, unemployment, deficits in the government budget etc.

In conclusion it seems that all the measures mentioned and many others made the Swedish governance system unadaptable to the ongoing internationalisation and globalisation. These rigidities could have hampered structural change and adaptation, with slow economic growth as a result. However, this hypothesis is in urgent need of further exploration. Then it would be desirable to study the problems in an internationally comparative setting. Thereby, an assessment would be possible of whether and to what extent the special Swedish features can explain the economic retardation.

Have things changed?

Has the situation changed in the last years? The 1990s started with a deep economic crisis that hit Sweden very hard. GDP declined steeply and unemployment rose to levels unknown since the 1930s. Then a recovery came with rapid increases in GDP, particularly in comparison with the preceding decades. It is sometimes maintained that the current economic development is similar to that in the 1950s and 1960s and that Sweden once again has become a fast-grower. The reasons for this are said to be mainly institutional changes; a radical transformation of the economic policy has occurred, which has been summarised as follows:

Monetary policy: Deregulated financial markets, floating exchange rates, inflation goals, an independent central bank.

Financial policy: Reformed government budgetary process, restrictions on government expenditure, goal for budgetary surpluses.

Structural policy: Deregulation, abolishment of state monopolies, a stricter competition law, a radical tax law.

Political decision rules: EU membership, four-year election periods (instead of three).[25]

The other reason could be that Sweden has done very well in 'the new economy'[26] which is to a large extent built on mobile telephony, the internet, etc. or – more generally – on information and communication technology (ICT or IT). Sweden has an old tradition in this field. One of the liveliest IT-regions in Europe is for instance situated in Stockholm. Furthermore, Sweden can show what in international terms is a very high density of computers, internet connections, and mobile telephones.

All this should have significantly influenced the growth figures. In Table 6, the percentage changes of GDP in recent years are shown for the same sixteen countries as used in the comparisons above. Compared to the average for the 1990s Sweden had a rapid growth, but compared to the growth engine for these years, the USA, it has been slow, and this is the case also in relation to Finland.

However, it is too early to say whether these growth figures are the outcome of temporary factors or if there is a change in the long-run performance. It is possible that the latter is true, but even so, it will take a long time to return to a top position in the income-per-capita league in OECD. In the early 1970s Sweden had a top rank, but in the year 2000 it was number 22 of 30 countries. Even if Sweden were to have a growth figure of 1 percentage point above the average of the rich countries, it would take up to 17 years for it to regain its 1970s position.[27]

Table 6. Annual percentage growth of GDP 1989–2000 in industrialised countries. Constant prices

	1989–1999	1997–1998	1998–1999	1999–2000	2000–2001	2001–2002	2002–2003	2003–2004
Australia	3.4	4.5	3.9	4.2	3.9	3.5	3.8	3.0
Austria	2.1[a)]	2.9	2.2	3.6	0.7	1.0	0.8	2.2
Belgium	1.9	2.7	1.8	3.8	0.8	0.7	1.3	2.9
Canada	2.1	3.1	3.7	4.8	1.5	3.4	2.0	2.9
Denmark	2.4	2.7	1.3	2.8	1.4	1.6	0.7	2.4
Finland	1.5	5.0	3.7	5.4	0.6	1.6	2.4	3.7
France	1.6	3.3	2.4	3.3	2.1	1.2	0.8	2.3
Germany	0.6[b)]	2.2	1.3	3.1	0.6	0.2	0.0	1.6
Italy	1.3	1.3	1.0	2.8	1.8	0.4	0.3	1.2
Japan	1.7	–2.8	1.4	1.9	0.4	0.3	1.3	2.7
Netherlands	3.4[a)]	3.7	3.0	4.5	1.3	0.2	–0.9	1.4
Norway	3.0[a)]	2.1	0.6	3.1	1.9	1.0	0.4	2.9
Sweden	1.6	3.0	3.9	4.0	1.1	1.9	1.5	3.6
Switzerland	0.9	2.1	1.4	3.3	0.9	0.1	–0.4	1.7
UK	1.9	2.2	1.7	3.0	2.1	1.8	2.2	3.1
USA	4.1[a)]	4.3	4.1	5.2	0.3	2.4	3.1	4.4
Arithmetic average	2.1	2.6	2.3	3.7	1.3	1.3	1.2	2.6

Source: *OECD in figures.*
[a)] 1995–1999 [b)] 1991–1999

Conclusion

In conclusion, the 'stylized fact' that Sweden's growth was extremely rapid in the period 1870–1970 can not be supported without strong reservations. The time when Sweden stood out as a fast grower is instead c. 1890–1950, when technological change and entrepreneurial talent had a positive impact on the development and the institutional setting did not hamper economic growth. The other 'stylized fact' – that Sweden had a comparatively slow growth from around 1970 to the 1990s – is, however, acceptable, although a relative slowdown had already set in by the 1950s. Over this period technological renewal did not contribute positively in the same way as before due to a rigid institutional framework. Whether this has changed once again in the 1990s to a long-term positive performance in international terms cannot yet be assessed. It is even possible that the different countries' economies will be integrated to such an extent that inter-country comparisons will be of less importance: perhaps comparisons of other types of economic areas or regions will attract more interest than those of small States.

1 For instance Bo Södersten, 'Inledning: svensk ekonomi inför år 2000', in Bo Södersten (ed.), *Marknad och politik* (Stockholm: SNS förlag, 1997), and Assar Lindbeck, *Det svenska experimentet* (Stockholm: SNS förlag, 1998).
2 The debate has mostly been conducted in Swedish, but an overview is found in *The Economic Journal* of November 1996 with the following articles: Jonas Agell, 'Why Sweden's Welfare State Needed Reform'; Steve Dowrick, 'Swedish Economic Performance and Swedish Economic Debate: A View from Outside'; Magnus Henrekson, 'Sweden's Relative Economic Performance: Lagging Behind or Staying on Top?'; and Walter Korpi, 'Eurosclerosis and the Sclerosis of Objectivity: On the Role of Values among Economic Policy Experts'. It should be no surprise that there are political undertones in this debate.
3 Simon Kuznets, *Six Lectures on Economic Growth* (The Free Press of Glencoe, Inc. 1959), pp. 89–100; Simon Kuznets, 'Economic Growth of Small Nations', in E. A. G. Robinson (ed.), *Economic Consequences of the Size of Nations. Proceedings of a Conference held by the International Economic Association* (London: Macmillan, 1960); Samuel Berrick Saul, 'The Economic Development of Small Nations: The Experience of North West Europe in the Nineteenth Century', in Charles Kindleberger and Guido di Tella (eds.), *Economics in the Long View, Essays in Honour of W. W. Rostow, Volume 2, Applications and Cases,* Part I (London: The MacMillan Press Ltd, 1982); and Carl Major Wright, *Economic Adaptation to a Changing World Market* (Copenhagen: Ejnar Munksgaard, 1939).
4 See for instance Angus Maddison, *Economic Growth in the West: Comparative Experience in Europe and North America* (New York: The Twentieth Century, 1964), *Dynamic Forces in Capitalist Development: A Long-Run Comparative View* (Oxford: Oxford University Press, 1991), and *Monitoring the World Economy 1820–1992* (Paris: Development Centre of the Organisation for Economic Cooperation and Development, 1995).
5 See e.g. Walter Korpi, *Halkar Sverige efter? Sveriges ekonomiska tillväxt 1820–1990 i jämförande belysning* (Stockholm: Carlssons, 1992).
6 The concept of 'the Swedish model' has gained a prominent place in Swedish political rhetoric, and perhaps this is why it is devoid of distinct meaning. Furthermore, it has chauvinist overtones and, therefore, it should be handled with great

care in scholarly contexts. There is a vast literature on 'the Swedish model'. See, for instance, Thomas Pettersson, 'I den svenska modellens skugga – Välfärdsutveckling i ett internationellt perspektiv efter 1930' in Lena Andersson-Skog and Olle Krantz (eds.), *Omvandlingens sekel: Perspektiv på ekonomi och politik i Sverige under 1900-talet* (Lund: Studentlitteratur, 2002), and the literature referred to there.

7 Peter Katzenstein, *Small States in World Markets. Industrial Policy in Europe* (Cornell University Press, 1985).

8 Comparisons of this kind are mostly based on GDP per capita. Another way of comparing economic performance is to use wage series. This has been done by (among others) Jeffrey Williamson in a number of publications: for instance, Jeffrey G. Williamson, 'The Evolution of Global Labor Markets since 1830: Background, Evidence and Hypotheses', in *Explorations in Economic History* (1995). However, the data problems are considerable in these comparisons, probably even more so than in the case of GDP per capita. Averages of wages are difficult to assess, and if the figure is said to represent the wages of a certain category, e. g. unqualified industrial workers, we must ask what is meant by the term and whether an identical category is to be found throughout the periods and nations discussed. However, a comparison based on Williamson's wage series shows a profile similar to that of the GDP per capita comparisons above.

9 Penn World Table (Mark 5.6). See further Robert Summers and Alan Heston, 'The Penn World Table (Mark 5)', *Quarterly Journal of Economics* 2 (1991). It should be emphasised that the series in the two data sets are different as to construction. Therefore it is not at all astonishing that there are clear differences in the percentages in tables 2 and 3. However, the tendencies shown are the same.

10 Here it is a question of productive technology. Some very small countries have reached very high income levels due to (for instance) financial transactions of various kinds.

11 Olle Krantz, *Small European Countries in International Organisations: A Perspective on the Small-State Question* (Umeå: Mimeo, 2004).

12 This implies that the rise of the foreign trade ratios in the 1950s and 1960s is interpreted as a recovery from the very low level in the 1940s.

13 Katzenstein, *Small States in World Markets.*

14 Lars Mjøset, 'The Nordic Economies 1945–1980', *ARENA Working Papers* WP 00/4, 2000, p. 1.

15 e.g. Angus Maddison, *Dynamic Forces in Capitalist Development: A Long-Run Comparative View* (Oxford: Oxford University Press, 1991), and *Monitoring the World Economy 1820–1992* (Paris: Development Centre of the Organisation for Economic Cooperation and Development, 1995).

16 The construction is described as follows: 'The A. T. Kearney / Foreign Policy Magazine Globalization Index encompasses nine key indicators of global integration. Globalization in goods and services is measured through the share of international trade (exports of goods and services plus imports of goods and services) in gross domestic product (GDP), as well as the convergence of domestic prices and world prices. Financial globalization is measured through income payments and receipts, the inflows and outflow of foreign direct investment, and the inflow and outflow

of portfolio capital, all measured as a share of GDP. The globalization of personal contact is measured with international tourists and travelers as a share of population, minutes of incoming and outgoing international telephone calls per capita, and transfer payments and receipts as a share of GDP. Finally, three elements comprise the Internet connectivity indicator – the number of Internet users, the number of Internet hosts, and the number of secure servers, all measured on a per capita basis.' (http://www.atkearney.com/pdf/eng/Rankings_S.pdf, 5 February 2001).

17 Belgium was not included in the globalisation measurement.

18 Sandro Sideri, 'Globalisation and Regional Integration', in *European Journal of Development Research* June (1997), 42.

19 These profound changes have been studied in international research, not least by political scientists and sociologists. One example is a volume very tellingly entitled *Organized Industrial Relations in Europe: What Future?* Colin Crouch and Franz Traxler (eds.) (Avebury, Aldershot, 1995). The introductory essay is called 'Farewell to labour market associations? Organized versus disorganized decentralization as a map for industrial relations' (Traxler) and the concluding chapter has the title 'Reconstructing corporatism? Organized decentralisation and other paradoxes' (Crouch).

20 It has to be emphasised that the following comments are made from the viewpoint of reaching high economic growth. The measures discussed below could be positive from other angles (for instance, welfare). Besides, they should be studied in an international perspective, which has not been done to a sufficient degree to allow firm conclusions. Therefore, as mentioned above, it is a question of hypotheses.

21 Needless to say, it is not possible to provide an extensive analysis of the Swedish political, institutional and economic performance in the second half of the twentieth century. Only some examples are given.

22 Lennart Jörberg, *Den svenska ekonomiska utvecklingen 1850–1990* (Ekonomisk-historiska institutionen, Lunds universitet, 1991), p. 47f.

23 After the last year in table 6 (1995) the share of government expenditure has gone down in Sweden to 60% in 1999. Probably the tendency was the same in other countries.

24 Åsa Hansson, *Limits of Tax Policy*, Lund Economic Studies 90 (2000), p. 111.

25 Hans Tson Söderström, Pontus Braunerhjelm, Richard Friberg, Victor Norman, Örjan Sölvell, *kluster.se. Sverige i den nya ekonomin* (Stockholm: SNS förlag, 2001), where a description of and opinions about developments in the last decade are given.

26 'The new economy' is in fact the same economy that has existed for a very long time, at least since the industrial revolution. Thus, it is a typical cliché or an expression devoid of analytical meaning.

27 Tson Söderström *et al. kluster.se*, p. 43.

Lars Svensson

Foreign Competition and Labour Market Institutions in a Small Open Economy: Sweden during the Short Twentieth Century*

Introduction

In 1968 chief economists G. Edgren of the Central Organisation of Salaried Employed (TCO), K.-O. Faxén of the Swedish Employers' Confederation (SAF), and C.-E. Odhner of the Swedish Trade Union Confederation (the LO) published a report with the title *Lönebildning och samhällsekonomi (Wage formation and the Economy)*, soon renamed 'the EFO report' after the initials of the three authors.[1] This was a collaborative study of wage formation in Sweden between 1952 and 1968 sponsored by the three major organisations in the Swedish labour market. The ultimate intention was to supply a normative model for wage policy within the wider socio-economic framework of 'The Swedish Model'. Ironically enough, the foundations of the EFO model were soon after eroded to the extent that the model eventually broke down, and the normative function of the EFO report became misleading. The EFO model worked successfully from around 1950 until the mid-1970s, a period which will in this chapter be called the extended EFO period.

The EFO report was based on a two-sector model with a competing sector (the C sector) and a sheltered sector (the S sector). It stated that 'relationships with abroad, given fixed exchange rates, and the development of productivity in the competing sector, have in fact controlled the determination of wages in the period studied, 1952–1968.'[2] This chapter goes a step further and claims that conditions in the competing sector have in fact determined the development of labour-market institutions in Sweden since the beginning of the twentieth century. The study uses the C sector vs. S sector dichotomy as the main framework of analysis. It demonstrates that the institutional development which eventually brought about 'The Swedish Model' in a broad sense, to a large extent was driven by C-sector agents, both employers and workers, as they tried to cope with 'small open economy constraints'. The approach is economic-historical in that it emphasises that conditions determining these constraints, as well as the potential means to manage them, have varied over time. More precisely, small open-economy constraints have varied in accordance with a regular and recurrent pattern of industrial dynamics which has characterised the Swedish economy since early industrialisation. Phases dominated by transformation and renewal have alternated with phases characterised by rationalisation within the established structure. Conditions in the labour market seem to have shifted in systematic accord with the alternation between these phases.[3]

Wage formation during the extended EFO period

The extended EFO period coincided with the 'Golden Years' when international relations were moulded by GATT and the Bretton-Woods system, i.e. characterised by relative openness, fixed exchanged rates, restrictions on capital flows but a reasonably free mobility of labour. Swedish national economic policy was Keynesian during this period and State interventionist. Government was in the hands of the Social Democratic Party, which was closely allied with the LO. However, as a distinguishing feature of the Swedish model, the government only interfered in labour-market affairs in exceptional circumstances.

The EFO report stressed that wage formation was subject to different conditions in the two sectors of the economy. It was a basic postulate of the EFO model that the competing sector was a price taker in the international market, while pricing in the sheltered sector was mainly determined by the development of costs. This had several implications.

Costs in the sheltered sector depended mainly on wages, profit requirements and productivity. Wage development in the sheltered sector tended to parallel development in the competing sector due to the fact that the latter was recognised as the leading sector in the wage-formation process. Consequently, wages were externally determined in the sheltered sector. Profits were, it was argued in the report, externally determined as well, since profit requirements were thought to be dependent on opportunities for financing in the capital market.[4]

Wage development in the competing sector was constrained by the necessity to stay competitive in foreign markets, i.e. to keep price increases within the limits set by the external rate of inflation. The room for wage increases was determined by the development of productivity in the sector. The EFO report stated that

> wages in competing industries could not in the long run rise so much above and beyond the limits fixed by productivity and price developments that the profitability and competitiveness of these industries became insufficient.[5]

The implication was that differences in productivity change would prompt deviations in prices between the two sectors. To the extent that productivity growth in the sheltered sector was below that in the competing sector, there would be pressure on the inflation rate to increase beyond the limits set by external conditions. It also followed that this threat to the model would be stronger if wage increases in the sheltered sector went beyond those in the competing sector, i.e. if the latter were not recognised as the leading sector in the wage formation process. As we shall see, this was a dilemma that had already attracted attention in the early 1920s and was a major force leading to centralisation of power within the trade-union movement as well as in the employers' organisations during the interwar period.

Problems that emanated from differences in conditions determining wage formation in the two sectors were obviously managed successfully in the period investigated in the EFO report. This was to a large extent due to the presence of a favourable institutional framework.

Central and nationwide collective agreements reached through centralised bargaining between the principal organisations of workers and employers, which possessed the power to implement such agreements, were an essential part of the institutional setting. Equally important, however, were the conventions that formed the ideological basis of the negotiations. These informal institutions included the recognition of the competing sector as the leader in the process of wage formation. Moreover, it was of vital importance that all parties acknowledged the superior role of productivity. This means that wage formation as well as income distribution between labour and capital should be subordinated to productivity growth. And finally, there was a wide acceptance of the doctrine of solidaristic wages, although interpretations could diverge.

Competition, rationalisation and wage formation

During most of the extended EFO period there was a sustained fall in the relative wage of workers in the competing sector. In the 1950s the average wage of male blue-collar workers in the metal and engineering industries was about fifteen per cent above the male wage in the food processing industry. During the next twenty years this wage differential was totally wiped out (see Figure 1).

This was part of a general levelling of wages between sectors that occurred during the 1960s and the 1970s. The same period also brought a considerable compression of wages within sectors.[6] Furthermore, female relative wages in manufacturing increased rapidly from around 1960 until the late 1970s.[7]

The wage equalisation process of the 1960s and 1970s has generally been regarded as a result of the successful realisation of basic ideological targets of the trade union movement, notably the solidaristic wage policy, which had been possible because the LO had gained in relative strength. The change in wage structure may, however, be given an alternative interpretation, which instead considers the solidaristic wage policy as a solution to difficulties that firms in the competitive sector encountered during the period. These were mainly related to the fact that Swedish firms faced increasingly fierce foreign competition from the late 1950s onwards, partly as a consequence of European post-war recovery and partly due to conditions created by the internal dynamics of Swedish industry.

The years around 1960 brought an end to a period of transformation and renewal that had characterised Swedish industry since

Figure 1: Ratio of male blue-collar wages in the competing sector to male blue-collar wages in the sheltered sector 1920–1939 (C-to-S) and ratio of male blue-collar wages in the metal trades industries to male blue-collar wages in the food and beverage industry 1920–1990 (Met-to-Food)

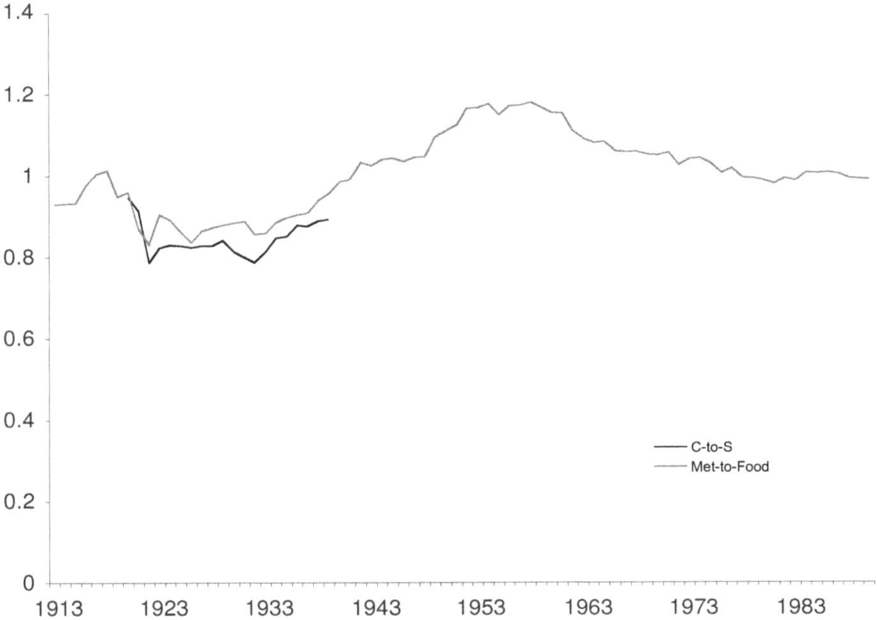

Sources: Author's computations from *Statistical Yearbook of Wages* (Stockholm: Social Welfare Board, 1928–1951), *Official Statistics of Sweden, Wages* (Stockholm: Social Welfare Board, 1952–1960) and *Official Statistics of Sweden, Wages* (Stockholm: Statistics Sweden, 1961–1990).

Note: Separate wage data for S-sector workers and C-sector workers are available only for the period 1920–1939. For the rest of the period we have used wages for workers in the metal trades (manufacturing of fabricated metal products, machinery and equipment plus basic metal industries, i. e. SNI 37 plus SNI 38 and their previous equivalents) as a proxy for the C-sector workers, and workers in the food and beverages industry (SNI 31 and its previous equivalent) as a proxy for S-sector workers. Figure 1 displays both series for 1920–1939. It demonstrates that the patterns of development were similar in the two series during that period. We have also experimented with other combinations. They all show a basically similar pattern.

the recovery from the Great Depression. In the terminology of Lennart Schön, the Swedish economy now entered a phase of rationalisation.[8] Rationalisation means concentration of resources to the most productive units and measures to increase efficiency within individual firms. In the rationalisation phase investments are thus primarily directed towards short-term and cost-reducing activities. This is partly a response to increased competition in wider international markets, which to some extent at least was a consequence of the diffusion of innovations over industries and firms as well as across national borders.[9] New technologies are increasingly easily adopted in different fields of production and in new geographical areas. Moreover, new technology now tends to form the basis of standardisation and specialisation, with considerable supply effects in core areas of production. Simultaneously, and due to the diffusion of technology, production spreads to new countries. This creates a need to expand markets, which triggers off a geographical extension of trade.

The specific conditions of the late 1950s had positive as well as negative impacts on Swedish firms in the competing sector. On the one hand, institutional development during the 1950s, notably the Bretton-Woods Treaty, GATT and the onset of European integration, supported the expansion of world trade. On the other hand, industrial recovery in Europe accentuated competition in European markets.

The ability of firms to survive in this highly competitive environment became dependent upon their ability to keep unit costs low. This is why rationalisation in the 1960s implied an extensive utilisation of Fordist modes of production in leading sectors of the Swedish manufacturing industry, e.g. the automotive industry. It included standardisation of products and production methods and the utilisation of special-purpose machinery that relied primarily on unskilled workers. Such a simplification of tasks tends to decrease productivity differentials between skill groups. It highlights the cost-saving function of wage-structure shifts and tends to increase demand for low-skilled workers at fixed relative wages.

Concurrently, expansion was mandatory in order to become and stay competitive by means of keeping unit costs low. Firms com-

Figure 2: Number of workers in the metal trades industries (see note to figure 1) as a proportion of the total number of workers in the manufacturing industry 1920–1990

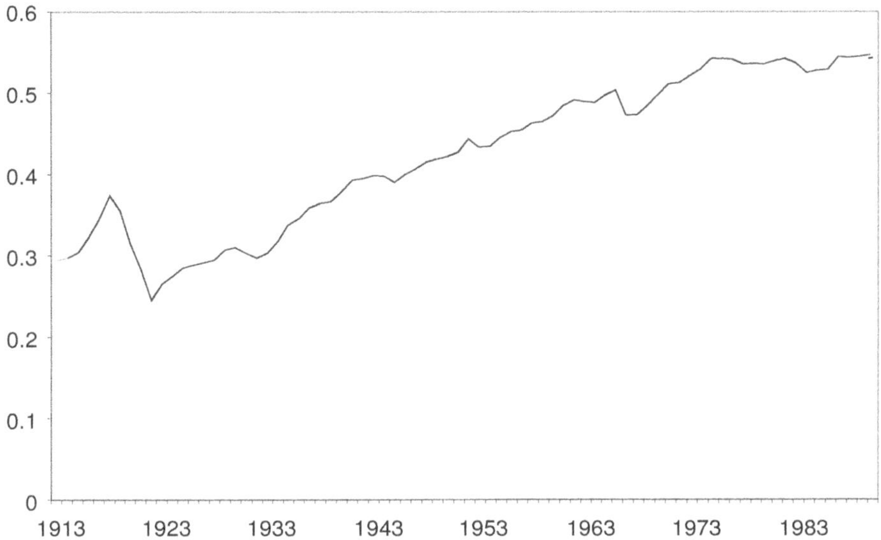

Sources: *Official Statistics of Sweden, Mining and Manufacturing*, (Stockholm: Board of Trade and Commerce, 1913–1960) and *Official Statistics of Sweden, Mining and Manufacturing* (Stockholm: Statistics Sweden, 1961–1990).

peting in international markets consequently faced the problem of attracting an additional amount of labour in a situation characterised by labour shortage, and simultaneously keeping labour costs down to a minimum. In some sectors this problem was not insurmountable, while in others world market shares gradually diminished. The textile and clothing industries regressed while the engineering industry, which had experienced a substantial growth in relative employment since the 1930s, continued its expansion at an unaltered pace. Its share of total industrial employment increased from thirty-three to forty per cent between 1960 and 1975 (see Figure 2), and its share of total exports increased from thirty-two to forty percent in the same period.[10] As shown above, relative wages in the metal trades fell substantially from around 1960. The simultaneous fall in relative wages and rise in relative employment call for an explanation.

Wage policy and the interests of competitive-sector agents

Firms in an expanding sector have basically two means to increase their labour force in circumstances of labour shortage: transferring labour from other sectors, or increasing the total labour force. Both seem at first sight to imply wage increases. I shall argue that the solidaristic wage-policy doctrine, which at the end of 1950s had gained wide acceptance within the LO, pointed to a way out of this dilemma and helped to exploit both these possibilities while still keeping wage costs down.

The solidaristic wage policy has a long history in the ideological as well as in the practical debates within the LO. An ideology of wage equalisation had been articulated already at the LO congresses in the 1920s.[11] The idea originated from workers in the competing sector, notably in the metal and engineering industries. In 1951 wage equalisation became an integral part of a new programme for the promotion of economic growth under full employment and price stability within the Rehn-Meidner Model.[12] It was a constituent part of the logic of the programme that solidarism would contribute to productivity growth in manufacturing. By applying the doctrine of equal pay for equal work, regardless of branch or geographical location, firms with low productivity were deprived of the possibility of surviving by means of paying low wages.[13] These firms would be presented with two alternatives: increase productivity and thereby be able to offer 'equal' wages, or close down. Both courses would increase average productivity. In the latter case labour would eventually be released and transferred to more productive units, making it possible for firms in leading sectors to expand their labour force at lower costs than would otherwise have been the case.

Agreements which featured provisions clearly designed to benefit the low-paid were signed from 1964 onwards, and were more pronounced between 1969 and 1974.[14] Considering the long history of the solidaristic wage doctrine, it is reasonable to ask why this policy was implemented only from the 1960s. The traditional view holds that this was because only then had the LO gained the power to force through equalising wage contracts, although a policy for equalisation had constituted a fundamental part of trade-union ideology for many years. Such a primarily political explanation is based on a 'capital-against-labour' framework of analysis. An alternative *cross-class alliance approach*[15] focuses on differences in conditions and interests between sectors rather than between labour and capital. This will be discussed in some detail below. Suffice it to point out at this stage that collective agreements between the Swedish Metal Workers' Union and the Swedish Engineering Employers' Association in 1961 already had a 'low-wage profile'.[16]

The solidaristic wage policy also became an efficient means of increasing the labour force by attracting new groups, notably women, to join its ranks. It is obvious that employers, particularly in expanding firms in the engineering industry, were seeking ways of filling job vacancies with low initial skill requirements by activating the labour-force reserve of married women.[17] In 1960 the LO and SAF agreed in central negotiations to abolish the separate wage tariffs for male and female workers over a period of five years from 1962. The effect differed between sectors, both with respect to magnitude and to pace. It was strongest and most rapid in the metal trades, which indicates that the growth of demand for female labour was related to the rationalisation process in industry. The highly Fordist organisation of production in parts of the engineering industry, e.g. the automotive industry, made it profitable to increase the proportion of women in the labour force. Productivity crests were short, which rendered negligible the drawback of higher expected female turnover compared with male. The advantage of lower female wages was of greater importance. Job vacancies with low initial skill requirements could be filled at relatively low costs by activating a labour reserve of married women.

Theory and evidence suggest that an increase in female wages became a successful means of taking women to the shop floor, but in male-dominated workplaces it was of vital importance that this could be achieved without increasing male wages. This implied a rise in female relative wages. Accordingly, the proposal to abolish separate wage rates for men and women furnished a golden opportunity to accomplish a favourable change in the wage structure.

The automotive industry provides an example.[18] While the female-to-male relative wage increased from seventy-three per cent in 1960 to ninety-six per cent in 1965, the male wage as a percentage of the average male wage in manufacturing as a whole decreased in the same period from 122 to 105 per cent. Between 1960 and 1975 the proportion of female workers rose from two to fifteen per cent of the total workforce. The changeover of the female relative wage to an upward trend occurred as early as 1959. Consequently, it was not an effect of the agreement to abolish separate female wage rates.

The divergence of interests among employers is further underlined by differences in how employers reacted to the agreements that introduced joint wage rates. This was qualified by a note stating that the occupational groupings were to be overhauled.[19] In several firms, particularly in the female-intensive and declining textile and apparel sectors, gender wage differentials were maintained through an extensive division into wage groups with differing duties.[20]

The examples demonstrate that equalisation of wages was in the interest of employers in expanding industrial sectors exposed to fierce foreign competition, where rationalisation was carried out by means of Fordist work organisation. It was compatible with the new production concept which implied substitution of low-skilled for skilled workers and female labour for male. Equalisation reduced total wage costs in the competing sector since wages initially were above the average of total manufacturing. At the same time it brought a labour-attracting increase in the relative wage of low-skilled, including female, labour. Consequently, an equalising wage policy was of direct interest to firms in the competing sector and was obviously clearly articulated and successfully accomplished by competitive-sector agents during the extended EFO period. This could happen because the export-oriented industry was a leading sector both quantitatively and qualitatively. The dominant engineering industry had expanded continuously since the early 1930s. In the mid-1960s engineering employment had accounted for nearly thirty per cent of total industrial employment, and engineering's share of total exports increased from twenty to forty per cent between 1950 and 1970.

Our analysis indicates that the renewal of labour-market institutions, wage-policy changes, and even the ideological re-orientation of the labour market organisations, conformed to established trends in wage-structure variables. The role of trade unions and employers' organisations was not independent of labour-market forces, especially the structure of labour supply and demand.

This does not mean that wage agreements merely reflected the market price of labour. Large organisations comprise not only divergent interests but, partly as a consequence of this, also competing ideological currents. The ideas actually articulated by an organisation are determined by internal power relations. Ideas that conform to trends in market forces appear to exert a greater influence than do ideas that are at variance with them. This enhances the persuasive power of such ideas within organisations, and assists their achievement of hegemonic status. But the relative autonomy of ideological structures may bring about a situation where the agents who originally introduced and supported the ideas lose their influence over current development. In other words, ideologies do not change overnight to immediately follow shifts in underlying material conditions.

The development and implementation of wage policies from the early 1960s demonstrates this. By that time the solidaristic wage-policy doctrine had gained wide support within the LO. It was eventually reformulated from 'equal pay for equal work' to a policy for general wage equalisation. At that point equalisation of wages was no longer of direct material interest to workers in the competing sector: they had already appropriated to themselves a considerable wage premium. However, equalisation conformed highly to the interests of – and was in practice supported by – powerful employers in progressive industrial sectors exposed to fierce foreign competition, who realised the possibility of using wage equalisation as a cost-reducing means of increasing their competitive capacity in international markets.

The history of labour-market institutions

The analysis in the previous section demonstrates that wage formation during the EFO period became subordinated to the interests of firms exposed to foreign competition. This was due to the increasing importance of the engineering industry, but also because a favourable institutional framework was at hand. That framework included both formal institutions such as the bargaining system and informal institutions such as the ideological foundation of the negotiations. They were all constituent parts of 'The Swedish Model' in a broad sense. They were rather the outcome of a drawn-out historical process than the results of normative modelling.

The metal trades agreement of 1905 and the principle of collective bargaining

The first nation-wide collective agreement in the Swedish labour market was concluded for the engineering industry between the Swedish Metal Workers' Union (Metall) and the Swedish Engineering Employers' Association (VF) in 1905. The agreement exercised a fundamental influence on the future development of industrial relations. Leading players in the manufacturing industry had, by signing the agreement, demonstrated that they accepted the principle of collective agreements and also recognised the workers' freedom of association. It also implied that the closed-shop principle was rejected.

One part of the agreement applied to the regulation of disputes between employers and workers and was in fact the first agreement on negotiation procedures in the Swedish labour market. In this sense it preceded and broke ground for the Saltsjöbaden Basic Agreement between the LO and SAF of 1938, which defined a set of rules for negotiation procedures and for conflict resolution that formed a basis for more peaceful labour relations.

Moreover, the negotiations that preceded the VF-Metall Agreement clearly revealed the problems of having two different parallel principles of organisation within the trade union movement. The Swedish Metal Workers' Union aimed at organising workers within the metalworking and engineering industries regardless of type of work, according to the vertical industry-association principle. Other unions such as the Founders' Union organised workers with certain skills according to the occupational-association principle. Eventually, and supported by pressure from the employers' organisations, the vertical industry-association principle was slowly adopted.

As early as the LO congress of 1912 a statement was made in support of this principle, but in practice the Swedish Metal Workers' Union was the pioneer in this matter.[21]

Centralisation of power among employers

The implementation of collective agreements presupposed a sufficiently centralised power structure within the organisations that concluded such agreements. SAF was founded in 1902. From the beginning mutual solidarity and support in labour conflicts were the fundamental objectives of the organisation. From 1905 SAF had the authority to approve collective agreements. From then on SAF's charter prescribed that no agreements were to be concluded unless they contained a paragraph which established employers' rights to employ and dismiss workers, to conduct and distribute work, and to use workers irrespective of union affiliation. In 1906 this was partly modified in the so-called December Compromise with the LO, which included the recognition of workers' freedom of association.

The development of labour relations in the engineering industry played a leading role in manufacturing at large. Collective bargaining and agreements rapidly spread to other sectors, and became an established institution in the Swedish labour market even before the First World War. In 1914 about 1000 agreements covered 142,000 workers; in 1940 there were 15,000 agreements covering almost one million workers.[22]

VF did not join SAF until 1917. By virtue of its size, but also because it organised firms in the most advanced industrial sector, it soon became the leading member organisation.[23] Sigfrid Edström, managing director of ASEA, a leading engineering firm, and chairman of VF since 1916, was elected chairman of SAF in 1931. He was a dedicated centralist and would play a major role in the further development of the organisation. So was Gustaf Söderlund, who was appointed SAF's managing director in the same year.[24]

However, their predecessor Hjalmar von Sydow, who had served as both chairman and managing director, had paved the way. From the early 1920s if not before the authority of SAF was used as a means of controlling the wage policy of the confederate organisations.[25] In the 1921 annual report of the SAF board, von Sydow pronounced a strong opinion in favour of central collective agreements. Moreover, in the 1924 report von Sydow also questioned the sectoral wage differentials that had developed in the early 1920s. He simply could not see any rational arguments why workers in the sheltered sector should be paid more than workers in the competing sector. Just as in the simultaneous debate within the LO, and in the EFO report much later, von Sydow noted that prices in the competing sector were determined in international competitive markets, while increased wage costs in the sheltered sector could be compensated for by adjusting prices in the domestic market. According to von Sydow SAF had not managed to solve the problem of employers in the sheltered sector that practised the law of least resistance instead of showing solidarity with their fellow employers in the competing sector.[26]

To keep wage growth in the sheltered sector, particularly the building trade, in line with the development in other industries was a problem that had attracted attention even before the war. The struggle within SAF ended in the mid-1930s when export-oriented employers established considerable power within the organisation. A major conflict in the building trades starting in 1933 caused the problem of wage differentials between sectors to come to a head. It prompted employers as well as workers in the competitive sector to fight eventually victorious internal battles against their fellow members in the sheltered sector. At the end of the 1930s, when the building-trade conflict had come to an end, power was centralised in the hands of representatives of the competitive sector both within SAF and the LO.[27]

Centralisation within the LO

Within the LO the centralisation issue was from the outset closely related to the problem of wage differentials between industrial sectors. Briefly put, the question was whether the workers in a single firm or sector should maximise their own wages regardless of the conditions of other workers, or whether solidarity among workers across firms and sectors should be taken into consideration. In his seminal work on the history of 'solidarsitic wage policy' Ullenhag holds that the three LO congresses in 1922, 1926 and 1931 brought a shift in ideological orientation towards solidarity with the low-paid workers.[28] According to its proponents, this implied a strategic move from defence to attack, which required the control of conflict weapons to be concentrated in the hands of the central body of the organisation.

A similar view on the causes of centralisation was put forward by Fregert,[29] who suggested that centralisation and wage equalisation in the interwar period might be explained by self-interest rather than ideology, since the campaign by low-wage groups for wage equalisation was an important factor behind centralisation.[30]

The unbalanced development of Swedish industry during the turbulent years following the First World War brought major shifts in relative wages between sectors, and a substantial wage premium emerged in favour of workers in the sheltered sector. The ratio of sheltered to competitive-sector wages moved from 95 to 125 per cent between 1916 and 1922.

Construction workers and workers in the food and beverage industry were among the least affected when nominal wages fell in 1920–1922. While blue-collar wages on average fell by thirty-two per cent, the decrease in these two sheltered sectors was limited to a mere half of that. The obvious reason was that employers could compensate themselves by adjusting prices, since the lion's share of their production was non-traded goods with low price elasticity.

This is precisely what was pointed out in debates at the LO congresses during the 1920s. In a motion to the 1922 congress the Stockholm section of the Swedish Metal Workers' Union declared:

> To the extent that the wages of other groups of workers exceed those of the workers in the export industry, the wages of the latter will be further reduced, something that can hardly be in accordance with the demands of class solidarity.[31]

The argument was that price increases of products from sheltered industries, which were often 'necessary also for the working class', directly reduced the real wage. The development of housing rents and nominal wages would eventually confirm this suspicion. The rent of a two-roomed flat increased from thirteen to twenty-three per cent of the average blue-collar worker's wage between 1920 and 1928.[32]

The metal workers repeated their claims at the 1926 congress, and were supported by the Sawmill Workers Union.[33] The call for a wage policy based on 'class solidarity' was now underpinned by proposals that would give the central organisation, the LO, the power to accomplish wage agreements on the basis of solidarity and with the aim of equalising wages. It was proposed that the board of the LO should be granted the authority to scrutinise all new agreements and, perhaps even more important, to control conflict funds.

Proposals for centralisation of power within the organisation did not, however, lead to any concrete measures until much later. Only at the 1941 LO congress were decisions taken that adapted the power structure of the organisation to centralised bargaining and central agreements. The congress granted the board of the LO the authority to scrutinise negotiations and agreement proposals of member federations, and also the power to deny a member organisation the right to conflict support if the terms at stake were not approved by the central organisation. Obviously, the conflicts in the building trades in the mid-1930s paved the way for the decisions at the 1941 LO congress. The arguments for centralisation were similar to those put forward in the motion from the metal workers almost twenty years earlier and by Bertil Ohlin in his 1926 article.

Attitudes towards rationalisation and productivity

The evolution of a positive attitude towards rationalisation and measures favourable to productivity growth has been described by De Geer[34] mainly from an employer's point of view, and by Johansson[35] from a trade-union perspective. These studies demonstrate that consensus was reached at an early stage in these matters and that trade unions in Sweden developed a comparatively positive attitude towards rationalisation.

It is worth pointing out that not only did the LO accept the ideas of rationalisation and scientific management as early as the 1920s, but the organisation also opted for a more active role in enhancing productivity. It is obvious that the Swedish Metal Workers' Union played a leading role in this process. At the 1931 LO congress there was a motion from the Gothenburg metal workers proposing the foundation of a department for 'the study of the development of the labour process' and 'for providing an information service on these matters'.[36] At the 1936 LO congress the issue was revisited by the Swedish Metal Workers' Union. A positive attitude towards rationalisation measures was combined with the aim of increasing workers' influence on industrial life: 'the trade union movement must contribute to the development and strengthening of industry, which is a prerequisite for better economic and social conditions. To this end the trade union movement must strive for social control over industry and increased influence on the management of firms.'[37]

The fact that the LO leadership had accepted rationalisation as the major means to improve economic and social conditions paved the way for the even more active role of the trade-union movement that was introduced by the Rhen-Meidner model at the 1951 LO congress. This brought a shift of the solidaristic wage policy's objective from wage equalisation to the promotion of growth. The Rehn-Meidner model was launched at a time when the centralisation process within the LO had been completed and the leading role of the Swedish Metal Workers' Union was uncontested. Since the early 1930s there had been a continuous increase in the relative wage of workers in the metal trades. The wage premium of sheltered-sector workers that caused the debate over solidaristic wages during the 1920s had turned into its opposite: to the metalworkers economic growth had become of greater direct interest than wage equalisation.

Decentralisation during the 1980s

Centralisation of power in the interwar period turned the Swedish labour market into an arena for trials of strength between two dominant organisations, the LO and SAF. Both were dominated by representatives of the competitive sector. Central agreements between the two dominant parties became the means of implementing the solidaristic wage policy that gained hegemonic ideological status during the period.

In the mid-1970s the two-part centralised model started to erode. One reason was, as was strongly emphasised in the follow-up of the EFO report in 1988, the growth of services, particularly public services, which shifted the balance of power in the labour market.[38] Another set of reasons that has less frequently been stressed was related to the structural crisis of the 1970s and the following transition into a phase of transformation and renewal of Swedish industry. In the previous discussion of the EFO period it was suggested that power relations in the labour market are to some extent determined by the structure of labour demand. Transformation means the introduction of new technology, which tends to increase productivity differentials between skill groups and prompt an increase in demand for high-skilled labour at fixed relative wages, which in turn may be assumed to enhance the relative power of white-collar workers.

Another consequence is that the function of the wage structure shifts over from cost reduction, which dominates in the rationalisation phase, to labour allocation. Wage differentials serve as an important means to attract and keep workers who possess the skills required to exploit the productivity potentials of the new technology. Just as in the 1960s when the engineering industry, squeezed by fierce international competition, took the lead in applying rationalisation measures to reduce production costs, so leading firms from that same sector led the way in applying the new technology of the electronic era. This may explain why the Swedish Engineering Employers' Association in the early 1980s came to question the value of central agreements, in particular the low-wage provisions and the 'wage development guarantees' which compensated groups with small or non-existent wage drift.

In the 1970s the previous consensus turned into severe ideological hostility between the LO and the SAF, the tensions eventually triggering a major conflict in 1980: some 900,000 LO workers were on strike or locked out for ten days.[39] This lent support to a strong opinion within the VF in favour of abandoning central bargaining, and in fact the VF managed to conclude a separate agreement with the Swedish Metal Workers' Union in 1983. Future policy formulations during the 1980s revealed that workers in the engineering industry also saw the need for change. At the 1989 congress of the Swedish Metal Workers' Union a document entitled *Solidaristic work policy* laid the basis for a shift from equalisation of wages to a wage policy that emphasised the importance of rewarding competence and skills. This shift represented a continuation of the arguments for a solidaristic wage policy as an engine of growth from the Rehn-Meidner report of 1951. The objective of the solidaristic work policy was to transform all work to 'good work'. The solidarity aspect would be satisfied by providing the prospect of developing the workers' competence and skills, rather than by wage equalisation. This would also contribute to productivity growth and thereby increase the room for real wage growth.[40]

The pioneering role of the VF and Metall in reshaping the bargaining system once again seems evident. Other organisations demonstrated a less determined attitude, and wage bargaining in other parts of the LO-SAF sphere oscillated between central coordination and free bargaining at the national industry level, although the central agreements were far from the detailed regulations that had characterised agreements in the 1970s.[41] The Swedish Metal Workers' Union was heavily criticised by other LO associations. The way out of this dilemma was to once more reinterpret solidarism. This implied a shift in emphasis from wages to work and competence, which seems to be perfectly compatible with the transformation of production during the electronic revolution.

A structural-economic interpretation of institutional change

Institutional development in the Swedish labour market during the twentieth century can be described as taking place in three distinct periods. From the beginning of the century and through the inter-war period power within both the SAF and the LO became more centralised, and collective bargaining became dominant. An ideology of solidarism evolved with the explicit aim of keeping wage increases in the sheltered sector in line with the development in sectors that were constrained by the need to stay competitive in international markets.

From the early 1950s the solidaristic wage policy was reformulated, and the main objective shifted from equalisation to growth. During the extended EFO period up to the mid-1970s the solidaristic wage policy was implemented within the institutional framework of centralised power and bargaining structures. The result was a considerable compression of the wage structure. Starting in the early 1980s employers and workers in the engineering industry broke away from central bargaining. Within the Swedish Metal Workers' Union the solidaristic wage policy was once again reformulated and a greater stress was laid on competence and skill as the basis of wage differentials.

Claims for wage equalisation and centralisation of power within the LO were a reaction to the wage advantage of workers in the sheltered sector that had emerged during the turbulent years following the First World War. Paradoxically enough, these claims were effective only in the 1940s, when the bulk of the wage advantage of sheltered-sector workers had already disappeared.

The turning point in the inter-industry wage-structure change came in 1933, and was related to the recovery of the Swedish economy after the structural crisis (see Figure 1). The 1920s, which bore the characteristics of a rationalisation phase, including fierce international competition, had not provided any room for wage increases in the competing sector. The upturn in the relative wage of the competitive sector coincided with the improvement of market conditions for the export industry. The volume of world trade took an upward turn in 1932 and Swedish foreign trade increased more than average.[42] It was linked to a favourable mix of Swedish exports and advantageous conditions in major markets, notably Germany and the United Kingdom.[43]

It is, however, important to note that the recovery was not export led. The export share of industrial production was higher in the 1920s than in the 1930s. But this does not imply a leading role for the traditional sheltered sectors of industry. The engineering industry experienced strong expansion in the domestic market, and annual growth amounted to 7.5 per cent between 1930 and 1950 compared with an average of 4.3 per cent for total manufacturing.[44] The metal industries increased their share of the manufacturing workforce from roughly thirty to forty per cent. Development blocks around electrification and the automobile, which became constituent parts of the successful transformation and renewal of Swedish industry after the structural crisis of the early 1930s, provided the scope for expansion.

The requirements of technical innovation demanded that employers in the engineering industry shifted their main concern from cost-reducing activities to adoption of new technologies. The importance of attracting labour with the ability to exploit those technologies triggered wage increases in advanced firms and sectors. A transformation phase is generally characterised by a relatively relaxed competitive situation, which can give room for wage increases. In sum, the fact that the Swedish economy, by international comparison, quickly recovered from the crisis can explain how there was room for relative wage increases in the competing sector during the 1930s. It also helps explain why both employers' and workers' organisations in the metal trades gained in relative strength and eventually forced through their interpretations of solidarism. The change in power structure, however, cannot be seen as a primary determinant of the wage-structure shift in the 1930s. Rather, the favourable economic development in the metal trades paved the way for increases in both wages and power.

The power of competitive-sector agents was consolidated and further strengthened during the extended EFO period. The cost-reducing function of wage-structure shifts became dominant in the rationalisation phase that commenced around 1960. The result was a continuous decrease in the relative wage of workers in the competitive sector during the 1960s and 1970s. It was suggested above that the solidaristic wage policy together with the centralised bargaining and power structures provided an effective solution to the conflict between the necessity for firms in the competing sector to cut wage costs and at the same time attract additional labour for unit-cost-reducing expansion. To workers in the competing sector, who had managed to turn the wage advantage of the sheltered sector into its opposite during the 1940s, wage equalisation was seemingly of no direct interest. However, in the Rehn-Meidner model wage equalisation was thought of as triggering economic growth to the benefit of the whole workers' collective. This may be a reason why the Swedish Metal Workers' Union in the end supported a wage policy that reduced wage differentials.

In 1980 the wage advantage of workers in the engineering industry had been totally eroded. To some extent this may explain the role of the Swedish Metal Workers' Union in dismantling the centralised bargaining model in the 1980s. The early 1980s were also the beginning of a transformation phase which brought a shift in the relations between skills and productivity that affected the attitudes towards wage inequalities – of workers as well as of employers – in leading industries, notably the engineering industry.

This analysis suggests that labour-market institutions, formal or informal, should not be looked upon as exogenous phenomena determined outside the labour market itself. The historical process that produced a highly centralised structure and a set of values that gained hegemonic status and became constituent parts of The Swedish Model grew out of a basic conflict between the sheltered sectors and those exposed to foreign competition. As the latter grew in strength, labour-market institutions increasingly developed to serve their interests. Their specific nature, and thus their effect on labour-market institutions, varied as the economy moved between phases with different characteristics. In some periods wage compression became a means of reducing costs in order to stay competitive in world markets, in others wage differentials increased to serve a labour-allocating function. The development of informal institutions largely centred around the idea of solidarity, which could be transformed into policy claims because it was appropriate to, and when necessary was re-interpreted to conform to, the interests of workers and employers in the competing sector. Changes in formal institutions, notably the bargaining system and power relations within the labour-market organisations, served to facilitate the implementation of these policies.

* This article is a product of the research project 'Technology Shifts and Regional Economic Development – Economic Transformation in Time and Space', which received financial support from the Bank of Sweden Tercentenary Foundation.

1 G. Edgren, K.-O. Faxén, and C.-E. Odhner, *Wage Formation and the Economy* (London: George Allen & Unwin, 1973). The first mimeographed Swedish version came out in 1968. After a slight revision it was printed in 1970. An English version was published in 1973.

2 Ibid., p. 13.
3 C. Lundh, 'Institutional Change in the Swedish Labour Market 1830–1990', in C. Lundh, J. Olofsson, L. Schön and L. Svensson (eds.), *Wage Formation, Labour Market Institutions and Economic Transformation in Sweden 1860–2000*, (Lund: Almqvist & Wiksell International, 2004); L. Svensson, *Closing the Gender Gap. Determinants of Change in the Female-to-Male Wage Ratio of Blue Collar Workers in Swedish Manufacturing 1913–1990* (Lund: Ekonomisk-historiska föreningen, 1995).
4 Edgren *et al.*, *Wage Formation and the Economy*, p. 23.
5 Ibid., p. 21.
6 D. A. Hibbs Jr. and H. Locking, 'Den solidariska lönepolitiken och produktiviteten inom industrin', *Ekonomisk Debatt*, årg. 23, nr 7 (1995), pp. 537–548.
7 Svensson, *Closing the Gender Gap*, p. 9.
8 L. Schön, *En modern svensk ekonomisk historia* (Borås: SNS Förlag, 2000), p. 33.
9 L. Schön, 'Industrial Crises in a Model of Long Cycles: Sweden in an International Perspective', in T. Myllyntaus (ed.), *Crisis and Restructuring in Small Countries* (Berlin: Scripta Meracaturae, 1998), pp. 410–411.
10 SOS Utrikeshandel, *Official Statistics of Sweden, Foreign Trade,* (Stockholm: Swedish Board of Commerce, 1913–1960, Statistics Sweden, 1961–1995).
11 J. Ullenhag, *Den solidariska lönepolitiken i Sverige. Debatt och verklighet* (Stockholm: Scandinavian University Books, 1971), p. 32.
12 The Rehn-Meidner model was named after the two LO economists who launched the programme in a report to the 1951 LO congress.
13 *Fackföreningsrörelsen och den fulla sysselsättningen* (Malmö: Tiden, 1951), pp. 159–162.
14 *De centrala överenskommelserna mellan LO och SAF 1952–1987* (Stockholm: LO, 1986).
15 P. Swenson, 'Bringing Capital Back in, or Social Democracy Reconsidered', *World Politics* 43 (July 1991), pp. 513–544.
16 *Verksamhetsberättelse 1962*, Svenska Metallarbetareförbundet (Stockholm: Tiden, 1962), pp. 23–24.
17 A conference entitled 'Women as a labour resource' and arranged jointly by the LO and the SAF in Saltsjöbaden outside Stockholm in 1964 serves as an example of these efforts. Four out of five representatives of individual firms represented big firms in the engineering industry. See *Kvinnorna som arbetskraftsresurs*. En konferens i Saltsjöbaden anordnad av Arbetsmarknadens Yrkesråd (Stockholm: Arbetsmarknadens Yrkesråd, SAF and LO, 1965), p. 34.
18 This was one of the most successful parts of the engineering industry, with an increase in share of total exports from 1.5 per cent in the early 1950s to 6 per cent in 1960 and 11 per cent in 1970; SOS Utrikeshandel, *Official Statistics of Sweden, Foreign Trade.*
19 *De centrala överenskommelserna mellan LO och SAF 1952–1987*, p. 21.
20 E. Magnusson, 'Långt kvar till förverkligande av likalönstanken', *Fackföreningsrörelsen* (1/1966), p. 23.
21 Styrman, *Verkstadsföreningen* (Stockholm: P A Norstedt & Söner, 1946), p. 65.

22 Landsorganisationens femtonmnnakommitté, *Fackföreningsrörelsen och näringslivet* (Stockholm: Tiden, 1941), p. 39.
23 Törnqvist, 'Verkstadsindustrin, ett maktcentrum i svensk avtalspolitik', *Statsvetenskaplig tidskrift* (1954: 3).
24 K. Treslow, *Verkstadsföreningen under 90 år* (Stockholm: VF, 1986), pp. 19–22.
25 K.-O. Faxén, C.-E. Odhner and R. Spånt, *Lönebildningen i 90-talets samhällsekonomi* (Simrishamn: Rabén & Sjögren, 1989), p. 70.
26 Ibid., pp. 73–74.
27 Swenson, 'Bringing Capital Back in', 521–522.
28 Ullenhag, *Den solidariska lönepolitiken,* pp. 26–33.
29 K. Fregert, 'Relative Wage Struggles during the Inter-War Period, General Equilibrium and the Rise of the Swedish Model', *Scandinavian Economic History Review*, Vol. XLII, No. 2 (1994), pp. 173–186.
30 Ibid., p. 186.
31 'Motion från Svenska Metallindustriarbetareförbundet avd. 1', in Protokoll, Landsorganisationens kongress 1922 (Stockholm: LO, 1922), p. 382.
32 *Framtida bostadspolitiken, SOU 1945: 63* (Stockholm: Socialdeparrtementet, 1945).
33 Ullenhag, *Den solidariska lönepolitiken,* pp. 28–29. Incidentally, there was a similar line of reasoning presented in an article by the economist Bertil Ohlin in *Verkstäderna*, a journal published by VF, also in 1926.
34 H. De Geer, *Rationaliseringsrörelsen i Sverige* (Stockholm: SNS, 1978); idem, *Job Studies and Industrial Relations, Ideas about efficiency and relations between the parties of the labour market in Sweden 1920–1950* (Stockholm: Almqvist & Wiksell International, 1982).
35 A. L. Johansson, *Tillväxt och klassamarbete. En studie av den svenska modellens uppkomst* (Stockholm: Tiden, 1985).
36 T. Karlbom, *Den svenska fackföreningsrörelsen* (Stockholm: Tiden, 1955), p. 242.
37 Quotation from Karlbom, *Den svenska fackföreningsrörelsen*, p. 244.
38 Faxén *et al.*, *Lönebildningen i 90-talets samhällsekonomi*, pp. 26–27.
39 N. Elvander, *Lokal lönebildning* (Kristianstad: SNS, 1991), p. 36.
40 *Solidarisk arbetspolitik för det goda arbetet*, Svenska Metallindustriarbetarförbundet Kongress 3–9 september 1989 (Stockholm: Metall, 1989).
41 N. Elvander, and B. Holmlund, *The Swedish bargaining System in the melting Pot, Institutions, norms and outcomes in the 1990s* (Solna: Arbetslivsinstitutet, 1997), p. 15.
42 E. Lundberg, *Ekonomiska kriser förr och nu* (Stockholm: SNS, 1983), p. 91.
43 Schön, *En modern svensk ekonomisk historia*, p. 352.
44 Ibid., p. 337.

Herman de Jong and Jan-Pieter Smits

Changing Patterns of Competitiveness in Dutch Manufacturing during the Twentieth Century: Factor or Technology Driven?

Introduction[1]

From an economic point of view nations do not need to be large in order to survive. In a recent publication Alesina and Spoleare provide a framework within which they analyse the costs and benefits of being 'large' or 'small'.[2] It is argued that small nations can prosper in a context of a free movement of goods and production factors. The case we present here is the Dutch economy between 1913 and 2000. This 'short twentieth century' incorporates both World Wars and the Great Depression with related economic dislocations and fierce protectionism. But it also incorporates the post-1945 era which was characterised by a strong liberalisation of international trade and, to a lesser extent, the free movement of labour and capital.

This chapter systematically explores how economic agents and institutions in the Netherlands reacted to international economic circumstances during the twentieth century. How did firms as well as governments respond to the problems posed by protectionism in the 1930s, and how was the Dutch economy able to reap the fruits of the gradual liberalisation of the international economy in the period after World War II? This question is primarily dealt with within a production-function framework. We will analyse which strategies Dutch firms and policymakers employed in order to enhance competitiveness, mainly focusing on broad industrial policies designed to protect and to improve the performance of firms and industries.[3] Central in our approach will be the question of whether strategies focused primarily on the cost-effectiveness of resources such as labour and energy, or on technological competence such as innovation and technological change.

In section 2 we will supply a brief overview of the changes in competitiveness over a long perspective by charting the share of Dutch exports in world trade. Section 3 explores the factor-price-related phenomena, concentrating on exchange-rate policies and policies influencing the cost-structure of firms through wage moderation and cheap energy supply. The relationship between technological change and economic growth and the way these processes are related to institutional developments are primarily studied at a macro level.[4] The evolutionary economic literature, however, also stresses the sector- or even firm-specificity of institutional and technological change: so we turn to the sector/branch level in order to identify which segments of the Dutch economy show competitive strength.[5] Section 4 focuses on changes in competitiveness at branch levels, where the figures seem to indicate that technology-related factors indeed play a large role in explaining patterns of competitive strength. Section 5 focuses on the role of multinational companies which, due to the importance of foreign direct investments, are important 'carriers' of technology creation and diffusion. Here we will show that in the chemicals and electrical-engineering sectors the patterns of change in competitiveness are closely related to differences in innovative activity, measured by investments in R&D as well as by foreign direct investments.

The long-term pattern of competitiveness

One of the main characteristics of the Dutch economy in the long term is its openness to flows of goods and factor inputs. This gives a strong international dimension to the economy, as it forces firms to face international competition. Most of the goods-producing branches are price takers on exports markets. But in order to be internationally competitive, the domestic market is inadequate to support efficient producers. The exports/GDP ratio as well as the ratio between foreign direct investments and GDP are among the highest in the world.[6]

We therefore will analyse to what extent Dutch firms were able to sell their products on the world market and to what extent these firms were able to compete with foreign producers. In order to measure changes in the international position of Dutch businesses we have calculated the share of Dutch exports in international trade, which we see here as an indicator of competitiveness.[7]

Figure 1: Share of Dutch exports in world trade, 1910–1996 (in %)

Sources: Jan-Pieter Smits, Edwin Horlings and Jan Luiten van Zanden, *Dutch GNP and its components, 1800–1913* (Groningen: Groningen Growth and Development Centre Monograph Series no. 5, 2000). I. Svennilson, *Growth and Stagnation in the European Economy* (Geneva: OECD, 1954). B.R. Mitchell, *European historical statistics, 1750–1970* (London, 1975). IMF, *Trade Statistics.*

Note: Natural gas exports are included in these figures.

Figure 1 shows the increasing share of Dutch exports in world trade in the first two decades of the twentieth century. Although we do not have precise figures for the 1910s there is ample information on rapid Dutch export growth during the First World War.[8] With the exception of a sharp fall shortly after 1920, Dutch exports boomed until 1931. In fact, during the 1920s the share of Dutch exports in world trade showed a considerable increase. During the depression of the 1930s and in the period of the German occupation between 1940 and 1945 there was a large decrease in market share, due to international trade restrictions in many forms. During the post-war boom of the 1950s and 1960s economic growth was to a large extent driven by exports. Export growth coincided with a strong growth of Dutch products' share of the world market. Figure 1 shows that the post-1945 expansion was not just confined to a recovery from the difficulties of the depression years and the consequences of the war. Especially after 1967 the level of relative exports became much higher than during the interwar period, and it peaked during the early 1970s. However, from the late 1970s onwards the share of Dutch exports in international trade showed a permanent decline. Obviously, the Dutch economy lost some of its competitive strength during the 1980s and 1990s.

How can we explain these movements in levels of competitiveness? Economic-historical literature suggests that long-term changes in competitiveness are primarily related to changes in the levels of comparative labour productivity and for that matter to choices related to changes in technology.[9] Looking purely at costs two other factors are of influence, namely the exchange rate and the costs of production factors (labour and other inputs). Together, these three variables determine the prices at which products can be sold on the world market. Of course the number of possible institutional variables influencing competitiveness is countless. We restrict our analysis to the institutional arrangements that influenced the relative price of factor inputs as well as the policies that affected technological progress. In other words the institutional factors are studied within a production-function framework. We start with exchange-rate policies, as they may influence the levels of export prices to a considerable degree.

Exchange-rate policies and policies influencing the cost-structure of firms

We identify three areas where macro policies could have influenced the price level of Dutch exports: (1) exchange-rate policies, (2) wage policies and (3) energy-price policies. For example, low exchange rates and low comparative wages were deliberate goals of post-1945 reconstruction policies to stimulate exports. But we believe that Dutch monetary and wage policies hardly had any direct influence on the development of competitive strength. On the contrary, we observe that the rising share of Dutch exports in world trade in the 1920s and 1960s occurred in a context of an appreciation of the Dutch guilder as well as of a strong increase of relative labour costs in the Netherlands.[10] However, we do think that these policies influenced the behaviour of firms and their accumulation strategies, and so in an indirect way the long-run international competitiveness of sectors.

Table 1: Real exchange rate of currencies to the US dollar. Netherlands, Belgium, Germany, United Kingdom, 1913–1995 (Neth. = 100, 1913 = 100, 1950 = 100)

	Netherlands	Belgium	Germany	U.K.
1913	100	100	100	100
1925	100	74	89	104
1935	100	63	114	82
1950	100	100	100	100
1960	100	90	103	91
1970	100	80	92	77
1980	100	71	97	87
1990	100	70	103	92
1995	100	69	104	75

Sources: I. Svennilson, *Growth and Stagnation in the European Economy* (Geneva: OECD, 1954), pp. 318–319; OECD, *Historical Statistics*, various issues; World Bank, *World Tables*, various issues.

Table 1 shows the real exchange rates of the Dutch guilder and of the currencies of the Netherlands' main trading partners – Belgium, Germany and the UK – to the US dollar. For each country the official exchange rate of a particular year was multiplied by the domestic level of the wholesale price index of the same year, creating an index of real exchange rates to the US dollar. The years 1913 and 1950 were taken as starting years from which the development of exchange rates and domestic price levels were measured. Next the Dutch rates against the US dollar values were used as a base and set at 100. The general picture shows that levels of Dutch real exchange rates have been high compared with Belgium and the UK and low compared with Germany. Combining the results in Table 1 with Figure 1 we find that both in the 1920s and the 1960s high real exchange rates were accompanied by higher shares of exports in world trade. Competitiveness of Dutch exports had increased in periods of rising real exchange rates. In the 1920s the evidence may be less strong, because the increase in Dutch competitiveness coincided with a relatively low real exchange rate vis-à-vis the United Kingdom. But during the 1960s there was a clear combination of relatively strong performance of Dutch exports accompanied by rising real exchange rates.

The most characteristic years of Dutch exchange-rate policies during the interwar period were without doubt the early 1930s. Dutch policymakers saw no reason to devalue the guilder to follow the British pound, which was already off gold in 1931: the Dutch gold reserves were high, Amsterdam had to remain a safe haven for international financial interests, and there was a strong belief in classical economic prescriptions.[11] Paradoxically, the depression of the 1930s and the decision to stick to gold had structural effects on the Dutch economy, giving way to the forces of rationalisation and industrial renewal. From 1930 demand for industrial goods and agricultural exports declined. Therefore the decision to maintain an external balance shifted the burden to lowering domestic levels of prices and wages. However, real wages remained high and firms started to cut back heavily on costs, resulting in a huge layoff of workers and closures of obsolete plant. Firms shifted more towards best-practice production methods, resulting in high productivity growth in all branches of industry. But productivity growth was also driven by substitution of capital for labour, resulting in a reduction of labour requirements and consequently fast-increasing unemployment rates. Between 1925 and 1935 productivity growth was more than 5 per cent per year, real value added increased by

4.2 per cent annually, whereas labour input declined by 1.1 per cent annually. Data on capital indicators reveal an annual increase on capital and machinery goods of 4 per cent. Thus, unit capital requirements hardly changed during the depression years. Total factor productivity (TFP) growth during these years was about 3 per cent annually against an average TFP growth rate for the total period 1913–1965 of 1.9. Although the Great Depression hit the Dutch economy very hard and saddled the country with an extremely high unemployment, modernisation of Dutch manufacturing was visible in a whole range of industries.[12] This acceleration in productivity growth and modernisation was an unintended outcome of the hard-currency policy of the interwar years, because price levels in the goods market had declined much faster than in the labour market.

Wages and wage policies

Did the level of wage costs influence the degree of competitiveness of the Dutch economy? Table 2 shows relative wages in the Netherlands and its major trading partners during the twentieth century.

Table 2: Hourly wages in manufacturing. Netherlands, Belgium, Germany and the United Kingdom, 1913–1995 (Index, Neth. = 100)

Year	Netherlands	Belgium	Germany	United Kingdom
1913	100	118	182	318
1930	100	64	104	128
1950	100	140	96	146
1960	100	127	112	134
1970	100	98	99	73
1980	100	107	89	63
1990	100	104	108	78
1995	100	106	116	65

Sources: Jan Luiten van Zanden, *The economic history of the Netherlands, 1914–1995* (London: Routledge, 1998); Herman de Jong, *Catching Up Twice. The nature of Dutch industrial growth during the 20th century* (Berlin: Akademie Verlag, 2003), p. 85; Bureau of Labor Statistics, *Office of Productivity and Technology*, September 1998.

Note: Wages converted with official exchange rates.

In general high Dutch relative wages tended to coincide with high export shares in world trade and vice versa. Between 1913 and 1930 Dutch relative wages increased considerably, together with the share of Dutch exports in world trade. After the Second World War, however, wages were initially extremely low compared with Belgium and the UK, as was the export share. During the second half of the 1960s wages reached a level comparable with Belgium, Germany and the UK. At the same time international competitiveness was still increasing. During the 1980s and 1990s wage costs declined relatively, but this obviously did not go hand in hand with an improvement of the share of Dutch exports in world trade.

After the Second World War wage restraint became a major characteristic of Dutch economic policy. The frustrating experience of the extremely high unemployment levels in the interwar period paved the way for a post-war labour market that was geared towards wage compression and wage moderation enforced by policies and legislation. Between 1945 and the early 1960s policy makers focused on such measures to make sure that employment opportunities in manufacturing would improve and investments and exports would grow. This can be illustrated by the fact that between 1945 and 1951 real-product wages declined to a level not much different from that of 1921. But what were the effects of these measures on the international competitive position of the Dutch economy?

We believe that the low wage policies had a profound effect on relative factor prices by making capital the expensive production factor. This triggered off a change in the process of factor accumulation. Contrary to the 1930s, when investments were directed at the substitution of capital for labour, we observe an economy-wide substitution of labour for capital during the 1940s. This was strengthened by the fact that capital goods were hard to get directly after the war. Delayed depreciations and low wage levels retarded the replacement of obsolete plant. Furthermore, low wage levels weakened incentives for both workers and employers to apply efficient work practices. Consequently, the macro economic situation was totally different from that of the early 1930s. Between 1930 and 1935 the Dutch economy had suffered from an overvalued currency and high real wage rates. After 1945 the Dutch government experienced an external-payments problem and devalued the Dutch guilder twice to improve competitiveness (in 1944 and 1949). At the same time real wages were kept on a low level through centralist wage policies and wage control, which resulted in a cut in living standards for workers: these measures transformed the country into a low-wage economy fuelled by cheap labour.

The most important consequence of wage moderation policies, intended or not, was the preservation of an industrial structure characterised by high employment levels in low-productivity industries such as clothing, hosiery and shoemaking, and in many branches of the metal industry, such as shipbuilding. During the 1950s, however, industrial growth was so strong that labour scarcity became a serious problem in an increasing number of industries, which resulted in an upward movement of wages and the collapse of existing wage policies. The low-productivity sectors suffered severe problems, because wage levels increased in all sectors. This seriously undermined the economic viability of a number of labour-intensive sectors of industry, such as textiles and shipbuilding, resulting in an unavoidable process of labour shedding in 'old' industries from 1965 onward.

After a long decade with no voluntary agreements on the general wage level, the early 1980s saw the return of wage moderation as a central theme in economic policy. Urged on by the government, employers' organisations and labour unions agreed on moderating wage growth in exchange for a shorter standard working week. Although there were positive effects on employment growth, there was no improvement in international competitiveness. Therefore we conclude that the recurring pleas among government officials and employers' organisations in the post-war period that low wage costs would stimulate competitiveness are not supported by the evidence we present here.

Energy-price policy

The third way in which the Dutch government attempted to improve the international performance of Dutch firms was by keeping down the costs of energy, especially in metallurgy, chemicals and oil-refining. After the Second World War the petrochemical industry developed into one of the biggest branches within manufacturing. Low energy prices were not the only driving force behind the strong growth of the petrochemical sector: locational factors, such as the importance of the port of Rotterdam as one of the main centres of international oil trade, should also be mentioned. However, there is ample evidence that the Dutch government was able to influence energy prices to a considerable extent, and this policy had important implications. The policy was made possible because of the exploitation of a large natural gas field that had been discovered in the late 1950s in the northern part of the country. From the early 1960s onward, domestic energy prices were among the lowest in the world. In 1992–1993 the price of natural gas for the industrial sector in the Netherlands was 20 US cents per cubic metre, which was very low in comparison with energy costs in other countries such as Belgium (30 cents), Denmark (40 cents) and Germany (45 cents).[13] It became therefore quite rational for Dutch firms to concentrate on energy-intensive spheres of production.

Table 3: Energy/GDP ratio, 1913–1987 (annual average compound growth rates)

	1913–1950	1950–1973	1973–1987
France	–0.74	–0.51	–1.24
Germany	–1.26	–1.12	–1.52
Japan	–0.25	–0.07	–2.83
Netherlands	–0.73	1.88	–0.81
United Kingdom	–1.24	–1.52	–2.18
United States	–0.90	–0.50	–2.17
Arithmetic average	–0.85	–0.31	–1.79

Source: Angus Maddison, *Dynamic Forces in Capitalist Development*, (Oxford: Oxford University Press, 1991), p. 156.

The impact of the low level of Dutch energy prices becomes strikingly clear when we analyse the changes in the energy-intensity of output. In fact, the Netherlands is the only country in which the amount of energy per unit of GDP showed an increase in the period 1950–1973. Furthermore, it can be demonstrated that the energy-intensive sectors were responsible for almost 75 percent of labour-productivity growth in the period 1950–1973. The oil crises of 1973 and 1979 revealed how vulnerable the Dutch economy had become to the exogenous price shocks of energy products. The Dutch productivity slowdown in the 1980s can to a large extent be ascribed to the bad performance of the energy-intensive industrial branches. It should be pointed out that the decrease of market shares of energy-intensive products is not just confined to natural gas. In the period 1973–1990 the revealed comparative advantage witnessed a decrease of 32.1 percent, which is less than the fall in competitiveness of crude oil (–92.9 percent), oil products (–45.5 percent) and electricity (–90.7 percent). These data show that the loss of competitiveness is not simply the effect of changing export trends of natural gas, but that this tendency can also be discerned in a great number of energy-intensive sectors of the economy.

We conclude here that Dutch government policy after 1945 was for various reasons focused more on the nation's resource endowments in the form of cheap labour and low energy prices and only in a very indirect way on the technological competence of the economy. The same tendency can also be seen at company level: in their analysis of Dutch competitiveness, Jacobs *et al.* conclude that Dutch entrepreneurs and businesses are primarily focused on low-cost production and less on innovation.[14] We will continue with this topic in section 5 below, but first we will analyse the long-term competitiveness of the Dutch economy at branch level.

Revealed comparative advantage in the Dutch economy

The determinants of competitiveness can to a large extent be found at sector or even branch level. In order to better understand the nature of Dutch competitiveness, we first analyse which industries or products displayed comparative advantage. We used export data to trace the revealed comparative advantage (RCA) of the Dutch economy, using the formula

$$RCA = [X^{NL}{}_i/X_i]/[X^{NL}/X],$$

where X = world exports, X^{NL} = Dutch exports and i stands for industry i.

Table 4: Revealed comparative advantage in Dutch industry, 1906–1950. National average = 100

	1906	1928	1938	1950
Food processing	95	121	243	147
Raw materials	51	51	31	66
Metals	16	52	41	95
Machinery	4	55	36	73
Transport equipment	n.a.	87	75	54
Chemicals	616	385	201	194
Textiles	48	106	89	151

Sources: For 1906 see: *Statistical Abstract of Foreign Countries. Parts I–III: Statistics of Foreign Commerce* (Washington, 1909). Data for the period 1928–1950: I. Svennilson, *Growth and Stagnation in the European Economy* (Geneva: OECD, 1954), p. 293, with the exception of the Dutch data that were taken from the *Jaarcijfers*, various issues.

Note: 'world exports' are exports from the USA, Belgium/Luxemburg, France, (Western) Germany, Italy, the Netherlands, Sweden, Switzerland and the United Kingdom. For 1906 transport equipment is included in the category of machinery.

In order to identify the comparative advantage of a particular Dutch industry (say textiles), its share in the world textiles trade is compared with the share of total Dutch exports (i.e. all products) in total world trade.

Table 4 shows that before the First World War the Dutch economy had a clear comparative advantage in chemical products (initially mainly fertilisers). On the other hand, the metals, machinery and textiles industries showed a relatively poor performance. Unfortunately, we do not have similar data on agricultural exports. However, for 1906 additional information could be derived from the *Statistical Abstract of Foreign Countries* (see sources mentioned below Table 4). These data indicate that the Netherlands showed low achievements in arable production (with an RCA of 56), but had a high revealed comparative advantage in livestock (an RCA of 172). During the first half of the interwar period the key players in the second industrial revolution (the metal and machinery industry) displayed strong growth, whereas in the second half of the interwar period the food-processing industries became highly competitive on the international market.

For the period 1961–1990 we can use very detailed trade statistics from the OECD. Tables 5 and 6 summarise the main findings for the first and last years of this period.[15]

Table 5: Revealed comparative advantage 1961 and 1990. Ten highest product groups in the Netherlands (average = 100)

1961		1990	
1 Coffee, tea, and cocoa	622	1 Natural gas	532
2 Dairy products	584	2 Animal and vegetable oils and fats	419
3 Crude oil products	347	3 Dairy products	404
4 Meat products and preserves	347	4 Meat products and preserves	323
5 Fruit and vegetables	234	5 Coffee, tea, and cocoa	320
6 Animal and vegetable oils and fats	233	6 Fruit and vegetables	308
7 Fodder for livestock	217	7 Fodder for livestock	294
8 Telecommunications apparatus	175	8 Tobacco products	263
9 Electrical machinery	173	9 Livestock	257
10 Natural gas	156	10 Crude oil products	232

Source: OECD, *Foreign Trade Statistics, 1960–1990.*

Note: Exports related to all OECD countries.

Table 6: Revealed comparative advantage, the Netherlands 1961 and 1990. Eight product groups with declining (–) and increasing (+) value between beginning and end years, percentage change

Largest *decrease*		Largest *increase*	
1 Coal	–77	1 Tobacco products	+436
2 Telecommunications apparatus	–67	2 Natural gas	+242
3 Electrical machinery	–63	3 Artificial resins	+155
4 Coffe, tea, and cocoa	–49	4 Livestock	+118
5 Furniture	–48	5 Inorganic chemicals	+110
6 Textile yarn	–44	6 Animal and vegetable oils and fats	+80
7 Crude oil products	–33	7 Office machines	+89
8 Dairy products	–31	8 Rubber	+80

Source: OECD, *Foreign Trade Statistics*, 1960–1990.

Note: Exports related to all OECD countries. Only product groups above the average value (100) in beginning or end year.

Ranking the industries according to world-market share we find that during the early 1960s the top10 were dominated by agricultural and food products: indeed, six out of the ten most competitive product groups are to be found amongst the agricultural-products and food industries. Both the petrochemical sector and the electrical-engineering and telecommunications industries also stand out as highly competitive during the 1960s.

Table 6 maps the largest changes in revealed comparative advantage between 1961 and 1990. The decrease in competitive strength was concentrated in coal, which is explained by the rapid increase in natural-gas exports, electrical engineering (characterised by a high RCA before 1970), and labour-intensive industries, for example furniture and textiles. The last mentioned low-productivity branches witnessed a strong relative decline throughout the period 1960–1990. Most of the industries had expanded rapidly during the 1950s because of the policy of wage moderation. However, rising labour costs per unit of output in the 1960s and 1970s undermined their economic viability.

At the end of the twentieth century the Dutch economy was much less diversified than it was during the 1960s. The electrical-engineering cluster lost much of its strong export position, while in the petrochemical sector a decline in competitiveness could be discerned as well. These losses were not compensated by the increases in competitive strength in relatively small branches such as inorganic chemicals or office machines. The export strength of the Dutch economy had become more and more focused on agricultural and food products, and natural gas.

The data in Tables 5 and 6 clearly indicate that the general rise of the Dutch export share in world trade (or: the rise in competitiveness) in the period 1913–1970 was largely concentrated in three clusters: agriculture/food, chemicals and electrical engineering.

These three clusters composed the bulk of Dutch exports, as can be seen in Table 7; but the emphasis shifted from agriculture/food towards chemicals/electrical engineering. This is not very surprising as far as the period 1921–1970 is concerned. The chemical as well as the electrical engineering industry can be seen as key sectors of the second industrial revolution. Yet, the continuous rise of the share of these branches and the relative decline of agriculture/food in the

Table 7: Share of agriculture/food, chemicals and electrical machinery in total value of exports (in current prices, 1921–1995, in %)

	All three clusters	Agriculture/food	Chemicals and electronics
1921	67.4	53.9	13.5
1929	63.4	45.3	18.1
1938	62.0	43.9	18.1
1950	48.2	34.1	14.1
1970	62.8	24.3	38.4
1980	70.5	19.7	50.8
1990	63.1	17.9	45.3
1995	61.0	18.0	43.0

Source: CBS, *Jaarcijfers voor het Koninkrijk der Nederlanden.* Various issues.

period after 1970 stand in contrast with the decline in the Dutch RCA of electrical engineering and bulk chemicals. In the most recent period the commodity structure of exports shows a specialisation structure that one would not predict from the analysis of the revealed comparative advantages. This is due to the fact that the industries in which the Netherlands lost its comparative advantage (chemicals and electrical engineering products) experienced a rise in world exports, whereas the industries in which the Netherlands experienced a stronger comparative advantage (such as food) declined in total world exports.[16] The explanation for this unexpected pattern of specialisation can be found in the changing structure of international trade during the second half of the twentieth century: in the mid-1950s food products still constituted 22 percent of world trade, but by 1995 this share had declined to a mere 9 percent.[17]

The technology factor: the role of multinationals

Technological advance and innovation can have profound effects on a nation's competitiveness by reducing production costs and thus prices, by increasing quality, and by creating unique products and consequently monopoly profits. Can we explain the Dutch movement in trade patterns in terms of technological competence and/or sector-specific accumulation? Although the importance of medium- and small-sized companies should not be underestimated, it was the large companies that played the leading role in the creation of new technologies in the Netherlands.[18] About 75 percent of Dutch investment in research and development (R&D) occurred in the five largest multinational companies.[19] Besides, these multinationals can be found in sectors in which the Dutch had a clear comparative advantage, such as the food-processing industries (Unilever), the oil and chemical sector (Shell, DSM) and the electrical engineering industry (Philips).

These companies not only played a major role in the creation of technological knowledge, but were also instrumental in the diffusion of foreign knowledge.[20] Through the presence of these companies the Dutch domestic market was in a way enlarged, creating international user-producer relationships across the country's borders. The additional learning effects and demand-induced innovations from beyond the Dutch borders fostered domestic suppliers. For example, Royal Dutch/Shell, a Dutch/British oil company carried out detailed research into technologies related to oil exploration and exploitation, and this was undertaken in a large number of countries. In the period preceding the First World War the board of directors of Shell became aware of the fact that a lot of technical know-how that had been gained in the Dutch East Indies remained unknown in Europe and the United States. So the organisational structure of the firm had to be changed in order to facilitate (and stimulate) the diffusion of technological knowledge. In 1913 a new organisational structure was introduced which, among other things, stated that all relevant technological information was to be reported to a central scientific staff at headquarters in The Hague, enabling all relevant technological information to be used by all subdivisions of the company.

The multinationals were of great importance for the Dutch economy. Yet how can the strong position of the multinational companies be understood? According to Chandler, multinationals emerge in a context of large markets, which stimulate firms to increase production.[21] In order to cope with this upscaling, the distribution of products also needs to be reorganised. The multinational company is supposed to be the best organisational entity to cope with the problems of upscaling.

Although this line of reasoning may be adequate to explain the American experience, it certainly does not apply to many of the continental European countries. For example, if we take the share of foreign direct investment in GDP as a measure of the economic significance of multinationals, it becomes clear that these companies have been of crucial importance for open economies like Switzerland and the Netherlands. We can therefore conclude that the emergence and further development of multinationals may have followed different growth paths than the one described by Chandler. On the basis of the analysis of the emergence of Shell, Unilever and Philips we find that the rise of the multinational companies in the Netherlands was encouraged by several factors. Firstly, the Netherlands is an open economy, with a large share of output that is exported and with a net export of capital. Secondly, this openness was important in the light of the small home market. Both Unilever and Philips produced for the international market from the start, which enabled them to escape from demand constraints: only at a later stage did the domestic market become important for these firms. Thirdly, there was enough capital available to finance the internationalisation of Dutch industrial enterprises: in fact, there was more financial capital available than could be absorbed by the domestic economy.[22] In the fourth place the Netherlands did not have a patent law: innovations were not protected in the Dutch economy. This institutional characteristic certainly favoured knowledge-intensive modes of production.

As foreign direct investment (FDI) undertaken by multinationals provides us with a lot of information about their development, in Table 8 we have compared the size of Dutch FDI with that of other countries. First of all we compare the share of a country's FDI investments in total (world-wide) FDI investments (see column 1). The share of these countries in world GDP (column 2) was added in order to see whether the importance of multinationals surpassed the levels that could be expected on the basis of the size of a country's economy in terms of its GDP level. Finally, column 3 presents information on the share of multinationals in GDP.

Table 8: FDI activities from and by selected OECD countries, 1980, 1992 and 1995 (in %)

	1980	1980	1980	1992	1992	1992	1995	1995	1995
	(1)	(2)	(3)	(1)	(2)	(3)	(1)	(2)	(3)
G	8.3	7.3	10.1	9.2	7.8	17.2	9.2	8.7	17.7
F	4.5	6.2	7.0	8.3	5.7	21.2	6.4	5.5	21.4
UK	15.5	5.0	26.7	11.4	3.9	43.7	10.8	4.0	55.8
NL	8.1	1.6	35.7	6.8	1.4	67.3	5.9	1.4	70.0
I	1.4	4.2	3.6	3.6	5.3	10.7	3.5	3.9	14.8
S	1.1	1.2	7.4	2.6	1.0	29.3	2.5	0.8	47.2
No	0.4	0.6	13.7	0.6	0.5	18.4	0.8	0.5	28.9
Jap	3.6	9.8	2.1	13.0	15.9	7.9	10.9	18.3	6.4
US	42.4	25.1	11.2	25.3	25.7	15.3	25.2	25.0	18.3

Source: A. Hogenbirk and R. Narula, 'Globalisation and the small economy: The case of the Netherlands', *Research memorandum/MERIT* 2/99-002 (Maastricht: MERIT, 1999).

Note: Based on UN and World Bank data. (1): share of a country in total outward foreign direct investment stock; (2) share of country in world output; (3) ratio of share of sales of foreign multinationals affiliates and domestic MNE's in country GDP. G = Germany, UK = United Kingdom, NL = Netherlands, F = France, S = Sweden, No = Norway, I = Italy, Jap = Japan, US = United States.

First of all, these data clearly reveal the large position of Dutch multinationals in the world economy. The share of Dutch outward foreign direct investment by multinationals in 1980 (8.1 percent) is high, especially when compared to the much lower share of the Dutch economy in world GDP (only 1.6 percent). The large level of multinationals' sales vis-à-vis the Dutch GDP is clearly reflected in column 3 of Table 8; in 1980 the ratio already amounts to 35.7 percent of Dutch GDP, but increases even further in the period 1980–1995. In 1995 the ratio of sales to GDP was as high as 70 percent: such high levels cannot be found in any other country. Nevertheless, Table 9 shows that the strong position of the multinationals on the world market has decreased after 1980. In 1980 Dutch multinationals were responsible for 8.1 percent of the total outward FDI, but by 1995 this share had decreased to 5.9 percent. The same slowdown is reflected in the development of R&D. On the OECD ranking list the Netherlands occupied a second place in terms of indus-

Table 9: Sectoral division of Dutch outward FDI stock, 1973–1995 (in %)

	1973	1975	1980	1985	1990	1995
Agriculture	0.3	0.3	0.5	0.1	0.1	0.1
Food	13.3	11.3	7.9	8.4	8.9	9.6
Chemicals	47.3	46.5	51.0	42.6	33.0	27.0
Metals etc.	24.1	25.3	19.0	13.9	12.0	10.0
Miscellaneous	1.8	2.0	2.1	1.4	3.3	4.8
Construction	1.1	1.6	1.3	0.8	1.3	0.7
Trade	5.4	5.4	7.3	4.1	7.0	11.0
Transport	3.0	3.1	1.7	1.2	1.5	1.7
Financial serv.	3.8	4.6	8.7	27.4	34.0	36.0
Total	100	100	100	100	100	100

Source: A. Hogenbirk and R. Narula, 'Globalisation and the small economy: The case of the Netherlands', *Research memorandum/MERIT* 2/99-002 (Maastricht: MERIT, 1999).

trial R&D in 1967 (with a level of 1.12 percent). In 1991 the Dutch position had deteriorated: the Netherlands then occupied a ninth place with a figure of 0.91 percent. So, contrary to the growth experience of almost any other OECD country, industrial R&D intensity witnessed a decline in the Netherlands.[23] And this decrease was concentrated in exactly those multinationals that had been responsible for about 75 percent of industrial R&D in the late 1960s, against a mere 40 percent in the 1990s.

It is too early to give a reliable explanation of the decrease of the share of the multinationals in R&D investments and of the fall of the Dutch share in world FDI. Yet, some tentative conclusions can be drawn. First of all, the multinationals suffered from the *penalties of the pioneer*. Many of these firms had been successful in mastering the technologies of the second industrial revolution, which were based on energy-intensive and mass-production processes. It seems that this technological regime had reached the limits of its growth potential during the 1960s. Further scale increases in business organisation proved to be unproductive. The 1970s and 1980s were a period of intensive downsizing. This process coincided with a return of these multinationals to their core business. In many cases the reformulation of business strategies was accompanied by a disposal of research activities. Furthermore, the energy-intensive industries were severely hit by the two oil crises of the 1970s.[24] The downsizing of the multinationals resulted in a considerable slowdown of the growth of output and productivity.

The implications of the slow growth of multinationals on different sectors of the economy can be demonstrated by looking at the sectoral division of the Dutch outward FDI stock.

These data clearly reveal the decreasing FDI (and technological) activity of multinationals in the chemical sector and in the cluster of metal products (the cluster in which electrical-engineering equipment is classified).[25]

Neoclassical economic theory expects small economies to specialise in technological diffusion and not in technology creation because of scale limitations: yet our research points at the importance of technology creation rather than just diffusion in the Dutch economy. The years between 1920 and 1970 were characterised by an increasing share of Dutch exports in world trade. This growth phase was to a large extent induced by technological innovations. From the 1970s onwards technology diffusion became much more important. For small and open economies it may be easy and profitable to use technologies which are developed elsewhere. However, additional investments need to be made in order to be able to implement these new technologies in the production process, especially in the realm of on-the-job-training: that is why the formation of 'human capital' seems to be of vital importance.

As far as schooling and vocational training are concerned, the Netherlands is among the highest-developed OECD countries. In the late 1980s the proportion of high technicians and of people with a university degree in total employment was high (27 percent) compared with Switzerland (20 percent), Germany (18 percent), Great Britain (17 percent) and France (14 percent).[26] Despite this high level of schooling, growth-accounting experiments by Van Ark and De Jong show that human capital only played a modest role in the Dutch growth process.[27] Also research by Jacobs, Nahuis and Tang indicates that human capital has not been instrumental in the process of technology diffusion.[28] These authors claim that total-factor productivity (TFP) growth can be largely explained by domestic R&D and the spillovers stemming from these investments. The TFP elasticities for domestic spillovers are about 0.14, and for foreign spillovers approximately 0.03. As far as human capital is concerned, this research does not show any evidence on the existence of positive external effects of human capital.

Even if the possible role of human capital in facilitating the assimilation of foreign as well as domestic technologies is considered, no positive relationships are found. Therefore Jacobs, Nahuis and Tang conclude that 'innovation driven growth theories are perhaps better vehicles to describe the growth process than human capital based growth models'. This conclusion has important policy implications, as normally much of the Dutch technology policy is aimed at increasing the assimilation of technology, rather than stimulating processes of technology creation.[29]

Conclusion

In this article we have tried to show that the international competitiveness of the Dutch economy during the twentieth century manifested very positive progress during the 1920s and the 1960s. Policies in the Netherlands focused mainly on cost reduction of important resource endowments. However, we find that these policies showed no direct positive effects on longterm competitiveness except insofar as there were unintended secondary effects through their influence on firms' accumulation strategies. Technology is probably the crucial factor. To use Porter's terminology, Dutch economic growth is more factor driven than investment or innovation driven. This means that the Dutch economy faces considerable difficulties when it comes to defending its position on the world market. Despite its success in terms of technology creation, the electrical engineering industry suffered an export collapse in the 1970s and 1980s. Just as in the case of textiles, this branch of industry suffered from the emergence of low-wage production in other regions: for example, Philips shifted many of its labour-intensive activities to South-east Asia.

The focus on processing industries is one of the characteristic features of Dutch manufacturing. This may be attributed to a 'tradesman' mentality among Dutch entrepreneurs, who focus less on increasing productivity levels through innovation than on trying to minimise production costs by keeping input prices low. To a certain extent Dutch firms are encouraged in this behaviour by a government policy that is aimed more at the lowering of factor prices than on strengthening the economy's technological basis.

1 Parts of this chapter were presented at conferences in Helsinki, Zürich and Oxford. Part of this research on competitiveness has already been published in J.P. Smits, 'Technologie, productiviteit en welzijn', in Johan W. Schot *et al.* (eds.), *Techniek in Nederland in de Twintigste Eeuw*, vol. VII. Zutphen: Walburg Pers, 2003, pp. 233–256. The authors would like to thank participants who commented on earlier versions.

2 Alberto Alesina and Enrico Spoleare, *The Size of Nations* (Cambridge, MA [etc.]: The MIT Press, 2003).

3 Here we follow Federico and Foreman-Peck, who make a distinction between three types of policies designed to influence industrial activities. Firstly, policies creating an environment for successful entrepreneurship such as the enforcement of property rights. Secondly, policies modifying the technology and markets for inputs and outputs. Thirdly, policies directed at changing the structure of the economy, that is, the relative importance of the industries and firms by 'picking winners' and 'helping losers'. We concentrate here on the second type of policies. Gianni Federico and James Foreman-Peck (eds), *European Industrial Policy* (Oxford: Oxford University Press, 1999), pp. 4–6.

4 See for example the literature on national systems of innovation: Charles Edquist, *Systems of innovation: technologies, institutions and organizations* (London [etc.]: Pinter, 1997); Bengt-Ake Lundvall, *National systems of innovation: Towards a theory of innovation and interactive learning* (London [etc.]: 1992); and Chris Freeman and Luc Soete, *The economics of industrial innovation* (London [etc.]: Continuum, 1997).

5 Richard Nelson and Sidney Winter, *An evolutionary theory of economic change* (Cambridge, MA.: Belknap Press of Harvard University Press, 1982).

6 Angus Maddison, *The world economy: A millennial perspective* (Paris: OECD, 2001); Ben Gales and Keetie Sluyterman, 'Outward bound: The rise of Dutch multinationals', in Geoffrey Jones and Harm Schröter (eds.), *The rise of multinationals in continental Europe* (Aldershot [etc.]: Elgar, 1993), pp. 65–98.

7 Jan-Pieter Smits, 'Economische ontwikkeling, 1800–1995', in Ronald van der Bie and Pit Dehing (eds.), *Nationaal Goed. Feiten en cijfers over onze samenleving, (ca.) 1800–1999* (Voorburg [etc.]: CBS, 1999), p. 17.

8 Ronald van der Bie, *'Eene doorlopende groote roes'. De economisch ontwikkeling van Nederland, 1913/1921* (Amsterdam, 1995); Herman de Jong, 'Between the Devil and the Deep Blue Sea. The Dutch economy during World War I', in Stephen

Broadberry and Mark Harrison (eds.), *The Economics of World War I* (Cambridge: Cambridge University Press, 2005), pp. 137–168.

9 Recent research on the Dutch economy has stressed the influence of technology specialisation (in terms of patents) on trade specialisation. This research corroborates a 'technology-gap' account of trade flows. See G. Amendola, P. Guerrieri and P. C. Padoan, 'International patterns of technological accumulation and trade', in Daniele Archibugi and Jonathan Michie (eds), *Trade, growth and technical change* (Cambridge: Cambridge University Press, 1998), pp. 141–167.

10 Smits, 'Economische ontwikkeling', p. 21.

11 Hein Klemann, *Tussen Reich en Empire. De economische betrekkingen van Nederland met zijn belangrijkste handelspartners: Duitsland, Groot-Brittannië en België en de Nederlandse handelspolitiek, 1929–1936* (Amsterdam: NEHA, 1990).

12 Herman de Jong, 'Dutch manufacturing performance in comparative perspective 1913–1965', *Jahrbuch für Wirtschaftsgeschichte* (Berlin: Akademie Verlag, 2000/1), p. 50.

13 Ministerie van Economische Zaken, *Toets op het concurrentievermogen. Achtergrondrapportage* (Den Haag, 1995), p. 45.

14 Dany Jacobs *et al.*, *De economische kracht van Nederland: toepassing van Porters benadering van de concurrentiekracht van landen* ('s Gravenhage: SMO-boek, 1990).

15 The data for the post-1961 period are significantly higher than the results presented in Table 4. The figures for the first half of the twentieth century are clearly understated, because the RCAs are calculated for aggregated categories, whilst RCA data are only reliable when calculated at a more detailed level. Despite the fact that the data for the earlier period cannot be directly compared to the figures for the last part of the century, they provide the same picture. Food-processing as well as the chemical industries can be considered as the most competitive clusters within Dutch manufacturing.

16 After all: $[X^{NL}_i / X_i] / [X^{NL} / X] = [X^{NL}_i / X^{NL}] / [X_i / X]$.

17 GATT, *International trade,* various issues. A final note should be made on the possible compensating effect of exports of services on the decline in world share of goods exports in the Netherlands. We do not have detailed international statistics at our disposal in order to chart the changes in competitiveness in this sector. The estimates of changes in export volume, however, show a much slower increase in those for services compared with commodities. Hence the decline in competitiveness in agriculture and manufacturing is not compensated for by the exports of services. For a more detailed account on services see Bart van Ark, 'The productivity problem of the Dutch economy: Implications for economic and social policies and business strategy', *Research Memorandum GD-66* (Groningen: Groningen Growth and Development Centre, 2003).

18 K. E. Sluyterman and H. J. M. Winkelman, 'The Dutch family firm confronted with Chandler's Dynamics of Industrial Capitalism, 1890–1940', *Business History* (1993), pp. 152–183.

19 CBS, *Kennis en economie 1999. Onderzoek en innovatie in Nederland* (s. l., 1999), pp. 89–90.

20 For a case study about the mechanisms of technology diffusion in Shell see Jan-Pieter Smits and Ben Gales, 'Olie- en gas', in Johan W. Schot *et al.* (eds.), *Techniek in Nederland in de Twintigste Eeuw*, vol. II. (Zutphen: Walburg Pers, 2000), pp. 67–89.

21 Alfred D. Chandler, *Scale and scope. The dynamics of industrial capitalism* (Cambridge, MA [etc.]: Belknap Press of Harvard University Press, 1990).

22 J.P. Smits, *Economische groei en structuurveranderingen in de Nederlandse dienstensector, 1850–1913* (Amsterdam, 1995), chapter IX.

23 P. Patel and K. Pavitt, 'Uneven (and divergent) technological accumulation among advanced countries: evidence and a framework of explanation', in Daniele Archibugi and Jonathan Michie (eds.), *Trade, growth and technical change* (Cambridge: Cambridge University Press, 1998), p. 58.

24 J.P. Smits, 'Omvang en oorsprong van de milieuschade, 1910–1995', in Ronald van der Bie and Pit Dehing (eds.), *Nationaal Goed. Feiten en cijfers over onze samenleving, (ca.) 1800–1999* (Voorburg [etc.]: CBS, 1999), pp. 235–256.

25 Although the share of services in total outward FDI has increased substantially, this did not stimulate productivity growth in this sector to a great extent. Increases in service productivity in the Netherlands are clearly below OECD average. See B. van Ark, L. Broersma and G. de Jong, 'Innovation in services. Overview of data sources and analytical structure', *Research Memorandum GD-44* (Groningen: Groningen Growth and Development Centre, 1999).

26 Patel and Pavitt, 'Uneven', 61.

27 Bart van Ark and Herman de Jong, 'Accounting for Economic Growth in the Netherlands Since 1913', *Economic and Social History in the Netherlands* vol. 7 (1996), pp. 199–242.

28 B. Jacobs, R. Nahuis and P.J.G. Tang, 'Human capital, R&D, productivity growth and assimilation of technologies in the Netherlands', in B. van Ark, S.K. Kuipers and G.H. Kuper, *Productivity, technology and economic growth* (Boston [etc.]: Kluwer Academic Publishers, 2000), pp. 293–316.

29 Ibid., p. 311.

MARGRIT MÜLLER

From Protectionism to Market Liberalisation: Patterns of Internationalisation in the Main Swiss Export Sectors

Introduction[1]

Small countries are heavily dependent on foreign markets, and consequently their economy is particularly vulnerable to changing conditions in international trade and capital flows. In the fields of exports and foreign direct investments (FDI) Swiss firms have from the nineteenth century pursued a strategy of internationalisation. Furthermore, the main export branches (textiles and watches, and later machinery and chemicals) have all been highly dependent on imported raw materials and intermediate products, but providing the needed supplies was no particular problem throughout the period under discussion except during wartime. Switzerland's high dependence on imports is underlined by the fact that import shares were usually higher than export shares. If we compare the share of trade in GDP the interwar years were a period of deglobalisation (Figure 1). The share of industrial exports declined from almost 30% before World War I to 10% in the midst of the depression of the 1930s. After World War II the export share increased again, and since the 1970s has been about the same as in the early twentieth century, while import shares have been lower. Clearly, the domestic economy with its sheltered sectors gained in importance during the second half of the century.

With a rather strong domestic sector and several export-oriented branches the Swiss economy shows in an especially pronounced form the dual structure typical of small countries: the outward-oriented sectors were interested in free trade and a liberal economic order, while the inward-oriented sectors advocated protection from for-

Figure 1: Growth rates of GDP and nominal industrial imports and exports in % of nominal GDP 1896–2000

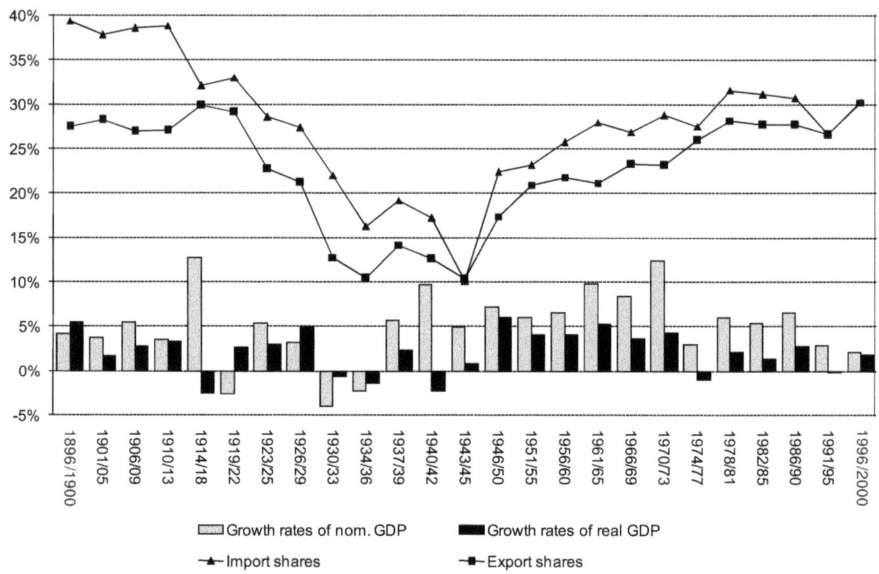

Sources: growth rates: computed by Heiner Ritzmann-Blickenstorfer based on Heiner Ritzmann-Blickenstorfer (ed.), *Historical Statistics of Switzerland* (Zurich: Chronos, 1996), Table L. 3 and Q.1.a, pp. 668–669 and p. 866; imports and exports 1896–1992: Ritzmann-Blickenstorfer, *Historical Statistics*, Tables L. 3 pp. 668–669; imports and exports 1993–2000: Swiss Federal Statistical Office (ed.), *Statistical Yearbook of Switzerland* (1995), Table 6.6, and (2002), Tables 6.5.2/3.

eign competition. In the literature on small countries the features usually emphasised are strong incentives towards consensus and compromise:[2] but in fact the diverging economic interests of the inward- and outward-oriented sectors were a constant source of conflict and a major constraint upon economic policy.

In comparison with large countries, the autonomy of small countries with regard to foreign-trade policies has been clearly restricted. What needs to be stressed is that such size-specific disadvantages do not necessarily apply to firms located in small countries. Expanding sales to foreign markets is often a necessity, and early internationalisation can lead to a competitive advantage in comparison with firms located in large countries.[3] Firms may exploit forms of internationalisation which are less prone to protectionist interventions, such as licensing agreements, joint ventures with foreign firms or FDI. Of course, these forms of internationalisation are linked with different advantages and disadvantages for the development of the firm and of the national economy. Even if they may function as substitutes, the resulting economic structure and performance will differ considerably.

The main objective of this chapter is to understand the interactions between the strategies adopted at company level and the rules and policies implemented on the political level. Firms view a given situation differently: their aims and capabilities, their visions for the future and experience gained in the past will shape the opportunities perceived and influence their choice.[4] The different strategies of growth pursued will lead to firm-specific capabilities and mould the firm's path of development in the future. To some extent shared beliefs, traditions and social norms will define their space for manoeuvre, and we will see that such restrictions have been mainly related to the economic sector in which they were active. Economic policies and institutional change may support or impair the branch-specific strategy for coping with changed conditions for international trade, and the behaviour of the firms will in turn influence political decision-making.

The next section deals with the impact of the interwar disintegration of the world economy on the main outward-oriented branches and the reactions of some of their leading firms: these reactions are then linked with the economic policies pursued during this period. In the fourth section the analysis is extended to the second half of the twentieth century.[5] The aim is to trace continuities and discontinuities in response to a context of reglobalisation.

Coping with economic disintegration

The interwar years were marked by two economic recessions: their impact was especially pronounced in the export industries, while the domestic industries fared better.[6] Some years with considerable

Figure 2: Nominal industrial exports and imports 1900–1950, in mill. CHF

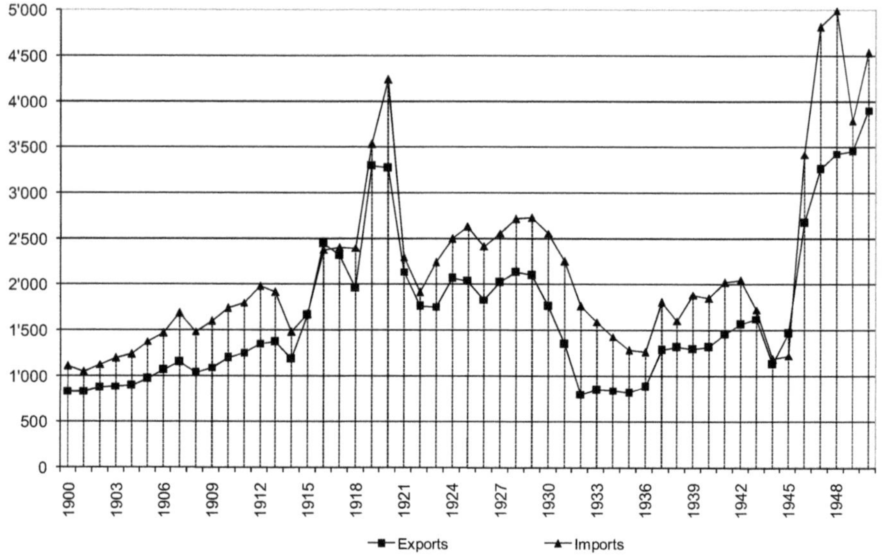

Source: Ritzmann-Blickenstorfer, *Historical Statistics*, Tables L. 3, pp. 668–669.

growth of industrial exports followed the sharp downturn in 1921/1922 (Figure 2). Between 1929 and 1932 total nominal industrial exports declined by almost two-thirds and remained flat until 1935. Total industrial imports declined to less than half the nominal value between 1929 and 1936.[7]

If we consider the geographical diversification of exports, the categorisation of the interwar period as one of deglobalisation is less evident, because exports clearly shifted to new markets. In the 1920s the average export shares to the Americas reached 20% and to Asia 10%. Between 1929 and 1935 nominal exports to all overseas regions were in decline, while export shares to Europe increased from an average of 70% to 80%. Export shares to North America declined considerably from 12% to 7%, to Latin America they stagnated at around 5% and to Asia they declined by about a fourth to 6%. But the share of exports to the near-eastern countries increased and in Latin America, where the main markets were Argentina and Brazil, exports were expanded to new countries during the eco-

Figure 3: Exports to Clearing- and Non-Clearing countries in % of total exports to Europe 1921–1940

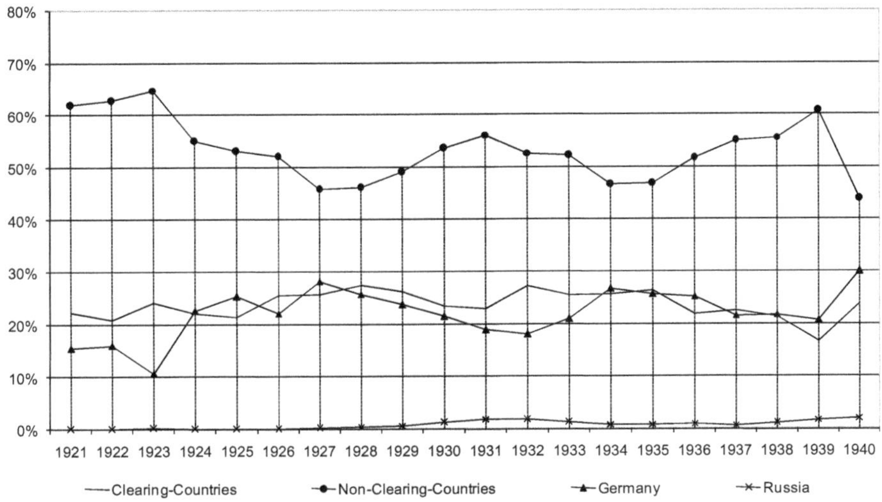

Source: Ritzmann-Blickenstorfer, *Historical Statistics*, Table L.22, p. 706.

nomic crises of the early 1920s (Peru, Ecuador, Columbia) and in the 1930s (Uruguay, Venezuela, French Guyana, Cuba). In Europe, the share of exports to Germany and the other clearing countries increased, while those to the free-currency area declined. This movement was reversed after the devaluation of the Swiss franc in September 1936 (Figure 3).[8]

The geographical distribution of industrial imports was more stable. Imports from European countries continued at around 75% except during and immediately after World War II, when imports from Europe declined to a minimum of 50% and those from North and Latin America increased from about 15% in the 1930s to 40% at the end of the war.[9]

Aggregate estimates on other forms of internationalisation, especially outward and inward FDI, are not available for the interwar years.[10] The general view is that, in line with the development in other countries, outward FDI slowed down.[11] But with regard to capital flows the situation in Switzerland differed considerably, because there were practically no restrictions for capital exports.[12]

Figure 4: Nominal industrial exports 1900–1950, in mill. CHF

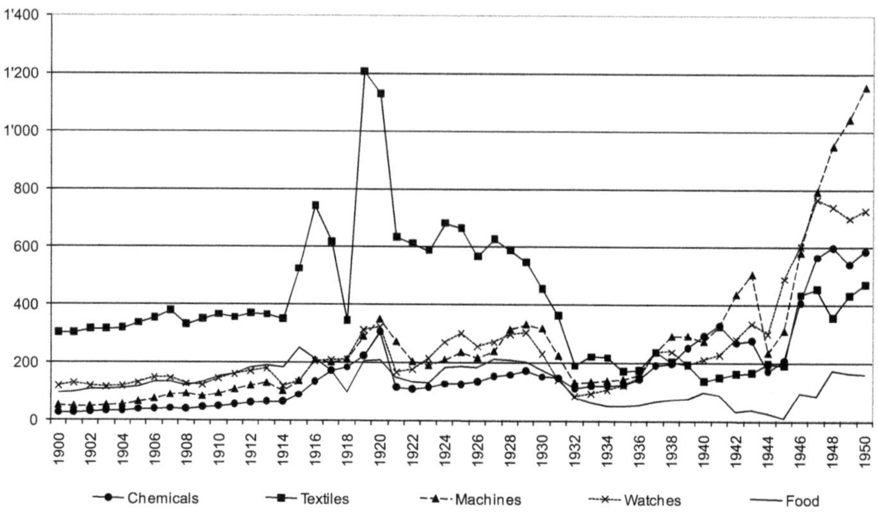

Source: Ritzmann-Blickenstorfer, *Historical Statistics*, Tables L.11b, pp. 683–687.

Further more, the late devaluation of the Swiss franc in 1936 was a favourable condition for investing abroad, and the number of Swiss multinational enterprises (MNEs) was higher than in other small European countries.[13] With regard to inward FDI, a defensive attitude progressively replaced the openness that had prevailed before the First World War.[14]

The most striking feature is the uneven development of the main export industries (Figure 4). Exports of textiles, the leading industry since the nineteenth century, stagnated in the early 1920s and then declined rapidly, while other industries' exports increased.

The depression of the 1930s affected all export industries, but in relative terms we can clearly distinguish between rising industries (machines and chemicals) and declining industries (textiles and food); the watch industry was able to regain its share of exports (Table 1).[15]

Why did some branches fare so much better during the interwar period? What strategies did these firms pursue, how did they perceive their room for manoeuvre and in what way were their reactions linked with economic policies?

Table 1: Distribution of industrial exports 1900–1949 (in %)

Year	Textiles	Watches	Food	Machines	Chemicals	Other Industries
1900	57.61	13.14	10.37	5.64	3.10	10.14
1910	57.24	10.39	10.96	6.73	3.68	11.00
1919	55.41	8.63	5.72	8.02	6.19	16.01
1925	42.86	14.19	8.98	11.19	6.03	16.76
1930	32.27	12.90	9.86	17.72	8.57	18.68
1935	25.47	14.94	6.44	17.55	15.19	20.41
1939	18.69	14.90	6.13	22.49	19.48	18.32
1949	17.92	19.62	4.70	29.16	15.20	13.41

Source: Ritzmann-Blickenstorfer, *Historical Statistics*, Tables L.11b, pp. 683–687.

The traditional export industries

In the interwar period the textile industry's share of total exports fell from over 50% to less than 20% by 1939 (Table 1). There were various reasons for the rapid decline of this industry. On one hand, the traditional textile centres were challenged by the expanding textile industries in central Europe and the Far East. On the other changing tastes, the mechanisation of production and rising customs duties drastically reduced demand for embroidery – especially in Great Britain and the United States, previously the main export markets. Swiss textile manufacturers had developed routines for coping with location-specific disadvantages from the nineteenth century,[16] and we may assume that firms reacted according to established practice by concentrating and reducing manufacturing capacity in Switzerland, shifting production to foreign countries or creating technologically demanding novelties for niche markets.

Superficially, the textile industry shows some striking similarities with the watch industry: both were regionally concentrated, both consisted of a large number of small enterprises, and the outwork system was still widely used. Any major fall in demand resulted in economic crisis for the whole region and called forth the intervention of the public authorities.[17] But the two industries differed considerably with regard to the opportunities perceived and the policies pursued. In the textile industry the loss of international competitiveness was largely accepted as inevitable. The policy of the business associations and the political authorities was to offer incentives for downsizing. By contrast, the watch industry strongly believed in the competitiveness of watches 'made in Switzerland', and their overall policy was to defend this location-specific advantage and keep production within the national borders:[18] this response was very unusual, not only when compared with that of other Swiss export industries, but also in light of the history of the industry itself. Collective efforts supported by the federal authorities had already played a prominent part in the short post-war crisis of the early 1920s,[19] and the beginning of the 1930s saw the establishment of the super-holding ASUAG, which was entitled to buy, dissolve and modernise factories and to reorganise the whole industry: but reorganisation was slow and not very effective. Price competition continued, and some firms tried to avoid high customs duties by assembling the watches abroad. Such practices were prohibited, and measures were even taken against the emigration of qualified workers, notwithstanding the large number of unemployed.[20] Coping with the depression by restricting companies' areas of discretion continued, although exports increased from 1935 onwards. Results show that the protective policy was successful to the extent that the decline of the watch industry was stopped (Table 1).

The food-processing industry consisted of firms which were highly export-oriented – producing, for example, canned food products and chocolate – and firms which concentrated almost exclusively on the domestic market – for example, breweries.[21] The share of food exports in total industrial exports increased during the 1920s and exceeded pre-war levels. During the depression of the 1930s, export values declined rapidly (Figure 4). Exports of the main products – condensed milk and chocolate – fell from 43 and 34 million CHF respectively in 1928 to 8.7 and 1.6 million CHF in 1933. The broadly shared view was that in Switzerland food processing had no future as an export-oriented industry.[22] But the leading firms survived and even achieved considerable growth, partly by taking over the smaller domestic food producers, but mainly by increasing production abroad. The most prominent example is Nestlé, but smaller firms, especially in the chocolate industry, pursued similar strategies.[23] During World War I Nestlé acquired several foreign firms in order to compensate the downsizing of production capacity in Switzerland. The rapid international expansion of the firm at a time of inadequate managerial capacities and organisational structures resulted in heavy financial losses and a considerable dependence upon its bankers, but the subsequent managerial and financial restructuring process, involving several disinvestments, was successful. From 1925 onwards the firm's sound financial situation and the enhanced competence and coherence of its top management allowed to pursue a strategy of controlled step-by-step expansion. The firm reacted to the depression of the 1930s by launching new products, searching for new foreign markets and expanding production in foreign countries. A thorough change of perspectives with regard to the most adequate strategy of growth can be observed in 1932. By then it had become clear that the State policy of sheltering the agrarian sector from import competition would continue in force.[24] Consequently, employment in Switzerland was reduced, some factories were closed and the production of new specialities was taken up abroad, mainly to avoid paying duties twice – on the imported agricultural goods and again on the exported processed food.[25]

The rising export industries

The exports of the machine industry increased before and during World War I, but collapsed after the war and again in the early 1930s after having increased from the mid-1920s (Figure 4). Their share in total industrial exports reached 17% in 1930 but then stagnated until 1935, while the share of chemicals continued to increase (Table 1). But by 1939 the machine industry had become the leading export industry. To provide some insight into the different strategies pursued by the firms in this rather heterogeneous industry, three companies manufacturing the main export products of this industry have been chosen: Sulzer Unternehmungen AG (hereafter Sulzer) produced mainly steam and diesel engines and pumps; AG Brown Boveri & Cie. (hereafter BBC) had been a pioneering firm in the electricity sector and was an important manufacturer of steam turbines; the Aktiengesellschaft Jh. Jacob Rieter & Co. (hereafter Rieter) was one of the leading textile-machine manufacturers. Sulzer and BBC, with five to six thousand employees in Switzerland the two largest firms in this industry, were diversified, multinational companies, while Rieter (about 900 employees) concentrated on spinning machines produced at its home base in Winterthur.

Before World War I the main markets of the Swiss machine industry were France (19%), Germany (16%), Russia (15%) and Italy (9%),[26] and the companies' geographical expansion after the war can be understood as an offensive reaction to compensate the loss of traditional markets. Sulzer transformed its most important sales agencies into subsidiary companies, new sales agencies were established overseas and licensing agreements concluded with foreign manufacturers.[27] BBC had manufacturing affiliates in several European countries and sales agencies all over the world, but was reluctant to conclude licensing agreements with other manufacturers.[28] The number of foreign affiliates needing financial support and the losses incurred during the crisis of the early 1920s were larger than in the case of Sulzer. Tight liquidity restricted BBC's room for manoeuvre throughout the interwar period.[29] Rieter had established a wide network of sales agencies and agents in practically all countries with a substantial textile industry. The downturn of demand in its main export markets – Germany, Austria and Italy – in the early 1920s was compensated by shifting exports to other countries, occasionally even to the Far East.[30]

All firms experienced a few years of rapid growth until 1929. The textile machine industry was not seriously affected by the progressive decline of the textile industry in Switzerland during the 1920s: for Rieter these years were marked by an increasing stock of orders and long delivery dates.[31] Obviously, any supportive links that may have existed previously between the two industries had become unimportant. In effect, relations with the textile firms were strained because in their view the firms exporting textile machines strengthened the position of their competitors in eastern and central Europe, Turkey and Japan. Sulzer increased the number of licensing agreements, but no new manufacturing companies were established abroad. BBC established manufacturing companies in Romania and Poland in the late 1920s, notwithstanding the strain on liquidity. The BBC management even decided to take up production in the United States. The American Brown Boveri Electric Corporation (ABBEC) was founded in 1925, but in 1931 production was abandoned and replaced by a licensing agreement.[32] This first overseas investment had encountered difficulties from the start because of conflicting interests and a profound lack of trust between the management of the parent firm in Baden and its US partners. Sulzer had planned to establish a manufacturing company in the United States in the early 1920s, but the project was not realised. Both firms perceived the United States as a very promising but difficult market. The American methods of mass production were admired and carefully studied, but imitated rather selectively.

All firms were highly dependent on foreign markets. Rieter exported 75% of its spinning machines to more than a dozen countries, but the bulk of exports still went to Germany and Italy, the main pre-war markets.[33] In the case of Sulzer, about 45% of total orders came from Great Britain and overseas countries, and only some 25% from domestic customers. Unfortunately, we have little information on the share of BBC's exports in its total production and none at all on the distribution of exports to the different countries though in some product lines export shares reached as much as 80%.[34] The traditional orientation towards central and eastern Europe – especially the Soviet Union – persisted, but exports from Switzerland remained marginal (Figure 3). Both firms exploited the opportunities in this market through their German affiliates, and in the case of Sulzer also by concluding licensing agreements.[35] Usually the sales area of the foreign subsidiaries was confined to their domestic market in order to avoid competition with the parent firm. In the case of Russia an exception had to be made for political reasons.

The impact of the depression on the machine industry was quite strong (Figure 4). In the case of Sulzer the yearly inflow of orders dropped from almost 70 million CHF in 1929 to 25 million CHF in 1934, and the number of employees declined by about a third.[36] For the management of BBC, the real extent of the crisis became visible in spring 1931, when the total stock of orders was down 50% on the previous year: their workforce in Switzerland dropped from almost 7500 in 1929/30 to 3500 in 1934/35.[37] Both firms questioned the viability of an export-oriented machine industry located in Switzerland, and alternative forms of internationalisation (FDI and licensing agreements) became more important. However, BBC's scope for action was restricted by liquidity problems. Up to 1935 the management focused on reducing costs by wage cuts, redundancies, cancelling investments and finally also by cutting expenditures for R&D. This economising and downsizing strategy culminated in a proposal to stop manufacturing turbines, BBC's core product line. But confronted with such a drastic decision, the attitude of the leading decision-makers changed. To gain a sound basis for the firm's future prosperity a thorough restructuring was initiated with the aim of preserving and developing accumulated company-specific know-how and competencies. Sulzer's liquidity was high throughout the period, and this certainly influenced the firm's room for manoeuvre. Priority was given to R&D and to maintaining the network of foreign subsidiaries at a lower level of capacity. The firm even ventured into a completely unrelated product line and developed a technically demanding, innovative type of weaving machine.[38] The policy of establishing manufacturing companies abroad and making licensing agreements continued: but 'expatriation' had its limits when it threatened to seriously reduce production and employment at home.[39]

For Rieter, a specialised firm without production bases in foreign countries, the options were different.[40] The routine reaction to the downturn of demand in 1929 was to intensify R&D and search for new markets. Sales were extended to Turkey, Romania and Bulgaria, countries that had been neglected in the past because of payment risks. The inflow of business became highly volatile – large but infrequent and unpredictable orders from varying countries. The devaluation of the pound sterling in autumn 1931 was countered by price cuts in order to defend competitiveness in overseas markets. This aggressive move led in 1933 to an agreement on prices and payment conditions with the firm's main competitors, the English manufacturers of textile machines:[41] the immediate effect of joining this cartel was that prices were stabilised, and by the end of 1933 the inflow of orders had increased, more workers were employed and investments in buildings and equipment began to rise again. The main concern of the management from then on was the functioning of the clearing system. Complaints about export quotas being too small were quite frequent, but the clearing system functioned satisfactorily most of the time. Sales to the clearing area increased from less then a third to over 50%, while domestic orders declined from 14% to 6%.

The international cartel of textile-machine manufacturers certainly facilitated Rieter's early recovery. The involvement of BBC in international cartels is not clear. In the late 1920s and early 1930s, attempts by foreign firms to establish some form of cooperation were given a welcome that was at best unenthusiastic and at worst downright suspicious: BBC feared losing control over its technical know-how.[42] The company history mentions several occasions to enter into association with important foreign groups, all of which failed within a few years.[43] It seems that Sulzer had no links with international cartels, probably because the firm was too diversified. With regard to their Swiss competitors, both firms tried repeatedly to reduce competition by segmenting product lines or by sharing large orders among the major firms of the machine industry. But the context of depression did not favour cooperation. Competition rather increased, because most firms tried to raise their domestic sales and to diversify into product lines suited to the domestic market. Consequently turning to the domestic market was, as a rule, not a promising strategy for the export-oriented firms in the machine industry. But there were some exceptions to this rule. Saurer, for example, the main manufacturer of trucks and buses, decided to concentrate on the domestic market, since the firm had largely lost its competitiveness in foreign markets during the 1920s.[44] This decade marked the end of automobile production in Switzerland.[45]

Unlike the watch industry machine-industry firms were rather reluctant to request government support, although both the main schemes for export promotion had been primarily intended to support this industry (see the section on economic policies below).

Up to World War I the share of the chemical industry in total industrial exports was very small. Its relative importance increased during the war and the interwar period, especially in the 1930s (Table 1). Throughout the period dyes were the main product, but pharmaceuticals gained in importance.[46] All the major dye manufacturers (Ciba, Geigy and Sandoz) were located in Basle. With the conclusion of the 'Interessen-Gemeinschaft' (IG) in 1918 competition among these firms was eliminated. Together they established some chemical works and sales organisations abroad in order to secure supplies and promote sales.

For this analysis the Gesellschaft für Chemische Industrie in Basel (Ciba) has been chosen as example.[47] By the 1920s the management was already pursuing a policy of shifting mass production to foreign subsidiary companies in order to take advantage of lower production costs, and by the end of that decade Ciba had manufacturing companies in Poland and France as well as sales agencies in several European and overseas countries. Together with its partners in the IG the firm owned factories for the production of dyes in England, the United States and Italy. About two-thirds of the total production of dyes was manufactured abroad, but the majority of the work force (about 60%) was still employed in Basle. In 1929 turnover and profits reached record heights; but there were first signs of an economic downturn, and the IG joined the German-French cartel which had been set up in 1927. This agreement regulated exports and stabilised prices for dyes. Furthermore, due to the regular information exchange production capacities could be allocated more evenly and production costs were reduced. In 1930 Ciba initiated a costly restructuring of its premises for the production of high quality, non-fading dyes: being linked to the cartel was an incentive to diversify and intensify R&D in non-regulated product lines.

The impact of the depression on the chemical industry was less severe than in the machine industry. The number of employees was much lower and, consequently, also the number of unemployed.[48] The drop of sales in 1931 and 1932 was attributed to the relocation of the textile industry and to the expansion of the domestic production of dyes in the main foreign markets. The worsening conditions for international trade due to protective tariffs, export and import quotas, international-payment restrictions, as well as the high production costs in Switzerland, were topics of major concern.[49] Apart from insisting on the necessity of reducing domestic prices and wages in order to restore international competitiveness, the firm did not turn to government support. The main strategies for compensating the loss of demand were expanding sales to new markets, product diversification and innovation. Sales agencies were established in South America, mainly in Argentina, Chile and Brazil. For pharmaceuticals – which contributed about 25% to total turnover and were less affected by the depression – England and the United States, two countries with high income levels, were perceived as the most promising markets. But high customs duties as well as the devaluation of the pound sterling and the US dollar caused large price increases for exports from Basle, and consequently exports to these countries and to the highly protected French market decreased steadily. In the early 1930s the packaging of pharmaceuticals was partly transferred to foreign sales agencies, and in 1935 it was decided to establish production facilities for pharmaceuticals in the United States and in England, France, Italy and Germany.

From the end of 1935 sales, profits and investments increased, but production was mainly expanded abroad and not in Switzerland. In November 1937 Ciba took up production in Summit, USA, and the year after in Horsham, England. The planned establishment of manufacturing firms in France, Italy and Germany had to be postponed because of the unstable political situation. Reallocating production and sales areas changed the role of the parent company. The rule that the foreign works produced only for their home market was loosened. Still, the number of employees in Basle did not decline, because the production of specialities increased. Research and the development of new products were still confined to the parent company.

The reaction of Hoffmann-La Roche, the largest Swiss manufacturer of pharmaceuticals, to increasing protectionism and the depression of the 1930s was quite similar: geographical diversification, FDI and intensification of R&D.[50]

The service sectors

The main branches of the service sector active on an international level were banking and insurance. There were also some quite important trading firms, but their history is scarcely known yet.[51] From the late nineteenth century the main Swiss insurance firms had pursued a strategy of internationalisation by establishing or taking over foreign subsidiaries, and these activities were intensified in the interwar years.[52] The standard explanation is that the loss of trust in

German insurance firms offered an opportunity for Swiss firms to take over a large part of their business. But such an argument misses important aspects, because only a few firms were able to seize this opportunity successfully in a very competitive and, to some extent, hostile foreign environment. The reinsurer Schweizerische Rückversicherungsgesellschaft and the primary insurer Zurich Versicherungs-Gesellschaft went through a period of rapid growth in the 1920s, expanding to new markets and diversifying into new categories of insurance.[53] With the latter company (Zurich) the process of acquiring and establishing new subsidiary companies was interrupted between 1931 and 1933 but then resumed, whereas with the former (Schweizer Rück) the main period of rapid growth, both in the domestic market and abroad, was between 1910 and 1930. In the 1930s the firm focused on maintaining its position in foreign markets, since its international network was already quite large. In both cases, firm-specific capabilities which had been acquired by experience before World War I were more important for expanding successfully to foreign countries than location-specific advantages.

Compared with the insurance sector, the internationalisation of the banking sector was less pronounced and largely confined to the geographical diversification of financial investments. Other forms of internationalisation remained exceptional.[54] In the 1930s the major Swiss banks active on an international level shifted the bulk of their foreign investments from Europe (mainly Germany and France) to the United States. Some of these banks established a subsidiary company in the United States just before the outbreak of World War II.[55] These steps towards new forms of internationalisation were mainly a measure to protect customers' assets and not the result of a strategy of internationalisation. Similarly in the chemical and food-processing industries multinational companies (for example Nestlé, Ciba, Roche) turned to holding structures in order to separate and protect their subsidiary companies overseas,[56] and from 1938 onwards the decisions taken by companies within the main export sectors were increasingly influenced by political events and the threat of war.

Economic policies

In the 1920s measures aiming at promoting exports were still rather unusual. The Schweizerische Zentrale für Handelsförderung (SZH) was founded in 1927 with the objective of strengthening official representations abroad (Swiss embassies and consulates), but its activities remained, at first, largely ineffective. Only in the summer of 1936, ten years after its foundation, did the federal government grant the financial means needed to establish trade agencies in those countries where the official representation was weak.[57]

During the depression of the 1930s the conflict of interest between the domestic and the export sectors of the economy became very pronounced. Furthermore, given the broad range of outward-oriented concerns with differing interests, the politically influential leading business association, the Swiss Federation of Commerce and Industry (Schweizerischer Handels- und Industrieverein SHIV), was unable to pursue a clear policy in favour of particular branches or sectors of the economy:[58] only measures favouring some groups without obviously harming others had a chance of gaining broad support. In December 1931 import restrictions were introduced to protect Swiss domestic industries from cheap German imports. The export industries fiercely opposed such trade restrictions, because they feared higher costs for raw materials and intermediate products; but subsequently, within the system of bilateral clearing agreements, import restrictions were considered a means of promoting industrial exports.[59] In fact the export industries benefited from the system of clearing agreements to varying degrees, while merchants and businesses operating on the domestic market complained that their economic interests had been neglected or sacrificed to the export industries.

The two main export-promotion schemes were the 'productive unemployment benefits' of 1932 (subsidies granted to firms by the federal and cantonal authorities to enable them to reduce prices for exports and keep their workers employed) and the State-backed 'insurance of export payment risks' introduced in March 1934. Compared with similar institutions established in other European countries during the 1920s and early 1930s this enactment came somewhat late, and its coverage was restricted to producer goods.[60] Both schemes were mainly intended to support the machine industry, but even there firms were rather reluctant to use them. Sulzer began to apply for unemployment benefits only in 1934 whilst Rieter had by then resumed recruitment, so that it had no need to ask for government support; we do not know whether BBC made any use of this type of export promotion. The insurance of export-payments risks was mainly intended to facilitate exports of machines to the Balkan countries, South America and (especially) the Soviet Union. But even the firms in the machine industry disagreed with regard to its advantages, and the scheme achieved only moderate success during the depression.[61] Sulzer had exerted considerable influence in promoting its implementation, expecting that it would facilitate exports to the Soviet Union. BBC was also interested in that area, but its management disliked the idea of having export risks insured; none the less, it gave political support to the scheme as a gesture of solidarity with the other firms in this industry. Rieter did not intend to make any use of this new facility.[62] The chemical and watch industries were not interested in or even opposed this new type of insurance when it was discussed within the SHIV.[63] The textile industry claimed insurance coverage for sales to less developed countries with higher payment risks, but only in 1939 was the insurance extended to all industries.

Quite generally, in the rising export industries (machines and chemicals) the demand for governmental protection remained weak. This was due to the wide spread aversion to government intervention in business affairs and to the fact that turning to the small domestic market was hardly an attractive option. Consequently, firms re-established competitiveness by reducing costs, intensifying R&D, diversifying product lines and shifting production to foreign countries to evade trade barriers. The practice of 'expatriating' production was widely criticised and accused of being a major cause of Switzerland's high rate of unemployment, whilst the firms involved replied that in a protectionist world FDI and licensing agreements with foreign firms were inevitable. In their view, foreign manufacturing facilities helped to preserve employment in Switzerland because they helped to bear the high costs of R&D. In fact, success in overcoming the depression did not depend only upon the different strategies of internationalisation and the degree of market control. As mentioned above, product innovations were a major contribution to recovering lost positions in the world market. The widely shared belief in technical progress and innovation as a means to compensate location-specific disadvantages was not shaken during the years of depression.

The most frequent complaints of the export-oriented firms were about the failure of the government to pursue a deflationary policy. In their view, only a general fall of prices and wages would have a lasting effect and restore their competitiveness in world markets. Their grievances focused mainly on the government's failure to reduce wages, tariffs and fees in the domestic and public sectors of the economy whilst the export industries had reduced wages considerably. Devaluation, the alternative means to restore competitiveness, was fiercely opposed. The fact that the leading export industries did not favour devaluation is really a puzzle. When domestic and foreign demand increased rapidly after devaluation in September 1936, the positive impact came as a surprise. Even then it was attributed to the fact that the capacities of the main foreign competitors were increasingly absorbed by the domestic military sector, and not to devaluation. Given the apparent lack of economic rationality, it is often argued that the attitude towards devaluation was marked by norms and values which precluded the perception of its economic advantages. But from the firms' perspective there were sound economic reasons for the scant interest shown in devaluation. With regard to sales to the clearing countries devaluation was of little value, because it only meant that the clearing agreements would have to be renegotiated:[64] it was also expected that import prices for raw materials and semi-finished products would increase, alongside wages. The management of BBC, for example, immediately raised export prices by 20% in order to counter the expected increase of import prices and wages.[65] Other firms, for example Sulzer, were concerned about the fact that 'productive unemployment benefits' would be cancelled. Furthermore, international cartel agreements and the practice of quoting prices in foreign currencies restricted the possibilities for reducing export prices.[66] The disappointment of the export-oriented firms at the government's failure to reduce prices and wages by other means was recalled in the comment of the SHIV on the devaluation of the Swiss franc in September 1936.[67] Obviously, the concerns mentioned above must have been widely shared. It should also be borne in mind that a strong Swiss currency was an undoubted advantage for firms in the chemical and food-processing industries which had pursued a strategy of shifting production abroad. The scant interest of the watch industry in devaluation may be accounted for by the fact that export values in this sector had almost recovered by 1935.

In the textile and watch industries, where government interventions were strong, the dominant strategy was to adapt supplies to decreased demand by downsizing capacities, impeding the establishment of new firms, reducing competition among firms and having further recourse to import restrictions. Such restrictive policies were also applied in the shoe industry and the domestic retail trade. They favoured self-regulation in the form of horizontal and vertical cartels, but the impact of these cartels differed considerably. In the case of some national cartels the firms completely neglected opportunities to expand into foreign markets, whereas in other branches national cartelisation went along with the rapid international expansion of their leading member firms.[68] An unintended consequence of protecting the domestic market from imports was the establishment of manufacturing companies in Switzerland by foreign firms anxious to defend their market share despite high production costs and the less than friendly response of domestic manufacturers.[69]

Continuity and change in the post-war decades

Regulated trade and capital flows with foreign countries as well as materials shortages marked the years after World War II. In Switzerland promoting exports was no longer a priority for economic policy. On the contrary, rapidly rising exports were blamed for causing bottlenecks for firms in the inward-oriented branches, especially with regard to employment. By 1946 the usefulness of the insurance of export payment risks was brought into question; it con-

Figure 5: Exports and imports 1951–2000, in mill. CHF

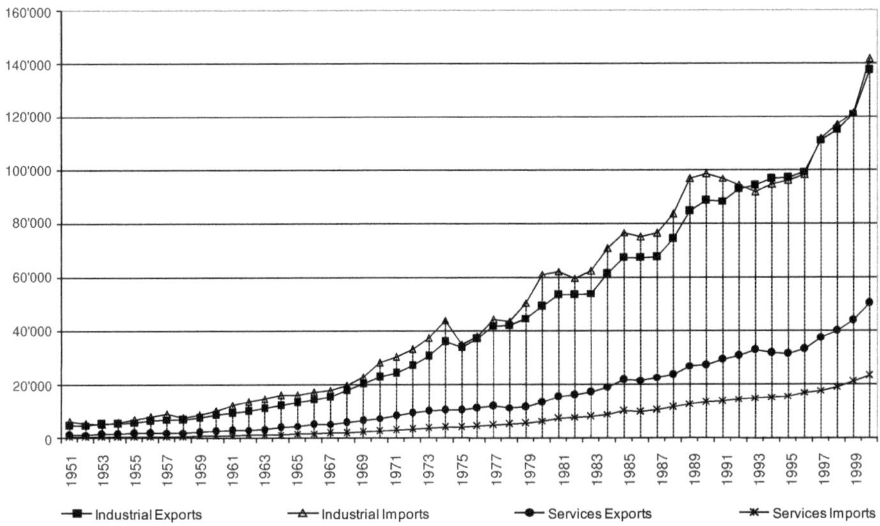

Source: Swiss National Bank, *Statistisches Monatsheft* (April 2006), Table Q1a.

tinued only on condition that its costs were covered by the export industries themselves.[70] Most foreign trade agencies, established in the late 1930s to promote exports but mainly concerned with facilitating imports during the war, were closed in the course of 1947.[71]

From the 1950s onwards exports increased rapidly and continuously, hardly affected by the economic recessions of the mid-1970s and the 1990s (Figure 5).[72] A comparison with the development of industrial exports in the previous period (Figure 2) clearly shows the impact of different international trading regimes on a small open economy: while exports fell drastically during the depression of the 1930s, they continued to increase in the recessions of the mid-1970s and the 1990s. The share of services in total exports increased only slightly from about 22% in the 1950s to about 25% in the 1990s, but its composition changed considerably. The share of tourism in total services exports declined from about 50% in the mid-1960s to a mere 25% in the late 1990s, while banking and insurance services increased to over 30%.

The geographical diversification of exports continued in the post-war decades and mirrors the uneven participation of world regions

Figure 6: Regional distribution of industrial exports in % of total industrial exports

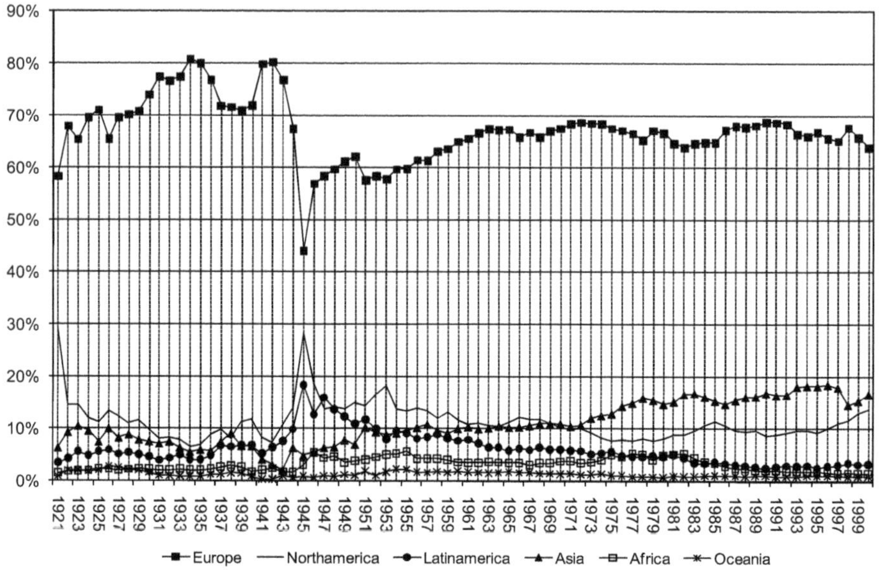

Sources: 1921–92: Ritzmann-Blickenstorfer, *Historical Statistics*, Tables L. 22–26 pp. 706–14; Swiss Federal Statistical Office, *Statistical Yearbook of Switzerland* (1993–2000), Table 6.6, and Swiss Federal Statistical Office, *Statistical Yearbook of Switzerland* (2002), Tables 6.5.2/3.

in the process of reglobalisation following World War II (Figure 6). The share of exports to Europe was lower than during the interwar period, while to North America it was about the same. The main new aspect was the marked increase of the share of exports to Asia since the 1970s, while exports to Latin America and Africa were lower at the end of the century than in the 1950s.[73] Industrial imports were geographically less diversified. From the 1960s onwards imports from Europe reached the pre-war level of 80%, while the share from Latin America fell rapidly from 20% in 1945 to less than 2% at the end of the century. The share of North America declined continuously from a maximum of 24% in 1949 to about 7% in the last decades of the century. Asia was the only region from where import shares increased after the 1970s.[74]

In contrast to the interwar period, the main export industries developed quite steadily and without major structural shifts (Fig-

Figure 7: Industrial exports 1950–1987, in mill. CHF

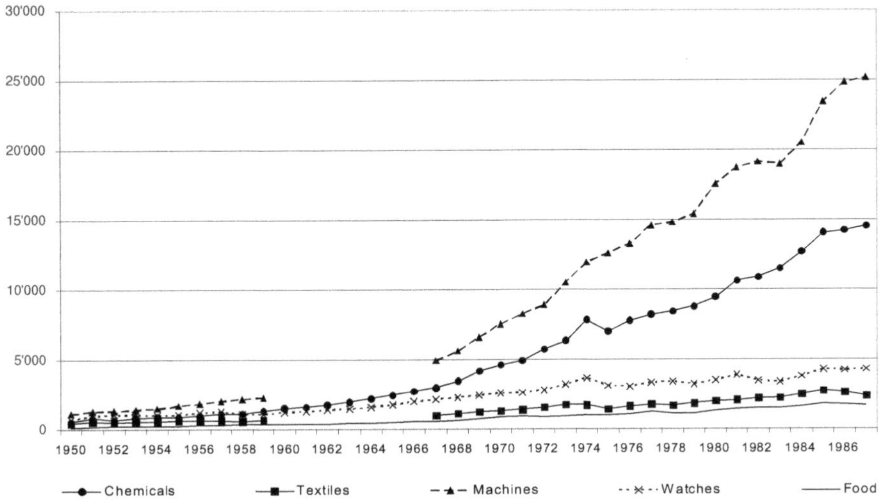

Source: Ritzmann-Blickenstorfer, *Historical Statistics*, Tables L.11b and L.13, pp. 683–687 and pp. 691–692.

Note: Aggregate data on the distribution of industrial exports after 1987 are not comparable, because the product group classification changed.

ure 7): all – in relative terms, the rising (machines, chemicals) sectors as much as those that were in overall decline (textiles, watches, food) – enjoyed increasing trade (Table 2).[75]

Table 2: Distribution of industrial Exports 1949–1985 (in %)

Year	Textiles	Watches	Food	Machines	Chemicals	Other Industries
1949	17.92	19.62	4.70	29.16	15.20	13.41
1959	9.50	15.85	5.70	32.62	19.03	17.29
1970	6.22	12.14	4.03	34.94	21.37	21.30
1975	4.48	9.66	3.11	38.79	21.64	22.32
1980	4.26	7.52	2.78	37.11	20.03	28.30
1985	4.29	6.69	2.84	36.41	21.88	27.89

Source: Ritzmann-Blickenstorfer, *Historical Statistics,* Tables L.11b and L.13, pp. 683–687 and pp. 691–692.

The declining export industries

In the textile industry some innovative firms began to specialise in technologically demanding high-quality products, whilst those companies competing at the low-price end of the market turned to cheap immigrant labour and then gradually abandoned production in Switzerland.[76] The various measures introduced during the 1930s to protect the watch industry from 'expatriation' were successively loosened, but exports remained the dominant form of internationalisation. In the 1970s and early 1980s the industry had to cope with a severe crisis. A new technology and new competitors, especially from Japan, threatened the still remarkable competitive advantage of Swiss firms, and the economic recessions of the mid-1970s and early 1980s in Europe and the United States aggravated the crisis.[77] After a thorough restructuring orchestrated by the major Swiss banks with the support of the federal government and the establishment of SMH Schweizerische Gesellschaft für Mikroelektronik und Uhrenindustrie AG (later SWATCH) the rapid decline of the watch industry was arrested. The belief that competitiveness was based on the location-specific advantage of being 'made in Switzerland' led firms to stick to the strategy of innovation and home-based growth, which resulted in a remarkable recovery during the late 1980s and 1990s in the expensive end of the market.[78] Even the largest firms expanded their activities – mainly by acquiring other Swiss firms and establishing a worldwide network of distribution companies – but established few production bases outside Switzerland.[79] In the food-processing industry the outward-oriented MNEs continued to expand production abroad, while the highly protected market for agricultural goods favoured the rapid growth of a food-processing industry focusing on the domestic market and to a large extent vertically integrated with the dominant retail chain stores. The origin of the high concentration of the retail trade and its exceptionally strong links with production can be traced back to the protective agricultural policy adopted in the 1920s.

The rising export industries and services

The available evidence shows that forced internationalisation in the form of FDI during the interwar period turned out to be an advantage for Swiss businesses and was not discontinued. Reorienting activities to the home market and closing foreign subsidiary companies remained exceptional and due to special causes, such as the political changes in eastern Europe or the nationalisation of the electricity industry in European countries.[80] Experience in doing business in various foreign countries became a major advantage in a period of slow but persistent economic liberalisation. The firms usually continued to stick to a rather demanding strategy, namely geographical expansion combined with product diversification, both intended as means of spreading risks and widening the basis for continuous growth.

In the chemical and machine industries the incentives to shift production abroad persisted.[81] But compared with the interwar years, the objectives pursued had changed radically. Whereas overcoming trade barriers had been the main motive during the interwar years, the main push and pull factors in a context of rapid economic growth were the extreme shortage of labour in Switzerland and the advantages of producing in specific foreign countries such as gaining easier access to large markets or being able to participate in advanced scientific research: increasingly, R&D activities were taken up by foreign subsidiaries. With the main insurance companies too a continuous pattern of internationalisation can be observed: business in the markets where the firms had been active before the war was maintained or expanded. Companies also ventured into new and promising markets in Asia, Latin America and Africa; only in the Eastern Bloc were activities reduced or abandoned completely.[82] The number of foreign subsidiaries of the Swiss banks increased somewhat slowly up to the late 1960s; but in the following decade the pace of internationalisation accelerated and large Swiss banks extended their foreign branch network considerably.[83]

The process of European integration had little effect on the geographical pattern of internationalisation. Shares of exports to EFTA countries and to other world regions (mainly North America and Asia) somewhat increased, but fears that European integration could

Figure 8: Stocks of FDI 1985–2005 (in mill. CHF) and FDI intensity 1980–2003 (in %)

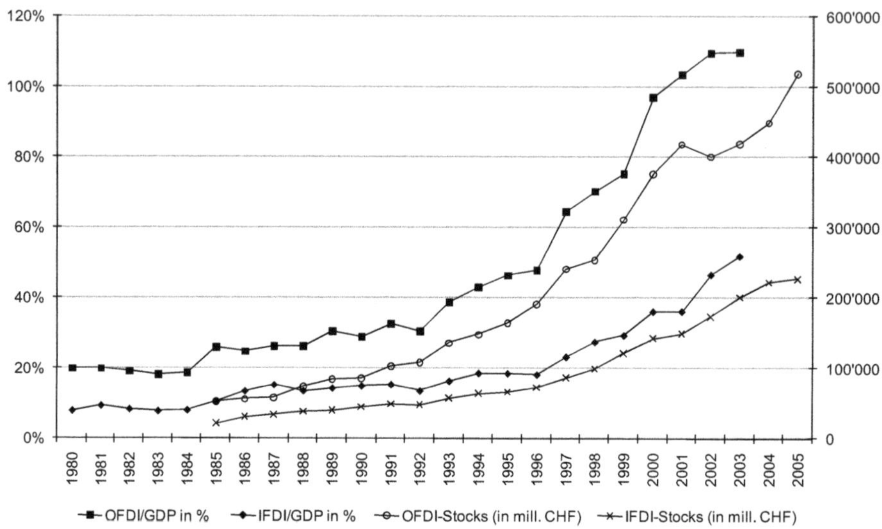

Sources: OFDI 1985–2005: Swiss National Bank, *Statistisches Monatsheft*, Table R2; IFDI 1985–2005: Swiss National Bank, *Statistisches Monatsheft*, Table R3; FDI/GDP 1980–2003: UNCTAD United Nations Conference on Trade and Development, *Foreign Direct Investment Database* (Online: http://stats.unctad.org/fdi/ReportFolders/ReportFolders.aspx, visited June 2006).

lead to new trade barriers soon disappeared. The overall tendency towards liberalisation continued on the basis of trade agreements between the EFTA and the EC as well as within the GATT (later WTO). Furthermore, Swiss firms were already well placed with FDI in the large European countries (Figure 8). In comparison with other small European countries the main difference has been the relationship between the stock of outward FDI/GDP and inward FDI/GDP. In 2003 this relationship was 2.22 for Switzerland (111/50%), 1.14 for the Netherlands (75/66%), 1.33 for Sweden (63/47%), 1.48 for Finland (42/29%), 1.03 for Denmark (37/36%), 0.98 for Austria (23/24%) and 0.17 for Ireland (23/130%).[84]

In the last decade of the twentieth century the comfortable lead of Switzerland's per-capita GDP began to shrink. Other small European countries showed considerably higher growth rates, especially in the late 1990s.[85] An analysis of the market shares of industrial exports compared with the structure of OECD exports confirms that the competitive advantage of the Swiss economy in watches and chemicals/pharmaceuticals still remains, but the share of exports in electrotechnical and electronic products is clearly below average.[86]

Major discontinuities marked the development of firms in the main export industries. In the period of accelerated globalisation the broad product diversification of most MNEs became a burden:[87] companies gradually reduced their product lines and focused more on what they perceived as their core competencies. The investments of Swiss firms in foreign countries increased considerably, mainly in the new form of international mergers and acquisitions, which were usually combined with disinvestments. The internationalisation of R&D also accelerated. By the 1990s Swiss total annual overseas corporate expenditure on R&D regularly exceeded that at home, whilst in the chemical and electrotechnical industries home-based R&D registered an actual decline although increasing abroad.[88] Given the large number of small and medium-sized firms in Switzerland, the large increase of enterprises with less than 500 employees taking up R&D activities in foreign countries is a remarkable new dimension of internationalisation.[89]

With the exception of the emergency measures introduced in the early 1970s in order to limit immigration and reduce inflation, government intervention in the export sector remained marginal. From the 1970s onwards the focus was on a policy aiming at price stability coupled with a largely autonomous monetary policy. The still dominant aversion of business elites to government involvement reinforced the traditional attitude of the political authorities to interfere only exceptionally in the economic sector, and then usually by indirect means. Business interests were taken into account, since the main business associations were integrated into the preparliamentary political decision-making process, the 'Vernehmlassungsverfahren'. But except for the undertakings considered of national importance (watches, banking) particular interests received – as a rule – little support. The mutually discrepant targets of the domestic and outward-oriented sectors of the economy – not to mention those between the export sectors themselves – resulted in a strong preference of the dominant business federation, the SHIV, for compromise solutions which implied levelling out group-specific interests and tolerating the widespread cartels of the domestic sector. As had been the case in the previous period, national cartels in the industrial and also in the service sectors (insurance and banking) were no obstacle to the successful internationalisation of leading firms.

Significant Swiss policies not shared with other small European countries included the maintenance of a liberal capital market for direct investments throughout the post-war period and the rejection of membership of the European Economic Area (EEA) in 1992. The absence of capital restrictions widened firms' room for manoeuvre, and could also be considered a necessary condition for overcoming the location-specific disadvantages at home and exploiting successfully the chances for growth on an international level. Switzerland's outsider policy with regard to European integration certainly weakened the external and internal forces aiming at enhancing competition through deregulation and privatisation: only since the 1990s have the highly regulated domestic industries and services been gradually exposed to international competition, partly because State monopolies were broken up, partly because self-regulation in the form of cartels was dissolved.[90] When cartels and State regulations began to crumble, firms which had concentrated on the domestic market were often unable to compete on the international front and failed or were taken over by domestic or foreign MNEs. Some firms ventured into foreign markets with inadequate experience and inappropriate managerial capabilities, and found themselves faced with costly reorganisation and restructuring processes.

Conclusions

Throughout the period discussed in this chapter export-oriented firms in Switzerland had strong but differing incentives to expand their activities in foreign countries and to engage in various forms of internationalisation. During the interwar years they had to cope with new competitors and increasing protectionism: to some extent deglobalisation on the international level was compensated by globalisation at company level. The specific constraints perceived within the industry, the necessity to adapt to the international reallocation of activities (textiles), to branch-specific forms of regulation (national and international cartelisation) or to a shared vision of comparative advantage in the future (watches, machines, chemicals) clearly constrained firms' freedom of action and influenced economic policies.

For several export industries apart from watches the question arose whether there was a future for the firms if they remained located in Switzerland. The textile industry suffered major closures, their remaining operations being reduced to niche production. The export-oriented food-processing industry definitely shifted the bulk of production abroad. In the machine and chemical sectors confidence returned as orders picked up in the course of 1935 and 1936. This economic upturn was due to developments and decisions taken at various levels of the economy: the overall recovery of demand in foreign countries, the devaluation of the Swiss franc together with the efforts undertaken by firms to restructure and rationalise production, to diversify sales markets and to intensify the search for innovations. R&D was a major contribution to recovering lost positions in foreign markets. The strong belief in innovation as a means of overcoming the depression can be observed in all export industries and was not shaken during the 1930s. This consensus, coupled with the experience of the firms in foreign markets, certainly constituted a national competitive advantage in Porter's sense of the term, implying that at the core of explaining national advantage in an industry must be the role of the home nation in stimulating competitive improvement and innovation.[91]

The extensive measures of control applied in the watch and textile industries remained exceptional and did not spread to the other export industries. The schemes employed for promoting exports were not very effective and contributed only marginally to these sectors' recovery. The strategies of internationalisation pursued by the firms and the insistence of the main export industries on a deflationary policy as the only means to overcome the depression certainly delayed the devaluation which, with hindsight and from a comparative perspective, would have been the more effective policy.

In most export branches, firms exploited their limited room of manoeuvre largely without recourse to governmental support. Consequently government interference in business affairs remained limited, and corporate tendencies to depend upon self-organisation were strengthened. Both international and national cartels were a means to stabilise prices and output, but the impact of international cartels on the further development of firms was much weaker, probably because these cartels were limited to specific products and in any case collapsed at the outbreak of World War II. National cartels were no obstacle to the successful internationalisation of single firms, but for most firms in regulated branches the incentives to expand to foreign markets were considerably reduced.

The strength of the path-dependence which can be observed in the post-war decades is quite remarkable. The enduring impact of the choices made for coping with the difficulties encountered during the interwar years and especially with the depression of the 1930s becomes evident in the decades after World War II. Internationalisation continued, although for other motives, and no rupture in the forms or the industry-specific pattern of internationalisation can be perceived up to the 1980s. While the forced internationalisation of the interwar period proved to be an advantage for companies, protectionism turned out to be a disadvantage because firms failed to develop the capabilities needed to cope with the intensified global competition of the 1990s.

The pressure to expand foreign-based business activities increased in the last decades of the twentieth century. Included were activities which had long been understood as belonging to the central function of the parent firm and had therefore mainly been kept within the home country, such as R&D and ownership control. The large multinational enterprises in the industrial and service sectors invested heavily abroad, while investment and employment within Switzerland declined. The views of these firms about location-specific advantages at home and in foreign countries must have changed considerably. The fact that compared with other small European countries the relationship between the stock of outward and inward FDI is much higher reinforces the notion that traditional location-specific advantages in Switzerland have weakened over the last decade of the twentieth century. The impact of the new type of global competition on the options and constraints perceived within the economic and political sphere – and consequently on the performance of the Swiss economy in the future – can hardly be evaluated yet.

1 Parts of this article were presented at a conference on Globalisation and Deglobalisation of Small European Countries in Zurich, 15–17 March 2001. The author would like to thank participants who commented on the earlier version, as well as Claudia Bischof-Biotti and Manuel Hiestand for statistical work.
2 See for example the distinguishing characteristics of strong corporatism typical for small European states described in Peter J. Katzenstein, *Small States in World Markets. Industrial Policy in Europe* (Ithaca and London: Cornell University Press, 1985), pp. 34–37.
3 John H. Dunning, 'Resolving some Paradoxes of the Emerging Global Economy: Small Nations as Trailblazers', in Daniel Van Den Bulcke and Alain Verbeke (eds.), *Globalization and the Small Open Economy* (Cheltenham, UK and Northampton, MA, USA: Edward Elgar, 2001), pp. 13–35.
4 See Mark Casson, *The Organization of International Business: Studies in the Economics of Trust*, Vol. 2 (Aldershot, UK and Brookfield, US: Edward Elgar, 1995).
5 Due to limitations of space it is not possible to deal with the special conditions pertaining during World War II.
6 See the contribution of Patrick Halbeisen in this volume.
7 Wholesale prices fell by about 40% and consumer prices by about 20% between 1928 and 1935. Heiner Ritzmann-Blickenstorfer, *Historical statistics of Switzerland* (Zurich: Chronos, 1996), H.10a., p. 492 and H.23, p. 504.
8 In the 1930s clearing agreements were concluded with Austria, Hungary, Bulgaria, Yugoslavia, Romania, Greece, Turkey, Germany, Italy, Spain and Poland. Peter Hug and Martin Kloter (eds.), *Aufstieg und Niedergang des Bilateralismus. Schweizerische Aussen- und Aussenwirtschaftspolitik 1930–1960: Rahmenbedingungen, Entscheidungsstrukturen, Fallstudien* (Lausanne and Zurich: Edition Payot/Chronos, 1999), pp. 55 ff.
9 Ritzmann-Blickenstorder, *Historical Statistics*, Tables L.18–26, pp. 698–714.
10 Ernst Himmel, *Industrielle Kapitalanlagen der Schweiz im Ausland* (Langensalza, 1922), estimated outward FDI of Swiss firms for the period 1895 to 1919.
11 Harm G. Schröter, 'Swiss multinational enterprise in historical perspective', in Geoffrey Jones and Harm G. Schröter (eds.), *The Rise of Multinationals in Continental Europe* (Aldershot, UK and Brookfield, USA: Edward Elgar, 1993), p. 56.
12 See the contribution of Patrick Halbeisen in this volume.
13 Harm G. Schröter, *Aufstieg der Kleinen. Multinationale Unternehmen aus fünf kleinen Staaten vor 1914*, Schriften zur Wirtschafts- und Sozialgeschichte, Band 42 (Berlin: Duncker & Humblot, 1993).
14 Gérald and Sylvia Arlettaz, 'La Première Guerre mondiale et l'émergence d'une politique migratoire interventionniste', in Paul Bairoch, Martin Körner (eds.),

Die Schweiz in der Weltwirtschaft (15.–20. Jh.), Schweizerische Gesellschaft für Wirtschafts- und Sozialgeschichte, Band 8, 8. Jg. (Zurich: Chronos, 1990), pp. 319–337, here 329f.

15 The main export industries are composed of the following categories listed in Ritzmann-Blickenstorder, *Historical Statistics:* textiles (cotton, silk, wool, embroideries), watches, food (excl. tobacco), machines (incl. metals, instruments, equipment, vehicles), chemicals (incl. pharmaceuticals). The main 'other industries' are: paper and wooden goods, leather, rubber and synthetic products, shoes, clothing.

16 According to Himmel, *Industrielle Kapitalanlagen,* pp. 124–127, in 1919 the stock of FDI of the firms in the cotton, wool and embroidery industry was about 500% of their investments in Switzerland; in the silk industry this relationship was about 250%.

17 See the contribution of Anne-Lise Head-König in this volume.

18 Marc Perrenoud, 'Contrastes et paradoxes de la crise dans l'horlogerie', in *La Crise des Années '30, Traverse,* Zeitschrift für Geschichte, 1997/1, pp. 108–116.

19 Thomas Perret, 'Un institut de recherche communautaire entre industrie et Etat. Le Laboratoire Suisse de Recherches Horlogères (LSRH) de Neuchâtel, 1921–1984', in Hans-Jörg Gilomen, Rudolf Jaun, Margrit Müller, Béatrice Veyrassat (eds.), *Innovationen. Voraussetzungen und Folgen – Antriebskräfte und Widerstände,* Schweizerische Gesellschaft für Wirtschafts- und Sozialgeschichte, Band 17, 17. Jahrgang (Zurich: Chronos, 2001).

20 Christophe Koller, *'De la lime à la machine': L'industrialisation et l'Etat au pays de l'horlogerie. Contribution à l'histoire économique et sociale d'une Région Suisse,* (Bern: Editions CJE, 2003), pp. 329–477. Germany, the US and UK were the main export markets in the interwar years, absorbing between 35% and 50% of total exports (p. 418).

21 From the beginning of the 1920s the estimated value of the foreign direct investments of the food processing industry, especially of the canning industry, was much higher than the value of domestic investments. See Himmel, *Industrielle Kapitalanlagen,* pp. 128–131.

22 Carl Koechlin, 'Handel, Industrie und Verkehr der Schweiz im Kampf um ihre Existenz'. Protokoll der Ordentlichen Delegiertenversammlung des Schweizerischen Handels- und Industrie-Vereins, 7. Juli 1934 in Zürich, pp. 9–35.

23 Martin Lüpold, 'Globalisierung als Krisenreaktionsstrategie. Dezentralisierung und Renationalisierung bei Nestlé, 1920–1950', in Hans-Jörg Gilomen, Margrit Müller, Béatrice Veyrassat (eds.), *Globalisierung – Chancen und Risiken. Die Schweiz in der Weltwirtschaft,* Schweizerische Gesellschaft für Wirtschafts- und Sozialgeschichte, Band 19, 19. Jg. (Zurich: Chronos, 2003), pp. 211–234.

24 The move to protection of the agricultural sector in the 1920s is described in Werner Baumann, Peter Moser, *Bauern im Industriestaat. Agrarpolitische Konzeptionen und bäuerliche Bewegungen in der Schweiz 1918–1968* (Zurich: Orell Füssli, 1999), pp. 38–149, esp. 130–143. At the beginning of the 1920s the Danish system of focusing on exports still seemed possible.

25 The firm diversified into the completely new product 'Nescafé'. Lüpold, 'Globalisierung als Krisenreaktionsstrategie', p. 215.

26 Swiss Federal Statistical Office (ed.), *Statistical Yearbook of Switzerland* (1926), pp. 186f.
27 Margrit Müller, 'Coping with barriers to trade: Internationalisation strategies of Swiss firms in the interwar period', in Hubert Bonin *et al.* (eds.), *Transnational Companies (19th–20th Centuries)* (Paris: PLAGE, 2002), pp. 239–254, here pp. 243f., with reference to Florian Adank, 'Die Unternehmensführung einer "Exportfirma par Excellence" im Ersten Weltkrieg und in zwei Wirtschaftskrisen: Die Sulzer Unternehmungen AG in Winterthur von 1914–1936', unpublished thesis, Philosophical Faculty of the University of Zurich (1999).
28 Müller, 'Coping with barriers', pp. 243f., with reference to Sibylle Veigl, '"Heute ist eben gar nichts mehr sicher." Das Unternehmen BBC Brown Boveri & Cie. Von 1927 bis 1938', unpublished thesis, Philosophical Faculty of the University of Zurich (2000).
29 *75 Years Brown Boveri 1891–1966*, published by Brown, Boveri & Co., Ltd., Baden, Switzerland, 1966, pp. 192–194. BBC's accumulated losses declared in 1923/24 were 25.5 million CHF. The nominal share value had to be reduced by 30%.
30 Müller, 'Coping with barriers', p. 241.
31 Margrit Müller, 'Patterns of Technical Innovation, Market Relationships, and Institutional Change During the Interwar Period', in Laurent Tissot, Béatrice Veyrassat (eds.), *Technological Trajectories, Markets, Institutions. Industrialized Countries, 19th–20th Centuries. From context dependency to path dependency* (Bern *et al.*: Peter Lang, 2001), pp. 306 and 315f.
32 Veigl, 'Das Unternehmen BBC', pp. 49–59, 71–76.
33 Müller, 'Patterns of technical innovation', pp. 306ff.
34 Müller, 'Coping with barriers', p. 243.
35 Ibid., p. 244.
36 Ibid., p. 307.
37 Müller, 'Coping with barriers', pp. 244f.
38 Müller, 'Patterns of technical innovation', pp. 309f.
39 Müller, 'Coping with barriers', pp. 244f.
40 Ibid., p. 242.
41 Ibid. Rieter also joined an agreement on minimum prices reached among the German producers.
42 Veigl, 'Das Unternehmen BBC', pp. 30ff., 108.
43 *75 Years Brown Boveri*, pp. 215f., refers to associations with AEG and Vickers. According to Harm G. Schröter, 'Small European nations: Cooperative capitalism in the twentieth century', in Alfred D. Chandler, jr., Franco Amatori and Takashi Hikino (eds.), *Big Business and the Wealth of Nations* (Cambridge: Cambridge University Press, 1999), p. 191, BBC secured its home markets from foreign competition and took part in international cartels.
44 Hans-Ulrich Wipf, Mario König and Adrian Knoepfli, *Saurer. Vom Ostschweizer Kleinbetrieb zum internationalen Technologiekonzern* (Baden: Hier+Jetzt, 2003), pp. 132–188. For the other main product lines (diesel engines and textile machines) the export orientation continued to prevail.

45 David Asséo, 'La Place de la Suisse dans l'industrie automobile mondiale d'avant 1914', in Bairoch and Körner, *Die Schweiz in der Weltwirtschaft*, p. 161.

46 In 1939 the share of dyes was 59% and that of pharmaceuticals (incl. scent and perfume) 28% of total chemical exports. The chemical firms in Basle were responsible for 70% of total chemical exports. Rudolf Baumgartner, *Die wirtschaftliche Bedeutung der chemischen Industrie in Basel* (Dissertation, Basel: 1947), pp. 67–69.

47 Müller, 'Coping with barriers', pp. 246–248.

48 In 1939 the chemical industry had about 22,500 employees, 1.7% of total employees in Switzerland. For Basle this share was almost 10%. Baumgartner, *Bedeutung der chemischen Industrie,* pp. 64–66.

49 Müller, 'Coping with barriers', pp. 246 f.

50 Hans Conrad Peyer, *Roche Geschichte eines Unternehmens 1896–1996,* (Basel: Editiones Roches, 1996), pp. 106–176.

51 Guex Sébastien, 'The development of Swiss trading companies in the twentieth century', in Geoffrey Jones, *The Multinational Traders*, Routledge International Studies in Business History 5, (London: Routledge, 1998), pp. 150–172.

52 For an overview on the development of the insurance business in Switzerland and its expansion abroad up to 1950 see Stefan Karlen *et al., Schweizerische Versicherungsgesellschaften im Machtbereich des 'Dritten Reichs'*, Vol. 12/1, Veröffentlichungen der Unabhängigen Expertenkommission Schweiz – Zweiter Weltkrieg (Zurich: Chronos, 2002), pp. 53–136.

53 Lars Feldmann, 'Die Schweizerische Rückversicherungsgesellschaft in der Zwischenkriegszeit 1918–1938', unpublished thesis, Philosophical Faculty of the University of Zurich (1998), and Elena Folini, 'Die Zürich Versicherungs-Gesellschaft in der Zwischenkriegszeit, 1918–1939', unpublished thesis, Philosophical Faculty of the University of Zurich (1999). The internationalisation of the Winterthur Versicherung is briefly described in Joseph Jung, *Die Winterthur. Eine Versicherungsgeschichte* (Zurich: Verlag Neue Zürcher Zeitung, 2000), pp. 116–123. The firm expanded its international activities considerably after World War I. The most important step was the decision to establish a branch office in the United States in 1936, pp. 82–87.

54 The Schweizerischer Bankverein (SBV) had established a branch office in London in 1898. Of all the Swiss banks it was the most internationalised. See Daniel Egger, 'Der Schweizerische Bankverein im Kontext der Internationalisierung: 1896–1939', unpublished thesis, Philosophical Faculty of the University of Zurich (2006), pp. 69–76.

55 Michel Fior, 'Globalisation et place financière. Les banques suisses et les Etats-Unis, 1931–1940', in Gilomen, Müller and Veyrassat, *Globalisierung*, pp. 251–262; Marc Perrenoud *et al., La place financière et les banques suisses à l'époque du national-socialisme. Les relations des grandes banques avec l'Allemagne (1931–1946),* Vol. 13, Publications de la Commission Indépendante d'Experts Suisse – Seconde Guerre Mondiale (Zurich: Chronos, 2002).

56 Lüpold, 'Globalisierung als Krisenreaktionsstrategie', pp. 217 f.

57 SZH, Jahresbericht, 1936. The first trade agencies were established in west Africa, the Near East, northern China and on the Antilles.

58 For a short history of this influential business association see Bernhard Wehrli, *Aus der Geschichte des Schweizerischen Handels- und Industrie-Vereins 1870–1970. Zum hundertjährigen Bestehen des Vorortes* (Erlenbach and Zurich: Rentsch, 1970).

59 Protokoll der Schweizerischen Handelskammer, 12.2.1932, pp. 2ff., p. 29: 29.4.1932, pp. 4ff. Vorort-Archiv des Schweizerischen Handels- und Industrievereins, Archiv für Zeitgeschichte, Zurich. See also note 8 above.

60 Lorenz Killias, *Die Export-Risikogarantie des Bundes als Mittel der Exportförderung; eine Orientierung für Exporteure* (Zurich: 1947), p. 48, gives an overview on the export insurance in other European countries. See also the contribution of Anne-Lise Head-König in this volume.

61 Between 1934 and 1938 insurance coverage was granted almost exclusively for exports of machines. On average, only about 2% of total exports were covered. The total amount of paid losses amounted to about 43,000 CHF and the sums covered to 71 million CHF (on a total amount of 142 million CHF). Killias, *Die Export-Risikogarantie*, pp. 145ff.

62 Müller, 'Coping with barriers', p. 249.

63 Protokoll der Schweizerischen Handels-Kammer, 26.9.1931, pp. 20 and 24; Vorort Protokoll, 3.7.1936, p. 157. Vorort-Archiv des Schweizerischen Handels- und Industrievereins, Archiv für Zeitgeschichte, Zurich.

64 For Rieter this was a major concern. The inflow of orders had been satisfactory, and devaluation destroyed this idyll. Müller, 'Coping with barriers', p. 242.

65 Veigl, 'Das Unternehmen BBC', pp. 130f.

66 Cartel agreements restricted Rieter's freedom to lower prices (see Müller, 'Coping with barriers', p. 242). Cartel agreements may have influenced Ciba's pricing policies also.

67 Schweizerischer Handels- und Industrie-Verein, 67. Jahresbericht und Mitteilungen über die vom Vorort im Vereinsjahr 1936/1937 behandelten Geschäfte, pp. 4ff.

68 Examples are Holderbank (now Holcim), the leading firm in the cartelised cement industry, or Zschokke in the highly regulated building sector. See Dominique Barjot, 'L'ascension d'un leader technologique européen: l'entreprise Conrad Zschokke (1872–1972)', in *Intérêts publics et initiatives privées. Initiatives publiques et intérêts privés. Travaux et Service publics en perspectives.* Actes du colloque international tenu dans le cadre des Onzièmes entretiens du Centre Jacques Cartier 7–8–9 décembre 1998, réunis par Sylvain Petitet et Denis Varaschin (Vaulx-en-Velin: ENTPE), pp. 417–438.

69 According to Koechlin, 'Handel, Industrie und Verkehr', p. 12. There has been no systematic research on the activities of foreign firms in Switzerland. An example is the establishment of a manufacturing company by the shoe manufacturer Bata in 1932, which had a considerable impact on the domestic shoe industry. Andrea R. Gadient, 'Bata in der Schweiz. Die Gründung und Entwicklung der Bata Schuh Aktiengesellschaft in der Schweiz 1928 bis 1936', unpublished thesis, Philosophical Faculty of the University of Zurich (1991).

70 Vorort Protokoll, 27.5.1946, pp. 12ff.; 22.11.1946, pp. 11f.

71 By 1965 all the remaining agencies were closed: Bogota in 1953, Havanna in 1962, Beirut, Algiers, Elisabethville and Bombay in 1965. SZH, annual reports 1947, 1953, 1962, 1965.

72 The wholesale price index increased from 100 in 1950 to 150 in 1974 and stagnated at around 200 from the 1980s onwards. 1950–1992: Historical Statistics, Tables HZ.10a, H.10b, H.11a, H.11b, H.8, H.9. 1993–2000: Statistical Yearbook of Switzerland (2001), T.5.3.1. The consumer price index doubled by 1973 (from 100 in 1950) and again by 1992. It reached almost 450 in 2000. 1950–1992: Historical Statistics, Tables H.18, H.20, H.21, H.22. 1993–2000: Statistical Yearbook of Switzerland (2001), T.5.2.1.

73 For an analysis of trade with developing countries see Bouda Etemad, 'Structure géographique du commerce entre la Suisse et le Tiers Monde au XXe siècle', in Bairoch, Körner, *Die Schweiz in der Weltwirtschaft*, pp. 165–181.

74 Ritzmann-Blickenstorfer, *Historical Statistics,* Tables L.18–21 and L.26, pp. 698–705 and p. 714; *Statistical Yearbook of Switzerland* (1995), Table 6.6, and (2002), Tables 6.5.2.3.

75 For a detailed statistical analysis of trade from 1946 to 1970 see Dominique Dirlewanger, Sébastien Guex and Gian-Franco Pordenone, *La Politique commerciale de la Suisse de la Deuxième Guerre mondiale à l'entrée au Gatt (1945–1966),* Contributions suisses à l'histoire internationale, vol. 6, (Zurich: Chronos, 2004), pp. 33–54. For a comparative analysis of the structure of industrial exports in the subsequent period 1964–2002 see Spyros Arvanitis, Heinz Hollenstein and David Marmet, *Internationale Wettbewerbsfähigkeit: Wo steht der Standort Schweiz? Eine Analyse auf sektoraler Ebene*, Konjunkturforschungsstelle Eidgenössische Technische Hochschule Zürich (Zurich: vdf Hochschulverlag AG an der ETH Zürich, 2005), pp. 71–77.

76 The number of textile manufacturers declined from 850 in 1966 to 421 in 1986, the number of employees from over 68,000 to about 31,000: Ritzmann-Blickenstorfer, *Historical Statistics,* K.25, p. 648.

77 Between 1970 and 1980 the number of employees in the watch industry shrank to a third or 30,000 persons, and almost 1000 establishments (58%) were closed. Erna E. Karrer-Rüedi, *Der Trend zum Wirtschaftsstil der flexiblen Spezialisierung. Eine Diskussion am Beispiel der Region der Schweizer Uhrenindustrie* (Bern *et al.*: Peter Lang, 1992), pp. 100ff.

78 Ibid., pp. 85ff. and 155. The share of the Swiss watch industry in the total value of world watch-production increased from 45% in 1986 to 60% in 2003, while its share in the total number of watches produced was less than 5%. SBG Schriften: *Die Schweizerische Uhrenindustrie*, (Zurich, 1986), p. 28; 'Wo Mehrwert geschaffen wird. Das grosse Schweigen der Uhrenbranche', *Neue Zürcher Zeitung*, 13.4.2004, Nr. 85, B 5.

79 According to the annual reports of SMH (1985–1997) and Swatch Group (1998–2000). In the 1980s the firm had manufacturing companies in Italy, France and the USA, and in the 1990s acquired two enterprises in France, two in Germany and established the first manufacturing plant in China.

80 Luciano Segreto, 'Les stratégie des sociétés financières suisses pour l'industrie électrique (1895–1939)', in David Gugerli (ed.), *Allmächtige Zauberin unserer Zeit. Zur Geschichte der elektrischen Energie in der Schweiz* (Zurich: Chronos, 1994), pp. 57–72.
81 The development of Ciba and Geigy is described in Margrit Müller, 'The Export-Dependence of the Swiss Chemical Industry and the Internationalisation of Swiss Chemical Firms (1950–2000)', in Louis Galambos, Takashi Hikino, Vera Zamagni (eds.), *The Global Chemical Industry in the Age of the Petrochemical Revolution* (Cambridge: Cambridge University Press, 2006). The continuous pattern of international expansion can also be confirmed for Roche and for firms of the machine industry (BBC, Sulzer, Schindler, Landis & Gyr) on the basis of annual reports and company histories.
82 Oliver Bärisch, 'Internationalisierung der Schweizer Rück 1950–1970', and Olivier Annaheim and Marcel Roth, 'Die Internationalisierung der Zürich Versicherungs-Gesellschaft 1950–1979', seminar papers, Institute for Empirical Research in Economics, University of Zurich (2002). See also Jung, *Winterthur Versicherungen*, pp. 101–111 and 129–149.
83 Youssef Cassis, 'La place financière suisse et la City de Londres, 1890–1990', in Bairoch and Körner, *Die Schweiz in der Weltwirtschaft*, pp. 342–345. Swiss banks had six foreign branch banks in 1943, eleven in 1965, 41 in 1975 and 79 in 1985.
84 See Arvanitis, Hollenstein, Marmet, *Internationale Wettbewerbsfähigkeit*, pp. 170–176.
85 Margrit Müller, '"Globalisierung" als vielschichtiger Prozess – Einsichten aus historischer Sicht', in Gilomen, Müller and Veyrassat, *Gobalisierung*, pp. 29ff.
86 Arvanitis, Hollenstein and Marmet, *Internationale Wettbewerbsfähigkeit*, p. 142.
87 On the changes in the chemical-pharmaceutical industry see Müller, 'The Export Dependence of the Chemical Industry'. Based on annual reports it can be shown that Roche also underwent a major restructuring process in the middle of the 1980s. Sulzer and ABB (the merger of BBC with the Swedish ASEA in 1986) were restructured several times during the 1990s. Rieter's performance was again exceptional: the firm diversified successfully into a new product line, acquired foreign manufacturing firms and became a truly multinational enterprise.
88 Müller, 'Globalisation', p. 30, with reference to Schweizerischer Handels- und Industrie-Verein und Bundesamt für Statistik (eds.), *Forschung und Entwicklung (F&E) in der schweizerischen Privatwirtschaft*, Zurich 1978, 1982, 1985, 1988, 1991, 1994, 1998, 2000.
89 According to Arvanitis, Hollenstein and Marmet, *Internationale Wettbewerbsfähigkeit*, p. 177.
90 See the contribution of Thomas David, André Mach and Tobias Straumann in this volume.
91 Michael E. Porter, *The Competitive Advantage of Nations* (London: Mc Millan, 1990), pp. 69ff.

EVEN LANGE and HELGE PHARO

Have your Cake and Eat it too. National Policy and Private Interest in a Small Open Economy: The Case of Norway

Traditionally Norway has been a highly trade-dependent country. From the sixteenth century onwards the structure of its industries has reflected the fact that in key sectors the country could not be self-sufficient. In the increasingly rapid modernization process from the 1840s the transformation of the Norwegian economy was closely related to the progress of international liberalization. By the end of the nineteenth century the export of goods and services constituted around a third of Norway's GNP. Income from shipping represented more than a third of that portion, giving Norway's foreign trade structure a salient feature that was maintained throughout the greater part of the twentieth century.[1]

The purpose of this paper is to discuss how Norway's dependence upon a liberal economic order in terms of trade and capital imports was handled by the political authorities. The desire to profit from an open world market had to be balanced against the need for protection of the primary sector and infant industry, and the fear of dominance by outside forces. We shall approach these issues by means of an analysis of the way that governments of different political colours and private economic interests have responded to the challenges of the international system. Changing governments have had to balance the forces opposing the mainstream liberal trend and to be seen to protect the weaker sectors against the perceived threats posed by openness and the influx of foreign capital. To a remarkable degree Norwegian governments have succeeded in these balancing acts, thus providing evidence that small States may in fact be seen to have considerable freedom of manoeuvre in the global political economy. Before analysing four distinct periods, we shall give a summary outline of the secular pattern of Norwegian trade and look at the significant changes that have taken place within this pattern of stability.[2]

Long-term stability and change in Norwegian trade patterns

Norwegian economic development from the 1840s was to a remarkable degree dependent on the upturn in European demand for the country's natural resources. The economic expansion was heavily oriented towards exports such as timber, fish and shipping, and domestic industrial expansion relied on finance and technical assistance from abroad. Exports of fish and timber to the European market, together with income from shipping, amounted to 80 percent of total exports from about 1850 to 1900, and a large fraction found its way to the British market.

This outward-oriented strategy served Norway well, and it became one of the small countries on the European periphery that managed to capitalize on opportunities stemming from increasing intra-European trade.[3] The export-oriented industrial expansion combined with a considerable dependence on imports of foodstuffs gave obvious incentives for pursuing liberal trade policies. In fact, the Norwegian government exercised the autonomy given within the union with Sweden to maintain significantly lower tariff rates than Sweden did. Faced with the protectionist surge in the last decades of the nineteenth century, Norway – to a higher degree than most other European States – maintained its free-trade stance, which contributed to Sweden's cancelling its free trade agreement with Norway in 1895. Entering the twentieth century Norway in many respects maintained an open economy: low tariffs, liberal immigration policies, and considerable openness with regard to the entry of foreign capital.

Throughout the twentieth century a desire for the most liberal international trade regime possible has characterized both Norwegian foreign economic policy and most of the country's major economic interest groups. Norwegian trade policies during the 1900s aimed at exploiting Norway's comparative advantages in an open world market, yet were at the same time geared towards shielding against sudden change those sectors unable to weather international competition due to climate, topography or settlement structure.

During the years preceding World War I this open-door policy was broadly maintained, though challenged both at home and abroad. In spite of some concessions to the prevailing economic winds in terms of somewhat higher tariffs and stricter concession laws to rein in foreign capital, the strong growth-period of the Norwegian economy after 1905 was characterized by increased internationalization. Total exports increased from around 30 to 40 percent of GNP in 1914, and during the speculative wartime boom the percentage reached 50 in 1916.[4]

The world economy in the interwar period provided a far less hospitable environment for a small open economy, in particular with regard to the mobility of the factors of production. The collapse of the gold standard undermined one of the pillars of the world market. The growing trade barriers in the shape of tariffs, quotas and clearing agreements also created serious obstacles to Norwegian foreign trade. Even so Norway maintained an export sector of some 30 percent of GNP throughout the period.

After World War II a process of liberalization was initiated. This subsequent openness greatly benefited most Norwegian industries but was at the same time met with considerable resistance from both the right and the left of the political spectrum. The post-war Labour governments coupled strong economic management with a drive for openness. This dual approach served simultaneously to promote an intended restructuring of the economy and to shield weaker industries. The resulting mix of policies provided for considerable domestic political freedom of action, while the value of exports increased to nearly 40 percent of GNP from the 1950s, and rose even higher fuelled by oil in the 1970s and 1980s.

In spite of the major upheavals in the international economic system during the twentieth century Norway's foreign economic relations display a remarkable stability throughout the period. This holds true also when we look at the country's relations with its main trading partners. Only the periods of the two world wars deviate from this pattern. During World War I imports from the United States increased dramatically, while the United Kingdom and Germany as well as Sweden increased their share of Norwegian imports. The German occupation during World War II caused Norway's trade with the western allies to be temporarily cut off, and occupation authorities made serious attempts to integrate the Norwegian economy into the German *Grossraumswirtschaft.*

Within this stable framework western Europe, primarily represented by the United Kingdom, Germany and Sweden, have been Norway's main trading partners throughout the period. As a market for Norwegian exports Europe, including the Nordic countries, has received a share varying between 70 and 90 percent of the total. The percentage was the lowest during the interwar period, when the United States took around 10 percent of Norwegian exports. Within the group of western European states the Nordic ones constituted a relatively modest market for Norwegian exports.

The underlying stability in Norway's trade patterns may be illustrated by aggregate figures for 1960s exports to the two areas respectively constituted by the European Economic Communities and the European Free Trade Area. After World War I exports to the EEC area remained, with the exception of World War II, stable at 25 percent until 1972. The EFTA area took around 38 percent from 1919 until 1960, and that share only increased to 44 percent in the years 1960–1972 when Norway joined these States in a free-trade area.

In an analysis of the foreign trade of a small country in the modern era imports deserve less attention than exports except for periods of extreme scarcity such as the two wartime periods and the years immediately following World War II. Under normal conditions import needs are relatively easily met, provided the country can satisfy its demand for foreign exchange by means of its exports. Even during the interwar period Norway managed to maintain – with the obvious exception of Germany – a multilateral trading system with its major partners.

After a situation where Norway was strongly oriented towards the United Kingdom and Germany as export and import markets respectively, the post-war period has been characterized by foreign trade between Norway and three to four partners of similar size. Throughout the entire period there has been a relatively equal balance between the share of exports and imports to the different regions. This holds true both for the Nordic area and for Europe as a whole. On a regional basis it has never been the case that large deficits in trade with one area has been compensated for by large surpluses with others.

A large and prevailing deficit in the trade in goods has remained a fundamental and characteristic feature of Norway's foreign trade during the greater part of the twentieth century. This deficit constituted around 10 percent of GNP from the turn of the century until World War I; it was somewhat smaller in the interwar period and in the 1960s and 1970s, and was somewhat higher in the reconstruction period and the 1950s. Until the 1970s the trade deficit in goods was compensated by a sizable surplus in services, mainly deriving from shipping earnings. The importance of shipping for Norwegian foreign trade during this period may be further illustrated by the fact that these earnings constituted between 10 and 15 percent of GNP before World War II and between 15 and 20 percent between 1947 and 1975. Thus, throughout most of this period between a half and a third of Norwegian foreign exchange earnings accrued from shipping.

From the end of the 1970s oil has taken over as the most important single source of foreign exchange, amounting to between 10 and 20 percent of total earnings. Oil came, so to speak, 'to order', as the international shipping crisis hit Norwegian shipowners hard. As a consequence of its extreme dependence on oil the Norwegian economy has become more vulnerable to the cyclical swings in oil prices and in the world economy. The large proportion of oil in its exports has also changed the export structure of the Norwegian economy away from that of a typical industrial State.

We shall consider four distinct periods of Norwegian adaptation to changing international trade regimes. The first spans the years from 1900 to the outbreak of World War I, and was generally characterized by the maintenance of relatively low tariffs in the face of an increasing protectionism among many of the main trading partners, and by the enactment of the concession laws which provided a legal framework for stricter control of foreign capital. The second period covers the period from the late 1920s until World War II, when Norway's basic liberal approach could no longer be upheld in an increasingly protectionist environment. The dual problem for Norway was to shield the primary sectors and small-scale manufacturing industry while at the same time maintaining exports and supporting Norway's global shipping interests. The third period of the early post-war years and the Marshall Plan further highlights the ever-present tension between the dependence on a liberal world order and the need to protect weak sectors. Finally, the period from the late 1950s to the early 1970s was characterized by accelerated liberalization and the search for capital for the modernization of the Norwegian economy. The exceptions are again represented by the primary sectors, which provided a breeding ground for opposition to Norway's joining the continental European integration process.

National independence and economic interdependence

During the last twenty years of the nineteenth century Norway's foreign-trade structure was fundamentally transformed. In terms of imports the ratio between consumer goods and capital goods plus industrial raw materials changed from 2:1 to 1:1. At the same time traditional fish and wood exports became more highly processed and new manufacturing industries entered the export trade. The open economy clearly stimulated growth. The export of goods doubled between 1875 and 1905, while imports as a share of GNP climbed from 29 percent around 1880 to 34 percent around 1900.

The constitutional struggles that in 1905 led to Norway abandoning the union with Sweden had significant repercussions within the sphere of foreign economic policy. Despite its liberal trade policy, the Norwegian government introduced several measures to ensure the country's economic independence. A series of concession laws were enacted from 1906 onwards to limit and control the considerable foreign investments in forests, mines and waterfalls. Foreigners were absolutely forbidden to own forests, and ownership of waterfalls and installations built to exploit them had to devolve to the state after 60 to 80 years. Laws also specified foreign companies' financial obligations, working conditions etc. These laws were above all to serve a domestic political function by reassuring public opinion and economic interest groups (above all farmers) that the national authorities were in charge and would not sacrifice local interests upon the altar of rapid growth.

The most vociferous proponents of these laws held high hopes that they would succeed in retarding the ongoing transformation of the Norwegian economy, whilst their principal opponents feared that this would indeed be the end result. In fact, however, the laws were enforced in such a manner that they appear not to have affected the influx of foreign capital or retarded industrial growth. Investment levels soared from 16 to 21 percent from 1900 to 1915, and share and bond markets expanded. To the political moderates in charge the laws served their political purpose without slowing down the economy.[5]

The perceived danger during the debates on the concession laws was that if foreigners gained control of much of Norwegian natural resources, Norway might be 'drawn into the spheres of influence of foreign powers, not just economically which was bad enough, but also politically', as the Conservative Party chairman put it.[6] The nationalist impulse also spilled over into the sphere of tariffs. In order to protect agriculture and the growing home-market manufacturing industries, the Storting approved tariff increases in 1905. These increases were, however, moderate in comparison with those of neighbouring Sweden and of Germany.[7]

The reasons for moderation are to be found in three opposing sets of interests that counterbalanced the protectionists. The highly export-oriented economy of the coastal areas was dependent on cheap imports for the fishing fleet and opposed significant tariff increases. On the Left the growing Labour Party as well small-scale farmers pointed to Norway's dependence on imported bread grains and anticipated an increase in prices. Labour was also concerned that higher bread prices would cause inflationary pressures and thus hurt Norwegian exports. Finally, the major manufacturing industries engaged in exports and shipping argued that Norway's further economic growth depended upon a liberal world order for the sake of Norwegian exports and international services. The Liberal government took note of this dependence to the degree that the export of timber products as well as shipping companies, such as the Norwegian American Line, were subsidized to maintain or increase market shares.[8]

Yet in certain respects the position of the new State, with its limited foreign-policy experience, was precarious. The combination of nationalist predilections with extreme dependence on foreign export and capital markets was to create serious problems in the years immediately preceding World War I as well as in the 1920s. Attempts by the prohibitionist lobby in Norway to limit alcohol consumption before the war by increasing tariffs on alcoholic beverages caused swift retaliation from France, where wine-growers feared that the Norwegian market would be closed. The French threatened Norway with cancellation of the trade agreement and the closure of French capital markets, which were of crucial importance for both private and public Norwegian borrowers.[9]

French retaliation to a proposed 10-percent increase in duties on alcoholic beverages would thus have had widespread repercussions which were formulated in the following terms by a leading politician: 'The fishing population of Norway will end up in dire need when they cannot dispose of their catch at an acceptable price, wood pulp will be excluded from the French and the Spanish markets and shipping will struggle even harder than is the case today.'[10] Faced with this threat the Norwegian government backed down and signed a new trade agreement promising to lower the import duty on wine. The French on their part promised to let Norwegian loans be quoted on the Paris stock exchange as long as Norwegian legislation was not changed to the detriment of French wine and liquor exports.

Turbulence and protection

The policies of moderate protectionism pursued before World War I represented an adjustment to internal as well as external pressures. A major tariff revision in 1927 did not alter this low-tariff approach, although Norway had to trim to the prevailing winds with a slight increase in the level of protection.

The upheavals in the international system of trade following the great depression had immediate consequences for Norwegian economic policy. Once Britain left the gold standard Norway, like the other Scandinavian countries, quickly decided to follow. Norway's decision to unpeg the Norwegian Krone from gold in the autumn of 1931 contributed to a relatively quick economic recovery from the depression.[11] Nonetheless, increasing balance-of-payments pressures for countries that remained committed to the gold standard meant that Norwegian exporters faced steep increases in import barriers, quantitative restrictions and monetary restrictions in continental Europe.[12]

By the early 1930s it was recognized even by those who favoured free trade in principle, i.e. primarily the non-union majority of the Labour Party, that for a country such as Norway it would be futile to try and go it alone. Free trade was removed from the Party platform in 1933, and in 1934 the Labour parliamentary spokesman on trade issues stated that its change of position was a matter of policy adjustment and not of principle; it was 'purely a matter of self-defence'. As long as a multilateral system prevailed Norway could pursue liberal policies.

> We are now in a different world. We cannot close our eyes to that, and in this field we have to be alert in order not risk great harm to our industries or even to risk shipwreck [...] On account of the current state of affairs we must [...] pay much more attention to national self-sufficiency.[13]

The smaller States of north-western Europe tried in a modest way to buck the new trends by entering into the Oslo Agreement in 1930 following a Norwegian initiative. While the agreement did not preclude tariff increases, parties to it were to be informed of such action and had the right to comment and propose changes. Once the United Kingdom in 1932 adopted new protective tariffs and joined the Ottawa Agreement Norway had to adjust by its own measures to the emerging system of bilateralism, quota restrictions and clearing agreements. In the subsequent negotiations, and even from a weak bargaining position, Norway managed to fend off British demands for tariff reductions but gained significant access to the British market. A Foreign Office negotiator noted that the Norwegians 'were living up to their reputation of being the least accommodating of the Scandinavian peoples'.[14] Liberal prime minister Mowinckel, reporting on the Anglo-Norwegian agreement to the

Storting in 1933, claimed that the negotiators had 'shot a hole in the wall of British protectionism'.[15]

The worldwide decline in agricultural prices that set in from 1927 had important long-term consequences for Norwegian trade policy. The agricultural sector, still employing 25 percent of the working population, had experienced a prolonged debt crisis during 1920s as a result of the Norwegian National Bank's attempt at restoring the Norwegian Krone to pre-war parity. When the crisis in the agricultural sector reached its zenith in the late 1920s, the Storting responded by increasing agricultural tariffs: this shielding of the agricultural sector received support from across the political spectrum. Significantly, Labour left their traditional position as champions of free trade in order to keep consumer costs down. Supporting the rural population was deemed necessary to fend off fascist tendencies in the countryside.

An important tool in a less liberal trade regime was the imposition of quantitative restrictions. In addition, protective tariffs were introduced on selected items. Within the field of agriculture the end result of these measures was to allow into the country only products that were of a supplementary character to those produced domestically. Import regulations were also used on selected industrial products such as shoes, cement and clothing. While agricultural regulations were generally imposed unilaterally, those on industrial goods were only applied after negotiations with the respective trading partners. The fear of countermeasures required the Norwegian authorities to proceed with great care. The end result, however, was not a reduction even for these items. In general, the government accepted annual imports that equalled the average volume of the preceding three years: moreover, the use of quotas affected only 12 percent of the total volume of imports. Comparable figures were 58 percent for France and 26 for the Netherlands.[16]

As for the third means of regulating trade, the use of clearing agreements, Norway took the initiative for such agreements with Spain and Italy mainly because Norwegian exporters experienced continuous problems with receiving payments for their goods. Exports to Italy and Spain consisted largely of stockfish and klipfish respectively, and the initiatives for clearing agreements reflect the importance to Norwegian governments of sustaining the coastal economies, which were facing increasing competition in foreign markets. The agreements served to improve Norway's position considerably vis-à-vis Icelandic exporters, as well as securing payments.[17]

Thus even under the extreme conditions of the interwar period Norway managed to maintain access for its most important exports, such as paper and pulp to the United Kingdom and dried and salted fish to southern Europe. At the same time agriculture was basically insulated from foreign competition, and selected consumer-goods industries were shielded. While also economically important, these sectors above all represented crucial political constituencies.

Norwegian trade and shipping, as the Liberal government had stated in 1933, 'had grown and developed shielded by the unlimited most-favoured-nation clause.'[18] This was assumed to be the system that would best work to the benefit of a small State like Norway. Still, Norwegian governments of the 1930s, which generally maintained such preferences, were able (under systemic conditions that must be presumed to have been far less favourable) to protect Norwegian trading interests to a significant degree, while also taking into account domestic pressure groups. It remains to be investigated whether they showed unusual skills in exploiting the possibilities of the new system or whether in fact the system may not have been as inimical to the interests of small States as the actors of the time professed to believe.

Liberalisation and special interests

The new multilateral system to be launched by the Bretton Woods agreement largely corresponded to the preferences of the Labour Party that had taken power in 1935 and that would, with the exception of World War II, continue to govern Norway until 1965. The greater part of the non-Labour opposition also professed to welcome it. So did the major exporting industries, shipping and the financial services. Labour was in fact intent on pursuing the modernization of the Norwegian economy by channelling investments into shipping and manufacturing industries and exploiting Norway's comparative advantages in terms of cheap hydroelectric power. For success, both sectors required a liberal world order in terms of export markets and access to capital. Foreign-exchange earnings from these sectors were deemed vital for Norway to achieve a higher standard of living and greater social equality.[19]

Furthermore, by the early post-war years Labour planners had decided that small States such as Norway were not viable economic entities in an era of industrial mass production: for greater efficiency larger markets than those provided by the small European nation states were required. Thus one could conclude that Norway would also welcome the processes toward economic integration that were launched in the years following World War II.[20]

For both internal and external reasons the situation was not that simple. The extreme shortages of food, fuel and investment goods after the war necessitated the continuation and further development of the bilateral system of controls and quotas that had developed as a consequence of the interwar crises and wartime conditions. Only the Marshall Plan speeded up the return to a multilateral system, and then only within the confines of the North Atlantic world.

The integration processes that gradually gained ground from the late 1940s, partly through European initiatives and partly as a consequence of American pressure, were dominated by States that were deeply distrusted by the political and economical elites in Norway, rather than by the north Atlantic States, and the United Kingdom in particular, that Norway looked to for economic cooperation as well as security protection.[21]

Norway's strong ties to the United Kingdom were to pose a challenge in the ongoing negotiations over liberalisation of intra-European trade. The Labour government rejected initiatives that would lead to a more closely integrated Europe. Its traditional strong ties with the United Kingdom even led leading politicians to consider Norway joining the Sterling Area, but this attempt came to nothing as the practical difficulties would have been considerable.[22]

While favouring a return to a multilateral trade regime, the government expressed reservations with regard to early attempts at liberalising intra-European trade. In the OEEC Ministerial Council Norway attracted heavy criticism for its expansive macroeconomic policy. In order to achieve its ambitious modernisation goals, the Norwegian government allowed the economy to run into heavy trade deficits. Erik Brofoss, then minister of trade and chief architect of Norway's economic policy, defended the Norwegian position by arguing that liberalisation was only a means to an end, namely to achieve high growth and low unemployment. Brofoss remained sceptical of an early return to convertibility. The principal argument presented by Brofoss and his advisers was that a quick return to convertibility would force the European governments into deflationary policies. Such policies would cause widespread economic contraction and lead to unacceptable social costs in the form of a higher unemployment rate.[23]

At the same time the domestic forces favouring a greater degree of self-sufficiency had gained strength since the interwar years. The spokesmen for agriculture inside and outside the Storting wanted to maintain the insulation from international competition achieved in the 1930s. Their spokesmen were also found in the Labour Party, which was dominated by an uneasy yet remarkably cohesive coalition of industrial workers, coastal fishermen from north Norway and small-scale farmers and rural workers. Parts of the fishing industry were also turning increasingly isolationist under the threat of foreign trawlers' closing in on Norwegian waters and of the resultant transformation of Norwegian artisanal fisheries.[24]

The consumer-goods industries had gained ground during the interwar period, and the shortages of investment goods for export industries in the immediate post-war period allowed them to gain further ground through the continuation of the system of quotas and regulations. The successes of the Soviet planned economy, the wartime radicalization of the Labour Party and the virtual rebirth of the Communist Party all added further strength to clamours for a more regulated and autarkic Norwegian economy. To top it all, even the internationalist leadership of the Labour Party saw dangers in exposing Norway quickly to a competitive international system. The wear and tear of wartime conditions, the lack of modernization as a consequence of many years of minimal investment and replacement had, the Labour government feared, rendered the Norwegian home industries incapable of withstanding international competition in the short term. A considerable part of Norwegian manufacturing industry was run down and antiquated, and Norway, as the Labour leadership saw it, was industrially underdeveloped. For a transitional period of unspecified length Norway was perceived to need continuing protectionist measures while preparing to face international competition in the longer run. We should bear in mind that the Labour government, while seeing Norway as highly dependent upon a functioning multilateral system, also was convinced that the State had to play a key role in relaunching Norway on the road to modernization. The interwar crisis had demonstrated that private capital needed the guiding hand of the government. Thus Norway entered the post-war period with a highly complex set of goals, highly dependent upon a favourable environment yet with a Labour government fearful that planning and liberalization might not be compatible.[25]

By the time the Marshall Plan was launched in the summer of 1947 the Labour government had concluded that the post-war scarcities would not disappear as expected. Food, fuel and investment goods would be hard to come by, capital for reconstruction remained hard to raise, and the multilateral system planned at Bretton Woods was nowhere near achievement. Labour's ambitious reconstruction and modernization goals were becoming harder to achieve as scarcities affected the expansion of export industries far more than home-market consumer industries. Already in the winter of 1946–1947 the Labour government as well as the opposition had cause to ponder the consequences of the scarcity of foreign exchange (i.e. dollars) for a small State. Norway in the autumn of 1946 had contracted a loan of $50 million from the American Export-Import (Exim) Bank. The Storting was reluctant to accept the terms of the loan, which included the proviso that 50 percent of goods purchased had to be carried on American ships. This represented a major threat to the earning power of the Norwegian merchant marine, by far the country's most important earner of foreign exchange. The net gain of the loan would thus be potentially far less than the total.[26]

The Labour government nevertheless decided that the need for dollars was such that the disadvantages had to be accepted. The opposition – the non-Labour parties on the Right and the Communists on Left, for a while joined by some Labour representatives – were unanimous in opposing the terms. The opposition had various grounds for opposing the Exim loan in particular and Labour's reconstruction and growth policies in general: the Conservatives and the Liberals were particularly concerned with Norway's shipping interests, the Farmers' Party were concerned that primary sectors which constituted the basis for 'our people's existence as a free, independent and culturally and morally advanced people' should maintain their key role in the Norwegian economy, and the Communists, certainly no opponents of industrialization, disliked both multilateralism and the American connection. They were unanimous, however, in their fear of great-power dominance and advocacy of the importance of small States' maintaining their independence and freedom of action. The Communists were briefly able to play credibly on such sentiments. As Jørgen Vogt said in the 1946 debate on the budget: 'I think the Farmers' faction is right to warn against the danger of putting our country into a fateful state of dependency upon foreign capital and influence.'[27]

The tensions between multilateralism and sector interests were notable during Norway's first 40 years of independence. They were for systemic reasons largely submerged in the 1930s. With the attempted return to a multilateral system they re-emerged more forcefully, for both political and economic reasons. Accelerated industrialization threatened the position of the primary sector and potentially also the political position of the non-Labour parties. Multilateralism also increased the pressure on these sectors: the anti-Hitler coalition broke apart and polarized into two opposing blocs, while the issue of non-alignment or Western alignment made Norway's foreign economic policy even more difficult to handle.

It is still not clear to historians how the Labour planners were able to square their growth plans with the assumption of a post-war crisis resembling that after the Great War. What is clear, however, is that the different problems they actually had to handle brought about a fundamental clarification. As Knut Getz Wold, a prominent member of the group, put it years later, a 'world depression or new foreign trade barriers would have played havoc with the economy.'[28] By the autumn of 1947 Norway's dollar reserves were running out and increasing tension between the great powers mandated a retreat from bridge-building to alignment with the West to secure Norway's independence and territorial integrity.[29]

Reconstruction policies could then be pursued within the framework of the Organization for European Economic Cooperation. The access to capital and the opening of markets that the Marshall Plan provided, facilitated the implementation of Labour's programme of export-led growth. Accession to the OEEC did not take place without some apprehension on the part of Labour, nor was the process of adjusting to the goals of fellow member States and the United States entirely painless. Norway was pushed into a more rapid reduction of quotas than would otherwise have taken place; the high investment rate was at times exposed to severe criticism, as was the latent inflationary threat. In spite of temporary setbacks and latent threats to established goals and policies the commitment to multilateralism remained unshaken amongst Labour's leadership. In the 1950 parliamentary debate on the budget party deputy chairman Trygve Bratteli in response to criticism from vocal supporters of more protectionism unequivocally stated that 'Norway is interested in an extensive exchange of goods and services with other countries.'[30] As the foremost architect of post-war Norwegian economic policy, minister of trade Erik Brofoss, put it in 1952: 'To solve Norway's foreign economic problems they have to be dealt with on the international level.'[31]

However, compromises at home were also necessary. Some went the way the Labour leadership wanted. Apart from the Communists and two representatives of the Farmers' Party the Storting supported the Long Term Programme that the government submitted to the OEEC in autumn 1948 despite the fact that it basically reflected Labour's industrialization goals. The explanation lies above all in the steadily stronger Cold War climate. Going against the programme would for the non-Labour parties also mean placing Norway's Western alignment in doubt. Foreign-policy consensus was becoming increasingly important. In this way domestic planning and liberalization within the OEEC represented compatible approaches to the overarching goal of modernization. On the other hand agriculture was gaining larger subsidies than Brofoss and the planners desired. The necessity of not antagonizing important voting blocs could work both ways.[32]

The need for consensus is also reflected in Norwegian attitudes towards the various attempts at European and Scandinavian integration. In the latter instance Norway's resounding rejection of a Scandinavian customs union in 1949–1950 and again in 1954 arose from fears that Norwegian agriculture could not face Danish competition and that those industries whose sales were reliant upon the domestic market would be unable to compete with Swedish imports. But the reluctance to enter customs unions also demonstrates that Norway's conception of multilateralism and larger markets did not imply supranational integration. The preference, as the government confided to the British, was for a more loosely and informally organized cooperation without the formal abdication of national sovereignty. Thus by the end of Marshall Plan period Norway had gone a long way toward accepting North Atlantic economic cooperation, and the government clearly recognized the need in the near future also to expose home-market industries to international competition. Agriculture was not to be touched, however, and the battle over fisheries was yet to be fought.[33]

Industrial modernisation achieved, primary sector protected

The traditional export-oriented manufacturing industry of Norway had during the first decades of the twentieth century increasingly been supplemented by firms producing consumer durables for the domestic market. This sector had developed behind the protective barriers that were introduced during the interwar period and maintained after the war. The result was a dual industrial structure.[34] The liberalization of the 1950s and 1960s to a large extent served to obliterate this distinction by exposing the shielded home-market-oriented sector to international competition. Non-competitive firms were forced out of business while those that managed to stay afloat mostly did so by also becoming exporters. The process was perceived and carried out as a dramatic turnaround involving substantial State support. The need to implement this transformation as quickly and painlessly as possible also involved the government in trying to bring more foreign investment to Norway.[35]

The scarcity of foreign capital had temporarily been alleviated by the Marshall Plan, and after its conclusion Norway still profited from American support from the Mutual Security Agency for the North Norway Plan from 1952, yet the need for capital was so pressing throughout the 1950s that the government in 1959 employed former secretary general of the United Nations Trygve Lie as a roving dollar ambassador for Norway. The need for capital, together with the continental European integration process, also lay behind the several Norwegian explorations of alternative forums for economic cooperation, such as a tentative plan for joining the Commonwealth and the third Norwegian initiative for Scandinavian cooperation, this time for a customs union launched in the fall of 1954.[36]

By the mid 1950s the government considered that the reconstruction and modernization process since the war had brought Norwegian home-market industries to the point where, supported by selective government measures, they would be able to face increasing international competition. The ruling Labour Party found that they could finally act on their guiding principle since the end of the war that the Norwegian home market was too limited for a rational organization of manufacturing industries.[37]

Integration into a more liberal world order by means of more general or limited free-trade agreements, or participation in a customs union, may be seen to be incompatible with the maintenance of national economic planning and a system of national controls and support. Norwegian historians of both conservative and radical bents have in fact concluded that Labour's planned economy could not be squared with liberalization. Members of the Labour government at times expressed the view that Norway was being pushed too rapidly towards liberalization, and came close to seeing the two strategies as incompatible. The left wing of the party was convinced that this was the case.[38] We would rather maintain that the policies pursued from the late 1940s represented, and were seen to represent, a pragmatic combination of planning and liberalization.[39] It may be considered another version of the ability to further broader national goals of economic policy while exploiting the strength of the export sector. The degree of liberalization and integration that was deemed acceptable above all depended upon the social and employment policies of the cooperating partners. The more similar these policies, the greater the degree of integration that was acceptable, as in the case of a Scandinavian (later Nordic) Customs Union from 1954. At the other end of the spectrum a large and heterogeneous group, such as the Wider Free Trade Area, would pose only a limited threat in terms of the imposition of undesirable policies.[40]

This combination of liberalization that took place within the European Free Trade Area, and at a more rapid pace than had been originally intended, together with the use of selective measures to transform Norwegian home industries, proved remarkably successful, and far more painless than anticipated. By 1964 a quarter of total exports originated from former home-market industries, and by the end of the 1960s these exports were responsible for nearly half of the growth of Norwegian manufacturing exports. The leading sectors were mechanical and electrical engineering, shipbuilding and furniture. The fear of the damaging effects of Swedish competition in particular, which had haunted Norwegian home-market industrialists during the Scandinavian and Nordic negotiations, had all but evaporated by the mid 1960s.[41]

Agriculture had been excepted from the internationalization process throughout the post-war period, and by the mid 1950s represented the main obstacle to a Nordic agreement. There is little indication that the Labour government at any time held any real hope of being able to involve agriculture in the internationalization process. On the other hand, the Government held high hopes of transforming the fisheries sector into a major exporter of frozen goods to expanding European markets. This would require the introduction of trawlers in large numbers and a rapid expansion of the freezing industry. These plans never materialized to the degree the Labour Party leadership envisaged, as the coastal population and the fishermen's organization opposed trawler expansion and were adamantly against the necessary concessions in terms of access to resources that were required for a major expansion of Norwegian exports. The political ramifications of a transformation of the Norwegian fisheries in the desired direction were simply too complex for the government to handle. Fisheries, in fact, came to represent the main obstacle to Norway's joining the European Community/European Union.[42]

With the partial exception of the fisheries sector the 1960s was characterized by a continuation of the traditional policy of having your cake and eating it too. There was an apparently successful mixture of maintaining and gaining market access and protecting the peculiarities of the primary sectors. The traditional staple export industries also managed to maintain their markets within the EEC and secured their positions through the 1973 free trade agreement between the EC and the rump of EFTA.

Not such a special case?

We may assume that there is nothing peculiar in the Norwegian desire to have it both ways: similar economic and political pressures and incentives are likely to have existed in most States. This does not make the Norwegian case less interesting. The freedom of action enjoyed by a small and relatively new State in a competitive environment invites closer investigation. By studying the processes and pressures in the Norwegian case and comparing it to other small States we may come closer to understanding how and why small European States managed the major economic upheavals of the first two-thirds of the twentieth century.

It is striking that the great powers and other trading partners with strongly opposing interests of an economic or political character have only rarely used or threatened to use forceful measures such as a trade boycott against what has been considered unacceptable Norwegian policies. The relatively few Norwegian staple exports were, as demonstrated by France before World War I, certainly vulnerable to such pressures. This indicates that the structure of the international system itself left Norway with considerable freedom of action, which may at certain times have been due to the implicit or explicit rules of the system and at others simply a consequence of Norway's geopolitical position and natural resources.

Norway covers a fairly large area endowed with a small population, relatively rich in terms of natural resources while short on investment capital and advanced technology during the period under investigation. From the point of view of foreign capital and the major powers Norway might have been considered an easy prey. The question then is how Norwegian governments of different political colours and generally in cooperation with indigenous economic interests have been able to combine an internationalist approach with a domestic regulatory system satisfying a strongly nationalist polity. Their attitudes to and regulation of foreign capital is a case in point. How has it been possible to maintain the dual approach of both inviting in foreign capital and at the same time keeping it under considerable control?

Policies have in fact been extremely flexible over time as between restrictive and liberal regimes and also in terms of periodically liberal interpretations of strict regulations. On the other hand Norway has been well served by sheer luck. After the long period of high investments in power-intensive industries around the turn of the last century heavy Norwegian indebtedness was relieved by the profits made during World War I. Similarly, the investments made during the 1960s and during the build-up of the oil industry were recovered by the price hikes engineered by OPEC in the 1970s.

Finally, we would like to look at the question of size from a different angle. Once the problem of a reasonable control of foreign capital has been solved, smallness may in some respects be an advantage. This may be the case both in terms of market access and with regard to the shielding of vulnerable sectors. When larger trading partners want reciprocal market access it may be easier for them, as was the case during the negotiations with the United Kingdom in the 1930s, to enter into compromises over relatively small markets. Small States may also draw proportionally larger advantages from international liberalization because their home markets offer too small a basis for efficient industrial production. Furthermore, a small economy may thrive if competitive in a very limited number of niches, since even a niche in the global market is so vast relative to the productive capacity of a country like Norway. It is notable that niche products such as horseshoe nails, aluminium automobile parts and furniture have in the case of Norway provided the base for relatively substantial industrial activity. The combination of crucial resource endowments, political skill and sheer luck in timing has made it possible to turn smallness to considerable advantage. Even before oil revenues Norway had achieved a very high standard of living while maintaining the settlement structure and a cultural identity closely linked to that of a pre-industrial society.

1 An earlier version of this paper was presented at a conference on Globalisation and De-globalisation of Small European Countries in Zurich, 15–17 March 2001. We would like to thank participants for comments. We would also like to thank Eivind Merok for valuable assistance in the final stages of preparing this article.
2 The historical literature on Norway in English is quite limited. For a recent survey with useful but brief bibliography see R. Danielsen *et al.*, *Norway: A History from the Vikings to Our Own Times* (Oslo: 1998); for a survey of Norwegian economic history in the twentieth century in Norwegian, F. Hodne and O.H. Grytten, *Norsk økonomi 1900–1990* (Oslo: 1992); see also F. Hodne, *The Norwegian Economy* (London: 1983); T. Bergh *et al.*, *Growth and Development. The Norwegian Experience 1830–1980* (Oslo: 1981).
3 K. O'Rourke and J. G. Williamson, 'Around the European Periphery, 1870–1913: Globalization, Schooling and Growth', *European Review of Economic History* 1 (1997), pp. 153–190; T. Bergh, T. Hanisch, E. Lange and H. Pharo, *Growth and development: The Norwegian Experience 1830–1980*, Norwegian foreign policy studies 37 (Oslo: 1981).
4 For all statistical information, *Historisk statistikk* (Oslo: 1968 and 1978).
5 E. Lange, 'The Concession Laws of 1906–1909 and Norwegian Industrial Development', *Scandinavian Journal of History* 2, no. 4 (1977), pp. 311–330.
6 F. Stang, *Erindringer fra min politiske tid* (Oslo: 1946), p. 93, quoted from R. Berg, *Norge på egen hånd 1905–1920. Norsk utenrikspolitikks historie. Bind 2*, vol. 2 in *A History of Norwegian Foreign Policy* (Oslo:1995), p. 106.
7 Berg, *Norge på egen hånd*, p. 101.
8 Berg, *Norge på egen hånd*, pp. 101–104.
9 Berg, *Norge på egen hånd*, p. 103; for the interwar conflict with Portugal and Spain, see O.-B. Fure, *Mellomkrigstid 1920–1940*, vol. 3 of *A history of Norwegian foreign relations* (Oslo: 1996), pp. 163–168.
10 Quoted from Berg, *Norge på egen hånd*, p. 103.
11 S. Broadberry, 'The North European Depression of the 1930s', *Scandinavian Economic History Review* 32 (1984); T. Hanish, 'The economic crisis in Norway in the 1930s', *Economic History Review* 31 (1983).
12 B. Eichengreen, *Golden Fetters. The gold standard and the great depression 1919–1939* (New York: 1995).
13 Qouted from Fure, *Mellomkrigstid*, pp. 172–173.
14 Fure, *Mellomkrigstid*, pp. 174–176, quote on p. 175.
15 Quoted from Fure, *Mellomkrigstid*, p. 175.
16 Fure, *Mellomkrigstid*, pp. 175 and 178.

17 Fure, *Mellomkrigstid*, pp. 173–179.
18 Quoted from Fure, *Mellomkrigstid*, p. 161.
19 H. Pharo, 'Bridgebuilding and Reconstruction: Norway faces the Marshall Plan', *Scandinavian Journal of History* 1, no. 1–2 (1976), 125–153; H. Pharo, 'The Marshall Plan and the modernization of the Norwegian economy', Comitée pour l'histoire économique et financière, *Le Plan Marshall et le relèvement économique de l'Europe* (Paris: 1993), pp. 591–604.
20 K. E. Eriksen and H. Pharo, *Kald krig og internasjonalisering 1949–1965*, vol. 5 in *A History of Norwegian Foreign Relations* (Oslo, 1997), pp. 108–112.
21 H. Pharo, 'Gjenreisning og utenrikspolitikk', in T. Bergh and H. Pharo (eds.), *Historiker og veileder* (Oslo, 1989), pp. 163–202.
22 L. F. M Øksendal, *En fast kurs. Norsk betalingspolitikk 1945–1958*, Master thesis at the Norwegian University of Science and Technology (NTNU), (Trondheim: 2001).
23 Øksendal, *En fast kurs*, pp. 172–174; Eriksen and Pharo, *Kald krig og internasjonalisering*.
24 Pharo, 'Gjenreisning og utenrikspolitikk'; Eriksen and Pharo, *Kald krig og internasjonalisering*, pp. 356–359.
25 Pharo, 'Gjenreisning og utenrikspolitikk'; Eriksen and Pharo, *Kald krig og internasjonalisering*, pp. 107–117.
26 Pharo, 'Bridgebuilding and Reconstruction'; Pharo, 'Gjenreisning og utenrikspolitikk'.
27 Pharo, 'Gjenreisning og utenrikspolitikk', quotes from pp. 176 and 178.
28 Pharo, 'Gjenreisning og utenrikspolitikk', quote on p. 168; interview with Knut Getz Wold, 21.05.1964, European Recovery Program, Harry S. Truman Library.
29 Pharo, 'Bridgebuilding and Reconstruction'.
30 Quoted in Eriksen and Pharo, *Kald krig og internasjonalisering*, p. 109.
31 Quoted in Eriksen and Pharo, *Kald krig og internasjonalisering*, p. 110.
32 Pharo, 'Gjenreisning og utenrikspolitikk'.
33 Eriksen and Pharo, *Kald krig og internasjonalisering*, pp. 123–168.
34 Hodne and Grytten, *Norsk økonomi*, pp. 127–145; E. Lange, *Samling om felles mål 1935–1970.* in vol. 11 of *Aschehoug's History of Norway* (Oslo, 1998), pp. 26–43.
35 Hodne and Grytten, *Norsk økonomi*, pp. 226–238; Lange, *Samling om felles mål*, pp. 178–183; T. J. Hanisch and E. Lange, *Veien til velstand* (Oslo, 1986), pp. 86–119.
36 Eriksen and Pharo, *Kald krig og internasjonalisering*, pp. 143–157, 287–326; H. Pharo, 'Marshallplanen sett fra amerikansk side. Norge i komparativt perspektiv', in *Historisk tidsskrift*, no. 2 (1989), pp. 184–229.
37 Eriksen and Pharo, *Kald krig og internasjonalisering*, pp. 107–114, 287–306.
38 Pharo, 'Gjenreisning og utenrikspolitikk'; Pharo, 'Marshallplanen sett fra amerikansk side', e. g. p. 200.
39 For a discussion of this issue see E. Lange and H. Pharo, 'Planning and Economic Policy in Norway, 1945–1960', *Scandinavian Journal of History* 16, no. 3 (1991), pp. 215–228.
40 Eriksen and Pharo, *Kald krig og internasjonalisering*, pp. 287–326.

41 Hanisch and Lange, *Veien til velstand*, pp. 112–114; Eriksen and Pharo, *Kald krig og internasjonalisering*, pp. 307–326.
42 Eriksen and Pharo, *Kald krig og internasjonalisering*, pp. 357–362; R. Tamnes, *Oljealder 1965–1995*, in vol. 6 of *A History of Norwegian Foreign Relations* (Oslo 1997), pp. 165–183, 219–246.

Section II

From an Open World Economy to Economic Disintegration and Protectionism

Maria Eugénia Mata[1]

A Forgotten Country in Globalisation? The Role of Foreign Capital in Nineteenth-Century Portugal

Introduction

The word 'Globalisation' is sometimes understood as the recent world integration resulting from contemporary transport and communication facilities, including computers, Internet and mobile telephones. In fact, the debate on globalisation concerns the 1990s, not the preceding decades. Sometimes, too, 'globalisation' is identified with the economic integration that occurred in the decades following the Second World War. From this perspective, economic integration and the rise of international organisations are the main globalisation indicators.

However, this view may be accepted only if we consider the generalised restrictions to free movement from 1914 to the early 1950s. The two World Wars presented not only desperate military struggles but also transport difficulties and economic rivalries. Blockades and other interruptions of the customary flow of international trade became the norm. Domestic consumption dominated markets, giving way to import-substitution mechanisms. The wars also put an end to large international flows of capital, as the economic normalcy prevailing in the nineteenth century disappeared and war needs pressed for the application of capital to military aims.

The interwar period did not see a resumption of nineteenth-century free-trade traditions. Europe experienced recovery during the 1920s but inflation (and in some countries hyperinflation) was the rule for a while, followed very soon by the Great Depression. Generalised unemployment throughout the Western capitalist economies required domestic consumption for national goods and gave way to tariffs on foreign trade. People's feelings against imports and foreign goods can explain policies aimed at protecting domestic markets. Closed markets and nationalism were widespread. Retaliation was the answer to trading partners' tariffs. In the small country of Portugal, Salazar's regime was no exception. Rural areas, traditionally detached from international markets, went on providing local needs. Portuguese industry enjoyed regulatory protection against free foreign competition.[2] The Portuguese economy experienced a closure in the interwar years, especially in the 1930s, to escape the effects of the Great World Depression.[3]

From this twentieth-century perspective, globalisation reached Portugal only after the end of the Second World War. Reconstruction was a shared aim across Europe. Portugal had maintained a neutral position during the war, although the Portuguese government ceded military bases to the Allies in the Portuguese islands of the Azores. Although there was no physical rebuilding necessary within Portuguese territory, when the United States of America offered funds through the Marshall Plan, Portugal accepted. An initial hesitation in 1947, fearing American hegemony over the world, gave way to a new government attitude in 1948. The threat of inflation and domestic difficulties in supplying urban markets with subsistence goods were responsible for this political repositioning.[4] Marshall foreign aid meant Portugal's participation in the OEEC, and is usually referred to as the beginning of Portuguese participation in international globalising institutions; but some studies prefer to stress the Portuguese decision to join the European Free Trade Association in 1959 and the European Economic Community in 1986 as her two main steps towards globalisation.

This, however, is a short-term perspective from a historical point of view. Portugal's participation in today's globalisation, which follows the government's decision to join the OEEC, EFTA and EC, has its roots in the pre-First World War period.

Portugal was a host country to European savings and businesses before 1914. Available data on foreign joint-stock companies suggest that the inflow of foreign investment in the second half of the nineteenth century cannot be neglected. Portugal, a small underdeveloped country, was no exception in hosting capital from the core European financial markets when nineteenth-century foreign capital movements dominated international economic relationships: poorer countries offered higher rates of return, and thus provided an attractive home for spare capital from their wealthier neighbours. Capital flows moved particularly 'to sparsely peopled areas where conditions for rapid growth along familiar Western lines were exceptionally favourable'.[5] Intensifying international trade, such investments could profit from the more favourable opportunities that existed in many economic sectors of the receiving countries, particularly in less industrialised countries around the world.

Helping to form the world market, they promoted the emergence of larger international financial markets. At the same time, the incentives to invest in public goods depended upon the new opportunities arising from the needs to finance local central State expenditures. Foreign loans supported public debts. The hope of small risks because of the pre-announced fixed interest rates on bonds may explain the preference for investing in public loans.

International analysis of foreign investment in the half century before 1914 ignores Portugal as a receiving country in the nineteenth-century network of capital outflows. Most studies consider the role of portfolio investment in Eastern Europe and the New World: few have considered the role of foreign investment in small countries. Portugal is supposed to have participated heavily in globalisation only through emigration flows, particularly to Brazil, an ex-Portuguese colony, and to the USA. Because of its smallness Portugal is a forgotten country in capital-flow studies.[6]

Portuguese historians assess the role of foreign capital in the Portuguese economy in a variety of ways. The dominant perspective views government bonds and railroad securities as the only two channels for foreign investment and the resulting picture is of high speculative flows, business failure and financial corruption. Other Portuguese historians ignore international funding initiatives entirely.

This chapter asserts the presence of foreign private capital in economic activities under normal business performance. It focuses on the role of foreign joint-stock companies working in Portugal in normal economic activities during the nineteenth century.

Available data on these foreign joint-stock companies suggests that the inflow of foreign investment may have been small. However, its role cannot be neglected by globalisation research, because the phenomenon of outsider investment in so small a country can illustrate how crucial getting new opportunities in peripheral areas was for maintaining the development of what turned out to be key modern economic sectors. In an underdeveloped society such as nineteenth-century Portugal the ideal of achievement was surely a decisive driving factor in the context of material progress. Corporations offered an institutional framework within which to propel business into modernity and progress.

One of the most important attractions to foreign capital in nineteenth-century Portugal was investment in the public debt.[7] Besides public bonds, foreign capital also arrived in the form of private foreign investment.

What do we know about foreign loans for Portuguese foreign public debt and private foreign investment? This is a vexed question in Portuguese historiography, as there are different opinions about the role of foreign investment in the Portuguese economy and its contribution to economic growth and modernisation. According to Vieira,[8] 'the role of British capital in the Portuguese economy during the second half of the last century was very relevant, whatever the perspective under which we would analyse it.' Besides discussing speculation and corruption as current features in foreign investment, Vieira argues that the capital inflow would have had a positive effect for Portuguese economic growth and modernisation.

On the other hand, Reis[9] argues that: 'capital inflows [in Portugal] played only a minor role in building up productive capacity, with the exception of certain special activities.' Although pessimistic, this idea runs contrary to traditional Portuguese history, which has often emphasised the dependence argument for Portuguese economic underdevelopment. Believing in the mechanics of foreign trade and foreign investment dependence, earlier dominant critical frameworks have pointed to exploitation, repatriation of profits and international dependence, particularly on England.

This chapter will regard the presence of foreign private capital in Portuguese economic activities and the British dominance there as not dissimilar to that of European foreign joint-stock companies wanting to operate in the country within the realms of insurance, mining, shipping, banks, telegraphs and telephones, water and gas provision, colonial business or even industrial activities. The history of international capital movements in the nineteenth century has a long tradition and has experienced a marked renewal and revision in recent years thanks to the growing interest in the question of globalisation. Socio-economic reasons justify the choice of the period studied. The 1860s opened a new era of business in Europe, with joint-stock companies in France, Spain, Italy or Belgium under a new juridical background: in Portugal the law changed in 1867. Moreover for earlier periods the basic sources are almost completely lacking (the first census in Portugal was organised in 1864 and the regular publication of foreign trade statistics began in 1865).

This chapter will examine a few important aspects of the socio-economic life of small countries in the nineteenth and early twentieth centuries as they endeavoured to attract foreign capital. New questions have been asked in this area, new methodologies have been followed and considerable amount of new data have been produced on many aspects. The context to which this chapter belongs is therefore highly dynamic and innovative. Potentially, it may help us to understand how capital movements did not reinforce divergence because they did not flow towards faster-growing economies but instead contributed to long-term convergence by flowing more toward the poorer economies.[10] Later in this chapter we will find an assessment of the impact of foreign direct investment upon business attitudes in Portugal. Perhaps the long-term value of this chapter will lie in the presentation and discussion of a relatively little known case as a piece, albeit a small one, of a far broader puzzle.

The dominance of investment in railways and foreign lending to Government

As is the case with other small countries, there is much historical evidence of foreign private investments in the nineteenth-century Portuguese economy. Individual foreign merchants or family businesses dominated the wine-production and export sectors. British families exported port and Madeira wines to European markets, particularly to England. Vieira[11] has described how British investments came to Portugal to fund the urban and suburban transport systems: but it was the Portuguese railway-building sector that achieved international prominence in foreign capital investment attraction, particularly from Great Britain.[12] In 1853 the Portugal Central Peninsular Railway Company was formed to build and run the Portuguese section of a Lisbon-Madrid line. As only 68 km of track had been laid and opened to traffic by 1857 the company failed, and the government purchased the line. In the same year Sir Morton Peto signed a new contract to build a line between Lisbon and Oporto; but no company was formed and no track was laid. In 1854 the Companhia Nacional dos Caminhos-de-Ferro do Sul do Tejo was formed to build a railway in the south to the Algarve. As only 70 km had been built and opened to traffic by 1861, the company failed and the government bought this line also. In 1864 a new South Eastern Portugal Railway Company was formed. It added 150 km of track, which were opened to traffic. The company failed in 1866, and the government built the rest of the line south to the Algarve (225 km). This picture of unsuccessful companies promulgated an image of business failure and corruption among Portuguese historians in the 1980s.

However, the Spanish entrepreneur José de Salamanca successfully formed the Royal Portuguese Railway Company in 1860. He bought the built line and extended it east to the Spanish frontier and north to the left bank of the Douro opposite Oporto. A total of 438 km track had been built and opened to traffic by 1864, and both lines were linked to Madrid in 1866.

During the 1870s and 1880s a new company, the Beira Alta Railway Company, built a 252-km line between the Atlantic coast and Spain: it crossed the north line and was linked to the Spanish network (and indirectly to the French and European network) in 1882. At the same time the Royal Portuguese Railway Company built two new lines. One was 212 km long: the other was the western line, which was 242 km long. Additionally a bridge over the Douro linked the northern line with Oporto in 1877, and a short cut in the Lisbon-Madrid line was ready in 1880.

The period from the 1890s and early twentieth century until the First World War witnessed a slowdown in railway building, with only regional lines being added to these main trunk lines.

The amount of capital invested in railways between the 1850s and the 1880s totalled £23.5 million, of which £10.6 million were public monies and £12.9 million came from private investment.[13] The sources of the latter were almost exclusively foreign, with the overwhelming majority coming from the core European economies. As a matter of fact, only £200,000 of investments in the Companhia Nacional dos Caminhos-de-Ferro do Sul do Tejo is clearly of Brazilian origin, and comes from the slave trade, as most contemporary scholarship suggests.

This effort to build railways and other public-service projects led the government to subsidise private builders or contractors and to buy out failed companies. The Portuguese government has a long-standing policy of large-scale borrowing in foreign markets due to persistent public deficits. London was a global financial market (as were Paris and Frankfurt). Available capital in European financial centres preferred stable returns, and Portuguese government bonds suited this purpose.

Portuguese government borrowing began with the securities of the 3% interest-rate loan of 1852. The government decided to lump all the previous foreign public loans into a single consolidated loan and to combine future foreign borrowing into this same loan through successive bond issues. This loan attained huge nominal amounts, although the securities' low market prices in the European financial markets brought much smaller amounts into the Portuguese exchequer. Available sources show that the market price of the Portuguese bonds in the London Stock Exchange was sometimes very low.[14] According to most historians, this fact spread in the markets an image of highly speculative opportunities for foreign investment in Portuguese bonds. Moreover, in the 1870s the government decided to borrow by soliciting redeemable loans. By the 1890s, six loans of this kind had been floated on foreign markets.

In 1892 the Portuguese government could not pay these loans' amortisation amounts, and paid only a third of total agreed interests. In response a partial bankruptcy was declared, and European markets suspended their lending to Portugal: it was necessary to renegotiate all the previously referred loans with the lenders. This was a difficult task which was only accomplished in the beginning of the twentieth century through a conversion in 1902 of all of them into a loan with a 3% interest rate. Meanwhile, only one new small 4.5% interest-rate loan was obtained in 1896 through the use of the monopoly tobacco rent to guarantee interest payments.

The Portuguese government also took out short-term loans throughout the second half of the nineteenth century from several foreign banks in Europe. This floating debt, owed in British pounds, French francs and Deutschmarks, enlarged the overall public debt.

Estimates of the inflows into Portugal[15] in Table 1 were based on the annual market values of the Portuguese bonds in London, at that time the world's main financial centre, and are unlikely to diverge significantly from what the government in fact received.

Table 1: Portuguese Net Government Borrowing.

1855–1859	1,575	1885–1889	9,893
1860–1864	4,768	1890–1894	4,722
1865–1869	1,758	1895–1899	1,620
1870–1874	3,900	1900–1904	0
1875–1879	3,504	1905–1909	0
1880–1884	9,029	1910–1913	0
Total			40,769

Source: Mata, *As finanças públicas*, p. 261.

Unity: amounts are in thousands of pounds.

The main conclusion of this essentially narrative accounting is that railways and public debt sought a huge amount of foreign capital. However, total gross flow investment also included a variety of other sectors.

The preference of foreign joint stock companies for insurance, mining, railways and banking before the 1880s

Individual foreign merchants or families may be found doing several kinds of business in Portuguese cities, particularly in Lisbon, the Portuguese capital and main economic centre in the country. On the eve of the First World War, Lisbon had 114 foreign firms.[16] Oporto and Funchal were two leading urban centres exporting Port and Madeira wines.[17] Foreign firms, mostly run by British families, dominated this export business.[18] As Hennart[19] explains, export-oriented business attracts foreign capital, with promoters usually belonging to the more developed country. The family character of the businesses may be understood if one considers the wish to allow relatives or close friends to share in a profitable opportunity.

During the decade following the law on joint-stock companies which was passed in 1867, the Portuguese economy attracted a large number of limited-liability companies: many more firms would come in the decades leading up to the First World War. This means that the definition of the juridical conditions for business regulation was a determining factor for private foreign investment in Portugal.[20] The law passed by the Portuguese Parliament on 22 June 1867 was based on liberal principles and brought freedom to the constitution of Portuguese joint-stock companies. In most European countries as well, mid-century laws removed many obstacles to company formation. This is what Timothy L. Alborn called 'a new "joint-stock politics" outside the pall of state intervention'.[21] Even so, the law retained the need for foreign joint-stock companies to gain authorisation from the Portuguese government to carry on business in Portugal. The law also obliged foreign companies already working in Portugal to obtain the same business licence. After selecting a Portuguese representative, the applicant company had to disclose its legal statutes in its country of origin. The applicant was required to agree to abide by the laws of Portugal – especially those of a fiscal nature – and to accept the decision of Portuguese courts in all legal matters. Applications for business licences preserved in the

Figure 1: Distribution of the number of Companies by countries of origin (1867–1875)

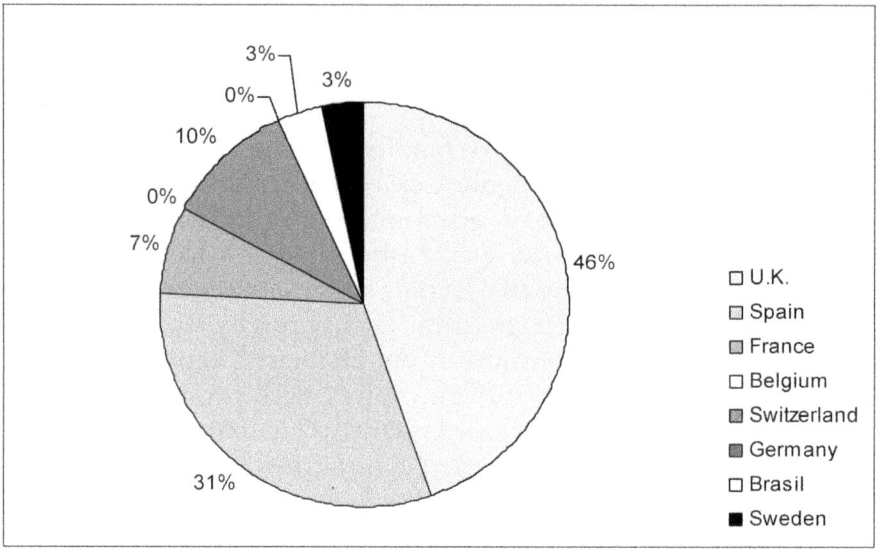

archives of the Portuguese Ministry of Public Works are a reliable source for data regarding the enterprises seeking authorisation from 1867 onwards. This paper explores this source for assessing the role of portfolio investment. Most was of British origin, as Figure 1 shows.

Some of these companies were multinational firms registered abroad that decided to open a branch in Portugal. Others were what Mira Wilkins calls 'free-standing companies'.[22] They were founded as joint-stock limited-liability companies purposely registered abroad to conduct business in Portugal, were legally independent and ruled by a board of directors. The stockholders purchased shares because the companies were presented as very attractive and generated confidence. Free-standing companies operated directly in the country, usually in a single economic sector. Vieira describes how British companies of this kind came to Portugal to operate in urban and suburban transport and to build railways during the second half of the nineteenth century.[23] There is no other available study comparable to Vieira[24] related to railway businesses during the 1890s and the early twentieth century up to the First World War, but the reason why these companies had this free-standing profile is because they needed capital to bring together profitable or potentially profitable businesses, although very often the prospectus of the companies might cloak this reality and the expected returns did not materialise. Most of the free-standing companies were short-lived. European investors looked for good investment opportunities, and few really appreciated the huge difficulties in managing distant businesses. Failures were very frequent in free-standing companies everywhere, and Portuguese railway building was no exception.

The following sections describe the presence of foreign private-portfolio investment in the Portuguese realms of insurance, mining, shipping, banks, telegraphs and telephones, water and gas provision, colonial business and other industrial activities. A difficult question is the possible doubt as to whether the announced capital was actually realized, but no information is available case by case. The approval of the application and granting of the licence to a company usually took a calendar year.

Some joint-stock companies were devoted to mining, a very risky sector. Their headquarters were abroad as well as their boards of directors. The Iron and Coal Company Limited had its home office in London and came to Portugal to operate ten mines for iron and coal in the Portuguese region of Leiria, which had been granted to George Croft. The Oporto Mining Company Limited was founded in London and was authorised in 1865 to run a lead mine near Oporto.

Some of the banks were binational, such as the London and Brazilian Bank Limited (or London, Brazilian & Maná Bank, the name prevailing at least until 1866). Its seat was in London and it was authorised to open local branches in 1863; it was renamed the New London and Brazilian Bank Limited in 1872. The Brazilian and Portuguese Bank Limited in London was also doing business in Lisbon and Oporto. Although foreign banking had no role comparable to that described by Lennart Schön for foreign banking in Sweden, capital applied in banking was much more substantial than that in mining (equity amounted to about £100,000 in mining companies and to £1 million in banks).[25] From the 1890s the most successful was the Crédit Franco-Portugais, which was linked to the French Crédit Lyonnais and still exists today under the name of Crédit Lyonnais Portugal.

Figure 2: Distribution of the number of Companies by sectors of activity (1867–1875)

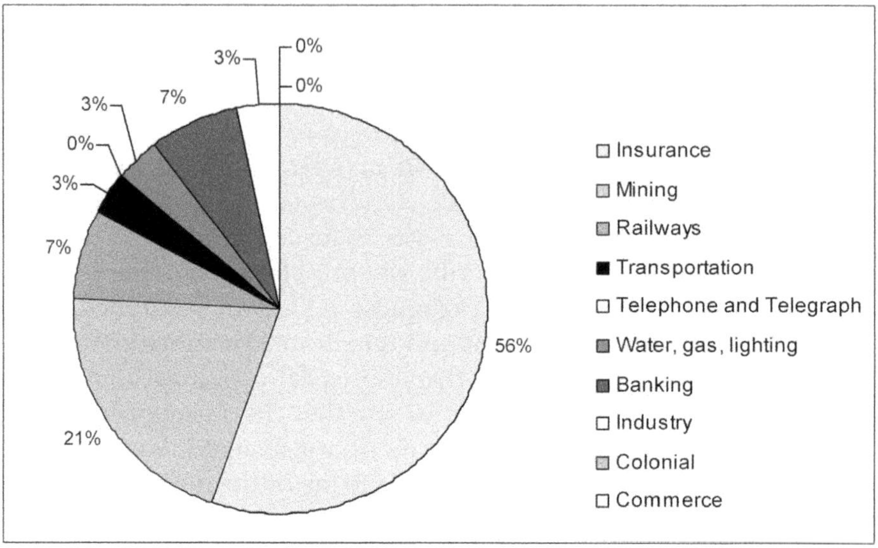

Shipping was another sector with bi-national companies. Evidence shows that during the 1850s and 1860s foreign capital was gaining an increasingly significant role in the Portuguese market. Compared with the long-established business traditions of British families in the port-wine export business since the eighteenth century, association of capital into formalised joint-stock limited-liability companies represented a higher sophistication of foreign capital for business in Portugal and strengthened relationships between Portuguese markets and foreign countries.

Until the 1870s insurance and mining were the preferred sectors, as Figure 2 highlights by indicating the number of companies in each sector: from the 1890s to the First World War favoured sectors also included water, gas or electricity provision, cork products, metallurgy and colonial business. Most insurance firms were branches of multinational companies. It is fair to say that insurance was a well-established corporate sector in most developed European countries. The search for larger international markets for their activities in order to profit from economies of scale was the main motive in bringing these companies to a small and less developed country such as Portugal. They could profit from the particularly privileged geographical position of the country on the sea routes from northern Europe to the Mediterranean countries, between the New World and Europe and between Africa or Asia and the old continent.

The first insurance companies to ask permission to come to Portugal were Spanish, going into business very early (1868). The Companhia el Fenix Español, based in Madrid for life, maritime and fire insurance, began business in Lisbon under the management of a wealthy Portuguese merchant Adolpho de Lima Mayer, and continued from the mid-1870s under the title Lima Mayer & Filhos. The Companhia de Seguros La Española from Madrid operated in Lisbon and Krus & Company was their representative; they had an office in Tenerife and say in their application to the Portuguese Ministry of Public Works that 'this company already has a lengthy history of operations in Portugal'. Krus was also the agent in Lisbon for the Companhia la Aseguradora which was based in Barcelona and operated only in maritime insurance. Two more Spanish maritime insurance companies began their business in Lisbon. La Companhia Catalana General de Seguros from Barcelona was from 1868 represented by Julio Possolo Hogan & Company. It was a short-lived company, as it was liquidated in 1879. Another short-lived insurance company from Barcelona, El Cabotage represented by João Baptista, also came to Portugal in 1868, but finished its activity in the country at the end of 1870.[26]

The British insurance companies arrived soon thereafter, choosing British firms with business in Lisbon as their agents in Portugal. The British and Foreign Marine Insurance Company Limited, the largest of all (with equity amounting to £1 million) was based in Liverpool and operated in Lisbon: Garland Laidley & Co. was their representative in Portugal. The Queen (with equity amounting to £500,000) was based in Liverpool, and Custance Son & Kendall ran their business in Lisbon. From 1874 on another £1-million equity company, the London and Lancashire Fire Insurance Company, also came to Portugal; Thomas Creswell represented it in Lisbon. In 1878 the Marine Insurance Company opened an office in Oporto, and in the same year the London and Southwark Insurance Company Limited opened an office in the Portuguese capital.

From England the Norwich Union fire office, administered in Lisbon by Abel Dagge & Company, had its home office in Norwich. The French L'Atlantique, from the Havre, with fr.1 million equity, operated in Lisbon and Oporto. Lima Mayer and Domingos Ribeiro dos Santos Junior were their agents, respectively.

The Schweiz, for transport insurance, from Zurich, had equity amounting to 5 million francs: Ernesto George was its operator in Lisbon. With a similar equity and role, Jeronymo Bobone ran the Swiss Neuchateloise from Neuchatel, while Lloyd from Winterthur was offering transport insurance under Wilhelm Dalheuer's management in Lisbon from 1873 on, with similar equity. Whise Dahl & Company represented the Swedish Neptunus from Stockholm for shipping insurance.

The German Magdeburger Allgemeine Versicherungs-Actien-Gesellschaft came in 1879, as well as the British Maritime Insurance Company Limited from Liverpool. In the next year Lisbon received an office of The Lion Fire Insurance Company Limited which had offices in London and Paris. Later on, the French La France Maritime also obtained authorisation to come to Portugal. For the insurance sector's share of total Portuguese business see Figure 3.

In mining corporate capital was entirely devoted to the activity in Portugal. A legal constraint of the law of 22 June1867 required proof that applicant companies were operational before coming to work in Portugal, in order to avoid fictitious firms. However, though each company was founded precisely to do business only in Portugal, the Portuguese Ministry of Public Works considered the authorisation necessary because 'after having been organised, it asks authorisation to work in this country where most of its operations are, according to its statutes'.[27] Drawing on its extensive experience in mineral exploitation since the beginning of the industrial revolution and resultant advanced technological knowledge and high engineering profile (as Figure 3 shows) a well-developed Europe could afford the move into a small and underdeveloped country such as Portugal. The Serrinha Tin Company Limited from London was established in Oporto under Maximiliano Shreck's direction. The British Marinha Grande Charcoal Ironworks Mining Company Limited opened an office in Lisbon in 1874 under William

Figure 3: Distribution of the number of Companies by sectors of activity (1867–1914)

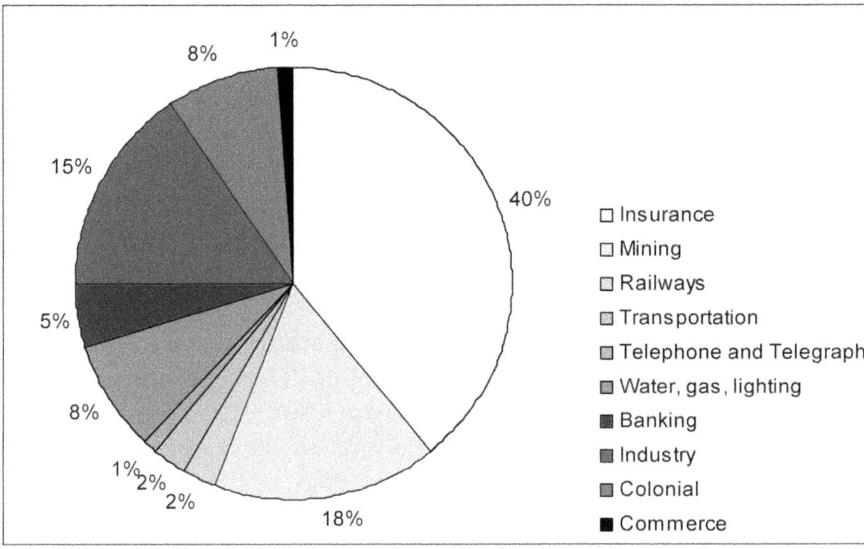

Medlicot's direction to work the Marinha Grande mine in the centre of the country. The Spanish Sociedade Mineira La Sabina preferred to work the mine of S. Domingos near Mértola from 1874 on, which was close to its headquarters in Huelva, but by 1880 the mine belonged to Mason & Barry Limited from London. The French Sociedade de Exploração de Minas em Portugal founded in Paris in 1874, was run by João Baptista Scola and Ferdinand Dietzch. The British Guadiana Company Limited opened an office at Lisbon in 1875 to work the Caveira mines (as well as some other Spanish mines near Huelva), bringing Francis George Claudet as administrator from London to Portugal. The San Thiago Iron Company Limited was founded in London in 1877 to work the iron mines of the southern Portuguese region of Alentejo. The Lusitanian Mining Company Limited came from London to work the mine of Palhal from 1879 on.

The only industrial company coming to Portugal about this period (1877) was the Spanish Sociedade Anonima Espanhola da Pólvora e Dinamite from Bilbao. A Brazilian company, the Companhia de Carris de Ferro de Lisboa, preferred urban transport business, operating the Lisbon tramways with a £45,000 capital base up to 1890, increasing to £200,000 due to electrification and company expansion. Brazil maintained strong relationships with Portugal: the ex-Portuguese colony had been independent since 1822 but cultural links remained very strong, including the use of the same language. Economic links were also very strong, including trade, emigration and regular capital transfers. This company is an example of successful diversification: founded in Rio de Janeiro in 1872 to institute a horse-drawn service in Lisbon in 1873, it was reorganised and re-founded in Lisbon in 1888 and obtained the monopoly of urban transport in the Portuguese capital in 1892 through a contract with the Municipality on very favourable terms. Before the end of the century the company was operating a 64-km network, and introduced electrical tramways from 1901.[28]

At this time, water provision was the business chosen by only one small British firm, the Oporto Waterworks Company Limited (represented in that city by A.M. Kopke de Carvalho). It is very interesting to remark that industry did not attract foreign companies to Portugal. With the exception of the gunpowder production only a cork-industry company came, the London and Lisbon Cork Industry Company Limited, operated in Lisbon by Henrique Mitchell, with £100,000 in capital.

Failures were frequent, as was the case in other small host countries. A well-known failure, The Lisbon Steam Tramways Company Limited, formed to build a Larmanjat railway system from Lisbon to Sintra, was founded in London in 1871 under the Portuguese Duke of Saldanha's patronage: it has been thoroughly studied in Vieira.[29] But it was only a case of speculative business, as its agent in Lisbon, E. Pinto Basto & Company, never laid any rails at all. Further speculative business occurred with the Spanish firm Sociedade Alcobenda & Company, which opened an office in Lisbon in 1882 under the name Construtora Hispano-Portugueza. The company advertised in Portuguese newspapers fixed interest rates from 12 to 18% or even 24%, guaranteed by land and capital. As it was not a joint-stock company, the Portuguese government could only forbid its business because of the exclusive rights previously given to the Banco de Portugal to establish savings banks in the country. In the banking sector another case occurred with the Banco Popular Espanõl, which obtained authorisation to do business in Portugal but never opened any office in the country.

Using the discretionary power in the law on joint-stock companies passed by the Portuguese Parliament, the Portuguese government refused authorisation to the French insurance company La Centrale to operate in Portugal in 1882. This company had been based in Paris since 1863. Permission was denied because its statutes did not allow for the possibility of establishing business abroad, and French authorities could use this fact as an argument to ignore any Portuguese diplomatic claim against the company. The company was founded in Paris and maintained offices in Italy from 1866 and in Spain from 1880.[30]

Despite these failures, many corporate companies were normal business cases achieving commercial success in Portugal. In the Stock Exchange Official Intelligence of 1908 fourteen nineteenth-century foreign companies are quoted, a fact that proves a strong rate of survival.[31] It is even surprising that the rise in the number of foreign joint-stock companies was greater than that enjoyed by Portuguese firms during the 1870s both in absolute and in relative terms. At the time of the law on foreign corporations (1867) there were 115 Portuguese joint-stock companies on the Portuguese mainland (and two more in the islands) and four foreign joint-stock companies. Ten years later, in 1877, 135 Portuguese joint-stock companies had begun new business (and one more in the islands) while the number of new foreign joint-stock companies now amounted to 29: the Portuguese had gained 20 (17% rise) and foreigners 25 (620% rise).

This means that the corporate economy in Portugal was being pushed from the outside, if one remembers that total investment was proportional to the numbers of companies, be they national or international. In fact, entrepreneurial initiatives to create new companies were predominantly from abroad. Great Britain, Spain and Switzerland were the leaders among the countries of origin, followed by France, Sweden and Brazil.

Diversifying into modern sectors from diversified countries of origin

During the 1880s foreign companies diversified into modern sectors and preferred telegraphs, telephones or gas and water provision. If one seeks to explain the determinants of capital inflow, it will be necessary to say that although a small economy has a weak pulling power, these were new economic sectors using modern technologies not available in Portugal at that time.

The Edison-Gower-Bell Telephone Company of Europe Limited was authorised in 1884 to install and operate telephone networks. The American British and Continental Cable Company Limited from London obtained immediate authorisation from the Portuguese government to lay the communication cable from Lisbon to the Azores and from there to America.[32] The Saint Michael Gas Company Limited was created to provide light to the city of Ponta Delgada in the Portuguese Atlantic island of S. Miguel (Azores) in 1886.[33] In the next year the British engineer Jonathan Ireland founded the Gas and Light Company of Portugal Limited in London to supply Portuguese cities in general particularly Vila Real de Santo António.

The Anglo-Portuguese Gas and Water Company Limited was established in London in the same year and obtained its licence to do business in the country providing gas and water to Portuguese cities, particularly to Figueira da Foz, under monopolistic conditions. The British engineer Frederic Briffault, living in Figueira da Foz, was the chairman of this company in Portugal.[34] Another British firm, the Anglo-Portuguese Telephone Company, was set up in London in 1887 to provide telephones and telegraphs in the country.[35] The Société Anonyme de l'Éclairage du Centre from Brussels was also authorised to do business in Portugal in the same year.

Of course, a few other companies preferred the more traditional and established sectors of insurance and mining. In mining, the British Barancannes Copper Mining Company Limited was based in London and received authorisation to work the Portuguese mine of Barancannes near Almodôvar under the governorship of Joseph Garland, who lived in Almodôvar. The Palhal Mining Company Limited was created in Glasgow in 1883 and began working the lead mine of Palhal in 1884, a business previously run by the Lusitanian Mining Company Limited. The British Lixa Mining Company was authorised in 1888 to operate mines in the environs of Lixa. The Tinoca, from Glasgow, obtained a similar authorisation for mining in the same year.

In the insurance sector the Commercial Union Assurance Company Limited, working in London since 1862, obtained authorisation in 1886 to do business in Portugal in life, fire and transport insurance. Francis Curteis Rawes, a British merchant living in Oporto, was its agent in Portugal.[36] The office of the insurance company opened in Oporto. From Paris, L'Urbaine opened an office in Lisbon for life insurance in 1883 and for fire in 1885. Two years later the Northern Assurance Company from London also received authorisation to come to Portugal.[37] From Hamburg the Nord-Deutsche Versicherungsgesellschaft was authorised in 1888 to run their insurance business in Portugal. In the same way, the Swiss transport-insurance company Federal, with home office in Zurich, was authorised to operate in Portugal in 1889 for 50 years: Sousa Lara & Company, whose business was mainly concentrated in the Portuguese colony of Angola, represented the company in Lisbon.[38]

Although foreign businesses also penetrated small countries' colonial empires because colonial businesses were flourishing at this time, this is not the subject of this chapter. We may remark, however, that Africa was becoming a coveted continent for all European countries, particularly after the Berlin Conference.

To sum up, there was a clear diversification. From three basic sectors, insurance, railways and mining, firms spread to new and sophisticated sectors including telegraphs, telephones, water, gas and electricity provision as well as urban transport. Most of these required modern technologies and engineering skills: Britain was the world leader in inventions and patents, while the splendid engineering schools in France and Germany were the envy of the world.

Spanish corporate firms were very numerous, but English companies were the largest and most powerful. French, Belgian, Swiss

Figure 4: Distribution of the number of Companies by countries of origin (1867–1914)

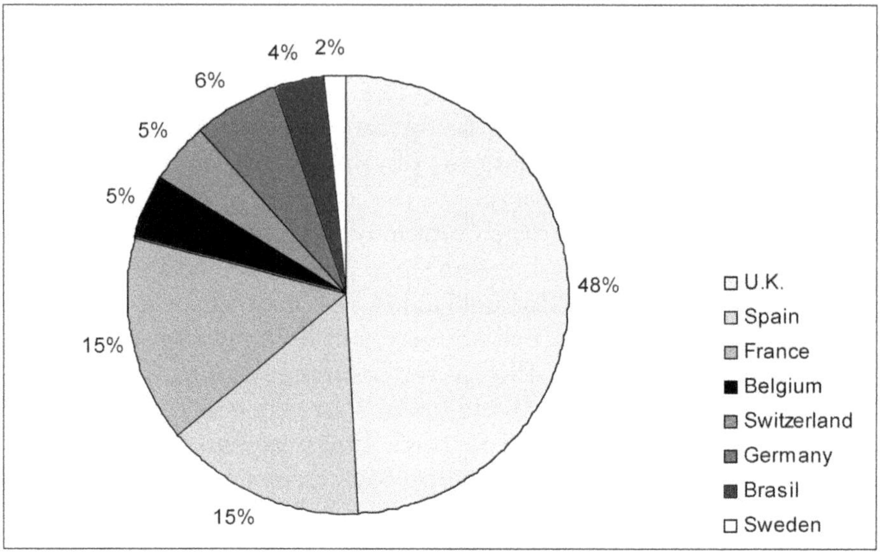

and German affiliations were also present in Portugal, but on a more modest scale (Figure 4). Geographical proximity to Spain, the only neighbour of Portugal, can explain why Spanish firms undertook the enlargement of their markets to the whole Iberian Peninsula, as economic relations had always been conspicuous, particularly throughout the border regions of northern and eastern Portugal. Good political relationships between the two countries reinforced these economic ties, although the plan for a political union under the single crown of Fernando II failed.

However, the role performed by Great Britain in globalisation explains the larger number (and greater importance) of British joint-stock companies in foreign countries. This is the case, moreover, in small countries having good relationships with the British Isles: one might consider the traditional commercial relationships between Portugal and England dating back to the Middle Ages which were accompanied by good political relations between the two countries under successive diplomatic alliances through the centuries. In the 1850s the two royal families had close family ties: Maria, the Portuguese queen, married Fernando of Saxe-Coburg, becoming a very close friend of Queen Victoria. Their long and detailed letters telling of their children, feelings and political concerns, regularly exchanged on a monthly or even weekly basis illustrate the excellent relationship between the two thrones which was echoed by the two countries' businesses.[39] These friendly political relationships persisted into the second half of the nineteenth century, and were only impaired in 1890 due to the political competition in defining colonial borders in Africa. The British Ultimatum gave rise to anti-British feelings among the Portuguese people, particularly in Lisbon, where the British consulate was stormed by a mob,[40] and also in Oporto where the Liga do Norte movement inveighed against British citizens living in Portugal.[41]

These events might indicate discouraging conditions for British companies working in Portugal, but it is difficult to assess their impact on the history and success of British firms. However, a complaint to Her Majesty's Minister in Lisbon from the Anglo-Portuguese Telephone Company is perhaps revealing. The complaint described ill will and persecution on the part of the Municipality of Lisbon, obliging the company to replace all the telephone cables hanging from the walls of the houses because they damaged private property. Predictably the company feared the costs involved in posts, labour and time to move them.

Despite these problems in Anglo-Portuguese diplomatic and political relationships, the British firms working in Portugal continued under the juridical background established in the law passed in 1867 for all foreign companies. No effects can be observed from the 1890 events in terms of British corporations coming out to Portugal, either in that year or in those that followed. In 1890 among eight foreign joint-stock companies authorised two were British, Henry Bucknall & Sons[42] and the Cork Company. Cork was a very important material, particularly since at this date artificial substitutes for it were still to be found. Portugal was (and is) one of the few world producers, along with Spain and Greece (the main Mediterranean European countries with a climate fit for cork trees).

Of the other six foreign companies three were French, two were German and one was Belgian.[43] Le Phénix from Paris[44] and La Nationale were devoted to the insurance business. The Parisian industrial company founded by Émile Roulet, Sociedade Geral Franceza de Conservas Alimentícias[45] came to Portugal to can sardines in olive oil. It used the currently available technology and enlarged its equity from 500,000 to 1,200,000 francs in order to operate in Portugal and on the Istrian coast. The main reason for the choice of the Portuguese and Istrian coasts was the lack of raw material along French coasts, due to the unpredictability of the sea routes of sardine schools. The Deutsche Lloyd Transportversicherungs-Actiengesellschaft from Berlin, existing since 1870, came to Portugal,[46] as well as the Preussische National Versicherungsgesellschaft from Stettin. They were both insurance companies. At last, a mining company founded in Brussels (although having its main office in Paris), the Sociedade Geral de Minas de Estanho de Bragança, with Portuguese, Belgian and French capital, was also authorised to work the mines of Bragança in Portugal for 30 years, an earlier company with those rights, the Sociedade Belga-Portuguesa Arrendatária das Minas de Bragança, having gone into liquidation.

The pattern of the foreign companies coming to operate in Portugal did not change in the 1890s. Among the traditional sectors, many insurance companies added their business to the other companies operating in Portugal. Good examples are Wilhelma from Magdeburg, the Alliance Insurance Company from London,[47] the Badische Schiffahrts-Assekuranz-Gesellschaft from Mannheim,[48] the Lloyd Bavaro from Munich,[49] L'Union Maritime from Paris, the British Palatina Insurance Company, Limited[50] and the Nouveau Lloyd Suisse from Winterthur.[51]

During the second half of the 1890s the Credit Franco-Portugais began managing exchange and banking operations in Lisbon, linked to the French Crédit Lyonnais, which proved successful.

The European and Azores Telegraph Company, Limited proposed to operate the telegraph business.[52] The Parisian Sociedade Torlades was accepted for commercial, industrial and financial operations, excepting discount and deposits.[53] As usual, only a small number of foreign industrial companies decided to operate in Portugal. Timothy L. Alborn suggests that 'most successful Victorian companies were in sectors like financial service, or transport and utilities'.[54] This fact may perhaps explain the larger presence of British companies working in these sectors in Portugal. Wilkin's theory on clusters seems to apply to the Portuguese case only in manufacturing, tropical colonial foodstuffs and cork. Distillation and sugar refining brought small companies and French technology: La Raffinerie Privilegiée du Portugal was founded in Brussels and in 1896 obtained a monopoly to refine sugar in Portugal. The Robinson Bros. Cork Growers, Limited came to process cork.

In the twentieth century before the First World War private flows of capital continued coming to Portugal. Two Brazilian companies based in Rio de Janeiro obtained authorisation for insurance business in Portugal: the Companhia Sul Americana and the Companhia de Seguros Marítimos e Terrestres 'Mercúrio'. For shipping and transport insurance La Marine Marchande was founded in the Havre. This company included Portuguese capital, particularly from the Azores-Lisbon firm Bensaúde & C°. The presence of Portuguese names in some companies mean that there was a participation of Portuguese capital in the business, but also a need for foreign partners to run it.

Technological innovation coming to Portuguese industry from foreign industrial companies can hardly be considered to be very significant, even though the country did not have a notable industrial tradition.[55] Foreign joint-stock companies came in a small number (13) to industry and preferred two specific labour-intensive industrial sectors, cork and canned fish, because of comparative advantages – exceptional raw material conditions together with abundant cheap labour. Portugal's abundant resources in cork, fish and olive oil can explain this foreign migration to Portugal, rather than any perceived need for commercial expansion or internationalisation in these sectors. It is possible to suggest a horizontal technology transfer in the introduction of the boiling-steam machine to replace the intensive male labour force in the cork industry: but in fish canning the boiling technology coupled with soldered tin cans and a female labour force were already the rule. Sometimes expertise was a relevant point. It seems to be the case with the British firm Baldwins, Limited, who came to Portugal for mining, smelting and amalgamation. Alfred Baldwin, an English MP,[56] founded this company with three steel-producers.[57]

The impact of foreign capital on the Portuguese economy

Foreign capital and emigrants' remittances played a decisive role in the Portuguese economy because of the seemingly permanent trade-balance deficits of the period. From 1850 to 1890, Portugal's accumulated trade deficits amounted to £44 million according to Lains,[58] and £80 million according to official data.

It is difficult to estimate foreign private investment. As less than 100% of sums invested actually reached Portugal (particularly in fields where free-standing companies did not dominate), a rough estimate may depart from Hobson. On showing that for all European countries together the British new capital publicly issued was about £200 million, Hobson attributes to Portugal some £8.136 million,[59] giving Portugal as much as France and a good deal more than Germany:

Table 2: Destination of British new capital publicly issued (Amounts in £)

Italy	12,440,000
Portugal	8,136,000
France	8,020,000
Germany	6,364,000

Source: Hobson, 'British overseas investments', p. 30.

Cramon is less optimistic over Portugal in his computation of British real amounts going abroad, but even disregarding Portuguese-issued external bonds and considering only corporate stocks and miscellaneous investments (except for railways), he concluded that mainland Portugal received accumulated direct private British investments amounting to £5 million with a £6.5 million market value.[60]

Sir George Paish[61] estimated[62] an annual British investment amounting to £100,000,[63] and his estimates were widely accepted and often repeated. Platt remarks: 'Paish's figures [...] are to be found behind nearly every stock figure for Britain's investments overseas (portfolio and direct) at the outbreak of the First World War.'[64] These data do not include investment in Portuguese colonies.

To sum up, foreign investment in Portuguese government bonds amounted to £40.769 million, in railways to £12.9 million and British investments in corporations, mines and miscellaneous undertakings to at least £6.5 million. According to Paish from the end of the century to the First World War a further £100,000 arrived from Britain annually (giving a total of £1.4 million). This does not include non-British foreign investment in sectors other than railways. A similar amount of £7.9 million (6.5 plus 1.4) can be postulated if we assume that non-British companies invested in the same proportion as the British (52% of the companies were non-British). For this estimate it is enough to remember that in this period the average per company did not depend on nationality. If Mark Casson[65] is right in his control theory, equity exercised control over foreign operations, and 'If such a control existed, then the statistics of [...] foreign investment should clearly be revised upwards' to more than £70 million in order to include the free-standing companies' equity as direct investment.[66]

Of course, repatriation of interest and wages may have made the net inflows of capital very small. Even so, globalisation effects were powerful because of technology spillovers. Perhaps a certain proportion of 'foreign investment' was actually domestic in the sense that it was amassed in Portugal, was remitted abroad and then returned as 'foreign': but in any case, if it was remitted abroad it was out of the Portuguese economy. So, any decisions to enter the Portuguese economy must be considered as foreign-portfolio investment. With joint-stock companies the accumulation of capital from small savers and its placement on international markets could supply the huge Portuguese needs for investment in most sectors. Limited liability made investment more attractive due to the limited risk involved: stock-exchange markets in the main European cities cleared the demand and supply of funds among shareholders. Internationalisation was the rule.

Considering the limited availability of savings in a small and underdeveloped country such as Portugal, the estimated average annual inflow of gross foreign capital of about £1 million was surely very significant and beneficial for compensating the permanent deficit in the trade balance. As a small country, Portugal received with foreign investment not only capital to stimulate economic growth in the globalisation context but also technical advice, technology transfer (railways and telephone technology, for example) and know-how on management and corporation culture. Cheaper transatlantic conveyance of goods and mail and access to export markets, insurance underwriters and financial institutions were made available as externalities. As economists like to say, vertical demand chains are channels of technology transfer.[67] Moreover, Portugal received corporations from a largely diversified group of European countries and from Brazil. On examining European entrepreneurial achievements, Alfred Chandler identified three European business cultures. According to him, the business culture of the Anglo-Saxon world emerged from the acceptance of inequality and the middle-class values of individualism, freedom and self-interest. The Germanic corporation developed a cultural context of co-operation, training and education. The Latin-area cultural environment seems more attuned to institutional potential. More recently Kalthoff *et al.* have added a Scandinavian corporate culture.[68] If we believe that Europe has a dense European culture, national differences in corporate culture become very relevant. Portugal tasted the entire range of business culture that the European corporate economies could afford. The USA was not yet exporting capital, technologies or cultural influences and was still receiving them from the old world, the great source of all relevant cultural influences at that time. The mixed national origin of foreign companies coming to Portugal afforded the country the benefits of plural approaches to business. Family-run firms may be regarded as typical European businesses, managed by the founder or by the entire family in a consensual way. Free-standing companies usually had decentralised leadership with prominent local Portuguese directors. The most successful firms needed to hold fast to firm political strategies and long-run goals, as well as maintain good relationships with central and local political authorities. In a certain way, the role of the State in defining the general legal framework and in imposing regulations gave rise to a close relationship between it and foreign companies working in Portugal. They depended on government authorisation to run their businesses and were very often facilitated thereby in decisive ways.

The principle of association of capital took on a number of faces: innovation is essentially creative and rational. For most of the companies, their coming to Portugal was itself an innovation, as they could achieve the aims of the firm in a different way by enlarging their geographical operations and by profiting from scale economies and interactions with a different society. They also spread the fundamental idea that a business needs a vision, a pre-understanding of market opportunities to raise money on the stock exchange, as well as a capacity for action, for putting information together. Domestic companies worked sometimes as agents for foreign companies (a good example is the shipping sector). Each company is a conceptualisation of an ideal following a meticulous reflection on opportunities. Insurance followed mainly the scheme of a multinational firm getting subsidiaries or affiliates, whilst railways, mining and colonial businesses followed the free-standing company model. All of these models were instrumental in satisfying investors' search for superior returns, and were attuned to the realisation of the social values included in the pre-World War I vision for business.

Conclusion

In a small peripheral economy such as Portugal nineteenth-century globalisation brought the ideal of achievement as a driving factor into material progress. Greater capital availability coupled with emigration made possible increasing labour productivity. Dreams and projects to emulate the core European businesses animated the Portuguese intelligentsia and the political parties of the day. Pragmatism and fascination for modernity were hallmarks of the epoch in Portugal.

Before 1892 a freer trade policy also eased competition, increasing the integration of Portugal into the nineteenth-century global market. A real free-trade policy would only be put in place during the prosperity of the post-Second World War years – in the 1960s when Portugal joined the EFTA and more recently with Portugal's entry to the EEC. In a long-term perspective this is, however, a recent push towards globalisation, as significant flows of labour and capital in the past, particularly before the First World War, had already provided strong ties with the core European countries. The implementation of these ties led Portugal into fifteenth place in the ranking of the most globalised countries in 2000, according to some globalisation indexes.[69]

1 Universidade Nova de Lisboa, Faculdade de Economia, Campus de Campolide, 1099-032 LISBOA. memata@fe.unl.pt.
I am grateful to the Portuguese *Fundação para a Ciência e a Tecnologia* and the *PRAXIS XXI* Programme for their financial support for travelling to European archives for the research. I thank the EUSSIRF programme for a visit to the BLPES. I thank Bruno Fritzsch, Lars Svenson, Jaime Reis, Pedro Lains, Nuno Valério, Maria Ioanis Baganha, Joaquim da Costa Leite and Jorge Alves for discussion in this issue. I thank the staff of the Archive of the Portuguese Ministry of Public Works for the assistance I received. I thank Dr. John Huffstot and David Edmonds for helping with the English. Errors, omissions or faulty interpretations are my own.
2 José Maria Brandão Brito, *A industrialização portuguesa no pós-guerra (1948–1965): o condicionamento industrial* (Lisboa: Dom Quixote, 1989).
3 Paula Fontoura and Nuno Valério, 'Foreign economic relations and economic growth in Portugal, 1840s–1980s: a long-term view', *Economies et sociétés*, 3 (2000), pp. 175–206.
4 José Maria Brandão Brito, 'The Portuguese response to the Marshall Plan', *Estudos de Economia* 10/4 (1990).
5 D.C.M. Platt, *Britain's investment overseas on the eve of the First World War: The use and abuse of numbers* (London: Macmillan, 1986).
6 Irving Stone, *The global export of capital from Great Britain, 1865–1914* (New York: McMillan Press, 1999).
7 Maria Eugénia Mata, *As finanças públicas Portuguesas da Regeneração à Primeira Guerra Mundial* (Lisboa: Banco de Portugal, 1993).
8 António Lopes Vieira, 'Investimentos Britânicos nos transportes urbanos e suburbanos em Portugal na segunda metade do século XIX: Fracasso e sucesso. A Lisbon Tramways Co. e a Lisbon Electric Tramways Co.', *Revista de História Económica e Social* 7 (1981), 81.
9 Jaime Reis, 'The historical roots of the modern Portuguese economy, the first century of growth 1850s to 1950s', in Richard Herr, *The new Portugal: democracy and Europe* (Berkeley: University of California, 1993), p. 129.
10 Kevin O'Rourke and Jeffrey Williamson, 'When Did Globalisation Begin?', *European Review of Economic History* 6 (April 2002); Kevin O'Rourke and Jeffrey Williamson, 'Once More, When Did Globalisation Begin?', *European Review of Economic History* 8 (April 2004).
11 Vieira, 'Investimentos Britânicos'.

12 António Lopes Vieira, *The role of Britain and France in the finance of the Portuguese railways 1845–1890. A comparative study in speculation, corruption and inefficiency*, PhD dissertation, University of Leicester, 1983.
13 Ibid.
14 Mata, *As finanças públicas*, pp. 210–215, 238–245, 249–250, 259–262.
15 Mata, *As finanças públicas*.
16 Annuario Commercial de Portugal, 1914.
17 Paul Duguid and Teresa da Silva Lopes, 'Ambiguous Company: Institutions and organisation in the Port wine trade, 1814–1834', *Scandinavian Economic History Review* 47/1 (1999), pp. 84–102.
18 Teresa da Silva Lopes, 'Brands and the evolution of multinationals in alcoholic beverages', *Business History* 44: 3 (2002), pp. 1–30.
19 Jean-François Hennart, 'Transaction-cost theory', in Wilkins and Schröter (eds.), *The free-standing company in the world economy, 1830–1996* (Oxford, New York: Oxford University Press, 1998), p. 76.
20 Maria Eugénia Mata, 'Sociedades anónimas: regulação e economia', *Boletim de Ciências Económicas* (1998), pp. 3–26.
21 Timothy L. Alborn, *Conceiving companies: Joint-stock politics in Victorian England,* (London and New York: Routledge, Explorations in Economic History, 1998), p. 3.
22 Mira Wilkins, 'The free-standing company 1870–1914: an important type of British foreign investment', *Economic History Review*, 41/2 (1988), pp. 259–282. See also Mira Wilkins and Harm Schröter (eds.), '*The free-standing company*'.
23 Vieira, 'Investimentos Britânicos'; Vieira, *The role of Britain and France*.
24 Vieira, *The role of Britain and France*.
25 Lennart Schön, *Wage Formation, Labour Market Institutions and Economic Transformation in Sweden 1860–2000*, Lund/Stockholm: Dept. of Economic History, Lund University/Almqvist & Wiksell International, 2004.
26 This company was founded in 1858 in Barcelona and continued for a quarter of a century.
27 Quoted from the decision of the Portuguese Ministry of Public Works on The Guadiana Company, Limited to work in Portugal. (Archive of the Portuguese Ministry of Public Works DGCI-RCI-1-S-*caixa* 2).
28 Vieira, *The role of Britain and France*.
29 Vieira, 'Investimentos Britânicos'; Vieira, *The role of Britain and France*.
30 The application to open an office in Portugal was submitted on 29 November 1881 (Archive of the Portuguese Ministry of Public Works, DGCI-RCI-1-S-*S.A. estrangeiras, caixa* 1).
31 Vol. XXVI, HG 4577 at BLPES, London, pp. 396, 1123, 1172, 1173, 1187, 1268, 1354, 1363, 1584, 1665, 1741, 1779.
32 *Diário do Governo*, 31-5-1884. The statutes were registered in Somerset House on 1 December 1883, when six British gentlemen and the French Count Alfred Xavier de La Chapelle founded the company in London. Simon Charles Hadley was the director of the company in London and Caetano Augusto de Sousa Carvalho (a merchant) his representative in Lisbon.

33 Decree 5-2-1886.
34 The directors were Robert Laidlaw and Herbert Percy Mundey, aided by John Milton Smith. The Public Record Office preserves the claims of the Company against Portuguese duties in 1889 (F. O. 63-1213, F.O. 63-1214, F.O. 63-1220).
35 Decree 3-1-2-1887.
36 The company was founded on 3 November 1862 according to the Act 748 Victoria c. 110, but became a joint-stock company on 8 August 1885.
37 Decree 10-2-1887.
38 Gervase Clarence Smith, *The Third Portuguese Colonial Empire*, pp. 127–134. This Swiss insurance company had equity amounting to fr. 5,000,000.
39 Ruben Andersen Leitão, *Novos documentos dos Arquivos de Windsor*, *Coimbra* (Coimbra Editora Lda, 1958).
40 This riot is documented in F. O. 63-1222, Public Record Office. The British consul in Lisbon reported this assault on the British Consulate at Lisbon in Rua de Santa Martha 94 to Her Majesty's Minister on 13 Jan. 1890. He wrote: 'Sir, I have the honour to report to you that last night about 9 o'clock, the British Consulate was surrounded by a numerous mob who pelted the windows with large stones breaking every pane of glass as well as part of the frame-work. The Coat of Arms was wrenched off from its place and dragged through the streets. The small force of police are at present guarding the Consulate, but as all the windows are broken, the shutters are being closed and a large number of people still about the building, and fearing fresh demonstrations of a similar nature. I have resolved to keep the office closed for the day, pending your instructions. C. O'Donnell'.
41 The British consul at Oporto reported to Her Majesty's Minister G. Petre in Lisbon the fears of British ladies to walk the streets of Oporto and told of a particular case concerning a lady: 'This lady was in a tram-car full of people when one of the mules fell. Upon which a passenger dressed like a gentleman said looking hard at the English lady: "Esta mula é uma ingleza: Todas as inglezas são mulas" [This mule is English, all English ladies are mules]. From a Portuguese with the habitual courtesy and *retenu* of the Portuguese – nothing could be more gross and insulting than these words, yet they elicited not a murmur of disapproval from the other passengers' (F. O. 63-1222, Public Record Office). The British consul at Oporto also referred to a letter of protest from the English Colonel Sandeman, as well as other cases published in *The Times*.
42 *Diário do Governo,* 29-11-1890. This company was founded expressly to come to Spain and Portugal to trade in cork and process it there and in England, using the necessary technological equipment. The equity of the company amounted to £1,000,000.
43 Maria Cristina Lourenço Cardoso, 'Investisseurs et investissements Belges au Portugal 1884–1914', in Michel Dumoulin and Eddy Stadell, *La Belgique et l'étranger aux XIX et XX siècles* (Bruxelles: 1987).
44 *Diário do Governo,* 31-10-1890. This was an old company founded in 1844 for life insurance in Europe for 99 years. The equity amounted to fr.4,000,000.

45 *Diário do Governo,* 24-10-1890. Émille Louis Roullet was a merchant living in Asnières (Seine) and adjusted this company to produce, in Portugal, canned fish using the traditional brand name for the sardines of De Saintange & C° or the new one of Émille Louis Roullet & C°.

46 *Diário do Governo,* 21-7-1890. The interest of insurance companies in coming to Portugal may be related to the opportunity to insure ships and their cargoes from Lisbon to the Portuguese African colonies. At this time the Portuguese government established the rules for regulating subsidies for monthly linked shipping routes. The equity of the company amounted to DM 3,000,000.

47 *Diário do Governo* of 14-5-1892.This life and fire insurance company was founded on 4 August 1824 to work in the U.K. and abroad.

48 *Diário do Governo,* 15-12-1893. This transport-insurance company was created in 1840 with equity of £500,000 which was enlarged now to DM 4,000,000.

49 *Diário do Governo,* 15-3-1892. This transport-insurance company had equity amounting to DM 4,000,000.

50 *Diário do Governo,* 23-4-1894. The company had offices in Manchester.

51 *Diário do Governo,* 10-1-1894. This land and sea transport-insurance company was founded on 14 June 1882 for 50 years. It had equity amounting to Fr. 4,000,000 and enlarged it to Fr. 5,000,000.

52 *Diário do Governo,* 1-8-1899. Carlos Ferreira dos Santos Silva ruled this small company in Portugal (equity amounting to £200,000).

53 *Diário do Governo,* 4-8-1899. The equity of the company amounted to Fr.1,000,000.

54 Alborn, *Conceiving companies,* p. 4.

55 A good example is the Raffinerie Portugaise from Brussels, which came for sugar refining. The company bought the previous Raffinerie Privilegiée du Portugal with its factory and surrounding lands in Junqueira, as well as the monopoly rights obtained by the previous Raffinerie Privilegiée.

56 Members of Parliament and other prestigious persons could spread confidence among investors.

57 *Diário do Governo,* 5-3-1903. The three producers were John Roper Wright (Glamorganshire), Isaac Buttler (Monmouthshire) and Roger Beck (Glamorganshire), who had founded Wright Buttler & Company, Limited. The equity amounted to £850,000.

58 Pedro Lains, *A economia Portuguesa no século XIX* (Lisboa: Imprensa Nacional-Casa da Moeda, 1995).

59 C. K. Hobson, 'British overseas investments, their growth and importance', *The Annals of the American Academy* 68 (Nov. 1906).

60 Edgar Cramon, 'British investments abroad', *Quarterly Review* 412 (July 1907) (London: John Murray, 1907-CCVII), pp. 245–272.

61 George Paish, 'Great Britain's capital investments in Other Lands', *Journal of the Royal Statistical Siciety* 72/3 (Sept. 1909).

62 George Paish, 'Great Britain's capital investments in Individual Colonies and Foreign Countries', *Journal of the Royal Statistical Siciety*, 74/2 (Jan. 1911).

63 George Paish, 'The export of capital and the cost of living', *Statist*, supplement, 14 (Feb. 1914).

64 D. C. M. Platt, *Britain's investment*, p. 6.
65 'An economic theory of the free-standing company', in Wilkins and Schröter (eds.), *The free-standing company*.
66 For an underestimation of private foreign portfolio investment, 'nearly all of it in railways and banks', see Jaime Reis, 'The gold standard in Portugal, 1854–1891', in *Monetary standards in the periphery: paper, silver, and gold, 1854–1933*, edited by Pablo Martin Aceña and Jaime Reis (Macmillan, 1999), pp. 76–77.
67 Magnus Blomström and Ari Kokko, *How foreign investment affects host countries* (World Bank International Economics Dept., International Trade Division, Washington, D. C., 1997).
68 Otto Kalthoff *et al.*, *The Light and the Shadow* (Roland Berger Foundation, Capstone, 1997). In this book Kersti Ullenhag explains how management education in Sweden encouraged new management practices.
69 'Measuring globalisation', *Foreign policy*, (January/February 2001).

Anne-Lise Head-König

The Process of Globalisation in the Swiss Labour Market Viewed in the Context of Three Major Export Industries (1880–1939)

Switzerland's economic development from the 1880s until 1939 and the resulting labour-market situation are an interesting example of the effects of globalisation. One can perceive two distinct periods in this process: the first, from the 1880s up to World War I, was characterised by a considerable degree of globalisation of the labour market and an increase in the labour force; and the second, developing after World War I, was characterised by a significant reduction in the size of the foreign workforce. Foreigners were excluded more and more from the labour market as time went on. Restrictive governmental measures were a major factor in this process. This new legislation, however, cannot be ascribed only to ideological considerations; it also reflects a deterioration in Switzerland's economic situation.

Between 1880 and 1913 Switzerland underwent fundamental economic changes which had a considerable influence on its labour market. A phase of growth began in the last two decades of the nineteenth century which required an ever-increasing number of workers who, for both demographic and socio-economic reasons, were not available in sufficient numbers within in the country.

In the first place, it must be remembered that Switzerland was a country with a comparatively low birth rate. To a considerable extent this was due to restrictive State and communal policies which had exerted a significant demographic influence upon certain parts of Switzerland up to the mid-1870s and which had the effect of preventing part of the population from marrying, with the result that the Swiss birth rate was low in comparison to neighbouring countries and lower still than that of the regions immediately adjacent to Switzerland.

Also, one must take into consideration the strong tradition of emigration, mostly to countries overseas. Work preferences played an important role here, and construction work – which was essentially seasonal – and factory jobs were particularly looked down upon. Thus, a large number of the inhabitants of rural areas who lacked the necessary skills to enter the labour market at an acceptable level consistently preferred to emigrate overseas rather than to work in a factory; and this was especially the case with the male workforce.[1] The differing behaviour of the male and the female parts of the population can be clearly seen in the far higher proportion of females working in factories in 1888. In relation to the total labour force, twice as many women worked there. The main factor deterring men from working in factories were low wages combined with long working hours, because such a combination, especially in regions which were still rural, prevented male workers from supplementing their income with earnings from a secondary activity.

It can be observed, then, that in the years 1900–1910 the number of Swiss factory workers increased by only 10%, whereas that of foreigners increased by more than 40%. Economic expansion required more labour, especially in the industrial sector, and from the 1880s the number of immigrants working in industry grew rapidly and came to represent an important factor for the economic growth of the country. By 1914 there were more than half a million foreigners in Switzerland, representing as much as 14.7% of the total population, compared to only 3% in France and Germany, 3.1% in Belgium and 1.2% in the Netherlands. Even when taking into account only those foreigners born abroad, there were still 7.4% foreigners in Switzerland in 1888, 7.5% in 1900 and 9.5% in 1910.

The war and the following post-war economic crisis brought with them a significant reduction in the number of foreign workers. In the population as a whole the proportion of foreigners declined to 11.8% in 1920, 8.7% in 1930 and then to 5.2% in 1941. This was because they had been employed in what were now declining sectors of the economy, and because of other structural changes in the interwar economy. In 1920 the agricultural sector employed a quarter of the nation's workforce, and this was to decline during the interwar period to a mere fifth. But the change in foreign demand also brought with it considerable structural shifts within the workforce in manufacturing industries. Some sectors expanded because they could also rely on the demand in the home market, as was the case with the engineering and the metal-processing industries, but massive adjustments were necessary in traditional industries such as silk, embroidery and watch-making, which had always been mainly dependent on world demand. These industries, which represented a major proportion of manufacturing jobs until the end of the 1920s, either ceased to be leading sectors in the 1930s or else had to be radically reorganised, entailing the laying off of thousands of workers in times of crisis with an accompanying massive reduction in the size of the foreign workforce.

The structure of the workforce

It was characteristic of the labour market up to World War I that the expanding economy created a dual market for the foreign workforce according to qualifications.[2] On the one hand, the economy required workers with low qualifications – or none at all apart from their physical strength – for work in the construction industry and comparable areas. On the other hand, there was a labour market for highly qualified people in sectors such as higher education, medicine and the civil service, where qualified Swiss nationals were scarce. The proportion of foreigners in these sectors increased from 11% in 1888 to 17% in 1910, with a high proportion of Germans due to the language requirements.

As mentioned above, within the traditional manufacturing sector foreigners were most numerous where it was a question of factory work. The proportion of foreigners subject to the Factory Act grew steadily to nearly a quarter by World War I, but then declined to 10% in 1923 with a further reduction to 6% of the workforce in 1930. In 1937 the Italian contingent was the largest, as it had been since the end of the nineteenth century. Cotton and silk mills and the construction industry employed a large proportion of foreigners, too. In the first two foreign labour increased from 11.9% in 1901 to 23.4% in 1911, whereas Swiss workers were more numerous in the weaving industry, where hygienic conditions, wages and working hours were far better. It must not be forgotten that in the cotton industry as a whole working hours were far longer than in any other sector.[3] Depending on the specific type of production within a single sector, however, huge differences existed in the proportion of foreigners employed. In the embroidery sector as a whole the foreign workforce represented 9.9% in 1911, but, whereas Schiffli-embroidery employed 34.3% foreigners, there were only 4% engaged in mechanical hand-embroidery.

But the physical presence of foreign labour within Switzerland varied not only in relation to the relevant economic sector and its methods of production, but also from one region to another, because until World War I there had effectively been no agreed single policy, no generally accepted practice on immigration, even though a federal legal framework did exist. Consequently, it was the cantons and not the central government that took the decisions, according to the needs of the local economy. This practice contrasts very markedly with that during the interwar period when the central government intervened sharply, especially with the aim of regulating immigration according to the needs of the domestic labour market.[4]

In the interwar period massive fluctuations, which were mostly the consequences of a reduced demand for Swiss products on international markets, characterised the labour market. But adjustments to reduce the resulting imbalance varied according to nationality, age and sex. Among the Swiss workforce, especially for the younger generation, there was the option of emigration. This possibility was frequently made use of, as can be seen in the significant increase of Swiss migrants to France, there being about 30,000 more Swiss in France in 1926 than in 1923; this movement affected not only the manufacturing and services sectors but also the primary sector, with a large proportion of Swiss migrant farmers settling in southern France. Also, discriminatory measures were in existence which prevented part of the Swiss female labour force from remaining in employment when married, with the exception of certain industrial sectors where pay was low or where the mode of production allowed married women to work from home. This explains why a large proportion of female workers subject to the factory legislation and working in low-wage sectors were in fact married;

for example, in the cotton industry where 48% of women workers were married in 1901 and as many as 40% in 1937.

However, part of the adjustment to the reduced demand for labour was effected by radically reducing the foreign labour force even in the more dynamic and innovative sectors. The number of foreign workers had already decreased during the war, but new restrictive legislation created at its end made it still more difficult for foreigners to re-enter the labour market and also prevented the employment of new migrants, except in certain sectors and then only temporarily. In the years 1917 and 1931 the legislation became significantly more restrictive; and 1921 saw the creation of a new status for foreign workers, that of 'seasonal worker'. It was hoped that with this new legislation, the authorities would be able to protect the domestic labour market better: in times of economic crisis fewer foreigners were to be granted long-term work permits and instead received only seasonal permits. The next step was to reduce the number of daily frontier workers. And when these methods were inadequate, as in the 1930s when Swiss exports were priced out of many markets, the number of work-permits overall was drastically reduced. As a result, from 1931 to 1934 foreign immigration declined by 60%, and the reduction in the number of work permits in the machine and metallurgy industries gives a clear picture of the deepening economic recession (Table 1).

Table 1: Types of work permits granted in the machine and metallurgy industries (1929–1936)

	Long-term permits	*Seasonal permits*	*Permits for frontier workers*
1929	600	797	2094
1930	437	1190	1975
1931	121	1102	1457
1932	76	526	761
1933	59	356	533
1934	62	293	407
1935	64	186	300
1936	38	131	244

Source: Annual Reports of the A.S.M. (Association patronale suisse des constructeurs de machines et industriels en métallurgie).

After World War I, the reduction in the size of the foreign labour force also had a huge impact on its demographic structure, including a drastic modification in the sex ratio of this population. Whereas in 1910 there had been 94 women per 100 men, this ratio changed to 128 women per 100 men in 1920 as a result of the transformation of the labour market during and after the war. Between 1910 and 1920 the proportion of female foreign workers declined by only 9%, but that of male foreign workers by as much as 41%. In 1911 there were 73,000 foreign male workers subject to the factory legislation, but only 41,000 in 1923, whilst the number of female foreign workers had not changed.

The reduction of the foreign workforce after World War I and the following crisis had an impact, too, on the overall age structure of the workforce in the manufacturing industries. In 1930 there were more than twice as many older foreign factory workers in Switzerland than in 1910.

The shift in the export industries and its impact on the workforce

The pressing need to export characterised all leading Swiss industries at the end of the nineteenth century. Also, there was no large home market behind tariff walls that could serve as a refuge, with the result that these industries were far more vulnerable to competition than would otherwise have been the case. This is the explanation for their difficulties in the 1890s when export opportunities, for instance to France and Germany, were reduced by tariff increases. However, from the mid-1890s there was considerable expansion of the export industries, with the opening of new markets such as the Russian market for the machine industry which by 1913 equalled 88% of the exports to France and 96% of those to Germany.

But from the end of World War I the loss of foreign markets, the higher costs of production and a shift in consumer demand to other types of textile coupled with the producers' failure to develop satisfactory replacements for them, as well as a waning demand for luxury products in general, contributed to a significant increase in the Swiss overall unemployment rate, with about a third of the labour force being made redundant. The intensity and duration of this crisis and its effects on the labour market can be compared to developments in Sweden. The disastrous decline in exports at the beginning of the 1920s was aggravated even in the more dynamic and innovative sectors, such as the machine and metallurgy industries and the chemical industry, both by the depreciation of clients' currencies and by the strategy of dual prices used by some of Switzerland's main trading partners in the sale of their raw materials.[5] The consequence was a sharp increase of unemployment in the leading export trades. The subsequent adjustment to normal conditions, added to the post-war depression, proved very difficult, as can be clearly seen in the case of the canton of Neuchâtel amongst others: the rate of unemployment in its watch- and clock-making industries increased very rapidly from 4.2% in 1920 to 35.7% in 1921 – and the unemployed then represented 15.5 of the total cantonal workforce[6] – to decline to 18.3% in 1922 and 4.1% in 1923. In the Swiss machine and metallurgy industries unemployment peaked in the last quarter of 1921 and the first three months of 1922 with more than 30,000 people completely or partly out of work.[7] To stimulate exports and to reduce unemployment, the policy adopted – despite the opposition of the trade unions – was a partial reduction in working hours in some sectors as well as a general reduction in wages. These measures came into force in 1921 and 1922. But there was a failure to find a more adequate solution for what in some industries was in fact structural unemployment due to the waning demand for their products.

To be sure, between 1913 and 1930 striking changes were taking place in the six main industrial sectors that were dependent on exports. In 1913 they contributed as much as 77.4% to the total value of Swiss exports, and still 65.4% in 1930. But there was a notable shift in their respective positions (Table 2).

Three industries increased the value of their exports (watch- and clock-making by 27%, chemicals by 137% and the machine industry by 153%), whilst there was a sharp contraction in the exports of the older industries where female employment dominated: –12%

Table 2: Contribution of the six leading export industries to the total value of exports in 1913 and 1930 (in percent)

	1913	*1930*
silk industry	20,7	13,9
Embroidery	19,4	4,6
watch and clock-making	16,9	16,5
machinery and metallurgy	9,2	17,9
chemical industry	6,0	10,9
chocolate industry	5,4	1,6
Others	23,4	34,6
Total	100%	100%

Source: Annual Report of the A. S. M., 26 (1931), p. 101.

in the silk industry, –61% in chocolate and –69% in embroidery. The consequences were not only a sharp increase in unemployment, but also an irremediable loss of job opportunities in these declining sectors.

The impact of international economic fluctuations and the shift in demand were felt all the more keenly due to the regional specificity and geographical concentration that characterize Switzerland. In effect, the textile industry was predominant in the German-speaking part of the country, whilst the watch- and clock-making industries prevailed mostly in the French-speaking part, and the metal-processing and engineering industries, which were to become leading sectors in the 1930s,[8] extended throughout both the German- and the French-speaking parts of Switzerland.

Even within a single sector there could be a marked geographical specificity. This can be seen in the silk and embroidery industries, Zurich being the centre for silk-weaving, Basle and its hinterland for the schappe and the silk-ribbons industries, and Lucerne for artificial silk. Similarly, embroidery production was localised in eastern Switzerland, with its main centres in the cantons of St. Gallen, Appenzell and Thurgau, whose workforce and economy were strongly dependent on export markets.[9]

The international division of work in the traditional industries: a trend towards globalisation in production rather than in the labour market

Up to World War I it was characteristic of the traditional and labour-intensive industries (embroidery, watch- and clock-making) that even though their expansion was regional within Switzerland, national borders were in no way an impediment to a transnational division of labour within the industry.[10] Proximity also played an important part in the migration of the labour force: thus, there was an important foreign labour force in the cantons situated nearest to Germany, Italy, and France. In addition, not only the workforce but also goods could be moved relatively freely from one country to another. This was the case for some of the most important industries, such as embroidery in the eastern part of Switzerland which functioned in a close relationship with German and Austrian regions, or the clock- and watch-making industry which collaborated with the neighbouring French regions or with other regions even farther afield.

As has been already pointed out above, globalisation in the Swiss context did not only signify the increased employment of foreign labour in Switzerland, but also an increased employment of foreign labour working abroad. Apart from the strategies of partial or total delocalization of firms abroad, as in the textile[11] (especially silk), food (especially chocolate) and machine industries, even in sectors with little or no delocalization, firms developed strategies which enabled them to some extent to exploit the advantages of low labour costs abroad for part of the production process and so to lower the overall cost of the finished product.

Various methods were employed of reducing the overall cost of production depending on the industry involved, and none of them was without its negative repercussions on the labour force within Switzerland. The watch-making industry used segmented production; it was mainly international production-process sharing[12] which allowed the industry to retain its lead on international foreign markets. The textile industry used tariff agreements which allowed a large range of goods to be temporarily imported and exported under a regime of duty exemption. The Swiss textile industry was mainly involved in 'outward processing',[13] and to a lesser extent in 'inward processing'. Outward processing was the designation for Swiss goods which were temporarily exported for processing in low-wage regions abroad and then reimported with a total or partial exemption from import duties and taxes. This principally concerned embroidery produced by the Swiss, which was then sent to Germany and Austria for processing before being reimported to Switzerland. 'Inward processing',[14] on the other hand, designated goods which were temporarily imported into Switzerland in order to be transformed there before being re-exported. This applied to certain products of the cotton industry, which were sent from Great Britain to Switzerland for the purpose of being imported only temporarily into Switzerland so that they could be conditioned or finished before being sent back to England. Clearly, there was little necessity for the workforce itself to move when the flow of goods was made relatively easy.

Embroidery, watch-making and the machine and metallurgy industries in the context of globalisation, production modalities and the division of labour

Embroidery and watch-making were two traditional leading industries up to World War I, and were both characterised by a large proportion of specialised workers employed in decentralised locations. Both industries also had contractual strategies with institutions for arbitration purposes with regard to tariff and work practices[15] even before World War I,[16] but these strategies could only be applied to a limited extent when exporting became difficult due to worsening market conditions. During the interwar period both of these industries lost out to foreign competitors as a result of the way in which their relevant markets evolved. But whereas the embroidery industry virtually ceased to exist despite private and col-

Figure 1: Workers in four industries working mainly for foreign markets

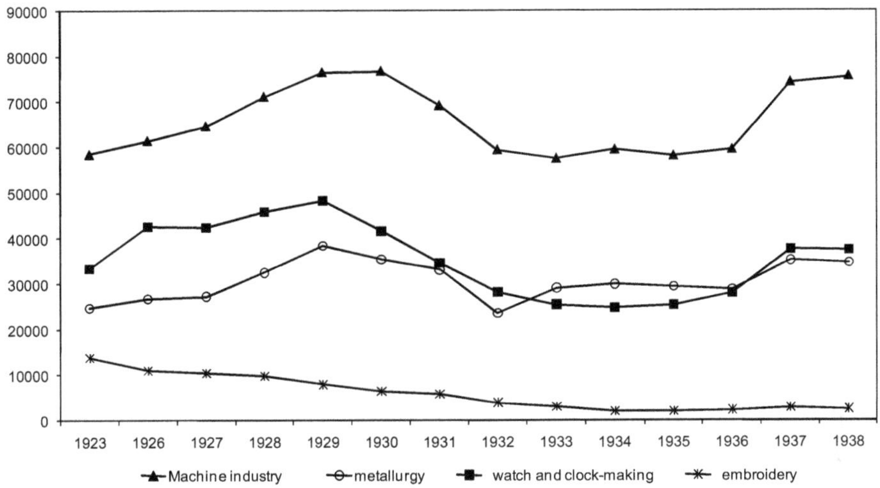

Source: Annual reports of the A.S.M.

lective efforts to the contrary as well as state intervention at a cantonal and federal level, the watch and clock industry managed to survive thanks to the draconian rules and regulations imposed by the State in the 1930s. In the interwar period, however, while embroidery (and, to a lesser extent, watch-making) were going into decline, the machine and metallurgy industries came to take a more dominant position in the Swiss economy (Figure 1). In contrast to the sectors in decline, these industries were characterised by greater centralisation of production and a well-qualified workforce composed to a large degree of male Swiss nationals. Nevertheless, in the 1930s State aid could not be dispensed with even here.

The embroidery industry

In terms of employment and exports, and like the silk industry, embroidery was one of the most important industries in Switzerland until World War I and subsequently during the first few years of the interwar period. It had its own specific methods of production, was characterized by a marked international division of labour and was also subject to cyclical patterns of demand depending on fashion. So, when mechanical production spread quickly in the 1870s,[17] there was a deliberate move back from manufacture to home production with the object of avoiding subjection to the new legislation on factory work which, as from 1878, forbade children under fourteen from taking part in paid employment and also limited the duration of work for all workers to a maximum of eleven hours daily.[18]

Similarly, a marked division of labour could be observed; and this was not only limited to the foreign region adjacent to the main producing area in Switzerland, namely the Vorarlberg in Austria, but also involved work contracted out to embroiderers in the region of Plauen (Saxony) situated some hundreds of kilometres away from the Swiss border. Plauen was itself also a region for the production and distribution of its own embroidery products, and thus competed with eastern Switzerland. This division of labour came about as a consequence of differences in skills and differences in pay.[19] However, the very existence of such a differentiated labour market and the dependency it created for the Saxon workforce, especially in times of crisis, nevertheless promoted general emulation and innovation. This was particularly striking in Saxony, and accounts for the continuing emancipation of its production from Swiss influence during the 1890s, and was particularly marked with regard to mechanical production. The crisis in export sales to the United States in 1890, which was due to a massive increase in that country's customs tariff, played a decisive role in the reorientation of production in Saxony. Within twelve months the production of Swiss embroidery to be exported for processing in Germany had decreased by 34% for all types of embroidery, but by as much as 76% for machine embroidery alone. In the latter case, trade was never to resume on its former scale, and for two main reasons. Firstly, the Saxon entrepreneurs managed to develop the production of new articles and specialised in specific types of goods, such as tulle embroidery – which later even came to be identified with the region in which it was produced and became known as 'Saxon lace'. Secondly, on the Swiss side there was a delocalization of firms to Saxony:

initially of a limited nature, this trend increased somewhat for technical reasons at the turn of the century.[20]

The reasons for the extensive finishing traffic involving 'outward processing' between Switzerland and Germany up to the First World War were twofold:[21] the wages in Switzerland were higher than in Saxony,[22] and there was a different structure in the relevant labour force. In Switzerland the embroidery industry employed a large proportion of males, nearly 45% of the total workforce, whereas in Saxony the very opposite was the case and, according to the German statistics, female workers predominated.[23] However, within the Swiss embroidery industry itself the structure of the labour force also varied depending on the type of production. In the mechanical hand-embroidery industry the labour structure differed markedly in sex ratio, age structure, marital status and nationality from that obtaining in Schiffli-embroidery production. In factories there were more women. With the subsequent decline of the industry, the feminisation of the workforce increased still further: there were 588 female factory workers per thousand workers in 1911, 656 in 1923, 755 in 1929, 774 in 1939.[24] These women were also younger, and there was a notable national segmentation of the workforce with a very high proportion of foreigners (Italians),[25] whereas only a small proportion of foreigners worked in mechanical hand-embroidery production. This structure of the workforce is also striking when one considers the economic relations with the Vorarlberg, the Austrian region adjacent to eastern Switzerland, where most of the outward processing took place, and whose role increased in importance once German firms were no longer available to carry out the necessary work. In 1910 more than 5,000 women in the Vorarlberg were employed by the Swiss finishing industry[26] out a total of about 12,000 embroiderers across the region,[27] and in the years 1911–1913 the volume of goods sent temporarily to the Vorarlberg for outward processing represented 24% of the total volume of exports. But it must be stressed that there was much the same reluctance to work in factories in the Vorarlberg as in Switzerland, with the indigenous workforce showing no desire to give up its traditional methods of production. As a result, there was a significant and increasing influx of immigrants from northern Italy into the Vorarlberg in search of work in the factories.[28]

This extremely intricate network of economic relations between Switzerland and the Vorarlberg survived into the 1930s, but to a much lesser extent from 1921 onwards. After World War I outward processing between these two regions was resumed in the face of vehement opposition by the Swiss labour force which can principally be ascribed to the catastrophic economic situation in the embroidery sector. State interventions and several agreements between Switzerland and Austria aimed at regulating the sector through the imposition of a minimum stitch-price for the workers of the Vorarlberg and in Switzerland, and this was coupled with regulation of the maximum number of hours that might be worked daily, to be enforced on both sides of the border.[29] After World War I, wages in the Vorarlberg were 70–90% lower than in Switzerland because of the depreciation of the Austrian currency. The imposition of a currency compensation amounting to 5% for every 100 stitches was insufficient to counterpoise the discrepancy that existed between the two regions,[30] and outward processing never returned to its pre-war levels. This was due firstly to the measures taken by both States to protect their respective workers by means of customs tariffs, and also to the protests from the Swiss workforce. The practice of temporarily exporting goods to be improved and finished abroad had always met with considerable opposition both from the Swiss embroiderers themselves and from those firms which produced entirely in Switzerland; and this opposition became all the more vocal in times of crisis when the proportion of unemployed was high as occurred in the 1890s, in the years immediately after World War I, and in the 1930s.[31] In the event, in the years 1921–1925 the above-mentioned export procedure accounted for only 5.8% of the total volume of exports, and in the years 1926–1930 for 6.8%.[32] This reduction of outward processing doubtless contributed to the development of a considerable autonomous production in the Vorarlberg: and the subsequent increase in its output in the 1920s represented direct competition for Swiss exports, which were thus priced out of many markets.

In the 1930s, however, both regions were seriously affected by the massive contraction of the market, and this contributed to the final decline of the industry, which was unable to compete with the production overseas and with that of the Indian subcontinent. The

Treaty on the Reorganisation of the Industry which was concluded between Austria and Switzerland in 1933 imposed on both countries the implementation of a policy of extremely restrictive measures in order to limit production drastically and so adapt it to the lower demand. Among these measures there was a limit to maximum working hours and the obligation to destroy embroidery machinery. Astonishingly, one clause stipulated that the Vorarlberg workforce could be paid up to 10% less than Swiss workers,[33] with the result that the Swiss industry was made completely uncompetitive and the conditions of employment for those working in Switzerland worsened markedly. Within the period from 1929 to 1939 the number of those still seeking employment in the embroidery sector reached new peaks in 1933 and 1934.[34] It comes as little surprise, then, that the agreement between the two countries did not survive the deterioration of the market and the increase in unemployment: it was denounced in 1935.

Several additional factors helped to hasten the demise of the embroidery industry in Switzerland, which at its peak in 1910 had employed 72,000 people (employed and self-employed), but provided employment for only five to six thousand in 1936,[35] in addition to six thousand people working from home.[36] In the Vorarlberg the situation was hardly better. From a maximum of 12,606 workers in 1910, the workforce had declined to only 853 in 1934.[37] For its part, the Swiss federal government was soon obliged to introduce several measures aimed specifically at improving the situation in the embroidery industry. A significant development here was the creation of a semi-official institution, the Stickerei-Treuhand-Genossenschaft,[38] in which the Confederation, the cantons, the communes and also private organisations were represented, and whose task it was to give help to firms that had got into serious financial difficulties.[39] Another measure was the obligatory destruction of embroidery machines in order to stop the overproduction of embroidery products and so adapt capacity more closely to the existing demand. Between 1922/23 and 1939 a total of 9,207 machines were destroyed, which entailed the payment of 5,700,000 million francs in compensation.[40] The consequences of this policy were disastrous for the workers concerned. With the destruction of their machines they had no way to make a living and such compensation as there was went principally to their creditors, since the machines had not been paid for in full.[41] Despite such widespread destruction, market forces proved ineluctable, since the interwar period was marked by irremediable changes not only in respect of fashion but also due to the introduction of new methods for decorating material. Ultimately, whatever measures the government took and in spite of the investment of more than eight million francs in aid to this industry in the course of the 1930s, the market for Swiss lace products never really recovered. The decline was further accelerated by new centres of production with significantly cheaper production costs having come into existence abroad shortly before World War I. In this context, the creation of the SASTIG (Schweizerisch-Amerikanische Stickerei-Industrie Gesellschaft) in 1911 with a significant Swiss participation gave the United States and its large-scale production an enormous advantage over all its competitors.[42] With its three huge factories in the US the SASTIG contributed to the progressive exclusion from the American market of most of the Swiss output. The American market absorbed 38% of Swiss embroidery exports in 1911, 29% in 1913, but only 9% in 1920, 7% in 1925, and 13% in 1931, and this at a time when total exports to the USA had declined by more then 90% since 1920.[43] Additionally, the sales of Swiss embroidery machines to competitors abroad during the 1920s served only to aggravate an already critical situation.[44] The rapidity with which the decline took place is all too evident when one considers the essentially downward post-war fluctuations in the value of exports (given in millions of Swiss francs) and the number of workers involved (Table 3). Due to the forms of organisation which characterised this industry, however, the number of factory workers employed tells only part of the story, as only a fraction of the workforce (between a half and a third) was subject to the Factory Act.

Table 3: Value of exports in millions of francs and numbers of factory workers in the embroidery industry

Year	*Value of exports*	*Year*	*Number of factory workers*
1885	90	1882	17.269
1890	91	1895	13.336
1895	77		
1900	119		
1905	137		
1910	204	1911	20.606
1919	410	1923	13.866
1920	392		
1925	129		
1930	65	1930	6.431
1935	12	1935	2.212
1939	25	1939	2.823

Source: Kuhn, *Aufbau und Strukturänderung*, p. 55; *Annuaire statistique suisse*, 1941; Saxer, *Die Stickerei-Treuhand-Genossenschaft*, pp. 219ff.

At the beginning of the twentieth century the danger of a monolithic development in the industry was recognised and attempts were made to remedy the situation by attracting other industries to the eastern part of Switzerland, but with little success until the middle of the 1920s.[45] The traditionalist modes of production and organisational structures of this industry – which had some features in common with other characteristic Swiss industries, such as clock- and watch-making – were deeply rooted in rural areas, where agricultural resources had cushioned the impact of the various crises preceding the First World War, because the workforce still derived some of their income from agriculture, or at least obtained some home produce from their own smallholdings. But in the 1920s the situation became desperate for those workers who no longer had any links with the primary sector. The impact of the successive crises – in 1920, 1926[46] and 1929 – brought about not only a large reduction in the workforce, but obliged much of it to emigrate due to lack of any paid employment. The impact on the overall population was enormous. The half-canton of Appenzell A. Rh. lost 22.8% of its population between 1910 and 1941, that of Appenzell I. Rh.

8.4%, the canton of St. Gallen 6.5%[47] and the cantonal capital lost more than 15% between 1910 and 1938 due to the fact that nearly two thirds of its foreign population left during this period.

The watch-making industry

The watch-making industry had similar problems to those of the embroidery industry because of its methods of production, and was likewise very much subject to economic fluctuations.

From 1890 to 1913 the export of watches increased year by year,[48] but the marked contraction of exports after World War I had considerable repercussions in the labour market, and this situation was aggravated by the fact that output no longer corresponded to current demand. Cheaper models were required, which foreign competitors were just as ready to provide. This was partly the consequence of an earlier international division of labour within this sector and of international production-process sharing. Also, small firms of up to 50 workers were the norm and in 1929 these still represented 81% of total watch- and clock-making businesses, and were widely spread geographically.[49] Following a strategy not dissimilar to that adopted by the embroidery industry before World War I, parts of the product were exported to be worked on abroad. But in the case of the watch industry this procedure meant that the exported components (chablons) were not infrequently built into the watches of foreign competitors, who were numerous both inside and outside Europe, and whose production increased substantially as a consequence.[50] Moreover, this policy of selling components abroad was part of a long tradition which rendered unnecessary the systematic delocalization of firms to other countries, notably to France or Germany, and served to a certain extent to keep skilled workers in Switzerland. But in the course of the severe crisis which affected the watch-making industry after World War I and which increased unemployment dramatically, there was a fear that skilled workers might emigrate, enabling the foreign competition to increase sales on foreign markets at the expense of Swiss exports. This concern, taken together with the high unemployment at the time, explains the willingness of the State to inject considerable sums in order to combat unemployment. For the canton of Neuchâtel alone the sum amounted to forty million francs (nominal value) between 1918 and 1924, which effectively represented more than twice the current annual cantonal budget.[51]

From the mid-1920s, however, watch and clock exports recovered, and this recovery was accompanied by a sizeable increase in the labour force of more than 44% between 1923 and 1929. There was an accompanying increase in output, with the sale of components abroad making the labour force extremely vulnerable to changes in demand and subject to unemployment when demand declined. Each component sold abroad represented a loss of about 30% in terms of value for the watch- and clock-making industry.[52] Drastic steps had to be taken to save the industry, and these resulted in further substantial job losses. The creation of the Fédération horlogère, Ebauches SA and of the UBAH represented the attempts of the employers from the mid-1920s to control production and the labour market in face of the industry's problems. Unfortunately these measures did not succeed, since they could neither be applied across the industry nor enforced with sufficient rigour: the scheme's basic flaw was its reliance on private rather than State intervention. The industry had planned to sell 31 million watches and watch movements abroad in 1929, but in fact managed to sell only 23 million.[53] Unemployment increased substantially in 1931 and 1932, but unregulated production was still a problem because some of the redundant workers now began to work from home, thus exacerbating the already existing overproduction.[54] The federal government found itself obliged both to increase its subsidies to unemployment funds, as these had accumulated completely inadequate reserves, and to extend the period for unemployment benefit.[55]

Further steps were taken in the course of the 1930s, this time principally by the State: these involved the creation of trade associations and of collective agreements regarding output and pricing, as well as the introduction of policies limiting the export of components. Finally, the government intervened to encourage the creation of a watch cartel whose function was to impose restrictions on output and technology.[56] Government intervention in the watch sector did succeed in stopping the decline of the industry, but the devaluation of the Swiss franc in 1936 represented the real turning point both for State intervention and for the recovery of the labour market. The day after devaluation the Swiss government, fearing the negative effects of the devaluation on the purchasing power of the workers and the potential for extensive labour conflict which would in turn exert an adverse effect on the economic life of the country as a whole, arrogated to itself the right to arbitrate ex officio and without a possibility of appeal in all wage disputes which involved the workforce of more than one canton and which could not be resolved by an agreement between the parties to the case.[57] Subsequently, in the dispute between employers and workers in the watch- and clock-making industry in the spring of 1937 over wages and holidays the government proposed the appointment of an arbitration tribunal drawn from both parties instead of a solution imposed upon them by the State. The resulting collective agreement in this industry signed in May 1937 was successful in establishing among other things the obligation to come to a peaceful settlement in labour conflicts. The agreement was concluded for two years, but was regularly renewed afterwards over a period of several decades. With regard to unemployment, though, the effects of devaluation were immediate. Within the space of a year the labour force had increased by a third from 28,000 to reach a total 38,000 workers once again.[58] This increase involved substantial additional female labour, however, and this entailed a reduction in wage costs for the employers when the trade union gave up their demand for equal pay for male and female workers. In effect, one can note the progressive feminisation of the factory workforce between 1911 and 1937, with a temporary reversal in this development in 1939: there were 387 females per 1000 workers in 1911, 436 in 1923, 474 in 1929, 509 in 1937, 490 in 1939, and 503 in 1941.[59]

In the case of the watch- and clock-making industry, and in contrast to embroidery production, the crisis had not been due to a fall-off in demand due to consumers' lack of interest, but can be ascribed to a general lack of purchasing power as well as in certain cases to the increase of customs duties.

The machine and metallurgy industries

Despite their growth as an export sector after the 1870s, the machine and metallurgy industries were responsible for only a small part of Switzerland's total exports until the end of the nineteenth century.[60] Throughout this period the export sector was essentially dominated by the watch-making and textile industries. However, the latter played an indirect and important part in the development of the machine industry as a result of foreign demand for textile machines. In the long run, the evolution of the different branches of the machine and metallurgy industries varied considerably. This is particularly evident in textile-machine production where exports declined by nearly 60% between 1929 and 1938 and the production of dynamos, electrical machines and transformers by nearly 50%, whereas the manufacture of tools for metallurgy increased by more than 150%.

The two decades before World War I and the interwar period were decisive for the expansion of the machine and metallurgy industries despite the major difficulties suffered at the beginning of the 1920s and during the great Depression, when the access to foreign markets was hampered by higher costs of production than those incurred by competitors. This is clearly demonstrated by the number of workers employed in the sector (Figure 2).

Clearly, production costs were also a major problem for the export industries and especially so in times of crisis. In the years 1923–1925 wages amounted to about 55–60% of the total cost of production in the machine and metallurgy industries.[61] According to the calculations made by the ASM in the interwar period most of their main competitors with the exception of Great Britain and Sweden up to 1930 and of the USA had the advantage of a lower wage structure in both their home and export markets. Table 4 shows the differences for qualified workers: and for unqualified workers these differences were even greater.

Figure 2: Number of factory workers in the machine and metallurgy industries (1882–1938)

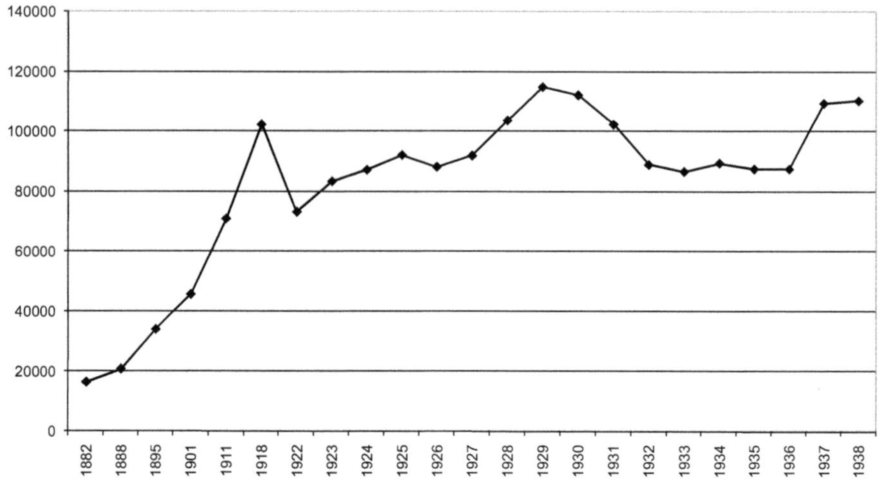

Source: Annual reports of the A.S.M.

Table 4: Wage index in the machine and metallurgy industries for Switzerland's main competitors (Switzerland = 100 %)

Years	*Germany*	*France*	*Italy*	*Great Britain*
1920 (Feb.)	25*	90	51	106
1926 (beginning)	80	53	55	104
1929 (end)	90	74	60	113
1930	89	77	56	112
1932 (beginning)	83	76	55	80
1934 (end)	88	72	56	81
1937 (beginning)	68**	101	–	128

* Germany: 1920 (end)   ** Germany: 1936 (end)

Source: Reports of the A. S. M.

Despite the usual entrepreneurial measures – wage reduction, part-time working, lay-offs (Figure 3) – declining demand on the part of Switzerland's main trading partners as well as the overvaluation of the Swiss franc produced a sharp fall in the volume of exports which had a massive impact on the workforce and contributed to the wors-

Figure 3: Number of workers in the firms affiliated to the A.S.M. working n hours per week

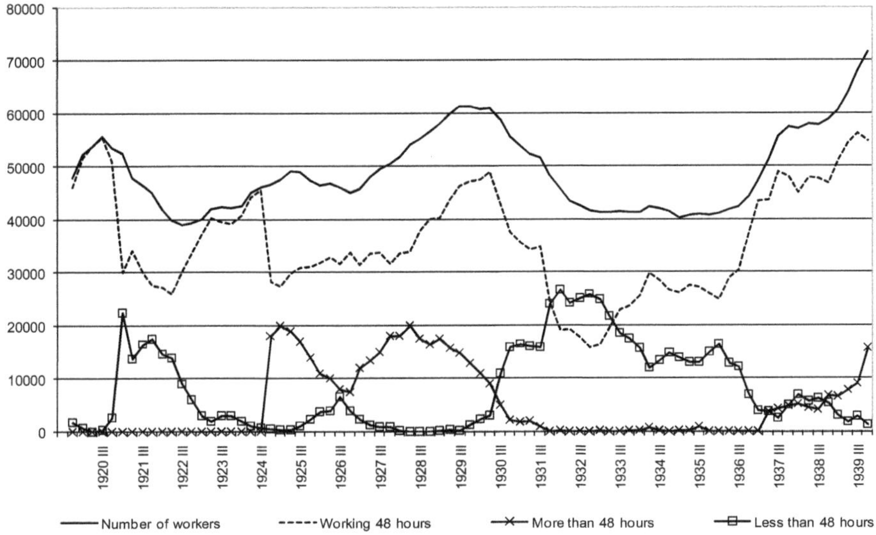

Source: Annual reports of the A.S.M.

ening of the financial situation of both the unemployed and of those who still had work.

The case of the Oerlikon factory illustrates the drastic repercussions the crisis had for its workers. From 1930 to 1935 their initial number (3400) was halved and all those remaining worked only part time.[62] In terms of full employment, this meant that when the available employment was at its lowest (the beginning of 1935), this level represented only 14% of the full employment of 1930. The drop in employment was similar in other firms of the machine and metallurgy sector, but the level of their employment did not fall so drastically. In the Oerlikon factory, interestingly, the rules for laying off workers were as follows: the incompetent first, then those who had worked in the firm from one to six years, then those who had relatives in the firm, and lastly workers who were over 65 years old.[63]

The tense situation in the labour market due to the increasing number of people out of work gave new impetus to discussions of the need for federal government to intervene by the introduction of manufacturing subsidies and risk guarantees in order to prevent a further decline in exports.[64] Since the end of World War I, and especially in periods of difficulties, a subject of frequently recurring discussions between the Vorort (the umbrella organization of the Swiss Federation of Commerce and Industry) and the government had been the lack of credit facilities for foreign customers for any period in excess of two to five years. Even among the major economic players a consensus could not be reached; opinions differed as to which the industries should benefit from such measures, the amount to be guaranteed and the foreign countries which should be taken into consideration.[65] In 1931 the machine industry favoured such a risk guarantee for the increasing exports to Russia as a means of reducing unemployment. The subject of exports to Russia was omitted from the discussions before the adoption in 1934 by Parliament of the risk guarantee for exports, doubtless for strategic reasons. As ultimately adopted by Parliament the guarantee aimed effectively at providing financial support for the machine and metallurgy industries both with a view to limiting unemployment as well as to preventing the delocalization of Swiss firms abroad. The State accepted the obligation to make good part of the loss incurred by firms engaged in the export of machine and metallurgical products when economic, financial and political conditions in the relevant foreign countries deteriorated.[66] In the event, the main beneficiary of the guarantee during the first two years of its existence was Russia, which took up 50% of the allocated funds.

The manufacturing subsidies which were introduced by central government in 1932 for those working in export industries took the form of so-called 'productive unemployment benefits'. In their addresses to Parliament government ministers repeatedly stressed the need to 'provide employment', to reduce the impact of the overvaluation of the Swiss franc on labour costs in export industries and to reduce the number of those who risked unemployment resulting from the insolvency of industrial firms obliged to operate in an environment of uneconomically high production costs.

Clearly, the government considered it more productive to use money which would have had to be paid in the form of unemployment benefits in order to help to reduce the production costs in Switzerland of those goods which otherwise would have been produced abroad by competitors. In 1934 labour costs in the machine industry represented about 40% of the price at delivery. Compared with the wage of a qualified worker in this sector in Switzerland official calculations showed that the wage of a qualified worker was 47% lower in Belgium, 38% in France, 18% in Great Britain and 16% in Germany.[67] The 'productive allocation' was thus intended to keep healthy firms alive so that they would not be forced to close down and lay off their workers. In fact, the subsidy was only granted when the firm could effectively prove that it had only accepted the orders placed with it in order to assure its own survival, and that it did not make any profit while benefiting from the State subsidy.[68] In addition to these conditions, the sums paid by the federal government had to be matched on the part of the canton by at least an equivalent subsidy to the firms concerned. In 1934 it was decided to fix the maximum subsidies at 20% of the price at delivery and exceptionally at 30%, with an obligation for the canton in which the firm was situated to contribute in those cases a further subsidy amounting to at least a third of the central-government subsidy.[69] When a firm was granted a guarantee it was required to furnish a monthly report regarding new orders coming in and the use made of the subsidies. For nine months of the year 1932 – the decree came into force on 18 March 1932 – the federal government estimated the number of those kept in employment due to this aid at some 3300 workers, not counting those in 'auxiliary' industries benefiting indirectly. Between March 1932 and the end of 1936, out of a total of 12 million Swiss francs, more than 80% of the 'productive allocation' was attributed to the machine and metallurgy industries, and only about 15% to the textile industry.[70] With the devaluation of the Swiss franc in September 1936, it was decided to give this allocation only in really exceptional cases, since the devaluation now made it possible for the export industry to compete with other industrialised States, whilst the risk guarantee became permanently institutionalised. The impact of the devaluation on the export sector was considerable, not only in terms of increased exports but also in terms of employment. Within a year, unemployment had declined by 50% in the export industries. Compared with the peak reached before the crisis, nearly three quarters of the unemployed were now back in work. Those still unemployed in the export sector represented no more than a fifth of those seeking work, whilst in the first year of the crisis they had formed the vast majority of those out of work.[71] But it is indisputable that the peace agreement concluded in 1937 in the Swiss engineering and metalworking industries on working conditions and the settlement of labour conflicts also contributed to the economic recovery of the sector, even if its influence has sometimes been overestimated.[72]

Conclusion

Compared with the marked openness of the labour market in Switzerland before World War I which led to its partial internationalisation, restrictive immigration legislation due to the deterioration of the economic situation at home and abroad was the notable characteristic of the interwar period. At the same time, the Swiss economy was obliged to undergo a fundamental reorganisation of all major sectors.

The considerable degree of structural flexibility which some historians have highlighted[73] can, however, be explained in terms of the difficult conditions prevailing in a number of these sectors. Embroidery, for example, whilst being the second leading export sector on the eve of World War I, had virtually ceased to exist at the end of the 1930s. Despite very low wages by Swiss standards, this industry became uncompetitive in foreign markets due to its inherent dispersion and its forms of production which traditionally allowed for workers' continued minor involvement in their family plot. Similarly, the watch-making industry ran into difficulties not only as a result of traditional methods of production, but also as a result of the outsourcing abroad of component manufacture. Only through stringent Malthusian measures to prevent changes in the size of firms and to control output, together with the devaluation of the Swiss franc, was this sector to some extent able to recover from the 1930s crisis. In addition – and in stark contrast to the 1920s – the composition of the workforce changed, with a recourse to an ever-increasing proportion of female labour. The third sector under consideration, that of machine and metallurgy industries, became a leading sector both in the domestic market and in foreign markets in the interwar period. Its role as main exporter, together with lobbying on the part of the main entrepreneurs concerned explains its privileged position with respect to government subsidies. But the fact that its workforce was mainly urban, well qualified and well organised also doubtless contributed to the government's awareness of the prevailing problems in this sector.

The partial closing of the labour market to foreigners, which inevitably led to a diminution in the number of foreign male workers, was an additional factor contributing to relatively peaceful reorganisation of the relevant sectors, as it was often these workers who had been at the forefront of industrial disputes with their persistent demands for improved conditions of work.

1 Up to the end of the nineteenth century some cantonal and federal authorities often asserted that the standard of literacy was adequate in Switzerland. Nevertheless it can be observed that the existing skills of the Swiss workforce were not infrequently unable to meet the needs of the economy.

2 Anne-Lise Head-König, 'Dynamique démographique, migrations, capital humain et secteurs d'activité. Le cas de la Suisse, 1870–1930', in Dominique Barjot, Olivier Faron (eds), *Migrations, Cycle de vie familial & Marché du travail* (Paris: Société de Démographie historique, 2002), p. 457.

3 In 1901 more than 70% of the workers in this industry still worked 64–65 hours a week, whereas in the watch-making industry less than 35% of the workforce had such a long working week (cf. *Swiss Factory Census*, 1911, p. LXIII).

4 Gérald et Silvia Arlettaz, 'Les Chambres fédérales face à la présence et à l'immigration étrangère (1914–1922)', *Etudes et Sources. Revue des Archives fédérales suisses*, 16/17 (1990/1991); 'Rapport du Conseil fédéral à l'Assemblée fédérale concernant l'ordonnance du 29 novembre 1921 sur le contrôle des étrangers, du 27 janvier 1922', *Feuille fédérale* (FF) (1922), I.

5 The coal market is a good example of this duality. Swiss industry had to pay 68% more for French coal, 79% more for German coal, and 52% more for British coal than the entrepreneurs of those countries had to pay in their own domestic market (cf. Eugène Dérobert, *La politique douanière de la Confédération suisse. Etude sur la politique douanière suisse depuis la constitution de l'Etat fédéral jusqu'à nos jours, et exposé du problème douanier actuel* (Genève: Jent S.A., 1926), p. 260).

6 Etienne Marguerat, *Les enjeux de la gestion du chômage en Suisse durant l'entre-deux-guerres. L'assurance-chômage et le développement des caisses de chômage à*

travers l'exemple du canton de Neuchâtel, unpublished mém. lic. histoire, Univ. de Lausanne (2001), p. 87.
7 *Ergebnisse der schweizerischen Sozialstatistik abgeschlossen auf Ende 1931*, Bern 1932, pp. 144, 157.
8 Its workforce then for the first time exceeded that of the textile industry.
9 According to the Swiss Population Census of 1920, 14% of the total population of these three cantons was employed in this sector.
10 Until World War I nearly three-quarters of Swiss investments were made in the border regions (cf. Harm G. Schröter, 'Etablierungs- und Verteilungsmuster der schweizerischen Auslandsproduktion von 1870 bis 1970', in Paul Bairoch and Martin Koerner (eds.), *La Suisse dans l'économie mondiale* (Genève: Droz, 1990), p. 400.
11 For a good example of the practice of investing abroad see Gisela Müller, *Die Entstehung und Entwicklung der Wiesentaler Textilindustrie bis zum Jahre 1945* (Schopfheim: Polygraphischer Verlag, 1965).
12 In French 'segmentation internationale du processus de production'.
13 In French 'trafic de perfectionnement passif'.
14 In French 'trafic de perfectionnement actif'.
15 Arnold Saxer, *Die Stickerei-Treuhand-Genossenschaft St. Gallen. Ein Beitrag zur Wirtschafts- und Sozialgeschichte der Stickereiindustrie* (St. Gallen: Tschudy AG, 1965).
16 Notably the 'Centralverband der Stickerei-Industrie der Ostschweiz und des Vorarlbergs'; cf. also Béatrice Veyrassat, 'Manufacturing flexibility in nineteenth-century Switzerland: social and institutional foundations of decline and revival in calico-printing and watchmaking', in Charles F. Sabel and Jonathan Zeitlin (eds.), *Worlds of possibilities: flexibility and mass production in Westerm Industrialization* (Cambridge: Cambridge University Press, 1997), pp. 216ff.
17 The number of embroidery machines in Switzerland doubled between 1872 and 1880.
18 This factor explains the fact that both factory and domestic types of production persisted in the embroidery industry up to its final decline in the 1930s.
19 It must be emphasized, however, that this traffic with Germany was not entirely one sided: Saxony also sent embroidery for improving and finishing to Switzerland, but on a far more modest scale (cf. Rudolf Jllgen, *Geschichte und Entwicklung der Stickereiindustrie des Voigtlandes und der Ostschweiz. Eine vergleichende Darstellung* (Annaberg: 1913).
20 Some Swiss entrepreneurs established factories in Germany so as to be able to take advantage of improvements made in the Schiffli-embroidery machines in Germany (cf. Jllgen, *Gechichte und Entwicklung*, p. 49).
21 This traffic did not survive World War I, and in the interwar period Swiss entrepreneurs were no longer able to compete with Saxony in this sector.
22 There was also a higher cost of living in Switzerland, which was partly due to the highly protected agricultural market.
23 Jllgen, *Gechichte und Entwicklung*, p. 82.
24 *Swiss Factory Census*, 1939, p. 29.

25 In 1905 Tablat, for example, a commune close to St. Gallen, employed a large number of foreign workers in its factories. In the embroidery sector 39% were foreigners, 28% being Italians.
26 *Berichte des Kaufmännischen Direktoriums St. Gallen über Handel, Industrie und Geldverhältnisse des Kantons St. Gallen* (St. Gallen: Fehr, 1910), annex, p. 279.
27 *Hundert Jahre Handelskammer und Gewerbliche Wirtschaft in Vorarlberg* (Feldkirch: 1952), pp. 188 ff.
28 Karl Heinz Burmeister, Robert Rollinger (eds.), *Auswanderung aus dem Trentino – Einwanderung nach Vorarlberg. Die Geschichte einer Migrationsbewegung mit besonderer Berücksichtigung der Zeit von 1870/80 bis 1919* (Sigmaringen: Thorbecke, 1995); cf. in particular the articles by Franz Mathis (pp. 116 ff.) and by Manfred A. Getzner (pp. 398 ff.).
29 *Hundert Jahre Handelskammer*, p. 191; Hans Nägele, *Das Textilland Vorarlberg. Werden und Wachsen einer alpenländlichen Industrie* (Dornbirn: Vorarlberger Verlagsanstalt, 1949), p. 191.
30 Hermann Häuptli, *Die Krisis der schweizerischen Stickereiindustrie mit besonderer Berücksichtigung der staatlichen Intervention. Ein Beitrag zur Geschichte der Stickereiindustrie* (Zürich: E. Gmünder-Zahner, 1929), pp. 142 ff.
31 Ibid., p. 212; Nägeli, *Das Textilland Vorarlberg*, p. 212.
32 Olga Bébié, *Der Zusammenbruch der Stickereiindustrie und der Aufbau der neuen Industrien in der Ostschweiz* (Zürich: Leeman, 1939), p. 145; Arnold Saxer, 'Der Stickerei-Veredlungsverkehr mit dem Ausland', *Revue suisse de statistique et d'économie politique*, 67 (1931), 426.
33 *Feuille fédérale* (FF), 1933, I, pp. 536 ff.; *Feuille fédérale* (FF), 1936, I, pp. 358–359.
34 *Swiss Factory Census*, 1939, p. 13.
35 *Feuille fédérale* (FF), 1936, I, p. 355.
36 *Swiss Factory Census*, 1939, p. 50. In 1905 out of a total of 66,000 workers more than 35,000 worked from home (ibid., p. 51). In contrast to the watch- and clockmaking industry, where there was a significant decline in the number of those working from home (from 24% in 1905 to 12% in 1929 and 9% in 1939) the home producers of embroidery continued to form a large proportion of the total workforce right up to World War II (47% in 1905, 51% in 1929 and still 46% in 1939: ibid., p. 52).
37 *Hundert Jahre Handelskammer*, p. 189.
38 See Saxer, *Die Stickerei-Treuhand-Genossenschaft St. Gallen.*
39 However, in view of the enormous scale of the task this activity was abandoned in 1926 and only resumed in 1936, and then limited to those firms considered to be viable (cf. Charles Lenz, *Les interventions de la Confédération en faveur des industries d'exportation* (Genève: Journal de Genüve, 1942), pp. 116 ff.).
40 Ibid. pp. 122–123.
41 Marcel Mayer, 'Das erste Jahrzehnt von "Gross-St.Gallen" , Stadtgeschichte 1918–1929', Neujahrsblatt. Hg vom Historischen Verein des Kantons St. Gallen, 136, 1996, p. 15.
42 Harm G. Schröter, *Aufstieg der Kleinen. Multinationale Unternehmen aus fünf kleinen Staaten vor 1914* (Berlin: Duncker und Humblot, 1993).

43 *Annuaire statistique suisse*, 1911 ff.
44 Rudolf Kuhn, *Aufbau und Strukturänderung der st.gallischen Industrie* (St. Gallen: Fehr, 1938), pp. 23, 25; *Hundert Jahre Handelskammer*, p. 192.
45 Peter Ullrich, *Der Standort der schweizerischen Industrie unter besonderer Berücksichtigung von Sinn und Möglichkeit einer schweizerischen Standortspolitik* (Bern: Stämpfli, 1951), p. 66.
46 In the embroidery industry the number of persons seeking work nearly trebled from March 1925 to February 1926, and while in March 1925 there was one job on offer for 10 people seeking work, this proportion had worsened a year later to one job for 47 persons (cf. *Informations de statistique sociale*, 4 (1926), p. 87).
47 Swiss Population Censuses.
48 David Landes, *Revolution in time: clocks and the making of the modern worlds* (London: Belknap, 1983), p. 326.
49 Marc Perrenoud, 'Contrastes et paradoxes de la crise dans l'horlogerie', *Traverses* 7 (1997), p. 109.
50 Landes, *Revolution in time*, p. 327.
51 It must be added that the canton was not alone in financing the unemployed in this instance (cf. Marguerat, *Les enjeux de la gestion du chômage*, p. 87).
52 Rudolf Schild, *Sanierungs-Bestrebungen in der schweizerischen Uhrenindustrie seit 1928 und deren Auswirkungen* (Solothurn: Vogt-Schild, 1936), pp. 30–31.
53 Ibid.
54 Marc Perrenoud, 'Corporatisme horloger et paix du travail (1926–1937)', in Ulrich Pfister, Brigitte Studer, Jakob Tanner (eds.), *Le travail en mutation. Interprétation, organisation et pouvoir, du Moyen Age à nos jours* (Zurich: Chronos, 1996), p. 305.
55 Marc Perrenoud, 'Entre la charité et la révolution. Les Comités de chômeurs face aux politiques de lutte contre le chômage dans le canton de Neuchâtel lors de la crise des années 1930', in *Pour une histoire des gens sans Histoire. Ouvriers, exclues et rebelles en Suisse, 19ᵉ–20ᵉ siècles* (Lausanne: Ed. d'en-bas, 1995), pp. 105–120.
56 Perrenoud, 'Corporatisme horloger'; Landes, *Revolution in time*, p. 326.
57 *Recueil officiel des lois* (RO), 1936, p. 766; Gabriel Aubert, *L'obligation de paix du travail* (Genève: 1981), p. 169.
58 *Swiss Factory Census*, 1937, p. 20*.
59 *Swiss Factory Census*, 1939, p. 29.
60 In terms of weight, from 94,000 quintaux in 1878 to 192,000 in 1890 and 343,000 in 1900.
61 August Reichlin, 'Die schweizerische Maschinen und Metallindustrie als Arbeits- und Verdienstquelle', *Zeitschrift für schweizerische Statistik und Volkswirtschaft*, (1926), p. 367.
62 Peter von Salis, *Die Maschinenfabrik Oerlikon in der Zwischenkriegszeit*, unpublished Liz.-Arb. Phil.I, Univ. Zürich, (2003), pp. 53 ff.
63 Ibid., p. 53.
64 See the contribution to this volume by Margrit Müller, 'From Protectionism to Market Liberalisation. The Internationalisation of the Swiss Economy in the Interwar and Postwar Period'.

65 See the Minutes of the Union suisse du Commerce et de l'industrie, especially those of the years 1926 and 1931.
66 Up to 1939 watch-making and chemical exports were excluded from this form of subsidy. Only the machine and metallurgy industries were beneficiaries of this system.
67 *La Vie économique* (1935), no. 1, p. 3.
68 *Feuille fédérale* (FF), 1932, 1, p. 611; Circulaire, FF, 1932, 1, p. 705.
69 *Feuille fédérale* (FF), 1934, 2, p. 850.
70 *Rapport du Conseil fédéral à l'Assemblée fédérale sur sa gestion en 1936*, Bern 1937, p. 234.
71 *Feuille fédérale* (FF), 1937, 3, p. 165.
72 Bernard Degen, 'Der Arbeitsfrieden zwischen Mythos und Realität', in *Arbeitsfrieden – Realität eines Mythos. Gewerkschaftspolitik und Kampf um Arbeit – Geschichte, Krise, Perspektiven* (Zürich: Widerspruch, 1987), pp. 11–30; Aubert, *L'obligation*, pp. 170ff.
73 Hansjörg Siegenthaler, 'Switzerland, 1920–1970', in *The Fontana Economic History of Europe*, vol. 6, part 2: *Contemporary Economies* (Glasgow: William Collins, 1977), p. 536.

Patrick Halbeisen

Open Financial Markets in Switzerland and their Impact on Monetary and Financial Policy[1]

Introduction

Considering its size, the Swiss economy has been characterised by a high degree of internationalisation for quite some time. This finds expression in its substantial foreign trade, direct investment and tourism. In the twentieth century, moreover, Switzerland has evolved into a major international financial centre. In addition to its political stability and neutrality, the Swiss economy's largely free capital movements and a stable convertible currency have been of decisive importance for its high level of international involvement. The Swiss export industry had already built up considerable production capacity in foreign countries prior to the First World War: Total capital holdings abroad were estimated at CHF 7.5 billion for the period before World War I, and in 1914, 160 Swiss companies had 265 productive subsidiaries abroad.[2] The export industry thus employed nearly as many people outside Switzerland as within the country.[3] By contrast, foreign assets in Switzerland amounted to CHF 1.8 billion, of which 1.4 billion were invested in securities. According to contemporary estimates, Switzerland's net assets abroad came to between five and six billion Swiss francs and constituted the same proportion of the nation's GDP then as at the end of the twentieth century.[4] Gottlieb Bachmann, who was then Chairman of the Governing Board of the Swiss National Bank (SNB), quoted a similar figure for the 1920s.[5]

This paper concentrates on the monetary environment. The main focus is on the period between the two world wars, when the major features of the financial centre gradually took shape. While the 1920s, after the gold standard had been readopted, were characterised by favourable monetary and economic conditions, during the deglobalisation of the 1930s, Swiss monetary policy came under considerable pressure; but the Great Depression was finally successfully overcome without any fundamental modifications to the liberal orientation of the monetary and financial system. This is all the more remarkable as Switzerland's strong international financial involvement played a definite role in exacerbating the crisis. The question thus arises why Switzerland, despite the costs, adhered to the gold standard for so long. In the past, Swiss historians have tended to explain this policy in terms of the overriding priority accorded to financial interests.[6] However, more recent research has cast doubt upon the validity of this interpretation. Although there was isolated support for devaluation from mid-1935, neither the business sector nor the trade unions made any serious political move in this direction. In the case of Switzerland it seems that the favourable economic developments of the 1920s, which were associated with the return to the gold standard, led to an economic and monetary consensus among the nation's major economic and political groupings. This consensus encompassed the desirability of a gold-based currency and free capital movement. The related concepts in terms of economic policy were so firmly entrenched that Switzerland was one of the last countries to devalue its currency. In Switzerland's case, however, the devaluation did not result in an abandonment of the gold-standard principles; even after the devaluation capital movements remained essentially free, and the Swiss franc continued to be convertible and firmly pegged to gold. Apart from some selective or temporary restrictions, Switzerland adhered to this position until the failure of the Bretton Woods system.

In the first section we will describe developments after the First World War which led to increased international acceptance of Switzerland as a financial centre. The income deriving from rising capital exports became an increasingly important item in the current account. Conversely, adverse effects also made themselves felt on the Swiss capital market. Notwithstanding initiatives on the political level, which went as far as calling for a prohibition on capital exports, capital movements were, in fact, only regulated to an insignificant extent. In the second part we will look at the effects of free capital movement and adherence to parity during the Great

Depression. Due to its strong international involvement, the Swiss economy was severely affected by the crisis. In the field of exports, trade barriers and declining demand exacerbated the problem posed by an overvalued Swiss franc. Moreover, frozen assets in Central and Eastern Europe (notably in Germany) and speculative attacks from various quarters launched against the Swiss franc, intensified the banking crisis. Finally, we will take a look at monetary and fiscal policy in the post-war era.

The 1920s

During the First World War, Switzerland – like other countries – had abolished the gold standard, but had found this to be unsatisfactory. Inflation soared to 25% per annum, and social tensions increased, finally culminating in the General Strike of 1918. In the early 1920s, the SNB conducted a monetary policy designed to bring the Swiss franc back to the parity of the pre-war years, which it achieved in November 1924. Subsequently, the central bank managed to maintain the gold parity of the Swiss currency without major difficulties right into the 1930s. Switzerland was thus one of the first countries to have returned to the gold standard.

After the return of the Swiss franc to its pre-war parity in November 1924, Switzerland, due to its political and monetary stability, saw an inflow of foreign funds. This strengthened the placing power of the Swiss banks and led to an increasing number of foreign bonds and shares being floated in Switzerland (see Figure 1).[7] France, the United States and Germany accounted for almost half of these issues, with Germany's share being especially large.[8] Some of these securities were acquired by foreigners. Switzerland became a conduit for international financial transactions and 'the Swiss capital market came to assume international importance.'[9]

A more cautious general assessment of Switzerland's role as a financial centre is appropriate;[10] as Hans J. Mast has emphasised,[11] the country did not become one of the three main financial centres in the world until the 1960s and 1970s. A comparison with the Swiss

Figure 1: Foreign issues in Switzerland in CHF millions, 1922–1934

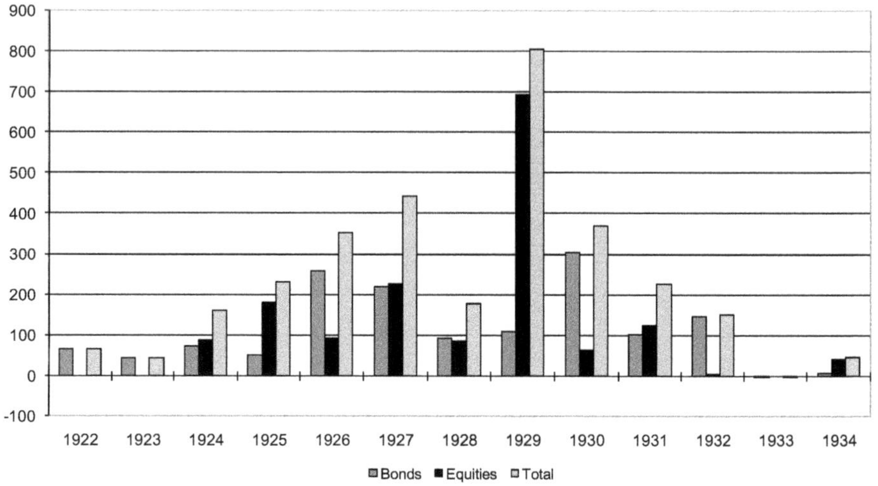

Sources: Computation by the author from various sources (see endnote 7).

financial system's development after the failure of the Bretton Woods system – in the aftermath of which financial transactions became increasingly detached from non-monetary conditions – must not, however, lead us to underestimate the significance of the Swiss financial centre or of Swiss banks in the interwar period. It is an undisputed fact, though, that Switzerland became more important as an international financial centre during, and especially after, the First World War, as can be seen for example in the development of equity. Between 1913 and 1929 the share of equity (paid-in capital + disclosed reserves) of the major Swiss banks, compared with their French competitors, increased from 28% to 124%.[12] If Switzerland's considerable off-balance-sheet transactions are added, the trend is even more impressive (see Figure 2).[13] As part of this development, the big banks also began to play a more important role among the internationally operating banks.[14]

The growing export of capital in the form of public bonds became a controversial topic during the 1920s, due to its effect on Switzerland's interest rates.[15] The farmers, merchants and leftists held capital exports responsible for rising interest rates.[16] A call was

Figure 2: Balance sheet totals and customer deposits of SKA and SBV in CHF millions in real terms (1914 = 100)

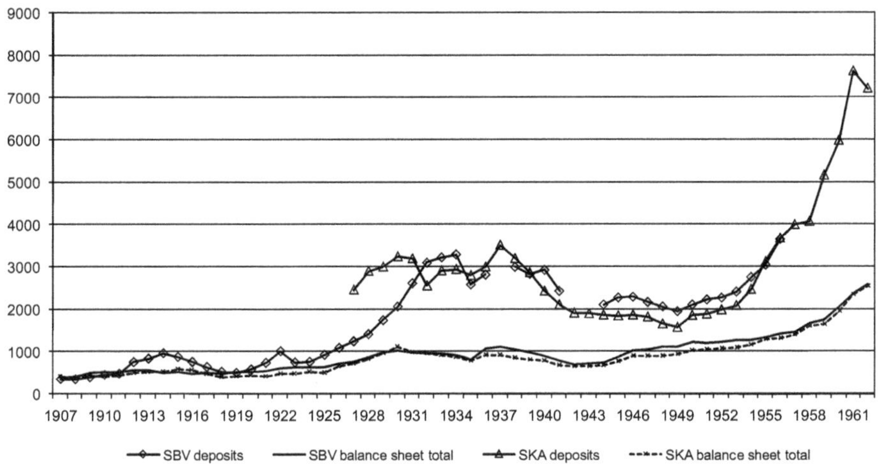

Sources: Computation by the author from various sources (see endnote 13).

even made for a ban on capital exports in the form of Swiss-franc issues. Surprisingly, only this particularly visible form of capital export was criticised.

Foreign bond issues in Swiss francs posed a potential problem for monetary policy, too, and the Swiss National Bank thus fought for its right to be informed by the banks regarding any planned issues, so as to be in a position to express any reservations with respect to monetary policy. However, the banks resisted all attempts to limit their room for manoeuvre. All the SNB could achieve was a verbal gentlemen's agreement concluded in 1927. In this agreement the banks undertook to notify the central bank of any planned bond issues and to take into account any misgivings the central bank or the Confederation might have, without, however, granting the authorities the right to veto individual bond issues. While the SNB assessed requests for capital exports in terms of the implications for interest rates and the exchange rate, the Department of Finance, the Department of Economics and the Political Department (foreign ministry) took into consideration foreign trade factors such as export opportunities for Swiss industry, customs and trade agreements, etc.

It was only in 1932, in the wake of discussions concerning banking supervision – a result of the banking crisis – that the gentlemen's agreement of 1927 was transformed into a more formal arrangement.[17] It was ultimately embodied in the Banking Law of 1934. Capital exports in the form of public bonds and bank loans that exceeded CHF 10 million, and with a term to maturity of more than two years, had to be approved by the SNB. All other forms of capital movement remained unregulated. Despite this statutory provision, the banks had various means of exporting capital against the will of the central bank. They were, for instance, able to restrict the duration or the amount of the bond, or to switch to other forms of capital export such as credits. Another possibility was to transact issues, or parts thereof, through foreign subsidiaries or business partners. This was apparently the role of *Effecten Maatschappij 'Amsterdam'*, the Dutch subsidiary of Schweizerische Kreditanstalt (SKA).[18] To date there has been no systematic study of the number of transactions that were aborted due to intervention by the authorities. What is clear is that there were a number of conflicts between the SNB and the commercial banks.[19]

The gentlemen's agreement was important not only because of its (limited) regulatory function in respect of the capital market but also because this form of paragovernmental regulation was, until the 1980s, taken as the model for governing relations between the central bank and the commercial banks.[20] As can be seen from various examples, the SNB often had trouble in asserting its interests against those of the commercial banks, and was often dependent on the latter's goodwill. The banks were able to maintain a good deal of autonomy vis-à-vis the authorities, which was not limited to any great degree by the 1934 Banking Law and which remained in force until well into the post-World War II period.

The balance of payments[21] trend shows that capital exports exceeded imports from 1924, resulting in a net capital export (see Figure 3).

In 1924, net capital exports resulted in a negative balance of payments.[22] However, just one year later this had been offset by rising capital income and increasing tourism revenues (see Table 1).

In 1929 the SNB drew up an internal study of the current-account trend in the 1920s.[23] In the SNB's opinion, the normalisa-

Figure 3: Balance of payments 1921–1929 in CHF millions

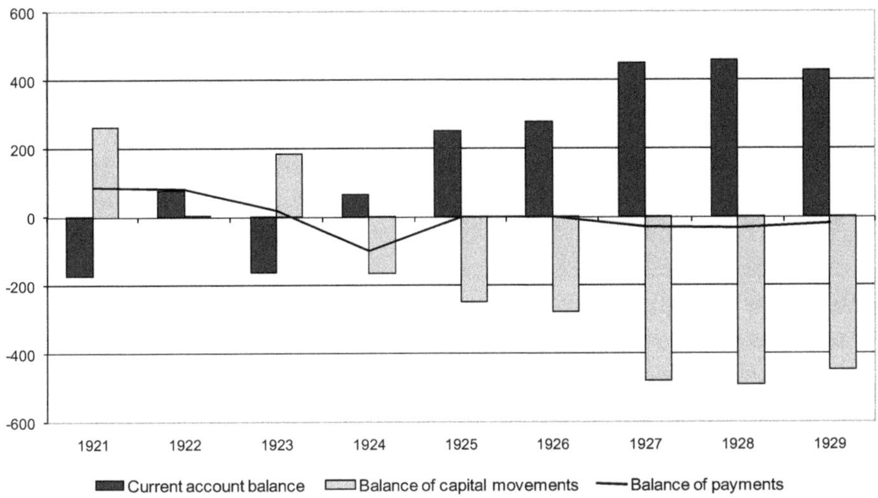

Source: Kellenberger, *Kapitalexport*, volume 1, pp. 155, 245 and 307.

Table 1: Current account 1921–1929, in CHF millions

	1921	*1922*	*1923*	*1924*	*1925*	*1926*	*1927*	*1928*	*1929*
Goods trade	–504	–233	–553	–481	–465	–553	–514**	–589**	–638**
Capital income	120	110	145	210	305	325	350	380	400
Tourism	180	150	180	250	320	380	470	520	510
Other services	30	40	65	88	83	126	145	148	156
Balance	–174	77	–163	66	250*	278*	451*	459*	428*

Source: Kellenberger, Kapitalexport, volume I, pp. 155, 245 and 307.
* Excl. trade in silver coins
** Corrected in each case by +15 CHF million for trade in merchandise not included in the statistics

tion of capital and money-market conditions in Switzerland and abroad had led to the positive development of the current account. From the point of view of the monetary authorities, capital export and the earnings resulting therefrom played a central role: Switzerland acted as an international creditor country of a size hitherto unknown, with the Swiss capital market gaining international significance. The SNB assumed that a considerable amount of capital had moved into the Balkan countries, the central European countries and also to Germany.

However, the SNB was aware that Switzerland's strong economic dependence on other countries also implied certain dangers. The trade deficit had to be offset by earnings from tourism and investment income. As tourism was weather-dependent, capital income took on a particular significance. The possibly negative implications of capital movements on the exchange rate and domestic interest rates were noted, but were not considered to be serious. The current-account balance, which had been positive since the mid-1920s, led to higher currency reserves, so that the parity of the Swiss franc was not endangered despite the capital exports. The pressure on domestic interest rates caused by capital exports was not denied by the SNB. It believed, however, that an appeal for moderation in fixing interest rates and relevant agreements between the banks would be sufficient to keep the problem under control.

With hindsight, it can be said that the SNB's assessment was correct. Once the currency had returned to pre-war parity, the SNB succeeded without any difficulty in keeping the franc at parity level by means of its discount policy, and interest rates were relatively low. This can be seen as testimony to the creditworthiness of Switzerland's political stability and monetary policy.[24] As can be seen from the balance-of-payments trend, Switzerland enjoyed the positive effects of a return to the gold standard after the First World War. A substantial increase in revenues from capital movements and tourism even overcompensated for the negative balance of trade, and the balance of payments was in equilibrium overall. However, with the outbreak of the Great Depression and the collapse of the international monetary system, Switzerland also began to feel the negative effects of this international involvement.

The 1930s

The world economic crisis and the collapse of the international monetary system at the beginning of the 1930s put an end to the favourable development of the current account. The traditional trade deficit widened, while at the same time, the two major items on the assets side of the current account, investment income and tourism, declined (see Table 2).

Table 2: Current account 1930–1939, in CHF millions

	1930	*1931*	*1932*	*1933*	*1934*	*1935*	*1936*	*1937*	*1938*	*1939*
Goods trade	–817	–915	–994	–776	–610	–488	–385	–521	–290	–592
Capital income	480	410	350	330	300	260	240	210	200	180
Tourism	400	300	250	240	200	120	110	180	170	130
Other services	150	121	112	92	105	110	87	97	89	95
Total*	213	–84	–282	–114	–5	2	52	–34	169	–187

Source: Eduard Kellenberger, *Kapitalexport und Zahlungsbilanz*, volume II (Berne: A. Francke AG, 1942), pp. 87, 244 f. and 364 f.
*Excl. trade in silver coins

The fact that the balance of payments remained positive until 1932 is due to the massive inflow of capital from both Swiss and foreign citizens, who, unsettled by the devaluation of sterling and the introduction of exchange-rate control measures in Germany and other countries, moved their money to Switzerland, which was viewed as safe from the threat of devaluation (see Figure 4). On account of this inflow of capital, it is not possible – in the case of Switzerland – to hold an excessively restrictive monetary policy responsible for the price decline. The monetary situation did not become tense until mid-1931. The prices for foreign goods fell very steeply. In 1934, the wholesale price index for foreign goods reached its lowest level, at 53.3 points (1929 = 100), while the index for domestic goods hit its lowest point – 70.7 points – in 1935. The consumer price index also fell to its lowest level of 79.5 points in 1935. Deflation was employed from 1929 to 1931; monetary conditions only became tighter after mid-1931 with the outbreak of the banking crisis (see

Figure 4: Balance of payments 1930–1939 in CHF millions

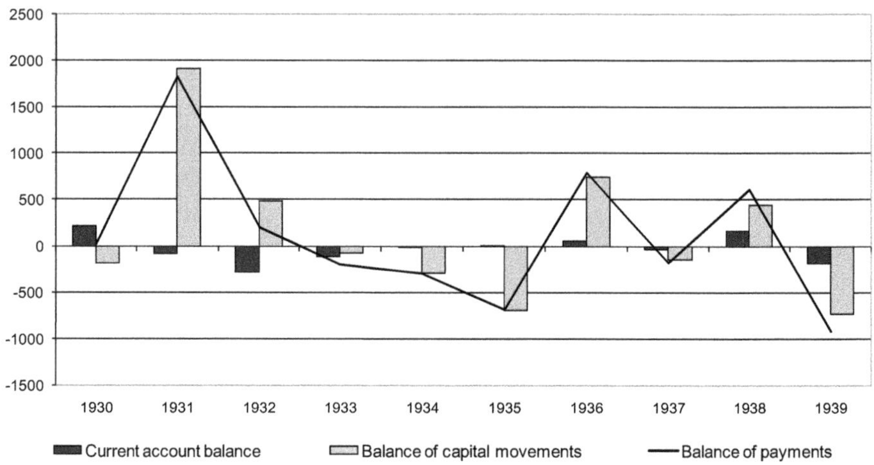

Source: Kellenberger, *Kapitalexport*, volume 2, pp. 87, 244 f and 364 f.

below).[25] Doubts concerning the security of the banks led the public to increase its cash holdings. In order to protect themselves from short-term withdrawals of funds, the banks had to increase their liquidity. Both these developments resulted in a lowering of the money-creation multiplier.[26]

The massive inflow of capital to Switzerland in the second half of 1931 served to delay the effects of the Depression there: In 1930 the economy was still growing slightly, and it was only in 1931 and 1932 that GDP declined sharply. 1933 and 1934 saw a recovery, but in 1935 and 1936 economic activity declined once more (see Figure 5 for progress in various sectors). Even if available estimates of real development of GNP underestimate the crisis, there is no doubt that although the recession in Switzerland lasted quite long, it was mild compared with other countries. According to official estimates, net national production fell by 5% between 1929 and 1933, compared with 33% in the United States, 10% in Germany and 12% in France.[27] Although unemployment statistics did not take account of the part-time unemployed (and there was little incentive for such persons to register as unemployed due to the lack of compulsory insurance), and hence underestimated the actual unemployment rate, the latter was – at a maximum of 6.4% at the beginning of 1936 – relatively modest compared with other countries.

As the economy continued to slow down and protectionism spread, the principles of laissez-faire were no longer followed in Swiss economic policy. The government introduced import restrictions and export promotion measures, together with benefits for the unemployed, subsidies for individual industries and statutory regulations aimed at limiting the money supply.[28] Monetary policy measures, however, were considered inappropriate until France devalued its currency. Despite its substantial export economy, Switzerland was thus one of the last countries still maintaining parity with the gold standard.The SNB justified its adherence to the gold standard in the years prior to devaluation by referring to Switzerland's special economic structure.[29] This implied that while export conditions could be improved by devaluation, imports would become correspondingly more expensive. There is a Swiss characteristic – aside from the threat of inflation – that led the SNB to consider devaluation inadvisable. This was the fact that Switzerland, with its considerable savings funds, was a typical 'pensioners' country' and would stand to suffer substantial damage as a result of such a step. This analysis convinced the SNB to continue adhering to the gold standard if at all possible, and to increase its gold reserves so as to be able effectively to counteract any withdrawals by other countries. The introduction of exchange-control measures, transfer moratoria and clearing systems in a number of countries induced the SNB to conclude that monetary policy was coordinated more closely with trade policy and the protection of capital than it had been previously. Switzerland was to acquire its goods primarily from those countries in which large amounts of Swiss capital were blocked, and economic negotiations were to insist on a part of the export proceeds in Switzerland being used for settling capital claims.[30] Beginning in the mid-1930s, the portion of foreign trade conducted as part of free-payment transactions declined.[31] In April 1934, the SNB repeated its arguments against devaluation in a memorandum addressed to the Political Department (foreign ministry). The SNB first of all stated that Switzerland, 'with CHF 392 in imports and CHF 210 in exports per capita', 'is the number one in foreign trade'. Economic dependence was thus particularly evident. Devaluation would result in an increase in prices and wages in Switzerland, thus destroying the initial positive effect for the export economy. According to the SNB, the devaluation would, moreover, spell the end of Switzerland's role as a financial centre. However, revenues from capital investment were indispensable for covering the trade deficit. A stable currency was thus 'of paramount importance for Switzerland'.[32] A further claim repeatedly brought forward by the guardians of the currency was that devaluation was morally reprehensible: It was unacceptable for a country to rid itself of part of its debts by devaluing its currency.

As long as Switzerland maintained the gold standard, it had very little room for manoeuvre on the economic-policy front. In order to return to international competitiveness, the authorities tried a policy of price and wage cuts. While prices declined significantly, nominal wages and salaries, seen overall, fell only moderately. The implication was that, in real terms, wages and salaries rose markedly, in particular during the first years of the crisis. Between 1929 and 1933, the increase amounted to 17%.[33] Even if wages and salaries in the export industry may have declined more rapidly, undoubtedly the development of real wages and salaries in Switzerland and in other countries that did not devalue their currency limited competitiveness. Import restrictions, export promotion measures, subsidies for the most hard-hit industries and unemployment insurance did not form part of this deflationary programme, although all these measures were held within tight limits due to the government's objective of balancing the budget. At that time, the SNB had neither the legal competence nor the technical ability to conduct an open-market policy. All it could do was to make it known beyond any doubt that it was prepared to defend parity and strengthen confidence in the currency.

However, this was made considerably more difficult as a result of the banking crisis that developed from mid-1931.[34] Notably the big banks, which, unlike the cantonal banks and the local institutions, conducted foreign business, ran into difficulties.[35] The crisis was triggered by the introduction of exchange controls in Germany. The Swiss banks now paid the penalty for their high level of lending to Germany in the 1920s. The Standstill Agreement between Germany and the foreign creditor banks on short-term loans revealed that

Swiss banks accounted for 16% (around CHF1 billion) of the total amount of standstill credits. This put Switzerland in third position after the United States (36%) and Britain (28%), and before the Netherlands (13%) and France (4.5%). In July 1933, Germany ordered a general moratorium on transfers for all financial payments to foreign creditors except for interest payments under the Standstill Agreement.[36] According to a report submitted to the Federal Department of Finance, the blocked Swiss funds (banks and non-banks) in Germany amounted to CHF3.4 billion on 28 February 1934. CHF970 million of the banks' combined total assets of CHF4.998 billion were subject to transfer restrictions at the end of 1934. Germany alone accounted for a full CHF736 million.[37] Though in the second half of the 1930s the banks succeeded in substantially reducing their assets in countries with transfer restrictions, the situation continued to be serious for individual institutions. In June 1939, the ratio of blocked foreign investment to capital resources at three out of the seven remaining big banks came to between 86% and 125%.[38] From the mid-thirties onwards, the banks increasingly began to orient their business policies to the United States.

The banks' liquidity problems caused by the transfer restrictions were further exacerbated as the public, worried by the banking crisis in Austria and Germany, started switching out of long-term into short-term deposits and began hoarding banknotes.[39] Switzerland, too, began to experience runs on its banks, and in the summer and autumn of 1931 the first two banks were forced to close their doors. This was followed by a sharp fall in the volume of bank lending. It was mainly the big banks, whose balance sheet totals were in a steep decline, who suffered from the crisis. Even the two most solid big banks exhibited this trend (see figure 2). The cantonal banks, however, which had a domestic-business focus, were able to benefit from the state guarantee and increase their balance-sheet totals.

Because of its legal status, the SNB was only able to provide the banks with a limited amount of liquidity support.[40] Moreover, any large-scale action to assist the banks might have been interpreted by domestic and foreign investors as a sign that all was not well with Switzerland as a financial centre, which could have led to further withdrawals and eventually to a general financial crisis.[41] Since there was a risk of a similar scenario developing if one of the major banks was permitted to fail, the SNB, the Federal Government and the banks joined forces to try and rescue two of the big banks. In one case, thanks to the injection of substantial amounts of public money, the plan was a success. In the other, the bank had to close its doors.[42] In order to ease the banks' liquidity problems a loan institution, the Eidgenössische Darlehenskasse (Federal Loan Agency), was set up in 1932. Unlike the SNB, this institution had authority to advance funds, within limits, against the security of assets subject to transfer restrictions. The conversion of the FLA into a relief institution 'which should also be able to exert a considerable influence on the management of the bank benefiting from support', was rejected by Parliament.[43] The liquidity situation of the banks became serious during each of the waves of selling of Swiss francs, but especially in the spring of 1935.[44] Thanks to the employment of public funds, the informal cooperation between the Confederation, the SNB and the banks, as well as to the latter's recourse to their own substantial reserves, the crisis was finally overcome.

Despite manifestations of resistance against the deflation policy on the political Left and among labour circles from 1933 onward, it is amazing that there existed in Switzerland a broad consensus concerning the parity of the franc. Up until 1935, exporters, Social Democratic politicians and the trade unions were unanimously against devaluation.[45] The same was true of the leading economists, who interpreted the crisis in terms of over-investment theory. Their critics, too, whose analysis derived from the under-consumption theory, were for the most part against devaluation.[46] On both sides there was a lack of awareness of the negative economic implications of deflation. Max Weber, economic adviser to the Swiss Trade Unions Federation, was – after the defeat of the so-called 'crisis initiative' (2 June 1935) – the proverbial lone voice in the wilderness. The initiative called for the following measures, limited to five years, to combat the economic crisis and its consequences: resistance to a reduction in salaries and wages and in the prices of consumer goods; work creation programmes; easing of credit terms; unemployment and emergency assistance; promotion of export and tourism; capital export controls; also, the associated necessary competences at a federal and cantonal level, as well as the procurement of the necessary public funds through the capital market (Confederation bonds). Devalua-

Figure 5: Index of industrial output by industry (1913 = 100)

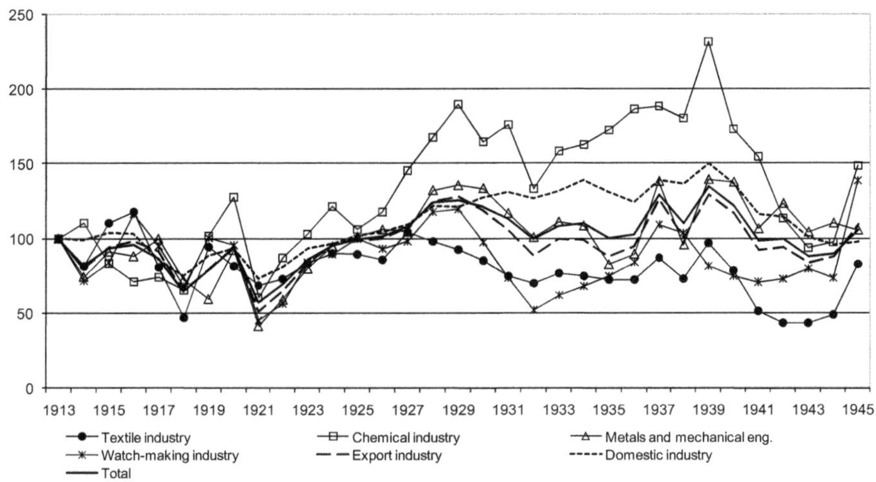

Source: Ritzmann (ed.), *Historical Statistics*, p. 629.

tion did not form part of the programme, however:[47] The Left was, in general, against devaluation, fearing inflation and the consequent erosion of real wages and incomes for employees and pensioners.

The export industry's proponents of devaluation were mostly textile manufacturers, who had been suffering from major structural problems since the 1920s, and representatives of the metals and mechanical engineering industries. Why did the export industry as a whole not assert its considerable influence in favour of devaluation? In this connection, Jakob Tanner has referred to the mythic status of the strong franc in the national consciousness of the 'unconquerable mountain people', which he believes became an *idée fixe* that in turn provoked a crisis mentality.[48] Looking at the output indices calculated by Thomas David, we inevitably come to other conclusions (see Figure 5).[49] It may be noted, for example, that individual industries showed diverging development. The chemical and watch-making industries, for instance, were back on a positive track as early as 1932. The other export industries also saw a small upswing in 1932, but this lasted only until 1934. It is also remarkable that domestic industry suffered only a minor downturn.

Margrit Müller's contribution to this volume demonstrates that firms in the main areas of export had various economic reasons to oppose devaluation, depending on their main export markets and the strategies they had pursued to cope with deglobalisation. In some areas, firms reacted to the crisis by intensifying their internationalisation through foreign direct investment (FDI). In view of protectionist measures in their main export markets, such as import restrictions, protective tariffs, etc. FDI seemed a more promising strategy than devaluation. Essential preconditions were a stable gold-based currency, low prices and interest rates and the free movement of capital. Against this background it is logical to conclude that the differing economic interests of the export industry were the reason why exporters did not call for devaluation.

The banks' position on the gold standard and the question of devaluation is also more complex and inconsistent than has generally been assumed.[50] On the one hand, in view of the inflow of foreign funds and as creditors of claims denominated in foreign currencies, the banks were in principle in favour of the gold standard as an international monetary regime, and of a stable convertible franc. On the other hand, they actively participated in speculation against the Swiss franc for profit considerations, thus jeopardising its parity. Despite public comments to the contrary, banking circles began to expect a devaluation of the Swiss franc after the United States had abolished the gold standard and the London World Economic Conference had failed, and they prepared for it by building up gold reserves. The Schweizerischer Bankverein (SBV) started to expect a devaluation profit as early as September 1933:

> However, should the currency really be devalued, which we all do not hope [*sic*] but which must be feared, we would have a sufficient margin on our gold – if we are allowed to keep it – to compensate for considerable damage, some of which has occurred already and some of which will certainly take place.[51]

These gold purchases weakened the Swiss franc and called the SNB into action. After various interventions by the SNB at individual banks and with the Federal Council had proved ineffective, the SNB concluded a gentlemen's agreement with the commercial banks on the restriction of gold and foreign currency transactions on 20 June 1935.[52] The authorities were obviously not convinced of the agreement's effectiveness, and on 19 June 1936 the Federal Council's decision on the protection of the national currency was passed, making any speculation against the Swiss franc a punishable offence. Despite these measures, the banks succeeded in building up large gold holdings, which generated considerable profits in the aftermath of the devaluation of 26 September 1936, as had already been anticipated in 1933. According to the calculations of the Independent Commission of Experts Switzerland – Second World War, the devaluation profit on gold and foreign currency of SBV and SKA amounted to CHF 22.5 and CHF 17.5 million respectively.[53] In the case of SBV and SKA, these amounts corresponded to roughly half of their gross earnings shown for 1935.

The adherence to the gold standard not only confronted the export industry with difficulties, but was also a challenge for the SNB. The inflow of capital of investors who had been thrown into a state of uncertainty by the economic development and the breakdown of the global monetary regime constituted a problem, as the SNB feared that this 'hot money' would leave the country just as quickly as it had arrived. In the 1930s, international investors were influenced both by the monetary policy of the major economies and by the associated expectations in terms of other countries' reactions. At the same time, problems with public finances (deficits) and in the financial sector (the banking crisis) inevitably led to speculation about the currency concerned and accordingly resulted in an outflow of gold, which could thus force a country to relinquish the gold standard: Figure 6 shows how the monetary policy of other countries had a direct effect on the gold and currency reserves of the SNB.

The aforementioned massive capital inflow prior to the British devaluation on 21 September 1931, and in reaction to the Central European banking crisis in the summer of 1931, can be clearly seen. Thereafter, until the United States abandoned the gold standard on 19 April 1933, the SNB's gold reserves remained stable. Evidently it was expected that Switzerland would also devalue, and this led to a flight of capital out of Swiss francs.[54] There was a renewed outflow of gold after a new parity for the dollar had been fixed on 31 January 1934. With the stabilisation of the dollar, gold flowed into the US 'because the dollar was being quoted in the market above the gold value' and the Swiss franc was subject to renewed speculation.[55]

Figure 6: SNB's gold and foreign exchange reserves 1928–1939 (in CHF millions)

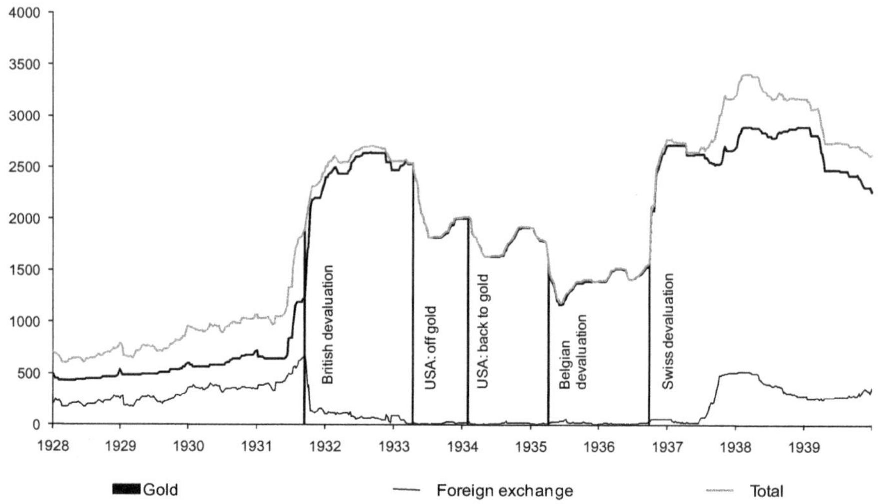

Source: Swiss National Bank return, SNB archive Statistics.

A final sharp decline was registered between February and June 1935, prompted by the Belgian devaluation on 1 April 1935 and an economic programme put forward by the left wing.[56]

The SNB adhered to the gold standard not only because of the aforementioned economic policy considerations, but also because it was convinced that gold provided the sole basis upon which an international monetary regime could function. It thus pressed for Switzerland to demand at the London Economic Conference that Britain and the United States should return to the gold standard. 'It [Switzerland] must form a united front together with France and the other gold currency countries and attempt to "force" this return.'[57] After this attempt had failed, France, Belgium, the Netherlands and Switzerland reacted by establishing the so-called 'gold bloc' together with Italy and Poland. The governments of these countries confirmed their intention 'to maintain the unhindered functioning of the gold-based currency in their countries at current gold parities and within the framework of valid legislation'. The central banks agreed to offer each other mutual support for the purpose of defending the gold-based currency and fighting speculation.[58] Given the contemporary economic and political pressures, however, this agreement was unable to prevent further countries abolishing the gold standard. In 1934, Italy introduced foreign-exchange controls; and at the end of March 1935 Belgium devalued its currency, as we have previously mentioned. The future of the gold bloc thus looked uncertain. Even the SNB began to plan for the possibility of devaluation and assigned an employee to consider the level of the devaluation rate.[59]

When, in spring 1936, the People's Front government came to power in France, the financial markets lost confidence and the French franc came under pressure. Although the government declared itself in favour of adhering to parity, it gave in to the pressure on 25 September, and France devalued the franc by 30%. Although the SNB did not consider the Swiss franc threatened by the French devaluation and was still in favour of maintaining parity, the majority of the government believed devaluation was unavoidable.[60] Its supporters argued that Switzerland should no longer remain a price island, and that while the devaluation would only be triggered by the renewed devaluation of the French franc, 'this could not be prevented and it was high time for Switzerland to keep pace with the world economy and to join in as well.'[61]

The fears expressed in the run-up to the devaluation of 26 September 1936 proved unfounded. The devaluation led neither to a renunciation of the principles of the gold standard nor to Switzerland's loss of significance as a financial centre. The opposite was true: The devaluation relieved the SNB of the obligation to redeem banknotes with gold or gold currency, but charged it with maintaining the value of the Swiss franc at between 190 and 215 milligrams of fine gold. The Federal Council issued a special directive instructing the SNB to fix the value of the Swiss franc at around 205 milligrams of fine gold, which corresponded to a devaluation of some 30%.[62] The financial centre experienced such a massive reflow of capital that the SNB was forced to reconsider the principle of free convertibility of the Swiss franc. Upward price pressures also proved to be not very serious and only short-lived. For Switzerland's economic development the devaluation was positive, although part of the recovery was due to the upswing in the world economy: a year later even the SNB was able to observe 'that the devaluation had a favourable influence on the cost/price relationship, mainly for the export industries.'[63]

The direction of capital flow was to change several times before and during the Second World War. Even though this sometimes posed serious problems for Swiss monetary policy and the SNB considered introducing currency controls on several occasions, Switzerland adhered as best it could to the principles of the gold standard, even during the war.[64]

Conclusion and outlook on the post-war period

In the 1920s, the view became established in Switzerland that the country's position as an international creditor was intimately connected with its close dependence on the external economy. The basic idea was as follows: Switzerland was a small country with few raw materials and therefore dependent on exports and imports. Despite their significance, Switzerland's exports were not sufficient to pay for its imports; but the resulting gap in the trade balance could be filled by income earned from tourism, services and capital transactions. For these mechanisms to operate effectively, not only must the conditions for international trading and capital movements be as liberal as possible, but it was also necessary to have a stable currency based on gold. When financial transactions threatened to have a negative impact on the Swiss capital market, economic actors, and especially the banks, were expected to subordinate their policies to the greater interest, in the pursuit of which the authorities would rely upon moral suasion rather than legislation.

Switzerland remained true to this guiding concept even during the difficult conditions of the 1930s, when exporters suffered from an overvalued currency, and increasingly common beggar-thy-neighbour policies and international capital flows were having negative effects on external and internal monetary policy. By supporting the export sector and segments of the domestic industry, Swiss economic policy endeavoured to alleviate the negative consequences of the deflationary policy which the authorities were forced to adopt through their adherence to the gold standard. Even though the economic crisis in Switzerland was comparatively mild, this did not prevent serious political tensions and even a government crisis.

Why did Switzerland adhere to the gold standard for so long? Of decisive importance was, in the first place, that Switzerland was a small and open economy that had had positive experiences with free capital movements and a currency pegged to gold. Besides the interests of the financial centre, the export industries' foreign direct investment was crucial in this context. Second, both decision-makers in the field of economic policy and economists lacked theoretical knowledge concerning the causes of the crisis and possible remedies. Finally, the authorities and, in particular, the SNB were convinced that there was no alternative to an international monetary regime based on the gold standard. This belief prevailed among central banks at the time. As long as there was some hope that the gold standard might be re-established internationally, the Swiss authorities regarded a devaluation as taboo – particularly also on moral grounds. As a creditor country with large gold reserves, Switzerland was one of the countries longest able to resist the pressure.

The devaluation of September 1936 did not change this belief. As the following summary will demonstrate, Switzerland tried to adhere to this monetary policy – convertibility and free capital movements – until the changeover to floating exchange rates at the beginning of the 1970s. Even though certain restrictions on capital movements necessarily had to be imposed in the interests of monetary stability, these were of minor importance compared with other European countries.

Despite the fact that after the Second World War Switzerland was one of the few countries with a convertible currency, and that free trade – the second major goal of the currency agreement of Bretton Woods – was also basically in the interests of Swiss economic policy, Switzerland did not join the Agreement until 1992.[65] In the early post-war period, economic exchanges with most trading partners in Switzerland were regulated by bilateral-payment agreements. As regards Switzerland, foreign currency loans played a significant role in enabling countries that had suffered the ravages of war to import her goods.[66] Such loans were not permitted under the by-laws of the Monetary Fund.[67] With the general changeover to current-account convertibility in Europe, payment agreements became obsolete, and Switzerland was for the most part able to observe the guidelines of the IMF.

After the war, Switzerland held considerable foreign currency reserves and – with a few exceptions – achieved an annual current-account profit until the demise of the Bretton Woods currency system. Switzerland was thus never forced to introduce foreign-exchange controls or to devalue the Swiss franc. Indeed, its difficulty was exactly the reverse. The regular current-account surpluses gave rise to an increase in the supply of central bank money, thus creating inflationary pressure. The Swiss authorities reacted to this problem by trying to restrict the inflow of capital through administrative measures (see below). Another possible step would have been to revalue the Swiss franc (an appreciation). Remarkably, it was not until 1971 that the authorities were prepared to do this.

After having suffered a marked decline in international financial-market transactions in the wake of the Great Depression and the Second World War, the Swiss financial centre gained a strong position in the post-war period. Due to foreign exchange controls and inflation, there was no real competition from the European financial markets, which were committed to the task of rebuilding their own economies. Until the mid-sixties, Switzerland played a prominent role in the issue of international bonds.[68]

Even though foreign exchange controls were never an option, the National Bank attempted, by various means at its disposal, to limit the effects of capital movements on monetary conditions in Switzerland. Thus it occasionally restricted the volume of foreign bonds in order to prevent excessive strains on the domestic capital market and a rise in interest rates. During the 1980s, globalisation of financial market capital export regulations were gradually liberalised, and in 1995, the authorisation obligation was changed into a reporting obligation serving statistical purposes.

Most of the restrictive measures in the domain of capital exports were merely temporary and partial: notably, direct investment was never subjected to restriction. Unfortunately, statistical data on the extent of Switzerland's direct investment abroad have only been available since the mid-1980s. While in the period from 1985 to 1995, annual direct investment fluctuated between CHF 2.7 billion and CHF 14.8 billion, the second half of the 1990s saw a steady and strong rise to a peak of CHF 75.4 billion in 2000. In 1997, the stock of direct investments abroad accounted for 62% of Switzerland's GDP: Switzerland thus took the lead within the OECD, followed by the Netherlands, Belgium/Luxembourg, Sweden and Austria.[69]

A problem for Switzerland in the post-war period was not so much capital exports as enormous capital imports at certain times. The worldwide economic upswing triggered a rise in the supply of funds for international capital transactions. As the liberalisation of these transactions proceeded, Switzerland proved increasingly attractive for foreign capital despite low-yield opportunities compared with other industrialised nations. The inflow of funds into Switzerland was due, apart from the country's political and economic stability and banking secrecy, to investors' need to spread risks.[70] The capital inflow significantly increased the supply of money, which, together with the favourable economic situation, jeopardised price stability; accordingly, the authorities introduced a number of monetary policy measures aimed at reducing money-supply growth. With a few exceptions (a stake in the transport and energy sectors and the acquisition of real estate), foreign direct investment in Switzerland was not restricted. As it had already done in the thirties, the SNB resorted to gentlemen's agreements, which were later replaced by legal measures in the form of Federal Parliament Decrees.[71] The agreements targeted either commercial bank money creation (gentlemen's agreement on holding minimum reserves at the National Bank and credit restriction measures) or the inflow of foreign funds (no interest paid on foreign balances). Kurt Schiltknecht came to the conclusion that the measures to ward off foreign funds introduced prior to 1966 did not suffice to effectively limit the inflow of capital from abroad.[72] Foreign-exchange controls would have been required in order to ward off foreign funds successfully.

When, at the beginning of the 1970s, the end of the Bretton Woods currency system was in sight, Switzerland was one of the countries that occasionally had to contend with massive speculative capital inflows. In May 1971, the SNB was compelled to suspend its intervention purchases on the foreign-exchange market for a few days and revalue the Swiss franc by 7.07%.[73] After the United States had abandoned the gold standard, there were various parity adjustments to the major currencies, leading to a revaluation of the Swiss franc on each occasion. However, these adjustments were no longer enough to save the system. After further measures for warding off foreign funds and new Federal Parliament Decrees had proved ineffective in the fight against inflation, the National Bank ceased its support of the dollar through foreign-exchange purchases at the end of January 1973. Switzerland was thus the first country to definitively adopt a floating currency. Subsequently the Swiss franc appreciated against the dollar by 24.8% between May 1971 and mid-February; it also appreciated by 9.7% against the currencies of its 15 largest trading partners.[74] The real trade-weighted CHF exchange rate rose by an average of 0.6% p.a. between the transition to floating and 2001.[75] The changeover to flexible exchange rates made it possible to fight inflation successfully; but the capital inflow continued, increasing particularly in economically and politically uncertain times, so that the National Bank faced repeated revaluation shocks. Since the 1980s the emphasis has been on monetary policy measures rather than dirigistic interventions.

In contrast to the interwar period, the post-war era saw prolonged economic growth. This, together with capital inflows, gave rise to inflation from the early 1960s. The Swiss authorities then tried to limit capital imports through administrative measures, but as all-embracing exchange management was out of the question, it was not possible to achieve price stability. Consequently, it was inevitable that the fixed exchange rate would be abandoned.

1 I would like to thank Jan Baumann, Sébastien Guex, Margrit Müller and Philipp Müller for their valuable input in numerous discussions.

2 Harm G. Schröter, 'Etablierungs- und Verteilungsmuster der schweizerischen Auslandsproduktion von 1870 bis 1914', in Paul Bairoch and Martin Körner (eds.), *Die Schweiz in der Weltwirtschaft (15.–20. Jh.)* (Zurich: Chronos, 1990), pp. 391–407, here p. 395.

3 Michael Bernegger, 'Die Schweiz und die Weltwirtschaft: Etappen der Integration im 19. und 20. Jahrhundert', in Bairoch and Körner (eds.), *Die Schweiz*, pp. 429–464, here p. 445.

4 Thomas Schlup, 'Kapitalverkehr', key word in the *Historisches Lexikon der Schweiz*.

5 Gottlieb Bachmann, 'Die Schweiz als internationales Finanzzentrum', in Neue Helvetische Gesellschaft (ed.), *Die Schweiz, ein nationales Jahrbuch* (Berne: Neue Helvetische Gesellschaft, 1931), pp. 29–38, here p. 34.

6 See, among others, Gérald Arlettaz, 'Crise et déflation. Le primat des intérêts financiers en Suisse au début des années 1930', *Relations internationales* 30 (1982), pp. 159–175.

7 For bonds, cf. Swiss National Bank (ed.), *Statistisches Handbuch des schweizerischen Geld- und Kapitalmarktes* (Zurich: Schulthess & Co., 1944), pp. 24 f. For the equity issues, see annex II to the speech by Ernst Ackermann at the Annual General Meeting of the Schweizerische Statistische Gesellschaft 1935, *Zeitschrift für schweizerische Statistik und Volkswirtschaft* I (1935), p. 209.

8 If we compare the figures published by Ackermann (see endnote 7) with a contemporary SNB survey of 'bonds available for public subscription and non-publicly placed bonds and share issues, to the extent that they can be established from newspaper reports', the result is a German share of the issuing volume of between 36% and 41%. See SNB archive 5.4/5147.

9 According to an internal SNB study. See also 'Notes on the Swiss balance of payments for 1927' (22.2.1929), SNB archive 5.4/5147.

10 For an assessment of Switzerland's role as a financial centre by the City of London in the 1920s, see Youssef Cassis, 'La place financière suisse et la City de Londres 1890–1990', in Bairoch and Körner (eds.), *Die Schweiz*, pp. 339–352.

11 Hans J. Mast, 'Der Bankenplatz Schweiz im Zweiten Weltkrieg', in Joseph Jung (ed.), *Zwischen Bundeshaus und Paradeplatz. Die Banken der Credit Suisse Group im Zweiten Weltkrieg. Studien und Materialien* (Zurich: Neue Zürcher Zeitung, 2001), pp. 767–790.

12 Sébastien Guex, 'La politique de la Banque nationale suisse (1907–1939): modèles, références et spécificités', in Olivier Feiertag and Michel Margairaz (eds.), *Politiques et pratiques des banques d'émission en Europe (XVIIe–XXe siècle): le bicentenaire de la Banque de France dans la perspective de l'identité monétaire eruopéenne* (Paris: Editions Albin Michel, 2003), pp. 526–548, here p. 526.

13 The figures on deposit balances are taken from Marc Perrenoud *et al.*, *La place financière et les banques suisses à l'époque de national socialisme. Les relations des grandes banques avec l'Allemagne*, Veröffentlichung der Unabhängigen Expertenkommission Schweiz – Zweiter Weltkrieg, vol. 13 (Zurich: Chronos, 2002), pp. 620 ff. For balance-sheet totals see Walter Adolf Jöhr, *Schweizerische Kreditanstalt 1856–1956. Hundert Jahre im Dienste der schweizerischen Volkswirtschaft*, (Zurich: Schweizerische Kreditanstalt, 1956), pp. 527 ff. and the Annual Reports of Schweizerische Kreditanstalt, and Hans Bauer, *Schweizerischer Bankverein 1872–1972*, (Basel: Schweizerischer Bankverein, 1972), pp. 485 ff. For the national consumer price index see Heiner Ritzmann-Blickenstorfer (ed.): *Historical Statistics of Switzerland* (Zurich: Chronos, 1996), p. 503.

14 Marc Perrenoud and Rodrigo López, *Aspects des relations financières franco-suisse (1936–1946)*, Veröffentlichung der Unabhängigen Expertenkommission Schweiz – Zweiter Weltkrieg, vol. 25 (Zurich: Chronos, 2002), p. 42.

15 Sancey, Yves, 'Place financière suisse et émergence d'une régulation para-étatique durant l'entre-deux-guerres', in Sébastien Guex *et al.* (eds.), *Krisen und Stabilisierung. Die Schweiz in der Zwischenkriegszeit* (Zurich: Chronos 1998), pp. 81– 93, here p. 83.

16 After the war, average mortgage rates in Switzerland rose from 4.82% in 1918 to 5.5% in 1921. In 1923 they dropped to 4.95% and rose again to 5.30% in 1924 and 5.40% in 1925. They dropped back to 5.25% in 1926 and to 5.20% in 1927. In 1928 and 1929 they stood at 5%. See Swiss National Bank (ed.), *Statistisches Handbuch*, p. 36.

17 Schweizerische Nationalbank (ed.), *Die Schweizerische Nationalbank 1907–1932* (Zurich: Schweizerische Nationalbank, 1932), p. 413.

18 Perrenoud *et al.*, *La place financière*, p. 218 and Perrenoud and López, *Aspects*, p. 47.

19 An example can be found in Jan Baumann and Patrick Halbeisen, 'Die Internationalisierung des Finanzplatzes Schweiz und ihre Folgen für die Währungspolitik: Konsens und Konflikte zwischen der Nationalbank und den Geschäftsbanken 1919–1939', unpublished paper for the conference 'Switzerland as a financial centre in international perspectives (1913–1965)', Lausanne, 1–2 October 1999, p. 22.

20 On the creation of the gentlemen's agreement in the interwar period see Sancey, 'Place financière suisse', pp. 81–93.

21 On the problem of balance-of-payments statistics in Switzerland and especially on the SNB's failed attempts – owing to resistance by the banks – to draw up balance-of-payments statistics in the 1920s and 1930s see Baumann and Halbeisen, 'Die Internationalisierung'. The figures stated here are taken from Eduard Kellenberger, *Kapitalexport und Zahlungsbilanz*, volume I (Berne: A. Francke AG, 1939), pp. 155, 245 and 307.

22 Negative figures indicate capital export.

23 See SNB archive 5.4/5147, 'Explanations on the Swiss balance of payments for 1927' (22.2.1929).

24 Eveline Ruoss, 'Die Anfänge der schweizerischen Geldpolitik', in: Youssef Cassis and Jakob Tanner (eds.), *Banken und Kredit in der Schweiz (1850–1930)* (Zurich: Chronos, 1993), pp. 29–52, here p. 48.

25 Sophie Faber, 'Die Ursachen der Deflation in der Schweiz in den dreissiger Jahren', unpublished paper for the annual meeting of the Swiss Society for Statistics and Economics on 20 and 21 March 1997.

26 Mathias Zurlinden, 'Goldstandard, Deflation und Depression: Die schweizerische Volkswirtschaft in der Weltwirtschaftskrise', *Schweizerische Nationalbank, Quarterly Bulletin* 2 (2003), 86–116, here 108.

27 Official estimates for 1929 to 1938 concern nominal net national income. By adding indirect revenue, net national product may be estimated. In order to calculate the customary gross national product, write-downs would also have to be added; these, however, are not known. A national product deflator, however, is lacking. Deflationing by means of the national consumer price index usually applied is a temporary solution, since this index also takes into account the price development of foreign goods and consequently shows greater deflation than a national pro-

duct deflator. This causes the decline in aggregate economic production to be underestimated. Cf. Zurlinden, 'Goldstandard', 94.

28 Wilfried Rutz, *Die schweizerische Volkswirtschaft zwischen Währungs- und Beschäftigungspolitik in der Weltwirtschaftskrise – wirtschaftspolitische Analyse der Bewältigung eines Zielkonflikts*, Diss. University of St Gallen (Zürich and St. Gallen: Polygraphischer Verlag, 1970), pp. 147 ff.; Martin Meier *et al., Schweizerische Aussenwirtschaftspolitik 1930–1948. Strukturen-Verhandlungen-Funktionen*, Veröffentlichung der Unabhängigen Expertenkommission Schweiz – Zweiter Weltkrieg, vol. 10 (Zurich: Chronos, 2002), pp. 75 ff.; and, with regard to the labour market, the contribution by Anne-Lise Head-König in this volume.

29 The following arguments are taken from an internal SNB study dated 3.3.1932 entitled, 'Krise, Wirtschaft und Banken. Beeinflussung der Zahlungsbilanz. Goldstandardfrage', SNB archive, 5.4/5147.

30 See report by the Governing Board to the Bank Committee on Switzerland's balance of payments and trade policy dated 6 October 1932, SNB archive 5.4/5147.

31 On the development of Switzerland's foreign trade in the context of restricted payments see Peter Hug and Martin Kloter, 'Der "Bilateralismus" in seinem multilateralen Kontext. Die Aussenpolitik der Schweiz zur Sicherung ihres Aussenhandels und Zahlungsverkehrs, 1920/30–1958/60', in Peter Hug and Martin Kloter (eds.), *Aufstieg und Niedergang des Bilateralismus. Schweizerische Aussen- und Aussenwirtschaftspolitik, 1930–1960: Rahmenbedingungen, Entscheidungsstrukturen, Fallstudien* (Zurich: Chronos, 1999), pp. 13–139, here pp. 58 f.

32 Commission Nationale pour la publication de Documents Diplomatiques Suisses (ed.), *Documents Diplomatiques Suisses. 1848–1945*, vol. 11 (Berne: Bentelli AG, 1989), no. 22, Annex II, pp. 73–75.

33 Zurlinden, 'Goldstandard', pp. 86–116.

34 On the development and scale of the banking crisis, see Daniel Bodmer, *L' intervention de la Confédération dans l'économie bancaire suisse* (Basel: Buchdruckerei National-Zeitung, 1948); Paul Ehrsam, 'Die Bankenkrise der 30er Jahre in der Schweiz', in Eidgenössische Bankenkommission (ed.), *50 Jahre Eidgenössische Bankenkommission* (Zurich: Schulthess, 1985), pp. 83–118; Patrick Halbeisen, 'The Banking Crisis and its Implications for Swiss Banking Legislation in the 1930s', in Manfred Pohl *et al.* (eds.), *A Century of Banking Consolidation in Europe. The History and Archives of Mergers and Acquisitions* (Aldershot etc.: Ashgate, 2001), pp. 102–120.

35 This may be derived simply from the development of the balance sheets. In 1930, at CHF 8.6 billion, the combined balance-sheet total of the big banks had reached a temporary peak. By 1935, total assets had dropped to less than half (CHF 4.2 billion). There is no doubt that a considerable part of this decline is attributable to foreign business.

36 Schweizerische Nationalbank (ed.), *Schweizerische Nationalbank 1907–1957* (Zurich: Schweizerische Nationalbank, 1957), p. 289.

37 SNB archive 4.1/4018, report and proposal by a committee of experts consisting of G. Bachmann, A. Dreyfus and E. Walch to the Federal Department of Finance concerning the release of banks from transfer restrictions on assets.

38 Halbeisen, 'Banking Crisis', p. 66.
39 See also on the following Faber, 'Die Ursachen'.
40 See Ehrsam, 'Die Bankenkrise', p. 92.
41 This problem is highlighted by Harold James. See Harold James, *The End of Globalization. Lessons from the Great Depression* (Cambridge MA: Harvard University Press, 2002).
42 On the efforts to rescue the Schweizerische Volksbank and Schweizerische Diskontbank see Ehrsam, 'Die Bankenkrise'; Halbeisen, 'Banking Crisis'.
43 SNB archive 4.1/4040, notes on the bank conference of 27 March 1933.
44 See statement in the SNB's Annual Report for 1935 (page 18): 'The economic stagnation, the increasing difficulties affecting foreign payments, *but particularly capital withdrawals* caused not inconsiderable problems for the banks in the year under review' [author's italics].
45 The only public support for devaluation came from the social movement of the 'Freigeldler'. This rather peripheral group of dissenters, founded by the economic autodidact Silvio Gesell, proposed to abandon the gold standard in order to introduce an index currency which was intended to adapt automatically, by a fixed mechanism, to the variations of the price index. For the history of the 'free economy' movement see Markus Schärrer, *Geld- und Bodenreform als Brücke zum sozialen Staat. Die Geschichte der Freiwirtschaftsbewegung in der Schweiz (1915–1952)* (Zurich: Zentralstelle der Studentenschaft, 1983).
46 For the theoretical background to the economic debate on the causes of the Great Depression and the economic-policy remedies see Elisabeth Allgoewer, 'Ueberinvestition oder Unterkonsum? Die Grosse Depression in der Schweiz. Beiträge der Wirtschaftstheorie zu ihrer Erklärung und Bewältigung', in Thomas Geiser *et al.* (eds.), *Arbeit in der Schweiz des 20. Jahrhunderts. Wirtschaftliche, rechtliche und soziale Perspektiven* (Bern etc.: Paul Haupt, 1998), pp. 187–216.
47 See Gaudenz Prader, *50 Jahre schweizerische Stabilisierungspolitik. Lernprozesse in Theorie und Politik am Beispiel der Finanz- und Beschäftigungspolitik des Bundes* (Zurich: Schulthess, 1981), pp. 100–102.
48 See Jakob Tanner, 'Goldparität im Gotthardstaat: Nationale Mythen und die Stabilität des Schweizer Frankens in den 1930er und 1940er Jahren', *Studien und Quellen* 26 (2000), pp. 45–85, here pp. 76–78.
49 Thomas David, 'Un indice de la production industrielle de la Suisse durant l'entre-deux-guerres', *Schweizerische Zeitschrift für Geschichte* 45 (1995), pp. 109–130. The figures are also contained in Ritzmann-Blickenstorfer (ed.), *Historical Statistics*, p. 629.
50 See Marc Perrenoud *et al.*, *La place financière*, pp. 54 ff.
51 Minutes of the managing board of Schweizerischer Bankverein dated 5 September 1933, quoted after Perrenoud *et al.*, *La place financière*, p. 631.
52 For the discussion concerning the gentlemen's agreement of the Swiss Bankers Association see Baumann and Halbeisen, 'Die Internationalisierung'.
53 Perrenoud *et al.*, *La place financière*, p. 64.
54 See SNB's Annual Report for 1933, p. 23.
55 See SNB's Annual Report for 1934, pp. 9 and 26.

56 The crisis initiative was an economic programme submitted by the political left in the form of a petition for a referendum, which was rejected with a slight majority. For the content and the monetary policy implications, see Baumann and Halbeisen, 'Die Internationalisierung'.
57 See Swiss Diplomatic Documents (SDD), vol. 10, no. 269, p. 664.
58 Schweizerische Nationalbank (ed.), *Schweizerische Nationalbank 1907–1957*, p. 318.
59 Archiv für Zeitgeschichte: estate of Rudolf Pfenninger, documents on the 1936 devaluation.
60 On the debate among the Swiss authorities after the announcement of the French devaluation see Tanner, 'Goldparität', pp. 54–57; Commission Nationale pour la publication de Documents Diplomatiques Suisses (ed.), *Documents Diplomatiques*, vol. 11 no. 297; and the excerpts from the private Federal Council minutes from which the Independent Commission of Experts Switzerland – Second World War quotes substantially (see Unabhängige Expertenkommission Schweiz – Zweiter Weltkrieg, *Die Schweiz und die Goldtransaktionen im Zweiten Weltkrieg*, Veröffentlichung der Unabhängigen Expertenkommission Schweiz – Zweiter Weltkrieg, vol. 16 (Zurich: Chronos, 2002), footnote 27, p. 89).
61 Commission Nationale pour la publication de Documents Diplomatiques Suisses (ed.), *Documents Diplomatiques* vol. 11 no. 297, 864.
62 Swiss National Bank, Annual Report 1936, p. 19.
63 Remarks by G. Bachmann, Chairman of the Governing Board of the SNB, on the development of the economic, monetary and financial situation of Switzerland since the devaluation; speech given at the Bank Council meeting of 17 December 1937, in SNB archive 2.3/2244.
64 On monetary policy during the Second World War see Vincent Crettol and Patrick Halbeisen, *Monetary policy background to the gold transactions of the Swiss National Bank in the Second World War* (n. p.: Swiss National Bank, 1999).
65 A useful brief overview of how the currency system of Bretton Woods functioned is provided in Barry Eichengreen, *Globalizing Capital. A History of the International Monetary System* (Princeton NJ: Princeton University Press, 1996).
66 In 1947, loans extended by the Confederation and by the private sector to other countries after the war amounted to CHF 696 million and CHF 477 million respectively. See Peter Hug and Martin Kloter, 'Der "Bilateralismus"', p. 89.
67 We cannot here enter into the other reasons brought forward against Switzerland's participation. For the discussions concerning Switzerland's adherence to the institutions of Bretton Woods, see Thomas Frings, 'Entre différence et différé: Quand le Sonderfall pousse la Confédération à une stratégie dilatoire face aux institutions de Bretton Woods', unpublished licentiate of the University of Lausanne, 2001.
68 With a few exceptions, the bonds were denominated in Swiss francs, the biggest borrower at the time being the World Bank. See Luc Berthoud, *Les emprunts étrangers en Suisse (depuis 1945)* (Zurich: Editions P. G. Keller, 1967), p. 22.
69 Fred Henneberger and Alexander Ziegler, *Internationalisierung der Produktion und sektoraler Strukturwandel: Folgen für den Arbeitsmarkt*, Study commissioned

by the State Secretariat for Economics (Berne: Staatssekretariat für Wirtschaft, 2001), p. 6 and literature listed.

70 Kurt Schiltknecht, *Beurteilung der Gentlemen's Agreements und Konjunkturbeschlüsse der Jahre 1954–1966 unter besonderer Berücksichtigung der Auslandgelder* (Zurich 1970), pp. 80 f.

71 On the individual measures see ibid.

72 Ibid., p. 164.

73 Schweizerische Nationalbank (ed.), *75 Jahre Schweizerische Nationalbank. Die Zeit von 1957 bis 1982* (Zurich: Neue Zürcher Zeitung, 1982), p. 103.

74 Swiss National Bank (ed.), *Monatsbericht*, February 1973, pp. 3 f.

75 Bruno Gehrig, 'Moving among currency giants – a Swiss perspective', speech given at the Swiss-American Chamber of Commerce, Zurich, 16. January 2001. http://www.snb.ch/e/aktuelles/index.html?file=referate/text_referate.html.

Ola Honningdal Grytten

A Small Country's Policy Response to Global Economic Disintegration during the Interwar Years of Crisis

Introduction

This chapter focuses on the disintegration of the world economy during the interwar period and examines its effects on Norwegian economic policy compared with those of other small European countries. Two very different patterns emerge. In the 1920s several western European countries aimed their policy at restoring the pre-war economic regime. More precisely their goal was to re-establish a liberal economic order, i.e. relatively free trade, fair competition and the gold standard at par gold values. This type of policy was pursued by the United Kingdom, the Netherlands, Switzerland, Denmark, Sweden and Norway. In the 1930s most countries responded to international economic disintegration by an inward-looking focus aimed at protecting their own industries, labour markets, and current-account balances. Monetary adjustments were a major feature. After Britain suspended gold redemption on 20/21 September 1931 several other countries followed, dropping gold in favour of a floating or pegged currency. Protectionism, cartelisation and subsidies were other new policies introduced by most western European countries to defend their domestic industries.

In 1920 Norway was a small open economy, and in the following decade the Norwegian government, parliament and central bank fought to retain the pre-war system of a liberal economic order. In the 1930s this policy was partly given up. Gold redemption was suspended by the end of September 1931, and measures were taken to protect domestic industries and labour markets, and the current-account balance.

In the 1930s a regime of moderate protectionism was introduced. The new order somewhat resembled a return to the mercantilistic system that had more or less prevailed until the 1840s. The new protectionism included both qualitative and quantitative measures. Import tariffs were reintroduced or raised: even the old mercantilistic element of import quotas was reborn. The reintroduction of protectionism had two main purposes. Firstly, as an answer to foreign protectionism: the government sought to protect its home markets for its domestic industries. In particular the authorities protected agriculture and major manufacturing industries, both facing severe competition from abroad. Secondly, the authorities sought to protect Norway's exchange reserves. Despite this new orientation, one should bear in mind that Norway was still under a more liberal trade regime than most countries in the western world in the 1930s.

Cartelisation was also positively encouraged: it was an attempt to protect the supply side from over-production with its inevitable drop in prices and profits. A negative consequence of this policy was the consumers' loss, as prices were kept artificially high. In addition to cartelisation subsidies were introduced in order to support some industries, in particular agriculture.

A semi-public campaign was also set on foot. The slogan was 'Buy Norwegian'. The aim was to stimulate the sale of Norwegian products in the domestic market and thus reduce the effect of the economic slump upon workers and producers.

In opposition Labour had initially agitated for inflationary fiscal policies. However, after having gained governmental power in 1935, they abstained from pursuing budget deficit expansion.

The deflationary monetary policy of the 1920s to restore, and after May 1928 to protect, the pre-war gold parities was given up in the early 1930s. Norway left gold, and a relatively more successful inflationary monetary policy was conducted by the central bank. This change in monetary policy had two major effects. Domestic demand increased. Thus, production rose, and unemployment fell. Also, the depreciation of the krone made Norwegian industry more competitive against countries that still maintained the gold standard. Norwegian products became affordable abroad: they were also cheaper than foreign goods in the Norwegian domestic markets. Accordingly, a significant increase in both exports and imports substitution took place. Thus, the new monetary policy enabled Norway to recover from the great depression quite rapidly.

Most measures against the crisis were introduced around 1930. The bulk of these became permanent, later even extended. Because of this my paper will argue that the shift from a mainly liberal economic regime to a mixed regulatory regime started around 1930. This is contrary to the conventional view, which holds that the turnaround started in 1935, when the Norwegian Labour Party came into office with a huge parliamentary majority together with the Farmer's Party.

Disintegration of the interwar economy

The interwar economy can best be characterised by its fluctuations between crises and spurts of growth. The international economy saw two major crises. The first, the post-war depression, was in the early 1920s. The second, the great depression, was in the first half of the 1930s. Both were characterised by steep falls in production and prices. The crisis of the 1930s was also accompanied by mass unemployment. In consequence of the collapse of the stock market on Wall Street from October 1929 onwards, American banks experienced heavy losses. Hence, American private banks could no longer offer short-term credits to Germany and Austria. Thus, Germany and Austria could not meet their obligations. International liquidity shrank rapidly.

On the international arena the national governments met the crisis of the 1930s by various protectionist measures. The first of these had in fact already been tried out in the 1920s, when in particular the USA and France, despite significant trade surpluses and undervalued currencies, decided to increase their tariffs. In the 1930s all western powers to some extent adopted some kind of protectionism, and international trade fell rapidly.

The lack of international liquidity, the collapse of the gold standard, the reintroduction of protectionism and the rapid drop in international trade are all factors of the disintegration or deglobalisation of the 1930s. This trend was not reversed until the post-World War II period. The collapse of the world economy forced governments to embrace protectionism. In turn, international trade declined even further. This process of disintegration and deglobalisation is described in the work of Hein Klemann, Olle Krantz and Ivan Jakubec. On the other hand, in Margrit Müller's survey of the Swiss case, we note that Switzerland followed a different course, meeting the problems of the interwar period by the internationalisation of several industries. The Swiss case reminds us of the fact that there were significant differences in policy choice among the European countries.

The Norwegian interwar economy

In Norway the economy suffered three major setbacks during the twenty years between the world wars. The first, in the early 1920s, was due to the international post-war depression. However, it was amplified by the introduction of deflationary monetary policies aimed at restoring the pre-war gold parity of the Norwegian currency, the krone.[1] This recession hit Norway harder than most other countries, and GDP per capita fell by eleven per cent over 1920–1921.[2] The fall in total production in the United Kingdom, Norway's most important trading partner at that time, was even bigger.[3] Also the two neighbouring economies, Sweden and Denmark, saw significant decline in output, equal or greater than in their recession of the 1930s.[4]

A new recession hit the Norwegian economy in the middle of the 1920s. This second slump is basically explained by the persistent national deflationary policy, and reflected domestic rather than international problems. The GDP did not fall significantly, but investments did, and unemployment reached peak levels.[5] Denmark, and to some extent Britain, who pursued a similarly stubborn monetary policy, also experienced slumps in the mid-1920s.[6] The two major setbacks in the 1920s resulted in high unemployment during most of that decade.

The third serious downturn came in the early 1930s, basically in consequence of the international depression: the Norwegian GDP

Figure 1: GDP, exports and imports for Norway 1918–1939 (1918 = 100)

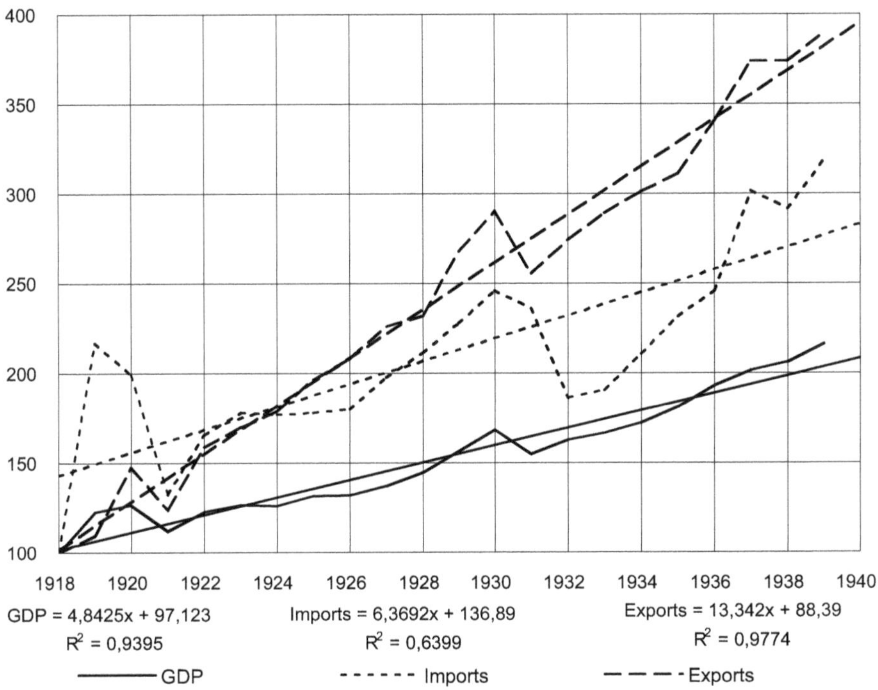

Source: NOS XII. 163, *National Accounts 1865–1960*, table 51, pp. 350–351.

per capita fell by 8.4 per cent in 1931.[7] This huge decline, however, was partly due to the year's widespread industrial unrest, with lock-outs and strikes. According to studies carried out by Professor Jan Tore Klovland, the 'natural' trough during the depression can be dated to the last months of 1932, a few months later than for most of Norway's principal trading partners.[8] At the same time unemployment reached peak levels: in 1933 one third of all insured labour-union members were laid off. The peak national rate of unemployment was around eleven per cent that year, and during the worst winter months of 1932–1933 it probably touched 15 per cent:[9] internationally unemployment met its peak level around 1933. This is noted by Anne-Lise Head König in her article on the labour markets during globalisation and disintegration 1880–1939, published in the present volume.

Figure 2: Foreign trade in per cent of GDP for Norway 1915–1939

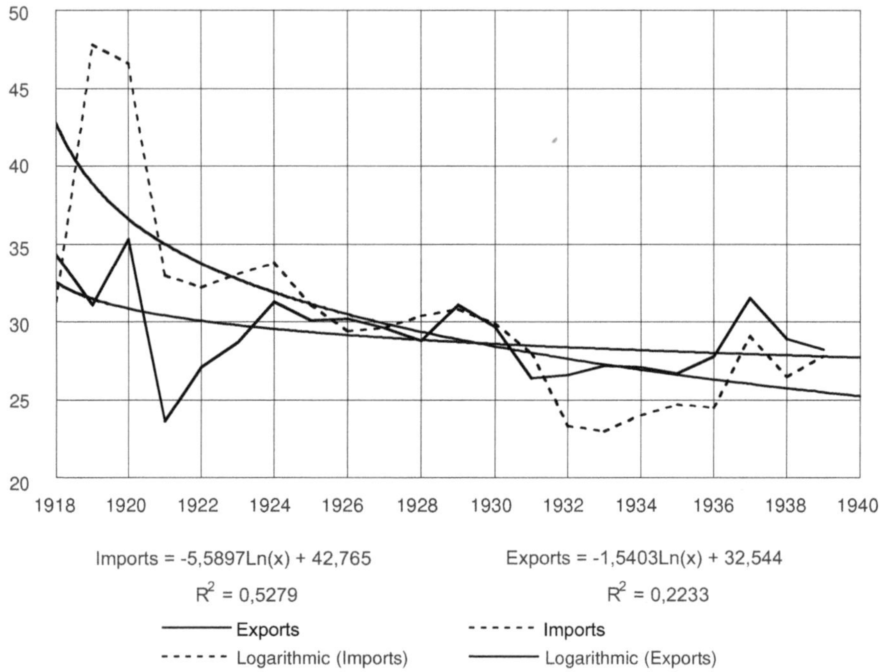

Source: NOS XII. 163, *National Accounts 1865–1960*, table 50, pp. 346–347.

In the remaining years of the interwar period significant economic growth took place. This was partly due to the adjustment introduced in response to the depressions. However, national accounts reveal that significant growth took place in the interwar period as a whole. In Norway the annual rate of growth in GDP per capita was 2.2 per cent over 1919–1939.[10] Prices fell almost constantly from the autumn of 1920 to 1934, and were reduced by about 50 per cent according to the consumer price index.[11] Thus, the setbacks in the interwar period certainly deserve to be titled depressions.

Following the disintegration of the international economy, the export and import sectors suffered. Yet despite years of serious setbacks, in terms of volume the Norwegian export sector gained ground during the interwar years. The national account series for Norway reports that annual growth in exports was 6.6 per cent in terms of 1938 prices, whilst the corresponding rate for imports was only 1.9 per cent.[12] However, the value of looking at these volume figures alone is limited. Terms of trade fell, since import prices rose compared to export prices. At the same time prices on international goods fell relative to domestic prices.

Current figures offer a better picture of the importance of foreign trade in this matter.[13] It is clear from Figure 2 that both exports and imports lost ground. The disintegration of the international economy obviously had a negative effect on Norwegian foreign trade.

The Norwegian policy response in the 1920s

Like many Western governments, the Norwegian government responded to the post-war crises of the 1920s by attempts to restore the institutional framework of the pre-World War I period, with a liberal trade order based on an international gold standard. The most visible action was the restoration of the old monetary system undertaken by several countries. For small open economies like the Norwegian it was natural to follow the example of their most important trading partners. These were first and foremost the United Kingdom, then Germany, and then the neighbouring countries of Sweden and Denmark.[14] Norway followed the course taken by the United Kingdom, and so did Sweden and Denmark. With the exception of Finland, the Scandinavian countries pursued very similar economic policies in both the 1920s and the 1930s, and, as we shall see, they were at that time closely connected to contemporary British economic policy.

Switzerland and the Netherlands also chose to restore their prewar gold parities. One aim was to regain confidence for their currencies and keep the financial markets open. This was particularly the case in Switzerland, as can be seen in Patrick Halbeisen's article published in this volume.

Monetary policy in the 1920s

Inflationary monetary policy in the period 1914–1920 and limited access to imported goods over 1914–1918 fuelled inflation and currency depreciation in Europe. Table 1 records inflation and currency depreciation in several Western countries 1914–1920.

The European countries followed three different paths with regard to monetary regimes and monetary policies in the 1920s. Most countries were unable to restore the pre-war parities. Some of these chose devaluation of their currencies (e.g. France, Italy, Belgium and Finland): others introduced new currencies (e.g. Germany, Poland, Austria, Hungary and the Soviet Union). The third alternative was to restore the old gold parities, as seen in the United Kingdom, the Netherlands, Switzerland, Sweden, Denmark and Norway. Of these latter countries Denmark and Norway had the longest way to go. In the case of Norway, the krone had depreciated more than 50 per cent from August 1914 to November 1920.[15]

Table 1: Inflation and exchange rates 1913–1920

	Consumer prices (1914 = 100)	Wholesale prices (1913 = 100)	Exchange rate (Par = 100)
Germany	989	1485	5.5
Finland	911	–	11.5
Belgium	459	–	33.0
France	341	509	31.1
Italy	313	624	18.7
Norway	302	377	49.9
Sweden	270	347	71.5
Denmark	262	374	50.0
Switzerland	253	–	80.6
United Kingdom	252	283	70.4
Japan	223	268	101.9
USA	206	243	100.0
The Netherlands	210	281	75.1
Canada	190	246	89.1

Source: NOS, *Statistical Yearbook for Norway 1921*, pp. 281–284.

In order to obtain this goal a deflationary policy was introduced. The first measures were taken by the central bank during the autumn of 1920. Granting of new credits was restricted and the central bank's interest rates were increased. Arguably, the increase in interest rates was marginal – only one per cent. However, the measures were carried out at the same time that the international depression, accompanied by rapid deflation, hit the economy. Thus, real interest rates rose dramatically, from – 30 per cent pre-tax in 1916 and 1917 to + 30 per cent in 1921, and almost + 40 per cent in 1922.[16]

The post-war setback basically had three effects on the economy. In the first place, restricted credits and higher real interest rates caused a contraction in the money stock. This contraction was followed by a reduction in product demand, and hence lower production, lower demand for labour and an increase in unemployment. Secondly, appreciation of the Norwegian krone from November 1920 to January 1921 and from October 1921 to November 1922 raised the price of Norwegian products on international markets. Thus overall demand for Norwegian products fell, as did production, whereas unemployment increased. Thirdly, significant deflation in the early 1920s made credits more expensive. This happened in two ways: real interest rates increased, and the real value of debts also increased. As a result a number of firms went bankrupt, and the banking sector sustained heavy losses. Both in 1923 and in 1925 Norwegian bank losses amounted to seven per cent of domestic GDP. More than a hundred Norwegian banks, about half of the then-existing commercial banks, went into liquidation during the 1920s.[17]

Economic crises, heavy bank losses and mass unemployment forced the central bank to call a halt to the deflationary policy in 1923 and 1924. At that time the international post-war depression had also come to an end. Thus, the international business cycle pointed upwards. As a result of the pause in the deflationary monetary policy the krone depreciated from 70 to 50 per cent of its par value. A trade surplus was finally achieved in 1926, and the krone started to appreciate in line with the trade surplus. The director of the Central Bank Nicolai Rygg now seized the opportunity to resume a deflationary monetary policy.[18] In 1926 a governmental commission proposed a formal devaluation of the krone by 25 per cent to return to the gold value. The suggestion, however, was approved neither by the government nor by the central bank. Healthy foreign trade and the continuance of a deflationary monetary policy made speculation in Norwegian money attractive. In a remarkably short time the krone rose to par.[19] In October 1926 it reached 95 per cent of par value. Finally, on the first of May 1928 gold redemption at par value was restored.[20]

A consequence of this second phase of deflationary policy was the onset of another slump. GDP only fell modestly, but investments and manufacturing output dropped significantly and unemployment reached peak levels.

Prices fell dramatically during the period of deflationary policy. Wages, on the other hand, were sticky and not brought down to the same degree. Thus real wages, and in particular product wages (i.e. nominal wages deflated by production costs) increased dramatically: in manufacturing they were almost four times higher in 1932 than in 1917. Labour-intensive production became too costly, and declined: capital-intensive production, however, increased in the 1920s.[21] Thus, the policy of 'back to normal' in response to the disintegration of the world economy resulted in mass unemployment (Figure 3).

Figure 3: Unemployment in per cent of labour force

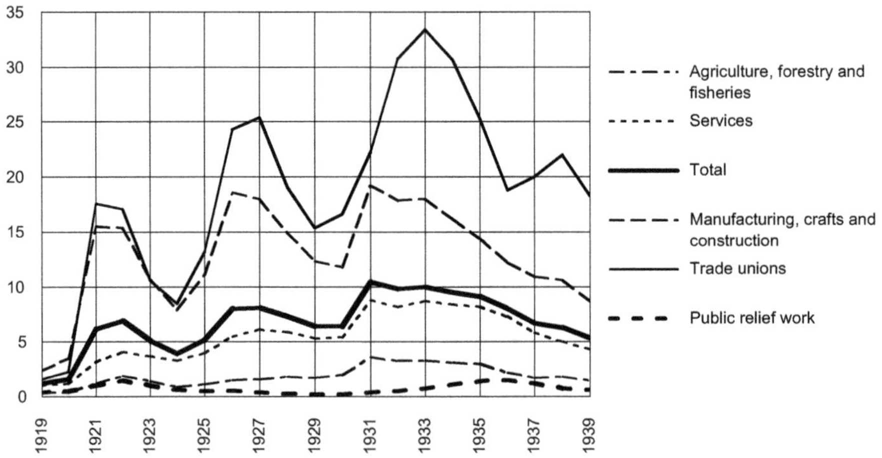

Source: Ola Honningdal Grytten, *An Empirical Analysis of the Norwegian Labour Market*, table 9.1, pp. 177–178.

International comparisons of the 1920s confirm that countries that pursued a deflationary policy were underachievers in the fields of investment and production. They also had higher unemployment than those that had adopted more inflationary policies.[22] This view is corrobotated in Patrick Halbeisen's article in this volume on monetary policy and international capital flows.

Competition laws

Further tools in the hands of the political authorities were the price, trust and cartel regulations. The new *Price Act* passed Parliament in 1920, the *Unfair Competition Act* in 1922, the *Act Controlling Trade Practices in Restraint of Trade*, commonly called the *Trust Law*, in 1926. When the ideas of these acts were first conceived the aim was to secure free competition and to free market prices. The Trust Law was meant to be an anti-trust law. The act provided for a permanent trust control board, an executive director and a secretariat. Mr. Wilhelm Thagaard was appointed its first director. He held the position until 1960.[23]

Political reactions to these laws differed significantly, and it was impossible to achieve majority support for any firm position. Thus, the final law texts became quite general, and fell victim to the interpretations of those charged with their implementation. Thagaard took the view that market regulations were necessary to overcome the problem of overproduction and falling prices. He argued that public price control boards could replace competition. When the price authorities found competition negative, firms could be compelled to register as trusts. By 1928 the number of cartels in Norway exceeded 100. By 1960 they exceeded 500.[24]

The political authorities also had other means of protecting markets from overproduction, falling prices and bankruptcy. In the 1920s steps were taken to regulate both fisheries and agriculture. The measures were taken partly by the organisations representing the supply side of the two industries and partly by the government and Parliament. However, these steps lacked efficiency. One important reason for lack of success was the problem of dealing with free-riders, taking adventage of other producers' output limitations. Thus, policy tools needed to be improved. That was basically carried through in the 1930s. In addition to the measures introduced in the 1920s, new and more powerful market regulations were brought into play in the last decade before the Great War.

The Norwegian policy response in the 1930s

During the depression in the 1930s a serious breakdown in international relations took place. The monetary system failed, and the gold standard had in fact been abandoned by almost every country by World War II. This rapid disintegration process is mirrored in the fact that international trade diminished in the early 1930s, and barely regained pre-World War I levels before World War II (Figure 4).[25]

The break down of international trade in the 1930s is also analysed in Hein Klemann's article in the present volume on international political development and international trade. The decade also saw a return to widespread protectionism in the form of quantitative and qualitative measures aimed at reducing imports. To protect the interests of producers and employees domestic and international cartels rapidly increased in number and size.[26] Again, the small open economies followed the great powers. As for the Scandinavian countries, they chiefly followed Britain.[27] However, due to their dependence on foreign markets and fear of retaliation the small and open economies practiced a cautious protectionism.[28]

Writers on the history of Norwegian economic policy claim that a change of economic policy regime took place *after* the great depression of the 1930s. More precisely, the shift is often dated from 1935 onwards, the year the Norwegian Labour Party came into office.[29] However, scholars concede that this shift was rather one of economic thought than of actual policy: according to the conventional view a permanent shift in politics came *after* the war. This

Figure 4: Imports of 75 countries January 1929–March 1933 in million US gold dollars

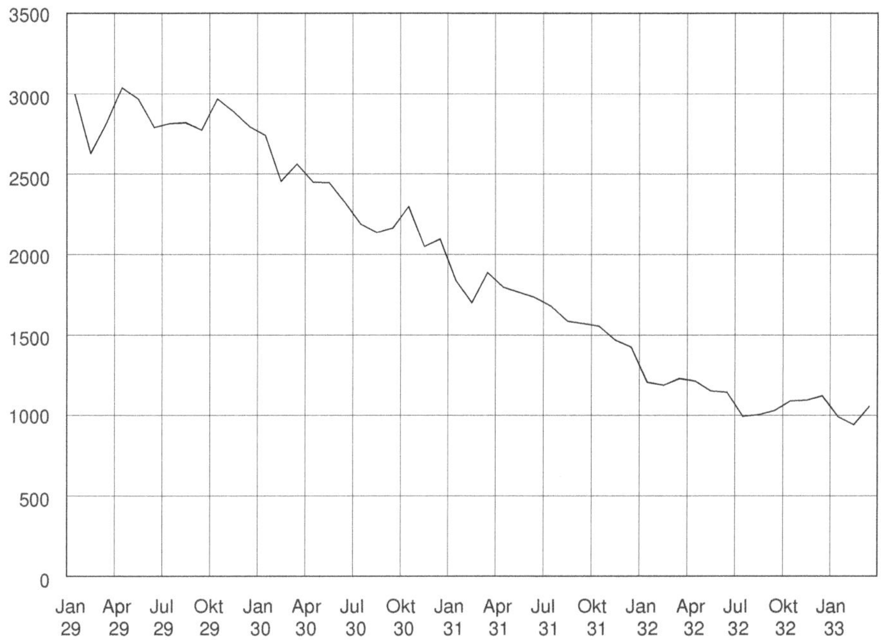

Source: League of Nations, *Monthly Bulletin of Statistics*, February 1934, p. 51.

chapter, however, argues that a real change started during the depression years, more precisely around 1930. This shift did not in its original form represent a reorientation towards Keynesian fiscal policy, but a change towards government interference in the markets. The Keynesian revolution did not influence Norwegian economic policies until the post-World War II era. And even at that stage classical Keynesian policy was not adopted, as the socialist government in Norway pursued a planning system more detailed than elsewhere, with direct company interference in the markets.[30] In addition several bilateral trade and payment agreements were set up, with Norway as an active participant.[31]

Protectionism

As a small open economy Norway did not benefit from an international return to protectionism. To protect domestic industries and the exchange reserves, however, Norwegian customs tariffs were increased. By 1933 the average tariff on imported goods was 16 per cent, against ten per cent in 1929.[32] Despite an increase of 60 per cent in three years, compared to other Western countries Norway, together with the two other small Scandinavian states Denmark and Sweden,still maintained relatively low tariffs in the 1930s (Table 2).

Table 2: Customs tariffs as a percentage of import values

	1929	1933/1934	1933/1934 in % of 1929
Finland	19	33	174
United Kingdom	12	30	250
Spain	18	29	161
Italy	11	26	236
Germany	8	25	313
USA	13	19	146
Norway	10	16	160
France	7	15	214
Sweden	9	10	111
Denmark	6	8	133

Source: H. Anstrin, 'Handelspolitikens avvägar och Nordens utrikeshandel', p. 21.

The Norwegian tariffs varied significantly for different kinds of goods. For traditional manufacturing goods they had been 18.3 per cent as early as 1930. They increased to 23.5 per cent in 1932 and to 24.8 per cent in 1937. For furniture, however, they were 7.8 per cent in 1930, 9.4 per cent in 1931, and were then reduced to 5.2 per cent in 1937.[33] Despite this fact, the Norwegian modern-furniture industry was a success in the 1930s.

In addition to the increase in tariffs on several import goods, import quotas were set up for some products that could be replaced by domestically produced goods. However, these quotas were high, surely, and it is not clear whether thay had any impact, since for several products the quotas were set higher than the actual imports.

Cartelisation

The interwar cartelisation wave began in the 1920s, both nationally and internationally, gathering force in the 1930s, notably in agriculture, industry, and international arrangements. The major problem for agricultural products was a steep fall in prices due to overproduction.[34] Since the demand for agricultural products was unresponsive to price change, a fall in prices tended simply to reduce the farmer's income. In the 1920s farmers tried to solve the problem by forms of cooperation organised amongst themselves. However, due to the problem of free-riders, the government and Parliament had to intervene. In 1928 a state-owned monopoly for imports of corn was revived. The monopoly was to buy all domestically produced crops. In general an excess price was paid to the producers, financed by selling imported corn at excess prices to consumers.

In the 1930s the government and the farmers' associations recommended local boards be set up to regulate the sale and distribution of milk. The regulation was approved by law as the so-called *Sales Act* passed by Parliament in 1930. The act regulated producers' sales of milk, egg, and bacon. The first milk board was set up the same year. From 1931 onwards, milk producers were to pay compulsory sales duties to these boards: this was deemed necessary to ensure equal production prices for milk.

Cartelisation of the milk market did not alone solve the problems of excess production of milk.[35] In June 1931 Parliament passed a law empowering the Ministry of Agriculture to order the incorporation of butter into all domestically sold margarine: thus the milk producers and their cartels received new markets for their products.[36] By the end of 1939 more than half of the milk produced for the national diary cartel was used for the production of butter, and 64 per cent of that butter was mixed into margarine.[37] This implies that about one third of the registered milk was by decree mixed into margarine.

Other cartels and market regulation bodies for agriculture were organised. The regulation of the milk market served as a prototype for the regulation of the egg, meat, and fruit and vegetable markets. Market regulation boards and cooperatives were set up on a large scale. The farmers gained from widespread regulation of the markets, but consumers lost through higher prices and reduced efficiency.[38]

As for fisheries (which accounted for about 25 per cent of the income from exports of goods in interwar Norway), a steep fall in international prices demanded immediate and effective action. The first steps towards cartelisation were taken as early as 1927, when the dockside sales of herring were organised by the fishing industry itself. In December 1929 the government gave this cartel legal status. Henceforth all fresh herring for export was to be handled by the cartel. In 1930 Parliament confirmed this decree by making it a law, the so-called *Herring Act*. From June onwards, similar acts for the export of other species of fish – basically cod – passed Parliament. In 1938 the *Raw Fish Act* came into being, regulating all commercial first-hand sales of fish and fish products in Norway through cartels.[39]

Norwegian industry also participated in international cartels (e.g. for nitrates, steel, and oil tankers):[40] the tanker pool may serve as an illustration of their operation. The International Tanker Owners Association Ltd. (Intertanko) was organised in London in 1934. Accounting for 95 per cent of the tonnage that competed in the free market for oil transports, the pool was in many ways a success for tanker-owners. Intertanko acted as a bargaining and hiring agency for oil tankers. The aim was to restrict the supply side of the market in order to maintain rates that covered the shipowners' costs of operating and laying-up their fleets.[41]

Subsidies

Maintaining producer prices and farm incomes was an important political aim in most European countries. Besides protectionism and cartelisation, subsidies to producers were common. According to the historical national accounts Norwegian direct subsidies increased from 28 million kroner in 1930 to 81 million in 1939, i.e. from 7.1 to 11.5 per cent of total State expenditure. The increase took place from 1934 onwards.[42]

In addition, indirect subsidies were even higher. From 1927 indirect subsidies were given to crop producers through price guarantees. In the 1930s interest rates in state-owned banks were subsidised, and farmers received government aid to switch their excess production from products with a supply surplus to products facing a demand surplus. Similar kinds of subsidies were offered to the fishing industry. Two State-owned banks were established, in 1921 and in 1938, to give subsidised loans for the renewal of fishing equipment and vessels. In 1936 a special State-owned bank was established to support the expansion of manufacturing by granting low-interest loans. The bank functioned as guarantor for manufacturing firms as well.

'Buy Norwegian'

A national organisation *Norwegian Work* was established in 1921. The purpose of the organisation was to promote import substitution, and it ran a series of slogans in the press calling on consumers to buy Norwegian products rather than foreign ones, provided price and quality were equal. The governor of the central bank Nicolai Rygg and the former prime minister Gunnar Knudsen were among the founders of this popular movement. However, the organisation made little headway in the 1920s, when the government's long-term agenda was still to restore pre-war international economic relations.

From 1930, however, attitudes changed. In October 1931, some weeks after the suspension of the gold standard, an appeal was published in all Norwegian newspapers. The appeal, under the heading 'Buy Norwegian' was signed by the prime minister, members of the cabinet, the president of the Parliament, the director of the central bank, the rector of the University of Oslo, representatives from both sides in the labour market and from 25 nation-wide organisations including the Churches. The message called on consumers to buy Norwegian goods, both to secure the balance of trade and to protect domestic labour from being laid off. That same month the king and the entire royal family became members of *Norwegian Work*.

The 'Buy Norwegian' campaign continued, and its importance was often emphasised by the prime minister and other members of the government or other officials. In 1933 even the crown prince, in the first broadcast speech by a member of the royal family, reminded the people of the importance of the campaign.

According to national newspapers, the campaign was a success. Imports of substitutable manufactures, including furniture, textiles and clothing, fell significantly in the 1930s, while domestic production of these goods increased.[43] However, as we will see in this chapter, monetary policy was probably a more important factor for import substitution in the Norwegian economy in the 1930s. Some protests against the campaign were heard: in particular, spokesmen for the export industries voiced criticisms, since they feared 'retaliation' abroad. However, these protests failed to change the work of the organisation, but the slogans became less stridently formulated in an attempt to avoid offending foreign interests involved in trade with Norway.

Fiscal policy

It is often argued that 1935 marks the beginning of a paradigm shift in Norwegian economic policy and economic thought. That year the first general agreement regulating the labour market was negotiated, and the Labour Party began a term of office that was to last for two generations. A common view at the time was that the shift of power marked the recognition of the failure of capitalism. Henceforth unfettered markets would be replaced by a regime of planning.

In my view there was no significant shift of paradigm in Norwegian economic policy in 1935. The Labour Party did not pursue an inflationary fiscal policy to stimulate demand in the 1930s. Public expenditure did increase, but so did taxes. The balance of the budget did not change in any direction. The late Professor Helge W. Nordvik examined the fiscal policy of interwar Norway using an IS-LM model. He concluded that the fiscal policy was neutral in the 1930s. In the period of Labour government from 1935 until the German attack on Norway in April 1940 the average annual effect of the fiscal policy is calculated to have been virtually nil, or more precisely: + 0.1 per cent of the gross domestic product.[44]

Most changes that did take place in economic policy in fact happened before 1935: changes in the monetary regime, the escalation of public subsidies, renewal of protectionism and public support of cartelisation. One may argue that the first general agreement between the employers' associations and the trade unions in 1935 marked an important breakthrough for labour-market planning. However, that first agreement bound only 220,000 trade unionists out of a total labour force of 1.3 million. The measures taken to regulate agriculture and fisheries earlier in the 1930s involved more people: according to the population census of December 1930 more than half a million people were engaged in the primary industries of the Norwegian economy at that time. In other words, agriculture and fisheries had already started the transformation process from free-market industries to regulated industries before the first general agreement came to being.[45]

Monetary policy

At the time of Britain's suspension of gold on 20–21 September 1931, speculation against the Norwegian krone forced the central bank to take action. Interest rates were raised. The official discount rate on private banks' borrowings from the Bank of Norway was increased from four to five per cent on 12 September, and then to six per cent on 26 September. On 27 September the Bank of Norway suspended redemption at par value. The high point occurred 28 September when the bank rate was raised to eight per cent.[46] This was deemed necessary to avoid large-scale capital outflow and to protect the krone from further speculation and possible depreciation.

The bank board may have entertained the idea that it would be possible to restore gold when the international currency markets had calmed down. However, it is clear that the decision to suspend gold was also made to benefit the export industries. The central bank feared they would lose competitive power, and since Britain was Norway's largest trading partner, the central bank wanted the krone to closely follow the pound sterling.[47] A tight monetary policy was pursued at first, and in September and October the krone depreciated against gold, but appreciated against sterling. However, the bank board feared the consequences of such a policy, and reduced the discount rate by two percentage points in October 1931.

As a result, in November and December 1931 the krone depreciated slightly against sterling. The mid-December exchange rate of that year when compared with the pre-September 1931 values reveals that the krone had depreciated by 45.2 per cent against the US dollar, 31.2 per cent against gold, and 0.4 per cent against pound sterling.[48] To protect its reserves, the Bank of Norway, the private banks and the business organisations voluntarily set up a currency committee to monitor and control the reserves through voluntary reporting.[49] During 1932 and 1933 the krone stabilised at an exchange rate that implied ten per cent depreciation against sterling, while it fluctuated significantly against the US dollar and currencies tied to the dollar or to gold.

The stabilisation of the krone against sterling along with a trade surplus from 1932 onwards permitted further reductions in the discount rate. On 1 September 1932 it was back on the four-per-cent level, and was subsequently cut to 3.5 per cent by the central bank in May 1933.

The countries which first suspended gold feared devastating consequences for their economies; but it soon turned out that abandoning gold had its advantages. In the first place, their currencies depreciated against those still clinging to gold, giving them a competitive edge as their products were now cheaper in international markets. Hence, exports did not fall as much as in the gold-standard countries. In addition, foreign-produced goods were now more expensive for Norwegian consumers. Thus, import substitution took place in those countries abandoning gold against those holding on to gold, and countries with depreciating currencies often experienced trade surpluses. Again, the suspension of gold allowed for a more relaxed monetary policy. In fact, the money stock started to increase. In Norway the money supply (M1) in current terms was stable from

1928 to 1933, having seen a steep fall in the 1920s: it started to grow at the end of 1934. In real terms the turning point was in 1932, resulting from the suspension of gold in September 1931.[50]

An increase in the money supply caused a positive shift in demand, resulting in higher production and lower unemployment. Deflation was replaced by moderate inflation. Nominal interest rates decreased as well, and this gave a boost to investments. In 1931 real interest rates before taxes reached almost 20 per cent in Norway. In 1937 they were close to minus ten per cent.[51] In the years 1931–1939 investment and export volumes grew by 60 and 52 per cent respectively: GDP by volume showed a growth of 39 per cent in the same period.[52]

Since those countries which left gold early in general experienced milder depressions and more rapid recoveries than the gold countries, both their central banks and their governments lost interest in restoring par values for their currencies. In 1933 the Sterling Area was established. Its members were countries that aligned their currencies to the pound sterling, and included most of the Commonwealth and the British colonies, several Middle Eastern countries, Portugal, and the Scandinavian countries. From July onwards the Norwegian krone was tied to the pound sterling at a value of 19.90 against 18.16 under the gold standard, a devaluation of ten per cent to the pound. In reality gold was not only suspended, but also abandoned. The new currency regime was in fact a Sterling standard. Econometric tests confirm that the member states of the Sterling Area were among the best economic performers in the 1930s with regards to gross national product, investments, exports, employment, and import substitution. In Europe the Gold Bloc countries were the losers.[53]

Table 3 offers the estimated correlation between currency depreciation and key variables including GDP, investments, exports, export surplus and unemployment for 15 Western national economies. The estimated regression coefficients are calculated as simple regressions in which currency depreciation is the decisive variable and the key economic macro indicators are the response variables. The data are based on percentage changes 1929–1935, with 1929 as 100 (here currency depreciation gives values lower than 100). All key macro indicators are in real terms except for export surpluses, which are in nominal figures. The 15 countries included in the calculations are eight small economies (Austria, Belgium, Denmark, Finland, the Netherlands, Norway, Sweden and Switzerland), and seven large economies (Canada, France, Germany, Italy, Japan, the United Kingdom and the United States). Regressions are run on data of all the 15 countries, of the 13 European countries, and of the eight small European Countries. The results are reported in Table 3.

Table 3: Regressions. Influence of monetary policy on macroeconomic indicators

	N	β_1	t	R^2
	15	–0.365	–3.159	0.434
GDP per capita (E)	13	–0.342	–3.580	0.538
	8	–0.476	–3.291	0.638
	15	–1.692	–5.919	0.729
Gross Investments (I)	13	–1.667	–8.291	0.862
	8	–1.223	–8.894	0.929
	15	–1.022	–5.219	0.677
Exports (X)	13	–1.011	–5.333	0.721
	8	–0.801	–3.003	0.601
	15	–0.953	–9.393	0.872
Export surplus (X-M)	13	–0.945	–9.304	0.887
	8	–0.889	–4.800	0.793
	15	6.374	3.936	0.544
Unemployment (U)	13	6.316	4.042	0.598
	8	9.914	10.562	0.949

N = 15: All 15 countries in the sample.
N = 13: All European countries in the sample.
N = 8: The eight small European countries in the sample.

The table confirms that there was a significant positive correlation between currency depreciation and economic growth, investments, exports and export surplus, and a negative correlation between currency depreciation and the scale of unemployment. More precisely, the estimated slopes of the regression lines between growth in GDP, investments, exports and export surplus on the one hand and the developments of the currency values on the other are negative. There is a positive slope of the regression line between currency values and unemployment.

On the basis of these tests for 15 countries we may conclude that monetary policy was a decisive factor for the economic development in the 1930s. Those countries that left gold had a milder recession and a more rapid recovery than those that remained on gold.

Apart from monetary policy, economic policies differed significantly between countries within the same monetary regime. However, the pattern of economic development followed that of monetary policy. This indicates that monetary policy may have been one of the most decisive policy factors for economic performance in the 1930s.

Conclusions

This chapter examines the Norwegian policy response to the disintegration of the interwar economy. In the 1920s the government's efforts were aimed at protecting the liberal trade order and the prewar monetary system, with the Norwegian currency, the krone, linked to the gold parity established in 1874. However, towards the end of the decade the first steps were taken towards public support for cartelisation.

In the 1930s the State's answer to international disintegration was quite different: Norway abandoned gold, and ran a more relaxed monetary policy. Voluntary currency controls were introduced to avoid large-scale capital outflow and countrywide cartels were established, in particular in agriculture and fisheries. These sectors were also subsidised to protect them from the negative consequences of over-production and the breakdown of the world economy. Protectionism was reintroduced, especially to support manufacturing industries.

Quantitative comparisons based on key macro variables confirm the view that monetary policy played a central role for economic performance in small, open economies. Sticking to gold had negative effects. Conversely, abandoning the fixed exchange-rate system and and pursuing a more inflationary monetary policy had a positive impact on economic performance. The lesson is that a flexible monetary response was, in the circumstances, the superior strategy.

Several writers on Norwegian economic history have claimed that a change in economic policy regime, from a free-market to an active-state philosophy, occured in 1935 when the Labour Party came into office. Admittedly, most changes were introduced after 1945. However, this chapter argues that significant changes in economic policy started earlier, around 1930.

1 Sverre Knutsen and Gunhild Ecklund, *Vern mot kriser? Norsk finanstilsyn gjennom 100 år* (Bergen: Fagbokforlaget, 2000), pp. 121–131 argue that the emphasis on deflationary monetary policy in Norway in the early 1920s has been exaggerated.
2 Ola H. Grytten, 'The gross domestic product for Norway', in Øyvind Eitrheim, Jan T. Klovland and Jan F Qvigstad (eds.), *Historical Monetary Statistics for Norway 1819–2003* (Oslo: Norges Bank, 2004), pp. 277–280.
3 Angus Maddison, *Monitoring the World Economy 1820–1992* (Paris: OECD, 1995), pp. 180–183 and 194–197.
4 Olle Krantz, 'Swedish Historical National Accounts 1800–1998 – Aggregated output series', memo (Umeå: Umeå University, 2001).
5 Ola H. Grytten, 'The Scale of Norwegian Interwar Unemployment in International Perspective', *Scandinavian Economic History Review* 43 (1995), pp. 226–250.
6 Maddison, *Monitoring the World Economy*, pp. 194–197.
7 NOS XII. 163, *National Accounts 1865–1960* (Oslo: Statistics Norway, 1968), pp. 350–351.
8 Jan T. Klovland, 'Monetary policy and business cycles in the interwar years: The Scandinavian experience', *European Review of Economic History* 2 (1998), pp. 309–344.
9 Ola H. Grytten and Camilla Brautaset, 'Family Households and Unemployment in Norway during Years of Crises. New Estimates', *The History of The Family* 5 (2000), pp. 36–37.
10 NOS XI. 143, *National Accounts 1900–1929* (Oslo: Statistics Norway 1953), pp. 128–129.
11 Ola H. Grytten, 'A Consumer Price Index for Norway 1516–2003', in Eitrheim, *Historical Monetary Statistics*, pp. 92–93.
12 NOS XII. 163, *National Accounts*, pp. 350–351.
13 *Ibid*, pp. 346–347.
14 Lennart Schön, *En modern svensk ekonomisk historia: tillväxt och omvandling under två sekel* (Stockholm: SNS, 2000); Hans C. Johansen, *The Danish Economy in the Twentieth Century* (London: Croom Helm, 1987), pp. 12–46; and Fritz Hodne, *The Norwegian Economy 1920–1980* (London: Croom Helm and St. Martin's, 1983), pp. 12–99.
15 Central Bank of Norway, *Annual Report 1924* (Oslo: 1925), p. 48.
16 Ola H. Grytten, 'Monetary Policy and Restructuring of the Norwegian Economy During Years of Crises, 1920–1939', in Timo Myllyntaus (ed.), *Economic*

Crises and Restructuring in History (St. Katharinen: Scripta Mercaturae, 1998), p. 112.

17 Sverre Knutsen, Even Lange and Helge W. Nordvik, *Mellom næringsliv og politikk. Kredittkassen i vekst og kriser 1918–1998* (Oslo: Universitetsforlaget, 1998), pp. 11–42.

18 Tore J. Hanisch, 'Om virkninger av paripolitikken', *Historisk tidsskrift* 58 (1979), pp. 244–247.

19 Tore J. Hanisch, Espen Søilen, and Gunhild Ecklund, *Norsk økonomisk politikk i det 20. århundre. Verdivalg i en åpen økonomi* (Kristiansand: Høyskoleforlaget, 1999), pp. 68–85.

20 Central Bank of Norway, *Annual Report 1927* (Oslo, 1928), p. 45 and Wilhelm Keilhau, *Den norske pengehistorie* (Oslo: Aschehoug, 1952), pp. 158–199.

21 Ola H. Grytten, *An Empirical Analysis of the Norwegian Labour Market, 1918–1939: Norwegian Interwar Unemployment in International Perspective* (Bergen: NHH, 1994), pp. 239–260.

22 Barry Eichengreen, 'Understanding 1921–1927: inflation and economic recovery in the 1920s', in Barry Eichengreen (ed.), *Elusive Stability. Essays in the History of International Finance* (Cambridge and New York: Cambridge University Press, 1990), pp. 24–56; Grytten, 'Monetary Policy and Restructuring', pp. 93–124.

23 Hanisch, *Norsk økonomisk politikk*, pp. 118–124.

24 Hodne, *The Norwegian Economy*, pp. 70–82.

25 Charles P. Kindleberger, *The World in Depression 1929–1939* (London: Penguin Books, 1987), p. 170; League of Nations, *Monthly Bulletin of Statistics* (February 1934), p. 51.

26 Charles P. Kindleberger, 'Commercial policy between the wars', in Peter Matias and Sidney Pollard (eds), *The Industrial Economies: The Development of Economic and Social Policies, The Cambridge Economic History of Europe* (Cambridge: Cambridge University Press, 1989), vol I, pp. 161–196.

27 Michael Kitson and Solomos Solomou, *Protectionism and economic revival: The British interwar economy* (Cambridge: Cambridge University Press, 1990); Forrest Cappie, *Depression and Protectionism: Britain between the Wars* (London: Allen and Unwin, 1983).

28 Helge W. Nordvik, 'Europeisk handelspolitikk i historisk lys: Proteksjonisme og frihandel gjennom 200 år', in Victor D. Norman (ed.), *Europa-forskning om økonomisk integrasjon* (Bergen: SNF, 1995), pp. 37–40.

29 Tore J. Hanisch, Espen Søilen and Gunhild Ecklund argue that the period 1930–1950 constitutes a transition period from a liberal to a planned economy in Norway: Hanisch, *Norsk økonomisk politikk*, pp. 91–94.

30 Espen Søilen, *Fra frischianisme til keynesianisme? En studie av norsk økonomisk politikk i lys av økonomisk teori 1945–1980* (Bergen: NHH, 1999).

31 Fritz Hodne and Ola H. Grytten, *Norsk økonomi i det 20. århundre* (Bergen: Fagbokforlaget, 2002), pp. 166–168.

32 H. Anstrin, 'Handelspolitikens avvägar och Nordens utrikeshandel', *Industria* (1937), 21.

33 Even Lange, *Krise og vekst. Norsk treindustri i begynnelsen av 1930-årene* (Oslo: UiO, 1974), p. 166.
34 Vladimir P. Timoshenko, *World Agriculture and Depression* (Ann Arbor, 1933), pp. 122–123.
35 J. Skeie, *Organisasjon og lovgivning til hjelp i jordbrukskrisen*, (Oslo, 1933), pp. 17–40.
36 Edgar Hovland, 'Smør og margarin blir ett fett', *Historisk tidsskrift* 58 (1979), pp. 305–325.
37 Rasmus Mork, *Melkeomsetning og meieridrift i Norge 1930–1940* (Oslo, 1941), p. 247.
38 Ola H. Grytten, 'The Consumers' Burden. What did regulations of the Norwegian milk market in the 1930s cost consumers', in Bjørn L. Basberg, Helge W. Nordvik and Gudmund Stang (eds.), *I det lange løp* (Bergen: Fagbokforlaget, 1997), pp. 143–164.
39 A. Hallenstvedt, *Med lov og organisasjon* (Oslo, 1982), pp. 89–93; Torvald Tande, *Norsk fiskeripolitikk* (Oslo, 1957), p. 195.
40 Trond Bergh, Tore J. Hanisch, Even Lange and Helge Pharo, *Norge fra u-land til i-land. Vekst og utviklingslinjer 1830–1980* (Oslo: Gyldendal, 1983), pp. 170–175.
41 Egeland, O. *Kongeveien* (Oslo, 1968), vol II, pp. 300–308.
42 NOS XII. 163, *National Accounts,* pp. 196–203.
43 Lange, *Krise og vekst*, pp. 145–164.
44 Helge W. Nordvik, 'Finanspolitikken og den offentlige sektors rolle i norsk økonomi i mellomkrigstiden', *Historisk tidsskrift* 58 (1979), pp. 223–237.
45 NOS IX. 61, *Population Census for Norway December 1st 1930* (Oslo: Statistics Norway, 1935), vol VIII, pp. 14–15.
46 NOS C. 188, *Historical Statistics 1994* (Oslo: Statistics Norway, 1994), p. 650.
47 Central Bank of Norway, *Annual Report 1931* (Oslo, 1932), p. 42.
48 Jan T. Klovland, 'Exchange rates 1819–2003', in Eitrheim (ed.), *Historical Monetary Statistics*, pp. 289–328.
49 Fritz Hodne, *God Handel* (Oslo: NHF, 1989), pp. 189–194.
50 This is the overall trend when looking at M0, M1, and M3.
51 Arne Jon Isachsen., 'Realrenten i Norge i et hundreårs perspektiv', *Bergen Bank kvartalskrift* 2 (1988), pp. 21–33.
52 NOS XII. 163, *National Accounts,* pp. 350–351.
53 Barry Eichengreen and Jeffrey Sachs, 'Exchange rates and economic recovery in the 1930s', in Eichengreen (ed.), *Elusive Stability*, pp. 215–238.

Hein A. M. Klemann

Political Development and International Trade: The Netherlands 1929–1941

Introduction

From the depression of the 1870s on, Dutch agriculture specialised in luxury products like meat, butter, cheese, eggs and vegetables. These products were sold in the industrial cities of the surrounding countries. Germany was the principal market, and Britain came in second place: only in the 1930s did these two countries temporarily exchange positions.[1] That the Netherlands was an important food-exporting country did not imply that it could feed its own population. The export of luxury agricultural products was based on the massive import of crude food commodities, in particular corn and seeds. Although some parts of the country were significant sources of grain, particularly rye, by the 1930s their output was scarcely sufficient to feed the poultry, let alone the other farm animals and the human population: in 1937 The Netherlands' 30 million fowls (including cockerels) consumed as much corn as the 8.7 million human inhabitants.[2] Apart from fowls there were 1.5 million pigs, 2.7 million cows, calves and bulls – principally for dairy products – and also a less significant number of sheep, horses, goats and ducks. All these herds and flocks were needed to produce the country's most important export products.

From the 1880s on, the Netherlands' huge production of animal foodstuffs and vegetables and the flourishing markets for them in the newly developed industrial areas of Germany and Britain created a vital export market. In 1937 49 percent – almost half – of Dutch exports were commodities aimed at two zones of the economy: food-processing and agriculture. In the same year, however, these two areas – accountable for 23 percent of the employment in private companies – were also responsible for 35 percent of Dutch imports.[3] In 1995 the American economist Paul Krugman wrote that nowadays, increasing trade results from the tendency to fragment the value chain 'to produce a good in a number of stages and a number of locations, adding a little bit of value at each stage.'[4] Dutch agriculture has produced luxury food for export markets since the late nineteenth century, but this was only possible by importing grain and edible fats for the livestock as well as for human consumption. In other words, in agriculture as well as industry, the Dutch produced only limited parts of the value chain. In his article Krugman writes that even in 1990 worldwide trade as a percentage of global output was only moderately higher than it was in 1913. The most trade oriented economies, however, have much higher trade shares than ever seen before. According to his data, there was no country in or before 1913 whose exports exceeded 50 percent of its GDP: today he finds six such supertrading economies, including the Netherlands and Belgium.[5] But in fact, between 1864 and the First World War Dutch exports had already exceeded 50 percent of GDP. From the 1890s exports were even more than 60 percent of GDP, and in 1913 exports were 62 and imports even 78 percent of domestic production, a level never reached again.[6] As it is 'virtually certain that at least 60 percent of the employment and value added even in small countries is generated in non-tradable sectors', it is also clear that 'a trade share of much more than 30–40 percent can only arise when exports involve adding a fairly small amount of value to imported intermediate goods.'[7] Already before the First World War, the Netherlands had average imports and exports of 76 percent of the GDP.[8] This made the country what Krugman calls a supertrading economy. Consequently, the war of 1914 and the protectionism and isolationism in the surrounding countries, cumulating in the collapse of the world economy in the 1930s, cut the Dutch economy – an economically fairly arbitrary part of a regional economy – off from its economic context.

As a result of the worldwide agricultural depression and the protection of food markets, in the 1930s the profitability of Dutch agriculture collapsed. As a consequence of the protection of the food markets in Britain and Germany and the agricultural depression that began in the 1920s, the Dutch government had to reassess its agricultural policy. For two reasons Dutch top officials thought it had no future:[9] firstly, the two most important European food markets were increasingly closed to Dutch produce, and there was no indication that this would alter in the near future. Britain gave preference to food imported from its Dominions, while in Germany nationalism, right-wing support for farmers and monetary problems worked together in supporting an autarkic agricultural policy. The second reason was internal: until the 1960s the Netherlands had a fast-growing population, faster than any other European country. In the 1930s this population growth resulted in an annual increase of the labour force by some 50 thousand persons (or about 1.5 percent). In agriculture, however, jobs were being lost: therefore industrialisation alone could create the jobs needed to employ the growing labour force.

From these reasons, farming had to be reorganised and downsized. Nevertheless, in the end The Hague decided to protect its farmers. In the short run this kept wages high and thus resulted in higher costs for industry. As a consequence of this, and of the policy to adhere to the gold standard until September 1936, Dutch industry could only defend its competitiveness by increasing productivity. Although from 1933 on industry grew again, increasing capital intensity prevented any growth of industrial employment.[10] The badly needed new employment was only achieved after the 1936 depreciation. Consequently, in the 1930s industrial employment never surpassed the 1929 level.

That the fast-growing population needed jobs was indeed a problem, but it is misguided to imagine that the long-lasting Dutch depression resulted from that demographic phenomenon.[11] As a consequence of neutrality during the 1914–1918 war Dutch competitiveness in the 1920s was strong enough to win increasing shares in world trade, giving full employment by the late 1920s; but when world trade declined during the 1930s depression, the Dutch share in it also fell. Only in 1941, during the German occupation, when German industrial orders came in freely, did employment rise above the 1929 level again: it is clear that during the 1930s the Dutch economy could not recover.[12] Stagnating employment was a symptom, not the cause, of the problem. Causes were the isolation resulting from foreign protectionism, but also the Dutch governmental reaction to this. The Hague decided to follow a policy that was thought to be in the interest of a certain part of the population, but proved scarcely beneficial to the country as a whole. Even in a small open economy with enormous interests in foreign trade – a supertrading economy – it is possible that for political reasons a decision may be taken that serves the interest of only a limited sector of society. In the 1930s this happened in the Netherlands. It was a consequence of political considerations: those who were unemployed – the working classes – hardly had any political influence, while the farmers were an electorate to be reckoned with.

The 1930s agricultural depression

During the interwar years the Netherlands was an important food-exporting country. Until the Great Depression this export went principally to Germany. In the late 1920s, however, for political reasons Germany had to protect its food markets. The severe suffering of the farmers in the Depression, and the radicalisation of Germany's Protestant rural areas where the Nazi farmers' leader Walther Darré won a majority of the people for his party and Fuehrer, put pressure on the crumbling republic. Berlin had to take the farmer's demands for protection of the food market seriously.[13] To their Dutch colleagues this protection seemed threatening. In fact, in the early 1930s it hardly resulted in any damage. When in 1929 and 1930 exports to Germany slumped dramatically, this was a consequence of the severe Depression, which had undermined German purchasing power. Actually, the Dutch share in German imports even increased, because Berlin started to protect its food markets by tariffs on grains and other raw foodstuffs, not on butter or vegetables.[14] Nevertheless, there also was an animated discussion about protection against the import of the type of luxury foodstuffs that came from the Netherlands or Denmark, especially butter, but this proposal encountered significant German opposition, even at cabinet level. The countries where Germany's meat, pork and dairy products came from – the Netherlands, Denmark and Sweden – were even more important – almost twice as important – as markets for

German industrial exports. Therefore industrial circles, fearing the vengeance of the small countries, opposed the tariffs the farmers demanded. Since trade in the Netherlands – and in all highly developed small countries – accounted for an exceptionally high proportion of their economy, these countries not only needed important markets, but also offered relatively important import markets. Consequently, there was a bitter political debate in Germany about butter tariffs and demonstrations in favour and against it. The situation finally began to constitute a real threat to Dutch exports during the financial crisis of the summer of 1931, when Berlin gave up the convertibility of the *Reichsmark*.

When in July 1931 the overvalued mark became inconvertible, the Reichsbank had hardly any gold or currency left; and after the destructive inflation of the 1920s devaluation was no longer an option. Consequently, no foreigner accepted Reichsmarks anymore, and Germany could only import as much as it earned in hard currency by its exports. As a result, however, of the increase of the overvaluation of the mark by the September 1931 depreciation of sterling and the world-wide depression, German exports diminished more and more. Consequently, Germany earned less hard currency and its capacity to import declined. Between 1930 and 1933 Dutch real exports to Germany fell by 37 percent.[15] In 1934 there was some recovery, but in that year important parts of these exports were paid for in blocked Reichsmarks. When the hope that these marks would be de-blocked proved false, The Hague had to prohibit such payments and exports declined again. Even in 1938, when the recovery in Germany was complete, Dutch real exports to Germany were only 58 percent of the pre-Depression level.[16] This had nothing to do with dwindling competitiveness, but with German isolationism. Germany's recovery was impressive, but isolated. By utilising its exchange control, Nazi Germany minimised the trade gap of the stimulus that governmental policy gave to its economy. This strengthened its internal development, but also kept German trade, and therefore the economies of some German trading partners, at a depression level.

After 1933 exports to Germany diminished further, resulting in immense problems in the countryside. Farmers, since the mid-1920s confronted with a setback in world market prices, now had to face the closure of their most important market. The German recovery of 1933 never resulted in any recovery of their export trade. On the contrary, the Nazi regime promoted recovery but ended any attempt to peg price levels to those in the outside world. As far as it was necessary to earn hard currency – that means, as far as the regime needed currency for imports vital to its targets – exports were subsidised. This, however, could not maintain real exports even at their 1932 Depression level. Thus, in 1933 and 1934 German real exports declined again by 9 and 8 percent. Nevertheless, as a result of recovery, real imports started to grow.[17] Because the price levels of German imports – food and raw materials – were more depressed than those of its exports – industrial products – this did not become a problem immediately. But in 1934, when growing German employment – a consequence of the recovery – resulted in growing demand, the Reichsbank lacked the currency to allow all importers to make payment in full. Foreign exporters however, very badly wanted to restart their exports to the Reich, and Dutch exporters even accepted payment into a *Sonderkonto* or special account which the Dutch central bank, the Nederlandsche Bank, held with the Reichsbank: in 1934 this resulted in an increase of real exports to Germany of 18 percent.[18] In Germany the opportunity to evade the rules of exchange control by paying for Dutch imports into an account of the Nederlandsche Bank without using hard currency was known as the *Loch im Westen* – hole in the West. As a result, 22 percent of Dutch exports to Germany were paid in blocked marks, but in December The Hague had to end this. It proved impossible to realise the blocked marks, which could only be used to pay for additional – more than normal – imports from Germany. Consequently only in 1937, four years after their deliveries, did the last Dutch exporters get their money.

In 1934 the critical situation of Germany's international payments and the rapid disappearance of the last gold and currency reserves caused Hitler's Reichsbankpräsident and Reichswirtschaftsminister Dr. Hjalmar Schacht to revise the allocation of international currency, and in September 1934 he introduced his *neue Plan*. Until then every importer received the same proportion of the currency he used before the Depression: but henceforth the availability of foreign currency would be decided on an individual-case basis. Because Schacht, a conservative economist and politician used by Hitler, combined the functions of minister of economics and bank president, it was the regime that controlled international trade. For The Hague and a number of other governments these German measures, together with growing blocked marks accounts, were reason to take steps against Germany.[19] The Dutch rightly feared that the monetary policy of the mistrusted Hitler regime would result in the selection of imports not on commercial, but on political grounds. German consumers liked the Dutch dairy products and vegetables, but the regime wanted the scarce hard currency to be spent on raw materials and raw foodstuffs. Because Berlin now controlled the allotment of foreign currencies, it was suspected that the Nazis would not be interested in cabbage, lettuce or butter.

For these reasons and to protect agriculture from the collapse of what was still its most important market, The Hague prohibited all payments to Germany and ordered those who had to pay anything to Germany to send their money to a new Netherlands Clearing Institute. In this way The Hague hoped to recover the blocked marks, and to start negotiations about bilateral clearing.[20] When in the last days of 1934 a clearing agreement was signed, The Hague managed to earmark a large part of the guilders Germany had earned in the clearing account for payment for Dutch agricultural products. No less than 39.5 percent of the German payment quotas in the clearing account that could be used by Berlin for imports from the Kingdom of the Netherlands, i.e. including the Netherlands Indies (Indonesia, Curacao and Suriname), were to be used for Dutch (non-colonial) agricultural products. In exchange Germany was allowed to use another 24.2% on strategic raw materials from the Indies. Dutch industry paid the price.

In this period a number of high-ranking officials advised the complete reorganisation of Dutch agriculture.[21] From an economic perspective they were right. In 1930 68 percent of the added value in Dutch agriculture was created in livestock breeding – 45 percent of this in dairy farming.[22] These areas produced a limited number of products in enormous quantities: it was impossible for the Dutch to consume all the butter and eggs themselves. The same was true for the horticultural products, especially vegetables. Only large-scale exports could guarantee sales on the necessary scale at profitable prices. Stock-breeding produced luxury products with imported fodder for the wealthy markets of the industrial cities, but the most important of these markets were hardly wealthy anymore, and in any case no longer sought Dutch products. Meanwhile Germany, the second largest European – and most important Dutch – market for food exports, seemed for an indefinite future to be reduced to a tiny part of its normal trading capacity. At the same time the only alternative market – Britain – was under strong pressure from its Dominions to receive their food exports on the same advantageous terms that British industrial exports already enjoyed on Dominion markets.

From 1933 London introduced preferential tariffs for meat, cheese and butter from Canada, New Zealand and Australia, which implied that the British home market was protected by import duties against non-Empire countries. 'Imperial free trade' was the slogan used by the Conservatives who in 1932 achieved de facto power, albeit in coalition with a part of Labour: only the British entrance into the European common market in the 1970s would end this preference policy. In 1932 horticultural import duties were also introduced, to give British farmers some protection: it was another severe blow to Dutch exports.[23] The agricultural depression and the protectionist reaction to it in Europe's important food markets seemed a fatal blow for the specialised Dutch agriculture. Stopgaps to save it could only result in high costs for other parts of the economy, especially industry. Nevertheless, agriculture was protected.

The Gold Standard policy

During the 1930s there never was a technical reason to devalue the Dutch guilder. Until September 1936 the guilder survived all crises. Although there was a growing but repressed opposition against the Gold Standard policy, most of the time devaluation was not only thought of as dangerous – in the early 1920s the paper currencies from the war period were very unstable – but also as immoral. 'We are no counterfeiters', the president of the Nederlandsche Bank, L.J.A. Trip, publicly declared.[24] The British Minister in The Hague,

Sir Hubert Montgomery was therefore absolutely right when he wrote that 'die-hards as Dr Trip would fight to the last trench'.[25] Religious parties enjoyed a significant influence in Dutch politics, and there has been a long-standing tradition of expressing political opinions in moral terms, but this did not always mean that there were no more practical arguments. In the first year after the depreciation of sterling of 1931 it was widely believed that the paper currencies of countries that had deserted the gold standard would cause inflation. When this proved not to be true, and when it became clear that the price level on world markets was more determined by the depreciated pound sterling than by gold,[26] the overvaluation of the guilder became not only a financial, but also a political problem.

According to some authors there was a degree of general economic illiteracy in Gold Standard countries. Many were unable to distinguish between inflation and devaluation.[27] This is probably right, but it seems unlikely that this economic illiteracy was a monopoly of governments and politicians in Gold Standard countries. Economics was not the central issue in politics, and among politicians all over the world theoretical economic knowledge was an exception. Therefore it was hard to find a country where the decision to devalue was a freely taken product of cool economic analysis. Everywhere it followed a financial or banking crisis. Therefore, to explain why some countries waited so long before devaluing, one should not analyse their political situations but explain why in these countries the international financial crisis of 1931 or 1933 did not result in a monetary or banking crisis. The enormous gold stocks of the central banks of the gold countries – in the cases of the Netherlands and Switzerland resulting from neutrality during the Great War, in the cases of Belgium and France from the undervalued francs after the stabilisation of 1926 – saved them for a long time from monetary collapse. In the Netherlands before 1936 only an explicit decision to devalue could have ended the gold standard, and such a decision would never have commanded a political majority.[28] Deflating price levels at home and hoping for some inflation in paper-money countries was the only way to recover some competitiveness. Industry also tried to improve its productivity: from 1934 on this resulted in some industrial growth, but it could not solve the depression as such.

It therefore seems unreasonable to blame politicians such as Trip or the Calvinist prime minister Hendrik Colijn, who became – even more than Trip – the champion of the Gold Standard.[29] However, in 1935, just after the devaluation in Belgium, the minister of economics M.P.L. Steenberghe, a politician from the Catholic south, decided that it was time for the Dutch to join the trend to devaluation and wrote a paper for the council of ministers concluding that only devaluing the guilder could bring economic recovery and the badly needed new jobs. There are good reasons to believe that Colijn himself now doubted his own policy, but went on with it for political reasons. Devaluing after years of propaganda for the gold standard would damage his prestige: he could avoid this by shifting the blame of a devaluation of the guilder on to someone else, for instance Steenberghe and his Catholic party, thus strengthening his position against his coalition partners and also getting rid of Steenberghe, whom he considered too independent. By creating a political crisis, which would probably result in a financial crisis and end the gold standard just in the same way as it was done elsewhere, he could let the Catholic Party (RKSP) – in social and economic matters a little more left wing than Colijn – feel that there was no alternative to him and that they had to accept his leadership. Everything went as Colijn planned it, with only one exception.

After Colijn forced a political crisis, monetary speculation started immediately. The only thing he misjudged was the duration of the crisis: it was all over and he was back in power in only a few days. Queen Wilhelmina, who thought a financial crisis would be disastrous – everybody always told her so and she knew nothing about economics – hurried to solve the problems, and since by the third day after the cabinet's fall it was already clear that it would be impossible for the Catholics to form a cabinet, Her Majesty ordered Colijn to resume the prime minister's post.[30] From the moment that this defender of the Gold Standard returned to office, the financial storms calmed down; indeed, the political crisis was solved too fast for the financial crisis to develop. This resulted in a rather ridiculous situation. The new Catholic minister of economics, the biggest party in Parliament, the highest officials of the ministries of economics and finance, and probably even the prime minister all believed that only a devaluation could solve the overvaluation of the guilder and restore Dutch international competitiveness, but for internal political reasons it was impossible even to discuss the matter. Only the September 1936 devaluation in France and Switzerland gave the long-awaited opportunity to do the same. Colijn, who started his career as a professional soldier in the colonial army – the type now called a war criminal[31] – made a radio speech proudly announcing that the Netherlands had defended the flag of the Gold Standard – although shot to ribbons – to the very last. He had only proved that even in a small country with enormous economic interests in the outside world, political decisions are not taken as a result of rational economic analysis, but are the consequence of internal political relations. Therefore the outcome of the political debate could very well be irrational or could only be in the interest of a limited group. The first was the case in the gold-standard policy, the second in the case of the agricultural policy, which had rendered an industrialisation policy – which was essential to solve the unemployment problem – almost unthinkable.

Even for those believing in the possibility of a deflation policy, it was clear that agricultural protectionism would destroy the only escape from the monetary problems. Nevertheless, it was during Colijn's term of office – the prime minister who during the 1920s had been chairman of the free-trade conferences of the League of Nations – that agricultural protectionism was introduced. That this champion of free trade, former director of the Royal Dutch Shell Group and a man with at least some theoretical knowledge of economics – he considered Keynes agreeable bedtime reading[32] – nevertheless opted for agricultural protection, suggests again that this part of his policy was not based on rational economic considerations: even in a small country with enormous interests in international trade, group interests could become dominant.

The political situation

In modern industrial societies agriculture often has a strong lobby.[33] That in the Netherlands during the 1930s this lobby could be strong enough to threaten overall employment and the export trade, resulted from the specific social and political situation during these years. Until recently the political landscape of the Netherlands was divided along religious and ideological lines: Conservatism among the Christian parties and right-wing liberals' fear of atheism and hate of socialism increased after the Russian revolution, and an internal incident in 1918 when the social-democratic leader J.P. Troelstra made clear that if it lay in his hands the German revolution would not stop at the border, resulted in a refusal to recognise the atheistic USSR and internally in a strong tendency to isolate left-wing parties.[34] That parties like the Communists or the Revolutionary Socialists were kept out of power went without discussion, but even the complete acceptance of the parliamentary system and of free enterprise by the SDAP, a party whose demand for economic and social reforms became increasingly muted, could not change the attitude of the right-wing parties towards the social democrats. The social-democratic SDAP was a political pariah. This did not mean that the social democrats were out of the coalition for a few years, but that the party was isolated on a national level – though not in local politics – and its members' opinions were completely ignored: decent people did not join forces with social democrats. Only in 1939, due to the ageing Colijn's political ineptitude, did a coalition between the Catholic RKSP and the social-democratic SDAP, that included some members of the liberal and Calvinist parties, become possible.[35] As long as the socialists were boycotted, more than a quarter of the seats in parliament were isolated by a coalition of all other parties. By doing so the right-wing liberal and Calvinist parties isolated their enemies, but the Catholics, the biggest party in the country and in economic matters the most left-wing of the accepted political parties, manoeuvred themselves into an impossible position. Because in 1933 the Catholics and Social Democrats together obtained more than half of the votes at the polls – and in most other elections got even more – the Catholics had no choice but to accept any other coalition. After the Second World War the renewed Catholic party – KVP – was always in the position to choose between a coalition with the also renewed Labour Party – PvdA – or with Calvinists and Liberals, and so the KVP itself became the centre of power. In the interwar years, however, by isolating the SDAP, the RKSP had to accept the leadership of the much smaller Calvinist parties. The reason for their acceptance of this situation is disputed. According to some it was because the Catholic leadership considered the ideological differences insurmountable, but this seems hardly an adequate explanation. Others think the leadership feared a disintegration of the party if a coalition with the Reds was formed. Recently it has been suggested that such a coalition was taboo because the Catholics were unwilling to admit that their ideological differences with the socialists were in fact surmountable.[36] Nevertheless, the Catholics had good reasons to defend the interests of labour. The southern and eastern parts of the country, where their power base lay, were still rather backward, but these also were the areas of rapid industrialisation. In the Netherlands most miners and workers in the textile industries were Catholics; but, as with most religious parties, the RKSP was a coalition of all kinds of social groups. It had farmers, employers and shopkeepers. What distinguished it from the Calvinist or Liberal parties was that it also had an important number of labourers in its ranks. In 1939 the Roman Catholic trade unions had almost 200 thousand members, the Social Democrat union little more than 300 thousand and the Calvinist union only 100 thousand.[37] Above that, the Catholics had the fastest population growth of all social groups, which probably resulted from the fact that this emancipating minority, since in 1917 universal suffrage was introduced, had great interest in not losing its position in society. As a result new jobs were of the highest importance, especially in the Catholic areas.

By accepting the isolation of the SDAP the RKSP, which in 1933 had had 28 of the 100 seats in the Second Chamber, had to accept that the much smaller ARP of Colijn (14 seats) would be the centre of power. Colijn, a former captain of industry and so a liberal in economic matters, was acceptable to the conservative liberal parties, as to the other conservative Christian party (CHU), which was in religious matters less orthodox, but in social and economic matters even more conservative. As a man of strong character he was also thought to be the ideal leader in a period of crisis. In this coalition, the RKSP was seen by its coalition partners as just acceptable provided it did not try to introduce too much social-security legislation and was willing to cooperate to keep the budget balanced. Because the Catholics thought it irresponsible to block every coalition, they had to accept this, and so it was Colijn who decided what happened. Nevertheless, they were probably in agreement with his decision to save agriculture.

The protection of agriculture

In 1933, when Colijn came to power, it was clear that agriculture had severe problems. Its foreign markets were closing, and nothing guaranteed that the old situation would ever be restored. Nevertheless, the idea of reorganising and downsizing agriculture was rejected. Protection of agriculture even started before 1933, during the ministry of Ruys de Beerenbrouck (1929–1933), a coalition of the RKSP and the two Calvinist parties. Although it is an exaggeration to say that the Netherlands in 1929 had an agricultural policy, nevertheless by 1930 some protection of sugar beet was in place, while in 1931 a clearly protectionist wheat bill was sent to Parliament. As a result the wheat production increased. Until the depreciation of Sterling these were all measures in favour of agriculture,[38] but after the monetary collapse, the introduction of protection in Britain and the even worse developments in Germany, agriculture underwent severe crises. As often in the Western world, farmers could reckon on moral support from other groups, even in the cities. When in 1932 German protectionism threatened Dutch agricultural exports, the Dutch reaction was a spontaneous boycott of German products, not only in the countryside, but also in urbanised areas.[39]

For the Christian parties in power, the agricultural depression seemed threatening. All had important support in the countryside; and farmers, their families and employees were still a quarter of the voters. Other voters in the countryside also were dependent on developments in this area of the economy. Because these people, in total almost a third of the electorate, supported the right-wing political parties currently in power, their real influence was even bigger, since the latter gained almost 45 percent of their support from the rural electorate. The Christian parties, however, also commanded an enormous amount of habitual support: these electors did not vote ARP or RKSP because they necessarily agreed with those parties' current policies, but because they were orthodox Calvinists or Roman Catholics. Farmers, however, made clear that they wanted to use their votes for more practical reasons. In 1933 the new farmers' organisation *Landbouw en Maatschappij* (Agriculture and Society) advised its members to vote for one of the Christian parties and not for the socialists and communists, nor – and this was new – for the Liberal Democrats of P.J. Oud. When this rather small party lost one of its seats at the elections, Oud blamed Agriculture and Society for it.[40]

Agriculture and Society had some of the characteristics of right-wing farmers' organisations of the 1930s. It not only wanted protection against foreign food imports, but in its circles it was also common opinion that agriculture suffered from urban parasites. Some leaders of it were even impressed by the ideas of the German Farmers' leader Walther Darré. When in 1935 the NSB, the *Nationaal Socialistische Bond* (National Socialist Association) – a more fascistic than really national socialist party – for the first time participated in local elections, Agriculture and Society recommended this party, which immediately gained its greatest success, obtaining more than 8 percent of the votes, and even more in Drenthe, the province where Agriculture and Society was founded.[41] Later Agriculture and Society developed in an even more right-wing direction; during the German occupation it would even merge with the farmers' organisation of the then collaborating NSB. For political reasons it was therefore understandable that the Christian political parties should fear the loss of their rural support – whence they obtained almost half of their votes – to the new organisation, which seemed to have enough influence to command the countryside vote: the Christian parties therefore endeavoured to allay the dissatisfaction that had given rise to these electoral developments.

When during the 1933 World Economic Conference in London it became clear that this conference would be another failure, that free trade was dead and that it was necessary to protect the economy because most foreign markets were closed already, it also became clear that agriculture in the Netherlands must have systematic support. That was not easy. The home market was too small to absorb all the dairy products, vegetables, meat and eggs the country produced. As a result of the closing of important markets, the trade system that underpinned Dutch agriculture broke down.[42] In reaction to this, the Agricultural Crisis Act of 1933 passed Parliament and the minister of agriculture[43] was empowered to decide for every agricultural product, whether it became a so-called crisis product. If so, he could prohibit the trade, transport, import or export, or even the keeping in stock, of this product without special licence. Further the government could subsidise production of some products, monopolise their trade, guarantee minimum prices, enforce the use of Dutch products, and demand levies on all kind of foodstuffs to build up an Agricultural Crisis Fund to finance the forgoing activities. From this source the dumping of superfluous food products, especially on the British market, was also financed.

The measures resulting from this legislation – which soon governed almost all foodstuffs – kept the internal price level high. As a result the idea of deflating Dutch prices in line with the depreciation in sterling countries – an idea already vitiated by the unexpectedly slow decrease of sterling countries' internal prices and their complete freedom from inflationary pressures – was now perceived as a total illusion. The Dutch cost of living, that by 1932 had declined to 83 (1929 = 100), in 1933 increased again by 2.4 percent to 85, while the GDP deflator (1929 = 100) that by 1933 had decreased to 82, now stabilised. In the same period, export and import prices almost halved.[44] From 1933 on the Dutch internal price level was not only much too high compared to international prices, but the agricultural policy even destroyed every attempt to adjust internal prices. It was clear from this moment that the gold-standard policy was absolutely incompatible with agricultural protection.

During the 1930s the agricultural-crisis policy saved farmers from ruin, but their income remained extremely low. Nevertheless, the consumers had to pay heavily for this policy. The annual support for agriculture amounted to roundabout 200 million guilder, or 4 percent of the GDP. Of this 75 percent was paid from levies on foodstuffs. As a result the costs of living were kept high. According to R. Laming, the well-informed British commercial attaché in The Hague, as a result of this policy the 1935 cost of living was 10 to 20 percent too high.[45] Even after the 1936 depreciation this persisted: according to calculations from 1938, the cost of living for those on lower and middle incomes was still 3 or 4 percent too high as a result of this agricultural policy.[46]

After the elections of 1937 the RKSP took revenge on Colijn. The party not only demanded that the dismissed minister of economics Steenberghe, an industrialist from the south, be returned to office, but even demanded that the new cabinet should be a Christian one. The reason for that was that Colijn, with his conservative outlook on social and economic matters and his strict financial opinions, found support with the liberal parties, while the Catholics, with their rather more left-wing social and economic ideas, hoped to find support with some parts of Colijn's own ARP party. For the same reasons, some members of the ARP also demanded a Christian coalition.[47] Although Colijn needed his liberal friends for his economic policy, as a leader of a Calvinist party he hardly could oppose a Christian coalition. When in the last period before the elections it became clear that his position in the new cabinet would be less strong and that his rival Steenberghe would return, by reintroducing the Oslo policy he tried to safeguard Dutch free trade in industrial matters and protectionism of agricultural products.

In the early 1930s the Oslo policy was an attempt of the small countries of western and northern Europe to preserve traditional free trade as far as possible. In 1931 it became clear that this was a complete failure. Now Colijn reintroduced this policy and in March 1937 invited authorities from Belgium and the Scandinavian countries to The Hague. Even the leader of the conference, the Dutch top-official H.M. Hirschfeld wrote in his memoirs that he did not know what to talk about, but Colijn wanted to use the positive economic developments after the depreciation to limit industrial protection. On Election Day, May 26, 1937, a treaty was signed by the delegations from the Oslo countries in The Hague, containing agreements about lowering industrial protection.[48] Steenberghe was furious. He was not, as Colijn was, a representative of the big Holland multinationals which needed the international and colonial markets, but an employer of local industry in Brabant, a rather backward but fast-developing part of the country. According to him the Netherlands should use the little economic revival to limit its agricultural protection and at the same time protect small-scale industry oriented towards the national market so as to increase employment. A government taking this course recognised that it could not reopen the international markets but had to find an alternative on the home market to create employment for the growing population. It was for this reason that Steenberghe demanded that he, as minister of an economic department, would be responsible for industry, agriculture and trade policy. The new Oslo agreement would not survive this minister.[49] However, he could not realise his idea to break down agricultural protectionism. There were new reasons to protect agriculture.

Economic preparation for war and the first years of the German occupation

Even in the Netherlands the German military occupation of the Rhineland in March 1936 was reason to worry.[50] Nobody immediately feared a military conflict involving the kingdom, but the experience from the last war proved that the position of a neutral power was also very delicate. Good economic war preparation therefore was a necessity. When in response to the Rhineland crisis it was checked whether the country was in any danger of shortages, it became clear that modern, quick transport facilities resulted in small stocks. There was much less wheat or rye in the country than only a few years before.[51] The experience from the Great War and the shortages in 1917 and 1918 resulting from the German submarine war and the British blockade proved that stocks were useful for surviving a period of transition. During a European war resulting in a renewed isolation of the continent, the country should be able to feed its own population after a limited period of time. Therefore agriculture could not be downsized for the present. At April 1, 1937, only one month before the elections that would bring Steenberghe back in office, the RVVO, the *Rijksbureau voor de Voorbereiding van de Voedselvoorziening in Oorlogstijd* (National Office for the Preparation of Food Distribution in Time of War) was founded.[52] If the country was to be neutral and would have to supply its population without imports, that would be problematic. Between 1913 and the late 1930s the population had grown from 6 to 9 million, and even in the last war food distribution had failed. Now it was calculated that only when agriculture was completely reorganised in the first year of war would it be possible to give the population a sufficient, albeit sober, diet. Then production should be concentrated on potatoes, cereals and other raw foodstuffs. All fowls should be slaughtered, together with 80 percent of the pigs and 20 percent of the cattle.[53] By offering good prices for the kind of foodstuffs needed and subsidising the slaughter of livestock, this could be realised. Of course in these last years before a new war, economic policy made it impossible to reduce agriculture and industrialise the country. That had to wait until the post-war years.

When in the first year of the occupation agriculture was reformed according to plan, it proved possible to feed the population from Dutch soil. Even a little export of food, especially of vegetables, was possible. Post-war stories about food shortages as a result of enormous German food exports from Holland do not derive from any actual experience of starvation. The idea about German food exports was based on Allied propaganda that was believed, while German propaganda denying it was disbelieved. This time, however, the Germans were right. There were hardly any exports, but the experience that before the German invasion everything was available while from May 1940 on, all luxury foodstuffs disappeared from legal markets, seemed to prove for those who did not believe the Allies for political reasons alone, that the London propaganda was right. However, that the people felt hungry had more to do with the diet they were used to, than with what they got. The comparative disappearance of meat, butter and other edible fats and the substitution of these products by potatoes and cereals were unpopular. People did not like their rations, but these were in some respects even healthier than the pre-war diet. Until 1944 black-market purchases were hardly necessary to increase the amount of food, but were employed to make the diet more agreeable. Therefore, cheese, eggs or meat were more important on the black market than basic foodstuffs like bread or potatoes.[54] When people remember real starvation, it is because the winter of 1944–1945, when the cities of Holland and Utrecht were isolated from all supplies as a result of the military situation and the crumbling of the Third Reich. This was such a severe experience that most survivors could scarcely remember that in the years before the food was sober but sufficient. Nevertheless, recent calculations confirm that food shortages were not dangerous until late 1944.[55]

As a result of the German occupation the most important market for the Dutch economy was open again. The export of agricultural products was not possible, because all food was needed to feed the local population, but industry was of importance for the Germans and had enough capacity. From the early summer of 1940 on industrial recovery, until then limited because of the closed German market, got under way; industrial employment vastly increased and in 1941 even surpassed the pre-Depression level. In the same period industrial profits peaked, and investments were growing. Only from 1942 on, when the exploitation of the occupied economies came in the hands of Albert Speer, who closed down all economic activity he deemed inessential, did industrial development suffer a setback. New research has made it clear that contrary to previous assumptions, after the war Holland's industrial capacity was even greater than it had been in 1940. This was not a bad starting point for post-war recovery and industrial development.[56]

Conclusion

During the war it was an advantage that Dutch agriculture had survived the Depression. When, however, the decision was taken to protect agriculture and not reorganise and reduce this sector, this was not done for rational economic, but for political reasons. The political parties in power had more connections with agriculture and with the big export-oriented industries in Holland, than with the smaller scale, developing industries in the other provinces. Unemployment was of course a problem, but the unemployed supported parties whose share in the country's governance was at best partial and at worst non-existent, and consequently had hardly any influence. Farmers, however, not only voted for parties who could help them, but also made it clear that these parties had to do something for them, or they would vote differently next time. The decisions not to devalue the guilder and to protect agriculture were damaging for international competitiveness and therefore for trade. Even in a supertrading country, however, policy is not only based on rational arguments, but also on the political situation and the interests of the dominant groups. If in 1933 the most rational decisions had been taken that were appropriate for a small open economy such as that of the Netherlands, not only would the guilder have been devalued, but agriculture would have been reorganised and its size adapted to that of the surviving markets. As a result industry would have gained space to develop the strength it showed in the 1920s and again in the 1950s, thus creating employment for the growing labour force. The fact that this was not done had little to do with the limited knowledge of economics of politicians. From 1935 on most of those who knew anything about it agreed that the guilder would have to be devalued, but nobody wanted to be blamed for it. From 1933 on it was clear that agriculture had lost its markets for an indefinite period of time. That this did not result in reorganisation, although this was the universal recommendation of those who at that time commanded respect within the state bureaucracy again indicates that political expediency had more influence on the decision than rationality. During the war it was an advantage that agriculture was still a substantial part of the economy, but only in 1937 and after, when the decision was renewed not to limit agriculture, did this become a bone of contention. Industry, in the 1920s a fast-growing sector that created badly needed employment, was confronted with internal costs kept high by the protection of other economic sectors. It survived, but could no longer create jobs. That industry commanded little support had to do with the fact that the industries that could have been supported had hardly any influence in The Hague. Only in 1940 and 1941, when German orders stimulated industrial development, did his sector revive and once more become a net creator of employment.

In 1945 the political situation changed completely. As a result of a coalition between the social democrats and the Catholics, the latter became the central party in the Dutch political scene. Therefore this party, for whom industrialisation made sound political sense, could stimulate its development.

1 Hein Klemann, *Tussen Reich en Empire. De economische betrekkingen van Nederland met zijn belangrijkste handelspartners, Duitsland, Groot-Brittannië en België en de Nederlandse handelspolitiek, 1929-1936* (Amsterdam: 1990). See about the development of agriculture in the late nineteenth century: Jan Luiten van Zanden en Arthur van Riel, *Nederland 1780–1914. Staat, Instituties en Economische ontwikkeling* (Amsterdam: 2000), pp. 362 ff.

2 Gerard Trienekens, 'The food supply in The Netherlands during the Second World War', in David F. Smith and Jim Philips, *Food, science, policy and regulation in the Twentieth Century. International and comparative perspectives* (London: 2000), pp. 117–133.

3 CBS, *Jaarcijfers voor Nederland.*

4 Paul Krugman, 'Growing World Trade. Causes and Consequences', in *Brooking papers on economic activities*, 1995 (1), pp. 327–377, there p. 334.

5 Krugman, 'Growing World Trade', pp. 334–335.

6 Jan-Pieter Smits, Edwin Horings and Jan Luiten van Zanden, *Dutch DNP and its components, 1800–1913* (Groningen: 2000); CBS, *Tweehonderd jaar statistiek in tijdreeksen, 1800–1999* (Voorburg: 2001); own calculations.

7 Krugman, 'Growing World Trade', p. 335.

8 Smits a. o., *Dutch GDP and its components*; own calculations.

9 See: Nationaal Archief (NA) Den Haag 1770 map 1: Nota van Ries en anderen ten behoeve van de commissie voor exportverruiming, 5 November 1932; Ministerie van Financiën, Archief 1918–1940, inv.nr. 227, doos 38: Nota van de Thesaurier-generaal aan de Minister van Financiën over de begroting van het Crisislandbouwfonds 1933 en 1934, 23 October 1933; H. M. F. Krips-Van der Laan, *Praktijk als antwoord. S. L. Louwes en het landbouwcrisisbeleid* (Groningen: 1985).

10 H. J. de Jong, *De Nederlandse industrie 1913–1965. Een vergelijkende analyse op basis van de productiestatistieken* (Amsterdam: 1999), p. 194.

11 J. W. Drukker, *Waarom de crisis hier langer duurde. Over de Nederlandse economische ontwikkeling in de jaren dertig* (Amsterdam: 1990), *passim*.

12 CBS, *Jaarcijfers voor Nederland*; Hein A. M. Klemann, '"Belangrijke gebeurtenissen vonden niet plaats"… De Nederlandse industrie 1938–1948' in *Bijdragen en Mededelingen betreffende de Geschiedenis der Nederlanden*, 114 (1999) afl. 4, pp. 506–552; Hein A. M. Klemann, *Nederland 1938–1948. Economie en samenleving in jaren van oorlog en bezetting* (Amsterdam: 2002), p. 266.

13 Klemann, *Tussen Reich en Empire*, pp. 119 ff.; Heinz Haushofer, *Die deutsche Landwirtschaft im technischen Zeitalter* (Stuttgart: 1963), pp. 254–255; Dieter Gessner, *Agrardepression und Präsidialregierungen in Deutschland 1930–1933. Probleme der Agrarprotektionismus am Ende der Weimarer Republik* (Düsseldorf: 1977), pp. 32–33; Dietmar Petzina, 'Hauptprobleme der deutsche Wirtschaftspolitik 1932/33', in *VJZG* (1967), pp. 18–55, there p. 32–33; P. A. Blaisse, *De Nederlandse handelspolitiek* (Utrecht: 1948), pp. 130–135.
14 Reichsstatistische Amt, *Monatliche Nachweise über den auswärtigen Handel Deutschlands.*
15 Klemann, *Tussen Reich en Empire*, p. 229.
16 Idem pp. 229 and 306.
17 Reichsstatistische Amt, *Monatliche Nachweise über den auswärtigen Handel Deutschlands.*
18 Klemann, *Tussen Reich en Empire*, p. 229.
19 Idem pp. 91 ff.; Dietmar Petzina, *Autarkiepolitik im Dritten Reich. Der nationalsozialistische Vierjahresplan* (Stuttgart: 1968), pp. 31–32; Allan Thomas Bonnel, *German control over international economic relations 1930–1940* (Urbana: 1940), p. 90.
20 C. A. Klaasse, 'Clearingverdrag met Duitschland', in *Economisch Statistische Berichten* 26 (September 1934), pp. 848–850.
21 Klemann, *Tussen Reich en Empire*, pp. 143 ff., see also: C. H. J. Maliepaard, *De Nederlandse landbouw* (Utrecht: 1949), p. 15.
22 Ministerie van Economische Zaken, *Beknopt overzicht van de totstandkoming van de Landbouwcrisiswetgeving in Nederland II* (Den Haag: 1938), p. 191; CBS, *Macro-economische ontwikkelingen*, pp. 55–56; see also: P. W. Klein, 'Depressie en beleid tijdens de jaren '30. Kanttekeningen bij de ontwikkelingen van de Nederlandse volkshuishouding in de jaren '30', in J. van Herwaarden, *Lof der historie. Opstellen over geschiedenis en maatschappij* (Rotterdam: 1973), p. 296.
23 Forest Capie, 'The British Tariff and Industrial Protection in the 1930s', in, *EHR*, 31 (1978) 399–409, there 399; G. Minderhoud, 'Crisis en crisiswetgeving', in Z. W. Sneller, *Geschiedenis van den Nederlandschen landbouw, 1795–1940* (Groningen / Batavia: 1940), pp. 510–511; H. M. Hirschfeld, *Actieve economische politiek in Nederland in de jaren 1929–1934* (Amsterdam: 1946), p. 113.
24 *Keesings Historisch Archief*, no. 98, 6 Mei 1933, 804 e.
25 National Archives London (Kew) T 160/725 Montgomery: From the Netherlands, 2nd April 1935, no. 4.
26 Ian M. Drummond, *The floating pound and the sterling area, 1931–1939* (Cambridge: 1981), p. 8.
27 R. T. Griffiths, *The Netherlands and the Gold Standard A study in policy formation and policy* (Amsterdam: 1988), p. 207.
28 'Economische kroniek', in *De Economist* (1935), 678–681, there 679.
29 H. M. Hirschfeld, *Herinneringen uit de jaren 1933–1939* (Amsterdam/Brussel: 1959), p. 53; A. van Schaik, *Crisis en protectie onder Colijn. Over economische doelmatigheid en maatschappelijke aanvaardbaarheid van de Nederlandse handelspolitiek in de jaren dertig* (Alblasserdam: 1986), pp. 32–33.

30 Klemann, *Tussen Reich en Empire*, pp. 62 ff. In his biography of Colijn, Herman Langeveld did not believe that Colijn forced the political crisis of 1935. Herman Langeveld, *Schipper naast God. Hendrikus Colijn 1869–1944* (Amsterdam: 2004), pp. 138 ff.
31 Herman Langeveld, *Dit leven van krachtig handelen. Hendrikus Colijn 1869–1944. Deel een 1869–1933* (SL 1998), pp. 58 ff.
32 Idem 149.
33 J. L. van Zanden and R. T. Griffiths, *Economische geschiedenis van Nederland in de 20^{e} eeuw* (Utrecht: 1989), pp. 149 ff.
34 P. J. Oud, *Honderd jaren. Een eeuw van staatvormgeving in Nederland 1840–1940* (Assen: 1961), pp. 253 ff.
35 Marcel Hoogenboom, 'De democratsiche paradox van de RKSP. De "leer van de uiterste noodzaak" als uiting van de groeiende eensgezindheid tussen katholieken en sociaal-democraten in het interbellum', in, *BMGN*, 120 (1995), pp. 521–545.
36 Ibidem.
37 CBS, *Jaarcijfers voor Nederland 1940*, p. 305.
38 Blaisse, *De Nederlandse Handelspolitiek*, pp. 130–131.
39 NA, Den Haag, Archief Handel en Nijverheid 723 map 5: De Chef der 6^{E} Afdeeling van de inspectie van den landbouw aan Handel en Nijverheid, 7 Augustus 1930, No. 4310; Ministerie van BuZa, DEZ 1924–1940, inv.nr. 110^{DUI} doos 491: Uittreksel notulen, Vergadering Commissie voor de herziening der handelsverdragen.
40 J. H. de Ru, '*Landbouw en Maatschappij*'. *Een analyse van een boerenbeweging in de crisisjaren* (Wageningen: 1979); Klemann, *Tussen Reich en Empire*, p. 206.
41 Jan Meyers, *Mussert. Een politiek leven* (Amsterdam: 1984), pp. 84–86; L. de Jong, *Het Koninkrijk der Nederlanden in de Tweede Wereldoorlog. Deel 1: Voorspel* (Den Haag: 1969), pp. 232–234.
42 See Hein A. M. Klemann, 'The international economic relations of Small Countries in the 1930s. Belgium and the Netherlands', in Timo Myllyntaus, *Economic Crisis and Restructuring in History. Experiences of Small Countries* (St. Katharinen: 1998), pp. 145–168.
43 Until 1933 agriculture was the responsibility of the Minister of the Interior: then until 1935 it became the responsibility of the Minister of Economics. From 1935 until 1937 it had its own minister, but in 1937 it became part of the department of economics again. This was a key decision of the RKSP, who wanted one minister responsible for all branches of the economy. Only then it was possible to make rational decisions about protection and economic stimulation across all sectors. On May 8, 1940, however, two days before the German attack, the food supply became such an important issue that it was necessary to split the department again and organise a new department of Agriculture and Food Supply.
44 CBS, *Macro-economische ontwikkelingen 1921–1939 and 1969–1985. Een vergelijking op basis van herzienen gegevens voor het interbellum* ('s-Gravenhage: 1985); CBS, *Jaarcijfers voor Nederland;* Klemann, *Tussen Reich en Empire*, pp. 169 ff.
45 NA, London (Kew) FO 425/410: Further correspondence regarding Western Europe. Part 31 January–June 1935: Memorandum. An appreciation of the economic position in the Netherlands, May 1935, Laming, pp. 162–165.

46 CBS, *Het aandeel van enkele indirecte belastingen en landbouwcrisisheffingen in de gezinsuitgaven* (Den Haag: 1939), pp. 7–9; Ministerie van Economische Zaken, *Beknopt overzicht van de Landbouwcrisiswetgeving III*, pp. 28–29.
47 P. J. Oud, *Het jongste verleden. Parlementaire geschiedenis van Nederland, 1918–1940, Deel 5* (Assen: 1949), pp. 1–3.
48 Hirschfeld, *Herinneringen*, p. 97.
49 Hein Klemann, 'Jacob Adriaan Nicolaas Patijn. Colijns marionet op het plein', in Duco Helleman c. s., *De Nederlandse ministers van buitenlandse zaken in de twintigste eeuw* (Den Haag: 1999), pp. 127–137, there 131–132.
50 J. L. van Zanden en R. T. Griffiths, *Economische geschiedenis van Nerderland in de twintigste eeuw* (Utrecht: 1989), p. 163.
51 NA, Den Haag, EZ, Archief H en N, inv.nr. 2.06.001, map 7306, Notulen e. d. CEVV en werkcommissies 1936–1938.
52 NA, Den Haag, EZ, Archief H en N, inv.nr. 2.13.68.06, map 25.
53 G. M. T. Trienekens, *Tussen ons volk en de honger. De voedselvoorziening 1940–1945* (Utrecht: 1985), p. 359; Hein A. M. Klemann, 'De legale en illegale productie in de landbouw 1938–1948', in *NEHA-Jaarboek voor economische, bedrijfs- en techniekgeschiedenis* 60 (1997), pp. 307–338.
54 Hein A. M. Klemann, '"Die koren onthoudt, wordt gevloekt onder het volk..." De zwarte markt in voedingswaren 1940–1948', in *BMGN* 5 (2000), 532–560.
55 Trienekens, *Tussen ons volk en de honger;* Klemann, 'De legale en illegale productie in de landbouw'; Hein A. M. Klemann, 'Discussie. Landbouw tijdens de oorlog en slachtofferschap in de historiografie', in *Tijdschrift voor Geschiedenis* 111 (1998), pp. 474–486; Merijn T. Knibbe, 'De Nederlandse landbouw tijdens de Tweede Wereldoorlog. Een reactie op het artikel "De Nederlandse economie tijdens de Tweede Wereldoorlog" van Hein A. M. Klemann,' in *Tijdschrift voor Geschiedenis* 111 (1998), pp. 75–94.
56 Klemann, *Nederland 1938–1948, passim.*

IVAN JAKUBEC

Czechoslovak Industry 1918–1938/1939: Outlet Problems for Goods

Preface

The following article focuses on the area of Central Europe after the break-up of the Austro-Hungarian Empire and the consequent outlet problems for Czechoslovak industrial goods in the period between the two world wars. In the inter-war years Central Europe witnessed the simultaneous processes of economic disintegration and national and international integration, which were a part of the creation of new frontiers between nations.

With the founding of the Czechoslovak Republic (or CSR) centuries-old economic ties were broken and the new state saw the union of two areas which had been developing differently: the Bohemian Lands (Bohemia, Moravia and Silesia) on one hand, and Slovakia and Ruthenia on the other.

While the Bohemian Lands had been from early twentieth century an industrial and agrarian territory with an economic development similar to western Europe (39.9% of the population were employed in industry and crafts), Slovakia and Ruthenia were backward agrarian territories with a high proportion of the population (63.5%) engaged in agriculture and forestry.[1] The process of integrating the western part of the republic with the East lasted for the duration of the entire inter-war period. It was influenced also by the small capacity of East-West transport connections, the insufficient density of transport, and the high tariffs of the former Hungarian state railways and numerous private railway companies in the east of the republic.

After 1918 industrial companies were forced to cope with many problems. One of them was the shift to peace production, another the lack of raw materials, or worn out machinery as a result of insufficient maintenance during the war. Many company branches and affiliated offices found themselves 'abroad' overnight, communication and transport connections were not functional, and so on. Economic life was consolidated after the establishment of a single customs territory, the separation of Czechoslovak currency from the Austro-Hungarian, the domestication of industrial, commercial and transport joint-stock and limited liability companies (when the headquarters of the companies were transferred to Czechoslovak territory), the repatriation of capital (when the shares of prominent companies situated in the CSR were purchased by banks and then resold to their clients), the stabilisation of currency, etc. While in the field of monetary policy post-war inflation was overcome and the currency became stabilized as early as 1923, i.e. much earlier than in other Central European countries, the process of domestication took much longer and was extended over decades. Domestication involved 235 industrial companies worth overall 2 billion Czechoslovak crowns of capital, which represented one-third of the commercial capital of the CSR.[2]

From the mid-1920s older companies enlarged their range of production and introduced new technologies. New companies focused primarily on technological progress and missing types of production, such as the electrical industry. Companies with large numbers of employees could be found in the mining and smelting industries, in metal processing, engineering, electrical and chemical industries. The category of middle- and small-size companies was more strongly represented, though.

Many issues surface when dealing with the outlet problems of Czechoslovak industrial goods:

1) Why were foreign outlets so important for the CSR?
2) How did the state encourage foreign trade?
3) Which other institutions encouraged foreign trade?
4) How did the process of connecting Czechoslovak foreign trade with European and global markets proceed?
5) Towards which territories was Czechoslovak industrial output directed?
6) What was the structure of Czechoslovak industrial production?

7) What was the technological level of Czechoslovak industry and how did it influence foreign trade?
8) Did the political orientation of the CSR influence the economic one?
9) Who influenced the economic policy of the CSR?

The first stage: The immediate post-war period and the restructuring processes in the 1920s

Czechoslovakia inherited approximately 26% of the population (14 million) and 21% of the area (140,000 square kilometers) of the Austro-Hungarian Empire, but also 60 to 75% of its industrial resources.[3] The Czechoslovak Republic is comparable to Greece in territory (127,000 square kilometers) and Yugoslavia in population (12 million inhabitants). After gaining political independence the essential task of the country's economic policy was to achieve economic independence, i.e. to create a new Czechoslovak economy. One of the main economic problems was to remedy the disproportion between the existing (inherited) capacity of industrial production and the potential demand of the domestic market.

By the establishment of an independent customs territory in 1919 Czechoslovak home trade was reduced to about a third of the former imperial home trade. It was consequently able to absorb less than half of the domestic industrial output. In this sense, the Bohemian Lands were actually 'overindustrialized'. The market of the Empire with its fifty million inhabitants was able to accommodate up to 75% of the production coming from the Bohemian Lands. For these reasons, Czechoslovakia was largely dependent on foreign export markets, especially in the case of its industrial products.

In economy, the decisive position was achieved by the group centred on the Trading Bank and politically connected to National Democrats. The Trading Bank exercised its influence by means of contracting and business organisations, such as the Central Union of Czechoslovak Industrialists, the Union of Czechoslovak Banks and the Chamber of Commerce in Prague. The Agrarian Party, concentrating primarily on agricultural issues, represented another important group.[4] The Agrarian Party's share in the formation of the country's economic policy resulted not only from the high number of the party's electorate but also the high share of agricultural production in the gross national production, especially through such crops as sugar beet, hops and malt.

The Czechoslovak trade policy in 1918–1922 was characterized predominantly by state regulation. On one hand, export was mildly stimulated by post-war inflation, on the other, it was hindered by the 1922–1923 deflation policy of the Finance Minister Alois Rašín. The main means of the state regulation of foreign trade were, foremost, licensing procedures, which were actually a war inheritance from the times of the Austro-Hungarian Empire, and, to a lesser extent, import taxes and trade treaties. Such measures, also customary in other countries, were necessitated by the state of the European markets and the lack of raw materials and goods. With regard to certain types of raw materials and products, the controlled economy still survived. International trade was complicated by problems in transportation and finance, but with the continuing economic consolidation of the Czechoslovak Republic import and export limitations were reduced.

The years 1923–1929 denote the period from the deflation crisis to the end of the economic boom. It is a time of economic stability and of trade liberalisation. The Czechoslovak economy required broader commercial ties with foreign countries both far and near. However, the 34% increase of customs rates on imported agricultural goods implemented in 1925 by the victorious Agrarian Party inhibited the export of industrial products to neighbouring countries and destabilized the 'natural' distribution of products in the region, including the Little Entente, an alliance formed in 1920–1921 by Czechoslovakia, Romania and Yugoslavia with the purpose of preventing the Habsburg restoration.

With the disintegration of the Empire, traditional outlets became foreign territories with their customs and import surcharges, and also tough competition. With the exception of wood and coal, the relatively highly developed industrial base of Czechoslovakia did not have sufficient supplies of domestic raw materials. For example, a necessary condition for machine-making and the production of iron was the import of quality iron ore, lead, zinc and tin; the leather and shoe industries were dependent on the import of animal skins and hides; the textile industry – the most important export industry – on the supply of cotton, silk and wool. Moreover, oil and chemical semi-manufactured goods were also imported. With such a structure of industry Czechoslovakia had an open, typically export-oriented economy, which, however, was also substantially dependent on the input of raw materials. During the economic boom, the value of exported goods represented about 30% of the national income. The production of certain industries was basically all targeted for export. In 1930 96% of all toys, musical instruments, stoneware and earthenware produced were intended for export, as were 95% of costume jewellery from Jablonec, 90% of household pottery, 85% of china ware, 79% of sheet glass, 69% of kaolin (china clay), 68% of silk goods, 61% of woollen goods, 59% of sugar and 54% of cotton goods.[5]

Table 1: The Czechoslovak Balance of Payments in 1925–1937 in Millions of Czechoslovak crowns (Kč)

Year	Export (Goods)	Import (Goods)	Balance of Foreign Trade (Goods)	Balance of Payments
1925	18821	17618	+ 1203	+ 144
1926	17857	15277	+ 2580	+ 621
1927	20135	17962	+ 2173	– 344
1928	21224	19208	+ 2016	+ 2
1929	20499	19988	+ 511	– 87
1930	17474	15715	+ 1759	+ 1099
1931	13149	11801	+ 1348	+ 1139
1932	7343	7487	– 144	– 33
1933	5853	5832	+ 21	+ 232
1934	7280	6382	+ 898	+ 143
1935	7418	6738	+ 680	– 66
1936	8008	7909	+ 99	– 817
1937	11972	10980	+ 992	– 258

Source: *Statistická ročenka republiky Československé* (Praha: Orbis, 1934), pp. 306–307; *Statistická ročenka republiky Československé* (Praha: Orbis, 1935), p. 288; *Statistická ročenka republiky Československé* (Praha: Orbis, 1938), p. 148; *Statistická ročenka Protektorátu Čechy a Morava I* (Praha: ÚSÚ, 1941), pp. 204–205.

Foreign trade represented the most important item in the balance of payments and was crucial for the acquisition of international currency (see Table 1). Consequently, the Czechoslovak economy was particularly sensitive to fluctuations in world markets. In spite of the development of heavy industry at the turn of the nineteenth century, light industry (the production of textiles, glass, pottery, and also sugar refining, wood processing etc.) still continued to be of crucial importance. In general, the development of Czechoslovak industry was influenced by regional differences in industrialisation, which was an inheritance from the imperial era, and by the structure of industrial sectors as well as the technological level of individual production plants. Both heavy and light industries were not highly specialized and consequently produced a broad variety of goods. This fact, together with the insecure situation in the world market and the low technological level of medium-size and small production plants, was inevitably reflected in the production of goods in small batches, or even as individual items. In the period 1919–1920 the process of transforming industry from war to peace production was well underway. Nevertheless, it was slowed down by a lack of raw materials and fuel, obsolete machinery, and low work morale. Pre-war levels were reached as late as 1924. During the boom, though, Czechoslovak industrial production showed greater progress than the majority of European countries. In 1927 it rose by 17%, and one year later by 10%.[6] This considerable growth was made possible by increased capital investment and the creation of new industrial resources. Although the share of the metallurgical, the machine and the chemical industries in Czechoslovak industrial production in general was smaller if compared to the developed countries of Europe, the growth of these sectors was higher than in Czechoslovak industry as a whole.[7]

Export was dominated by industrial products, especially textiles – cotton, woollen, jute and silk goods and clothing (hats, lingerie, garments). At over 7 billion Czechoslovak crowns the export of textiles in 1929 represented more than 30% of the overall export figures; 3.4% (700 million crowns) was the share of clothing. The production of iron maintained its position: in 1929 its share hovered around 8.8% (under 1.8 million crowns).[8] From 1926 there arouse the acute problem of German competition in the Balkans, where attempts were made to start an independent industry.

Low concentration, higher production costs of minor companies, and slow modernisation negatively influenced the productivity of labour, and, consequently, profit. In light of the shortage of domestic investment capital, modernisation of industry was to be enhanced by the Building and Construction Act (No 100; 1921) and by tax allowances for investment and retooling activities (Act No 102; 1921). Industry was further supported by the state in laws establishing lower customs rates on the import of machines not produced domestically (No 58; 1925: No 113; 1927: provision No 158; 1929), and in the legal statute concerning direct tax (§79), which provided a special deduction of 20% off machine and technical equipment costs for plants that exchanged old machinery for new.

The transport of raw materials to production plants for processing and of finished goods for export traditionally represented a substantial part of production costs in the Czechoslovak Republic. For this reason many companies and even whole industrial sectors were interested in their reduction. For example, the Bata company started to build its own sea, air and car fleets, to make parts of the Morava River navigable, to construct the Otrokovice Canal and to build a railway line between Vizovice (Moravia) and Horní Lideč (Slovakia). In the early 1930s the transport of one ton of wool from Buenos Aires to Hamburg (13,500 km) cost Bata only 194 Czechoslovak crowns, but from Hamburg to Zlín, the seat of the firm, (861 km) as much as 378 crowns.[9] Also, the import of rubber from the Dutch Indies to Zlín and the export of finished slippers from Zlín to Bombay or Calcutta cost Bata about 6.3 times more than their Japanese competition.[10] As estimated by the Czechoslovak Ministry of Industry, transport costs in 1929 amounted to 49% of the sales price; this was caused not only by the unfortunate geographical position of the Czechoslovak Republic but also by the fact that the transport tariffs of Czechoslovak transport companies did not reflect the worldwide drop in raw material prices.[11] Within the framework of its economic constraints the Czechoslovak Republic did attempt to support exports, e.g. by a tariff policy which included the enforced tariff cooperation of state transport companies –

Czechoslovak State Railways, Czechoslovak Airlines, Czechoslovak Postal Services – and of state-controlled transport companies – the Czechoslovak Elbe Shipping Company, the Czechoslovak Danube Shipping Co. and the Czechoslovak Oder Shipping Co. Nevertheless, transport costs were influenced by tariff rates, or, rather, by the degree of cooperation with the railway management of those countries goods were exported to and imported from, or, on whose territory they were in transit. Czechoslovak tariff policy deserves praise for exploiting the country's location to its advantage in the competition of Hamburg with Trieste, and from the 1930s also with Gdynia, Gdansk and other ports. The state directly or indirectly supported transport companies by means of legislative measures, loans, subsidies, tax deductions, etc. Increased industrial demands on transport frequently resulted from the insufficient transformation of the Czechoslovak economy's unsatisfactory structure, low productivity and high costs of production, as well as from the loss of outlets as a result of territorial changes etc.

Only very few Czechoslovak companies had any experience of international trade, as before World War I this was conducted for them by commercial companies and banks in Trieste, Vienna and Berlin. Also the new trade mark 'Made in Czechoslovakia' was unknown. Czechoslovak businesses established direct trade links only gradually and with difficulty. Many markets were unknown and uncertain. A few companies had their own export organisation, but before World War I most central export agencies were based in Vienna and their transfer to the Czechoslovak Republic was slow. For example, the silk industry's central sales office remained in Vienna.

Industrial companies were thus forced to establish their own direct links abroad, build export organisations, agencies, warehouses and even their own shops (e.g. Bata, Nehera, Rolný). Skoda Enterprises and Českomoravská-Kolben established in 1921 a common organisation called Čechomašina for export to Russia. Others, such as Bata, Waldes and Brno Wool Enterprises established companies in those countries where it was difficult or impossible for them to deliver their goods. When foreign trade was forced to have recourse to state subventions, Bata and Skoda Enterprises set up two independent companies Kotva and Omnipol. The most successful were companies such as Bata, Skoda Enterprises, the Mining and Metallurgical Corporation, the Czechoslovak Munition Works and the textile producers Rolný and Nehera.

The smelting, machine and chemical industries, and partly also the production of shoes (Bata) and clothing (Nehera), were on a higher technological level. The onset of the Depression brought a dramatic change to the structure of Czechoslovak industry as it had been formed in the late nineteenth century. The textile industry lost its dominant position and the significance of the food processing industry was also diminished. Metallurgy, the production of machines and construction materials, the chemical industry, wood processing, and the shoe and textile industries were on the rise. After the brief post-war depression in 1921–1923 demand shifted from consumer goods to means of production. The drop in the demand for textiles and some foods (sugar) was a sign of the ongoing industralisation of agrarian countries, the competition of Javanese and Cuban cane sugar, and consumer retrenchment. This drop affected the principal Czechoslovak export items. Consumer industries were moreover located in the border territories, where the dominant population was German. The structure of foreign trade was not sufficiently transformed. Despite a small drop in export figures, textiles kept their dominant position; although the share of woollen goods decreased, that of ready-to-wear clothing increased. Export figures of leather goods, including shoes, rose from 3.2% to 6.8%. The share of iron and steel products rose, but all too frequently these were only semi-finished products. Also the proportion of the main so-called 'new' industries gradually dropped: machines from 3.4% (in 1921) to 2.6% (1928–1929 average), chemical products from 1.6% to 1.5%. In general, the highest growth rate figures in the 1920s were those of the shoe industry, chemical and metal industries. Within these, electrical engineering and car production developed at the greatest speed. Smelting was also on the rise.[12]

Let us consider the structure of Czechoslovak exports in comparison to other selected countries. According to Table 2 below from the State Statistics Board in Prague (1929) the Czechoslovak Republic seemed to rank amongst the most advanced. The problem, though, lies in the structure of finished products because in the case of Czechoslovakia they are characterized by a smaller share of know-how input (53.7% of exports) whilst the share of technologically more demanding goods represented only 15.2%.

Table 2: Structure of Czechoslovak exports compared with selected European countries, and using main Brussels classifications, in % (1929)

State	I. Livestock	II. Food and Drink	III. Raw materials and semi-finished	IV. Finished industrial products
Sweden	0,3	9,2	49,8	40,7
Netherlands	0,8	36,9	18,7	43,6
Belgium-Luxemburg	0,4	7,8	33,1	58,7
Italy	0,1	24,7	12,5	62,7
France	0,7	11,9	19,5	67,9
Czechoslovakia	0,2	11,4	16,8	71,6
Germany	0,2	5,4	19,9	74,5
Austria	0,9	2,1	22,2	74,8
Great Britain	0,3	6,4	16,1	77,2

Source: E. Kubů and J. Pátek (eds.), *Mýtus a realita hospodářské vyspělosti Československa mezi světovými válkami* (Praha: Karolinum, 2000), p. 212 on *Statistická příručka ČSR IV* (Praha: Orbis, 1932).

On one hand, as an industrially advanced country Czechoslovakia exported its consumer goods and machine products to less developed areas, and imported raw materials and other goods with a smaller share of labour. On the other hand in its relations to the most advanced countries it played the role of a less developed, more dependent partner, exporting raw materials, semi-finished products, and light industrial products with a smaller share of labour, and importing technologically more demanding goods. In some fields, however, Czechoslovakia, or rather Czech industry, was actually capable of producing top quality products.

In 1925–1929 Czechoslovak industry had a 1.7% share in global industrial production (3.8% in Europe), which placed it tenth in the world (following Belgium). With its 110 dollars of industrial production value per capita it was comparable to Denmark (140 dollars) and Finland (110 dollars), and came twentieth globally.[13] The value of Czechoslovak production was higher than that of Austria and Italy but lower than of the developed countries of Western Europe, the USA and Canada. Czechoslovakia did not rate among the most advanced industrial countries, but it certainly belonged in the itermediate category of industrially developped countries, together with Austria, Finland, Italy and Norway. The Czechoslovak share in global export reached 1.9% in the years of economic boom.[14]

This relative success may be explained by a long-standing tradition of industrial enterprise, the good quality of the products, late 1920s' modernisation and investment trends (electrification, standardisation) and also the emancipation of Czechoslovak industry in the European and world-wide contexts.

The organisation of foreign trade also had to undergo a complex development. At first the newly created Czechoslovak Republic continued with the state control and regulation of foreign trade as implemented during the war. Instead of former headquarters in Vienna a Czechoslovak export and import commission was established shortly after the coup, further export syndicates were founded in 1919, the commission for foreign trade in November 1919, and in June 1920 the Foreign Trade Board, dissolved in 1922. Licensing procedures were within the competence of the Ministry of Industry, contracts in that of the Ministry of Foreign Affairs. Exporters were made to deliver acquired hard currency to the central international currency office. The exchange of goods was regulated by compensatory and contingent contracts. During the 1920s foreign trade was gradually liberalized and export-import licensing procedures removed. Twenty-two contracts with the most-favoured-nation clause were in effect by 1929. Although the customs system of the 1920s was protectionist and hindered export, the implementation of contracts with most-favoured-nation clauses selectively and reciprocally lowered customs rates.

Advanced countries along with ports (like Hamburg, Bremen, Trieste) took on the role of mediators for Czechoslovak access to more distant overseas markets, including those of dependent territories. Newly established and without experience and contacts, Czechoslovak industry right after the war was not able to place its products in such markets, and the re-import of overseas raw materials and so-called colonial goods to Czechoslovakia together with the re-export of Czechoslovak products overseas actually repre-

Figure 1: The Value of the Czechoslovak Import to the Continents in 1927–1937 in %

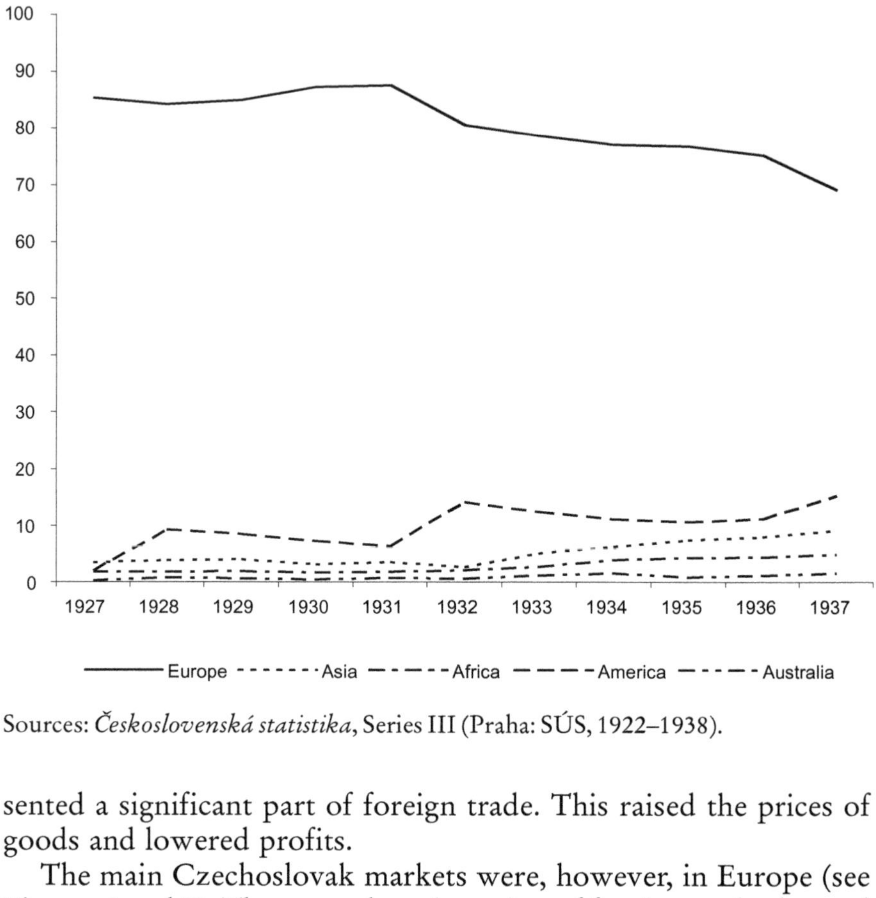

Sources: *Československá statistika*, Series III (Praha: SÚS, 1922–1938).

sented a significant part of foreign trade. This raised the prices of goods and lowered profits.

The main Czechoslovak markets were, however, in Europe (see Figures 1 and 2). There too the orientation of foreign trade changed between the wars. 1919–1925, the years of the formation of Czechoslovak economy, were characterized by close but increasingly looser ties with neighbouring countries (Austria, Hungary) and by attempts to build a stronghold in the Balkans. In the mid-1920s Europe had a 90% share in Czechoslovak export and import, North and South America about 6% and Asia approximately 2.5%.

One weakness of Czechoslovak export trade rested in its unfocused support by the state and interest groups. In 1927 a section was created at the Ministry of Industry with the task of promoting exports. Although the Ministry budget did include items for support-

Figure 2: The Value of the Czechoslovak Export to the Continents in 1927–1937 in %

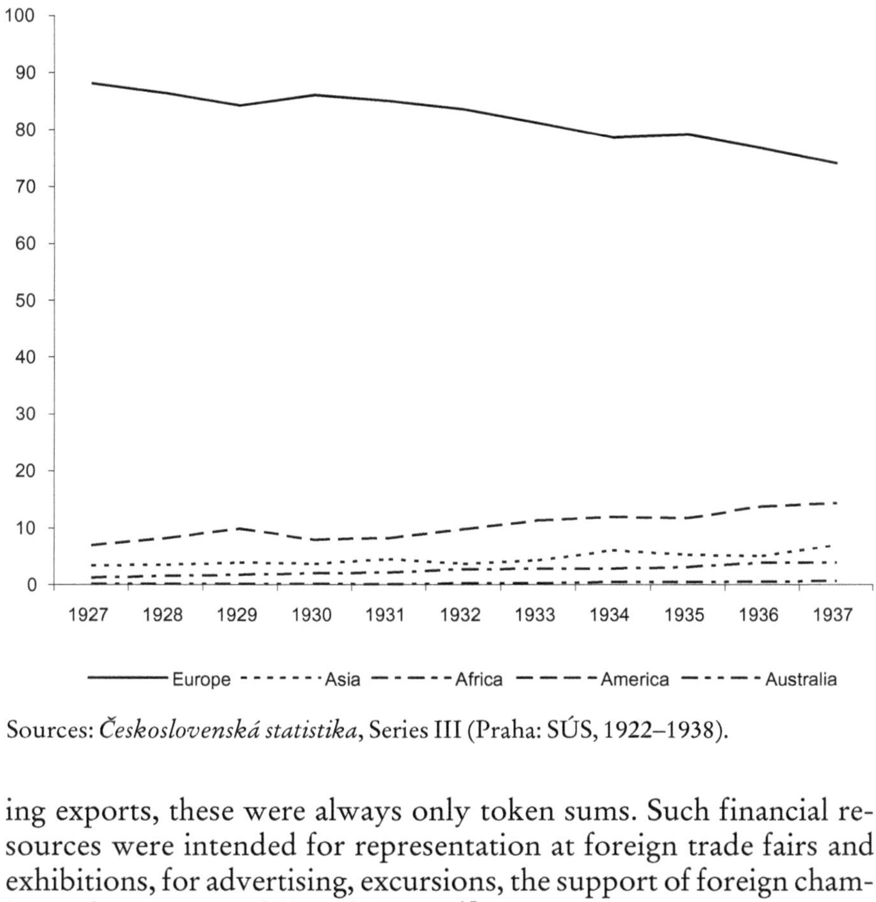

Sources: *Československá statistika*, Series III (Praha: SÚS, 1922–1938).

ing exports, these were always only token sums. Such financial resources were intended for representation at foreign trade fairs and exhibitions, for advertising, excursions, the support of foreign chambers of commerce, fellowships etc.[15]

In the 1920s the foreign trade policy of Czechoslovakia supported the export industries in various ways, from non-contractual commercial connections to quotas on high priority trade contracts. Export was also stimulated by tax reductions, export bonuses, and the organization of international trade fairs and exhibitions. On the other hand exports were impeded by the sudden revaluation of the Czech crown in 1922 and sliding agricultural customs rates from 1925 which became fixed in 1926, especially in relation to Hungary.

The second period: The growth of problems in the 1930s

This period is characterized by a new wave of protectionist policies during the Great Depression. Clearing trade emerged. On one hand, the export of industrial goods made from raw materials imported from countries with convertible currencies created frozen Czechoslovak debts and dead (unreproductive) capital for export companies. On the other, the clearing trade system pushed Czechoslovak exporters to markets in countries with convertible currencies, and this was a positive influence, as the markets of western Europe, Scandinavia and the USA required quality goods, which in turn required improved technologies and rationalized production. However, the new customs-rate tables of 1933 increased customs tariffs also for industrial products.[16]

The Geneva Conference on the economy in 1927 accepted the principle of free trade. The general convention signed in 1928 removed import and export prohibitions, but allowed numerous exceptions. The Depression in the 1930s erected new customs barriers, and renewed licensing procedures and the blocking of foreign currency.

Increasingly protectionist policies abroad provoked many companies and industrial branches to react by concentrating production, minimizing production costs (conveyor-belt production, introducing new production technologies), searching for new outlets in more distant regions, broadening the scope of supply, flexibly accommodating the customers' requirements and appealing to state institutions for export support etc.

As early as 1929 several industries met with export difficulties, for example malting, wood processing, sugar refining and textile production. In Czechoslovakia the economic Depression culminated in 1933 when the index figure of industrial production reached only 60.2%; the brunt was borne especially by the metal industry (dropped to 41%), glass-making (48.6%), wood processing (48.5%), production of cement and stone (53.1%), and textiles (63.3%).[17]

It is estimated that the share of industry in the overall amount of Czechoslovak production in 1938 was 65%, whilst its share in the national income in 1937 totalled 23.7 billion Czechoslovak crowns, i.e. 35%.[18]

The process of concentrating production and capital took on various forms in the 1920s and 30s, the principal ones being capital increase, the fusing of companies, or the swallowing of smaller companies by larger ones, and the creation of cartels (trusts and pools) and syndicates. With the passing of the Cartel Act (§141) in 1933 cartelisation was bound within a legal framework.

In sectors with scattered and unconcentrated production the state attempted to accelerate the affiliation and cooperation of individual companies by means of so-called forced syndicalisation, i.e. the establishing of a compulsory cartel for all producers in the same line of business. Forced syndicates were established in textile, glass, wood and food processing industries (beer brewing, distilling). Between 1933 and 1938 the number of cartels rose from 538 to 1,152; 212 of them were cartels of Czechoslovak and foreign partners. The economy of Czechoslovakia in the 1930s was practically all cartelized by processes of spontaneous cartelisation based on the free affiliation of interested companies, or as a result of state intervention. Although foreign producers, especially German ones, demanded the placing of their products on the Czechoslovak market, and imposed limits on Czechoslovak production or at least insisted on mutual registration of trade marks, it would not be correct to call the Czechoslovak Republic, in A. Teichova's words, 'a tennis ball between foreign financial groups'.[19] On the contrary, Czechoslovak participation in the cartels reflected a respect for the potential of Czechoslovak industry, its level and importance not only in Central Europe, but on the European market as such. Other positive results were the availability of production under licence and access to new technology. Between 1930 and 1933 Czechoslovak participation in international cartels steadily grew. This was a reaction to the depression, a tool for maintaining price levels, the result of more effective rationalisation of decreasing production, and an attempt to restrict competition. Czechoslovak iron and steel industries became the most concentrated not only on a nationwide scale but also internationally.

Part of the attempts to make Czechoslovak products more competitive were two proposals for introducing export bonuses, both of which appeared at the turn of 1933–1934. The central Union of Czechoslovak Industrialists proposed a refund on trade taxes (sales tax, coal tax, transport tax and the tax on water-power) at the rate of 15% of export value, which actually meant encumbering the state. Currency was not to be affected. Since returns from other taxes (income tax) would grow, customs revenue would increase. The other proposal (made by Karel Engliš, the former Minister of Finance) encumbered imports with a 10–20% foreign currency tax, the revenue from which was to be the source of bonuses for exporters. Critics of this proposal warned against the impending growth of prices, the danger of other countries' reciprocal measures and also the fact that more than 30% of the foreign trade was conducted in Czechoslovak crowns, i.e. the devaluing of the crown. At its 16 January 1934 meeting the board of the Central Union of Czechoslovak Industrialists demanded accelerating the process of entering into trade contracts, unifying decisions about export and import, introducing direct financial support for export, introducing tax refunds, and relaxing or reducing credit rates.[20] The Czechoslovak crown devaluation act of 17 February 1934 was the object of tough negotiation. Czech Agrarians and Social Democrats pushed for devaluation, which was also supported by National Socialists, the People's Party, German Agrarians and by industrial exporters. Staunchly against were National Democrats, the Trading Bank (•ivnobanka) and the National Bank. While Great Britain devalued its currency already in the autumn of 1931, Czechoslovakia devalued much later than its competitors, and at a time when Czechoslovak exports were already on the rise.

Only five days before devaluation Jan Matějček, the Czechoslovak Consul General in Hamburg, sent the Ministry of Foreign Affairs in Prague an analysis of the improving export situation and urging the deferral of devaluation. This quite extensive document mentions eleven points for improving Czechoslovak export. The author referred to his knowledge of export issues pertaining to Hamburg, as the naval port with the highest significance for Czechoslovakia. He pointed out that 'the worst moment of the Depression is over and global economy is showing signs of improvement; this is especially true for overseas markets where not only demand but also solvency are turning for the better'.[21] His suggestions advocated more flexibility in licensing the duty-free import and export of certain kinds of semi-finished products intended for further processing, tax deductions on exports (trade tax, sales tax and consumption tax), reducing the prices of postal services, coal and transport (especially on the Elbe), the sale of raw materials on the domestic market at global prices, the support of export-oriented factories, the founding of a state bureau for foreign trade and increasing the network of embassies abroad. After the first devaluation of the crown in February 1934 there was only a minor increase of foreign trade. Progress came after the second devaluation in October 1936. In 1937 the foreign trade turnover reached 57%, exports 58% and imports 55% of the precrisis level.

As a reliable indicator of a technologically advanced economy we may take the numbers of applications for patents and of patents granted.[22] As far as the number of patent applications is concerned, in 1929 (9,113) the Czechoslovak Republic was on a level comparable to Belgium (9,557), Austria (8,954) and Switzerland (8,643).[23] A certain idea of the significance of the volume of purchase and sale of patents and licences, from the commercial point of view at the international level, is provided by the ČSR's balance of payments. Despite the fact that between 1925 and 1937 the passive balance rose from 20 million (7,2% of balance) to 60 million Kč (0,3% of balance), i.e. tripled, the ratio of 1:3 changed to a more favourable 1:2,6. Earnings rose more rapidly than expenses.[24]

The largest number of applications made and patents granted was in the area of chemicals, the electrotechnical industry, and automobile production, i.e. the so-called new branches or branches representing progress and the second phase of the wave of industrialisation. In this respect the Czechoslovak economy was following European and world trends.[25] The large-scale participation of foreign applicants for patenting in the ČSR also shows that foreign interest in patenting ensures profitability and therefore the protection of generally binding and useful patents, and likewise the integration of the ČSR into the world community. At the same time Czechoslovak patents were registered abroad. Their number is comparable to those in such countries as Denmark, the Netherlands and Sweden.[26]

In some important branches of modern technology crucial to the development of such areas as electrotechnology and measuring technology, Czechoslovak research did not achieve results comparable with those gained abroad, or achieved them only in the initial phase (electrotechnology), and did not have the financial resources for further research development. The passive balance of the trade in patents and licences was linked to the efforts of Czechoslovak economic experts to acquire foreign technical knowledge and technology.

As far as structural changes in Czechoslovak industry are concerned, there was a marked move towards heavy industry at the expense of light industry. Despite the marked increase in Czechoslovak exports of technologically more demanding products their importation into the country was still higher. The most positive development took place in the export of vehicles (both for railway and road transport).

By 1937 textiles dropped to about 13% (2,199 million crowns) of overall exports, the share of clothing being 4.2% (506 million crowns). By 1937 production of iron rose to 15.2% (1.8 million crowns). On the contrary, the export of glass, glass ware, leather and leather goods, saw a rapid fall in figures.[27]

In 1937 Czechoslovak involvement in global industrial production dropped to 1.3%; whilst Europe's dropped to 3.3%. After the Depression the Czechoslovak Republic did not manage to penetrate world markets as it did in the 1920s. In 1937 export goods represented only 21–23% of the national income and the country's share in global exports dropped to 1.6%. Only the smelting, footware and partly also clothing industries kept apace with developments in the world.[28]

In the years 1929–1936 the share of overseas markets rose markedly. Europe dropped by 15% to 70–75%, both the Americas rose to about 15%, Asia to 7.9%. One reason is that Czechoslovak foreign trade was not able to compete with the German economic expansion to the Balkans. With respect to Czechoslovakia significant changes took place in the European market itself. Trade was transferred from Germany, Austria, Hungary and Poland to be distributed more evenly in other parts of Europe. The bulk of trade with Western Europe increased, although partly as a result of the new orientation towards non-clearing-trade countries with convertible currencies. Especially perceptible is also the positive emancipatory trend of Czechoslovak foreign trade which no longer relied on middlemen for access to more distant thirld-world markets. Due to its geographical proximity and advanced economy Germany maintained its position as the most significant trade partner.

The tight political and military-strategic orientation of Czechoslovakia towards the Little Entente was not reflected in economic terms. The Economic Council of the Little Entente established in 1934 was supposed to hinder the economic alienation of its members. The massive and simultaneously passive export of arms on credit has never been paid off by the countries of the Little Entente. The main problem of any economic understanding in the Little Entente was the structure of offered goods. Mutual economic ties were restricted solely to an exchange of goods, and the Economic Council dealt primarily with commercial questions. The marketing of Rumanian and Yugoslav wheat, maize, pigs, lard and bacon in Czechoslovakia was barred by the Agrarian Party. Czechoslovakia also imported tobacco, plums and hops from Yugoslavia, and crude oil from Rumania. Both countries imported from Czechoslovakia industrial consumer goods, investment units and arms. The clearing payment system impeded mutual trade cooperation. The Czechoslovak Republic could not absorb as much as did the agriculture of Germany. The position of Germany in relation to the Little Entente Balkan states was about two or three times stronger.[29]

Export to regions with convertible currencies which had not yet switched to clearing trade was to be facilitated by a commercial company created in 1932 under the auspices of the Central Union of Czechoslovak Industrialists and called the Central Office for the Compensation of Czechoslovak Producers and Importers. It was dissolved two years later.

Apart from a network of consulates and embassies foreign trade was also aided by the export department of the Chamber of commerce, the export section of the Central Union of Czechoslovak Industrialists, the Trade Chamber's Institute for the Support of Foreign Trade, and Chambers of Commerce which were established at home and abroad (e.g. the Czechoslovak-French, Czechoslovak-Polish, Czechoslovak- Italian Chambers etc.). Export was further assisted by state guarantees of export credits enacted in July 1931 and the provision of export bonuses, deductions and refunds for exporting producers.

The absence of an office oriented purely towards exports was acutely felt. Before World War I such institutes were established in Britain, the USA and France, and after the war also in Belgium, Switzerland and Austria; in the 1920s in Italy, Germany, Poland, Hungary and Yugoslavia. In Czechoslovakia it was as late as 1934. That year the Export Institute of Czechoslovakia was founded. In November 1938 it had seven agencies (in Casablanca, Shanghai, Bombay, Mexico City, Chicago, Sao Paulo and Osaka), fifty-five collective representatives who were commissioned by individual firms, ten trade correspondents and five reporters. In its attempts to centralize export services in the Czechoslovak Republic the Institute met with opposition from older sections, e.g. the Chambers of commerce. It was oriented towards medium and small-scale firms which could not afford their own foreign agencies. The Institute also constantly struggled with the shortage of finance.

Czechoslovak diplomats' international ambitions were expressed in prime minister Milan Hod •a's plan of Central-European integration. It assumed the participation of eleven countries including Germany and the renewal of exchange between the industrial West and the agricultural South-East and East. Hodza presented his plan at an interparliamentary conference in London in the year 1935. The countries of the Little Entente (CSR, Rumania, Yugoslavia) and the countries of the Roman Protocols (Italy, Austria, and Hungary) were to be brought economically closer. This nucleus was then to be joined by other Balkan and Baltic states. Mostly, their economies were of an agrarian character. The marketing of corn surpluses in member states and in Western Europe was to be coordinated by a special headquarters in Vienna, which was to perform the function of a broker. The plan was based on regional economic preferences. The plan counted on a multilateral treaty with Germany. However, Hodza's plan did not gain the required support either amongst the superpowers (Great Britain, France, Germany) or with the potential members of this group.[30]

Conclusion

Considering the economic importance of industry, the Czechoslovak state attempted to create favourable conditions for the promotion of industrial products on world markets. Elements of the pro-export measures were maintaining a stable currency, in 1934 and 1936 the devaluation of the crown, tax refunds, in 1931 state guarantees for export credits, and in 1934 the founding of the Export Institute of Czechoslovakia. The 1920s saw the implementation of a liberal economic and customs policy which was reflected in a series of trade contracts with the most-favoured-nation clause. In 1933 Czechoslovakia raised its customs tariffs in the new customs rates table and increased the customs protection of domestic industrial production. In the field of industry state regulation was actually an exception: regulatory measures were implemented by the Central Union of Industrialists after consulations with the Ministers of Industry and of Finance.

The First Czechoslovak Republic can be characterized as a Central-European industrial-agricultural state with an above-average proportion of agricultural production. Its neighbouring countries, with the exception of Germany and Austria, were of an agricultural-industrial character. Raw materials and semi-finished products purchased, or rather immediately paid for with hard currency, were used for the production of goods, which in turn were exported to the South-East and East of Europe, i.e. to areas with an insecure capacity for payment, later enhanced by clearing trade. The natural exchange of goods with neighbouring and more distant countries was impaired not only by the change in frontiers but especially by the erosion of the possibility to pay for Czechoslovak industrial exports by agricultural imports. This was the result, first, of the agrarian governing elite's policies, which were somewhat surprising for an industrial-agricultural country: a stubborn insistence on high agricultural tariffs, and on the partners' capacity for payment and later clearing trade. At the same time, these countries were going through a wave of industrialisation linked to autarky. The political orientation of Czechoslovakia towards the Entente and the Little Entente was not reflected in the economic sphere. It was

Germany which remained the most significant trading partner for Czechoslovakia during the inter-war years.

Czechoslovak exports were made expensive by transport costs (of raw materials, semi-finished and finished products), by the lack of domestic raw materials, the consequent dependence on their import, and a limited home market. Nevertheless, by the end of the 1930s Czechoslovak industry had clearly undergone significant changes in its outlets when foreign companies' control of access to more distant markets was removed. But any possibility of reaching better economic results was limited by the brief span of the period between the two world wars.

1 E. Kubů and J. Pátek (eds.), *Mýtus a realita hospodářské vyspělosti Československa mezi světovými válkami* (Praha: Karolinum, 2000), p. 91.
2 Ibid., p. 13; newly to the economic problems of the Czechoslovakia see V. Průcha *et al.*, *Hospodářské a sociální dějiny Československa 1918–1992*. Vol. 1: Období 1918–1945 (Brno: Doplněk, 2004).
3 60%: W. Lewit, *Die wirtschaftliche Lage der Tschechoslowakei seit dem Umsturz* (Wien: sine, 1936), p. 17; V. Průcha *et al.*, *Hospodářské dějiny Československa v 19. a 20. století* (Praha: Svoboda, 1974), p. 73;
60–70%: V. Lacina, *Velká hospodářská krize v Československu* (Praha: Academia, 1984), p. 29;
70–75%: J. Faltus, *Povojnová hospodárska kríza v Československu* (Bratislava: SAV, 1966), pp. 13–14.
4 V. Lacina and L. Slezák, *Státní hospodářská politika v ekonomickém vývoji první ČSR* (Praha: Historický ústav, 1994).
5 V. Lacina, 'Zahraniční obchod vletech první Československé republiky', *ČČH* [Czech Journal of History] 1 (1997), p. 116.
6 V. Lacina, *Zlatá léta československého hospodářství (1918–1929)* (Praha: Historický ústav, 2000), p. 104.
7 A. Teichová, *Wirtschaftsgeschichte der Tschechoslowakei 1918–1980* (Wien: Böhlau, 1988), pp. 35–37.
8 J. Chylík, *Vývoj zahraničního obchodu v našich zemích* (Praha: Jednota k povzbuzení průmyslu v Čechách, 1947), p. 47.
9 J. A. Bat'a, *Spolupráce. Výbor z článků a projevů v letech 1920–1936* (Zlín: TISK, 1936), p. 192.
10 Ibid., pp. 72–73.
11 The Natinal Archives Prague (NA Praha), Ministry of Industry and Trade (MPO •), c. 632, No. 24891/27, Význam vnitrozemské dopravy pro ČSR jako exportní stát.
12 V. Lacina, 'Problémy odvětvové struktury československého průmyslu vletech 1918–1930', *ČSČH* [Czechoslovak Journal of History] 6 (1976), pp. 821–849.

13 V. Lacina, 'K místu Československa v evropské a světové ekonomice v letech 1918–1938', *ČSČH* 6 (1978), p. 825.
14 Ibid., p. 830.
15 T. Jiránek, *Organisační základna podpory vývozu v meziválečném Československu* (Pardubice: Univerzita Pardubice, 1999), Appendix, p. 154.
16 I. Jakubec and E. Kubů, 'Veränderung der territorialen Orientierung des tschechoslowakischen Außenhandels zwischen den Kriegen', in A. Teichová and A. Mosser and J. Pátek (eds.), *Der Markt im Mitteleuropa der Zwischenkriegszeit* (Praha: Karolinum, 1994), pp. 257–293.
17 V. Lacina, 'Dynamika průmyslového rozvoje v meziválečném Československu', *ČČH* 2 (1996), p. 290.
18 *Statistická ročenka Protektorátu Čechy a Morava 1942* (Praha: ÚSÚ, 1942), p. 240; Lacina, 'Problémy', p. 822.
19 A. Teichová, *Mezinárodní kapitál a Československo v letech 1918–1938* (Praha: Karolinum, 1994), p. 46.
20 Lacina, 'Dynamika', pp. 18–19.
21 The Archives of the Ministry of Foreign Affairs Prague (AMZV Praha), The Political Reports (Politické zprávy), 14. 2. 1934, No. 106/34, Čs. konsulát Hamburk, p. 3.
22 See in more I. Jakubec, 'Patents and Licences in Interwar Czechoslovakia (1918–1938)', *Archives internationales d'historie des sciences* vol. 50, No. 144 (2000), pp. 152–159.
23 L. Špirk, 'Mezinárodní patentnictví', in B. Mansfeld et al., *Průvodce světem techniky* (Praha: Prometheus, 1938), p. 91.
24 *Statistická příručka republiky Československé* III (Praha: Orbis, 1928); *Statistická ročenka republiky Československé* (Praha: Orbis, 1935–1938); *Statistická ročenka protektorátu Čechy a Morava* I (Praha: ÚSÚ, 1941) and *Statistická příručka Československé republiky. Statistical Handbook of the Czechoslovak Republic* (Praha: MZV, sine).
25 J. Cantwell, 'The Evolution of European Industrial Technology in the Interwar Period', in F. Caron and P. Erker and W. Fischer (eds.), *Innovation in the European Economy between the Wars* (Berlin and New York: Walther de Gruyter, 1995), pp. 277–324; *Statistisches Handbuch für die Republik Österreich* 17 (Wien: Verlag des Bundesamtes für Statistik, 1937), p. 82.
26 L. Jeníček, 'O myšlenkovou původnost našeho průmyslu', in *Československý průmysl* II (1946), pp. 56–57.
27 Chylík, *Vývoj*, p. 47.
28 Lacina, 'K místu', p. 825; Lacina, 'Zahraniční', pp. 117–119.
29 V. Lacina and J. Pátek (eds.), *Dějiny hospodářství českých zemí od počátku industrializace do současnosti*, vol. III. Období první Československé republiky a německé okupace 1918–1945 (Praha: Karolinum, 1995), pp. 157–176.
30 D. Jančík, *Německo a Malá dohoda. Hospodářské pronikání Německa do Jugoslávie a Rumunska v první polovině 30. let* (Praha: Karolinum, 1990), pp. 73–80.

Section III

Trade Liberalisation, European Integration and Deregulation

Hans Otto Frøland

In Pursuit of Selective Protectionism: The Norwegian Experience, 1920s–1950s*

As part of their ambition to lower tariffs the League of Nations commissioned nationwide reports on tariff protection during the inter war period.[1] Not surprisingly, these indicated that small western European countries tended to apply relatively low tariffs. They found that these countries introduced policies of selective tariff protection as tariffs generally were raised in the late nineteenth century. The logical explanation for this is quite simple. Firstly, they depended more on imports to develop their own industrial output than larger countries did. Secondly, being also more dependent on foreign markets for their output, to gain access to these markets they opened up their domestic markets to foreign business. The league's tariff experts not only worked to unify customs terminology: they also refined the conceptualisation and measurement of nations' tariff protection policies, as measuring nominal tariffs was found to be inadequate.[2]

To determine the tariff protection of domestic producers the relative price effect of tariffs on imported raw materials also had to be taken into account. This approach has later been elaborated on as the quantitative concept of 'effective rate of protection'. The understanding on which this methodological approach is based says that parliaments tend to apply tariffs selectively.

This also applies to low-tariff countries, where Norway serves as a good example. This chapter describes Norway's pursuit of selective protectionism for its manufacturing industries from the Customs Tariff enacted in 1927 to the Customs Tariff of 1958. It excludes the tariffs introduced to protect agriculture as well as tariffs introduced for fiscal purposes.

Having established that parliament increased tariffs selectively in the Customs Tariff of 1927, this chapter will argue that the pattern was maintained in the 1930s. After import quotas replaced tariffs as protection in the wake of World War II, I will contend that the government deliberately dragged its feet to avoid quota liberalisation, following instead the policy of selective protectionism. Furthermore, it will show how tariffs were reintroduced as a means of protection in Norway in 1952 when the country was forced to surrender quota control over selected imports. The government deliberately reintroduced tariffs according to the principle of selective protectionism. The change in policy focus from quotas to tariffs was a response to international constraints: for this reason my chapter will also discuss the OEEC liberalisation of quotas and the liberalisation of tariffs in GATT. As Norway's tariff policy was, as mentioned, based on the principle of selective protectionism, the Customs Tariff of 1958 was simply a technical revision of existing tariff rates. It fixed tariffs *ad valorem* for items which previously had specific duties according to the Brussels nomenclature. It did not raise tariff rates.

The logic of moderate selective protectionism

To gain access to foreign markets, small countries' governments open domestic markets to foreign business. This cost-benefit calculation constituted the very foundation on which successive Norwegian governments based their international commercial policies throughout the twentieth century. Yet it often gave governments awkward political dilemmas as liberal import regulations might disturb domestic socioeconomic structures and give rise to political discontent.

Ever since the Customs Tariff of 1897, the general solution to this dilemma has been a policy of moderate and selective protectionism.[3] A large proportion of imports had few or no duties, as they functioned as input for domestic production. These imports were raw materials, semi-manufactured goods and machines which were not produced in Norway. The tariff authorities paid more attention to duties that served protectionist purposes. These duties were raised slightly in the Customs Tariff of 1905. Ranging from a low percentage to as high as 35 per cent, these duties were fixed to shelter weak and labour-intensive manufacturing industries according to the estimated need for protection. The textile industry serves as an example of this. The industry would import raw materials and machinery free of duty, while fabrics and clothing were charged import duties ranging from 5 to 30 per cent according to the estimated need.

The principle of moderate selective protectionism is visible in the tariff commission reports after 1905. A tariff commission appointed in 1915 was asked to assess whether tariff policy ought to be more liberal. Its report was submitted in 1923. Basically it supported nineteenth-century free-trade arguments, but accepted selective protectionism to avoid socioeconomic disturbances in a volatile international situation. Consumer loss was accepted as the price of producer stability. However, the fixing of tariffs must not eliminate competition.[4] When parliament enacted a new Customs Tariff in 1927, manufacturing tariffs were raised accordingly. Not until 1952 was another tariff commission appointed. Whereas the former commission worked for eight years, the latter was convened for just ten months. This was because it was asked only to report on the level of textile tariffs needed to avoid socioeconomic disturbances in what was perceived as an emergency situation. Although the mandate was selectively protectionist, the government instructed the commission that 'no commodity tariffs must be fixed so as to eliminate the domestic competition':[5] ever since 1897 a fear had lingered that tariff protection might cause domestic inflation and structural inefficiency.

The policy of moderate selective protectionism was based on the principle that although free trade was superior to protectionism, some manufacturing processes temporarily needed shelter. In the inter war period, the increase of tariffs and eventually import quotas was legitimised by allegations that trading partners had upset the economy by dumping commodities on the Norwegian market. In the 1950s similar protection found legitimacy in the notion that some domestic industries needed shelter to modernise before they were exposed to unrestricted imports. Tariff experts maintained that protective tariffs must be fixed according to the needs of the manufacturing process. The policy of moderate, selective protectionism called for fine tuning in tariff-fixing. As will be seen later, in the

1950s experts argued that textile industries needed a tariff protection equivalent to 20 per cent of value added.

Thorough accounts kept by the Ministry of Finance on the basis of import statistics from 1938 provide an illuminating picture of this policy of moderate selective protectionism. The value of duty-free imports as a share of total imports was 56.2 per cent. Tariff incidence (total value of import duty revenue as a share of total import value) was 14 per cent, which indicates a moderate tariff policy. The equivalent incidence for goods charged with duties was 32.1 per cent. Among this group of goods charged with import duties the accounts also distinguished between those charged with 'fiscal duties' and those with 'protective duties'. The import value of goods charged with 'fiscal duties' constituted 29.6 per cent of all imports charged with duties, while the tariff incidence was 59.5 per cent. The import value of goods charged with 'protective duties' constituted 66.1 per cent of all imports charged with duties whereas the tariff incidence was 20.1 per cent. The remaining 4.3 per cent of import value of goods charged with duties had combined duties and consequently did not fit into the two categories.[6]

As shown, some items were taxed simply for fiscal or social-policy purposes. In general, these were considered 'luxury goods', and were not produced in Norway. While customs revenue contributed about 30 per cent of total government revenue before 1914, it remained at 13–15 per cent in the interwar period and almost negligible in the years after 1945.[7]

The policy of moderate, selective protectionism meant a policy of fine-tuning tariff protection. The logical consequence of this basic principle was a bias towards tariff autonomy. Yet being a trading nation, successive governments always favoured basing multilateral agreements and bilateral treaties on most-favoured-nation treatment. In overall commercial policy there was a bias towards the promotion of export revenue.

Selective protectionism in the 1930s

When parliament in 1927 enacted the Customs Tariff it maintained a general 50 per cent increase in tariff rates that had been introduced between 1923 and 1926. A contemporary expert maintained they were increased by 250 per cent since 1913.[8] However, the majority of these were introduced for purely fiscal purposes. Parliament furthermore saw that specific industries needed further protection. The Customs Tariff introduced higher imposts on several labour-intensive items, e.g. textiles, clothing, furs, rubber ware, wood products, paper items, and glassware. Some semi-manufactured items needed as input for domestic production such as some wool and cotton items, ironware and nails were given lower tariffs. However, increases tended to be higher than reductions, giving a net effect in favour of protection.[9]

The logic of selective protectionism was further sustained in 1928 and 1929 as parliament enacted further tariff protection on wool and cotton.

This pattern was sustained as Norway also joined the general protectionism of the 1930s. Having implemented the policy of tariff truce since 1930 the parliament enacted a 20 per cent increase in tariff rates from 13 January 1932, yet mainly for fiscal reasons.[10] This additional tariff rate was extended to 33.3 per cent from 16 March 1940. In 1932 parliament also authorized the government to increase tariffs by 400 per cent.[11] Again the argument was reactive in its logic. The leader of the parliament's tariff committee maintained that 'All countries protect themselves by introducing restrictions. We cannot allow our country to remain open as this would destroy large parts of our economy.'[12] However, the government never used the authorization when negotiating international commercial agreements. Consequently, only in 1933 did parliament pass an act that increased tariffs selectively for purely protective purposes, which was, however, implemented only after the World Economic Conference.[13] In particular rubber footwear, crockery, feather and down received additional protection. In 1938 tariffs were further raised selectively on textiles, electrical equipment and glass ware.

Tariff increases were somewhat balanced by bilateral commercial agreements. Of most importance was the agreement with Britain in May 1933, which reduced tariffs on some items and confirmed them on 58 items,[14] though Norway had also to accede to British demands for a lower tariff on textiles.[15] Equivalent yet less important agreements were also negotiated with other States.

In 1929 the aggregate national tariff level was 10 per cent, while in 1937 it had grown to 16 per cent before falling to around 14 per cent in 1938. This was a modest increase compared with the large European countries, but larger than the other Scandinavian countries and the Benelux countries.[16]

Nonetheless, by 1937 import quotas also mattered in terms of protection. Basically, when negotiating international commercial treaties the most-favoured-nation principle was still Norway's ideal. For the most part quotas were introduced as a reaction to other States' commercial policies and not for protective purposes.[17] In 1933 quotas were introduced on some items as a result of the Anglo-Norwegian commercial treaty, of which coal was the most important.[18] In June 1934 parliament empowered the government to use quotas on a general basis, which continued until the German occupation in 1940. The Ministry of Trade argued that sustaining a liberal policy would be impossible in an increasingly unfriendly international climate. The empowerment might work as leverage in bilateral trade negotiations.[19] According to League of Nations accounts, in 1937 only twelve per cent of the total Norwegian import value went through quota regulations.[20] Yet on sensitive commodities quotas were introduced for protective purposes. Quota protection replaced tariffs on items such as footwear, furniture and crockery.[21] Thus the introduction of quotas in the 1930s did not remove the pattern of selective protectionism.

It was only after the war that import quotas mattered on a large scale in Norway's international commercial policy. In July 1945 imports were prohibited by a government decree, which in December 1946 was replaced by parliamentary legislation:[22] henceforth all imports needed a government licence. As with all countries in Europe, foreign trade was regulated by a web of bilateral trade and payment agreements which fixed quantitative quotas of exchange.[23] In the late 1940s tariffs did not matter at all in terms of protection.

Quota liberalisation in the OEEC

The OEEC Council of Ministers decided in November 1949 to set up an import liberalisation programme that obliged the 17 member States to remove their quota restrictions by the end of 1951: governments would have to present a cumulative series of 'free lists' of goods that were released from quota restrictions, and already by 15 December 1949 they were obliged to release goods equivalent to 50 per cent of the value of their private European imports in 1948. To avoid unequal burdens in terms of commodity composition, commodities were divided into three subgroups; manufactures, foodstuffs and raw materials. However, the governments preserved their bilateral balances of payments, and on the target dates they had attached conditions to their 'free lists'. It was evident that effective 'free lists' would depend upon a programme with multilateralised payments through clearing and which also provided deficit countries with cheap credits. Therefore, in January 1950 the council made further 'free listing' dependent on the establishment of the European Payments Union (EPU). After the EPU was established in September 1950 the quota liberalisation programme was embedded in the so-called Code of Liberalisation.

This code existed until the OEEC was replaced by the OECD in 1961, but had really lost its momentum by 1956. It compelled member States to liberalise quota restrictions in line with council decisions that set an index target and a target date calculated on the basis of total imports in 1948. The value of total private imports in 1948 was always used as the denominator in the fraction, not the value of private imports in the year referred to by the index. Table 1 shows the council's decisions, and also those taken before the EPU was established. After January 1955 the index target remained at 90 for the rest of the code's life. This was confirmed by the council's decisions of 26 October 1956 and 30 June 1959.

The programme faced severe setbacks. Very soon the original goal of quota-free trade at the end of 1951 became unrealistic. The council made no decision to extend the 'free lists' between October 1950 and January 1955. As the code provided for legitimate exemptions if reserves were threatened and as the Korean War had dis-

Table 1: Quota liberalisation schedule

Decision date	Index target	Target date
4 July 1949	As complete as possible	By 1951
13 August 1949	As complete as possible	1 October 1949
2 November 1949	50	15 December 1949
31 January 1950	60	After the EPU is established
15 September 1950	60	4 October 1950
27 October 1950	75	1 February 1952
14 January 1955	90	1 October 1955

Source: Wendy Asbeek Brusse, *Tariffs, Trade and European Integration, 1945–1957. From Study Group to Common Market* (New York: St. Martin's Press 1997), p. 82.

turbed international prices, several governments invoked the escape clause and reintroduced quota restrictions. The FRG suspended its 'free list' between February 1951 and April 1952, but then re-liberalised to an index of 75. Britain and France suspended their 'free lists' in November 1951 and April 1952 respectively. The British index was reduced from 90 to 61 in November 1951 and further to 46 in March 1952. The UK, however, expanded its 'free list' again by the summer of 1953, and reached an index of 75 by October. France did not reach the 75 target until April 1955. Table 2 shows the achieved indices for selected countries throughout the programme.

The programme was weak also in terms of reciprocity. Firstly, it excluded trade on government account. This in particular favoured Britain and France. Calculated on a 1948 basis, State agencies represented 27 per cent of British and 22 per cent of French imports in 1949.[24] Having expanded her 'free list' in 1952, Britain reached an index of 86. However, if State trade had been included in the basis for the calculations, the index would have dropped to 61.[25] This discrepancy between the official liberalisation index and actual openness was even greater for France. Whereas Britain reduced her share of State trade greatly by 1954–1955, and to only two per cent of total imports in 1956, France maintained her share. Secondly, as much of State trade was in agriculture, the programme affected agricultural exporters negatively. Approximately 30 per cent of Dutch and 70 per cent of Danish exports consisted of agricultural goods. Thirdly, it excluded tariffs. Thus, such high-tariff countries as France

Table 2: Achieved liberalisation indices by selected countries 1950–1959

A = June 30, B = December 31

Country	1950		1951		1952		1953		1954		1955		1956		1957		1958	1959
	A	B	A	B	A	B	A	B	A	B	A	B	A	B	A	B	B	B
BLEU	56	64	75	75	75	75	87	87	87	88	88	96	96	96	96	96	96	96
Netherl.	55	66	66	71	75	75	92	93	93	93								
Denmark	53	50	50	65	68	75	76	76	76	76	76	78	86	86	86	86	86	86
Sweden	53	69	75	75	75	85	91	91	91	91	91	94	93	93	93	93	93	93
Norway	39	45	51	51	75	75	75	76	76	75	75	75	75	78	81	81	81	81
Iceland	0	15	41	41	41	0	0	29	29	29	29	29	29	29	29	29	29	29
France	58	66	75	76	0	0	0	18	51	65	75	78	82	82	0	0	0	91
FRG	47	63	0	0	77	81	90	90	90	90	90	91	92	92	93	93	91	92
Italy	54	76	76	77	100	100	100	100	100	100	100	99	99	99	99	99	98	98
UK	57	86	90	61	46	44	59	75	80	83	84	85	94	94	94	94	95	97
OEEC	56	67	65	61	66	65	71	77	81	83	84	86	89	89	83	83	83	90

Base year: 1948, FRG 1949.

Source: Willy Andres, *Der Liberalisierungskodex der OECE für den Warenhandel* (Zurich: Juris-Verlag, 1964), p. 78.

and Italy could maintain their protection as they liberalised quotas, whereas such low-tariff countries as Denmark and the Netherlands could not. The difficult situation for Denmark and the Netherlands is illustrated by the tariff rates imposed by high-tariff countries on their export goods.[26] These two countries encountered tariffs of between 18 and 37 per cent in France, 15 and 26 per cent in the FRG, and 11 and 33 per cent in Italy. As agricultural exporters, Denmark and the Netherlands were continuously complaining that their exports were hit by restrictive State trading. The low-tariff countries, the Benelux, Scandinavia and Switzerland, complained that their exports were hit by high tariffs. All of them also maintained that simply because France and Britain imported less on private account in the base year 1948, they would reach the index targets more easily. This lack of reciprocity between the smaller and the larger States led to a high degree of intergovernmental tension, not only in the OEEC but also in GATT.

GATT was negotiated in 1947 to regulate old-fashioned tariff bargaining on a most-favoured-nation basis between contracting parties. It was an even weaker framework than the OEEC. It had no political powers, as members were allowed to invoke exemption clauses, and it authorised existing preference areas as well as quota restrictions on agricultural imports. It needed to be extended every third year. Several bargaining rounds were organised in the 1940s and 50s; in Geneva in 1947, Annecy in 1949, Torquay in 1951 and Geneva in 1956. During this period tariff negotiations were carried out on a product-by-product basis, which from a technical point of view hampered progress. As indicated in Table 3, GATT only modestly reduced tariffs during the period from the Annecy round in 1949 to the Dillon round in 1961. Having reached an average 19 per cent cut in Geneva in 1947 the subsequent average cuts remained at merely two to three per cent.

Table 3: Indicators of GATT efficiency 1947–1967

I: Total number of concessions exchanged.
II: The concessions' trade coverage in million $.
III: Percentage of average depth in tariff cuts *ad valorem*.

Conference	Year	I	II	III
Geneva	1947	45 000	10 000	19
Annecy	1949	5 000	n. a.	2
Torquay	1951	8 700	n. a.	3
Geneva	1956	2 700	25 000	2
Dillon	1961	4 400	49 000	7
Kennedy	1967	8 159	n. a.	35

Source: Wendy Asbeek Brusse, *Tariffs, Trade and European Integration, 1945–1957. From Study Group to Common Market* (New York: St. Martin's Press 1997), p. 118.

GATT failed basically because high-tariff countries would not relinquish their tariff protection. During the Geneva round in 1947 neither large nor small countries paid much attention to tariffs because, as they were levied by weight or volume and not by value, general price increases had rendered them ineffective. Governments knew that their protection was provided by quota restrictions. Consequently, they granted a high number of tariff concessions in addition to a 19-per-cent average depth in tariff cuts. Not until the quota 'free lists' started to make their presence felt did governments become more preoccupied with tariff protection. By enacting new customs tariffs, high-tariff countries replaced duties based on weight or volume with duties based on value to catch up with post-war price developments and thus render tariffs more effective. France had already decided this before the Geneva round in 1947, but did not put it into effect until the Annecy round in 1949. Italy also did this before the Annecy round and the FRG before the Torquay round in 1951. Britain did not have to do this because she relied on the existing Commonwealth preferences. Well aware that the high-tariff countries were less affected by the OEEC quota liberalisation programme, low-tariff countries soon voiced their discontent. By 1950 the OEEC secretariat had received 493 complaints that member States were applying protective tariffs. A vast majority of the complaints came from the low-tariff countries.[27] Switzerland entered into an informal coalition with the Scandinavian and Benelux countries, often referred to as the 'Low Tariff Club' (LTC), which lobbied to force the large States, notably Britain, France, Italy and the FRG, to reduce their tariffs.

Norway's selective liberalisation of import quotas, 1949–1957

Norway always complained that the OEEC liberalisation programme was implemented too early and too quickly, arguing that liberalisation would drain reserves, a consequence that could only be countered by deflationary policies. Liberalisation would jeopardise investment programmes as governments would loose control over the composition of private imports. It would furthermore expose sheltered industries to a competitive environment in which they would not survive. In 1952 the minister of trade defended import quotas before the OEEC Council of Ministers when he explained how Norway had achieved a bilateral balance with the dollar area:

> How did we achieve that? By giving top priority to shipping that can earn dollars; by giving top priority to new investments in industries that can produce dollar goods; let us say by using exchange controls, import controls to direct investments into the right fields. [...] In our case we can prove that by resorting to direct means we can come very close to closing the dollar gap.[28]

Norway continuously complained about the programme, but never actually vetoed extensions of the index target. The government was even forced to defend further liberalisation because those countries with which Norway had a bilateral surplus reintroduced their quotas. It considered the British and French suspensions of their 'free lists' of strategic importance for Norway. In 1953 the Ministry of Trade calculated a yearly loss of export revenue of NOK 30–40 million with France and NOK 100 million with Britain due to their reintroduction of import quotas. The argument in Oslo was based on the fact that an export surplus with Britain and France was needed to pay for the ever-increasing deficit with the FRG. Consequently, the government was forced to advocate re-liberalisation.

While thereby defending the programme, the government still sought to maintain as many national quotas as possible. Avoiding the liberalisation of ships, vehicles and machines was regarded as vital to sustaining targeted investment programmes. Avoiding the liberalisation of textiles was regarded as crucial because it would affect employment immediately. Free import of these items would also drain reserves. Therefore a policy of delay was implemented which aimed at maintaining quotas as long as possible while pleading balance-of-payments constraints. Consequently, Norwegian efforts for years lagged behind the Council's index targets. The 'free lists' were composed so as to produce the highest possible index while ensuring the least possible repercussions on investment programmes and sheltered industries. They were worked out in close cooperation with the national industry and labour organisations. The fact that Norway never deliberalised indicates the success of this policy.

Table 4 provides a record of the Norwegian index performance as compared with the OEEC index targets, and also displays the different calculations in Oslo and Paris.

Submitted on October 1, 1949 on the basis of a council decision reached on July 4, the first Norwegian 'free list' was deliberately composed to change neither the volume nor the composition of imports. In addition to being export commodities, the selected items were either de facto liberalised or had low domestic demand.[29] At that point in time there was no index target.

Aware that most lists were nominal, on 2 November 1949 the council decided to fix an index target for the lists to be submitted

Table 4: Quota liberalisation schedule and achieved indices by Norway, 1949–1955

Decision date	Target date	Index target	Norway's index calculations	OEEC's index calculations
4 July 1949	1 October 1949	–	33.6	20.5
2 November 1949	15 December 1949	50	52	38.2
31 January 1950	Establishing EPU (1 October 1950)	60	61.1	44.5
31 January 1950	After EPU (1 February 1951)	75	61.1	44.5
	12 May 1951	–	64.9	51
	1 May 1952	–	75	75
January 1955	1 October 1955	90	75	75

Source: Hans Otto Frøland, 'Norway's Liberalisation of Trade and Payments in the 1950s', *Scandinavian Economic History Review* Vol. 52, 2–3 (2004), 22.

by 15 December. The Norwegian list on this occasion contained some machine parts, but the government still kept machines off the list. The second list also aimed at avoidance of disturbances. The import growth following the two 'free lists' in 1949 was estimated at NOK 100–150 million on a yearly basis.[30] Considering that Norway's import surplus between January and October 1949 was NOK 1723 million, the impact of the 'free lists' was hardly critical.

As shown in Table 4, according to Norwegian calculations the two first lists contributed to 33.6 per cent and 52 per cent of private imports in 1948. Apparently, this was quite an achievement. However, when calculating the index the government excluded all ship imports in the base year 1948. This way of calculating the index came to be a crucial part of Norway's tactics to minimise and delay quota liberalisation. By omitting ship imports from calculations Norway could reach a higher index, if not necessarily the index target. The government argued that rebuilding a merchant navy after the war was an important reason why Norway was a structural debtor and, consequently, that ship imports had to be treated separately. If the Norwegian calculations had been accepted by the council, the government would have retained greater control of the composition of imports. Not surprisingly, it turned out that the OEEC calculations would include ship imports in the base year and consequently only gave an index of 20.5 and 38.2. Yet to the Norwegians, the controversy over technicalities and calculations caused welcome delays. According to the calculations in Paris, Norway lagged far behind the liberalisation schedule until May 1952.

Norway had no problems in reaching the index targets for raw materials (as these were needed anyway), nor those for foodstuffs (as imports of these were few) in 1948. As with most other countries the problem lay with manufactured goods. If these were liberalised too quickly, demand would explode. The third 'free list', aiming to achieve the index target of 60, was submitted in October 1950. On that occasion no new items were listed, as the government only removed its former discrimination against imports from Belgium, Switzerland and the FRG on manufactured goods. According to OEEC calculations this brought the index for manufactured goods to a modest 29.4.

By the autumn of 1950 the complaints against Norway's calculations had developed into serious discontent in Paris. In November the council appointed a committee to scrutinise Norway's liberalisation efforts. The committee demanded that Norway should bring its index for manufactured goods to 40 and the overall index to 52, which was still eight points below the official target.[31] In December the council urged Norway to submit an additional 'free list' by early February 1951 that would fulfil this demand.[32] The government in Oslo realised it would have to be accommodating. Senior officials argued for liberalising the import of dry-cargo ships to avoid further pressure to liberalise imports of machines, vehicles and textiles.[33] The government submitted an extra 'free list' on February 3, raising the index for manufactured goods to 37.9, and the overall index to 50.5. To avoid criticism it promised that further steps would be taken in May.[34] Of significance would be the liberalisation of dry-cargo ships, for which at least 50 per cent of the contract was financed by foreign loans. However, these promises were not enough to appease the experts in Paris. The council replied by demanding an index of 60 for manufactured goods and an overall index of 75 by 14 May 1951: this target was adopted by the council on 27 October 1950.

On April 7 1951 the council put textiles and clothing on the so-called 'common list', which was set up to harmonise the member countries' 'free listing'. The ECA mission in Oslo lobbied the Norwegian government to liberalise textiles. While the government liberalised the import of dry-cargo ships on 12 May 1951 it would still not release machines, vehicles and textiles. Norwegian calculations extended the index for manufactured goods to 57.6; and as raw materials and foodstuffs were at 84 and 75 respectively, the overall index now reached 64.9.[35] The council, meeting on 4 July 1951, accepted Norway's 'free list' in the short term, but shortly after another OEEC committee was appointed to scrutinise the Norwegian efforts. This committee rejected Oslo's condition that 50 per cent of ship contracts had to be based on foreign loans. It concluded that Norway's index for manufactured goods only reached 37.9 and the overall index only 51. In accordance with the council's concerns the committee suggested that Norway draw up new proposals by January 1952 as to how it would reach the official index target. The government realised that continued foot-dragging might cause more political problems, and to ward off another round of scrutiny by a Paris committee it promised that further steps would be taken. It transmitted a short but extended 'free list' at the end of December 1951 which stated that several items would be liberalised by May 1952. The council accepted Norway's measures on 11 February, and on 1 May 1952 dry-cargo ships and other commodities, including textiles, were liberalised. As displayed in Table 6, this gave an index of 75 in Oslo as well as in Paris. Raw materials showed 88, foodstuffs 79 and manufactures 70. If the OEEC had accepted the exclusion of ship imports from the calculations the overall index would have been 83. Apparently the two-and-a-half-year period of Norway's deliberate foot-dragging had come to an end.

Nonetheless, the government would only reluctantly liberalise the existing quotas. To give liberalisation further momentum, on 29 October 1953 the council asked member States to deliver so-called 'negative lists' in which each government justified which quota restrictions they would maintain as the OEEC took further steps towards full liberalisation. The Norwegian government handed in a short list in which the items covered only two per cent of private imports in 1948.[36] When the list was scrutinised in March and July 1954 the OEEC's Steering Board of Trade asked for the remaining 23 per cent, as according to the computations made in May 1952 Norway had only reached an index of 75. As in 1953, Norway started to run an increasing balance-of-payments deficit, the tactic in Oslo being to invoke balance-of-payments constraints to sustain quota protection for the remaining 23 per cent. This met with success. As a step towards reaching the index target of 90 the council decided in January 1955 that each member State must liberalise 10 per cent of their imports still under quota restrictions by 1 June 1955. Norway was exempted from this step because of her current-account deficit. However, having deliberately invoked the balance-of-payments argument for years, it was difficult to keep further liberalisation from the agenda when balance of payments improved strongly in 1956. Having taken no further steps since May 1952, the government liberalised further on 1 July 1956 and 1 April 1957. As shown in Table 5 these steps were minor. However, they consisted of commodities regarded as extremely employment sensitive, such as clothing, shoes and furniture.

Table 5: Achieved quota liberalisation indices by Norway, 1952–1957

	Overall	Manufactures	Foodstuffs	Raw materials
May 1952	75	70	79	88
July 1956	78	73.2	81.3	90.9
April 1957	81	76.5	83	93

Source: Hans Otto Frøland, 'Norway's Liberalisation of Trade and Payments in the 1950s', *Scandinavian Economic History Review* Vol. 52, 2–3 (2004), 26.

Norway never reached the index target of 90 because the import of tankers, which in 1948 constituted 13 per cent of total imports, was never liberalised. The argument that tankers and cars must remain under quota restrictions was eventually accepted by the council on 10 May 1957.

The reintroduction of selective tariff protection

Because post-war reconstruction was protected by quotas, tariffs received little attention from planners in Oslo in the 1940s. Well above 50 per cent of imports were duty-free. Customs duties as share of total government revenue were reduced from 26.7 per cent in 1938–1939 to 7.7 per cent in 1947–1948.[37] Tariff incidence for 'protective duties' (as opposed to 'fiscal duties') was reduced from 20.1 per cent in 1938 to 13.3 per cent in 1946.[38] Higher import prices had made customs duties insignificant as compared to quotas because, as most items had specific duties levied on the basis of weight or volume, the duty incidence as well as the protective effect of tariffs would diminish. Only a few items were fixed *ad valorem*, which would match the effect of price increases. In 1951 the Customs Tariff consisted of 1025 items; of these 800 items had specific duties, while only 34 items had duties fixed on the basis of value. The rest were mixed tariffs and were generally low except for those items which were fixed *ad valorem*. Not surprisingly, and in accordance with the principle of selective tariff protectionism, these were machines, tools and vehicles. From the general insignificance of tariff protection during those years it followed that the government would give priority to the export industries' interests for market access. During the first GATT rounds the government could easily trade off tariff concessions on most items without any serious risk to the sensitive industries at home, as these were guarded by the import quota control.

In the Geneva round in 1947–1948 Norway gave concessions on 140 items, of which 60 had their tariffs reduced, 35 were frozen at the existing level and 45 were confirmed as duty-free.[39] Most reductions concerned items which were not produced in Norway, and were levied for fiscal purposes. The duty-free items mainly consisted of raw materials for the manufacturing industry. Officials admitted that domestic businesses were unthreatened by the concessions.[40]

In the Annecy round in 1949 Norway negotiated more reluctantly. Again officials regarded the round as a success because they had negotiated important concessions for the export industries. A total of 116 items in the Norwegian Customs Tariff were negotiated, of which 34 involved reduced tariff rates.[41] But not even on this occasion would the concessions affect sensitive domestic industries. In terms of yearly loss of incidence the tariff concessions granted in Annecy was estimated at a modest NOK 770 000 on the basis of imports in 1938. The equivalent figures for the concessions given in Geneva were estimated at NOK 24 million.

These rather insignificant tariff concessions were redeemed before the freeing of quota protection started. When the Torquay round started in September 1950 the OEEC Council had already fixed the quota liberalisation index target at 60. From then on the government regarded domestic protection of weak industries as just as important as achieving concessions for Norway's export industries. A memorandum in the Ministry of Trade anticipated that the 'free lists' would increasingly jeopardise these industries, which should not be further attacked by Norway's simultaneously reducing her tariff protection.[42] Consequently, the government only reluctantly joined the efforts of the Low Tariff Club during the Torquay round to get the high-tariff countries to reduce their tariffs. Well aware that Norway selectively applied high tariffs on specific commodities, in particular within SITC 5 and 6, it was assumed that if the high-tariff countries complied with the low-tariff countries' demands, Norway might also be forced to reduce tariffs that provided effective protection to sensitive industries. The government offered few concessions at Torquay, although slightly more than in Annecy. Duty loss was estimated to be slightly more than NOK 1 million on the basis of imports in 1948. Again officials admitted that the Torquay round concessions would not harm the sensitive industries.[43]

While negotiating more reluctantly in GATT from the moment quota liberalisation was implemented, the government also deliberately took action to selectively raise Norway's tariff protection. As shown in Table 6 duty incidence, having decreased since the Geneva round in 1948, increased after the Torquay round in 1951.

Table 6: Norwegian duty incidence 1947–1954

1947	1948	1949	1950	1951	1952	1953	1954
5.9	4.2	4.1	3.9	3.3	5.6	5.0	5.3

Source: Hans Otto Frøland, 'Norway's Liberalisation of Trade and Payments in the 1950s', *Scandinavian Economic History Review* Vol. 52, 2–3 (2004), 29.

Well aware that Norwegian index calculations for quota liberalisation were under attack in Paris, government officials introduced the idea that before the Torquay round Norway should raise those tariffs which were not bound by GATT agreements.[44] As most items in the Customs Tariff had specific duties, the officials proposed to increase tariff protection by fixing the rates *ad valorem*.[45] Changing the Customs Tariff would take time. Therefore, an interministerial committee was appointed on 30 April 1951 to draw up a short-term plan for increasing tariff protection as quotas were removed. Machines, tools and vehicles, contributing to 12 per cent of total import value in 1949, were regarded as sufficiently protected, as these items already had *ad valorem* duties. Therefore, the committee's first idea was to increase specific duties by 200 per cent as called for by the textile, clothing and shoe industries. In its report on 26 November 1951 the committee proposed that specific duties be increased by only 100 percent.[46] This was adopted by the cabinet the next day.[47]

At this point in time the officials knew Norway soon would be under pressure to put textiles on the quota 'free list'. Their major concern in the short term was that Norway had fixed tariff rates on textiles and clothing under GATT. However, a GATT clause allowed tariff rates to be increased if the principles according to which they were fixed were changed. To raise tariff protection on textiles and clothing the interministerial committee proposed to immediately fix their duties *ad valorem*. The cabinet also adopted this proposal on 27 November 1951. Parliament, which also asked for higher tariffs to replace quotas,[48] enacted the government's proposals on 14 December,[49] and the act came into force on 2 January 1952. The general 100-per-cent tariff increase on specific duties applied to 509 out of 1025 items in the Customs Tariff. Before the act came into force only 34 of the 1025 items were fixed *ad valorem*. Afterwards, *ad-valorem* duties applied to 121 items. For textiles and clothing, tariff rates increased generally by between 100 and 200 per cent on fabrics, 250 per cent on bands and 400 per cent on knitting wool and thread. Estimates concluded that the measures would increase duty revenue by at least NOK 40 million on a yearly basis.[50] However, they were not introduced for fiscal but for protective purposes, as their quota protection would disappear by May. Tariff rates on a number of items were now established at between 20 and 30 per cent *ad valorem*. For the textile industry the measures provided a tariff protection equivalent to that of the highly protected Italian textile industry.

This general raising of tariffs in 1952 was considered a short-term measure in a difficult situation. On January 11 the government appointed a Customs Tariff Commission (Tolltariffkomiteen av 1952) to assess whether the raised tariffs should remain as a long-term measure. As textiles would be released from quotas by May 1 to meet the council's demand that Norway reach the index target of 60 the commission was instructed to concentrate in the short term on the textiles and clothing tariff rates.

Textiles was one of the fastest-growing industries in post-war Norway in terms of employment. Having employed 13500 people before the war, by 1951 it employed about 24000. The equivalent figures for the clothing industry were 10000 and 14000. Nonetheless, these industries were fundamentally weak. Having estimated total factor productivity growth in the 1950s, Klovland concludes that three out of every four textile industries had a negative record.[51] Under no circumstance would they survive quota liberalisation. As there was surplus capacity in the European textile industry, low import prices were expected if protection was removed. In retrospect, one account concluded that textile production dropped by 15 per cent from 1951 to 1952 because Norwegian producers anticipated devastating competition from abroad as textiles were included in the 'free lists'.[52] Not surprisingly, the textile and clothing industries were lobbying for alternative protection measures.[53]

The Customs Tariff Commission presented its report on 3 October 1952. The majority vote proposed fixing textiles and clothing tariff rates at 20 per cent of manufacturing costs, as the general rule, implying some reduction as compared with the rates fixed in January 1952:[54] but the cabinet and parliament adopted the committee's minority vote, which proposed the principle of fixing tariffs at 25 per cent of manufacturing costs.[55] When imposed on 1 January 1953 the reduction in textile tariff rates was estimated at about 20 per cent. Having raised tariffs by several hundred percentage points in January 1952, the reduction in January 1953 was minor. According to the Minister of Finance, the tariff rates would still provide sufficient shelter to modernise the textile industry before it was exposed to foreign competition.[56]

Whereas textiles were freed from import quotas in May 1952, clothing remained protected until April 1957. The tariff rates on textiles imposed in January 1953 were still considered a temporary measure. When they were enacted in December 1952 the minister of finance proclaimed that by 1955 a modernisation of the textile industries had to be completed and tariffs reduced accordingly.[57] In 1955 a committee (Tekstilutvalget av 1955) was appointed to assess whether the textile industry was still in need of tariff protection. Its report, submitted on 3 November 1955, answered in the affirmative, and furthermore argued that the cotton-based sector of the industry was in need of an increase. The committee said that current tariff protection only covered 21 per cent of the industry's manufacturing costs. The industry itself lobbied for 25 per cent, which was accepted by the committee. Parliament introduced this rate accordingly.[58]

The importance given to selective tariff protection since 1951 also led to a restrained bargaining policy during the 1956 Geneva round. The committee preparing Norway's bargaining policy was reluctant to offer concessions that would put pressure on sensitive industries,[59] with the result that concessions were few and largely conciliatory.[60] The government was prepared to reduce tariffs on 61 items, for which duty loss was estimated at NOK 4.5 million on the basis of imports in 1954.[61]

The increased importance of tariffs subsequently made the government more inclined to withdraw tariff concessions on sensitive items. Article XXVIII of GATT allowed the contracting parties to renegotiate these at any time. To avoid withdrawals they therefore regularly agreed to waive this right. Until 1954 Norway was one of the countries always waiving this right without reservation. However, in the GATT session running from October 1954 to March 1955, during which a waiver was agreed until January 1 1958, the government considered withdrawing tariff concessions. An expert committee (Den rådgivende komité for visse økonomiske spørsmål, særlig tollspørsmål) in February 1955 recommended withdrawing constraints on 23 items. As Norway would have been the only country not accepting the waiver, neither the government nor parliament approved the recommendation.[62] However, as the waiver expired on 1 January 1958, Norway renegotiated a tariff increase on cosmetics, glassware and earthenware as these industries were seriously threatened by imports. On that occasion Norway was not alone in asking for withdrawals, which made it easier from a political perspective.[63]

The policy of selective protectionism from 1951 never made Norway a particularly protectionist country. In general, tariffs were fixed according to the principle of moderate protection. Fifty-five per cent of imports in 1958 were bound by tariff concessions under GATT. Of the residual 45 per cent, 20 per cent was imported duty-free. Freedom to raise tariffs unilaterally would only cover 20 per cent of imports. The new Customs Tariff enacted in 1958 on the basis of the Brussels definitions fixed far more items *ad valorem* but was not intended to raise tariff protection.[64] The policy of selective protectionism enforced since 1951 was considered adequate.

Pursuing a policy of moderate tariff protection, Norway had good reason to join the Low Tariff Club in 1950. However, among the seven lobby members Norway in general maintained the highest tariffs and, as argued, reintroduced a policy of selective tariff protectionism from 1951. Not surprisingly, Norway kept a low profile within the Low Tariff Club and was quite ambivalent towards its endeavours. Its failures never really disappointed the government in Oslo, which was more concerned with encouraging trading partners to release their imports from quotas than from tariffs. While claiming 'membership' and continuously paying lip-service to the efforts of the Low Tariff Club, the government had its sympathies elsewhere. The situation in 1955–1956 provides a good illustration. In May 1955 the government signed a memorandum on tariff policy submitted jointly by the club. The memorandum called for the high-tariff countries to reduce their tariffs during the coming GATT round in Geneva. When the OEEC Council met in June 1955, all signatories threatened to refrain from implementing their 'free lists' to meet the index target of 90. However, at that point in time the Norwegian officials were more afraid that France and Britain would retaliate by not liberalising their quotas. A 1956 note from the Paris embassy stated that:

> Norway has participated in the endeavours of the Low Tariff Club but has let the others do the talking. [...] Norway has never maintained the demands of the Low Tariff Club and we have [...] no interest in encouraging them [the high-tariff countries] not to reach the index target.[65]

As Norway herself deliberately applied tariffs for protection, the government preferred the multilateral focus to be on the import quotas, not tariffs.

* Abbreviations in endnotes:

AAB	Arbeiderbevegelsens arkiv og bibliotek, Oslo (Norwegian Labour Movement's Archives)
AUH	Avdeling for utenrikshandel (A foreign trade division within the Ministry of Trade)
EB	Erik Brofoss arkivet (Erik Brofoss files. In AAB)
HAEU	Historical Archives of the European Union, Florence
HD	Handelsdepartementets arkiv (Archives of the Ministry of Trade. In RA)
HK/HA	Handelskontoret/Handelsavdelingen (A foreign trade division in the Ministry of Trade)
Innst.S	Innstilling til Stortinget (Report on ways and means by a select committee in the parliament)
NI	Norges Industriforbunds arkiv (Archives of the Norwegian Federation of Industry. In RA)
NOS	Norges Offisielle Statistikk (Norwegian official statistics)
Ot.prp.	odelstingsproposisjon (Bill for the larger division of parliament. In St.forh.)
RA	Riksarkivet, Oslo (Norway's national archive)
RK	Regjeringskonferansene (cabinet meetings. Filed under SK)
SA	Stortingsarkivet, Oslo (Parliament's archive)
SK	Statsministerens kontor (Prime Minister's Office. In RA)
St.m.	Stortingsmelding (White paper. In St.forh.)
St.prp.	Stortingsproposisjon (Parliamentary bill. In St.forh.)
St.forh.	Stortingsforhandlinger (official report of the proceedings of the parliament)
St.tid.	Stortingstidende (Verbatim parliamentary proceedings. In St.forh.)
UD	Utenriksdepartementets arkiv (Archives of the Ministry of Foreign Affairs. In RA)
VK	Valutakontoret (Currency division within the Ministry of Trade)

1 Cf. *Tariff Level Indices. International Economic Conference, Geneva May 1927* (Geneva: Publications of the League of Nations: II. Economic and financial, 1927 II); Heinrich Liepmann, *Tariff levels and the economic unity of Europe* (London: Allen and Unwin, 1938).

2 A. Loveday, 'The measurement of tariff levels', *The Journal of the Royal Statistical Society* 92 (1929). Mr Loveday was the Director of the Economic, Financial and Transit Department of the League of Nations.

3 H.O. Frøland, 'Norwegen', in Michael Neu, Wolfgang Gieler, Jürgen Bellers (Hrsg.), *Handbuch der Aussenwirtschaftspolitiken: Staaten und Organisationen*, Teilband 2 (Münster: LitVerlag, 2004) pp. 729–737.

4 Innst. S. nr. 100 (1927) Innstilling fra tollkomiteen om tollavgifter pp. 32–43, in Stort.forh. 6a, 1927.

5 RA, NI, Box 1780, Innstilling fra Tolltariffkomiteen av 1952 om tollsatsene for tekstil- og konfeksjonsvarer (første del), 3 October 1952, p. 5.

6 RA, UD, 44.2/13, Tollbeskyttelsen i Norge, 31 March 1947.

7 NOS, Historical Statistics 1978 (Oslo: Central Bureau of Statistics, 1978), tables 238 and 239, pp. 446–447.

8 I. Wedervang, 'Tollbyrden i Norge', *Statsøkonomisk Tidsskrift* 39 (1925), 3.

9 M. Tuveng, 'Norges ytre handelspolitikk i den senere tid', *Statsøkonomisk Tidsskrift* 53 (1939), 231–232.
10 St.prp. nr. 6, 1932 Om et ekstraordinært tillegg til den gjeldende innførselstoll, in St. forh. 2a, 1932.
11 St.prp. nr. 74, 1932 Bemyndigelse for Kongen til midlertidig å treffe bestemmelse om forhøielse av de i tolltariffen fastsatte tollsatser m.v., in St.forh. 2a, 1932; Innst. S. nr. 168 (1932) Innstilling fra finans- og tollkomiteen om bemyndigelse for Kongen til midlertidig å treffe bestemmelse om forhøielse av de i tolltariffen fastsatte satser m.v., in St.forh. 6a, 1932; St.tid. 1932, in St.forh. 7b, 1932, pp. 2504–2518.
12 SA, Record of secret meeting in parliament 29 June 1933, p. 12.
13 SA, Tilleggsbemerkninger fra utenriksdepartementets til hemmelig st.prp.nr. 6, 1934; Record of secret meeting in parliament 5 March 1934.
14 St.prp. nr. 74, 1933 Om godkjennelse av en handelsoverenskomst mellom Norge og det Forente kongerike Storbritannia og Nord-Irland med protokoll m.v., in St.forh. 2a, 1933; Innst. S. nr. 132 (1933), in St.forh. 6a, 1933; St.tid 1933, in St.forh. 7b, 1933, pp. 1870–1871.
15 RA, HD, HK/HA, Box 397, Anglo-Norwegian Trade Negotiations, 15 March 1933.
16 H. Anstrin, 'Handelspolitikens avvägar och Nordens utrikeshandel', *Industria* (1937), 21.
17 Tuveng, *Norges ytre handelpolitikk*, pp. 248–252.
18 Ot.prp. nr. 76, 1933 Om utferdigelse av en lov om forandring av lov av 22. mars 1918 om midlertidig innførselsforbud, in St.forh. 3, 1933.
19 Ot.prp. nr. 43, 1934 Om utferdigelse av en lov om midlertidige innførselsforbud m.v., in St.forh. 3, 1934.
20 League of Nations, *Quatitative Trade Controls. Their Causes and Nature* (Geneva: League of Nations, 1943), p. 19; League of Nations, *Commercial Policy in the Interwar Period: International Proposals and national Policies* (Geneva: League of Nations, 1942), p. 70.
21 J. Iversen, 'Bemerkninger om handelspolitikken efter 1930 med spesielt henblikk på Norge', *Statsøkonomisk Tidsskrift* 53 (1939), 110.
22 Ot.prp. nr. 139, 1945–1946 Midlertidig lov om innførselsforbud, in St.forh. 3b, 1945–1946.
23 W. Diebold, *Trade and Payments in Western Europe. A Study in Economic Cooperation, 1947–1951* (New York: Harpers & Brothers Publishers, 1952); St. m. nr. 32 (1952) Om varebytte og betalingsavtalene i tiden 1945–1951, in St.forh. 2c, 1952.
24 W. Andres, *Der Liberalisierungskodex der OECE für den Warenhandel* (Zürich: Juris-Verlag, 1964), p. 18.
25 A. Milward, *Britain's Place in the World. A Historical Inquiry into Import Controls 1945–1960* (London: Routledge 1996), p. 126.
26 W. Asbeek Brusse, *Tariffs, Trade and European integration 1947–1957. From study Group to Common Market* (New York: St. Martin's Press, 1997) p. 105.
27 Asbeek Brusse, *Tariffs, Trade and European Integration*, pp. 91–96.
28 HAEU, OEEC Council Minutes of the195th Meeting on 20 and 21 October 1952.
29 AAB, EB, Box 42, Norsk memorandum til OEEC av 5. oktober 1949, undated.

30 St.m. nr. 21, 1950 Om utarbeidelsen av de norske frilister, 8, in St.forh. 2b, 1950.
31 RA, HD, VK, Box 310, 'Liberalisering av vareimporten', 21 November 1950.
32 HAEU, OEEC, Acts of the Organization Vol. III, Decision of the Council on the position of Norway with regard to the 60% Stage of the Liberalization of trade, 19 December 1950.
33 RA, HD, VK, Box 310, Kommentar til eksaminasjonen av den norske liberalisering i Special Restricted Committee, 16 November 1950.
34 RA, HD, VK, Box 310, Om Norges liberalisering opp mot 60%, 17 February 1951.
35 RA, HD, VK, Box 310, Liberalisering av dry cargy skip, 9 November 1952.
36 The memorandum on the Norwegian 'negative list' is included in St.m. nr. 66, 1954 Om internasjonale handels- og betalingsproblemer og om Norges bilaterale varebytte- og betalingsavtaler i tiden 1952–1953, in St.forh. 2c, 1954.
37 RA, HD, AUH, Box 292, Tollforhandlingene i Torquey i 1950, 14 September 1950.
38 RA, UD, 44.2/13, Særskilt vedlegg til Innstilling 1 fra komiteen for forberedelse av den norske deltagelse i de internasjonale handels- og tollforhandlinger i Geneve, 31 March 1947.
39 St. prp. nr. 70, 1948 Om midlertidig tiltredelse av Generalavtalen om Tolltariffer og Handel, undertegnet i Geneve 30. oktober 1947, in St.forh. 2a, 1948.
40 RA, HD, AUH, Box 220, Rapport om tollforhandlingene i Geneve, 17 January 1948.
41 St. prp. nr. 35, 1950 Om ikraftsetting av norske tollinnrømmelser foreslått under de internasjonale tollforhandlinger i Annecy 1949 i samband med Genralavtalen om tolltariffer og handel., in St.forh. 2a, 1950.
42 RA, HD, AUH, Box 292, Tollforhandlingene i Torquay i 1950, 14 September 1950.
43 RA, NI, Box 1746, Rapport fra den norske delegasjonen til de internasjonale tollforhandlinger i Torquay, undated, 132; St. prp. nr. 120, 1951 Om undertegning av Torquay-protokollen til Generalavtalen om tolltariffer og handel og ikraftsetting av nye tollinnrømmelser som følge av de internasjonale tollforhandlinger i Torquay samt om forlengelse av de tollinnrømmelser somer tilstått under de internasjonale tollforhandlinger i Geneve og i Annecy i samband med GATT, in St.forh. 2a, 1951.
44 RA, HD, AUH, Box 292, Rapport fra arbeidsutvalget til DRK om forberedelsene til Norges deltakelse i de internasjonale tollforhandlingene i Torquay, undated.
45 RA, HD, AUH, Box 213, Spørsmålet om tollforhøyelse, eventuelt i forbindelse med overgang til verditoll, 12 March 1951.
46 RA, HD, AUH, Box 213, Innstilling fra Det interdepartementale utvalg til behandling av spørsmål om tollforhøyelser, eventuelt i forbindelse med overgangen til verditoll.
47 RA, SK, RK , 27 November 1951; St. prp. nr. 170, 1951 Om en midlertidig forhøyelse av visse tollsatser, in St.forh. 2a, 1951.
48 Innst. S. nr. 242, 1951 Innstilling fra den utvidede finans- og tollkomite om frigjøringen av den europeiske handel, in St.forh. 6a I, 1951.
49 St. tid., in St.forh. 7 b, 1951, pp. 2726–2754.
50 St. prp. nr. 170, 1951 Om en midlertidig forhøyelse av visse tollsatser, in St.forh. 2a, 1951; Innst. S. nr. 345, 1951 Innstilling fra Finans- og Tollkomiteen om midlertidig forhøyelse av visse tollsatser., in St.forh. 2a, 1951.

51 J. T. Klovland, 'Accounting for productivity growth in Norwegian manufacturing industries 1927–1959', Norwegian School of Economics and Business Administration, Discussion Paper 21, 1999, p. 12.
52 NOS, XI 326, *Productivity Trends in Mining and Manufacturing 1949–1955* (Oslo: Central Bureau of Statistics Norway, 1959), p. 51.
53 RA, HD, AUH, Box 213, Letter from De Norske Tekstilfabrikanters Hovedforening to Ministry of Finance, 4 May 1951; RA, NI, Box 1780, Innstilling fra Tolltariffkomiteen av 1952 om tollsatsene for tekstil- og konfeksjonsvarer, undated, 22ff.; cf. also H. Espeli, 'Protectionism, Lobbying and Innovation. Perspectives on the Development of the Norwegian Textile Industry, especially since 1940', *Scandinavian Economic History Review* 45 (1997), pp. 257–275.
54 RA, NI, Box 1780, Innstilling fra Tolltariffkomiteen av 1952 om tollsatsene for tekstil- og konfeksjonsvarer, 3 October 1952.
55 St. prp. nr. 190, 1952 Om visse nedsettelser av tollavgiftene for tekstil- og konfeksjonsvarer og om pålegg av toll på sinkplater, in St.forh. 2a, 1952; Innst. S. nr. 376, 1952 Innstilling fra finans- og tollkomiteen om visse nedsettelser av tollavgiftene for tekstil- og konfeksjonsvarer og om pålegg av toll på sinkplater, in St.forh. 6a I, 1952.
56 St.tid., in St.forh. 7b, 1952 , p. 3298.
57 Ibid.
58 St. prp. nr. 145, 1955 Om forhøyelse av visse tekstiltollsatser, in St.forh. 2a, 1956; Innst. S. nr. 310 Innstilling fra finans- og tollkomiteen om forhøyelse av visse tekstiltollsatser, in St.forh. 6a, 1956.
59 RA, UD, 44.2/13, Innstilling fra komiteen for forberedelse av den norske deltagelse i de internasjonale handels- og tollforhandlingene i Geneve, undated.
60 St. prp. nr. 107, 1956 Om ikraftsetting av norske tollinnrømmelser som følge av de internasjonale tollforhandlinger i Geneve 1956 i samband med Generalavtalen, in St.forh. 2a, 1956; St.tid, in St.forh. 7b, 1956, pp. 3303–3324.
61 Innst. S. nr. 258, 1956 Innstilling fra den utvidede finans- og tollkomite om ikraftsetting av norske tollinnrømmelser som følge av de internasjonale tollforhandlinger i Geneve 1956 i samband med Generalavtalen om tolltariffer og handel, in St.forh. 6a, 1956.
62 St. prp. nr. 48, 1955 Om Stortingets samtykke til å undertegne en erklæring om forlengelse til 1. januar 1958 av tollbindingene under Generalavtalen om tolltariffer og handel, in St.forh. 2a, 1955; Innst. S. nr. 314, 1955 Innstiling fra den utvidede finans- og tollkomite om Stortingets samtykke til å undertegne en erklæring om forlengelse til 1. juni 1958 av tollbindinger under generalavtalen om tolltariffer og handel, in St.forh. 6a, 1955.
63 St. prp. nr. 110, 1958 Om forlengelse av gyldighetsperioden for norske tollinnrømmelser, in St.forh. 2a, 1958; St. prp. nr. 112, 1958 Om endring av visse tollsatser som følge av forhandlinger under generalavtalen om tolltariffer og handel, in St.forh. 2a, 1958.
64 St. prp. nr. 121, 1958 Om teknisk revisjon av tolltariffen. – Overgang til Brüsselnomenklaturen, in St.forh. 2a, 1958.
65 RA, UD, 44.25/1b, Statsrådsmøtet i OEEC 28. og 29. februar 1956 – Generalsekretærens memorandum om OEECs fremtidige virksomhet, 17 February 1956.

Gudmundur Jonsson and Sigurdur Snaevarr

Iceland's Response to European Economic Integration, 1945–1960

The economic development of Iceland from the late nineteenth century to the 1960s offers an interesting example of how a small country can move from one extreme position to the opposite in its economic relations with the outside world. For the greater part of this period Iceland strove for export specialisation and embraced an outward-oriented trade regime. The 1930s marked a major shift in Iceland's foreign economic relations, as the country underwent a period of sluggish exports with growing protectionism which lasted until the 1960s. The export ratio (exports as a percentage of GDP) dropped from an annual average of 42 per cent in the 1920s to 30 per cent in the 1930s and, after a short recovery during the Second World War, fell still further to about 20 per cent in the 1950s, its lowest point in the twentieth century. This trend was only broadly in line with economic development in Europe as the contraction of foreign trade was more pronounced and protectionist policies more entrenched and longer-lasting than in most west-European countries.

The aim of this chapter is to examine why Iceland clung for so long after the war to protectionism at a time when most European countries were experiencing rapid growth of foreign trade, greater openness and increased economic integration. We will pay particular attention to Iceland's response to economic cooperation and integration in western Europe by discussing its participation in the Marshall Plan and its policies towards GATT and EFTA. Our main focus, however, will be on Iceland's participation in the OEEC Trade Liberalisation Programme and the European Payment Union. We will demonstrate how Iceland became one of the most reluctant amongst OEEC members to liberalise foreign trade and participate in the process of integration, and seek to explain the important factors determining Iceland's position.

Economic policy after the Second World War

In stark contrast with continental Europe, the special circumstances brought about by the war led to unprecedented economic growth in Iceland. The country was spared the destruction of war, apart from the loss of a considerable number of fishing vessels and freighters in the north Atlantic with consequent casualties. As early as the autumn of 1939 the trawler fishing industry was able to take advantage of increasing demand in Britain for fish and soon made good profits. The occupation of Iceland in May 1940 by British armed forces had an even bigger impact: the inflow of nearly 30,000 troops and trade concessions by the British government was an enormous boost to the economy. The economic problems of the interwar period – sluggish growth, unemployment and shortage of foreign currency – vanished almost overnight. The occupation force employed thousands of Icelanders in defence works, and its purchases of goods and services constituted significant additional demand in a society with a population of only 130,000. A year later, however, and at British request the American armed forces took over the defence of Iceland following an agreement between the Icelandic and US governments in 1941. The American activities were even more extensive, deploying some 50,000 soldiers at the height of their presence in 1943. Iceland had been one of the poorer countries of Europe before the war, but became the fastest-growing economy during the war, achieving an average growth rate of more then 10 per cent between 1938 and 1945. By 1945 Iceland had one of the highest GDPs per capita in Western Europe.[1]

Iceland was, therefore, in a uniquely advantageous position to embark upon a major economic revival after the war. A broad consensus across the political spectrum was reached in 1944 by the coalition government of the right-wing Independence Party (IP), Social Democratic Party (SDP) and the Socialist Party (SP). Economic policy was fundamentally reshaped around the central idea of economic and social security. With foreign-exchange reserves worth ISK 580 million at its disposal at the end of the war, which amounted to more than 40 per cent of the country's GDP, the government embarked upon a long-awaited economic reconstruction programme

Figure 1: The real exchange rate of the Icelandic krona 1915–1960 (1914 = 100)

Source: Gudmundur Jonsson and Magnus S. Magnusson (eds.), *Hagskinna. Icelandic Historical Statistics* (Reykjavik: Statistics Iceland, 1997), p. 695.

Note: Real exchange rate is calculated in terms of relative consumer prices against the US dollar, sterling and the Danish *krone*.

to compensate for losses and decline of productive capacity during the Depression and the war. The aim was to greatly increase production, bring the economy into line with 'the best international standards' and invigorate the export industries in order to maintain the living standards achieved during the war. Ambitious reconstruction plans were initiated by the government to replace outdated production facilities, the trawler fleet was renewed, herring-meal factories were built and agriculture provided with modern equipment and machinery. Promoting investment in the major sectors of the economy – fisheries and agriculture – became a policy priority of successive governments in the late 1940s and the 1950s.

The new-found wealth of the war years was, however, a mixed blessing for the economy. Living standards greatly improved, and vast reserves of foreign currency offered the nation a great opportunity to enhance its productive capacity; excess demand during the war had, however, led to rampant inflation, ranging between 26 and 31 per cent from 1940 to 1943 but dropping to below 5 per cent in the last two years of the war as inflationary pressures abated. The steep price rises far exceeded the inflation levels of Iceland's main trading partners, causing a real appreciation of the Icelandic króna by almost 90 per cent from 1938 to 1945 (Figure 1). Persistent shortage of labour and appreciation of the króna greatly strengthened the labour movement, in turn creating high purchasing power and a large monetary overhang once markets opened up. The government took various measures to halt wage and price rises, but without much success. In the field of monetary policy its hands were tied as far as the exchange rate was concerned. At the insistence of the British and, later, the United States governments, fixed exchange rates were negotiated in the wartime trade agreements, which covered most of Icelandic trade until 1946.

There were few signs of firm anti-inflationary measures in the immediate post-war period. On the contrary, the government added to the inflationary pressures with the implementation of its ambitious economic reconstruction programme. The enormous discrepancy in price developments between Iceland and its trading partners and the consequent imbalance in the external economy was one of the most serious and protracted problems of economic policy in the post-war period. The high real exchange rate caused severe balance-of-payments problems and discouraged exports. Since the price discrepancies were of such major proportions bringing domestic prices and incomes into line with those of the country's main trading partners posed a formidable challenge to the government. Until 1950 neither of the two possible strategies to tackle the problem – massive deflation or a large devaluation of the currency in conjunction with other measures – was adopted, and demand management, as far as that concept can be used to describe the haphazard public measures employed, was highly accommodating.

Implementation of the investment programme in 1945 and 1946 increased the inflationary pressures. Imports increased drastically in 1946, and for the first time in many years Iceland showed a current-account deficit on the balance of payments. The economic situation became critical as imports continued at previous high levels, bringing foreign exchange reserves to an all-time low. By March 1947 the sterling reserves had been exhausted and dollar reserves were also low. At the end of 1947 net foreign assets of the banks had shrunk to a mere 8 per cent of their position two years earlier. This situation was aggravated by a deterioration in terms of trade which started in 1947 and persisted until 1952: by 1951 they had deteriorated by no less than 30 per cent on 1947 levels. A deep-seated imbalance in the external economy continued for years, with the result that Iceland showed a deficit on current account of the balance of trade every year from 1946 to 1960.

The enormous imbalance in the external economy dictated foreign economic policy in the post-war period. Any chance of liberalizing trade depended on the success of dealing with this problem. In the spring of 1947 the government resorted to harsh measures including strict import quotas, sharp rises in tariffs and rationing of imported consumer goods in order to preserve a viable external balance in the overheated domestic economy. The rationing system, which was much harsher than during the worst years of the Depression, was in place from 1947 to 1950. The government was also forced to give financial support to the fish export industry which, in addition to facing lower prices in international markets, was squeezed between internal inflation and a fixed exchange rate for the króna. Export subsidies were introduced in 1946 and extended in 1948. These measures marked the beginning of a complex and a wide-ranging system of import levies and controls and export subsidies which was to characterise the Icelandic economy throughout the 1950s.

Apart from other factors, this peculiar system of economic management was detrimental to economic growth in at least two ways: the high exchange rate of the króna was detrimental to foreign trade and the huge distortions in both import and export prices led to inefficient allocation of resources. If the success of Iceland's economic policy is measured in terms of GDP per capita, it compares unfavourably with other west-European countries. Annual average growth was only 0.5 per cent as compared to an average of 6.1 per cent in 12 other western European countries over 1945–1950, while the same figures for the period 1950–1960 are 2.4 per cent and 3.5 per cent respectively.[2]

Patterns of foreign trade

Iceland's commitment to free trade and participation in European economic cooperation after the Second World War depended in the final analysis on the performance of the export industries and how they would fare in the rapidly changing international environment. The relatively large export sector was dominated by fish products, which accounted for no less than 85–90 per cent of all merchandise exports. Employing between 15 and 20 per cent of the workforce and requiring a wide range of goods and services for its operation, the fishing industry exercised a strong influence on other economic activities such as the manufacturing of inputs to the fisheries, services, and shipbuilding and repairing. Fish exports were very volatile, not only because of large fluctuations in catches but also due to changes in the rather narrow overseas export markets. Before the war southern Europe had been the main outlet for the single most important export article, salted cod, which alone accounted for 55–60 per cent of all exports. With the outbreak of the Civil War in Spain in 1936 the biggest market for Icelandic salted fish collapsed, leading to bankruptcies of fishing firms and a desperate search for new markets. In the following years the fishing industry went through a process of major restructuring and market adaptation, concentrating on the development of herring fishing and frozen fish production.

In response to greatly reduced exports and falling prices during the Great Depression, Iceland adopted extensive trade barriers in the form of quotas, tariffs and currency rationing. At first, the aim was to balance the external economy and tackle the urgent currency shortages, but in 1934 a comprehensive protectionist policy was adopted with the aim of staving off foreign competition and boosting employment.

As it had been a part of the Danish realm for centuries and then a sovereign state under the Danish king between 1918 and 1944, Iceland's biggest trading partner was Denmark. Political and economic ties, however, became weaker during the first decades of the century, while Iceland developed stronger commercial and financial links with Britain, which became the principal source of Icelandic imports during the 1930s. On the other hand, Britain was not as

Table 1: Geographical distribution of foreign merchandise trade, 1945–1965

Current prices	1945	1950	1955	1960	1965
Exports, million $US	41	28	52	73	129
Percentage distribution	100	100	100	100	100
The dollar area (U.S.)	10	14	12	16	17
Britain	71	12	8	15	20
Other EPU countries	20	49	35	41	45
Soviet Union	0	0	18	15	5
Other clearing countries	0	25	25	14	12
Imports, million $US	49	31	68	89	137
Percentage distribution	100	100	100	100	100
The dollar area (U.S.)	67	22	24	17	21
Britain	22	22	11	9	14
Other EPU countries	10	37	34	46	45
Soviet Union	0	0	14	14	9
Other clearing countries	1	18	18	15	12

Source: Gudmundur Jonsson and Magnus S. Magnusson (eds.), *Hagskinna. Icelandic Historical Statistics*, pp. 454–462.

important a market for Iceland's exports in the interwar period, receiving on average about 15 per cent of total exports. Iceland moved further into the British sphere of influence during the Second World War, when the country was not only occupied by Britain but also became a member of the sterling area and conducted most of its trade with Britain and, to lesser extent, the United States.

Traditional patterns of Icelandic foreign trade were only partially restored after the war. Exports of fresh fish to Britain were bound to decline with the restoration of the trawler fishing industry on the Humberside, and the volume was greatly reduced compared to that of the war years. A further blow to British-Icelandic trade was a ban imposed on landings of Icelandic fish in British ports in 1952, the result of a dispute between the countries over the extension of the Icelandic fishery limits from 3 to 4 miles that year. The markets for salted fish in southern Europe gradually improved, but the volume was far below pre-war levels. On the other hand, Germany again became an important market for fresh fish. Icelandic fish exporters pinned their hopes on the relatively new technology of freezing fish, which promised a higher value added than either salted fish or fresh fish production. But this strategy encountered various problems requiring big investments in plant and equipment and market development from scratch in Europe, where facilities were lacking for handling frozen fish. The American market was, on the other hand, technologically advanced.

Expansion on the continental fish market proved to be a slow process for Icelandic exporters. The problem was not only how to sustain existing levels of demand for fresh fish, but also how to meet increasing competition from other fishing nations and food producers in general, together with the consequent fall in international prices. Producers also had to respond to growing protectionist tendencies in other fish-producing countries aimed at staving off foreign competition.[3]

One of the few positive signs in the fish-export sector during the immediate post-war period was a major bilateral trade agreement with the Soviet Union in 1946, which entailed the provision of considerable amounts of frozen fish fillets, herring and herring meal in exchange for mainly lumber and oil. The trade agreement was, however, only temporary, for the Soviets lost interest in trade with Iceland in the coming years, a change which may have been primarily politically motivated.[4] Between 1946 and 1949 Iceland became firmly aligned with the United States and its western allies, which ruined the Soviet government's hope of Iceland maintaining its neutrality policy. In any case, Icelanders were unable to renew the trade agreement with the Soviet Union in 1948.

Iceland and the Marshall Plan, 1947–1953

From the autumn of 1945 to the autumn of 1946 a fierce political debate took place in Iceland over the request of the United States government for three military bases in Iceland on a long-term basis. The request caused a deep split in Icelandic society, but the issue was resolved by the Keflavik agreement in 1946 under which the United States government was to withdraw its military forces from Iceland in exchange for landing rights in Keflavik for a period of

6½ years. The government coalition collapsed as a result because the Socialists were unwilling to accept any United States military presence in the country. The Cold War split not only the broad political consensus between Left and Right, but also left the labour movement mostly outside economic policy making, setting Iceland apart from the more corporatist Nordic countries.[5]

Foreign economic policy was also greatly influenced by the political divisions engendered by the Cold War. The attitude of the Independence Party and the Social Democrats towards closer economic cooperation with the United States was fairly positive while the Socialist Party was hostile to it, viewing it as yet another move towards the American domination of Iceland. Given the strong nationalist feeling among the public and the importance all political parties attached to Iceland's economic sovereignty, it is hardly surprising that government and parliament were initially reluctant to participate in the Marshall Plan.

Pressing economic problems were gradually to soften the government's stance. Balance-of-payments problems continued to grow and were compounded by increasing marketing difficulties in Europe, partly because of growing European problems with balance of payments and partly because of Icelandic exporters' reluctance to adjust to lower price levels after the war. In the spring of 1947 foreign minister Bjarni Benediktsson and the Icelandic ambassador in Washington Thor Thors urged the United States administration to assist Icelandic exporters in the sale of fish to the Allied zone in Germany as a reward for the landing rights at Keflavik: failing this, Iceland would have to become still further dependant on trade with the Soviet Union, or even face the collapse of its foreign trade.[6] Not wanting to jeopardise their long-term objective of gaining permanent military bases in Iceland the United States government responded positively to Iceland's request, and an agreement was made with the military authorities in the Allied zone in Germany for the sale of 70 thousand tons of fish and a smaller amount of herring meal in 1948 at above-market prices. The United States government also facilitated the sale of 20 thousand tons of salted fish to Greece and Italy by subsidising its price.[7]

These were the economic and political circumstances under which the Icelandic government agreed to participate in the Paris conference on European Economic Cooperation in the summer of 1947. All the political parties except the Socialist Party were in favour of sending a delegation to the Paris conference.[8] Three of the four political parties had newly formed a coalition government, the Socialist Party being replaced by the rural, middle-of-the-road Progressive Party. The policy of the new government towards the Marshall Plan and increased economic cooperation was cautious and not at all clear. Publicly, the government claimed that the purpose of participating in the conference was not to ask for aid but to promote Iceland's export interests and to stress the importance of fish products in the future organisation of food production in Europe.

In a parliamentary debate on the Marshall Plan in October 1947 Benediktsson said that the main purpose of Iceland's participation had been to avoid foreign loans.[9] The remark did not necessarily mean that Iceland would reject American aid. From Benediktsson's point of view the greatest advantage of the European Recovery Programme (ERP) for Iceland was its strengthening of international trade, which provided the country greater opportunities to sell its products to Europe for US dollars. But Benediktsson's emphasis on the link between the ERP and US assistance in fish sales to Germany and Greece earlier in the year lends support to the interpretation that the Icelandic government was expecting further favours from the United States in marketing their products in Europe.

The Americans also linked assistance to Iceland with the ERP, referring to it as 'the introduction to the Marshall Plan'.[10] The United States government wanted the Icelandic government to join the ERP in the hope that it would promote political and economic stability in the country and increase the possibility of acquiring military bases on a long-term basis.[11] Iceland belatedly decided to take part in the Marshall Plan and was one of the 16 founding-member countries signing the OEEC treaty on 16 April 1948. On July 3 of that same year Iceland and the United States signed a bilateral treaty, and an Economic Cooperation Administration (ECA) office was opened in Iceland shortly afterwards. The United States ambassador Richard P. Butrick also became the head of the ECA office. In October 1948 the legislation on the Marshall Plan was passed after a long and heated debate in the Althingi, the Icelandic parliament.

The Icelandic government soon developed a more positive attitude towards the Marshall Plan, and even started to press for aid. However, it resisted being incorporated into a more general aid programme formulated within the OEEC, and made instead direct representations about aid to Washington. In a letter on 4 December 1948 to Benediktsson the outspoken ambassador in Washington Thor Thors said that 'from the European Institution we have nothing to expect but trouble. [...] It is my firm opinion that our main policy should be to ignore and avoid OEEC to the utmost possible.'[12] By turning directly to the United States government and appealing to its strategic interests in Iceland the Icelandic government succeeded in obtaining very generous aid, amounting to a total of $38.7 million between 1948 and 1953. Grants accounted for no less than 77.2 per cent of the total, conditional grants 13.7 per cent and loans 9.1 per cent. In addition, a sum of $141 thousand was granted through the Technical Assistance Programme. In *per capita* terms, no member of the OEEC received as much in grants as Iceland – $209 – with the Netherlands coming second at $109.[13]

The fact that Iceland, one of the very few countries of Europe emerging not only undamaged but also much richer from the war, should receive more in *per capita* grants than any other nation participating in the Marshall Plan is certainly one of 'history's ironies'.[14] How did the Icelandic authorities justify their claims for no less aid than the war-battered countries on the continent? Foreign minister Bjarni Benediktsson made no effort to hide the fact that Iceland had prospered during the war and 'enjoyed higher living standards than any other country in Europe.' Nevertheless, he added, Iceland was in real need of assistance because it was the country with the 'harshest natural conditions and fewest resources'.[15]

The Marshall Aid was a substantial injection into the Icelandic economy, amounting to nearly 6 per cent of GDP at its peak in 1951. It was of crucial importance in the short run, as it cushioned the impact of the prolonged slump between 1948 and 1952. Without doubt the aid averted a crisis in foreign trade, financing on average 17 per cent of imports between 1949 and 1953, an injection that was instrumental in reducing import quotas and rationing in 1950 and 1951. It also had some long-term impact as it enabled Iceland to continue economic reconstruction at a fast pace by furnishing capital for heavy investment in the fishing industry and for a number of industrial projects aimed at the diversification of the economy (hydroelectric power stations, a fertiliser plant and a cement factory).[16]

In more critical appraisals of the aid scholars have contended that its effects on macroeconomic management were negative, giving the government leeway to postpone unavoidable but unpopular corrective policies and thus further aggravating the imbalance in the external economy.[17] In the two following sections Iceland's external trade policy and its links with the ERP will be examined more closely.

Liberalizing foreign trade

The introduction in 1949 of the Trade Liberalisation Programme (TLP), a major plank in the ERP, came at a bad time for the Icelandic economy. In the face of deteriorating terms of trade, harsh rationing and an ever more elaborate system of import taxes and export subsidies, the government felt it had little room to manoeuvre. That autumn the government reported to the OEEC that it was not prepared to start trade liberalization, due to a balance of payments deficit and foreign currency shortages. The economic difficulties were partly blamed on the failure of the herring catch that year, but it was also pointed out that the imports programme for the current year had already been implemented and currency licences granted.[18] The OEEC accepted Iceland's policy but the government was encouraged to reduce import barriers as soon as the foreign-currency position improved.[19]

The political situation was unstable throughout the year, with the parties of the coalition government unable to reach agreement on measures to tackle the imminent economic crisis, acute currency shortages, increasing operational losses in the fishing sector and ever costlier subsidies to fishing-boat owners. The government coalition had broken up in the summer and elections were called in October. As the political parties were unable to form a majority government after the elections, the IP formed a minority government in December, while talks continued between the parties to seek a solution to the political crisis.

It therefore became the task of the IP minority government to formulate policy in response to the OEEC Trade Liberalization Programme at the end of 1949. In a report by two prominent economics professors appointed by the Ministry of Trade to study the matter, a frank analysis was presented of the economic situation and the management of the economy.[20] Its main conclusion was that Iceland was in the present circumstances unable to free imports because 'fundamental preconditions for taking such steps are not at hand'. The main obstacle, in the view of the authors, was the high exchange rate of the króna, which caused demand for currency far in excess of supply, making any relaxation of import controls impossible without creating chaos on the foreign-exchange market. The second major obstacle was the fact that foreign trade was largely channelled through bilateral agreements in inconvertible currencies which could not be used in trade with other countries. While this situation persisted, Iceland would be forced to direct its purchases to countries which were willing to buy Icelandic products. Furthermore, the authors of the report pointed out that since currencies of the 'clearing countries' tended to be overvalued, exporters were encouraged to direct their sales to them.

The question of devaluation in order to liberalize imports is addressed in the report. An effective devaluation, the authors argue, would need to be on a very large scale and would not alone be sufficient to create conditions for wide-ranging liberalization because other important economic problems needed to be tackled simultaneously, notably the pressure on prices and wages, a lax credit policy and budget deficits. Tackling these central problems would inevitably arouse strong political opposition from the trade unions and other interest groups.

The Ministry of Trade intended to send the report to the OEEC as a clarification of Iceland's policy in relation to the TLP; but it was never sent to Paris, presumably because of its frank assessment.[21] To justify Iceland's poor performance within the TLP in the years to come Icelandic authorities chose to emphasize factors outside their control: trade barriers and market difficulties in other member countries, dependence on trade with the clearing countries and, not least, persistent failures of herring fishing. Internal political restraints were hardly mentioned.

On 14 March 1950 the two largest political parties, the IP and the PP, finally succeeded in forming a majority government, which held power until 1956. The parties agreed on radical stabilisation measures, including a devaluation of the króna by 42.6 per cent against the dollar, restrictions on price rises and a ban on wage indexation. The main objective of these measures was to invigorate the fishing industry and restore profitability in the export sector. Secondly, the devaluation was to curb excess demand and promote stability in the external economy. Trade liberalization was, however, not of primary concern, although the devaluation gave some room for reducing import controls. But room to manoeuvre was limited because of extremely low exchange reserves and small stocks of imported goods. Only with the granting of an 'initial balance' worth $4 million in conjunction with the establishment of the European Payments Union (EPU) in the summer of 1950 was Iceland able to take firmer steps towards liberalization.

On 4 August 1950, the Ministry of Trade issued a free list of goods exempted from currency and import licensing, including such items as cereals, fishing gear, fuels and salt. One of the primary concerns in composing the free list was to protect trade with the clearing countries.[22] It was estimated that these measures would lead to the release of a mere 14 per cent (calculated on the basis of 1948 imports) of private imports from OEEC countries.[23] In December a small addition to the free list was announced to include a greater variety of goods. This action brought the percentage of imports on private account to 22 per cent of the total imports in 1948, which amounted to 17 per cent of imports from the OEEC the same year.[24]

The government's stabilization programme allowed considerable relaxation of import controls and rationing. The reduced demand caused by the devaluation and a more balanced budget resulted in a greater internal stability towards the end of 1950 than had been seen for many years. A balanced budget was attained in 1950 and 1952, while in 1951 there was a substantial budget surplus. Nevertheless, inflationary pressures persisted, although at a diminishing rate, due partly to external inflation but also to a lax credit policy.

The government came under pressure from the fishing industry, which was facing higher costs and marketing problems, especially in the OEEC countries. In March 1951 an agreement was concluded between the government and vessel owners allowing them to dispose of 50 per cent of the foreign-exchange proceeds of parts of their produce (cod liver oil, herring and herring products excluded), which they were allowed to sell at a premium in a 'free market'. The purchasers were only allowed to use this currency for purchases of certain goods outside the liberalized sector. This was a special sector of imports designed for these purchases, the so-called 'conditional free-list' or 'boat list'. Dollars and EPU currencies were sold at a 60-per-cent premium while currencies of clearing countries traded at a 25-per-cent premium. These measures entailed both a veiled subsidy to the boat owners and a double exchange regime.[25]

The dollar inflows under the Marshall Plan paved the way for further liberalization of trade. The government seems to have aimed at releasing 60 per cent of imports to the free list and 15 per cent to the conditional list, in total 75 per cent. But due to the balance-of-payments situation a much more modest target of 41 per cent was notified with a new free list issued on 6 April 1951.[26] Iceland was forced to apply for exemption from further liberalization.[27]

In 1952 the economy started to pick up at long last and during the following three years, 1953–1955, Iceland experienced rapid economic growth. Little progress was made, however, with regard to trade liberalization. There were increasing marketing difficulties for fish exports to Europe, the most serious one caused by a dispute between Iceland and Britain over the decision of the former to extend her fishery limits from 3 to 4 miles. A boycott on Icelandic fish was organized by private individuals with the tacit agreement of the British government. During the boycott, in force until 1956, the most important market for fresh fish remained almost closed. Iceland had to retreat even from the limited degree of liberalization hitherto granted to imports from Europe. New restrictions on imports were set up in 1952, aimed at previously liberalized imports from the OEEC countries, with the result that the liberalized sector shrank from 41 per cent to 26 per cent that year.[28] About 70 per cent of total imports in 1952 were, however, exempt from import licences, of which 13.6 per cent were goods on the conditional free list. OEEC recognized Iceland's retreat as legitimate, 'primarily on account of its exceptional position as an exporter of only one class of commodity, fishing products.'[29]

Exporters looked increasingly to markets outside the OEEC countries, i.e. the promising market for frozen products in the United States, but even more importantly to the markets of eastern Europe and some other clearing countries. Iceland made important bilateral agreements with Finland, Czechoslovakia, Poland, Spain, Austria (until 1952) and Brazil, covering on average a fifth of total exports 1948–1952. A further step down this road was taken with a major bilateral agreement with the Soviet Union in 1953, welcomed by the Icelandic government and fish export industry as compensation for the loss of the British market. The agreement marked the beginning of decades of extensive trade between the countries. As early as 1953, more than 13 per cent of all exports went to the Soviet Union, which would accept on average 17 per cent of total exports for the rest of the 1950s. This figure was close to the level of Finnish exports to the Soviet Union at that time. This raised the share of the clearing countries (mostly from the Warsaw Pact group) to 40 per cent on average between 1953 and 1959.

The increase in bilateral trade restricted imports still further, as the government was forced to direct purchases to these countries by using various policy instruments such as import quotas, lower premiums on currencies of the clearing countries than on those of the EPU countries or the United States, and controls of currency licences through the banks. One of the direct consequences of the Icelandic-Soviet trade was a considerable shift in imports from the United States to the Soviet Union, including almost all oil imports.

Trade relations with the EPU area were, on the other hand, fraught with difficulties, and throughout the 1950s Iceland continued to have serious balance-of-payments problems with western Europe, its main supplier of general manufactures. The export trade's dependence on fish made it extremely difficult for the country to balance its books against its most important trading partners in the OEEC, particularly Britain. As already mentioned, adverse developments in the continental market for fish products, coupled with the boycott of Icelandic fish in Britain, aggravated Iceland's unfavourable trade position with the EPU. Iceland found itself unable to maintain exports to the EPU area, the share of exports going to the area dropping dramatically from 75 per cent of total exports 1945–1949 to 44 per cent 1955–1959.

Officially, the OEEC showed sympathy towards Iceland and the economic problems which blocked further liberalization of its foreign trade. In OEEC reports the fact is also acknowledged that increased import restrictions on agricultural products, including fish products, in some member countries made it more difficult for countries like Iceland to improve their trade balance with the OEEC countries. Still, the OEEC was critical of various aspects of Icelandic economic policy and urged the government to take stronger measures to curb excess demand and control investment and bank lending. The expansion of trade with eastern Europe from 1953 onwards and its effect on trade relations with member countries was also a cause for concern, as the shift of trade not only meant a deteriorating position against the EPU area but also encouraged the Icelandic authorities to impose further controls on imports from western Europe.

The Steering Board of Trade took the view that although Iceland did not discriminate between individual member countries, its policy entailed discrimination vis-à-vis member countries as a whole by its imposition of quantitative restrictions on imports from the OEEC whilst encouraging purchases from important buyers of fish and fish products in eastern Europe.[30] Furthermore, the multiple-exchange-rate system, which became ever more elaborate during the 1950s, discriminated against imports from member countries since a much higher premium was levied on imports from EPU countries than on imports from clearing countries.

Iceland's special position within the OEEC became even more evident in the mid-1950s when her trade with non-member countries increased at the same time as she was lagging far behind in the Trade Liberalization Programme. Iceland's performance is presented in Table 2, which shows TLP targets achieved by Iceland according to government papers and OEEC reports. The table also shows free imports as a percentage of total imports in the same year instead of in 1948, the base year used in the OEEC calculations. Icelandic authorities complained from the start that 1948 was not representative of the Icelandic import trade because of unusually high imports

Table 2: Progress of trade liberalization 1950–1960

	TLP index end of year[1] %	Imports on the free list as % of all imports
1950	17	
1951	41	43
1952	26	46
1953	29	48
1954	29	52
1955	29	51
1956	29	53
1957	36	66
1958	36	69
1959	36	67
1960	(85)	n.a.

Sources: *Twelfth Annual Economic Review* (Paris: OEEC, 1961), p. 185; *Arsskyrsla Landsbankans* 1950, p. 67; General Economic Review 1953. Memorandum for OEEC, August 1953, p. 17; General Economic Review 1953. Memorandum for OEEC, August 1953, p. 18; *ÞI.* Vskrn. 1994-B7259. Sixth Report, p. 3; *ÞI.* Utanrikisraduneytið 1998-B/431 1 1956–1958. Efnahagssamvinnustofnun Evropu. Position of Iceland with regard to liberalization of trade. Memorandum from the Icelandic delegation, p. 5; *ÞI.* Vskrn. 1994-B/260 1956–1960. Periodical Report on Iceland, p. 2.

Note: With 1948 as a base year.

of investment goods from OEEC countries in that year, and argued therefore that it was not a suitable base year. When compared with the TLP indices for other OEEC countries the Icelandic figures are staggeringly low, with only Turkey trailing behind. Even with such low targets the quota removal included a lot of sham liberalisation, as the government retained other trade and exchange controls. The targets for 1957 and 1958, for example, are unrealistically high since foreign exchange was heavily rationed.

More attention was given to Icelandic economic problems within the OEEC from the mid-1950s, and in the following years two strategies especially were explored with the aim of improving trade relations with the OEEC. One was to examine every possibility of increasing fish exports to the area, and a special committee was set up to examine the OEEC fish market and its potential. The other was to encourage Icelanders in their pursuit of a more diversified economy and to assist them to reduce the country's reliance on fish exports. Hydroelectric power production in conjunction with power-intensive industries was considered to be the most promising strategy in this respect. These investigations did not, however, lead to any concrete policy action in the short term.

The EPU and the development of balance of payments

Shortly after the British occupation of Iceland in May 1940 an agreement was signed between the two nations on trade and economic affairs, wherein various restrictions on foreign currencies in Iceland were adopted, the exchange rate fixed and Iceland granted conditions similar to those enjoyed by sterling-area members. In April of 1941 Iceland became a formal member of the sterling area.[31] Monetary relations with the UK had been close, as the króna had been pegged to sterling since 1925 with the exception of a devaluation in 1939, which was aimed at improving profitability in the fishing industry. Iceland's position within the sterling area changed in the autumn of 1941 when the British troops were replaced by United States personnel, and Iceland no longer had to pool its dollar reserves. Iceland clearly benefited from its membership of the sterling area in terms of current transactions and, it seems, in terms of access to credit.

Because of Iceland's membership in the sterling area there were some uncertainties as to whether she should become a signatory to the agreement on Intra-European Payments and Compensations (IEPS) signed in October 1948. This was an entirely bilateral system by which a creditor country received conditional aid from the ECA and a debtor country gained drawing rights on those funds. Finally it was decided that Iceland, along with Ireland, another sterling-area member, should take part independently, although it was made clear that the Bank of England would act as central bank vis-à-vis the BIS on behalf of Iceland and Ireland. At this time there was no independent institution entrusted with the central banking function in Iceland; instead the National Bank of Iceland, a commercial bank, was in charge of fundamental central-bank operations such as issuing of notes and coins.[32] When the IEPS was negotiated Iceland did have a payment surplus against the rest of OEEC, and membership of the sterling area ensured easy transfer to other countries. Because of the surplus Iceland did not qualify for 'indirect aid', but Britain issued drawing rights to Greece for the purchase of Icelandic fish products.

Iceland decided to apply to become a signatory to the EPU agreement, even though the deadline was already past. In the negotiations Iceland sought overdraft facilities from the EPU, as her access to credit in London was limited. Pointing to a hastily downward-revised forecast of trade deficit, the Icelandic authorities applied for an initial balance of $5.5 million against an uncovered forecast deficit of $6 million. The negotiations also revealed the plans of the ECA not to grant recipients of initial balances any quotas; but applying the common rule for deciding such a quota would have given Iceland $15 million.

The ECA administration was very sceptical about Iceland becoming a member. They argued that Iceland's deficit could easily end up much higher than expected, and pointed out that Iceland might be forced to settle some of its debts in gold should the deficit exceed swing margins plus initial balances, an obligation she could under no circumstances fulfil. Implicitly, they argued, the Icelandic authorities assumed that when the gold threshold was reached further import restrictions would be imposed.

In the end Iceland was granted an initial balance of $4 million. These balances were quickly used to repay debts and ease imports. When the balance-of-payments difficulties persisted in subsequent years 'special resources' were made available to the structural debtors, from which Iceland received $11 million. Iceland was, furthermore, allowed to draw on its EPU quota from June 1952, as it was established that the ECA's plan to block quotas was at variance with the EPU agreement.

During the immediate post-war period the deficits were covered by running down the foreign-exchange reserves accumulated during the war. The Marshall Plan came to the rescue in 1948 and was vital for maintaining the external balance between 1949 and 1952. Most of the aid was in the form of grants, about half of which were

Table 3: Balance of current transactions and currency flows through EPU

In million *kronur*

	Balance on trade in merchandise and services			Grants and credits through EPU			Per cent of	
	Against all countries	Against sterling area	Against EPU	Against sterling and EPU	Initial balance and special resources	EPU credits	Total	EPU deficit covered, %
1951	–138	–163	–13	–175	88		88	50.3
1952	–123	–157	24	–133	39	29	68	51.4
1953	–104	–105	–84	–189	69	29	99	52.3
1954	–24	–40	–104	–144		91	91	63.2
1955	–142	–57	–196	–253		91	91	36.0
1956	–162	–80	–136	–216		85	85	39.1
1957	–166	–57	–139	–196		86	86	44.1
1958	–91	–45	–154	–198		86	86	43.5

Source: Central Bank of Iceland and BIS.

channelled by the ECA and MSA through the EPU ($15.15 million) by the use of Iceland's initial position in the EPU ($4 million) and of 'special resources' at the disposal of EPU ($11.2 million).[33] The purpose of the initial position was to balance Iceland's trade with other member countries, but later contributions were primarily used to restore import reserves and to finance imports from OEEC countries for three investment programmes.[34] Table 3 shows the balance in Icelandic krónur of current transactions and currency flows through the EPU.

When the Marshall Plan ended in 1953 Iceland relied increasingly on its drawing rights with the EPU, which had reached $6 million in October 1954.[35] Of even greater importance during these years were military receipts derived from the United States base in Keflavik which had been established in accordance with the defence agreement between Iceland and the United States in 1951. Between 1953 and 1955 net receipts from the base accounted for almost a fifth of total foreign-exchange receipts. In the following years the United States military activities in Iceland were, however, greatly reduced, especially after the Althingi had passed a resolution in 1956 calling for a revision of the defence agreement with the United States, including the withdrawal of United States forces from Iceland. This resolution became the official programme of the left-wing coalition government of 1956–1958. Diminishing incomes from the base forced the government in the late 1950s to resort increasingly to foreign borrowing to balance its payments which, as a result, increased the burden of foreign-debt repayment.

The balance-of-payments position varied greatly between the main trading areas. Throughout the 1950s the position vis-à-vis the OEEC countries was negative, while the position vis-à-vis the clearing countries and especially the dollar area was favourable, the latter due to Marshall Aid, significant expansion of exports of frozen fish to the United States in the early 1950s and military receipts from the United States base from 1952 onwards. Iceland had to import dollar cereals, oil and machinery for many years, but the United States never became one of its main trading partners.

The exhaustion of the multiple-exchange-rate system

In 1956 economic growth started to slow down, and remained sluggish during the following years. Balance-of-payments difficulties became more severe, with exchange reserves in 1955 at their lowest level since 1939. Inflationary pressures persisted, with the rate of inflation far exceeding those of Iceland's main trading partners in the first half of the 1950s. Between October 1949 and June 1956 the cost-of-living index rose by 82 per cent, as compared to 50 per cent in Norway, 40 per cent in Britain, 28 per cent in Sweden and 36 per cent in Denmark. The overheating of the economy seriously undermined the operation of the export industries, which were kept going by fast-increasing government subsidies financed mainly by levies on most imports. The elaborate system of multiple exchange rates, import controls, subsidies and selective levies of varying rates produced enormous price distortions and inefficiencies. Subsidies helped keep the fishing industry at a high activity level even though many enterprises were operating at a loss.

The government concentrated its efforts on various measures to counteract the inflationary pressures, i.e. by temporarily freezing wages and prices and subsidising consumer goods. Devaluation was not regarded as a realistic option for two reasons. The huge devaluation in 1950 had produced mixed results, only temporarily restoring external balances while pushing up prices. Secondly, devaluation was politically unacceptable to both of the left-wing parties, the SDP and the SP, and to the trade unions. The option of stabilisation through devaluation was ruled out when a left-wing government took power in 1956 with the participation of both the left-wing parties and the PP.

A comprehensive overhaul of the subsidy system was undertaken in 1957 in order to improve the profitability of the export industries, based on a compromise between the trade unions, farmers and the fishing industry. The import certificate system of 1951 was abolished and the subsidy system simplified by the founding of the Export Fund, through which all export subsidies were paid. The level of subsidies was raised by 40–50 per cent and financed by raising sales and excise taxes and import levies. The free list was moderately increased, with imports by private individuals now raised from 29 per cent to 36 per cent.[36] The Icelandic Chamber of Commerce called the measures 'a special form of devaluation' and criticized the new system for its price distortions.[37]

Increased government support did not solve the export industries' problems. With foreign aid not as forthcoming as before, the balance-of-payments deficit on the current account rose from 24 million krónur in 1954 to 166 million krónur in 1957, accounting for nearly 3 per cent of GDP every year 1955–1957. To cover the balance-of-payments deficits the government increasingly turned to foreign borrowing. Under these precarious circumstances in the external economy and with the acute shortages of foreign currencies the free list was scarcely effective, as many goods on the global free list were in reality reserved for the clearing countries.[38]

New economic measures in May 1958 aimed at restoring the external balance by yet another increase in export subsidies and import levies coupled with tighter budgetary policy. These measures resulted in a moderate improvement for the export industries and a more balanced budget, but they did not address the problems of the economy on a broad front, passing over important fields such as investment, bank lending and incomes policy. Bank advances rose significantly and the rise in import levies led, through the indexing of wages, to a new wage-price spiral. On 1 December 1958 a wage compensation increase of 9.2 per cent was due. The government was unable to negotiate a postponement of this increase with the trade unions and resigned after the wage increase had taken effect.

The current-account deficits of the balance of payments in 1958 were considerably lower than in previous years as a result of better terms of trade and good fish catches. In 1959 there was a sharp deterioration in the foreign-exchange position, partly caused by the accumulation of inventories and partly by inflationary pressures. The growing deficit was financed by drawing exchange reserves down to a minimum, increasing the banks' foreign overdrafts and by heavy public and private borrowing. Public debt was at an all-time high and the burden of repayments one of the heaviest in the world.[39]

A return to freer trade

The left-wing government was replaced by a minority government of the Social Democrats, whose main task was to reform the electoral law with the support of the Independence Party and the Socialist Party and avert runaway inflation. By applying wide-ranging measures to reduce prices and wages in early 1959, it managed to halt inflation for the rest of the year. A new electoral law was enacted, installing a system of proportional representation in all the 8 large constituencies and replacing 20 smaller constituencies with mixed voting methods. The new system led to a more equitable distribution of parliamentary seats, giving the more densely populated areas more weight and shifting the balance of political power from the predominantly rural Progressive Party to the other three parties. The change also furnished the basis for a political realignment, as the Social Democrats and Independence Party now gained a majority in the Althingi. In December 1959 these two parties formed a government with a slim majority in the Althingi.

The IP-SDP government embarked on sweeping changes in economic policy. A comprehensive stabilisation programme was launched during the first months of 1960. On 20 February the system of multiple exchange rates was abolished and a uniform exchange rate was introduced, coupled with a devaluation of 34 per cent against the US dollar.[40] All special compensations to exports were discontinued and the Export Fund was closed down, while a uniform export tax of 5 per cent was enacted to finance the fund's arrears. The system of linking wages to the cost-of-living index was made illegal and the government declared that from now on unions and employers would have to shoulder responsibility for wage settlements. In order to mitigate the expected price rises following the devaluation and other increases in the cost of living, the government increased family allowances and old-age pensions and sharply reduced income taxes. Consumer subsidies were increased, financed to some extent by a new general sales tax of 3 per cent and by other tax rises. Measures taken to tighten monetary policy included raising interest rates and discontinuing automatic Central Bank loans and overdraft facilities to fisheries and agriculture.

A law on imports and foreign exchange transactions took effect on 1 June, liberalizing the major part of imports and invisibles. About 60 per cent of imports, based on 1958 figures, were liberalized while 40 per cent remained subject to licence, most of them coming from countries with which Iceland maintained bilateral payment arrangements. These included potatoes, flour and sugar, coal, oil, iron, steel and lumber and most cotton textiles. Liberalising these goods would have had serious repercussions on imports from these countries, which in turn would have reduced their purchases of Icelandic goods. Thus the share of liberalized goods varied greatly between countries and areas; only 14 per cent (on the 1958 base) of imports from the OEEC were under licence while 72 per cent of the total imports from the clearing countries were.[41]

The stabilization programme was viewed with satisfaction within the OEEC, which had for years encouraged the government to undertake fundamental reform of its economic policies. Committees of high-level OEEC officials visited Iceland in 1958 and 1959, among them secretary-general René Sergent, who came twice to urge the government to reform, pointing to the example of the French who had belatedly opted for fundamental change at the end of 1958. During the transition period Iceland received substantial financial aid through the OEEC in the form of drawing rights corresponding to the gold tranche made on the IMF, and $5 million was drawn on the European Fund.

In a broader perspective the stabilization programme of 1960 marked a distinctive turning point both in foreign trade and in post-war economic policy, installing a more liberal framework for the economy with emphasis on abolishing trade restrictions. The programme marked the beginning of an era in which devaluation, instead of direct controls, became the standard tool for keeping balance in the external economy. The massive devaluation of the króna was an indication both of an enormous disparity in price levels between Iceland and Europe and also of a political boldness on the part of the government. It led to deep cuts in real wages for a while and to years of clashes with the labour movement. These economic measures also brought Iceland onto a new path in its foreign relations; external balance was restored and foreign-exchange reserves at long last exceeded the next few weeks' requirements for imports. Exports grew only slowly, but luck was with the government: in late 1961 herring-fishing at last began to revive, with favourable results for the external balance.

Furthermore, the 1960 stabilisation programme contributed to a significant change in the direction of trade away from the clearing countries towards the OEEC countries. This shift was the result of a combination of factors. Icelandic exports became more competitive in OEEC markets as a result of devaluation at the moment when fish prices were rising in hard-currency countries. Imports also shifted to west-European countries as exports to them expanded. After the artificial subsidy system was abolished and the import regulations to preserve Icelandic export interests in the clearing countries were eased, east-European countries found it increasingly difficult to compete with west-European industrial and consumer goods.[42]

Tariffs, GATT and EFTA

Given the special system of economic management in Iceland up until 1960 it is not surprising that the government was less than enthusiastic over participation in international efforts to reduce tariffs.

Iceland was invited to take part in the third General Agreement on Tariffs and Trade (GATT) round in Annecy in 1949, but the government declined the offer on the grounds that it was impossible for Iceland to reduce tariffs for fiscal reasons.[43] Since the 1930s Iceland had maintained a high level of protective tariffs. The devaluation of the currency had been more modest than in the other Nordic countries in the 1930s, but instead the government had introduced high protective tariffs, causing a rise in the incidence of import duties to about 16 per cent in the late 1930s and even above 18 per cent after 1940. In 1947 tariffs were increased sharply to finance increasing export subsidies. Thus, the nominal rate of protection rose from about 18 per cent to above 30 per cent in the 1950s.

The system of import levies and export subsidies blocked all hopes of Iceland joining GATT, and it was not until after the stabilisation measures in 1960 that preconditions for participation were in place. Hoping to further Iceland's trade interests by negotiating reductions in tariffs on fish products in the main trading countries, the Icelandic government accepted the invitation to join GATT as a temporary member in 1964. Iceland participated in the Kennedy round that year and became a full member of GATT four years later.[44]

Iceland watched closely and was involved in the discussions on a Free Trade Area within the OEEC in the late 1950s, but because of its special trade structure dominated by fish exports which were treated as agricultural products and therefore not included under the terms of the Free Trade Area, the country did not become a member of the European Free Trade Association (EFTA) when it was founded in 1960. The extensive system of trade restrictions and another serious dispute with Britain over the extension of the fishery limit to 12 miles, the 'cod war' of 1958–1961, compounded the problem. However, with the abolition of the multiple-exchange-rate system in 1960 and closer economic and political ties with the OEEC countries in the 1960s the question of joining EFTA became urgent and was much debated in the late 1960s. In 1970 Iceland finally joined EFTA, and only then abandoned the high tariff policy that had been in force for 40 years.

Conclusion

Few, if any, west-European countries took as cautious a position on post-war European cooperation and integration as Iceland. The new republic of Iceland was admittedly eager to secure and enhance its standing as a fully independent State within the international community by joining the major international economic institutions set up at the end of the war. Its commitment to a more open economy and closer economic integration with Europe was, however, at best half-hearted. Thor Thors' previously quoted remark that 'we have nothing to expect but trouble' from the OEEC may be a somewhat-exaggerated expression of received opinion in government circles, but it illustrates well the reluctance to adhere to the common framework of the OEEC. Participation in the OEEC's Trade Liberalisation Programme was the clearest example of this, where Iceland had the lowest score of all the OEEC countries except Turkey. As Europe was adopting a more liberal economic framework, reducing trade barriers and experiencing unprecedented growth of foreign trade, Iceland was moving in the opposite direction. Foreign trade was at an all-time low during the 1950s and the major thrust of economic policy was to develop an increasingly elaborate system of import levies and export subsidies coupled with very high protective tariffs.

Why was Iceland's foreign economic policy so out of touch with the rest of western Europe after the war? We can point to three different but related explanations to that question. First, the economic problem that confronted Iceland in the immediate post-war period was not how to get the economy running again, as it was for the war-torn countries of Europe, but how to scale down the level of its economic activity and incomes in such a way as to avoid impairing the growth potential of the economy. Excess demand and galloping inflation during the war had created huge price disparities between

Iceland and its main trading partners, leading to a real appreciation of the currency. Severe balance-of-payments problems and currency shortages emerged with the transition to a peacetime situation, compounded by a deterioration in terms of trade between 1947 and 1952. The government failed to bring the economy into line with peacetime conditions and instead imposed severe restrictions on imports, together with an increasingly complex system of import levies and export subsidies from 1947 which lasted until the end of the 1950s. This type of economic management gave little room for trade liberalisation and a more open economy in general. The 1950 stabilisation programme was the only serious effort to bring Iceland into step with its main trading partners during the period under review. They largely failed, however, due to inflationary pressures from abroad and lack of coordinated fiscal and monetary measures at home.

Secondly, Iceland's structure of output and trade was very different from most of the OEEC countries, and its commercial interests therefore did not fit well with those of most of the other member states. Iceland's economic structure was based on a complementary pattern of trade, exporting mainly fish products and importing a range of manufactured goods, fuel, raw materials and even foodstuffs. Iceland needed trading arrangements which opened up foreign markets for its highly competitive fishing sector, but unfortunately fish products were classified as agricultural products and hence increasingly protected in the OEEC member countries. Exporters therefore turned their attention to other areas and found outlets for frozen fish in the US market but even more importantly in eastern Europe and the Soviet Union, which became one of Iceland's principal trading partners during the 1950s. Conversely, trade with the OEEC countries was at its lowest during the 1950s, about 44 per cent on average in 1955–1959 compared with 76 per cent in 1945–1949. In order to protect its export interests Iceland directed its purchasing of imports away from the OEEC countries and towards eastern Europe.

Iceland's failure to liberalise its economy in the 1950s was not only a result of structural restraints but also of policy priorities. Commitment to trade liberalisation was of secondary importance to what can be described as a 'policy of growth', which was carried out through various more or less public investment programmes with the aim of sustaining high levels of growth and employment. Highest priority was given to investment in fisheries, agriculture and residential housing, but efforts were also made to diversify the economy with a number of industrial projects.

From a political point of view, Iceland was able to shy away from its international commitments to freer trade and closer integration for two principal reasons. The Icelandic economy was too small to matter to anybody other than the Icelanders, and the government was therefore able to pursue its own commercial policies without serious fear of retaliation. Secondly, because of its military-strategic interests in Iceland the United States government was reluctant to put pressure on its government to adhere to the Trade Liberalisation Programme, participate in GATT or adopt economic policy in line with the ERP. The Marshall Plan and the generous treatment of Iceland within the EPU made it easier for the government to carry out ambitious investment plans and postpone painful measures to extinguish the chronic balance-of-payments deficits and the system of multiple exchange rates, import levies and export subsidies. Iceland, along with Austria, Turkey and Greece did not have to play by the same rules as the rest of the OEEC, since a large part of its trade debts with the EPU was financed by American aid through the granting of 'initial balances', 'special resources' and, in the case of Iceland, by the use of its drawing rights with the EPU and from military receipts from the US base in Keflavik.[45] Not until the stabilisation programme of 1960 was Iceland able to break out of the deadlock of low growth and balance-of-payments restraints and abolish the peculiar system of economic management that had characterised the 15 years immediately following the war.

1 Gudmundur Jonsson, 'The Transformation of the Icelandic Economy: Industrialisation and Economic Growth, 1870–1930', in Sakari Heikkinen and Jan Luiten van Zanden (eds.), *Exploring Economic Growth. Essays in Measurement and Analysis* (Amsterdam: Aksant, 2004), p. 147.

2 Angus Maddison, *Monitoring the World Economy 1820–1992* (Paris: OECD, 1995), pp. 194–197; *Thjodhagsreikningar 1945–1992*, National Economic Institute (Reykjavik, 1994), p. 117.

3 *Fish Marketing in OEEC Countries* (Paris: OEEC, 1951); *The Economics of Fisheries* (London: FAO, 1956).

4 Petur Thorsteinsson, *Utanrikisthjonusta Islands og utanrikismal. Sogulegt yfirlit* I (Reykjavik: Hid islenska bokmenntafelag, 1992), pp. 470–471.
5 Thor Whitehead, 'Leidin fra hlutleysi 1945–1949', *Saga* XXIX (1991), 63–121; Idem, *The Ally Who came in From the Cold. A Survey of Icelandic Foreign Policy 1946–1956* (Reykjavik: University of Iceland Press, 1998); Valur Ingimundarson, *I eldlinu kalda stridsins. Samskipti Islands og Bandarikjanna 1945–1960* (Reykjavik: Vaka-Helgafell, 1996); Idem, *The Struggle for Western Integration. Iceland, The United States, and NATO during the First Cold War*, Forsvarsstudier 3/1999 (Oslo, 1999).
6 Thor Whitehead, 'Leidin fra hlutleysi', pp. 78–79.
7 Cf. Ingimundarson, *I eldlinu kalda stridsins*, pp. 149–150.
8 *Althingistidindi* 1947 D, p. 118.
9 *Althingistidindi* 1947 D, p. 120. See also Ingimundarson, *I eldlinu kalda stridsins*, p. 148.
10 *Althingistidindi* 1948 B, p. 1937.
11 Ingimundarson, *I eldlinu kalda stridsins*, pp. 150–151.
12 Quoted in Sigurdur Snaevarr, 'Island og alþjodaefnahagsstofnanir 1945–1960' in Gudmundur J. Gudmundsson and Eirikur K. Björnsson (eds.), *Islenska söguþingid 28.–31. mai 1997. Radstefnurit* I. (Reykjavik, 1998), pp. 247.
13 Gunnar A. Gunnarsson, 'Island og Marshallaaetlunin 1948–1953', *Saga* XXIV (1996), 96.
14 Ingimundarson, *I eldlinu kalda stridsins*, p. 141.
15 *Althingistidindi* 1948 B, d. 1940–1941.
16 Thorhallur Asgeirsson, 'Efnahagsadstodin 1948–1953', *Fjarmalatidindi* 2, mai–juni (1955), pp. 69–71.
17 Sigurdur Snaevarr, 'Iceland' in Hans H.J. Labohm (ed.), *The Fiftieth Anniversary of the Marshall Plan In Retrospect and in Prospect – Report of the Seminar organised by The Clingendael Institue in Cooperation with the Netherlands' Atlantic Commission, The Hague, 15–16 May 1997;* Gunnar A. Gunnarsson, 'Island og Marshallaaetlunin 1948–1953'.
18 *National Archives* [NA], Maryland, Record Group [RG] 469. Records of the U.S. Foreign Assistance Agencies, 1948–1961, Mission to Iceland, Office of the Director, Subject Files 1948–1953, Telegrams relating to the Recovery Program, 1949–1950, Box 1. U.S. embassy in Paris (Harriman), 23 November 1949.
19 *Arsskyrsla Landsbankans* 1949, p. 80.
20 *ÞI*. Vskrn. 1994-B/308 1949–1958, Friverslunarmalid, unsigned and without date.
21 *ÞI*. Vskrn. 1994–C/16 1950–1950, Brefabok, Thorhallur Asgeirsson to Petur Benediktsson, 3 February 1950.
22 *ÞI*. Vskrn 1994-B/158 1950–1962, Frilistinn, Greinargerd um frilista.
23 *NA*, RG 469. Records of the U.S. Foreign Assistance Agencies, 1948–1961, Mission to Iceland, Office of the Director, Subject Files 1948–1953, Telegrams relating to the Recovery Program, 1949–1950, Box 1. American embassy to State Deptm, 10 November 1950.
24 *Arsskyrsla Landsbankans* 1950, pp. 66–67; *Boksafn Hagstofu Islands*, Icelandic Report for the Fourth Quarter of 1950, Prepared by the Ministry of Commerce, p. 22.

25 The scheme was not in conformity with the IMF's Article of Agreements from 1946. The Icelandic authorities struggled with the IMF on the issue for most of the 1950s: cf. Snaevarr, 'Island og alþjodaefnahagsstofnanir 1945–1960'.
26 *Verslunarrad Islands. Skyrsla um starfsemi þess* 1951, p. 14.
27 *Arsskyrsla Landsbankans* 1951, p. 57; Icelandic Report for the Fourth Quarter of 1951, p. 1.
28 General Economic Review 1953, Memorandum for OEEC, August 1953, p. 17.
29 OEEC C(53)263/07, Council, Present Economic Situation and Problems of Member Countries, Report by the Economic Committtee, Iceland, p. 8.
30 *ÞI.* Vskrn. 1994–B/ 259, OEEC C(54)282, Invocation of articles 3(c) and 20(a) of the code of liberalisation by the government of Iceland, Report by the Steering Board for Trade to the Council, 25 October 1954.
31 This agreement has never been published.
32 The Central Bank of Iceland began operation as an independent institution in 1961.
33 Graham L. Rees, *Britain and the Postwar European Payments System* (Cardiff: Wales University Press, 1963), p. 113.
34 Thorhallur Asgeirsson, 'Efnahagsadstodin 1948–1953', p. 65; *ÞI.* Vskrn. 1994-B/ 259. Iceland; Graham L Rees, *Britain and the Postwar European Payments System*, pp. 111–118.
35 Asgeirsson, 'Efnahagsadstodin 1948–1953', p. 65.
36 *ÞI.* Utanrikisraduneytid 1998-B/431 1 1956–1958, Efnahagssamvinnustofnun Evropu, Position of Iceland with regard to liberalization of trade, Memorandum from the Icelandic delegation, p. 5.
37 *Verslunarrad Islands. Skyrsla um starfsemi thess* 1956, p. 13.
38 See *Fjarmalatidindi* januar–juni 1950, p. 28; *ÞI.* Vskrn. 1994–F1/6 1952–1969 OEEC-skyrslur, The new regime of imports and foreign exchange.
39 *ÞI.* Vskrn. 1994–B/ 260, 1956–1960, OEEC-skyrslur, Iceland, General Economic Review 1959 and a Report on the Stabilization Program, June 1960, p. 11; Jonmundur Gardarsson, 'A Reluctant European: Iceland, EFTA, and the EEC 1956–1963'. M. A. thesis, Jesus College, University of Oxford (1994), p. 43.
40 Accounting for the abolition of import levies. However, the nominal devaluation was much greater with the US dollar shooting up to 38 kr. from 16.26 kr which equals 57 per cent devaluation.
41 *ÞI.* Vskrn. 1994–F1/6 1952–1969 OEEC-skyrslur, The new regime of imports and foreign exchange; *ÞI.* Vskrn. 1994–B/ 260. 1956–1960. OEEC-skyrslur, Iceland, General Economic Review 1959 and a Report on the Stabilization Program, June 1960, p. 26.
42 *Verslunarrad Islands. Skyrsla um starfsemi þess* 1960, p. 17.
43 *NA*, RG 469, Records of the U.S. Foreign Assistance Agencies, 1948–1961, Mission to Iceland, Office of the Director, Subject Files 1948–1953, Telegrams relating to the Recovery Program, 1949–1950, Box 1. Lawson to Secstate ECA, 23 November 1949.
44 Thorsteinsson, *Utanrikisthjonusta Islands* II, pp. 781–785.
45 Rees, *Britain and the Postwar European Payments Systems*, pp. 111–124; Alan S. Milward and George Brennan, *Britain's Place in the World. A Historical Enquiry into Import Controls 1945–1960* (London: Routledge, 1996), p. 67.

Isabelle Cassiers and Philippe Ledent

Belgian Monetary Policy under Bretton Woods*

The Bretton Woods era, lasting from 1944 to 1971, was characterised by a very particular way of handling international monetary relations: the whole system rested on a regime of fixed parities between numerous currencies, on a central position secured by gold and the US dollar, and finally on the desire for a speedy return to free international trade. At the end of the 1940s the European economies which had been so badly shaken by the Second World War had still to face several important challenges: reconstruction, mutual understanding and coordination. Their success in these undertakings seems to have contributed significantly to the extraordinary recovery period known as the 'Golden Age'.

Nevertheless, the realisation of the agreements made at Bretton Woods in 1944 was a lengthy process. The return to currency convertibility and to free trade was so complex that it could only be implemented in successive stages. The creation of the European Payments Union (EPU, 1950–1958) is a good illustration of the numerous stages that were planned to facilitate the transition of European economies from a war footing to a regime of international cooperation.

In this global mindset, Belgium wasted no time in demonstrating its strong desire to open up its economy to international trade, reintroduce currency convertibility and play an active part in setting up institutions to regulate trade at European and international levels. As early as 1944 Belgium took radical measures to balance its money supply and stabilise prices and exchange rates. The keystones of its economic policy, founded on a firm commitment to the values of a market economy, were its monetary and exchange rate policies. At first sight Belgium's choices appeared to be in line not only with the principles laid down at Bretton Woods, but also with the characteristics of a small and open economy.

However, there were several factors which made these monetary and exchange-rate policies very difficult to put into practice: firstly, the slow resumption of international free trade caused by the time required for the relevant Bretton Woods agreements to come into effect. Moreover, the way the EPU had been set up stood in opposition to the direction Belgium had taken in expectation of a rapid return to free trade and to the total convertibility of all major currencies. Secondly, the size of Belgium's public debt at that time and the persistence of substantial deficits thwarted any positive outcome from the restrictive monetary policy. Finally, the complex nature of Belgian money-market institutions, which were the fruit of compromise on various sensitive internal issues, did not provide fertile ground for the development of an unambiguous monetary policy.

Overall, the achievements during the years in question cannot be considered as a total success. On the positive side, there is no doubt that some of the targets were achieved: the establishment of an open economy, international cooperation and stable exchange rates and prices. But a price had to be paid for these successes: in the 1950s the choice of a restrictive monetary policy could be perceived as slowing growth and domestic investment, whilst the opening of markets in the following decade was accompanied by a reduction in Belgium's leverage in the decision-making process.

The purpose of this chapter is to examine these interpretations, with a major focus on the 1950s, by highlighting the complex interactions between the external and internal constraints imposed by a network of complex institutions. The chapter is divided into four sections. The first offers a view of economic-policy decisions taken in the aftermath of the Second World War, and of the way that these decisions shaped the context for growth. The second part analyses the 1950s by emphasising the difficulty economic policymakers had in adapting to external and internal pressures. The third section outlines the way that negative events in the 1950s finally turned into a 'virtuous circle' in the 1960s, marked by an extraordinary growth rate. Section 4 concludes.

The initial choices: a strong franc and stable prices

During the Second World War two opposing schools of thought became apparent in discussions on preparing for a return to a peace-time economy.[1] On the one hand there was the school of thought represented by Paul Van Zeeland, Prime Minister of Belgium from 1935 to 1937. He had opposed the deflationary policies of the early 1930s and had brought the Belgian economy out of depression through a combination of substantial devaluation and the implementation of Keynesian principles.[2] Van Zeeland proposed gearing post-war monetary policy to furthering economic recovery. He opposed the implementation of deflationary measures and advocated a relatively low currency parity together with a high level of liquidity so that civil demand could rapidly take over from wartime expenditure.[3]

The second school of thought, supported by Maurice Frère, Governor of the National Bank of Belgium and advocated by the Finance Minister Camille Gutt, proposed the opposite approach: a drastic reduction in the amount of money in circulation as soon as the war was over, in order to avoid any risk of inflation and to maintain a high exchange rate for the Belgian franc. According to this theory, which reflected the orthodox policy adopted at the beginning of the 1930s, exchange-rate manipulation should never be used as a means of reviving an economy.

The first school of thought was rejected and a strict monetary reform – the Gutt plan – was implemented as soon as Belgium was liberated. This proved to be extremely significant for economic policy during the whole post-war period. Despite the very complex situation at the end of hostilities Belgium was the first country to reform its monetary system – eight months before France, one year before Holland and four years before Germany.[4] The adoption of this reform was reflected in the establishment of an ordered programme for the aims and instruments of economic policy, with a strong franc and stable prices being the prime targets and monetary policy the preferred instrument to achieve them. Indirect control over total expenditure in the economy (by means of limiting the cash available to fund such expenditure) was intended to make it possible to abolish direct controls and reinstate market-economy mechanisms as quickly as possible.[5]

The reforms of October 1944 reduced the amount of money in circulation by about two thirds, bringing it down to approximately the pre-war level.[6] Banknotes were withdrawn from circulation and partly replaced by new notes. Surplus fiduciary money and bank deposits were frozen either permanently or provisionally. In the case of permanently frozen deposits (37% of the money stock) the assets were converted a year later into debt securities *(Emprunt d'assainissement monétaire).* Provisionally frozen deposits (26% of the money stock) were paid back gradually between 1944 and 1949 as the economy recovered, so as to keep a tight control over the growth of the money stock and maintain a fixed exchange rate with the United Kingdom.[7] Sterling remained the basic reference, and the pre-war exchange rate for the pound was used to set the exchange rate for the Belgian franc, which was then declared to the IMF in implementation of the Bretton Woods agreement.

The period immediately following the implementation of the Gutt plan was an exceptionally prosperous time for Belgium, and the success of the monetary reform was a cause for general self-congratulation. In fact numerous other factors also contributed to the rapid recovery, such as the limited extent of war damage, the rapid liberation of the port of Antwerp and, above all, the structure of European demand. In the post-war reconstruction period this demand was heavily accentuated towards commodities such as coal and metals, which were the Belgian industrial sector's speciality.[8] Finding itself in such a favourable position, Belgium was not obliged to follow the United Kingdom, which devalued sharply (by 30.5%) in 1949. The Netherlands and the Scandinavian countries devalued to the same extent, closely followed by Germany (25%) and France (22%); but Belgium, backed by its current-account surpluses with its European trading partners, limited itself to 12.5%. This was one of the lowest devaluation rates at that time, and in practice was equivalent to a revaluation. More than ever before, the National Bank of Belgium could pride itself on having a strong franc.

Thanks to this policy choice Belgium subsequently enjoyed particularly low levels of inflation. As a result of social dialogue becoming part of the institutional framework, the index-linking of wages to the cost of living became more or less standard practice. With inflation under control, this meant that wage increases were kept relatively low. But there were disadvantages, as well as advantages, to this situation. On the one hand, those countries which had opted for a major devaluation gained an additional share of the export market, whilst Belgium saw its share decline.[9] And on the other hand, the fact that income grew slowly depressed private consumer demand, which throughout the period increased much more slowly in Belgium than elsewhere.[10]

From 1950 onwards Belgium was firmly committed to a system of fixed exchange rates. It made no more applications to revalue its currency and steadfastly retained a parity of 50 francs to the dollar until the end of the Bretton Woods arrangements.

The two aims of a stable exchange rate and stable prices were therefore achieved very rapidly, but monetary policy constantly came up against two constraints, one external and the other internal. First, the return to currency convertibility proved much slower than expected. The Belgian authorities' options were based on a very liberal concept of international trade but in practice international trade was still subject to countless controls and restrictions, with the result that throughout the 1950s the Belgian economy found itself forced into a position where it constantly had substantial claims on other European countries. Second, the significant weight of the State debt and the persistence of high public-sector deficits made it very difficult to implement a coherent monetary policy.

The initial choices that shaped Belgian economic policy should therefore be submitted to crucial questions: was the choice of a very strict monetary policy well adapted to the 1950s context of slow return to convertibility and high public debt? and to what extent did this context hinder the implementation of such a policy? In the next section we will examine both of these questions.

Restricted economic growth in the 1950s

However eye-catching the Belgian economic recovery was, the 1950s were nevertheless marked by a relatively slow rate of Belgian growth compared to that enjoyed at that time by most of its neighbouring countries (Table 1). Several analyses have stressed the losses in Belgium's share of the export market, the relative weakness of its investment, and the slow growth of public and private consumption.[11] These undesired effects seem to result directly from the economic-policy choices of the time and their match (or mismatch) with the economic environment.

The logic underlying a system of fixed exchange rates is that it offers a mechanical means of correcting a balance-of-payments surplus by issuing paper money. Swollen by the monetary multiplier, the money supply boosts domestic demand for goods and services, encourages imports and, as a result, reduces the initial balance-of-payments surplus. During the 1950s the current-account surplus should have resulted in an increase in the money supply, more vigorous economic growth and an eventual correction of the initial imbalance.

The restrictions on capital movements that existed at that time should, in theory, have helped that adjustment mechanism by lessening the risk of the compensation of a current-account surplus by a capital outflow. Controlling capital movements also allowed the Central Bank to use the interest-rate instrument for domestic policies.

The mechanisms described above should have dealt with high public deficits and let expansionist Keynesian policies (analogous to those implemented elsewhere) develop: modulating expenditure according to the economic cycle should have sustained domestic demand, while funding the Treasury requirements should have increased the amount of basic currency and so boosted demand further. But in the 1950s these factors did not have the expected knock-on effect. On one hand, the currency inconvertibility and the desire to liberalise capital movements as quickly as possible both nullified any chance of an 'automatic' correction of the current-account balance taking place. On the other hand, the system adopted for the funding of public deficits and the set-up of the monetary market affected the efficiency of monetary policy.

The inconvertibility of currencies and capital flows

The Belgian authorities considered a stable currency as a requirement for promoting foreign trade in the context of fixed-exchange rates and the return to currency convertibility. This in turn required monetary stability. For the Bank indeed monetary stability enables the internal balance of prices and wages to be guaranteed and any potential discrepancy with other competing countries to be reduced. This is why the strict control of the money supply and the holding of large gold reserves – two necessary conditions to achieve monetary stability – were the primary objectives of the central bank.[12]

Whatever the theoretical justification behind this argument might be, its implementation was frustrated by the 1950s' international context, which was characterised by the slow pace with which the Bretton Woods principles were applied. Let us explore how upholding currency inconvertibility distorted the whole process.

The swift post-war recovery of its economy and its industrial sector's specialisation in basic commodities meant that Belgium rapidly found itself in a position where it could supply other European countries with the coal and steel they needed for post-war reconstruction. As a result Belgium became the major creditor of western Europe, to the extent that the Belgian franc was referred to as the 'European dollar'. It would have been very useful if Belgium had been able to convert its substantial claims on other European countries into a means of payment for the American capital goods it needed to modernise its own industry, thus effecting both the correction of the initial surplus on the current-account balance and the modernisation of its industry. But these claims were not convertible into dollars, since the currency-convertibility principles established at Bretton Woods had proved difficult to put into practice.

The EPU, which was set up in 1950 to facilitate multilateral payments between member states of the Organisation for European Economic Cooperation (OEEC), only provided a partial solution to Belgium's payment problems. The system set up by the Union was basically structured in such a way as to support intra-European trade and increase debtor countries' access to credit, but it worked to the disadvantage of creditor countries (a criticism levelled at the system by Robert Triffin).[13] As Belgium had a chronic surplus over its EPU partners and a chronic deficit towards the United States, it was hampered by the fact that the European currencies were not convertible into dollars. The country was forced into a position where it was building up claims on the other EPU countries and consuming its dollars and gold reserves to pay for imports from the USA. This situation was contrary to the objectives followed by the Central Bank since 1944, and in particular its strict control over monetary expansion.

In response to this situation Belgium adopted a package of restrictive measures in 1951 with a view to limiting its trade surplus.[14] The Central Bank clarified the reasons behind its decision by explaining that the EPU had imposed on Belgium the heavy burden of an excessive debt volume that went far beyond the quota voluntarily accepted at the beginning of the system by the Belgian authorities. This fact forced the country either to opt for a risky course of monetary expansion or to take restrictive measures that directly contradicted the principal objective of free international trade and exchange.[15]

The particular structure of the international monetary system forced Belgium to backtrack on its initial policy of liberalising trade. The harsh terms of the monetary policy linked to an international background of imperfect currency convertibility worked against the expansion of the export sector and goes some way towards explaining the lack of industrial modernisation in Belgium and consequently the relatively slow growth of the Belgian economy in the 1950s.

A second aspect of the external constraints that influenced the direction of Belgian monetary policy was the acceptance of relative capital mobility. Most countries continued to implement strict capital controls in order to protect themselves against speculation on exchange rates. The parities determined in the Bretton Woods' agreements remained fragile and could have collapsed at any time if there were a speculative attack on currencies. This meant that the Belgian authorities were faced with a dilemma. On the one hand the widespread restrictions on capital movements were diametrically opposed to their free-trade approach and difficult to put into practice in a very open economy. On the other hand, if there were no restrictions on capital movements, their prime objective of maintaining a stable franc would force the Central Bank to deal with variations in its foreign-exchange reserves, paralyse the expansionist effect of the current-account surplus on the economy and remove the possibility of manipulating interest rates for purposes of domestic economic policy.

As early as 1951 Belgium found a way out of this problem in the form of a free-exchange market for certain types of capital transactions. In 1955 the Belgium-Luxembourg Economic Union introduced a major innovation by creating an official two-tier exchange market. Current-account payments were to be made via the regulated market, whereas financial capital movements were to be effected on the free market. This was tantamount to a subtle deviation from the Bretton Woods agreement, and as such was frowned upon by the IMF[16] but it was nonetheless tolerated.[17]

After the creation of the two-tier exchange market defending the Belgian franc exchange rate seemed to be much less onerous for the Belgian monetary authorities. On the one hand, they accepted the IMF (and later, the European Monetary Agreement) rules governing current-account payments, which meant that they were obliged to intervene on the regulated market to keep exchange rate fluctuations within a band of 1% either side of the official rate. But on the other hand the authorities refused to maintain exchange rates for purely financial movements of capital within the same margins. It should also be noted that only fifteen currencies were traded on the regulated market.[18] This meant that two exchange systems were operating in parallel, with the second system mitigating the monetary constraints of the first.

Obviously there was no question of condoning a prolonged and significant deviation of the free-market rate of a currency from its official parity – a deviation that could have been perceived by economic agents as an unavoidable parity modification on the official market and would, in consequence, have triggered speculation. This meant that the Central Bank – or more precisely the Belgium-Luxembourg Exchange Control Institute – was still potentially obliged to intervene on the market in response to capital movements, although it could restrict its interventions to crisis periods. As the segments of the exchange markets were not totally separate, the authorities could relax or tighten the constraints as the situation demanded by increasing or reducing the number of transactions permitted on the free market. The Central Bank wanted to avoid the occurrence of such crisis periods, and so its conviction was reinforced that the only useful objective was to maintain monetary stability by a strict control on the money supply.

Finally, the basic principles of Belgium's economic policy (giving priority to stable prices, a stable exchange rate for the franc and liberalising capital flows) appear to have led to a policy of restricting exports and of imposing relatively high interest rates on lending. As the inflation rate was kept within bounds, real interest rates, albeit occasionally negative, were generally higher than those in neighbouring countries (Table 2). This may have restricted the domestic demand for credit and contributed to the relatively slow rate of growth in domestic demand.[19]

Financing the public debt and the configuration of the money market

The implementation of Belgium's monetary policy was strongly influenced by the existence of a particularly high public debt, equivalent to approximately 80% of GNP at the end of the war (see Table 1): due to the more or less permanent annual deficits, this high level of indebtedness declined only slowly. Part of the State's borrowing requirement was covered by bank loans: following the 1935 reform which abolished the so-called 'mixed banks' deposit banks were no longer authorised to hold equities and bonds issued by industrial companies. As a result of the war economy they had allocated a significant part of their assets to the State: in 1944 a record 84% of the total value of bank loans was granted to the State.[20]

Following the post-war monetary reform Treasury certificates held by banks were frozen, as were banknotes and deposits. Under the Gutt plan the frozen assets were only to be released very slowly. This meant that banks had to be forced to keep treasury certificates; otherwise they could have submitted them for redemption and used the funds raised to grant loans to companies whose assets were provisionally frozen. This would have obliged the State to resort to the National Bank of Belgium, and the issue of new banknotes would have frustrated the reduction in the money supply brought about by the Gutt plan. This is why a special regulation was passed in 1946 obliging deposit banks to comply with a cover ratio and keep a large proportion of their deposits (50 to 65%) in the form of public-sector securities.

This regulation achieved two objectives: controlling the money supply and financing the public sector. A series of monetary reforms introduced over the course of the next fifteen years were all geared to the same targets and created a long-term partnership between the banks and the State. It is striking to note that most of the new money-market regulations and institutions were directly or indirectly linked to financing the public debt. The gradual relaxation of the mandatory ratios between 1949 and 1957 and their eventual abolition in 1961–1962 went hand in hand with measures designed to encourage the banks to keep a large part of their assets in the form of public-debt securities. As a result, Belgian banks only allocated a small proportion of their resources to financing the private sector: at the end of the 1950s bank loans to companies and individuals represented only 36% of deposits in Belgium, compared with 43% in the United Kingdom, 72% in Germany and 81% in France.[21]

This made monetary policy less efficient. Changes in the discount rate only had a limited impact on the volume of bank loans since a significant proportion of these loans were made to the State and the State's demand for credit was less sensitive to interest rates than that of corporate and private borrowers. Given that only a fraction of lending activities was influenced by interest rates, a major stimulus was required if these activities were to generate significant variations in the volume of loans.[22]

In addition, banking regulations and the structure of the money market weakened the multiplier effect of basic currency issued by the central bank.[23] It is well known that the multiplier effect is greater if banks' reserve coefficients are low and the general public shows a limited preference for banknotes. The fact that banks were obliged or actively encouraged to hold substantial stocks of State paper had exactly the same effect as maintaining banks' reserve coefficients *(r)* at a very high level. This was compounded by the general public's particularly marked preference for banknotes *(b)* throughout the period.[24] In fact, the volume of money of account did not exceed the volume of notes and coins in circulation until 1968.[25] Monetary policy had undoubtedly become less efficient due to the combined impact of these two (high *r* and high *b*) – not totally unconnected – factors. The general public was disinclined to deposit money with the banks because the interest rates being offered were ridiculously low. The banks argued that this was justified as they themselves were receiving a very low return on Treasury certificates, which made up a large portion of their assets.[26] In fact before 1957 interest rates on Treasury certificates did not follow market trends, and offered a stable but extremely low return.

This vicious circle created another vicious circle in its turn. The general public increasingly turned to public credit institutions, which offered a better return on their savings deposits. These institutions were able to do this because they were not considered as banks and so were not obliged to comply with the same constraints as banks with regard to their lending activities. The extraordinary expansion of these non-controlled institutions, which attracted 65% of deposits made by the general public in 1960,[27] limited the degree of control the monetary authorities were able to exercise over the development of quasi-money.

There was also very little scope for using an open-market policy to regulate the money supply. Open-market transactions were effected by the Fonds des Rentes, which was set up in 1945 under the auspices of the National Bank of Belgium and the Finance Ministry. However, this institution's main duty was to stabilise public-debt securities. In the opinion of some observers of the Belgian money market, stabilising securities' prices in this way made monetary policy even less efficient; any attempt by the Central Bank to reduce the money stock could be counteracted by the opportunity offered to holders of State debt securities to redeem their assets with the Fonds des Rentes without the risk of losing any capital, and so to rapidly replenish their liquid assets.[28]

Clearly the implementation of a coherent monetary policy was not made any easier by the complex structure of the different institutions which played a role on both the money and the exchange market (Figure 1). At the time, after examining the respective roles played by the National Bank of Belgium and the Banking Commis-

Figure 1: The main players in the Belgian money market in the 1950s

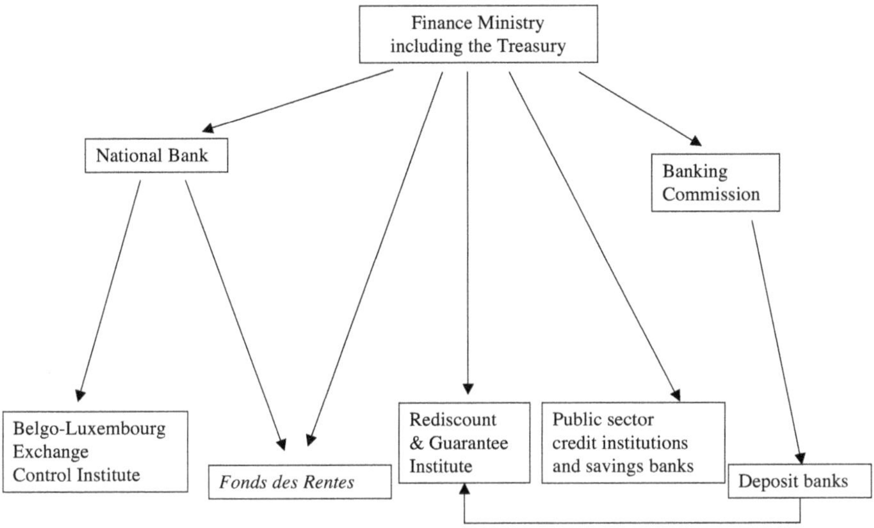

sion, one observer condemned the 'existing two-headed organisation', saying: 'A logical mind might well wonder whether it is really necessary to have two institutions, whose respective competencies are bound to overlap.'[29] This comment could have been extended to the complex and multi-faceted set of institutions (Figure 1).

The way in which the structure of the money market developed at that time seems to have been conditioned more by the public-sector borrowing requirement than by the dictates of a coherent monetary policy. This was a constant source of complaint from the National Bank of Belgium, which jealously guarded its prerogatives and scrupulously implemented the limits it was empowered to impose on the funding of government expenditure in accordance with the terms of an agreement dating back to 1948.[30] Throughout this period the National Bank of Belgium's advances to the public sector remained stable at around 10 billion Belgian francs, which represented a steadily decreasing proportion of both public-sector expenditure and the central bank's assets. This fixed ceiling on monetary funding appears to have deprived the State of the resources it needed to implement an efficient contracyclic policy.[31] We cannot exclude the fact that this ceiling reflected a latent power struggle between the Central Bank and the government. The monetary history of this period is rich with other symptoms of this conflict.

The outcome of these perceptible tensions was a radical reduction in economic policy instruments, as has been emphasised by several scholars. Finet stated that

> the state is constantly short of funds. The question must therefore be asked whether, under these circumstances, the State can engage in contracyclic policy. [...] The State has no real freedom in the management of its finances. It often borrows where and when it can, and even then only to meet its immediate needs.[32]

More generally, Morissens concluded that

> the Governments have enjoyed only a limited freedom of choice which compelled them to use relatively few instruments. [...] By a process of elimination, the Governments were led to rely as much as possible on the instruments of money and credit.[33]

It is against this background that we should view of the law of 1957, which laid down a new gold-based status for the franc. This law seems a strange anachronism when compared to the international monetary system which had been drawn up at Bretton Woods: it defined the Belgian franc in terms of a given quantity of gold and reinstated the obligation to provide cover in gold. This unusual return to the gold standard seems to have been motivated by a desire on the part of the governor of the National Bank of Belgium, Maurice Frère, to prevent the government from using a devaluation of the franc as a means of boosting the economy. Since the value of the franc was defined by law, any manipulation of the exchange rate had to be approved by Parliament.[34] This was a further step taken by Belgium in its unreserved commitment to a stable franc, but it cut still further the flexibility of the economic policy tools at its disposal.

To sum up the argument: the 1950s monetary policy based on stable prices and a strong currency did not in fact deliver the strong growth it had promised. Keeping in mind the external and internal pressures, it seems more likely that a vicious circle set in (see Figure 2):

- current-account surpluses were partially offset by net outflows of capital (Figure 3) with the result that the issue of basic currency was limited;

Figure 2: Negative knock-on effects of Belgian monetary policy during the 1950s

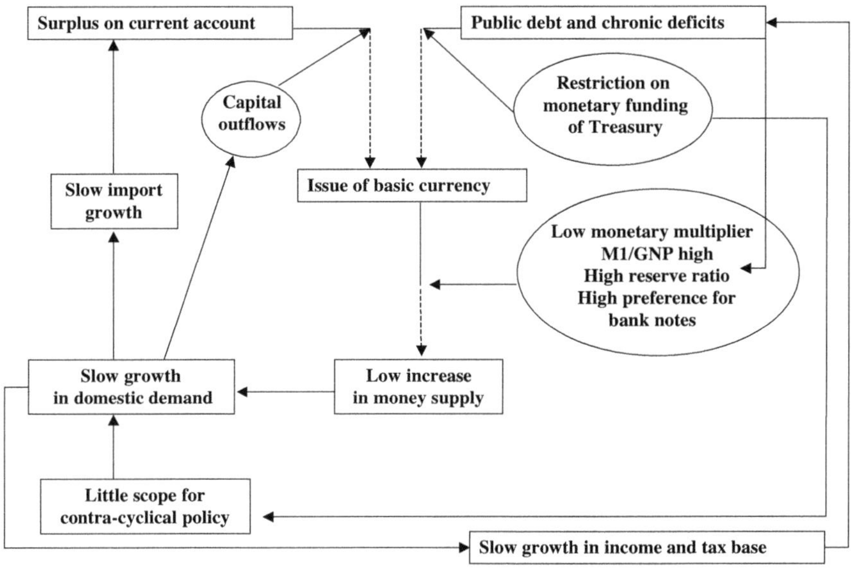

- restrictions on funding Treasury requirements also limited the issue of currency by the National Bank of Belgium;
- the banks were obliged to hold substantial reserves in the form of treasury certificates (since the public debt still had to be financed), which meant that the effect of the monetary multiplier, already diminished by the general public's marked preference for banknotes, was reduced still further.

As a result, the slow growth rate of the overall money supply frustrated domestic demand. This had three significant consequences:

- the import sector languished; imports were already restricted by the imperfect currency convertibility arrangements (see above);
- tax revenue was too low, giving rise to high deficits, despite the slow increase in public expenditure;[35]
- there were too few attractive investment openings for domestic savers, who preferred to invest their funds abroad, giving rise to a chronic private-capital-account deficit.

Figure 3: The balance of payments for the Belgium-Luxembourg Economic Union (BLEU)

a) Overall analysis

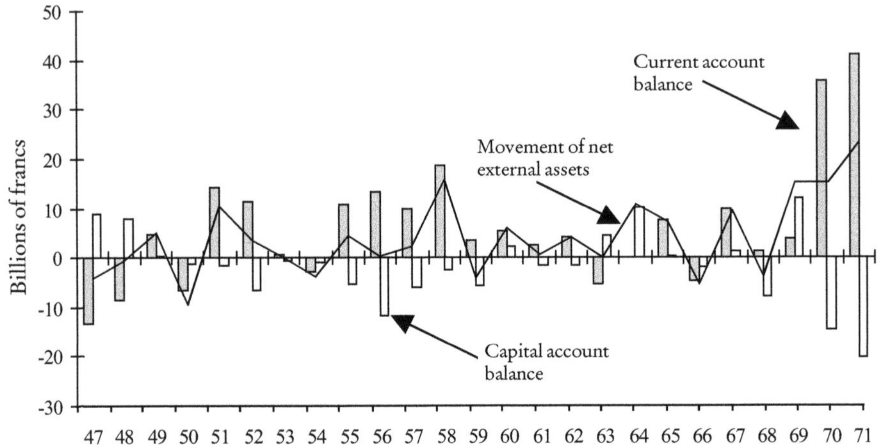

b) Details of balance on capital account

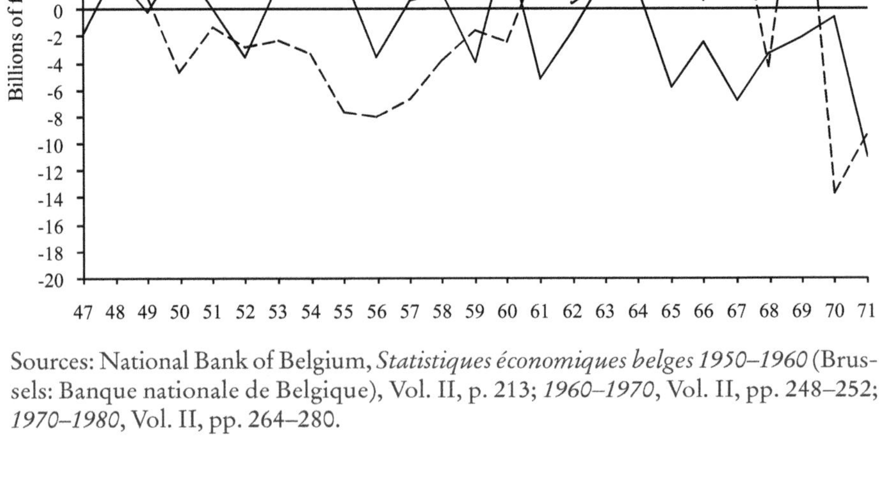

Sources: National Bank of Belgium, *Statistiques économiques belges 1950–1960* (Brussels: Banque nationale de Belgique), Vol. II, p. 213; *1960–1970*, Vol. II, pp. 248–252; *1970–1980*, Vol. II, pp. 264–280.

The 1960s: from a vicious to a virtuous circle?

A combination of various factors finally broke this vicious circle at the end of the 1950s: the return to full currency convertibility in 1958 marked the end of the more restrictive EPU period and the beginning of the heyday of the Bretton Woods arrangements. This enabled Belgium to lift its export restrictions and to freely use its claims on other European countries to revive its imports from the United States. The creation of the Common Market boosted European trade, much to Belgium's advantage, situated as it was in a prime position at the heart of Europe. This was a significant contributory factor in attracting foreign investors to Belgium.[36] On the domestic front, the discussions as to why the economy grew relatively slowly[37] in the 1950s led at the end of the decade to the adoption of the 'expansion laws', which granted preferential conditions to foreign companies setting up business in Belgium.[38]

From this time on the rate of economic growth picked up substantially, stimulated by both exports and investments.[39] The particular conjunction of growth factors contributed to defusing the latent conflict between monetary and budgetary policy, and between the Central Bank and the government.

Growth was mainly initiated by direct foreign investment, and this led to a reduction in current-account surpluses and even to deficits. From 1958 onwards the current-account surpluses of the Belgium-Luxemburg Economic Union (BLEU), which had been particularly high in the period 1955–1958, started to decline. Imports increased significantly, rising by an average of 10.3% per year between 1959 and 1970, compared with 4.7% during the period 1950–1958.[40] Direct investments also led to a decline in net capital outflows, which eventually gave way to net capital inflows. Figure 3 illustrates the very marked reversal in private-capital balance which occurred at the beginning of the 1960s. A detailed analysis of the balance of payments reveals that this shift was clearly due to inward direct foreign investment, given that outflows of Belgian financial investments abroad, which were first noted in the 1950s, continued.[41] The appearance of deficits on the current account cancelled out the potentially inflationary impact of net capital inflows and automatically limited the issue of basic currency, thus obviating the need for the Central Bank to intervene to stabilise prices.

The increasing rate of economic growth also helped to fill the State's coffers and contributed to a marked reduction in the public debt, which in terms of GDP dropped from 70% in 1959 to 48% in 1970 (Table 1). This relative decline in public-sector borrowing enabled a series of reforms to be implemented, the sum total of which was a reduction in the banks' reserve ratio. Pressure on the money market eased, the use of money of account became more widespread, and the growth rate of the money stock increased. These factors all underpinned expansion without generating excessive inflationary pressure. Subsequently, the combination of several elements seems, with a mainly unchanged policy, to have enabled a virtuous circle to begin, fuelled by outstandingly dynamic growth (Table 1) which allowed external and internal constraints to be relaxed.

However, this situation did not have only positive effects: it also induced a loss of various economic levers in the decision-making process. First, the development of current and capital movements multiplied the number of operations on both the exchange markets. This situation necessitated more interventions by the Central Bank, not only on the official market, but also on the free market.[42] This left little scope for using interest rates as an instrument for controlling the money supply, since they had to be used to reduce the gap between the official and the free exchange rates; that is, to manage the flow of capital and the stability of the Belgian franc, as explained above.[43] Figure 4 illustrates the spread between the official and the free exchange rate on the Belgian market for the US dollar, German mark and Dutch guilder. It shows a surplus demand for dollars, particularly at the beginning and end of the period, and market anticipation of the revaluation of the mark and the guilder in 1961 and of the mark in 1969. By comparing Figures 4 and 5 it can be seen that sharp rises in the discount rate and Treasury-certificate rate occurred at times when free-market exchange rates diverged from the official rate, i. e. in 1957–1958, 1961, 1967 and 1969. Higher interest rates were designed to encourage capital inflows through the free market and so boost demand for the Belgian franc and halt the decline in the exchange rate. It can clearly be seen that there is a

Figure 4: Exchange rates on the Belgian market

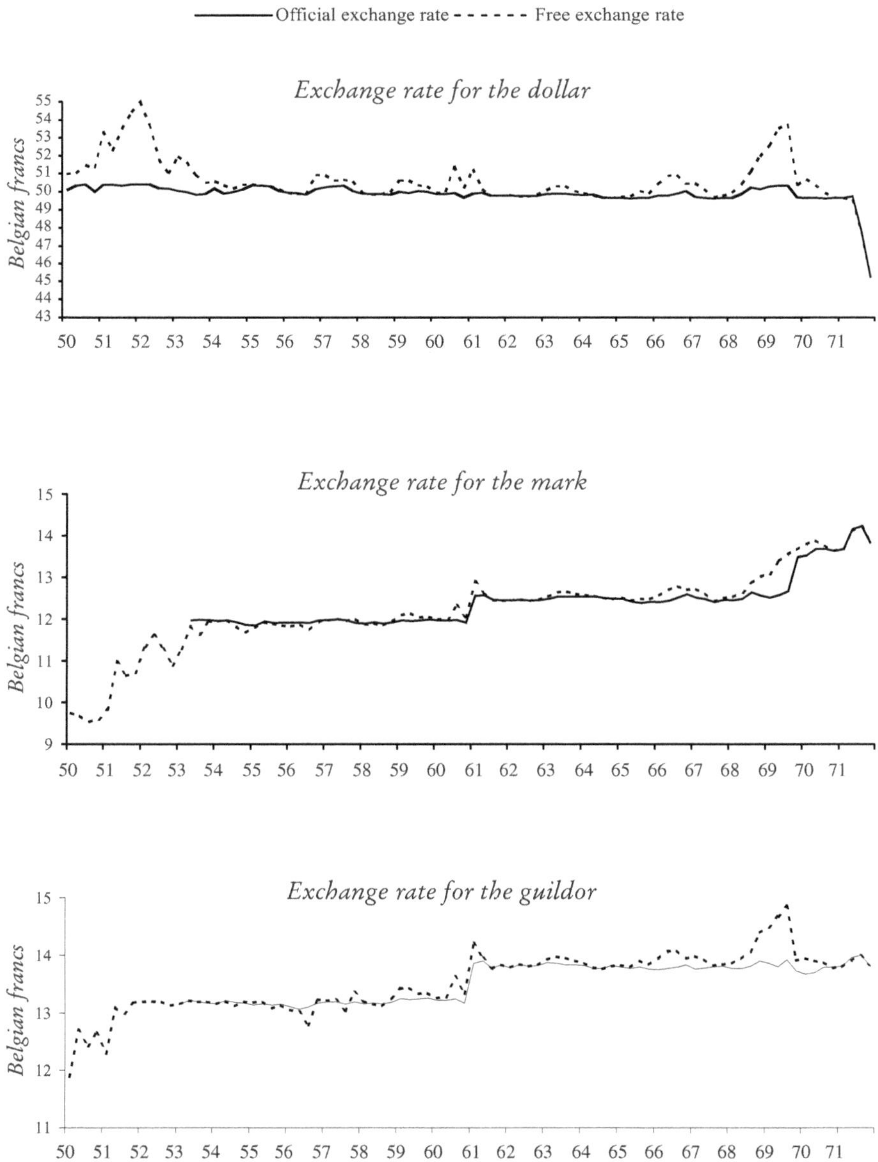

Sources: National Bank of Belgium, *Statistiques économiques belges 1950–1960*, Vol. II, pp. 233–236; *1960–1970*, Vol. II, pp. 321–331; *1970–1980*, Vol. II, pp. 320–333.

fairly close correlation between the dates on which official interest rates were increased and the dates on which the balance of private capital showed an improvement (Figures 3 and 5). As a consequence, the Belgian Central Bank lost an essential lever for controlling monetary policy.

Figure 5: Interest rates

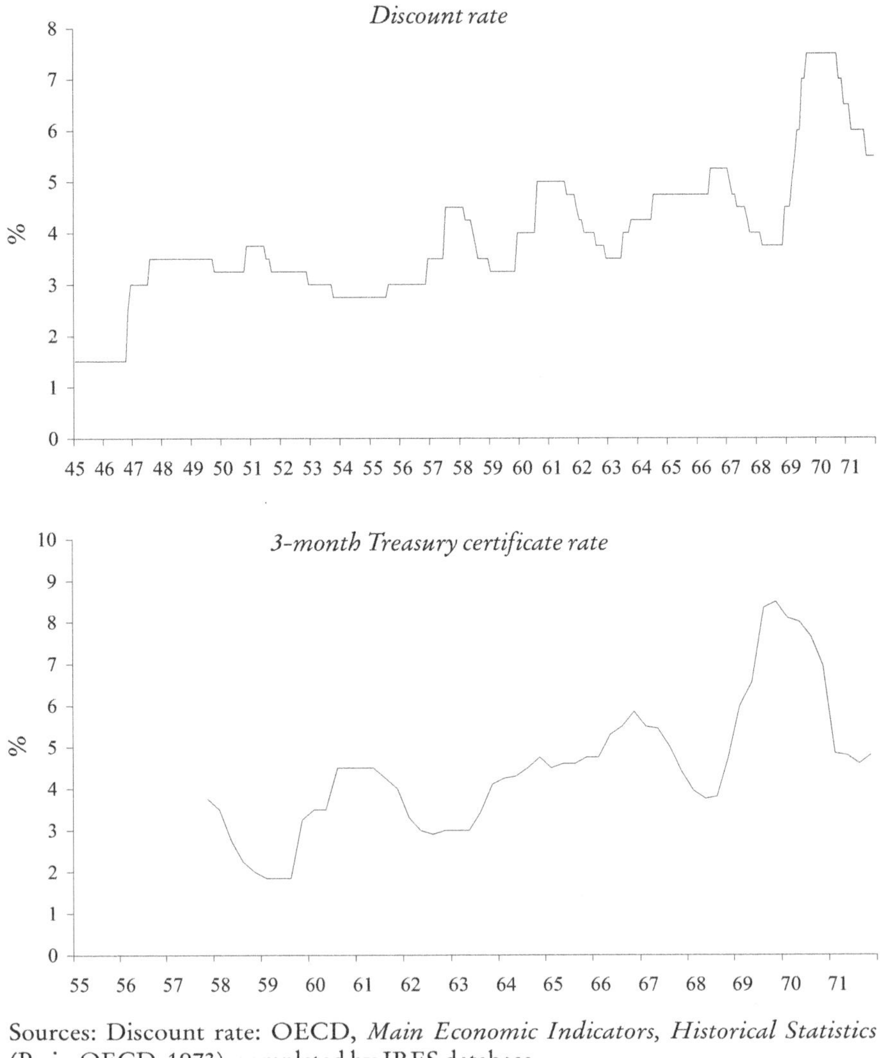

Sources: Discount rate: OECD, *Main Economic Indicators, Historical Statistics* (Paris: OECD, 1973), completed by IRES database.

Second, the large movements on the free market diminished the capacity of the Central Bank to maintain a strong currency: indeed, on the analogy of the previous decade it might have been expected that Belgium would emulate Germany and the Netherlands and revalue in 1961 and 1969. It did no such thing. This was a consequence of the substantial gap between the exchange rates on the official and the free markets at this time.[44] Another explanatory factor is a boomerang reaction to the 1957 law which defined the Belgian franc in terms of a given weight of gold. This law was devised by the National Bank to make devaluation less attractive to the government; but it also restricted the bank's own scope for revaluation. Whether deliberate or not, the depreciation of the Belgian franc against the currencies of two of its neighbours further boosted the growth rate of Belgian exports.

Third, the opening of the Belgian economy to foreign capital also had consequences on the private sector: the exceptional growth rates enjoyed in the 1960s significantly enhanced its outward orientation. At the end of the Bretton Woods era the Belgian economy's degree of openness was even greater than that of the Dutch (Table 1). In addition – and this might be a greater cause for concern for the future – the dynamic growth of the economy became even more reliant on foreign investment, with foreign investors controlling – at least in part – the management of the companies which they had financed:[45] from 1960 to 1972 foreign investment in the manufacturing sector accounted for one third of gross capital formation, and for one half of this sector's net capital formation.[46] Did this growing vulnerability amount to a major breach in the virtuous cycle of growth that seemed so well established during the 1960s?

Conclusions

After the end of Second World War policy choices had been clearly defined: in complete contrast to the French vision of a planned economy and even to the Keynesian economic-policy principles that were widespread in the western world, and in a clean break with its own experience of the late 1930s, Belgium manifested complete faith in the merits of a market oriented economy. Belgium wanted to pursue these virtues via a policy of universal – even deflationary – price stability.

This course was maintained without any concessions throughout the 1950s, despite the difficulties created by currency inconvertibility, capital flows and the public-sector debt. Under these constraints, the implementation of a policy of price stability and the opening of markets led to deflationary tendencies, increasingly complex institutional set-up and power struggles that sometimes appeared to be paralysing the economy.

During the 1950s slow growth and investment weakness became major sources of concern. 'The expansion of production asserted itself only gradually as an objective of economic policy,' noted Morissens in 1962, 'but the promotion of internal competition and the increased mobility of factors of production were pursued only through scattered measures, while co-ordination was not considered as an objective.'[47] A decade later, Finet could still claim that 'the tradition of economic liberalism affects domestic policy […] The Government has never succeeded in applying an overall economic policy.'[48]

Despite a largely unchanged policy, a series of predominantly external events made it possible for a virtuous circle to kick in at the beginning of the 1960s. But an assessment of this period of growth cannot neglect the long-term effects of the increasing openness of the Belgian economy and its mounting dependence on foreign capital. The 1970s crisis destroyed a third of industrial jobs, and the 1980s and 1990s saw the buying-up of Belgium's leading companies by foreign firms. However, the small size of the Belgian economy is not sufficient to explain these trends: other small open economies – such as The Netherlands – seem to have defended their economic autonomy better.

The evidence presented in this paper can therefore legitimately raise questions as to whether the Belgian economy's growing vulnerability to external decisions was linked to economic policy choices made in the 1940s and 1950s. The strong belief in the principles of economic liberalism, the absolute priority given to stable exchange rates and prices, the resultant slow economic growth, the lack of structural reforms, the predominance of short-term targets: all these factors encouraged outflows of Belgian capital in search of foreign investment openings. This trend probably increased the Belgian economy's financial dependence on outside sources. In this situation, the sharp rise in growth in the 1960s could not be funded from internal sources. The idea of supporting economic growth by making calls on foreign investors was merely another short-term device. As a French commentator noted at the end of the period under review, 'the liberal tradition, which to date has been strongest in Belgium, has prevented detailed medium- and long-term plans from being drawn up and implemented'.[49] The cost of this 'short term to short term' strategy could only be measured decades later, once the decision-making centres had moved out of Belgium.[50]

Table 1: Structural data for the Belgian economy and its main trading partners

a. Real GDP per capita: annual average rates of growth

	1944–1950	1950–1960	1960–1971	1944–1971
Belgium	4.8%	2.4%	4.3%	3.7%
Netherlands	14.6%	3.3%	3.7%	5.9%
West Germany	–6.1%	7.1%	3.4%	2.5%
France	13.8%	3.6%	4.4%	6.1%
Italy	6.0%	5.4%	4.7%	5.3%
United Kingdom	–0.5%	2.3%	2.2%	1.6%
Total of 5 partners	1.6%	4.3%	3.6%	3.8%

Sources: A. Maddison, *L'économie mondiale 1820–1992 analyse et statistiques* (Paris: OCDE, 1995): Countries: Table D 1a, pp. 206–209; Total of 5 partners: Table A 3a pp. 110–113 and Table C 16a pp. 192–195.

b. Degree of openness (X / (GDP + M))

	1953	1960	1973
Belgium	24.6%	26.1%	36.2%
Netherlands	35.4%	35.6%	31.9%
West Germany	16.8%	20.4%	18.4%
France	12.7%	13.9%	14.4%
Italy	10.6%	14.7%	14.6%
United Kingdom	18.6%	18.7%	18.8%
Average of 5 partners	18.8%	20.7%	19.6%

Source: Kredietbank, *Bulletin hebdomadaire de la Kredietbank* (1996).

c. Money

	Money stock (M1/GNP)			Percentage of fiduciary currency in M1		
	1950	1960	1970	1950	1960	1970
Belgium	45.8%	38.6%	29.3%	58.2%	57.1%	50.2%
Netherlands	36.0%	26.7%	22.6%	48.1%	52.1%	40.5%
West Germany	17.1%	15.7%	15.4%	67.9%	74.1%	65.4%
France	30.8%	31.8%	29.5%	54.8%	44.2%	37.1%
Italy	–	31.9%	49.4%	–	44.5%	34.1%
United Kingdom**	–	25.6%	18.6%	–	41.6%	48.9%
Average of 5 partners*	27.9%	26.3%	27.1%	56.9%	51.3%	45.2%

Source: International Monetary Fund, *International Financial Statistics*, Yearbook 1984.

d. Public finances

	Public debt / GNP			National surplus (+) or deficit (–) / GDP		
	1950	1960	1970	1950	1960	1970
Belgium	73.0%	69.3%	48.0%	–	–3.8%	–1.8%
Netherlands	–	44.0%	28.7%	1.6%	0.7%	–1.1%
West Germany	7.4%	7.4%	7.0%	–0.8%	–0.6%	–0.1%
France	–	28.4%	12.6%	–5.7%	–1.4%	0.5%
Italy	–	39.9%	36.7%	–	–1.6%	–5.1%
United Kingdom**	–	1.8%	1.3%	2.5%	–1.9%	1.4%
Average of 5 partners*		24.3%	17.3%		–0.8%	–0.9%

Source: International Monetary Fund, *International Financial Statistics*, Yearbook 1984.
* the average is calculated on the basis of available data.
** internal debt only.

Table 2: Inflation rates and interest rates in Belgium and neighbouring countries

a. Inflation rate

	1945–1954	1954–1959	1959–1971	1945–1971
Belgium	3.2%*	2.0%	3.2%	3.0%
Netherlands	5.5%	2.2%	5.4%	4.8%
West Germany	4.4%	2.5%	4.1%	3.9%
France	21.4%	5.1%	4.4%	10.1%
Italy	10.3%	2.3%	4.7%	6.1%
United Kingdom	4.1%	3.8%	4.4%	4.2%
Average of 5 partners	8.1%	3.0%	4.3%	5.3%

Annual average growth rates.
* from 1946 onward.

Sources: 1945–1954: consumer price index, according to B. R. Mitchell, *International Historical Statistics Europe 1750–1988* (New York: Stockton press, 1992); 1955–1971: GDP price index, according to International Monetary Fund, *International Financial Statistics* (Washington:International Monetary Fund), Yearbook 1984 and 1985.

b. Real short-term interest rate

	1946–1954	1955–1959	1960–1971	1955–1971
Belgium	–	1.5%*	1.6%	1.6%
Netherlands	–	0.3%	–1.6%	–1.0%
West Germany	–	0.9%	–0.4%	0.0%
Italy	–	1.7%	–0.4%	0.2%
United Kingdom	–	0.6%	1.2%	1.0%

Average rates.
* from 1957 onward.

Sources: Nominal rate from OEEC, *General Statistics, OEEC Statistical Bulletins*, January (1955), No.1 and OECD, *Main Economic Indicators*, inflation: see above.

c. Real long-term interest rate

	1946–1954	1955–1959	1960–1971	1946–1971
Belgium	1.4%*	3.2%	3.2%	2.7%
Netherlands	–2.2%	2.0%	0.4%	–0.2%
West Germany	n. a.	4.0%**	2.7%	3.1%
France	–1.7%***	0.5%	1.3%	0.3%
Italy	–3.0%	3.9%	1.1%	0.2%
United Kingdom	–0.5%	1.1%	2.6%	1.2%
Average of 5 partners	–1.8%	2.3%	1.6%	0.9%

Average rates.
* from 1947 onward; ** from 1956 onward; *** from 1949 onward.

Sources: see part b.

* This chapter is based on a broader research carried out by the authors for the National Bank of Belgium: I. Cassiers and Ph. Ledent, *Politique monétaire et croissance économique en Belgique à l'ère de Bretton Woods (1944–1971)* (Brussels: Banque nationale de Belgique, 2005).

1 H. Van de Wee and M. Verbreyt, *De Nationale Bank van België, de Emissiebank en de Belgishe regering van 1939–1945* (Brussels: Banque nationale de Belgique, 2005).
2 I. Cassiers, *Croissance, crise et régulation en économie ouverte, la Belgique entre les deux guerres* (Brussels: De Boeck Université, 1989). See chapter 5.
3 V. Janssens, *Le franc belge: un siècle et demi d'histoire monétaire* (Brussels: Service Interentreprise, 1976), p. 304; 'La Banque Nationale de Belgique', in *Les Banques de l'Europe de l'ouest de 1920 à nos jours* (Paris: Comité pour l'histoire économique et financière de la France, 1995), p. 265.
4 J. G. Gurley, 'Excess liquidity and European monetary reforms, 1944–1952', *American Economic Review*, XLIII (1), March 1953, 76–100.
5 Cassiers and Ledent, *Politique monétaire*, chapter 3. See also F. Bismans, *Croissance et régulation, la Belgique 1944–1974* (Brussels: Académie royale des sciences, des lettres et des beaux-arts de Belgique, 1992), p. 451: Janssens, 'La Banque nationale de Belgique', p. 265.
6 M. Frère, 'La restauration monétaire en Belgique', *Revue d'économie politique*, Paris, LXX, No. 6, November–December 1960, 82–108, 83 and 88.
7 For a detailed description of the monetary reform see Van der Wee and Verbreyt, *De nationale Bank*; R. Brion and J-L. Moreau, *La politique monétaire belge dans une Europe en reconstruction (1944–1958)* (Brussels: Banque nationale de Belgique, 2005); Cassiers and Ledent, *Politique monétaire*; L.H. Dupriez, *Les réformes monétaires en Belgique* (Office international de librairie, 1978); Janssens, *Le franc belge*; Frère, 'La restauration monétaire'.
8 We will not elaborate on these points, which have been dealt with elsewhere: see I. Cassiers, '"Belgian miracle" to slow growth: the impact of the Marshall Plan and the European Payments Union' in B. Eichengreen, (ed.), *Europe's Post-war Growth Revisited* (Cambridge: Cambridge University press, 1995).
9 United Nations, quoted by B. Eichengreen, *Reconstructing Europe's trade and payments: The European Payments Union* (Manchester: Manchester University Press; Insight from Economic History, 1993), p. 50: Cassiers, 'Belgian miracle', p. 279.
10 Cassiers, 'Belgian miracle'.
11 These point have already been explored in Cassiers, 'Belgian miracle'; I. Cassiers, Ph. De Villé and P. Solar, 'Economic growth in post-war Belgium', in Crafts, N. and Toniolo, G. (eds.), *Economic growth in Europe since 1945* (Cambridge: Cambridge University Press, 1996).
12 For a complete description of the Central Bank's objectives in the aftermath of WWII see Cassiers and Ledent, *Politique monétaire*, chapter 3; Brion and Moreau, *La politique monétaire belge*. The objective is also explicitly explained in the 1954-annual report of the National Bank of Belgium, pp. 8–9.
13 R.Triffin, *Europe and the Money Muddle. From Bilateralism to Near-Convertibility, 1947–1956* (London: Oxford University Press, 1957). See also Eichengreen,

Reconstructing Europe and Janssens, *Le franc belge* for concrete measures concerning Belgium.

14 Cassiers, 'Belgian miracle'.

15 See for example the 1952-annual report of the National Bank of Belgium, p. 9.

16 A. Lamfalussy 'Stratégie et politique monétaires', *Reflets et Perspectives de la vie économique, Que nous est-il arrivé? Un demi siècle d'évolution de l'économie belge. Sous la direction d'Isabelle Cassiers*, Tome XXXIX, No. 1. (2000), p. 147.

17 In a general decision dated 15 July 1956 the IMF recognised that two-tier exchange markets which did not constitute an infringement of the current-account-transactions settlement system and which were only designed to facilitate the control of capital movements were not contrary to the Fund's regulations and did not even require the approval of the Fund. See P. Fabre, 'Le double marché des devises dans l'Union Economique Belgo-Luxembourgeoise', *Banque*, Paris, No. 285, May 1975, pp. 465–470, p. 469.

18 Fabre, 'Le double marché des devises', p. 466.

19 See Cassiers, De Villé and Solar, 'Economic growth', p.186: throughout the period under review the average growth rate of domestic demand was lower than the growth rate of exports.

20 I. Cassiers *et al.*, 'Les banques belges face à l'Etat: une rétrospective (1935–1993)', *Revue d'économie financière*, No. 48 (1998), pp. 125–155.

21 M. Grosfils, 'L'Efficacité de la politique monétaire. Le cas de la Belgique', *Recherches économiques de Louvain*, XXVII, No. 8, December 1961, pp. 815–839, p. 823.

22 Grosfils, 'L'efficacité de la politique monétaire'.

23 J. Finet, 'Monetary Policy in Belgium' in K. Holbik (ed.), *Monetary Policy in Twelve Industrial Countries* (Boston: Federal Reserve Bank, 1973), pp. 39–69, p. 45.

24 In 1960 the ratio of banknotes to total money stock was 58% in Belgium, 21% in the USA, 32% in Italy, 37% in the United Kingdom, 42% in France, 44% in Germany and 45% in Holland. See Commission gouvernementale pour l'étude des problèmes de financement de l'expansion économique, *Rapport* (Brussel: Banque nationale de Belgique, 1962); International Monetary Fund, *International Financial Statistics* (Washington: IMF, 1984).

25 National Bank of Belgium, *Statistiques économiques belges 1950–1960* (Brussels: Banque nationale de Belgique, 1960), p. 164.

26 For further details on this topic see Cassiers *et al.*, 'Les banques belges'.

27 Association belge des Banques (selected issues).

28 Grosfils, 'L'efficacité de la politique monétaire', p. 826; Finet, 'Monetary policy in Belgium', pp. 60–61.

29 Grosfils, 'L'efficacité de la politique monétaire', p. 827 (author's translation).

30 National Bank of Belgium, *Statistiques économiques belges 1950–1960*, p. 164.

31 Grosfils, 'L'efficacité de la politique monétaire', p. 823.

32 Finet, 'Monetary policy in Belgium', p. 58.

33 L. Morissens, 'Economic Policy in Belgium, 1949 to 1961', in *Economic Policy in our Time*, Vol. III (Amsterdam: North Holland Publishing Co., 1964), pp. 1–67, pp. 8–9.

34 For further details see Bismans, *Croissance et regulation*, pp. 433–438 and Janssens, *La Banque nationale de Belgique*, pp. 265–266: 'The fact that the law was unanimously approved by Parliament illustrates the authority enjoyed by the bank and the bank's governor in particular at that time. "Such a case of mass hallucination is quite rare," wrote an observer a few years later.'
35 Grofils, 'L'Efficacité de la politique monétaire'.
36 See in particular Secrétariat Général du Gouvernement, 'Le franc belge et le florin', *Notes et études documentaires*, No. 3747–3748, 21 décembre 1970, pp. 3–54, p. 14.
37 See Commission gouvernementale pour l'étude des problèmes de financement de l'expansion économique, *Rapport*.
38 This list is far from exhaustive. The major drivers of change also included the decision to abandon support to the coal mines, and the independence of the Congo. These two factors both triggered structural reorientations of the Belgian economy. These points have been dealt with elsewhere. In this chapter we restrict ourselves to factors which clearly affect the logic of Figure 2.
39 For further details see Cassiers, De Ville and Solar, 'Economic growth'.
40 National Bank of Belgium, *Statistiques économiques belges*.
41 National Bank of Belgium, *Statistiques économiques belges*.
42 Brion and Moreau, *La politique monétaire belge*, p. 314.
43 Grosfils, 'L'efficacité de la politique monétaire'.
44 Lamfalussy, 'Stratégie et politique monétaires', pp. 146 and 148.
45 The definitions of the balance of payments items/headings state that 'direct investment is characterised by the fact that the investors exert a certain degree of control over the management of the company in which the investment has been made' (Banque nationale de Belgique, *Statistiques économiques belges, 1970–1980*, (Brussels: Banque nationale de Belgique, 1980), vol. 1, p. 124).
46 W. Van Rijckeghem, 'Benelux', in A. Boltho (ed.), *The European Economy: Growth and Crisis* (Oxford: Clarendon Press, 1982), pp. 592–593.
47 Morissens, 'Economic policy in Belgium', p. 5.
48 Finet, 'Monetary policy in Belgium', p. 39.
49 Secrétariat général du Gouvernement, 'Le franc belge et le Florin', p. 14.
50 See G. Kurgan-Van Hentenryk, 'Propriété et contrôle des entreprises', *Reflets et Perspectives de la vie économique*, pp. 121–132; G. Kurgan-Van Hentenryk, 'The Banque nationale de Belgique and the Belgian economy during the XXth century', *Journal of European Economic History*, Special Issue: Financial systems in Europe in the XXth-Century: Factors of Crisis, Stability and Growth (2000), pp. 45–85.

Timo Myllyntaus

Unharnessing Capital: Deregulation of International Capital Movements and Finnish Monetary Policy in the 1980s

Strategy

The Finnish economy managed fairly well during the pressures of the Second World War. This success was partly attributed to a regulative economic policy. Because the governments did not hurry to liberalise the economy, Finland remained a quite regulated economy up to the 1980s. The State institutions intervened in the functioning of the market mechanism, particularly in the financial sector.[1] When the economy, and especially the external world, were changing to a greater openness and liberalisation, the successful system of the past finally became a burden.

During the postwar decades, however, Finland was not the only regulated economy. Dismantling regulation was a major goal in various western countries from 1945. Between countries, central differences consisted in the timing and pace of liberalisation. National policies can be described by three models. Gradual dismantling of currency regulation within a long timespan formed the first model, which was chosen by countries such as Denmark and Japan, who started their deregulation in the early 1970s and completed it in the mid-1980s. A rapid deregulation within only few months characterises the second model, called the 'big bang': Canada chose this model as early as 1950, and West Germany in 1958;[2] Britain followed suit in 1979 and New Zealand in 1980.[3] Late liberalisers generally chose the third model – a gradual deregulation within a medium-long period: in the 1980s Finland and Sweden gave up currency regulation over five years. Various other countries of the late deregulation wave, such as Norway and France, can also be included in this group.[4]

This chapter focuses on the Finnish case and analyses factors behind the change of financial policy and also the consequences of deregulation.

Corporatism and economic growth

Finland's geopolitical situation in the Europe of the cold war period affected its economic policy. Deliveries of war reparations, refusal to receive Marshall Aid, membership of the Pact of Friendship, Cooperation, and Mutual Assistance (FCMA),[5] and bilateral trade with the Soviet Union all complicated opportunities to liberalise foreign trade. Nevertheless, there were also internal reasons for regulating the exchange rates of currencies and movements of capital in a country where State regulation and intervention had expanded into various sectors.

Regulation fitted well with social corporatism, which is an institutional arrangement to change the economic and political framework by organising communication and negotiations between various political interest groups. In the postwar period social corporatism emerged in all Nordic countries,[6] where the government, employers' associations and trade unions were the major partners in the negotiations. These interest organisations have annually agreed on wages, salaries, taxes and the main lines of economic policy. In the Europe of the 1980s, the small EFTA countries were the most corporatist economies, and their unemployment levels were only one third of those of the rest of this continent. In aiming at high growth rates in the postwar period, small European countries have applied corporatism as an instrument to adjust their economies to external changes.[7] In contrast, big economies such as the USA have preferred market and macroeconomic instruments to solve economic difficulties. Their measures have often included protection of exports by foreign price adjustments, whereas small countries have avoided protectionist solutions and sought internal compensation.

In small European countries high dependence on foreign trade has fathered sophisticated industrial adjustment strategies and a reactive and flexible economic policy. Corporatist organisations in

Table 1: Economic Openness Index: Exports plus Imports as % of GDP, 1988–1992

Country	1988	1990	1992
Belgium	117.8	124.0	137.2
Ireland	–	–	116.0
Netherlands	88.6	92.4	100.1
Norway	50.9	57.8	79.1
Austria	53.1	57.1	77.9
Switzerland	58.2	59.4	68.5
Portugal	–	–	67.8
Denmark	49.3	51.6	66.4
Germany	47.7	50.6	59.9
Greece	–	–	56.1
Sweden	52.6	49.2	54.0
Finland	42.0	39.0	52.6
United Kingdom	40.6	42.1	48.9
France	35.8	37.1	44.9
Italy	32.2	32.3	39.6
Spain	29.6	29.1	38.0
United States	15.9	16.5	21.9
Japan	15.9	17.8	18.0

Sources: *OECD Historical Statistics 1960–1989* (Paris: 1991), pp. 138–140; *OECD Economic Survey on Austria 1993, Annex on Basic Statistics: International Comparisons* (Paris: 1993); *OECD in Figures: Statistics on the Member Countries* (Paris: 1994), pp. 24–25, 62–63; Calculated by Olli Rehn, *Corporatism*, p. 27.

small countries tend to regard free trade as a policy to which there is no alternative. Under free trade, prices of imported goods remain lower and competitiveness of exports higher than in a protectionist milieu.[8] Small European countries belong to the most active foreign traders in the world, and the openness of their economies achieves high scores on the economic openness index, shown in Table 1.

Her separation from Russia and achievement of political independence in 1917 had various economic consequences for Finland. One of them was that her range of exports narrowed: agricultural goods and the products of the wood-processing industries accounted for about 90% of exports in interwar Finland. The competitiveness of Finnish sawn wood and paper in world markets was maintained by frequent devaluations, whose advantages were undermined by subsequent high inflation. Tight currency regulation and administrated exchange rates were instruments to boost economic growth and exports. Frequent and considerable devaluations of the Finnish mark (*markka*, FIM) affected the distribution of income in favour of the export industries. Finland's special geopolitical position contributed to keep the Finnish financial market separate from the international financial markets.

Finnish economic policy led to considerable business cycles but also to rapid economic development. The 1970s were a difficult time for Finns: a steep rise of living standards was interrupted and a postwar record in the unemployment had to be faced. In contrast, the repercussions of the second oil crisis were mild and a rapid recovery began.

In the 1980s Finland experienced perhaps the longest growth period in its economic history. Business life began to globalise, the economy was booming and living standards rose remarkably: by the end of the decade: OECD statistics indicated that Finland was one of its wealthiest member countries, with only Switzerland, Luxemburg and Japan surpassing its GNP per capita. Although that claim was partly an illusion caused by the overvaluation of the Finnish currency, the prosperity of the Finns was unprecedented.

Capital movements made the internationalisation of Finnish firms much easier than earlier. Finnish investment in foreign countries increased tremendously, whereas only a few firms were interested in Finnish markets. When interest rates were rather high in the home country, especially in the 1980s, many Finnish companies and institutions took up foreign loans.

Interest groups and the Finnish financial markets

In principle the framework of the Finnish financial markets remained the same from the late 1940s to the early 1980s. In practice, however, the influence and power of various institutions changed within this period, when Finnish financial markets were quite undeveloped and the stock of exchange insignificant. Three features affected the entire economy: the level of interest rates was high, while the rate of inflation surpassed the western European average: rapid economic growth and a high rate of investment were feeding each other.

Catching up with western neighbours by further industrialisation was a major goal of the Finnish postwar governments, which together with the parliament and the central bank were the prominent actors on the financial markets. Although the Bank of Finland has formally been the 'bank of the parliament', it has enjoyed considerable influence and independence. It controlled financial markets, decided exchange rates, regulated the capital movements over the border and kept accounts of the bilateral trade with the Comecon countries.

By its operations the Bank of Finland was able to regulate the interest rate of credits in the economy and control the banking sector. In the relation to the GNP, the financial markets accounted for a much smaller proportion in Finland than in the USA or western Europe. The exceptionally central role of banks has been regarded as an idiosyncrasy of the Finnish financial markets. A very high proportion of transactions in the economy flowed through banks. The institutional structure of banks varied from local cooperative and savings banks to national commercial banks and state-owned Post Bank.[9] Although the European banking sector has in general been very centralised, Finland, with the Netherlands, was a special case, being at the top of the list within the OECD countries: Table 2 indicates that the five biggest banks possessed more than half of the total savings in eight of the fifteen countries.[10]

Table 2: The share of the five biggest banks of the total savings in some countries in 1984

Country	%	Country	%
Finland	97	Belgium	45
Netherlands	97	Spain	43
Sweden	89	Austria	36
Greece	83	Italy	36
Ireland	69	Japan	33
Australia*	64	West Germany	26
Denmark	57	United States*	13
Portugal	55		

Source: Vesa Vihriälä, 'Rahoituslaitokset rahoitusjärjestelmässä', *Suomen rahoitusmarkkinoiden kehitys 1980-luvulla*, Bank of Finland A: 78 (Helsinki: 1990), p. 95.

* Including only national claims.

At the turn of the 1970s and 1980s, managers of commercial banks began to criticise currency regulation. They claimed that its significance in economic policy had considerably decreased because of the internationalisation of the economy. Foreign trade on goods had gradually been liberalised, but the movement of capital remained regulated. Purchases of foreign companies and portfolio investments abroad ought to be liberalised, they urged, because they did not include large risks. Currency regulation was also alleged to restrict the operations of Finnish banks abroad, while these banks competed vigorously for market shares at home. The main arguments of bank managers were that regulation hampered the internationalisation of Finnish companies, jeopardised their competitiveness and paralysed the function of the market mechanism.[11]

Companies' main arguments against currency regulation were that it restricted credits and particularly worsened the position of small and medium-size companies. The system was also perceived as favouring the open sector, which could include credits in its transactions with foreign markets. In contrast the closed sector – companies working only in the home market – was excluded from cheaper foreign credits. In addition, the CUI considered the Finnish banking sector old-fashioned and inflexible, driving companies to seek financial services elsewhere. Finally, business circles considered that the liberalisation of the early 1980s was too little and too late.[12]

Although Finnish trade unions were doubtful and precautious, they were never active opponents of currency deregulation. Most of their representatives considered that Finland could not close its borders, and that in the long run regulation would endanger its competitiveness in the world market. Only the economists connected with trade unions criticised arguments presented by the opponents of regulation. From macroeconomic viewpoints, they proposed a slower and more planned deregulation of the financial market. There were also economists within the trade-union movement who claimed that a competitive export industry would boost real wages and guarantee higher employment.

The deregulation of the financial markets received its most trenchant criticism from the *Maataloustuottajien keskusliitto* (MTK), the central union of farmers and forest owners, and its economic research institute *Pellervon Taloudellinen Tutkimuskeskus* (PTT). The chief economist of the latter, Pertti Kukkonen, considered the contemporary international currency system unstable, and for him the primary goal of currency regulation should be to enable small open economies to maintain fixed exchange rates, whereas deregulation would force the abandonment of this goal. Fighting against inflation would become ever more difficult, and as a result unemployment would rise. The degree of independence in monetary policy was thus directly related to currency regulation. Kukkonen forecast that deregulation would lead to an unstable monetary market, a fluctuating exchange rate, speculation on exchange rates, expansion of credit and a marked outflow of currency reserves.[13]

For decades MTK had supported the old line of Finnish economic policy, and its members had benefited from successive devaluations. Currency regulation was used as an instrument to prevent the escape of capital before anticipated devaluation. Therefore, liberalisation endangered the cornerstones of established economic policy. In the corporatist system of postwar Finland, the political power of MTK had been great at first, but as a result of urbanisation and industrialisation it was in a clear decline. The rise of income policy in the late 1960s pushed MTK gradually aside from the centre of power, and the organisation's resistance did not prevent the liberalisation of the financial markets.

Deregulation

Afterwards – since the late 1980s – it has been asked how Finland could have continued its regulation of financial markets for forty years after World War II even though liberalisation in the other economic sectors had started much earlier and in some cases proceeded quite far. Furthermore, why had the Finnish governments stuck to this regulative policy for such a long time?[14]

This State intervention was a principal cause of Finnish financial markets remaining 'simple and undeveloped'. From the 1940s the market mechanism was replaced by administrative control, and the following instruments were the most vital and characteristic of the Finnish regulation system:[15]

1) an administrative interest-rate system composed of regulation, recommendations and agreements. The central bank had an unchallenged mastery of interest rates in the banking system.
2) regulation of capital movements to and from foreign countries. This was another activity of which the Bank of Finland took charge.
3) control of bond issues and bonds' emission rates. The State had a privileged position in the capital market because for all bond issues governmental permission was required.
4) a tax system that favoured the administrated sector of the financial markets.
5) compulsory savings schemes were set up to support the public sector and expand the statutory pension system. The funds amassed were directed by the State apparatus into selected investments.

During the regulation era those companies and households that received loans were privileged. The nominal interest rate was often reasonable, while the real, deflated interest rate was low and in the 1970s and 1980s sometimes even negative: Table 3 shows the difference of interest rates between the free market and the regulated sector. Because of the tax exemption and rising prices of flats and other real property, loans were often used for housing, which proved a good investment. Because the regulated financial system provided funding for large companies, there were strong vested interests to support the system. The general rate of investment remained high in postwar Finland, but because of the lack of real competition between various projects, investments were carried out inefficiently and conservatively.[16]

The system of financial regulation withstood the pressures of the 1970s. However, the recovery in the end of that decade stimulated the demand for credits beyond the regulated supply. The system started to leak when companies began to lend money to each other and small brokers, so called 'attic banks', emerged to transmit funds. Banks counteracted by setting up subsidiaries and investment banks to operate on market money, which returned a positive real interest rate.

Table 3: Administrative and market interest rates in Finland, 1980–1985, annual averages

	1980	1981	1982	1983	1984	1985
Free market sector	%	%	%	%	%	%
Daily interest rate (Dir)	12.4	11.5	11.6	15.4	16.5	13.4
Dir plus marg. supplements	15.1	14.8	14.3	15.8	16.5	13.4
Interest rate for FIM-futures of 3 months	13.8	12.7	13.7	14.2	15.7	13.0
Interest rate for market loans	11.2	11.6	12.8	13.9	15.6	13.2
Int. rate for debenture loans	11.6	12.0	12.2	13.1	14.0	12.7
Regulated sector						
Bank credits	9.8	9.8	9.3	9.6	10.5	10.4
State bonds	10.5	11.0	10.9	11.1	11.1	10.7
Bank deposits for 24 months	8.9	9.0	8.6	8.7	9.2	8.8

Source: Juha Tarkka, 'Kahlitun rahan aika: Suomen rahoitusmarkkinoiden säännöstelyn vuosikymmenet', in Seppo Honkapohja and Antti Suvanto (eds.), *Raha, Inflaatio ja talouspolitiikka* (Helsinki: 1988), p. 223.

Companies trading in futures could control their short-term liquidity. In 1980 the Bank of Finland withdrew from the futures market of exchangeable currencies and transferred futures contracts to currency banks to be serviced according to certain instructions. Next year it set currency quotas to banks for providing credits for imports and for transmitting Finnish bonds and debenture loans to foreigners. After that, the gradual liberalisation of financial regulation continued into the next decade.[17]

Free financial markets emerged quickly from the beginning of the 1980s. The issue of debenture loans increased, and transactions of stocks, bonds, and debenture loans at the Helsinki Stock of Exchange grew rapidly. Finnish businesspeople quickly learnt the new rules of the liberalised financial market. Capital imports quadrupled in the four-year period 1982–1986 compared to the previous four-year period, as shown in Table 4.

The sharp change in financial policy had several causes. It would be an exaggeration to claim that leakages of the old system broke financial regulation and forced the authorities to accept liberalisation. At the same time, the doctrines of policy-makers changed.

Table 4: Capital imports subject to licence in Finland, 1977–1986, Finnish marks

Type of imports	1977–1981		1982–1986	
	Billion FIM	%	Billion FIM	%
Under special licence	3.8	36	7.0	16
Under general licence	6.7	64	36.1	84
Total	10.5	100	43.1	100

Source: Jorma Hietalahti and Ahti Huomo, *Pääomaliikkeiden säätely Suomessa ja muissa OECD-maissa,* Bank of Finland A: 67 (Helsinki: 1987), p. 31.

Special licence: Companies long-term credits, direct investments, portfolio investments, transmitted credits by special financial institutions, and directed issues of shares.
General licence: currency banks' long-term credits, short-term credits related to exports or imports, temporary funding, funding of futures transactions, sales of FIM-debentures through the Helsinki Exchange Stock.

They did not cling to the past, but began to emphasise competition and the market mechanism in order to boost economic efficiency. A new slogan was that market forces knew better than government officials what were the most promising investment objects. In any case, 'grey-money' financial markets were already a reality, and the coexistence of the regulated market alongside these new markets was seen to be impossible in the long term, and speculative profits could be made by transferring funds from one market to another. Hence, the Bank of Finland and the government did not see any realistic alternative to deregulation.

One of the epochal decisions was to abandon regulation of the average interest rate in June 1986. After that market forces decided the interest rates of both savings and loans. By that time, the strict official regulations on the proportions of self-funding and bank loans in purchases of flats and estates were also repealed.

On the free markets inter-bank competition vastly increased the scale of loans to households, whose demand for mortgages had been constricted by the previous regulation: participants spoke of these years as 'the casino economy', 'dwelling roulette', and 'the consumption feast'. The prices of dwellings almost doubled as the imports of cars, motor boats, and consumption goods soared. The imbalance of commodity trade worsened, and the competitiveness of Finnish industry weakened.[18]

The deregulation of the financial market was carried out during one of the longest-ever upturns in the Finnish economy. Pouring domestic and foreign credits into a rapidly growing economy led in the late 1980s to overheating, a deficit in the balance of payments and a shortage of employment in certain sectors. Foreign capital came to Finland, but much more Finnish capital was invested abroad. The internationalisation of Finnish companies increased quickly, while on the home market dozens of mergers took place. For example, the entire wood-processing industry was reorganised between the mid-1980s and the late 1990s.[19]

Depression

In autumn 1990 the 'consumption feast' came to the end.[20] The deepest peacetime depression of the twentieth century began. It was even worse than the Great Depression of the 1930s. No other western industrialised country experienced such a severe slump in the 1990s. The rate of unemployment rose from 3.4% in 1990 to 18.4% in 1994. In 1990–1993 private consumption dropped by 11% and GNP in fixed prices decreased by 11.4%. The construction sector had to face the hardest blow. In 1989–1993 the prices of housing fell by 39.2% and private investments by 53.4%. After a three-year downturn the economy began to recover in late 1993.[21]

The early 1990s were a sharp contrast to the 1980s: in the worst year (1994) nearly half a million Finns were unemployed. Hundreds of firms went into liquidation and the whole banking sector was in crisis. The central organisation of savings banks and a part of the local savings banks network were absorbed by other banks under the government's guidance. Thousands lost their homes and tens of thousands faced repayment difficulties. Yuppies and extravagant lifestyles disappeared; flea markets, simple homemade food, and gardening became the fashion of the day. The contrast to the situation in the previous decade was unbelievable; Finland, 'the Japan of Europe', was humiliated. Only tatters of the former glorious 'success-story of Finland' were left.

Concluding remarks

The slow deregulation of the Finnish financial market derives from the continuity of the Finnish economic policy, and is partly the result of strong vested interests behind the old system and also of the strong position of the State bureaucracy in Finnish policy-making. Internal opposition carried insufficient weight and the external pressures before the 1970s were not compelling enough. The oil crisis had caused such severe problems in both Finland and Sweden that their policy-makers considered it necessary to adjust their financial markets to the rules of the outside world in order to guarantee the growth of foreign trade and development in the rest of economy.[22] In the economic debate, the liberalisation of the financial market during the boom of the 1980s was considered the main cause of the exceptional depression of the 1990s. The deregulation of a pivotal sector of the economy was carried out without any advance planning or calculation of its consequences upon the rapidly growing economy.[23] The banking crisis aroused particular anger because in the 1990s the government had supported the banking system with handsome subsidies from the taxpayers' money.[24]

The deregulation was carried out partly because of the external pressure; globalisation was taking a big step forward at the time. The internationalisation of the Finnish economy was seen to be unavoidable. Some of the cornerstones of postwar growth, such as the wood-processing industry and trade with the Soviet Union, were losing their dynamism. The falls in the prices of sawn timber, pulp and paper in the early 1990s formed another cause of the Finnish depression. The third factor was the disintegration of the socialist camp in eastern Europe. The end of bilateral trade with the USSR in December 1990 and the collapse of the Soviet Union in the following year were unexpected shocks to the Finnish economy. Trade with the big eastern neighbour had been in decline since 1986, and between 1989 and 1991 its share of Finnish exports fell from 15 to 5 per cent. Nevertheless, it has been claimed that the psychological impact of the Soviet collapse on the Finns was greater than its economic impact. The sequence of events in the east created an atmosphere of uncertainty that greatly discouraged investment throughout the Finnish economy.[25]

The harsh experience of opening their financial market to international transactions did not make the Finns loose their nerve: the crisis was attributed to bad luck and bad policy,[26] and confidence in the benefits of internationalisation and globalisation survived. In 1994 they voted to join the European Union, switched from their national currency, the *markka,* to the European *euro,* and during the ten year period 1995–2004 Finland (like Sweden, which had endured similar experiences of a recent slump and banking crisis) became one of the most globalised economies in the world.

1 Juha Tarkka, 'Kahlitun rahan aika: Suomen rahoitusmarkkinoiden säännöstelyn vuosikymmenet,' in Seppo Honkapohja and Antti Suvanto (eds.), *Raha, inflaatio ja talouspolitiikka* (Helsinki: 1988), pp. 189–250.
2 West Germany dismantled the regulation of interest rates in the banking sector in 1966. Tarkka 1998, p. 229.
3 Britain gave up quotas of bank credits in 1971, while a traditional cartel on interest rates was dispersed. The cartel had tied its interest rates to the basic rate of the Bank of England. A similar system was applied in Finland to the mid-1980s. Tarkka, 'Kahlitun rahan aika', p. 229.
4 OECD, *Exchange Control Policy* (Paris: 1993), p. 20; Ahti Huomo, 'Valuutansäännöstelyn talouspoliittinen käyttö eräissä OECD-maissa', in Jorma Hietalahti and Ahti Huomo, *Pääomaliikkeiden säätely Suomessa ja muissa OECD-maissa,* Bank of Finland A: 67, (Helsinki: 1987), pp. 40–47, 51–56, 62–64.
5 The Finno-Soviet Pact of 'Friendship, Co-operation, and Mutual Assistance' (FMCA) was signed in 1948, continued until Finland revoked it in 1991 when the Soviet Union collapsed.
6 The Nordic countries include Denmark, Finland, Iceland, Norway and Finland.
7 Andrei S. Markovits, 'Austrian Corporatism in Comparative Perspective,' *Austro-corporatism. Past, Present, Future,* in Günter Bischof and Anton Pelinka (eds.), Contemporary Austrian Studies, vol. 4 (New Brunswick: 1996), pp. 5–20; Olli Rehn, *Corporatism and Industrial Competitiveness in Small European States: Austria, Finland and Sweden, 1945–1995,* (Pori: 1996), pp. 68–75.
8 Peter J. Katzenstein, *Small States in World Markets. Industrial Policy in Europe* (New York: 1985), pp. 39–40.
9 Rehn, *Corporatism,* pp. 230–231.
10 Jaana Rantama, 'Rahoitusmarkkinoiden keskeiset muutokset', *Suomen rahoitusmarkkinoiden kehitys 1980-luvulla,* Bank of Finland A: 78 (Helsinki: 1990), pp. 15–17; Vesa Vihriälä, 'Rahoituslaitokset rahoitusjärjestelmässä', *Suomen rahoitusmarkkinoiden kehitys 1980-luvulla,* Bank of Finland A: 78 (Helsinki: 1990), pp. 57–102.

11 Antti Ilmanen, *Valuuttasäännöstely ja valuuttalainsäädäntö Suomessa vuodesta 1939 lähtien,* Master's thesis, Faculty of Law, University of Helsinki 1986, pp. 70–72.
12 Rehn, *Corporatism*, pp. 229–230.
13 Pertti Kukkonen, Kansainvälinen raha- ja valuuttajärjestelmä ja Suomen rahoitusmarkkinat, *Kansantaloudellinen aikakauskirja* vol. 82 (1986) no 1, pp. 4–11.
14 Tarkka, 'Kahlitun rahan aika', p. 190.
15 Tarkka, 'Kahlitun rahan aika', p. 190.
16 Matti Pohjola, *Tehoton pääoma: uusi näkökulma taloutemme ongelmiin* (Helsinki: 1996).
17 Rantama, *Suomen rahoitusmarkkinoiden*, pp. 53–56.
18 Jaakko Kiander and Pentti Vartia, *Suuri lama. Suomen 1990-luvun kriisi ja talouspoliittinen keskustelu*, ETLA B 143 (Helsinki 1998a), pp. 69–73.
19 Juha Näsi, Pasi Ranta and Pasi Sajasalo, *Metsäteollisuuden megamuutos. Pelinäkökulmainen analyysi suomalaisen metsäteollisuuden kehkeytymisprosesseista vuosina 1985–1996,* Jyväkylän yliopisto. Taloustieteen osasto, julkaisuja no 114 (Jyväskylä: 1998); Pertti Kukkonen, *Rahapolitiikka ja Suomen kriisi,* (Helsinki: Pellervon taloudellinen tutkimuslaitos, 1997).
20 Rolf Kullberg, *…ja niin päättyi kulutusjuhla* (Porvoo: 1996).
21 Kiander and Vartia, *Suuri lama*, p. 380.
22 Jukka Pekkarinen, 'Keynesianism and the Scandinavian Models of Economic Policy,' in Peter A. Hall (ed.), *The Political Power of Economic Ideas: Keynesianism across Nations* (Princeton, 1989), p. 323; Christina Telasuo, *Småstater under internationalisering. Valutamarknadens avreglering i Sverige och Finland på 1980-talet. En studie i institutionell omvandling* (Göteborg, 2000), pp. 250–255.
23 Kustaa Hulkko and Jorma Pöyrä, *Vakaa markka. Teot ja tarinat* (Jyväskylä: 1998), p. 462.
24 Jaakko Kiander and Pentti Vartia, 'The Great Depression and the 1990s in Finland', *Finnish Economic Papers* 9 (1996), pp. 72–88.
25 Kiander and Vartia, *Suuri lama*, pp. 185, 369; Jaakko Kiander and Pentti Vartia, 'The Depression of the 1990s in Finland: A Nordic Financial Crises or a Result of the Collapse of the Soviet Union', in Timo Myllyntaus (ed.), *Economic Crises and Restructuring in History. Experiences of Small Countries* (St. Katherinen: Scripta Mercaturae Verlag 1998b), pp. 379–396.
26 Seppo Honkapohja and Erkki Koskela, 'Finland's Depression: A Tale of Bad Luck and Bad Policies', *Economic Policy* 29 (1999), pp. 401–436.

Thomas David, André Mach and Tobias Straumann[1]

The Questioning of Selective Protectionism in Switzerland: Cartel Law Reform and Corporate Governance Changes in the 1990s

Introduction

In the mid 1980s Peter Katzenstein pointed out that small European states had succeeded in combining good economic performance with generous social policies during the post-war period.[2] To explain the roots of their success, he convincingly highlighted those features of small European states that were specifically aimed at coping with their external environment: international liberalisation, domestic subsidies and flexible adjustment to fluctuations in international markets through a democratic corporatist framework. Thus small European countries might be expected to be less vulnerable to the current trend of economic globalisation, as they had already been exposed to international competition, at least in product markets. However, in the 1990s many small European states experienced important changes in their economic and social policies, and especially in their domestic 'compensation policies'.

Switzerland, certainly one of the most internationalised economies among the small European states, is a typical case. Like other small European countries, Switzerland developed some 'compensation policies'; however, they were quite different from those of other small European states because of the dominant political coalition in power. In contrast to other countries like Sweden, Austria or the Netherlands, social policies and state interventionism remained less developed in Switzerland. Instead, various forms of selective protectionism took a central place in the development of the Swiss economy: a generous and protectionist agricultural policy, a lax anti-cartel legislation which left ample room for private self-protection, various public regulations to attenuate any over-intensive foreign competition. These policies favoured mainly the economic sectors producing for the domestic market, but other regulations also benefited the more internationalised sectors of the economy. These political arrangements and economic policies that had existed for a long time – since the 1930s, and in some cases since the late nineteenth century – were, however, called into question with increasing intensity from the end of the 1980s.

In this chapter we will present two case studies of aspects of selective protectionism which have been increasingly challenged during the 1990s: cartel legislation and corporate governance structures. The former mostly benefited domestic sectors of the economy, whereas the latter also protected the most internationalised Swiss companies against foreign takeovers. Our aim is to explain the changes that occurred in these two fields during the last decade and to show in which ways these traditional policies have been called into question. To explain these changes we will highlight both external pressures (economic globalisation and the acceleration of European integration) and domestic political demands for a new orientation in economic policies, arguing that the interaction between external pressures and the changing positions of major national actors was decisive in triggering these reforms.

Selective protectionism and globalisation

It has lately become a commonplace to observe that a new globalisation wave has changed international and national economic policies. But there is still a lot of debate on how these changes can be measured and qualified, in particular for small European countries, since the latter have always been very open to and dependent on the world economy.

Nevertheless, small European countries have been shaken by this new wave of globalisation just as much as larger countries. Even Switzerland, a country with a long tradition of open borders for goods and capital, has had to redefine some of its national economic policies. Two reasons were mentioned to explain the unexpected Swiss vulnerability in the 1990s: the loss of competitiveness of the Swiss economy during the previous decades and the fact that the Swiss economy had not been as open as was claimed by many politicians and observers. The second argument seems to fit events during the 1990s far better than the first one. In this chapter we shall show how the Swiss economy developed a certain system of selective protectionism and why the current new wave of globalisation called it into question.

Selective protectionism in Switzerland

Selective protectionism in Switzerland emerged during the late nineteenth century.[3] The long economic depression of that time favoured the institutionalisation of close links between the weak central government and the major economic associations of the day. The depression also forced the state to introduce several 'domestic compensations' in order to protect some sectors from global competition and to stabilise the domestic economy in order to sustain local development: agricultural subsidies, creation of public cantonal banks, the regional consolidation of the railways network, and the formation of the first cartels. These measures transformed the Swiss political economy in a fundamental way. Although still open to many imports and to international capital, it ceased to be liberal in a strict sense. In particular, it reinforced the dualist structure of the Swiss economy: sheltered domestic sectors and competitive sectors oriented toward international markets (textiles, mechanical engineering, watches, chemicals, banks and insurance).

Selective protectionist measures were reinforced during the first half of the twentieth century and particularly during the 1930s, which also saw the progressive integration of the Social Democratic Party and the trade unions into the decision-making process. In 1936 company law was reformed in order to protect Swiss corporations from foreign takeovers: the purpose was to ensure that large Swiss companies remained under the control of a native elite. Thus, selective protectionism not only concerned the domestic sectors of the economy, but also the sectors active on international markets.

After the Second World War the adoption of the new economic articles of the Constitution included the formal recognition of the role of organised interests in the decision-making process and the implementation of economic and social policies. This amendment also recognised the legal character of cartels and the importance of maintaining a rural population.

The gradual liberalisation of trade and capital movements after 1945 did not touch the Swiss system of selective protectionism. The main reason was World War II: Switzerland had survived the war without great damage and could easily return to normal times. The Swiss franc was one of the few freely convertible currencies at the time, and Swiss trade relations were among the most liberal in Europe. This gave Switzerland an enormous lead over the rest of Europe, which lasted until the 1980s. It always belonged to the group of countries that demanded more liberalisation of trade and capital movements. Although selective protectionism was still in place, the Swiss economy was clearly more liberal than that of most other countries.

Globalisation and the reform of Swiss economic policies

With the increasing liberalisation of trade and financial markets since the mid-1970s things started to change. Whilst other OECD countries had achieved at least partial reform of their central economic policies during the 1980s, Switzerland only started to adjust its economic policies to these new international pressures during the following decade:[4] instead of leading, she became a latecomer on the international scene, especially in Europe. The main reason for this transformation was the changed nature of globalisation: nations no longer simply agreed on a gradual liberalisation of trade and capital, but had created new powerful institutions and had included economic sectors that had been omitted from earlier negotiations. At the same time, new communications and transport technologies enabled a dramatic reduction in transaction costs and accelerated the liberalisation of financial markets. A good yardstick for the new nature of global capitalism is the increase of portfolio investment: in the 1970s net portfolio inflows and outflows were about half as large as foreign direct investment across the OECD, whereas by the 1990s they were 2.5 times as large.[5]

As a result, managers of multinational corporations and the diplomats of the Office of Foreign Economic Affairs (OFEA) increasingly called selective protectionism into question. Under the intensifying international competition subsequent upon technological changes and markets liberalisation, these managers became increasingly impatient with Swiss domestic economic policies and demanded radical measures to lower the costs of industrial production. They started to question the special treatment of the domestic sectors and the agreements between labour and capital. The diplomats of the OFEA were confronted with the fact that the new initiatives at GATT and European levels included economic sectors that had been protected for a long time: for example, the GATT negotiations included the agricultural tariffs of member states. And the aim of the Single European Act, launched in 1985, was to abolish most regulations designed to protect domestic firms against their foreign competitors.

In the late 1980s most Swiss politicians began to realise that a new era had begun. The unexpected dynamics of the negotiations forced them to rethink the traditional system of selective protectionism. In January 1989 Jacques Delors, the President of the European Commission, explained that the cooperation between the European Community and the European Free Trade Association (EFTA), of which Switzerland was a member, was supposed to become closer. The negotiations were concluded in October 1991, with the adoption of the European Economic Area Treaty,[6] and in 1994 the GATT negotiations achieved a similarly smooth resolution. These new international pressures were reinforced domestically by a systematic campaign organised by managers of multinational corporations, neo-liberal economists and some leading right-wing politicians. It created the general perception that radical change was needed if the country wished to maintain the high levels of prosperity it had known in the past.

This general perception was reinforced by the recession of the early 1990s, when Switzerland experienced a steep increase of its unemployment rate – from below 1% to more than 5%. In comparative perspective this was still a small percentage, but in the Swiss context such unemployment had been unheard of since the depression of the 1930s. In the political debate these developments were interpreted as a symptom of the declining competitiveness of Swiss firms.

Paradoxically, the rejection by a slim margin of the European Economic Area Treaty in December 1992 led the Swiss authorities to act as if Switzerland had in fact joined the EEA. Switzerland began in 1993 to realise a so-called autonomous adjustment ('autonomer Nachvollzug') to EC laws. The government, now under even greater pressure from managers of multinational companies, launched an 'economic revitalisation programme' that was intended to liberalise and deregulate the Swiss economy. Its success was not overwhelming, but it did achieve a series of economic–policy reforms that had been unthinkable for decades: a readjustment of the agricultural policy (in line with the Uruguay Round of the GATT), a reform of the cartel law, a new law on the internal market, the introduction of value added tax (VAT), the liberalisation of the telecommunications market and the partial privatisation of the state-owned post and telecommunications company.[7]

Cartel law reform in the 1990s

One of the major components of the economic revitalisation programme launched by the government in 1993 just after the rejection of the EEA Treaty was the reform of the cartel law, which was adopted in 1995 and clearly inspired by EU rules. This reform can be considered as a turning point in the field of the regulation of domestic markets and stands in sharp contrast with the then-prevalent tradition: it was described by some competition law specialists as a 'paradigm change' or an 'economic purification' of the Swiss competition law.

Figure 1: Number of Cartels by their year of creation (per decade)

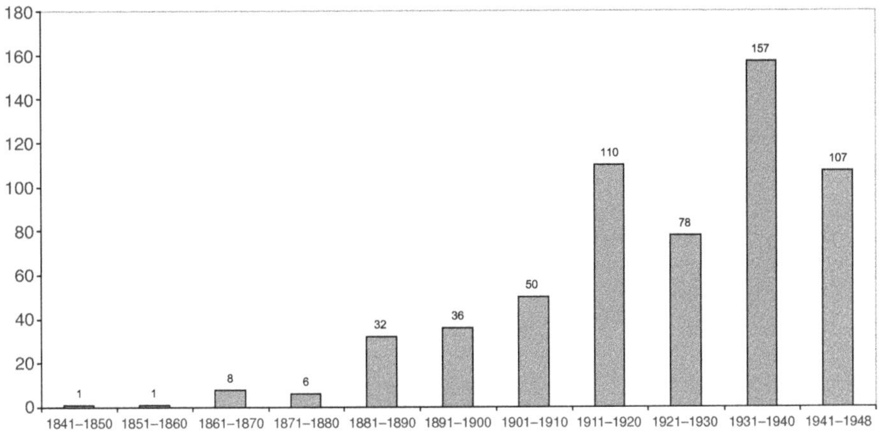

Source: Commission fédérale des prix 1957: 47ff.

Permissive cartel law as a mechanism of self-protection for domestic industries

Historically, the early organisation of economic interests during the second half of the nineteenth century went hand in hand with the formation of cartels between private companies. The first cartels were created during the world depression at the end of the nineteenth century, at the same time as the introduction of protectionist measures for different economic sectors. After the end of the world depression, cartels were even more tolerated and consolidated as a result of certain decisions of the Swiss federal court.[8] As Figure 1 shows, the timing of the creation of cartels was particularly important during wars and economic crises: this was especially true for the domestic sectors of the economy, but much less so for the export-oriented sectors.[9]

After the Second World War and the adoption of the new economic articles of the Constitution, cartels were officially recognised and tolerated; only their 'economically and socially harmful effects' were to be fought. It then took 15 years to adopt a cartel law to implement the general principles of the Constitution. This law, adopted in 1962, gave only minor investigative powers to the Cartel Commission, which was composed of representatives of the major economic associations and of law specialists appointed by the government. This kind of 'militia institution', partly private and partly public, is very common in Switzerland.[10]

Organised economic interests were very reluctant to transfer too much power to a public authority responsible for promoting competition in domestic markets; and, as Rentsch emphasises,

> the resulting anti-cartel legislation can be viewed as a trade-off: domestic industries and trades did not get the expected amount of government protection against international liberalisation; in exchange, they got a mild anti-cartel legislation that left ample room for self-protection.[11]

In this perspective, the weak Swiss cartel legislation can be considered as a form of selective protectionism for those economic sectors mainly producing for the domestic markets.

After the Second World War Swiss competition policy remained very weak and permissive towards anti-competitive private practices, as pointed out by Schröter:

> the Swiss were called 'the unmatched world champions of cartels'.[12] Switzerland proved to be the country least touched by the change of economic theory. In this sense, after the Second World War, Germany handed over its function of acting as a prototype of cooperative Capitalism to Switzerland.[13]

At the beginning of the 1970s a first reform of the law was addressed: this attempt took 15 years, and the initial draft proposal, which aimed to strengthen the cartel law, was successfully fought by the Small Business Association (USAM) and the Federation of Commerce and Industry (USCI), the two major business associations. The new law adopted in 1985 remained ambiguous and very tolerant toward anti-competitive practices, and at the beginning of the 1990s Switzerland was still considered a cartels' paradise.[14]

The 1995 reform of the cartel law

To understand the rapid changes in policy content and economic practice during the 1990s we have to take into account the profound changes at international level, especially the acceleration of

European economic integration and the negotiations on the EEA Treaty, which involved Switzerland directly. The Swiss authorities steadily pursued a bilateral and pragmatic foreign economic policy which allowed them to preserve the political particularities of Switzerland (neutrality, direct democracy and federalism), but also to promote the expansion of the export-oriented sectors and to tolerate diverse forms of selective protectionism for domestic sectors. This pragmatic strategy of economic integration 'without political participation' was increasingly questioned with the emergence of such issues as the EEA Treaty and the Uruguay round of the GATT.[15] These international changes profoundly affected the perceptions and the positions of some central actors in the Swiss political and business communities.

Since the adoption of the Single European Act in the mid-1980s which reinforced the integration of European markets, European competition policy under the direction of neo-liberal commissioners (Peter Sutherland 1985–1989 and then Leon Brittan 1989–1993) became one of the most efficient instruments for the promotion of competition and the liberalisation of European markets. Because of its direct applicability, the European competition policy became one of the most supranational policies of the EU: 'Competition policy is thus the most direct example of the industrial policy of the 1970s being replaced by a neo-liberal free market policy in the 1990s.'[16] In addition, all member states began to change their national competition law in line with the European regulations, even though there was no formal requirement to do so.[17]

Despite Switzerland not being a EU member, several Swiss companies active on European markets had already been sanctioned during the 1970s and 1980s by the European Commission because of the external application of the European competition rules, and were thus directly affected by EU competition policy. During their negotiations on the EEA Treaty, the Swiss negotiators tried to exclude the European competition rules or to include only a part of them; but Switzerland had to accept that the EEA Treaty would include the complete European competition legislation. Even though this would not have required a reform of the national cartel law because of the direct applicability of the EU rules, the adoption by Switzerland of the EEA Treaty would have threatened the position of Swiss national cartels,[18] and would have allowed the European commission to conduct its investigations in Switzerland with the cooperation of the Swiss authorities.[19]

In addition to the changes at European level, the increasing liberalisation of economic exchanges and the effects of the economic recession of 1991–1994 destabilised some national cartels, which had more and more difficulty in preserving their internal discipline. Furthermore, because of increasing international competitive pressure, the export-oriented sectors of the economy put more pressure on their domestic subcontracting partners to reduce their costs. Moreover, the strength of the Swiss franc during the 1990s also induced some companies to prefer foreign subcontracting possibilities instead of local ones.[20] In this context of increasing international pressure (economic and institutional) and because of the changing attitude of some members of the business community, several famous cartels were dismantled at the beginning of the 1990s (banks, insurance companies, concrete, cigarettes, beer) and a new attitude towards competition policy emerged among the Swiss political and business elites.

This changing behaviour of some Swiss major economic actors is reflected in several publications by representatives of the most internationalised economic sectors,[21] but also in studies by Swiss economists[22] and by the OFEA.[23] These publications for the first time openly criticised the negative economic impact on Swiss domestic markets of the lack of competition. One of their major conclusions was that the liberalisation of domestic markets would considerably improve the competitiveness of the Swiss economy, leading them to propose a radical revision of Swiss competition policy. In addition we must remark that under the partially revised cartel law of 1985 the practice of the Cartel Commission became more severe against cartels and clearly adopted a more critical attitude toward them.

After the rejection of the EEA Treaty in 1992, the complete reform of the cartel law became one of the central propositions of the governmental reform programme. The political process which led to this reform is illustrative of the changing coalitions between the different economic actors. Whereas all representatives of the business community (USAM and USCI) had been strongly opposed to a reinforcement of the cartel law during the 1980s, a new coalition appeared at the beginning of the following decade which advocated the complete reform of the cartel law. We can distinguish three leading actors behind this reform: an informal group of representatives from the most internationalised export-oriented sectors, some neoliberal economists and the OFEA.

The first actors consisted of an informal grouping around Fritz Leutwiler, former CEO of ABB, and David de Pury, new CEO of ABB. This group did not feel sufficiently represented by the traditional business associations and openly criticised the various 'compensation policies' benefiting mostly the domestic sectors of the Swiss economy (the agricultural policy, the cartel policy and the foreign-worker policy). They asked for radical changes in various economic policies. In 1992 the Department of Economic Affairs appointed an informal experts' committee, chaired by David de Pury, to define the major orientation of the government's future economic policies. The 'de Pury report' proposed to change the Constitution by introducing a means of dismantling cartels; this option was eventually abandoned because of the lengthy legislative process it entailed and the possibility of tightening the law without resorting to constitutional reform.

Some economists also played a central role in the inspiration and the promotion of the government's economic revitalisation programme. Two economists, Heinz Hauser from the university of St. Gallen, who had already been involved in the preparation of the first 'white paper' of the business representatives, and Silvio Borner from the university of Basel were both members of the 'de Pury committee'. In several publications, they repeatedly underlined the necessity to liberalise Swiss domestic markets and to strengthen anti-cartel legislation.

The third central actor was the OFEA, which was directly involved in the decision-making process through its vice-director's presidency of the experts' committee on the reform of the cartel law. In its reports on Swiss foreign economic policy at the beginning of the 1990s the OFEA had severely criticised the lack of competition in the domestic markets and pleaded for more competition there. The traditional business associations (USAM and USCI) were excluded from the committee, which was entirely composed of competition-law specialists; this exclusion would have been completely unthinkable a few years before. The cartel commission, even though it was closely associated with the reform process, did not play a central role in the elaboration of the initial draft proposal or in the decision-making process. Internally divided between the business representatives and the law specialists, the cartel commission gave up its leading role to the experts' committee for the elaboration of the new law.

All the major issues on the content of the new cartel law had already been negotiated in the so-called pre-parliamentary phase. Parliament played only a minor role in the reform process and merely gave its general approval to a text that had been drafted by the experts' committee and subsequently refined by government: a coalition between economists and representatives from the most internationalised sectors of the economy and from the OFEA was the driving force behind the reform. The Left and the trade unions were in favour of the reform, but did not play an important role in the decision-making process.

The reform of the cartel law faced strong opposition from the USAM and by a large part of the USCI, where it gained the support of export-oriented members (machine and chemical industries especially) but the determined opposition of those producing for the domestic market. The political representatives of these sectors tried to change the orientation of the reform in Parliament, but were outvoted by a large majority. At first the USAM announced they would fight the reform by demanding a referendum, but eventually abandoned this because of their political marginalization.[24] In 2002 Parliament adopted a new partial reform of the cartel law, which further strengthened the power of the Competition Commission.

Although the new law does not forbid cartels,[25] it provides clearer guidelines and decision competencies to the new Competition Commission to combat anti-competitive practices in domestic markets. It also gives decision competencies to the new Competition Commission; a much clearer and more severe approach to cartels and the abuse of dominant position is introduced, as well as a merger-control mechanism. Rigid cartels on prices, quantity and geographical area are considered harmful and hence forbidden. Beside that, the number of employees in the secretariat of the Commission has increased from 10 to around 50 since the adoption of the new law.

The new law can be described as a Europeanisation of Swiss competition regulations.

Transformations of Swiss corporate governance[26]

It is common to distinguish two types of corporate governance: the Anglo-American model and the Continental European one. The first displays three characteristics: large and liquid capital markets, an important role played by powerful institutional investors and an active market for corporate control where outside shareholders can dislodge poorly performing managements. The continental European model is a network-oriented system where large corporate groupings (banks, insurance and industrial companies) are intertwined in a structure of cross-shareholding and have generated relative managerial autonomy from financial interests. The management is thus more able to resist the claims and interests of the company stakeholders. Since the end of the 1980s, due to the liberalisation of financial markets and their growing importance, some authors claim that a converging trend is under way in which the continental European model is undergoing a radical transformation and beginning to look like the Anglo-Saxon model.[27]

As we shall see below, Switzerland, with its high degree of ownership concentration and cross-shareholding, clearly belongs to the continental European model. In addition, Switzerland has also introduced several mechanisms which enable national companies to protect themselves against foreign takeovers. These provisions have been increasingly called into question over the past fifteen years.

The Swiss model of corporate governance

Despite its high degree of internationalisation, which goes back to the nineteenth century,[28] the Swiss economy has maintained a strongly nationalistic flavour: power of decision, equity dominance and tenure of key posts were kept in the hands of Swiss nationals. Major firms were even able to introduce selective protectionist mechanisms to shield themselves against foreign takeovers.[29] Two central elements were at the heart of this policy and characterised the Swiss corporate-governance model: first, the concentration of ownership, and second, the close relations between banks and industry.

The first feature of Swiss corporate governance is the concentration of corporate ownership amongst a small number of persons (see Table 1 below). According to Windolf and Nollert, only Germany had a higher degree of ownership concentration:[30] the economic wealth of the country is thus also concentrated among a small number of persons. The concentration of ownership is closely related to the importance of individual/family ownership. Schröter already mentioned this point when describing multinational companies of small European countries at the eve of the First World War.[31] These characteristics persist today: many large Swiss companies are still dominated by a single shareholder or by a small group of shareholders. At the beginning of the 1990s the proportion of large firms controlled by families or individuals in Switzerland was much higher than in other developed countries (Table 1).

Table 1: Ownership concentration and Types of owners in the early 1990s

Proportion of stock owned (%)	SWI	NL	GER	FR	UK	US
0–4.9	17.8	23.7	9.5	37.3	48.6	95.0
5–9.9	17.6	30.0	7.8	14.2	31.0	3.5
10–24.9	17.9	9.6	17.8	15.1	10.5	1.4
25–49.9	15.6	10.1	13.9	9.4	2.6	0.1
50–74.9	8.0	6.8	12.9	8.1	2.4	–
More	23.1	19.7	38.1	15.8	4.9	–
Types of owners						
Individual/Families	31.1	8.3	18.9	18.0	10.1	1.8
N = 100%	614	603	821	1224	1859	5925

Source: Windolf and Nollert, Institutionen, Interessen, Netzwerke, pp. 64–65.

This concentration is strengthened by the exclusion of other groups from the decision-making processes. Minority shareholders have few rights; their position comparing badly with that enjoyed under other jurisdictions such as the US or the UK.[32] In addition, there is no mechanism of codetermination in Switzerland that allows employees to exert some direct influence over the allocation of corporate resources.[33]

Second, the close ties between international banks and industry in Switzerland make its corporate governance system look more like the German than the Anglo-Saxon model. In the early 1990s banks in the UK and the US held less than 1% of the shares of quoted firms, against 4.7% in Switzerland and 10% in Germany.[34] Swiss and German corporate governance structures share another characteristic: the system of proxy voting which allows banks to cast votes for other shareholders. Private shareholders authorise the banks that hold their shares to represent their interests at the companies' annual general meetings.

Finally, the interrelation between big banks and industries is strengthened by the role of the former in company financing.[35] In Switzerland between 1973 and 1990 bank loans were an important source of finance for most Swiss corporations, even if self-financing remained the main source of capital: the contribution of internal funds to the financing of industrial companies is around 50%, bank loans account for around one third and corporate bond issues represent 15%.[36] Thus, Swiss management has often been able to arrange external financing through private transactions with banks and other lenders without recourse to the capital market, thus circumventing the pressure of capital markets on management performance.

These close relationships between banks and industry explain the fact that bank representatives can be found on the boards of most important companies. Network analyses expose the high density of interlocking directorates and cross-holdings in Switzerland, which is due partly to the small size of the country. Representatives of the banks sit on the boards of non-financial companies, and conversely industrial firms appoint representatives onto the boards of banks.[37] This tight network implies a high degree of autonomy and self-regulation in the corporate sector, which in turn facilitates long-term cooperation and control over the markets.

The concentration of ownership, and more generally the high degree of cohesion of the business community, combined with the early buoyancy of the economy, favoured the adoption of selective protectionist measures over the control of national companies. The regulation called '*Vinkulierung*' constitutes the main instrument of this policy of selective protectionism. This term is codified in Swiss company law; it was first introduced at the end of the nineteenth century and subsequently reinforced in 1936.[38] It refers to limitations on the transferability of Swiss registered shares. Swiss company law recognises three categories of participation paper: bearer shares, registered shares and dividend-right certificates:

> Registered shares differ from bearer shares mainly in the way they are transferred from seller to purchaser. As far as the company is concerned, it recognises as shareholders only those whose names are registered in the stock ledger [...] The company has the right to restrict or refuse entry in the stock ledger on a great variety of grounds. Registered shares whose transfer is restricted in this way are said to have been "vinkuliert".[39]

For a long time, registered stocks were only held by (domestic) investors accepted by the management. Foreign investors could only trade freely in the bearer shares. Both possessed voting rights (generally one vote per share). However, the par value of registered stock is never higher but often lower than the bearer stock. More votes can be thus controlled with the same capital by buying registered stock rather than bearer stock. This kind of voting-rights distortion was very common among Swiss companies. Loderer and Jacobs in a study of 42 firms conclude that registered shares control a mean of 71% of all votes and claim an absolute majority in more than 75% of the firms, while making up only 48% of the market value of equity.[40]

The practice of *Vinkulierung* helped to reinforce and stabilise the concentration of ownership. This system allows a small ownership group – often members of a single family – to retain control of the firm and the right to determine its strategy even when they have floated the company on the market in order to attract public funding.[41] Monks and Minow summarise these features as follows:

> Swiss corporate governance has traditionally been characterised by management's acutely conservative attitude towards investors. Switzerland has often been dubbed 'the fortress of the Alps' by the international financial community.[42]

The destabilisation of the 'Fortress of the Alps'

The increasing liberalisation of product and financial markets during the last twenty years has effected a profound change in the external environment with which Switzerland has to deal. This recent trend of market liberalisation was triggered on the one hand by the strategies of multinational companies that expanded abroad and on the other by the decisions of national political authorities to suppress barriers to trade and capital flows. These two dynamics are tightly intertwined.[43] In addition, with the liberalisation of markets the financial sector has gained an increasing importance. This change has favoured the emergence of new actors (investment funds, for example) within the financial sector, who imposed new constraints on large Swiss companies by developing aggressive strategies to increase the return on equity of their portfolio investments. Moreover, it has also impelled 'traditional actors' (notably banks) to change their preferences and strategies. This internationalisation of capital markets and the increasing influence of investors who demanded financial liquidity, shareholder protection and accounting transparency, has imposed increasing pressure on Swiss corporate governance and threatened the defensive mechanisms designed to separate capital contribution from control.

The pressure exercised by the growth of foreign direct investment (FDI) and portfolio investment is combined with the increasing importance of the Anglo-Saxon financial centres. However, this evolution is mediated by regional (economic objectives within the European community) and domestic factors.[44] It is thus important to focus on three developments: the rise of the Anglo-Saxon financial centres and their impact on Swiss multinationals; the changing strategies of domestic actors; and regulatory changes during the 1990s.

1. The Swiss economy has been deeply involved in the recent trend of economic globalisation. Since the end of the Bretton Woods system the foreign expansion of Swiss multinationals has been facilitated by the devaluation of the dollar and the appreciation of the Swiss franc. This further internationalisation of Swiss industry was not without implications for the Swiss corporate governance system at the national level, as can be shown by the example of Nestlé.

In 1988 Nestlé was the first Swiss company to lift the embargo against foreign buyers of its registered stock. One of the reasons put forward by the board was the company's international image: Nestlé's takeover practices abroad during the 1980s had been somewhat controversial: Nestlé had expanded abroad through the acquisition of foreign companies, while shielding itself from unwanted suitors. In 1988, for fear of reprisals in other countries, Nestlé took the decision to open itself to foreign investors.[45] However (and more important than the public image), the extension of the foreign activities of multinational companies in the 1980s meant that Nestlé needed to increase its equity in order to finance its own development, which implied raising more equity abroad and thus opening itself to foreign shareholders.[46]

The requirements imposed by the London Stock Exchange (the SEAQ International), where 15% of the trading activity in Swiss blue-chip stocks takes place, also played a role in changing the practices of Swiss multinational companies. The distinction between bearer shares and registered shares as well as the ownership restriction with respect to registered shares were indeed important obstacles that prevented Swiss shares from becoming traded abroad to any degree.[47] Thus, in order to be listed on foreign stock exchanges (London or New York) large Swiss multinationals had to abandon some of their restrictions against foreign investors and introduce more transparency in their corporate practices. In 1993 Nestlé simplified its capital structure by introducing a share reunification which was subsequently followed by other large Swiss firms. 'International pressure for reciprocity' fostered among some of the largest export-oriented Swiss companies an alignment with Anglo-Saxon investment criteria that stressed greater transparency and the simplification of the capital structure.

2. At the domestic level, the emergence of new actors such as investment funds or new 'raiders' willing to increase the valuation of Swiss companies also contributed to modify Swiss corporate behaviour. One of the consequences of the institutionalisation of the *Vinkulierung* process had been the substantial price difference between bearer and registered shares. Thus, between January 1985 and September 1987 the price ratio between these two types of shares for

19 of the most important Swiss companies was 1.71 to 1.[48] This difference implied that the market capitalisation of Swiss firms was very often undervalued in comparison to their assets. Swiss companies being protected against foreign takeovers, the first attacks upon the traditional functioning of Swiss corporate governance came from some Swiss investors attracted by their undervaluation. Since the beginning of the 1980s there were repeated attempts by Swiss 'raiders' to take over famous industries: Werner K. Rey and Bally; Karl Schweri and Usego-Trimerco Holding AG; Tettamanti and Sulzer; and more recently Ebner and the UBS.[49] This last episode deserves our attention. During the first half of the 1990s BK Vision, an investment bank created by Martin Ebner in the mid-1980s, accumulated a significant block of shares in UBS, one of the three big banks in Switzerland at that time, in order to gain some degree of effective control over it. BK Vision – whose aims are, according to its corporate charter, to create value for its shareholders by buying and managing investment portfolios – would thus be in a position to influence UBS management decisions. In September 1994 the UBS board proposed a share reunification plan in order to prevent a control change. This plan was narrowly accepted after a fierce battle. The UBS proxy fight is a landmark in Swiss corporate-governance history:

> Hostile takeovers were essentially unheard of, and criticism of management by shareholders was highly unusual and thoroughly unappreciated. Mr. Ebner's activities have had the merit of stimulating public debate about shareholders' rights and shareholder activism. Also, they have contributed to making shareholder value a politically correct goal for firms to pursue and made it more acceptable for shareholders to criticize management.[50]

Due to the increasing competition on the financial markets, the major Swiss banks have redefined share ownership as an asset-management and investment business. These large institutions have been very active in attempting to promote an 'equity culture' or a 'shareholder value ideology' in Switzerland; and after fierce debates and some famous cases of mismanagement, the business community increasingly accepts its principles.[51] This ideology, which stresses the primacy of shareholders' interests, implies an important change in the traditional model of corporate governance in Switzerland. The activism of institutional investors and their insistence on transparency over strategy, performance and the company's financial situation together with the definition of a core set of markets offering above-average growth potential was relatively unknown in Switzerland.

During the 1970s and 80s the conservative attitude of the Swiss companies towards minority and foreign shareholders was also made possible by the passivity of Swiss pension funds. As in the US and the UK, but unlike Germany, France or Italy, the second tier of the Swiss pension system is based on a private capitalisation system. This means that Swiss pension funds manage a huge amount of capital investments, which in 1998 exceeded the Swiss GDP. However, one of the features of these funds has been the over-representation of interest-rate-linked assets (bonds in particular).[52] Moreover, until the 1990s pension interests had been usually represented by a bank or some other third party rather than by a direct and active shareholder presence at shareholders' meetings. There have been some changes recently. One of the first measures was to introduce (in 1995) the option of penalty-free transfers from one pension fund to another, which has forced these establishments to adopt a more profit-oriented management. Effectively, pension funds have increased the proportion of stocks in their portfolio from 3.3% in 1978 to 6.8% in 1987 and 10.4% in 1991; in 1996 it was around 16%.[53]

3. During the last decade several regulatory reforms were adopted in Switzerland in the areas of financial markets and corporate governance. Although they did not constitute a quantum shift in the national regulatory framework and were themselves the upshot of compromises between the principal actors, these new regulations did impose some changes in traditional corporate-governance mechanisms. The reform of company law (1992) and the new law on Stock Exchange and Securities Trading (1995) both demanded more transparency in disclosure rules and accounting presentation.[54]

The pressures for these reforms came from the admitted need to assimilate the Swiss national rules to European norms (or at least to reduce the differences: see Experts' Report 1993 on the future prospects for company law), and were demanded by representatives of the largest and most internationalised companies which had already, on a voluntary basis, largely adapted their practices to the requirements of the international financial community. These reforms were thus a reflection of the changing international environment but also introduced new rules which directly affected the functioning of Swiss domestic companies.

Transformations of Swiss corporate governance mechanisms

The transformation of the international environment (liberalisation of financial markets and the new rules established at European Union level) and the increasing importance of actors from the financial sector (investment funds, the changing role of banks) have affected the traditional functioning of Swiss corporate governance, as noted by *The Economist*: 'A lot of the old complaints about the Swiss way of running companies are losing force.'[55]

First, the 'process of *Vinkulierung*' tends to disappear. The decision of Nestlé to allow foreigners to hold registered stock in 1988 was followed by other important companies. There is also an increasing pressure on quoted companies to introduce a 'single share'. In 1989 only 13.1% of the companies listed at the Zurich Swiss Exchange had a 'single share': by twelve years later this proportion had reached 70.7% (out of 198 companies, see Figure 2).

However, this does not mean the end of family ownership and the victory of the shareholders. There are still other measures which allow Swiss corporations to control the evolution of their shareholding structure: they may fix ceilings for voting rights at shareholders' meetings or introduce a percentage limit for each individual shareholding.[56]

The deregulation of financial markets, the increasing power of institutional investors, the relaxing of the *Vinkulierung* process and the priority given to the equity market largely explain a second feature of these last twenty years: the increasing number of mergers and acquisitions (see Figure 3).[57] Three elements should be stressed. First, not surprisingly, the proportion of foreign firms acquiring Swiss firms almost doubled between 1983 and 1999. Some flagships of Swiss industry changed owners.[58] Second, the sharp increase in mergers and acquisitions included huge mergers between some of the largest Swiss multinationals who were threatened by potential foreign acquisition: Ciba and Sandoz into Novartis, UBS with SBS,

Figure 2: Proportion of Swiss quoted companies with a 'single share', 1989–2001 (in %)

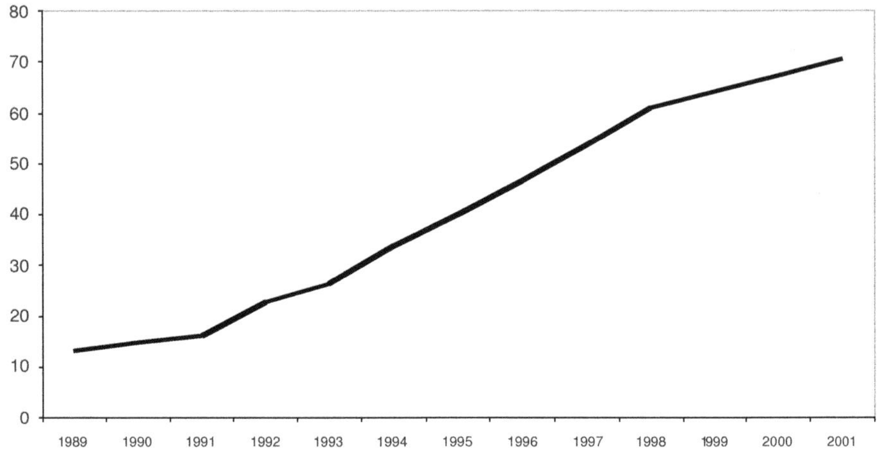

Sources: R.M. Kunz, *Shareholder Value durch Financial Engineering. Stimmrechte, Einheitsaktien und Aktiensplit* (Bern: Haupt, 1998) and R.M. Kunz, 'Simplification of Equity Capital Structure and Market Value', *Financial Markets and Portfolio Management* 16/1 (2002), 30–52.

Figure 3: Mergers and acquisitions in Switzerland, 1980–1999 (1980 = 100)

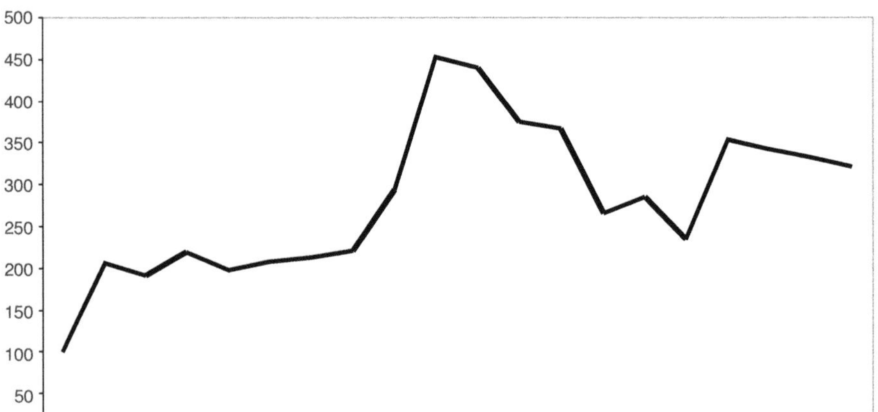

Source: *Schweizerische Handelszeitung* 2000.

Note: This publication is based on inquiries and estimates and is not wholly reliable.

Crédit Suisse with Winthertur insurance. A third significant element is the foreign expansion of Swiss multinational companies through mergers and acquisitions. In 1983 the proportion of these activities to total Swiss mergers was only 13%, but by 1999 it had risen to 36%.

Third, numerous restructurings of important industrial companies also took place: these were generally motivated by a desire to concentrate on core activities and abandon less profitable segments. This was the case for ABB, Sulzer and Algroup, some of the largest Swiss industrial firms. In the chemical and pharmaceutical sector too, the largest companies (Novartis and Roche) outsourced their chemical specialities by the creation of Ciba CS and Clariant. These changes were completely consonant with the pursuit of shareholder value.

Fourth, one of the leitmotivs of the proponents of the shareholder-value ideology has been the professionalisation and downsizing of boards. This has been a clear tendency with large companies, where it has been accompanied by the recruitment of new board members through a more formal selection process instead of according to the dictates of group representation and personal relations, as was formerly the case.[59] This has resulted in a sharp decrease in the density of the company network between 1990 and 2000 but has not achieved its removal.[60]

Conclusions

For Swiss economic policies the 1990s were a decade of political and institutional innovation unequalled since the Second World War. The initial pressures came from abroad: the structural change in the global economy and the emergence of new multilateral institutions (WTO, EU) forced Swiss managers and policymakers during the last decade of the twentieth century to rethink some traditional politico-economic arrangements, especially what we have termed the selective-protectionist regulations.

The innovations of the 1990s were more than simple incremental reforms. They changed basic mechanisms of Swiss economic policies, provoking much opposition from those who were on the losers' side. Changes in the international environment (economic and institutional) affected the political preferences of economic actors and deepened the cleavages between the different economic sectors. It favoured the most internationalised exports sectors rather than the less flexible concerns producing for the domestic markets. This holds true for the various reforms aimed at domestic-market liberalisation and at the strengthening of competition policy, but also for fiscal policy (introduction of VAT, the reduction of stamp duties on financial transactions and the reform of business taxation, which all mainly favoured the export-oriented and financial sectors). However, in the field of corporate governance, large Swiss companies were also destabilised by the increasing involvement and influence of national and foreign institutional investors. We can point to a trend toward a more market-driven corporate-governance system which calls into question traditional characteristics of Swiss corporate governance: ownership concentration, cross-shareholding and the protectionist mechanisms of the traditional managers.

Nevertheless, due to the political resistance of the potential losers and the inertia of extant institutions, these changes did not achieve radical innovations. Although the new cartel law of 1995 strengthened the competition authority and introduced more severe regulations against anticompetitive practices, the significant role played by the latter will be largely unimpaired for the foreseeable future. The same is true for the evolution of corporate-governance structures: even though the new economic environment and legal framework opened up many Swiss firms to foreign investors, the two major pillars of the Swiss model of corporate governance (tight networks between companies and the relative autonomy of the management toward the shareholders, as expressed through the importance of concentrated ownership) are still largely valid.

1 Parts of this paper were presented at conferences in Zurich, Lausanne and Gothenburg. We would like to thank Peter Solar, Margrit Müller, Harm Schröter, Ola Grytten, Lars Svensson, Isabelle Cassiers, Willem Hulsink, Magnus Henrekson, Andrew Gamble, Hanspeter Kriesi, Guido Pult and Joakim Reiter for helpful comments. We also would like to thank Frederick Kermisch for research assistance.

This research was partly funded by a grant of the Swiss National Foundation (Grant No 1214-068112.02/1).

2 P. Katzenstein, *Small States in World Markets: Industrial Policy in Europe* (Ithaca and London: Cornell University Press, 1985).

3 And even during the first part of the nineteenth century. See U. Menzel, *Auswege aus der Abhängigkeit. Die entwicklungspolitische Aktualität Europas* (Frankfurt am Main: Suhrkamp, 1988), who has emphasised that the adoption of selective protectionist economic policies through state interventions (*selective-dissociative* in his terms) during the first phase of industrialisation favoured an economic development in Switzerland that was less dependent on the initial export sectors.

4 G. Bonoli and A. Mach, 'Switzerland: Adjustment Politics within Institutional Constraints', in F. Scharpf and V. Schmidt (eds.), *Welfare and Work in the Open Economy. Diverse Responses to Common Challenges*, Vol. II (Oxford: Oxford University Press, 2000), pp. 131–173.

5 B. Simmons, 'The Internationalization of Capital', in H. Kitschelt *et al.* (eds.), *Continuity and Change in Contemporary Capitalism* (Cambridge: Cambridge University Press, 1999), pp. 36–69.

6 The EEA Treaty implied the adoption of 60% of EU regulations by the EFTA countries.

7 For more details see A. Mach (ed.), *Globalisation, néo-libéralisme et politiques publiques dans la Suisse des années 1990* (Zurich: Seismo, 1999).

8 E. Gruner, 'Die Handels- und Gewerbefreiheit und die Staatsordnung von 1874–1914', *Wirtschaft und Recht* (1960), pp. 149–155.

9 However, large Swiss companies were frequently involved in international cartels. On this issue see H. Schröter, 'Cartelization and Decartelization in Europe, 1870–1995: Rise and Decline of an Economic Institution', *Journal of European Economic History* 25 (1996), pp. 129–153; H. Schröter, 'Small European Nations: Cooperative Capitalism in the Twentieth Century', in A. Chandler *et al.* (eds.), *Big Business and the Wealth of Nations* (Cambridge: Cambridge University Press, 1999), pp. 176–204.

10 On this law see F. Rebmann, *Une Economie autogérée sans intervention de l'Etat? Le rôle et la position du Vorort dans le processus de législation sur les cartels (1950–1962)* (Lausanne: Mémoire de licence, Université de Lausanne, 2006).

11 H. Rentsch, *Cartels and Wealth: A Paradox in the Swiss Economic System* (Zug: FSW Forschungsinstitut für Wirtschafts- und Sozialpolitik, 1989).

12 Schröter, 'Cartelization', p. 149.

13 See also B. Hotz, *Politik zwischen Staat und Wirtschaft* (Diessenhofen: Rüegger, 1979); P. Tercier, 'Du droit des cartels au droit de la concurrence', *Zeitschrift für Schweizerisches Recht* 112 (1993), pp. 399–418.

14 OECD, *Economic Survey: Switzerland* (Paris: OECD, 1992).

15 J. Tanner, 'Die Schweiz und Europa im 20. Jahrhundert: wirtschaftliche Integration ohne politische Partizipation', in P. Bairoch and M. Körner (eds.), *La Suisse dans l'économie mondiale* (Genève: Droz, 1990), pp. 409–428.

16 S. Wilks, 'Regulatory Compliance and Capitalist Diversity in Europe', *Journal of European Public Policy* 3 (1996), 545. See also L. Mac Gowan and S. Wilks, 'The

First Supranational Policy in the European Union: Competition Policy', *European Journal of Political Research* 28 (1995), pp. 141–169.

17 On this issue see H. Dumez and A. Jeunemaître, 'The Convergence of Competition Policies in Europe: Internal Dynamics and External Imposition', in S. Berger and R. Dore (eds.), *National Diversity and Global Capitalism* (Ithaca: Cornell University Press, 1996), pp. 216–239.

18 The European commission had already sanctioned purely national cartels, because they were deemed to 'affect trade between member states' as stipulated in the articles 85 and 86 of the Rome Treaty (new articles 81 and 82).

19 For more details see M. Baldi, 'Bemerkungen zum EWR-Wettbewerbsrecht aus grundsätzlicher Sicht', in O. Jacot-Guillarmod (ed.), *Accord EEE. Commentaires et réflexions* (Zurich: Schulthess, 1992), pp. 285–300; A. Mach, *La Suisse entre internationalisation et changements politiques internes: législation sur les cartels et relations industrielles dans les années 1990* (Zurich: Rüegger, 2006).

20 See the chapter on Switzerland in OECD, *Globalisation and Small and Medium Enterprises* (Paris: OECD, 1997).

21 F. Leutwiler and S. Schmidheiny (eds.), *La Politique économique de la Suisse face à la concurrence internationale. Programme pour un ordre plus libéral* (Zurich: Orell Füssli, 1991); Groupe de Travail Informel (Commission 'de Pury'), *Rapport final du groupe de travail informel 'Ordnungspolitik'* (Bern: Federal Department of Economic Affairs, 1992); D. de Pury *et al.*, *Ayons le courage d'un nouveau départ. Un programme pour la relance de la politique économique de la Suisse* (Zurich: Orell Füssli, 1996).

22 S. Borner *et al.*, *Schweiz AG. Vom Sonderfall zum Sanierungsfall?* (Zurich: Verlag Neue Zürcher Zeitung, 1990); H. Hauser and S. Bradke, *Traité sur l'EEE, Adhésion à la CE, Course en solitaire: Conséquences économiques pour la Suisse* (Chur: Rüegger, 1992).

23 Report on the foreign economic policy (Berne: Federal Department of Economic Affairs, 1991).

24 For more details see Mach, *La Suisse*.

25 The change from an 'abuse principle regime' to an 'interdiction regime' similar to the EU would have required a constitutional amendment and a compulsory popular referendum, and would have taken many years more.

26 An extended version of this section can be found in T. David and A. Mach, 'The Specificity of Corporate Governance in Small States: Institutionalisation and Questioning of Ownership Restrictions in Switzerland and Sweden', in R. Aguilera and M. Federowicz (eds.), *Corporate Governance in a Changing Economic and Political Environment. Trajectories of Institutional Change on the European Continent* (London: Palgrave, 2004), pp. 220–246.

27 F. Morin, 'A Transformation in the French Model of Shareholding and Management', *Economy and Society* 29 (2000), pp. 36–53. For a critique see M. O'Sullivan, *Change and Continuity in the French System of Corporate Governance* (Conference Paper: European Project: Corporate Governance, Innovation and Economic Performance in the EU (CGEP), 2001).

28 Bairoch and Körner, *La Suisse*.

29 See David and Mach, 'Specificity'.
30 P. Windolf and M. Nollert, 'Institutionen, Interessen, Netzwerke: Unternehmensverflechtung im internationalen Vergleich', *Politische Vierteljahresschrift* 42 (2001), pp. 51–78. On Germany see U. Jürgens *et al.*, 'Shareholder Value in an Adverse Environment: the German Case', *Economy and Society* 29 (2001), pp. 54–79.
31 H. G. Schröter, *Aufstieg der Kleinen. Multinational Unternehmen aus fünf kleinen Staaten vor 1914* (Berlin: Dunker & Humblot, 1993).
32 F. R. Ehrat, 'Switzerland', in M. W. Stecher (ed.), *Protection of Minority Shareholders* (The Hague: Kluwer Law International, 1997), pp. 223–239.
33 In 1976 the 'Mitbestimmung' popular initiative of the trade unions which proposed a system of codetermination was refused by the Swiss citizens in a popular vote.
34 U. Birchler, 'Aktionärsstruktur und Unternehmenspolitik – Bedeutung für die Sicherheit des Bankensystems', *Quartalsheft der Schweizerischen Nationalbank* 13 (1995), 266.
35 Big banks (Credit Suisse and UBS) and state-owned cantonal banks are the main lenders to firms, with a combined market share of over 75%. See G. Hertig, 'Lenders as a Force in Corporate Governance. Criteria and Practical Examples for Switzerland', in K. J. Hopt *et al.* (eds.), *Comparative Corporate Governance. The State of the Art and Emerging Research* (Oxford: Clarendon Press, 1998), pp. 809–835.
36 Birchler, 'Aktionärsstruktur', 269.
37 P. Rusterholz, 'The Banks in the Centre: Integration in Decentralized Switzerland', in F. Stokman *et al.* (eds.), *Networks of Corporate Power* (Oxford: Polity Press, 1985), pp. 131–147; M. Nollert, 'Interlocking Directorates in Switzerland: a Network Analysis', *Revue suisse de sociologie* 24 (1998), pp. 31–58; M. Nollert, *Unternehmensverflechtungen in Westeuropa. Nationale und transnationale Netzwerke von Unternehmen, Aufsichtsräten und Managern* (Münster: Lit Verlag, 2005); G. Schnyder *et al.*, *The Rise and Decline of the Swiss Company Network during the 20th Century* (Travaux de science politique No. 22, Institut d'Etudes Politiques et Internationales, Université de Lausanne, 2005a).
38 For more details see H. Kläy, *Die Vinkulierung. Theorie und Praxis im neuen Aktienrecht* (Basel: Helbing & Lichtenhahn, 1997); M. Lüpold, *Schutz vor wirtschaftlicher Überfremdung oder Abwehr unfreundlicher Übernahmen? Die Vinkulierung von Namenaktien in der Praxis der Unternehmen und die Veränderungen des rechtlichen Rahmens (1929–1961)* (Zürich: Lizenziatsarbeit Universität Zurich, 2004); G. Schnyder *et al.*, 'The Clash of Paradigms: Switzerland's Long March towards a Shareholder–Oriented Conception of the Firm', in Dusan Isakov *et al.* (éds.), *Le Gouvernement d'entreprise en Suisse. Dynamiques externes et stratégies internes* (Zurich: Schultess, 2005b), pp. 41–68.
39 H. Kaufmann and B. Kunz, *Shareholder Restrictions in Switzerland* (Zurich: Bank Julius Baer, 1991), p. 5.
40 C. Loderer and A. Jacobs, 'The Nestlé Crash', *Journal of Financial Economics* 37 (1995), pp. 315–339. Swiss companies are not the only ones to use this mechanism that allows shareholders to control a firm while holding only a small fraction of its equity. See R. La Porta *et al.*, 'Corporate Ownership Around the World', *Journal of Finance* 54 (1999), pp. 471–517; L. A. Bebchuk, 'Stock Pyramids, Cross-owner-

ship and Dual Class Equity. The Mechanisms and Agency Costs of Separating Control from Cash-flow Rights', in R. Morck (ed.), *Concentrated Corporate Ownership* (Chicago: University of Chicago Press, 2000), pp. 295–314.
41 M. Anderson and T. Hertig, 'Institutional Investors in Switzerland', in T. Baums *et al.* (eds.). *Institutional Investors and Corporate Governance* (Berlin and New York: Gruyter, 1994), pp. 489–529.
42 R. A. G. Monks and N. Minow, *Corporate Governance* (Cambridge and Oxford: Blackwell, 1995), p. 320.
43 Simmons, 'Internationalization of Capital'.
44 For a general argument see T. H. Block 1998, *Financial Market Liberalization and the Changing Character of Corporate Governance*, Center for Economic Policy Analysis, Working Paper Series III.3 (1998).
45 Loderer and Jacobs, 'The Nestlé Crash', pp. 320–322.
46 Anderson and Hertig, 'Institutional Investors'.
47 T. Helbling, 'The Effects of Foreign Competition on Stock Markets: SEAQ International vs. Switzerland', in N. Blattner *et al.* (eds.), *Banking in Switzerland* (Heidelberg: Physica-Verlag, 1993), pp. 216–217.
48 R. Stulz and W. Wasserfallen, 'Foreign Equity Investment Restrictions, Capital Flight, and Shareholder Wealth Maximization: Theory and Evidence', *Review of Financial Studies* 8 (1995), pp. 1019–1057 (see table 2).
49 Kläy, *Vinkulierung*, pp. 32–34.
50 C. Loderer and P. Zgraggen, 'When Shareholders Choose not to Maximize Value: the Union Bank of Switzerland's 1994 Proxy Fight', *Journal of Applied Corporate Finance* 12 (1999), 101.
51 See for example NZZ, *Shareholder Value* (Zurich: Verlag Neue Zürcher Zeitung, 1996) and NZZ, *Corporate Governance. Kompetenz, Kontrolle und Verantwortung in den Unternehmen* (Zurich: Verlag Neue Zürcher Zeitung, 2001). More generally see W. Lazonick and M. O'Sullivan, 'Maximizing Shareholder Value: a New Ideology for Corporate Governance', *Economy and Society* 29 (2000), pp. 13–35.
52 Anderson and Hertig, 'Institutional Investors', pp. 503–504.
53 Office Fédéral de la Statistique (OFS), *La Prévoyance professionnelle en Suisse. Statistiques des caisses de pensions 1998* (Neuchâtel: Office Fédéral de la Statistique, 2000), p. 49.
54 For more details see P. Forstmoser *et al., Schweizerisches Aktienrecht* (Bern: Stämpfli, 1996); Schnyder *et al.*, 'Clash of Paradigms'.
55 *The Economist*, October 13, 2001, p. 69.
56 Anderson and Hertig, 'Institutional Investors'.
57 Figure 3, which takes into account the number and not the value of the mergers and acquisitions, undervalues the importance of the phenomenon in the 1990s. See Handelszeitung, *Wer übernahm wen? Fusionen und Beteiligungen 2000* (Zurich: Handelszeitung, 2000): UNCTAD, *World Investment Report 2000: Cross-Border Mergers and Acquisitions and Development* (Geneva: UNCTAD, 2000).
58 For several examples see Handelszeitung, *Wer übernahm wen?*, pp. 5 f.
59 P. Böckli, 'Corporate Governance: The "Cadbury Report" and the Swiss Board Concept of 1991', *Revue suisse du droit des affaires* 4 (1996), pp. 149–163.
60 Nollert, *Unternehmensverflechtungen*; Schnyder *et al.*, 'Clash of Paradigms'.

Kersti Ullenhag

Globalisation, Management Education and Management Practice: The Case of the IFL, Sweden[1]

Introduction[2]

In the late nineteenth century Swedish companies began to move abroad. A century later, at the threshold of the new millennium, Sweden had one of the world's most globalised economies. Multinational corporations had turned global primarily in the last decades of the twentieth century. Industrial corporations increased their investments abroad and had in the late decades of the twentieth century been followed by retail chains: IKEA sold furniture and Hennes & Mauritz clothes across the globe.

Deregulation of Swedish capital markets in the 1980s facilitated international capital movements. Swedish investments abroad grew rapidly. Massive Swedish investment abroad was in the 1990s followed by a flow of foreign investments into Swedish economy. Thirty-nine per cent of the market value on the Stockholm stock exchange was in foreign hands early in the year 2000.[3] Mergers crossing the Swedish border had been frequent. Anne Wibble, who represented the Liberals in parliament and had been minister of finance from 1991 to 1994, commented on the new situation in the spring of 1995: 'In the 1970s we were convinced that everything was possible to attain by economic policy. Since then we have learnt this is not the case.'[4] To her, it was obvious that the deregulation of Swedish capital markets and the strategies adopted by Swedish multinationals had decisively changed the prerequisites of Swedish economic policy. Swedish multinationals had taken the lead in Swedish globalisation, and the options for national economic policy were reduced. Kåre Willoch, a prominent leader of the Conservatives in

Norway and Norwegian prime minister from 1981 to 1986, has in his memoirs (1990) expressed a similar conclusion on the shifting scope for national economic policy. He found that the big oil corporation Statoil had become 'a State in the State'.

From this perspective an understanding of the process of globalisation calls for studies of big corporations and their management strategies. By the end of the millennium management practice in the global business world had become more and more uniform and Americanised. Thus, the development of a homogenous management practice went hand in hand with the process of globalisation. Multinational corporations served as worldwide channels for management ideas. Managers tended to 'follow their leader' in big business. Management education, consultants and media helped them.[5]

Aim and scope

The aim of this chapter is to study management education in the process of globalisation. It is inspired by the view that management education may have a crucial influence on business performance. It has been argued that 'Many visitors were persuaded that American management success' in the decades following World War II 'depended on the thriving system of academic business education. [...] So convinced, they launched the business studies movement in Europe.'[6] The positive relationship between university-linked management education and economic development was – as noted above – taken for granted when American business prospered during the decades after World War Two. Robert R. Locke has emphasized that management education was viewed as a powerful force behind American business expansion.[7] On his scenario Europe followed suit and imported the American model of management education. From another point of view, however trends in modern management practice have been attributed to Japanese management practice, sometimes labelled Toyotism.[8]

This chapter will report upon my examination of the Swedish Institute of Management (Institutet för företagsledning, IFL), founded in Stockholm in 1968 by men in trade and business and the leading institute of management education in Sweden for decades to follow. Before the end of the millennium more than 30 000 leaders had participated in the IFL programmes.[9] Management education given by IFL has already been the topic for research in studies written by Åke Jerkedahl, Dag Björkegren and Jörgen Sandberg.

Åke Jerkedal in the early 1960s evaluated a programme that was to be integrated into the new Institute. He analysed the change in attitudes resulting from the training. It turned out that the outcome was open to different interpretations. Initial attitudes and degrees of motivation seemed to be of crucial importance.[10]

Dag Björkegren – in his doctoral dissertation – analysed IFL top management courses in relation to 'governing values', 'acting', 'learning climate', and 'learning and professional relevance'. Björkegren was disappointed with what he found. He was not impressed by the academic approach. According to him participants in need of improved social competence were instead given technical information of little practical value.[11]

'Management construction' and management practice are the topics of an essay by Jörgen Sandberg. He compares a case study on 'management construction' in programmes launched by the IFL with the 'dominating construction of management' as presented in scientific literature on management performance in the Western market economy. He concludes by questioning the 'capitalistic system' as such as a context for a desirable management education.[12]

Focus in the following is on the IFL's relation to Swedish industry, its linkage to international surroundings and the content of education launched by the IFL. To what extent has globalisation in the last decades of the twentieth century meant an Americanisation of Swedish management education, and to what extent is management education adapted to local surroundings? Is it possible to argue that management education in Sweden leads to the development of management practice and management strategies adapted to national surroundings, or do managers in Swedish corporations just follow their international leaders?

I have not been able to find anyone else who has looked into European management education from this point of view, which means that I have not had the opportunity to make comparisons with educational programmes established by other European countries. Nevertheless, I do think that the Swedish case I have chosen has something to say about the role of management education in general. Further, the global setting in which the IFL operated indicates that the development was not unique.

This chapter contains two parts and a summary. The first part focuses on the organization of the IFL and the structure of clients and programmes on international markets. The second discusses the content of the IFL top-management education and its relation to Swedish industry and American management education. The summary deals with the IFL, the clients and the content of education in a global context, in other words the IFL management education in globalisation.

Structure and markets

An international background

In the 1960s the course of international events meant that public debate in Sweden shifted to the Left. The spirit of the times was formed by protests against the American war in Vietnam, by liberation movements in Africa and by an admiration for Communist China. Students in particular pursued left-wing arguments. Students and workers were supposed to join in a struggle against capitalist society. Socialist views dominated Swedish media.

To the business community the left-wing critique was unexpected. Men in trade and business needed a new way to defend their position. The establishment of the IFL in 1968 was one expression of their reaction. The immediate cause for this establishment was to be found in a new economic programme launched by the ruling Social Democrats: Social Democrats and labour-union members were to undertake ideological training, and Swedish university education was to be restructured. The traditional form of degrees based on freely chosen courses was to be replaced by structured programmes adapted to 'the needs' of society. Departments of Business Administration were introduced into the universities. The continuing role of the private schools of economics and business administration was questioned. Thus, the existence of the Stockholm School of Economics was threatened. This school had been founded in 1909 as the first business school in the Nordic countries.[13] Behind its establishment lay a group of leading male industrialists headed by vice managing director (in 1911 managing director) of Stockholms Enskilda Bank, Marcus Wallenberg.[14] In the late 1960s his son Marcus Wallenberg Jr left his position as managing director of this family bank to become chairman of its board. To the left-wing movement he and the Wallenberg bank became the symbol of imperialism and capitalistic society. He himself and the bank were abused in the media and in demonstrations.[15] To strengthen the position of businessmen and to 'save the Stockholm School of Economics', Marcus Wallenberg initiated the establishment of the IFL.[16]

Courses in management education were at the time offered by Svenska Arbetsgivareföreningen (SAF, the Swedish Employers' Federation), Svenska Civilekonomföreningens Institut för Vidareutbildning (SCIV, the Institute for Further Education owned by the Swedish Association for Graduate Business Administrators) and by Teknologföreningen (the Swedish Association of Graduate Engineers). A six-week Executive Programme given by SAF was one of the first European courses launched for in-service management.[17]

Wallenberg felt that residential courses given by SAF and SCIV ought to form the basis of a new organization. The idea was to reshape and strengthen advanced management education on a national level. In 1967 Wallenberg engaged Per-Jonas Eliœson to lay the groundwork for a new institute: since 1963 Eliœson had been head and director of studies at SCIV, but he was still a young man of thirty-two when Wallenberg approached him. He had gained his Licentiate of Economics in 1966, had been teaching at the Stockholm School of Economics and also had links with the Institute for Economic Research (Ekonomiska Forskningsinstitutet, EFI).[18]

Negotiations and structure in 1969

The creation of a new institute presupposed negotiations for support from various sources. Folke Haldén, director of management education of the SAF, was unwilling, as were the faculty at the Stockholm School of Economics. The former wanted to keep his own courses and the latter contemplated starting advanced management programmes of their own. From the Federation of Swedish Industries, however, Eliæson received a positive reaction. Tryggve Holm and Curt-Steffan Giesecke, president and managing director respectively of the Federation – after discussions at the Wallenberg Bank – persuaded the SAF to join the project. Thus, the launching of a new institute for advanced management education was made public just before midsummer 1968.

In the following autumn the composition of the first board of directors was a delicate matter for Eliœson. It was decided that all members of the board had to be 'agents of progress' and be no more than forty-five years old. The SAF, the SCIV, the Swedish Federation of Industries and the faculty members of the Stockholm School of Economics all wanted to have influence on the new institute. To these demands was added a special requirement from the Social Democratic government. Marcus Wallenberg had – following the Swedish tradition of negotiation – discussed the foundation of a new institute for advanced management education with prime minister Tage Erlander, minister of finance Gunnar Sträng and minister of education Olof Palme. They had declared that the Social Democratic government would accept the establishment of the new institute if the board included two public-sector representatives.

The negotiations were successful. Ragnar Söderberg, the leading figure in the Söderberg group, a family group that had diversified holdings in Swedish industry, provided important support. Ragnar Söderberg was a board member of a number of large Swedish firms and was in the beginning of the 1970s vice-chairman of the Stockholms Enskilda Bank. He had been married to a member of the Wallenberg family.[19] The Swedish Institute of Management was established as a foundation on 13 November 1968.[20]

Its founders were Handelshögskoleföreningen (the Stockholm School of Economics Association), the SAF, Sveriges Industriförbund (the Federation of Swedish Industries) and the SCIV. These four founders each had to provide 200000 Swedish crowns and were allowed to appoint five trustees each to get the Institute started. These twenty trustees were to appoint board members and accountants and to supervise the board's activities. The trustees held their first meeting on 26 November 1968, when Ragnar Söderberg was elected chairman of the board. He was also appointed to convene and chair further trustee meetings until 1972.

The men representing the trustees at the initial meeting held leading positions in their organizations. They were Marcus Wallenberg (the Stockholm School of Economics Association); Curt-Steffan Giesecke and Folke Haldén (the SAF); the managing director of the Federation of Swedish Industries Axel Iveroth; Per Lindberg, who held the chair of the SCIV; and Per-Jonas Eliæson.[21] Among the elected trustees were Marcus Wallenberg, Tryggve Holm and Ingmar Eidem, who was elected chair of the Federation of Swedish Industries in 1969, and Claes A. Palmers, who held the chair of Svenska Civilekonomföreninge (the Swedish Association of Graduate Business Administrators).[22]

The trustees appointed nine board members: Per Lindberg, managing director of ASEA; Sten Gustafsson, managing director of Incentive AB; Per G. Gyllenhammar, vice managing director of Skandiakoncernen: Björn Rosén, managing director of AGA AB; Karl-Axel Linderoth, administrative director of the Swedish Cooperative Wholesale Society; Ivar Löfqvist, director general of the Swedish Agency for Administrative Development; and Hans Nordmark, administrative director of LKAB.[23]

Four of the board members – including the elected chairman Per Lindberg – thus came from the private sector; one represented the cooperative movement, two the public sector; and two were engaged in management education in the SAF and the SCIV: these were Folke Haldén, director of management education of the SAF, and Per-Jonas Eliæson from the SCIV. There had been no room for the faculty of the Stockholm School of Economics, and so to give them a platform in the IFL a development council was formed. In planning the IFL activities, the board, according to the IFL bylaws, had to confer with this council chosen 'primarily' from 'academic teachers experienced in training executives'.[24] The board had a strong foothold in Swedish industry, and opened up links with the State and to the cooperative sector. Thus the composition of the first board of the IFL illustrated 'the Swedish model' of mutual understanding; it meant that the IFL was to serve the private, state and cooperative sectors.

In the centre of the IFL network was its promoter Marcus Wallenberg. He was in the 1960s looked upon as the leading representative of Swedish trade and industry, not only in Sweden but also outside the country. In the late 1960s the Wallenberg bank group was in a class by itself in the Swedish economy. The group had 181 000 employees and the Wallenberg family exerted a strong influence in Swedish multinationals; in ASEA, Electrolux, Ericsson, SAAB, Alfa Laval and Atlas Copco. It has been calculated that twenty-three per cent of the Swedish industrial workforce were employed within the Wallenberg group in 1969.[25] Marcus Wallenberg himself – the foremost representative of the group – had traditionally had good relations with the labour unions and with members of the Social Democratic government, not least with the minister of finance, Gunnar Sträng. His commitments were not only Swedish but also international. During the years 1960–1963 he was chairman of the Council of the European Industrial Federation; in 1962 he participated in the establishment of the Business Advisory Committee to the OECD and served as its first chairman until 1964. In 1965 he was appointed for a three-year period to be president of the International Chamber of Commerce (ICC).[26]

Marcus Wallenberg's influence in the shaping of the IFL is underlined by the composition of the board. Two of the four IFL board members representing private industry were taken from within the Wallenberg industrial sphere: the chairman of the board Per Lindberg (managing director of ASEA) and Sten Gustafsson (managing director of Incentive AB, a development company).

When on 1 January 1969 the residential courses in advanced management education that had previously been offered by the SAF and the SCIV were transferred into the IFL, the SCIV was dissolved. Its mother organization the Swedish Association for Graduate Business Administrators substituted as a trustee for the SCIV.[27] During the first year of the IFL's activities the formal linkage to professional economists was complemented by a linkage to professional engineers: the Swedish Association of Graduate Engineers was formally invited to be a fifth trustee of the IFL. Inspired by a wish to combine technology and economics in management education, this association had since 1956 provided courses of its own. In September 1969, however, the Association of Engineers accepted an invitation to join the IFL. The association was to elect five trustees and supply 200 000 Swedish crowns.[28]

The IFL took on the shape of a network organization. The aim of the organization according to the by-laws established in November 1968 was to'pursue and promote the education of staff in leading positions and to carry on activities attaching thereto. To this end, the foundation may also support scholarly research suited to the advancement of such education. It is to be a non-profit organization.'[29]

The staff of the IFL was limited. At the end of the first year, the institute had ten employees headed by Per-Jonas Eliæson, who had been appointed director. Four had full-time positions, while six were employed half-time. Five of them worked on programme development.[30]

It is obvious that IFL's management-education operation had at the time of its establishment a strong foothold in Swedish society. Leading male industrialists who could offer a client market for advanced management education, not least in Swedish multinationals, supported the establishment. There were links with the public and the co-operative sectors. Teachers at the Stockholm School of Economics wanted to participate in the teaching. It is also obvious that the IFL was connected to international markets, not only by way of Swedish multinationals but also by way of personal networks.

International cooperation 1969–2000

The initial shape of the IFL proved durable: the trustee structure of the first year was still in place at the turn of the millennium, and the institute remained a network organization with a small staff. Per-Jonas Eliæson continued as director of the IFL for more than two decades until 1993. During the years 1970–1986 he combined this position with that of head of the Stockholm School of Economics.[31] As time went by the premises of the IFL were adapted to expanding activities. The first office was located at Saltmätargatan 26. The Stockholm School of Economics had provided accommodation for the IFL.[32] The office stayed in the centre of Stockholm, but in 1982 the IFL could inaugurate Kämpasten – premises of its own adapted to residential courses – in Sigtuna north of Stockholm.

The IFL established a formal connection with international management education right from the start. The trustees transferred their memberships of the European Association of Management Training Centres (EAMTC) and the International University Contact (IUC) to the IFL. In 1971 those organizations merged into the European Foundation for Management Development (EFMD) in Brussels. In the following year the Swedish membership in the International Council for Scientific Management (CIOS) was transferred to the IFL. The CIOS was formed by members from three regions: Europe, the US and Latin America.[33] Three decades later in the 1990s the IFL was represented on the EFMD board, as so often before. During this decade the IFL had research connections within the European Institute for Advanced Studies in Management (EIASM) and the Institute for Management of Innovation and Technology (IMIT).[34]

Markets 1969–2000

The IFL followed its clients into international markets, offering courses that answered their needs. In 1978 the IFL and the Stockholm School of Economics formed a partnership with ten large Swedish multinationals totalling some 556000 employees – AGA, ASEA, Atlas Copco, LM Ericsson, Euroc, Saab-Scania, Sandvik, Tetra Pak International, Unilever and Fläkt – and launched an international programme, Training for International Operations (TIO). This programme was initiated because of the rapid growth of international business. It was said that 'The prospect of waking up one morning and finding that established business procedures can no longer cope with demands is a particularly frightening one for export-dependent Sweden.'[35]

Experienced managers in parent companies and subsidiaries from within the partnership participated in IFL seminars at Kämpasten for a period of six weeks. Only a third of the participants in each TIO programme were allowed to be of Swedish nationality. The course language was English. By 1984 no less than some 300 managers from 47 countries had participated in the TIO programme, which created an international network of exchange embracing the involved companies. The programme was still running in the 1990s, but its schedule had been reduced from six to five weeks.[36]

There were also smaller internal corporate courses running at Kämpasten directed at managers working in subsidiaries in many parts of the world, but also – starting in 1984 – training courses in international management for Chinese managers in Beijing. These programmes were to establish contacts between Swedish managers in China and their Chinese counterparts.[37] Programmes in China were financed for a decade by the Wallenberg group and the SIDA.[38]

Cooperation between the IFL and the State brought about another broad international IFL course, the Applied International Management Programme (AIM). This six-week programme that was launched in 1982 and was still running in the 1990s was financed by Swedish government grants channelled through the Swedish International Development Authority (SIDA). The course was directed towards managers from the developing countries. Participants were recruited from Africa, Asia and Latin America. They represented management in private, cooperative and State-owned firms as well as in government offices and national organizations. Scandinavian managers with a special interest in developing countries were also invited to participate. The course was given at Kämpasten and involved fieldwork in Nordic corporations; contacts with Swedish companies were an integral part of the programme, and the course language was English. In the 1990s some twenty countries were usually represented in each programme.[39]

In the 1990s the time had come to establish a training centre in Brussels. In 1986 half of the production of Swedish corporations abroad was to be found within EC, and in the following years Swedish investments in Europe grew heavily. Uncertainty about Sweden's future relation to the Common Market stimulated investments in Europe.[40] When the industrial interest in Europe grew, the IFL followed suit. In the late 1980s the IFL offered seminars in international management in Brussels. The seminars were primarily directed towards Swedish corporations. At the same time, parts of Swedish-based courses were given in Brussels and devoted to the development of the EC and its relation to Swedish trade and industry.[41] In 1991 the IFL opened up a training centre of its own in Brussels at Passage du Nord, located in an old wing of Hotel Metropol in the neighbourhood of the Grand Place. Here you will also find the IFL Brussels office.[42] The aim of the Brussels operation has been 'to offer Swedish management a broad international insight and an increased understanding of European integration, as well as Sweden's role in it.'[43]

The IFL in Brussels offered courses directed at companies, organizations and the public sector.[44] Programmes running at Kämpasten in many cases had a week located in Brussels. After the fall of the Berlin Wall, Russia had become a new market, and programmes were organized in cooperation with the Kaliningrad International Business School and the Management Institute of Karelia: these courses were run in Kaliningrad and Karelia, and included the search for commercial partners in Scandinavia.[45] Other development programmes were by the end of the millennium located far away from Sweden – in the US, China, Japan, South America and Africa.[46]

A global market

At the end of the millennium the IFL was part of an international network of management-education institutions, and the IFL programmes were running within a globalised market. Clients were European, American, Asian and African. The IFL activities had a Swedish framework, however: clients were followed abroad. Swedish multinationals had offered a client market for IFL programmes within their subsidiaries all around the world, and Swedish government grants had opened up a market in developing countries. The globalisation of the Swedish economy brought about the globalisation of the IFL.

The framework constituted by Swedish multinationals was not the same as it had been, however. The deregulation of Swedish capital markets and new institutional investors – in the last decades of the millennium – meant greatly increased activity on the Stockholm stock exchange and a new focus on share capital value. Through mergers and acquisitions Swedish multinationals were transformed into corporations 'related to Sweden'. The dominant position held by the Wallenberg family disappeared. The family bank, Stockholms Enskilda Bank, merged with a considerably bigger bank, Skandinaviska Banken, in 1971, and Skandinaviska Enskilda Banken (SEB) was established. Marcus Wallenberg – the initiator of the IFL – died in 1982 and the family lost some of its influence.[47]

Investor, an investment company, now controlled the Wallenberg industrial group. In order to retain control of important corporations, the Wallenberg family had to concentrate its ownership. In 1971 there were thirty different companies in the Wallenberg portfolio in which it held long-term ownership. At the threshold of the 1990s the figure had been reduced to thirteen. ASEA, who provided the IFL with its first chairman of the board – Per Lindberg, the managing director of this multinational – was still amongst those.[48] ASEA was no longer the same, though. In 1988 ASEA and Brown Bovery in Switzerland merged into Asea Brown Bovery (ABB). At the turn of the millennium the company's headquarters had moved from Västerås in Sweden to Zürich in Switzerland.[49]

In February 2001 plans for a new merger within the Wallenberg financial sector were presented. The SEB and Föreningssparbanken (the Swedish United Savings Banks) were to join forces and merge into SEB Swedebank, hopefully in the autumn of 2001. The new bank was to follow industry abroad. The plans were to have eleven million clients served by 35 000 employees, of which no more than 19000 would be employees in Sweden. Slightly more than ten per cent of the share capital was to be in the hands of the Wallenberg group, the largest shareholder: it was said that national frontiers had fallen down. The new bank was to be a European financial corporation based in Sweden.[50] This merger did not come about, however.

Thus, at the turn of the millennium the IFL market within Swedish private industry and in the Wallenberg industrial group was not what is used to be. Not only had Swedish industry become globalised and its structure transformed, but the field of Swedish management education had changed as well. The IFL faced new competition in an expanding trade on a global market. New centres of management education had been established. Most important, within the same field as the IFL was Executive Education, a wholly-owned subsidiary of the Stockholm School of Economics. This subsidiary was established in the 1980s, and by the turn of the millennium had a strong position around the Baltic. In 2004 the IFL and Executive Education united to meet new challenges on international markets for management education. The new unit was integrated into the Stockholm School of Economics but kept the name of the IFL.[51]

Content of education

An American background

University-linked management education in the US had its roots in the war administration. Courses in military leadership instituted by the American administration during the war were transformed at Harvard into courses in advanced management. Thus, management education in the US turned towards scholars. A university-linked management education expanded. At the same time American industry prospered. In general terms business education was seen as a force for progress.

In Europe – not least in Sweden – there was a strong belief that social-science research could provide solutions to social problems. The Swedish prime minister Tage Erlander was one of those who perceived that such research provided a strong basis for policy-making. The Swedish Employers' Association (SAF) adopted this idea. In 1952 the director of management education at the SAF, Folke Haldén, launched the first course in Sweden that followed the Harvard system of advanced management education. It involved three-week courses in Yxtaholm, an estate bought by the SAF in 1948.[52] On 1 January 1969 this programme was transferred to the IFL, as were the courses run by the SCIV, where Per-Jonas Eliæson had been head and director of studies since 1963.[53] In this capacity, he visited the US. In his own words: 'In 1966 I travelled 5500 miles in

America. I visited all important business schools. I inquired about their plans and their actual operations.'[54]

Thus the IFL, when it started, adopted the Harvard model of case studies to strengthen the linkage between practice and theory. The case-study model has been used ever since but adapted to Swedish surroundings; participants and teachers discuss the strategies adopted by Swedish firms in the presence of relevant actors.[55]

A Swedish context

The men behind the IFL were convinced that management could be taught. In addition they saw education as a continuous process, and they accepted the idea that scholarly work was needed to support it.[56] To Per-Jonas Eliœson – head of the IFL for more than two decades – the creation of the IFL was a demonstration of strength in a small country. The institute would meet the growing need for leadership training in private, cooperative and State organizations. The education pursued would produce knowledge, as well as new attitudes and social and intellectual competence. Management education would develop human capital. Interplay among men, surroundings and society was needed. At the first meeting with the IFL development council on 9 September 1969 Eliœson expressed his high regard for management education. In his presentation he said:

> The priority given to rapid growth practically all over the world calls for, and brings about, a rapid change in many different directions and on many levels. The claims on those who hold leading positions are indeed great and will certainly not be less in the future. The shortage of qualified and well-educated people in trade, industry and administration is an acute problem not just in Sweden. It is a major problem also internationally [...] A fundamental assessment is that management skills can be learned. Another is that education must be viewed as a continuing process throughout a person's active life. Basic education is not enough. [...] Leadership is essential in order to direct and guide development in the proper direction, to establish goals and guide developments towards these goals continuously balancing, reconsidering and revising.[57]

Thus, rapid growth, according to Eliœson, called for leadership, and good leadership called for management education. Management practice was of crucial importance in economic development, and good management practices could be learned through management education.

Experiences from management practice were to be discussed and analysed by scholars. The teachers had to awaken knowledge unconsciously held by participants, who were to be encountered in their own real working situation. According to Eliœson, a professor of business administration is always at a disadvantage. Planning should be ongoing. 'Planned improvisation' was the key to a successful programme. Teachers should live with the clients long enough to get to know them. It was all about learning, not about teaching.[58]

During the discussion following Eliœson's presentation at the first meeting with the IFL development council in September 1969, it was emphasized that the IFL should pay more attention to the behavioural sciences. A special case in this connection was the curriculum in the planned IFL school. Engineers were said to lack an understanding of the interplay between roles in companies. They ought to learn to communicate with economists and – on a higher level – to be trained in critical thinking and analysis.[59]

This discussion reflects the spirit of the times. Swedish managers had to cope with left-wing critique and new demands from society. When encountering new attitudes, they needed a capability to deal with antagonistic voices. This required an understanding of the workings of society. In the IFL development board the linkages to American management education were strong. In this connection, however, it was felt that an uncritical acceptance of American views was dangerous.[60]

Top management seminars in the 1970s

The IFL management education contained programmes dedicated to different types of corporations and clients on different levels of management. New courses were launched as time went by. The following analysis will be restricted to the content of programmes dedicated to managerial strategies. Only programmes that involved the top executives responsible for overall strategic decisions will be dealt with here.

Seminars directed towards board members and managing directors having a great need to follow rapid change have been a constant feature of IFL's work. The first seminar had strong US connections, and was held at Yxtaholm on 23–26 November 1969 conducted by three specialists from the Harvard Business School: Professor Neil C. Churchill, Professor Richard F. Meyer and Dr Norman Zachary. Its theme, 'The Computer: Concepts for Management', pointed towards the future. The Harvard case-study model was adopted.[61] Cooperation with Harvard meant the future involvement of Harvard professors in different fields. This was the case when Marcus Wallenberg called attention to the need for education in international financing. Specialists from Harvard were engaged as teachers in new IFL courses.[62]

In the 1970s associate professor Lennart Strömberg was in charge of the IFL seminars. He found facts and managerial problems to be of more interest than attitudes and patterns of behaviour. He felt that the content of the seminars should mirror changing needs. They were supposed to give support in crisis situations and in internationalisation and help to solve problems when creative management was needed. The content of the seminars was chosen in a dialogue with clients. If a seminar met with good response, the content and the views of the participants were transferred to other courses for which the participants chose pupils from among their employees. The idea behind the casework was that you ought to bring 'the real world' into the classroom. The choice of cases was dependent upon personal relations and experiences.[63]

In 1971 the IFL collaborated with the Stanford Research Institute in the seminars 'Planning for Corporate Growth' and 'Decision Analysis': the latter also involved cooperation with Stanford University.[64] In 1976 a seminar examined the need for engineers as managers; in 1977 the time had come to discuss 'Companies in crisis. Diagnosis and treatment' and in 1978 'Diversified corporations. Strategies and Control'.

How to deal with companies in crisis was discussed at an IFL seminar at a time when there were problems in Swedish industry, with heavy losses in the shipbuilding and the iron and steel sectors. The non-socialist government elected in 1976 gave massive State support to these industries. The case to be analysed in the IFL seminar was Kalmar Verkstads AB, a State-owned company in the engineering industry. According to Lennart Strömberg, Karl-Erik Linderoth probably initiated this case. Linderoth was managing director of the Swedish Cooperative Wholesale Society and a member of the IFL board from the start. In the late 1960s Kalmar Verkstad had experienced severe problems. A reconstruction was carried out in 1970, and in 1977 – when the seminar was held – the company was characterized as one of the few bright spots in the group of State-owned companies in Sweden. The question for the seminar was, How did this come about? In the discussions, assistance was given by people directly involved with the company, such as the secretary of state in the Department of Industry and executives from Kalmar Verkstad. Teachers and researchers gave theoretical perspectives from Vanderbilt University, Nashville, and the University of Milwaukee in the US, from the Scandinavian Institute for Administrative Research in Helsinki and London, and from the Stockholm School of Economics.[65]

In the seminar 'Diversified corporations. Strategies and Control' that was given the following year (1978) the case study had a higher degree of actuality: the topic was Esselte AB, where Lennart Strömberg had personal connections at management level. The company had been established in the printing industry in the early twentieth century. In 1978 the managing director of Esselte, Sven Wallgren, was not happy with the company's organizational structure. Between 1974 and 1978 Esselte had diversified and bought no less than twenty-one companies of different sizes. The greater part of these investments was made abroad. The questions for the IFL seminar were what strategy to choose to increase internationalisation. Assisting in the discussions were executives from Esselte and other Swedes with practical or theoretical experience of diversification, but there was no input from America.[66]

A comparison between the seminar on crisis and that on diversification illustrates the transformation of the IFL seminars in the 1970s. In the beginning the IFL seminars were based on theoretical questions: later the starting point was company-related problems in Sweden, and theoretical questions were addressed only when they were seen to be central to the solution of the problem. Thus, the need for American expertise at the seminars was reduced. In the choice of content the organizers had passed from new theoretical knowledge to important problems in Sweden.[67]

Top management programmes in the 1980s and 1990s

Lennart Strömberg had left the IFL in the 1980s and his responsibilities were transferred to Lennart Lundkvist, who had been recruited to the IFL from the Stockholm School of Economics in 1969: Lundkvist had collaborated with Strömberg. For a couple of years Lundkvist shut down the seminars. He wanted to find a new concept for top-management education to attract top executives who no longer participated in IFL activities. Lundkvist appointed a new faculty of four persons to reconstruct the seminars. The faculty defined the target group as managing directors and board members in leading Nordic companies listed on the stock exchange and Nordic top executives in other big corporations, in major organizations and in public administration. Clients were to receive personal invitations; a vice managing director might be accepted, but ought to come together with his managing director. The subject of the seminars was to be questions concerning corporate leadership, corporate control and corporate organization.

In 1983 a new series of seminars was launched. This series was still running at the end of the millennium. As the permanent course leader, Lennart Lundkvist found that the core business was to find development questions that had a high degree of priority. In discussions with the faculty that was responsible for the seminars, he defined the subject to be elaborated, discussed the details of the agenda in interviews and invited some managing directors to give introductory speeches and take part in the planning process. In the 1990s one seminar ran two days in a row on three different occasions. Specialists might be present, but not during the first part of the seminar. At the end of the seminar the discussions were summarized by the course leaders. The idea was to create a select meeting place, where experienced top executives would feel free to exchange experiences and debate on urgent corporate problems. That meant that there was to be no written documentation.

To exemplify the work, Lennart Lundkvist mentioned in an interview a seminar from 1998. The subject of the seminar was 'The interplay between owners, board members and managing directors'. Well-known managing directors of big corporations representing different ownership structures introduced the subject. Represented were a big Finnish family corporation (Ahlströms), a big Swedish family-owned corporation (Ax:son Johnson), the Wallenberg investment company (Investor) and a corporation that was owned by large institutions (Skandia).[68]

The seminars are part of a Top Management Programme that in the 1990s also gives partnership courses, open courses and – in cooperation with a research institute at the Stockholm School of Economics – a research programme focused on corporate governance. As a result of this research programme two books were published in the 1990s by the faculty responsible for the IFL top-management seminars: two professors at the Stockholm School of Economics (Sven-Erik Sjöstrand and Lars Östman), an assistant professor at the IFL (Bengt Brodin) and Lennart Lundkvist.[69] The first book *Styrelsearbete i koncerner* (Corporate Governance) was published in 1995. Fifteen group executives that had been involved in the IFL seminars participated in the writing of the book.[70] The second book *Koncernchefen och ägarna* (The Group Executive and the Owners) was published in 2001. Fifteen retired group executives constituted a consultative group. The focus on shareholder value in the late twentieth century is debated and is found to be too strong; the authors stress that short-sighted financial perspectives have overruled realities on the workshop floor in a harmful way. In addition it is emphasised that owners tend to be a homogenous group which means that strategies become more uniform.[71]

Tailor-made programmes

Anders Aspling succeeded Per-Jonas Eliœson as managing director of the IFL in 1993. According to Aspling 95 per cent of the IFL programmes in 1999 were developed to clients' order. The corresponding figure a decade earlier had been 50 per cent.[72]

The first tailor-made programmes were launched in the middle of the 1970s. Many of these were in response to problems or opportunities caused by internationalisation. A course created in partnership with Esselte provides an illustration. As mentioned above, Esselte had bought quite a few subsidiaries abroad. The corporation had 20000 employees and many small profit centres. Leaders on different levels had to cope with different cultural surroundings in a decentralized organization. There was a need for leadership development.

Esselte decided to organize a leadership course in cooperation with the IFL. The IFL was – according to Lars Lidén, director of Esselte – chosen as a partner because the institute had access to teachers at the Stockholm School of Economics. The course, which started in 1977 and went on for a semester, was run several times. The participants were aged 30–35. Division managers suggested their names and they were invited to take part by the group executive Sven Wallgren. The programme started with a classroom week in Sweden or abroad. This week dealt with internal information as well as theory. Then the participants were divided into groups that had to work out solutions for real Esselte problems, often problems on the corporate level. The project solutions were presented and discussed in a concluding classroom week in Stockholm in the presence of staff members. Sven Wallgren himself thus gained awareness of employees who showed promise in leadership.[73]

By the late 1990s Leif Lundkvist and the IFL top-management faculty had run some thirty internal company programmes. The initiative had come from corporations and organizations in the IFL network who were looking for new strategic solutions. The need for a new vision or the choice between a local strategy and internationalisation might be the reason for a new programme. The partnership was built on confidence and the courses were closed to outsiders. The absence of ready-made solutions is seen as a prerequisite of the IFL's success.

In 1990 a new contribution to the Top Management Programme was the 'Voyages of Discovery'. Leif Lundkvist and his assistant travelled to Boston in the US with board members and staff of a company listed on the stock exchange. The group was to study 'the new economy', IT and entrepreneurship.[74]

Management education in globalisation: a summary

Markets

The establishment of the IFL had a background in Swedish trade and business. In the 1960s Marcus Wallenberg – the prominent leader in the Wallenberg bank and in the Wallenberg group of industries – initiated the IFL to strengthen the position of Swedish business. The establishment of the institute was supported by leading men in trade and business but also by men from the political world. Networks within Swedish multinationals and the Swedish International Development Authority (SIDA) opened up a global market for the IFL. The IFL became part of the globalisation of Swedish society in the last decades of the twentieth century.

Swedish clients were followed abroad. A major private venture was the launching of the programme 'Training for International Markets' (TIO) at the request of ten Swedish multinationals in 1978. Also, the State opened up international markets to the IFL, above all through the Applied International Management Programme (AIM) introduced in 1982. In the first step, clients from Swedish subsidiaries abroad and clients in development programmes received management education at Kämpasten in Sweden; later on the IFL courses were run in Brussels – where the IFL established a centre of its own – in Russia, US, China, Japan, South America and Africa. Almost all commissions were, even in the 1990s, originated in Sweden, however.

Thus Swedish trade and business constituted the IFL market from the first, but this market was greatly transformed. Swedish multinationals were, through mergers and acquisitions, transformed into corporations 'related to Sweden'. Foreign capital had entered Swedish trade and business in a new way. Foreigners as managers replaced Swedish men. The Wallenberg group no longer had a dominant position. The family bank, Stockholms Enskilda Bank, merged with a considerably larger bank, Skandinaviska banken, into Skandinaviska Enskilda Banken, (SEB) in 1971. In February 2001 plans for a new merger were announced: SEB and Föreningssparbanken (the Swedish United Savings Banks) were to become SEB Swedebank, a European financial corporation based in Sweden. This merger did not take place, however.

Not only its clients but also management education as such offered an international network for the IFL. At the end of the millennium the institute was involved with international organizations in management education and in management research. The institute was a member of such organizations as the European Foundation for Management Development (the EFMD), the European Institute for Advanced Studies in Management (the EIASM) and the Institute for Management of Innovation and Technology (the IMIT). Added to these networks were different types of cooperation with management education centres abroad and personal networks. Some years later the IFL followed the trend towards bigger units and merged with Executive Education within Stockholm School of Economics.

Content of education

The launching of European management education in the decades after World War Two had an American background. When the IFL was established, management education in the US was of crucial importance. The first director of the IFL, Per-Jonas Eliœson, was one of many Europeans who went to the US to study and to learn how to deliver successful management education and to establish connections with American centres of management education and management research. The Harvard case-study model was adopted from programmes transferred from the SAF.

In the early days the IFL launched ready-made American programmes as top-management seminars. The first seminar in November 1969, 'The Computer: Concepts for Management' was conducted by three specialists from the Harvard Business School, and the IFL adopted the Harvard case-study model. Two years later the Stanford Research Institute was invited to participate in the seminar 'Planning for Corporate Growth' and, together with Stanford University, in the seminar 'Decision Analysis'. American specialists continued to be needed as teachers, as for example when a course on international financing was introduced at the request of Marcus

Wallenberg. Strategies on international markets came to be an important part of the IFL portfolio.

As time went by the content of the IFL courses was to an increasing degree adapted to Swedish surroundings. The Harvard case-study model was transformed into a Swedish model. The close connections with their clients meant that the IFL teachers got access to internal information in partner programmes. Representatives of companies involved and university professors worked together as teachers in project groups: recommendations were given and discussed in the presence of managers. This method of work evidences a strong managerial confidence in the institution supplying the education. This method was not possible in the US (and was met by surprise by the Americans), and is supposed to be extremely difficult in Europe as well.

In the 1990s courses were launched to help clients to find new strategies. The focus in top-management education had shifted from American decision theory to company-related problems. A faculty connected to the Stockholm School of Economics furnished top-management education with a theoretical approach. The task of the faculty was not to present theory but to apply it when needed. Thus, the dependence on American management education was greatly reduced. In the top-management seminars and the partner programmes the IFL did not act as a traditional management institute, but rather like a consultant. Thus, recommendations given in the IFL programmes may have been a driving force in the globalisation process.

The leaders of top-management education at the IFL launched courses that had been requested by Swedish corporations. In the 1990s Swedish corporations asked for courses on corporate governance, and the IFL top-management portfolio focused on the interplay between owners, board and managers. These questions were of course being addressed not only in Sweden but also all over the world, and the relation between owners and managers and the focus on shareholder value could be debated in a global context.

Lennart Lundkvist and members of the IFL faculty none the less considered that the IFL had a special mission – the mission to protect 'the Swedish model'. They found that this model had a different balance of power from the American, and a culture of its own. In this Swedish model there are checks and balances between levels of power within business and trade, whereas in America managerial and board levels are merged into each other. In this Swedish model the culture is informal. Managerial leadership is based on a short distance between different levels of power. A great number are involved in the decision-making process and decisions are taken by consensus.

The founders of the IFL wanted to strengthen the position of Swedish trade and industry by management education within the IFL. Three decades later Sweden had quite a few management education centres. In the 1990s the IFL was working in a competitive market and the old clients were no longer what they used to be. The director Anders Aspling found that the IFL – 'to be able to work for Sweden' – had to find a new role on the global market. The IFL looked about for foreign clients.[75] Three years later the IFL united with the Executive Education section of the Stockholm School of Economics. The new unit went out to capture new international markets.

1 Thanks to Rådet för arbetslivsforskning (RALF, The Working Life Research Board), which financed this study of the Institute of Management (IFL). For proof-reading this chapter I have – as so often before – the pleasure to thank Lynn Karlsson. Quotations are translated from Swedish into English.

2 For an overview of Swedish economic history see Lennart Schön, *En modern svensk ekonomisk historia: Tillväxt och omvandling under två sekel* (Stockholm: SNS förlag, 2000).

3 Bengt Brodin, Leif Lundkvist, Sven-Erik Sjöstrand and Lars Östman, *Koncernchefen och ägarna* (Stockholm: Ekonomiska forskningsinstitutet vid Handelshögskolan i Stockholm, EFI, 2000), p. 22.

4 Interviews with Anne Wibble, April 1995.

5 The spread of management ideas is being analysed in the programme 'The Creation of European Management Practice' (CEMP). This research programme had financial support from EU. Research was carried on at the University of Reading, the University of Uppsala, the Norwegian School of Management in Oslo and the management school IESE in Barcelona. Professor Lars Engwall at the department of Business Administration, Uppsala University coordinated the programme, and the contents of the present chapter originated as part of it.

6 Robert R. Locke, 'Management in Higher Education since 1940' in Lars Engwall and Elving Gunnarsson (eds.), *Management Studies in an Academic Context* (Stu-

dia oeconomiae negotiorum 35. Uppsala: Universitetet; Stockholm: Almqvist & Wiksell International [distributor], 1994), p. 158.

7 Ibid.

8 See for example Leda Gitahy, *A New Paradigm of Industrial Organization: The Diffusion of Technological and Managerial Innovations in the Brazilian Industry*, Comprehensive summaries of Uppsala dissertations from the Faculty of Social sciences, 93 (Uppsala: Acta Universitatis Upsaliensis: Univ.-bibl.[distributor], 2000).

9 'Välkommen till IFL Bulletinen', *IFL Bulletin* 1 (1998), 3.

10 Åke Jerkedahl, *Top Management Education: An evaluation study* (Stockholm: Meddelande/PA-rådet, 0480-080X; 50, 1967), pp. 219 and 226–229.

11 Dag Björkegren, *Företagsledarutbildning: En fallstudie* (Stockholm: Ekonomiska Forskningsinstitutet vid Handelshögskolan, EFI, 1986), p. 171.

12 Jörgen Sandberg, 'Utbildningsretorik eller ledarskapspraktik' in Sven-Erik Sjöstrand, Jörgen Sandberg and Mats Tyrstrup (eds.), *Osynlig företagsledning* (Stockholm: Ekonomiska forskningsinstitutet vid Handelshögskolan, EFI: Studentlitteratur, 1999).

13 Aspects of the creation of the Stockholm School of Economics are analysed in Eva Wallerstedt, *Oscar Sillén, professor och praktiker: Några drag i företagsekonomiämnets tidiga utveckling vid Handelshögskolan i Stockholm* (Studia oeconomiae negotiorum 30. Uppsala: Universitet; Stockholm: Almqvist & Wiksell International [distributor], 1988).

14 See Magnus Söderström, 'EFI 60 år. Historien om ett forskningsinstitut' in *EFIs årsbok* (Stockholm: Ekonomisk forskningsinstitutet vid Handelshögskolan, EFI, 1989), p. 30.

15 Ulf Olsson, *Furthering a fortune: Marcus Wallenberg Swedish banker and industrialist 1899–1982* (Stockholm: Ekerlid, 2001), pp. 341 ff.

16 Interview with Per-Jonas Eliœson 11 September 1999.

17 Anders Lindström, 'Sweden' in Alan Hayle, Martine Plompen and Sybren Tymstra (eds.) *Management Education. A handbook* (Brussels: European Foundation for Management Development, cop. 1995), p. 102.

18 Interview with Eliœson and 'Eliæson, Per-Jonas' in Hans Uddling and Katrin Paabo (eds.), *Vem är det: Svensk biografisk handbok* (Stockholm: Norstedt, 1992), p. 283.

19 Interview with Eliœson and Jan Glete, *Nätverk i näringslivet: Ägande och industriell omvandling i det mogna industrisamhället 1920–1990* (Stockholm: Studieförbundet Näringsliv och Samhälle, SNS, 1994), p. 135.

20 Stadgar för stiftelsen Institutet för Företagsledning', § 2. IFL.

21 'Protokoll fört vid bildandet av stiftelsen Institutet för företagsledning den 13 november 1968' and 'Protokoll fört vid sammanträde med huvudmännen för Institutet för företagsledning den 26 November 1968 i Stockholms Handelskammares lokaler Västra Trädgårdsgatan 9, Stockholm', § 3. IFL.

22 Protokoll 26 November 1968. IFL.

23 Information taken from Swedish biographies.

24 Interview with Eliæson and Protokoll 26 November 1968, bilaga. IFL.

25 Ulf Olsson, *I utvecklingens centrum: Skandinaviska Enskilda Banken och dess föregångare 1856–1996* (Stockholm: Skandinaviska Enskilda banken, 1997), p. 207.
26 Olsson, *Furthering a fortune,* pp. 339, 345 ff. and 291.
27 'Svenska Civilekonomföreningens Institut för vidareutbildning. Årsberättelse (förslag till)', pp. 2, 3 and 4; Per-Jonas Elicœson till Broder 18 February 1969, IFL; interview with Eliæson.
28 IFLs programme 1999 samt 'Civilingenjörsförbundet' in *Nationalencyklopedin: ett uppslagsverk på vetenskaplig grund utarbetat på initiativ av Statens kulturråd,* bd 4, (Höganäs: Bra Böcker, Cop. 1990), p. 162.
29 Stadgar, § 2. IFL.
30 'Institutet för Företagsledning. Årsberättelse 1969. Första verksamhetsåret, p. 8'. IFL.
31 Interview with Eliæson.
32 Institutet för Företagsledning. Årsberättelse 1969, p. 8. IFL.
33 Programme 1973, p. 15. IFL.
34 'IFL – Institutet för Företagsledning. Din partner för ledarutveckling' 1998 [Information sheet], p. 9. IFL.
35 'Managers in training for international operations', *Atlas Copco. Contact 1* (1979), 4.
36 Programme 1995, p. 28, Programme 1984, p. 2 and Programme 1999, p. 36. IFL.
37 Programme 1995, p. 28, Programme 1984, p. 3 and 'Institutet för Företagsledning 1988' [Presentation], p. 83. IFL.
38 Interview with Anders Aspling 15 April 1999.
39 Programme 1984. p. 3, Programme 1982, p. 14, Programme 1995, p. 28 and Programme 1999, p. 14. IFL.
40 Birgitta Swedenborg, 'Svenska multinationella företag' in *Sveriges Industri* (Stockholm: Sveriges Industriförbund: Industrilitteratur, 1992), pp. 89–94.
41 'Från IFLs horisont', *Tidskriften Företagsledning* 1 (1988) Special issue; Anders Lindström och Peter Bratt (eds.), *Institutet för företagsledning*, 83.
42 *IFL Bulletin* 1 (1998), 12.
43 Programme 1995. IFL.
44 Ibid.
45 Anders Aspling, 'IFL idag', *IFL Bulletin* 1 (1998), 4.
46 Programme 1999. IFL.
47 Olsson, *I utvecklingens centrum*, pp. 216–227.
48 Håkan Lindgren, *Aktivt ägande: Investor under växlande konjunkturer* (Stockholm: Institutet för ekonomisk-historisk forskning vid Handelshögskolan, EHF: Investor [distributör], 1994), pp. 235 and 269.
49 'ABB' in *Nationalencyklopedin*, supplement band 1, pp. 2–3.
50 Press conference on Swedish TV, 22 February 2001.
51 'Bildandet av IFL vid Handelshögskolan' Presentation on the IFL at the Stockholm School of Economics in January 2006: http://www.ifl.se/templates/index.aspx? Page id=12.
52 Stadgar and Årsberättelse 1969, p. 3. IFL.
53 'Eliæson, Per-Jonas' in *Vem är det*, p. 283.
54 Interview with Eliæson.

55 Sandberg, 'Utbildningsretorik eller ledarskapspraktik' in Sjöstrand, Sandberg and Tyrstrup (eds.) *Osynlig företagsledning*, p. 173.
56 Stadgar and Årsberättelse 1969, p. 3. IFL.
57 Per-Jonas Eliœson, 'Företagens ledarutbildning och ledarutveckling – Diskussionsunderlag för sammanträde med IFL: s utvecklingsråd tisdagen den 9 september 1969,' p. 1. IFL.
58 Interview with Eliæson.
59 'Protokoll fört vid sammanträde med IFL: s utvecklingsråd tisdagen den 9 september 1969', §§ 1, 3 och 4. IFL.
60 Ibid., § 3.
61 Årsberättelse 1969, p. 8. IFL.
62 Interviews with Lennart Strömberg 10 and 21 August 2000.
63 Ibid.
64 'IFL 1971' [Information sheet]. IFL.
65 Unprinted documentation from the IFL seminar 1978. IFL.
66 Unprinted documentation from the IFL seminar 1978. IFL.
67 Interview with Strömberg.
68 Interview with Lennart Lundkvist 23 August 2000.
69 Ibid.
70 Bengt Brodin and Rune Andersson, *Styrelsearbete i koncerner* (Stockholm: Ekonomiska forskningsinstitutet vid Handelshögskolan: Institutet för företagsledning, IFL, 1995).
71 'Koncernchefen och ägarna' and 'Högste chefen tappar makten', *Dagens Industri* 19 August 2000, pp. 8–9.
72 Interview with Aspling 15 May 1999.
73 Interview with Lars Lidén 12 October 2000.
74 Interview with Lundkvist.
75 Interview with Aspling 15 May 1999.

L'UDOVÍT HALLON

Slovakia's International Economic Integration from 1993

Introduction

The entrance of the Slovak Republic after its establishment in 1993 into the process of economic globalisation was a direct result of the political changes in central Europe at the end of the 1980s. The break-up around 1989–1991 of the bloc of totalitarian states at that time under the political and economic control of the communist regime of the Soviet Union was the basic precondition for the spread of economic globalisation into the whole of central Europe. This is why the position of these particular countries in the world economic globalisation after the year 1989 depended primarily on their overall political development and especially on the orientation of their economic policies. Some forms of globalisation had already occurred within the Soviet Bloc, in the environment of a command economy and totalitarian political system. The outcome of this was that the small countries of central and eastern Europe with a totalitarian past – in contrast to small countries with free-market economies – had to cope with the disintegration or transformation of their old economic systems and at the same time engineer their penetration into the present structures of the world free-market economy. The break-up of the economic affiliations of the countries of the Soviet Bloc formerly integrated by the Council of Mutual Economic Help (COMECON), with which the former Yugoslavia also cooperated, actually happened very fast – in only a few months. However, the building of new-style mutual economic relations, achieving participation in the market of developed capitalist countries, as well as coping with the arrival of international corporations and of foreign capital – that is, direct foreign investments into the post-Communist countries – meant a long-term and complicated process. The continuity, rapidity and depth of this process again depended mainly on the nature of the economic policies of individual post-Communist states.

The economic situation in central Europe after the year 1989 had a number of parallels with the situation after the end of the Austro-Hungarian monarchy in 1918. However, there were some qualitative differences. The main common feature was the sudden ending of long-term economic connections over a large economic area and the change of orientation of business relations from less demanding markets in central and eastern Europe to the markets of developed western European countries with strong competition from high-quality production. The common features also include the disintegration of older countries and the establishment of new small states heavily dependent upon external economic relations, which led to currency reforms, sharp inflation and the resultant restructuring of the economy accompanied by economic losses and social crises. The main difference can be said to be the fact that the difficult economic transformation of the post-Communist countries was complicated by their transition from an economy of centralised regulation to a free-market economy and from state ownership to private over the whole structure of the economy, from small-scale production to mass production. Ownership also changed after 1918. Basically this involved shifts of capital more or less influenced by the state, while keeping the continuity of the development of a free-market economy. The process of internationalisation of the economies of the transition countries after 1989, therefore, overlapped with the process of privatisation and partly depended on its character. The conscious attempts of the small countries in central Europe to develop mutual economic liaisons through newly established organisations, as well as common goal-oriented progress towards Western economic structures, were a positive change from the situation in the 1920s and 1930s, when a tendency to autarchy prevailed. Among the transition countries after 1989 we want to focus, apart from Slovakia, especially on the group of central European countries: the Czech Republic, Poland, Hungary and Slovenia.

In the case of Slovakia the main difference between the circumstances in the 1920s and the 1990s is that after the break-up of Czechoslovakia in 1993 the two resultant states did not become part of a larger state unit as was the case after the break-up of the Austro-Hungarian Monarchy, but created an independent economic area with separate external economic relations. On the other hand, there are some common aspects, including the pursuit of greater independence from standing business relations and from disadvantageous economic structure. For evaluation of the causal context of independent Slovakia's participation in international economic globalisation after 1989, an analysis of the economic policies of its government institutions is of prime importance. The development and results of the internationalisation of the Slovak economy itself can be demonstrated through basic data about foreign trade and inflow of foreign capital, as well as on the activities of multinational capital groups in Slovak enterprise sphere. The development of economic policies in Slovakia after the fall of the totalitarian regime took place in several phases which approximately corresponded to the electoral mandates of individual governments. These phases were defined by the periods 1990–1992, 1993–1994, 1995–1998, 1999–2002 and 2003–2006. The greatest influences on Slovakia's entry into international economic processes were exercised by state policies on foreign trade and privatisation as well as by implementing legal, financial and taxation rules which allowed the state to attract foreign investments on one hand and to discourage unwelcome speculators on the other.

The role of economic policy in Slovakia's international economic integration

From centrally planned economy to free market economy (1989–1992)

In the short period from 1990 to1992 – from the fall of the totalitarian regime in former Czechoslovakia to the nation's split into two separate states – basic conditions were created for Slovakia's transition from a centrally planned command economy to a free-market economy. The opening of the Slovak economy to the world was enabled by measures of revolutionary importance such as the decentralisation of economic regulation, liberalisation of foreign trade and prices, achieving internal convertibility of the currency, and establishing the concept of privatisation. Similar economic reforms were carried out in other post-Communist countries at this time.

These reforms carried out by the method of so-called shock therapy resulted in the immediate collapse of the mutual economic relations of the post-Communist countries and a reorientation towards states with a free-market economy – especially those of the European Union. These processes had an even sharper and quicker development than the break-up of traditional markets and reorientation of foreign trade in central Europe after the end of Austria-Hungary. This resulted in a deep economic slump in 1991–1993 compared with the year 1989, ranging in the industry of the five monitored countries from 29% to 39%. This development was very similar to the situation at the beginning of the 1920s. Similarly, inflation led to hyperinflation in some countries, in particular Poland and the countries formed from the former Yugoslavia. The amount of mutual trade between Hungary, Poland and Czechoslovakia decreased by 42% in the years 1988–1992. GDP fell in nine countries of the former eastern bloc by approximately 23% in 1989–1991. Unemployment went up to approximately 9%.[1] The following table shows the results of foreign trade development in the central European countries in the 1920s after the demise of Austria-Hungary, and the basic changes of its orientation after World War Two and after the fall of totalitarian regimes.

The position of the transition countries in foreign trade relations influenced development in the currency area. A common sign was sharp inflation caused mainly by price liberalisation. In former Czechoslovakia where inflation was lowest, currency devaluation started in 1990. In 1991 inflation started in the Czech and Slovak Republic, peaking at 65%. In the following year the situation was stabilised.[2] The character and tempo of the privatisation of state property had an especial influence on the entrance of international capital. After vigorous discussion of several privatisation programmes, Czechoslovakia accepted a scheme based on the coupon method (that is, by dividing state property among a wide stratum

Table 1: Changes in foreign trade orientation of the central European transition countries (Share of western Europe and central-eastern Europe in the foreign trade in %)

Year	Czechoslovakia		Hungary		Poland		Roumania	
	western Europe	central Europe	western Europe	central Europe	western Europe	central Europe	western Europe	central Europe
1928	55,2	19,8	30,9	37,3	62,7	14,2	54,9	24,0
1989	37,6	47,2	46,2	40,1	44,9	39,4	32,5	31,1
1992	63,2	25,4	68,9	21,3	72,1	15,9	51,8	19,5

Source: 'Zmeny strategickej orientácie obchodu postkomunistických krajín', *Trend* 45 (1993), 4.

of citizens on the basis of coupons representing a certain capital share). The direct selling of enterprises to foreign investors was to be only of secondary importance.

The main purpose was accelerated privatisation and obtaining popular support for economic reform. According to the plan privatisation was to be carried out in several phases. The first started in August 1991 and was to be completed in March 1993. In Slovakia 678 enterprises were registered for privatisation in the amount of 169 billion crowns out of which 48% was privatised by the coupon method and only 7% was sold to investors. Another 28% was placed under the authority of a new institution: the Fund of National Property.[3] At the same time, from February 1991 the so-called 'lesser privatisation' was carried out by means of public auctions. Foreign capital was not allowed to enter the first round of auctions. There were changes in finance as well. The centralised financial institution, the State Bank of Czechoslovakia, which was both a currency-issuing and commercial institution, was divided into a national bank and several state commercial banks. These also started arranging foreign trade transactions in foreign currency.

The profit of the inhabitants of Slovakia from the first round of privatisation was not high enough to outweigh the negative social impact of economic reform. While in the Czech Lands unemployment reached 2.6% in 1991, in Slovakia it was 10.4%. The main cause of the problem was the structure of the Slovak economy. Its share in the industrial production of Czechoslovakia in 1989 rose in comparison with 1937 from 8.5% to 29% of the approximately eleven-times-higher production of the Czech and Slovak Republic.[4] Thus, the core of Slovak industry came to be energy-intensive heavy industry depending on raw material imported from foreign countries, especially the Soviet Union. After the break-up of the Eastern Bloc the armament industry totally collapsed. These industrial difficulties were used as propaganda by opposition Slovak nationalist movements with the aim of undermining the foundations of the united state. They demonised the role of international capital, claiming that its aim was to dominate and exploit the Slovak economy. The central government and Czech economic sphere were presented as the agents of these manipulations. The June 1992 elections were won by the party led by the populist Vladimír Mečiar, which united nationalist and post-communist elements. In the Czech Lands, the right-wing party led by V. Klaus took power, with the aim of accelerating the reforms. The new national governments were not able to agree on two basic questions, namely the constitutional organisation of the Czech and Slovak Republic and the basic principles of economic reform. This is why the country split by mutual agreement.

Initial economic stabilisation of independent Slovakia (1993–1995)

The economic development of the separate Slovak Republic in the first years of its existence from January 1993 till about the end of 1995 was quite successful, after overcoming some initial difficulties. Slovakia achieved positive trends in almost all macroeconomic indicators. Rational precautions in the currency and financial domain, as well as a boom in world markets with western developed countries finding new possibilities for trade exchange with the transition countries, contributed to this. These factors had a positive influence on the growth of foreign trade. A significant shift occurred in the orientation of exports towards countries with developed free-market economies, but transformation of its inner sectional structure fell behind. Negative trends prevailed especially in the process of privatisation and consequently in the entry of foreign investors.

The situation in foreign trade is very important for Slovakia because after the separation, the Slovak economy became the most open of all the economies of the transition states in central Europe. This is evident from the indicators of openness of the economy in 1997 (Table 2). In the sphere of economic policy, devaluation of the new currency, the Slovak crown, by 10% in July 1993 and implementation of a 10% import surtax helped the successful balance of foreign trade exchange in the years 1993–1995. After the devaluation the government guaranteed stable development of the currency by implementing a fixed exchange rate for the crown set against a basket of seven world currencies. From July 1994 the basket was simplified to DM and USD at a ratio of 60:40%. Through these economic tools, complete liberalisation of the foreign currency regime and complete convertibility of the balance of payments was achieved from October 1995.[5]

Table 2: Degree of openness of transition countries of central Europe in the year 1997 (Export/GDP in %; Export plus import/GDP in %)

Country	Slovakia	Czech Repub.	Hungary	Poland	Slovenia
Export/GDP	49,5	43,8	41,8	18,0	46,0
Turnover/GDP	109,6	96,0	88,2	47,6	97,4

Source: M. Jakoby, 'Zahraničný obchod'. in Anton Marcinčin and Miroslav Beblavý (eds.), *Hospodárska politika na Slovensku 1990–1999* (Bratislava: Slovenská spoločnosť pre zahraničnú politiku, 2000), p. 140.

Table 3: Average annual inflation rate in transition countries in the years 1993–1998 in %

1.	Slovakia	10.6	5.	Poland	23,6
2.	Czech Repub.	11.3	6.	Roumania	123,7
3.	Slovenia	15.6	7.	Russia	244.3
4.	Hungary	20.9	8.	Bulgaria	282.1

Source: M. Beblavý, 'Monetárna politika', in Marcinčin and Beblavý (eds.), *Politika na Slovensku 1990–1999*, p. 103.

In 1994–1995 Slovakia achieved a surplus of imports over exports. The main items of the export commodity structure were cheap raw products, especially iron and steel: this commodity's share of total exports grew from 14% in 1993 to 16% in 1994. The biggest Slovak metallurgical concern was also the most important Slovak exporter.[6]

Although the first government of independent Slovakia verbally advocated integration with developed free-market economies and claimed interest in Western economic and military structures, Slovakia's actual movements in economic policy were directed to other ends. This double-faced policy was notably evident in the spheres of privatisation and of Slovakia's unfriendly attitude towards foreign investors. In May 1993 the first stage of privatisation ended, a little late. In the Czech Republic they immediately started preparing and carrying out the second stage of privatization, once again by the coupon method. The Slovak government rejected coupon privatisation and opted for the standard method of direct sale of enterprises. In September 1993 the second stage of privatisation officially started in Slovakia too: in reality the privatisation process almost stopped. Popular discontent with the progress of privatisation grew to the extent that in March 1994 the Slovak parliament dismissed V. Mečiar's government and appointed a temporary government, which was assigned two main tasks, namely announcing early parliamentary elections and quickening the privatisation process. It made a new plan for the coupon method of privatisation. After the early elections in September 1994, V. Mečiar's party once more came to power. The government formed by this party and its allies cancelled almost all the privatisation plans of the previous government and prepared a completely different scheme. The coupon method was replaced by bond privatisation in a nominal value of 33.3 billion Sk. with interest set at the discount rate of the national bank. The real privatisation of enterprises, including property represented by government bonds, progressed by the method of direct sale. The leaders of privatisation were to be domestic entrepreneurs, with the alleged goal of strengthening the Slovak entrepreneurial sector and preventing the sale of national property abroad. In reality the enterprises were more or less given away to top representatives of the state and the former management of privatised concerns. The small share of foreign investors in government-driven privatisation grew even smaller. Their share in the purchase price of sole concerns went down from 24% in 1993 to 21% in 1994 and 11% in 1995. In the monitored three years, 13 foreign firms acquired companies with a total purchase price of 4.604 billion Sk.[7]

Unbalanced economic growth and the trends against economic integration (1996–1998)

The positive factors which brought the Slovak economy back to life in the mid 1990s stopped working after 1995. This had a very serious impact on the development of the foreign-trade balance of Slovakia. Conditions in world markets worsened and interest in Slovak raw materials deteriorated sharply. The only possibility was accelerated sectoral restructuring of the economy. Its development, however, being influenced by the financial and privatisation policies of the government, continued to fall behind. The government tried to support economic growth with expansionist financial policies. Capital was gained from expensive short-term foreign credits, which increased the country's debts. The companies privatised by their former management profited especially through so-called rent seeking on the basis of their close links with government circles. This is why their interest in structural change was minimal. Restrictive precautions in the financial sphere were introduced in 1996, but without any significant effects. Another key factor with a negative impact on the balance of foreign trade was in the area of currency policy. The original positive influence of the fixed rate of the Slovak crown eventually became counterproductive. The currency was overvalued, which resulted in preference for imports and the competitive ability of the Slovak Republic in the world market was lowered. Over 1995–1998 the surplus of the foreign trade balance of Slovakia gradually changed into a large deficit.[8] The new deepening of the disproportion in external economic relations prevented enforcement of at least partial structural changes, although these met with some success, especially in connection with the activities of foreign capital, namely in the automobile and electric industries, despite a very narrow inflow of foreign investments. The activities promoted by foreign capital resulted in a changed import structure, especially in an increased share of technologically advanced equipment goods. The government measures to extend exports such as establishing the Fund to Support Foreign Trade in 1996 or the Bank of Exports and Imports in 1997 were not very effective. This is why the government introduced administrative anti-import actions.[9]

In the period 1996–1998, privatisation was actually limited only to the first half of the year 1996, when the last part of the second stage of privatisation was implemented. Its object was 610 enterprises with a book value of 136.8 billion Sk. The greater part of this property, which in terms of sale price comprised 67% of all privatised state property, fell into the hands of persons from government circles and of managers with pro-government sympathies. Government economic circles also got hold of companies from the first stage of privatisation by gaining control of or liquidating the investment funds and investment companies which controlled 73% of the businesses assigned to the first stage of privatization. In this situation the share held by foreign investors in the process decreased to less than one percent of the purchase value of the companies concerned. From the beginning of the privatisation process in 1992 to the elections in the autumn of 1998 companies with a total purchase price of 7.7 billion Sk. (which was 9.9% of the total purchase price – 77.6 billion Sk. – of the privatised concerns) were sold to foreign firms. Their share in the original price of 291.4 billion Sk. was even lower. It was 4.7 billion Sk., or 1.6%. On the basis of a law of July 1995, certain more important companies having between them a total asset value of 150 billion Sk. were completely excluded from privatisation as so-called 'strategic' (communication, transport etc.) companies.[10]

Restoration of economic balance and expedition of economic integration (1999–2002)

The pro-reform government of Mikuláš Dzurinda, which came to power in October 1998, declared that its first task was to quicken economic reforms with the aim of getting Slovakia into the first group of transition countries on the way to the European Union. In the interest of these goals it introduced a few measures and decided to accelerate restructuring, renew the privatisation process and support the entrance of foreign capital. It repealed the law on strategic companies, which made privatisation of monopolies, larger banks and key industrial companies possible. Foreign capital was to be attracted by motivating measures in the form of the law on establishing industrial estates and especially the law on investment stimulus. This law included tax holidays for 10 years, state benefit for staff requalification and the creation of new jobs. Reliefs were provided from a fixed investment threshold, and subsidies according to the proportion of unemployment in the region. Motivation was also expected from the general improvement of the country's image in the world, to which the signing of the agreement with the EU in 1999 and entry to the OECD in 2000 contributed. An invitation to join the NATO was imminent.[11] Immediately after its appointment the government replaced the fixed currency rate with a fluctuation zone of +/– 7% by means of a floating rate for the crown. This resulted in a currency devaluation of 19% in October 1998 and by increased annual inflation in the following period. This measure had a positive influence on the development of foreign trade. The foreign trade deficit decreased in 1999–2000.[12] The activity of foreign capital, which flowed into Slovakia in considerably greater quantity after 1998, especially contributed to the sectoral restructuring of the economy. The accumulation of foreign investments was largely the result of the sale of strategic state enterprises to international corporations through open tender. Privatisation was successful in the banking sector. In this respect Slovakia caught up with the other transition countries of eastern Europe. It also satisfied the conditions for the entrance process into the EU. All these factors had a basic influence on the further development of the integration of Slovakia into the international economic structures of developed free-market economies.

Economic growth restoration and EU entrance (2003–2006)

Contrary to predictions of gains by the anti-reformist parties the parliamentary elections in the autumn of 2002 again returned a government led by Mikuláš Dzurinda and exclusively composed of representatives of right-wing and liberal parties. The new government even intensified the reformist trend of economic policies established in the previous period. The main programme of the government was the preparation for entrance into western economic and military structures, i. e. the EU and NATO. Among the main economic goals were the completion of privatsation of strategic enterprises in the field of power generation, water supply and transport, as well as further enlargement of the flow of foreign investments. Part of the reform efforts was a plan for the reform of the pension, health, and school systems, which partially depended upon the entrance of foreign investments. The economic legislation was gradually adjusted to norms valid in the EU, which was one of the conditions of the so-called admittance process. In order to comply with EU entry conditions the government had to abandon some of its foreign-investment incentives, especially the tax reliefs and state financial support which had served as a principal motivation to foreign investment. More recently a change in state-support philosophy has occurred. The state contribution to investors is now graded according to the technological level of the incoming investment, while before the key criterion was the proportion of unemployed persons in the investment region. Where top-level technology is concerned the state share in investment can even reach 40%. The change of entrepreneurial environment had according to current results an even greater importance for investors, especially in connection with the tax reform which took place in 2003. A so-called equal income tax was introduced for both corporate and individual tax-payers, as well as a unified value-added tax rate of 19%. By this means the tax burden of all enterprises was reduced to a level that was ranked among the lowest in Europe.[13] The greatest motivation element for foreign investment influx was the entrance of Slovakia into NATO in April 2004, and especially its entrance into the EU together with five other CEFTA countries, thc Baltic States, Malta and Cyprus on 1 May 2004. Its entrance into the EU and NATO gave Slovakia increased credibility in the eyes of investors and at the same time removed customs barriers to the markets of western Europe and of the new EU-member countries. While the previous period of M. Dzurinda's first government in the years 1999–2002 is labelled a period of economic stabilisation at the price of economic growth, with weakening employment and decreasing real wage-levels, the years of Dzurinda's second ministry 2003–2006 became a period of gradual renewal of economic growth and increasing foreign investments. Inflation dropped from 12% in 2000 to 3.3% in 2002. In the years 2003–2004 it temporarily increased to 8.5% and 7.5%, principally as a result of fuel, energy and water price deregulation. The positive trends of economic development could be seen in the exchange rate of the Euro against the Slovak crown. From January 2001 till January 2006 the approximate Euro exchange rate against the crown dropped from 43.80 Sk. to 37.50 Sk., which is about 14.4%. The enterprise sphere used the beneficial rate to buy cheaper technology. The central bank, though, strangled the strengthening of Slovak currency by continual interventions, so that the export ability of the economy would not be lowered. The main aim of currency policy became the transition to the common European currency on January 1, 2009, according to the Currency Programme of the central bank. A great turning point in fulfilment of this programme was the entrance of the Slovak crown into the Mechanism of exchange rates ERM II on November 25, 2005. Central parity of crown against Euro was set 38.455 Sk. with a fluctuation zone of +/– 15%. Slovakia and its currency entered the ERM II as the first state out of the Vysegrad 4 (V4) economic bloc formed in 1992 with the aim of integrating central Europe. Also the adjustment of the public finance deficit towards norms necessary for the transition to a common European currency was more favorable in Slovakia than in the other V 4 countries. The development of other main economic indicators has been quite successful, too. The average annual growth of VAT increased from 3% in the years 1999–2002 to 5% in the years 2003–2005 and further growth is anticipated.[14] Principal among the key indicators of quickened globalisation of the economy was the growth of direct foreign investments. While in the years 1990–1999 investments of about 2.3 billion USD came to Slovakia, in the years 2000–2005 they reached almost 10 billion USD. In the yearly growth of foreign investments per inhabitant, since 2000 Slovakia has overtaken Poland and Slovenia and has caught up with Hungary. However, a significant role has been played here by the privatisation of strategic enterprises. The greatest share in the influx of investments was held by German capital, followed by Dutch, Austrian and French. In the last few years Slovakia has seen a great expansion of South Korean investment capital, mainly in automotive concerns. As for the quality indicators overall labour productivity made progress, growing by 53% in the years 1989–2004. Less favorable are the slow growth of added value, the slow increase of the share of sophisticated areas of production and especially of top information technologies, though the situation in these areas has started to change lately. The foreign trade deficit – caused mainly by substantial imports of technical equipment for new plants established by foreign investors, especially in the automotive industry – persists. The social side of economic development still remains a thorny problem. The entrance of investors is mostly motivated by Slovak labour costs, which are the lowest in the CEFTA countries. While the GDP grew in the years 1989–2005 by about 33%, the real wages in 2005 were still under the level of the year 1989. The growth of real wages and decrease of unemployment, which was 19.2% in the year 2001, have both made progress since 2003, but not by much.[15] This slow social progress is grist for the mill of the anti-reformist opposition parties.

Slovakia's position in the international economic integration of central European transition states

Privatisation and foreign investments

The preceding pages have shown that in the transition countries the main factors influencing the inflow of capital and the process of globalisation were their starting situation at the end of the 1980s, the strategy of privatisation and its implementation, the level of stability of the overall economic development and the political development, which together contributed to the transition state's image in the outside world. The starting circumstances for privatisation were more positive in Hungary, Poland and Slovenia, which already had small-enterprise private sectors and received foreign capital through loans. Hungary and Poland were already discussing some forms of so-called spontaneous or nomenclatura privatisation. Slovenia had covered a greater part of the journey to a free-market economy: it had more developed trade relations with western countries and a higher quality level of industry. State ownership was dominant in all areas of the Czechoslovak economy. Czechoslovakia had the advantage of long-term stable economic development and low inflation.[16] After overcoming economic recession and inflation at the beginning of the 1990s all the transition countries of central Europe managed to stabilise their economic development. Hungary, the Czech Republic and Poland, which proceeded directly towards association agreements with the EU and NATO, were successful in the political sphere. Slovenia soon caught up with the first group. After its creation, Slovakia was integrated into the first group, but as a result of the nationalist and totalitarian trends in the politics of V. Mečiar's governments it was excluded. A fundamental change in the assessment of Slovakia came in 1998. In the privatisation process, the way of Hungary, based on gradual but deliberate progress and a transparent direct sale of concerns, was found to be the most effective. In 1990, the companies to be privatised by gradual seeking of strategic and mainly foreign investors were already identified. The Czech Republic and Slovakia started with the controversial coupon privatisation, which led to the enterprise sphere being dominated by privatisation investment funds. In the Czech Republic the investment funds changed into holding companies which enabled the entrance of foreign capital in more transparent forms. After the split the Slovak coupon privatisation changed into ineffective managerial privatisation by domestic-government-friendly subjects and individuals. In Poland the privatisation process developed to its full extent only in the second half of the 1990s. Similar methods of mass privatisation by domestic candidates as in Czechoslovakia were used, but certain restrictions were accepted by the privatisation fund to prevent the mistakes of the Czech and Slovak procedure. Since the restrictions were not very efficient privatisation was implemented with imperfectly transparent forms and a small share for foreign investors. In Slovenia privatisation fell behind till the end of the1990s because managerial and employee privatisation without an important role for foreign investors was preferred. It was supposed to organically continue the specifically Yugoslav model of autonomous leadership of the companies from before 1990, which allegedly created certain forms of ownership relations.[17] In the years 2000–2005 privatisation in most central European transition countries came to the closing phase. Mostly it took the form of direct sale of enterprises to foreign investors through searching for a new strategic partner. The main privatisation targets in this period were the so-called strategic enterprises, or natural duopolies from the field of fuel, electricity, water, transport, and telecommunications. For instance, in the Czech Republic foreign capital entered the gas company, in Hungary partially into the electric power industry; and in Poland the state railway was being prepared for privatisation. In these countries the process was partially limited by the economic policies of left-wing governments. In the privatisation of strategic enterprises the fastest development was seen at the hands of the right-wing Slovak government, mainly with the participation of German, Austrian, French and Italian capital. Telecommunications for example were taken over, as in the neighbouring countries, by the daughter company of Deutsche Telekom, the central electric power company was privatised by an Italian group, Enel, and Austrian capital has tried to privatise airports. The privatisations, though, were not entirely free of favouritism and intrigue, a fact which was used by the anti-reforms opposition to try to stop the whole process.[18]

The central European countries also tackled the problems of economic restructuring after the fall of the Austro-Hungarian market in 1918 by means of an inflow of foreign capital. The basic difference was specifically that the process of privatisation of state ownership influenced the development of foreign investments after 1989. In some successor states of the Habsburg monarchy (Czechoslovakia and Roumania) there were property shifts called nostrification. This did not mean privatisation of state property, but reprivatisation of capital property of foreign (especially Austrian and Hungarian) firms by domestic capital. From the view of the structure of foreign capital, international loans played a greater role in central European countries after the First World War.

On the basis of assessment of the major factors, Hungary received the largest amount of foreign investment per inhabitant, followed by the Czech Republic, Slovenia, Poland and Slovakia. This is also confirmed by the facts in the table, which also shows the inner structure of foreign investments when divided into portfolio and direct foreign investments as well as investment in the loan forms

Table 4: Total value of foreign loans of central European countries in the year 1937 in million USD

Country	Czechoslovak.	Yugoslavia	Hungary	Poland	Roumania
Foreign loans in million USD	243	388	400	484	584

Source: Jaroslav Pátek, 'Die Stellung der Tchechoslowakei auf dem internationalen Kapitalmarkt in der Zwischenkriegszeit 1918–1938', in Alice Teichová, Alois Mosser and Jaroslav Pátek (eds.), *Der Markt im Mitteleuropa der Zwischenkriegszeit* (Prague: Vydavatelství Karolinum, 1997), pp. 173–176.

Table 5: Participation of the Czech, Slovak and foreign capital in the capital of Slovak industrial, trading and transport companies in the year 1936 in million USD

Capital total	Czech capital	in %	Slovak capital	in %	Foreign capital	in %
58.4	40.1	68.5	5.7	9.7	12.8	21.8

Source: *Statistická ročenka Republiky československé* (1938), p. 107.

Note: Values for the Czech and Slovak capital are approximate.

Figure 1: Foreign direct investment into Slovak Republic by country of investor in 2000 (The total value 3 497 million USD in December 2000)

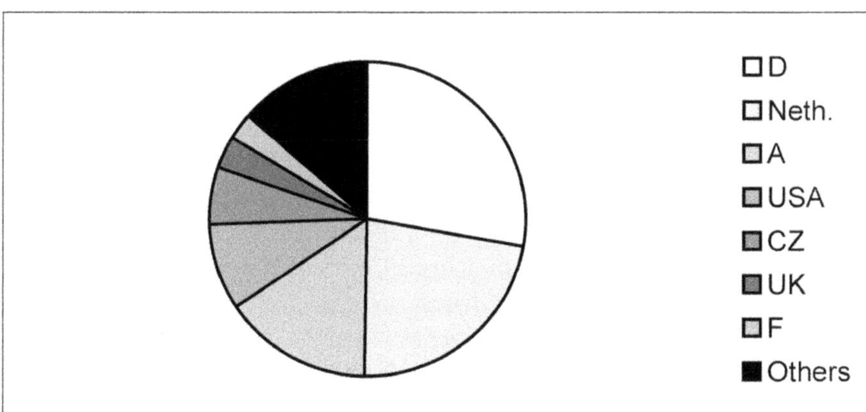

Source: *Štatistická ročenka Slovenskej republiky* (2001), 117.

Figure 1a: Foreign direct investment into Slovak Republic by country of investor in 2003 (The total value 10 248 million USD in December 2003)

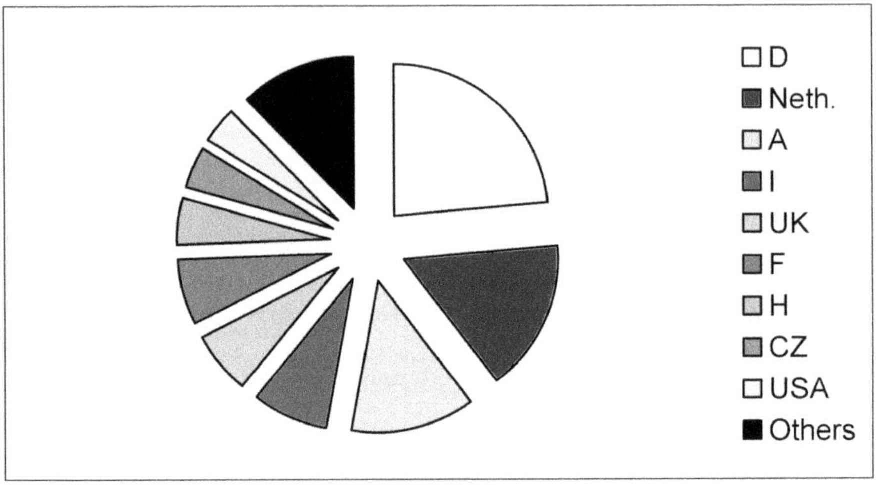

Source: *Štatistická ročenka Slovenskej republiky* (2004), 149.

labelled as 'other'. Table 7 presents data from four central-European countries and two so-called newly industrialised countries of South America and eastern Asia. While until 1989 the former socialist countries lagged behind and in the years 1990–1994 investment activity was in the process of development, after 1995 the increase of foreign investment was so sharp that the amount per inhabitant was greater than in the other two monitored countries. After 1999 the activities of foreign investors in the CEFTA countries grew substantially. In the overall volume of incoming investments Poland and the Czech Republic took the lead. In the years 1999–2003 alone the influx of foreign direct investments (FDI) into the monitored group of states grew from 71.8 billion to 150.6 billion USD, an increase of more than a hundred percent. In the sum of foreign investments per inhabitant Hungary was the leading country till 2003. Closely behind was the Czech Republic, then on a similar level Slovakia and Slovenia, and some way after them Poland.The purpose and role of foreign investments in the economy of central European countries and particularly in Slovakia can be illustrated through more indicators. Figure 4 maps the share of

Table 6: Share of joint ventures in total Slovak exports and imports by a selected population of organisations in %

Year	1994	1995	1996	1997	1998	1999	2000
Export	37	34	36	37	32	31	31
Import	42	36	39	44	35	34	40

Source: Hošková, 'The economy of Slovakia', p. 36.

Table 7: Financial account of the balance of payments for selected emerging markets in the period 1985–1999

	USD million			Per capita, USD		
	1985–1989	1990–1994	1995–1999	1985–1989	1990–1994	1995–1999
Czech and Slovak Republik, Hungary and Poland						
FDI net	235	14519	52339	3.7	218.6	811.9
Portfolio net	0	8139	15134	0.0	126.4	234.9
Other invest.	−17789	−19679	22260	−257.6	−290.8	345.2
Total	−17534	2979	89742	−253.9	54.2	1391.1
Argentina, Brasil and Mexico						
FDI net	19469	44248	189263	77.7	162.6	648.0
Portfolio net	−8771	180168	101451	−35.3	656.4	350.7
Other invest.	−69889	−69124	−58285	−277,6	−251.3	−198.1
Total	−59191	155292	232429	−235.2	567.6	800.6
Korea, Malaysia, Thailand						
FDI net	7275	26014	37144	64.0	217.2	287.3
Portfolio net	4101	30251	60587	38.0	249.1	474.8
Other invest.	−15373	55553	−47101	−137.8	463.9	−351.8
Total	−3997	111818	50630	−35.8	930.1	410.3

Source: V. Baláž and A.M. Williams, 'Capital mobillity in transition countries of central Europe', *Ekonomický časopis* 2 (2001), p. 244.

Notes: Current US dollars. Diferences due to rounding.

FDI in the GDP of the monitored countries. After 2000 this indicator changed significantly in the Czech Republic and Slovakia, where at the end of 2002 it was 57% and 43%. In other monitored countries there were only slight changes. The role of foreign capital in the Slovak economy is documented by the share of the companies with foreign investments in imports and exports. The figures indicate the great importance of companies with foreign investments

Figure 2: Per capita foreign direct investment influx to transition states of central Europe in USD

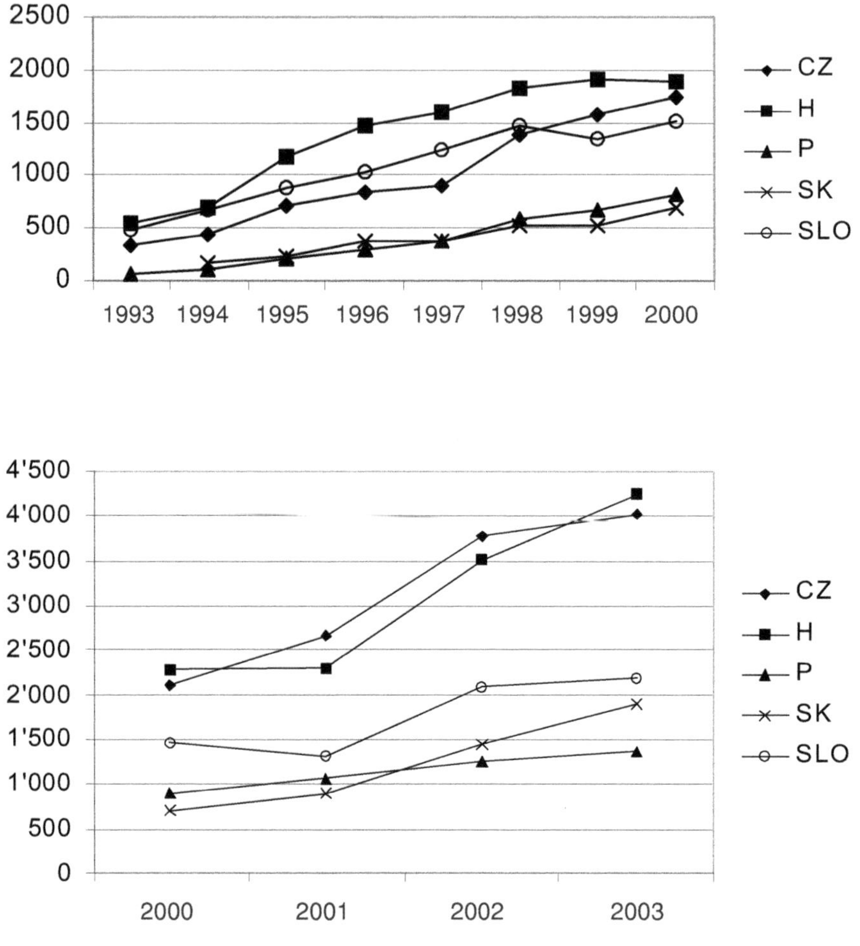

Sources: G. Hunya and J. Stankowski, *Foreign direct investment in central and east european countries and the former Soviet Union* (Wien: WIIN – WIFO, 2001), pp. 6–8; A. Hošková, 'Impact of foreign direct investment on the economy of Slovakia', *Biatec* 9 (2001), 35–36; A. Hošková, 'The Effects of foreingn direct investment on domestic industry', *Biatec* 1 (2001), 32–36; Soňa Ferenčíková and Marek Vážan, 'Nové trendy vo vývoji priamych zahraničných investícií v krajinách strednej a východnej Európy', *Hospodárske rozhľady* 4 (2005), 523–524.

Note: CZ = Czech Republik, H = Hungary, P = Poland, SK = Slovakia, SLO = Slovenia.

Figure 3: FDI Influx to transition States of central Europe in USD million

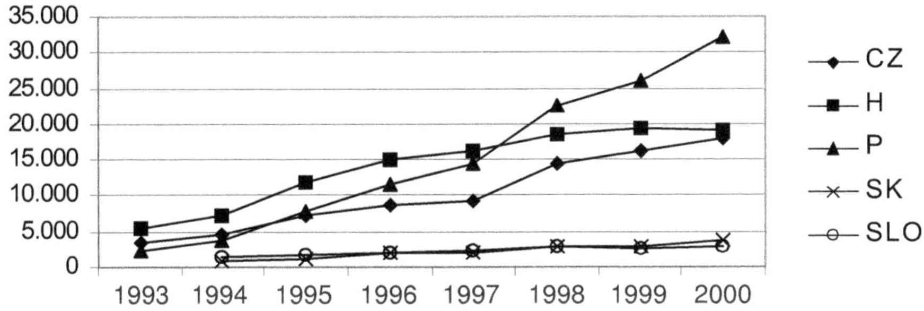

Source: Hunya and Stankowski, *East european countries and the former Soviet Union*, pp. 6–8; Hošková, 'The economy of Slovakia', 35–36; Hošková, 'Investment on domestic industry', 32–36.

Figure 4: FDI to GDP Ratio in Transition States of Central Europe in %

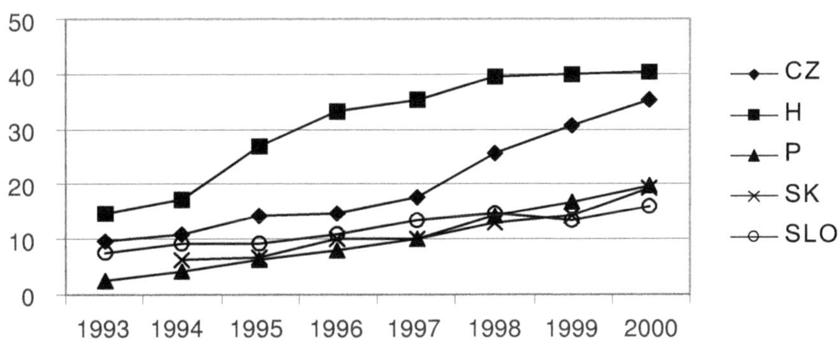

Sources: Hunya and Stankowski, *East european countries and the former Soviet Union*, pp. 6–8; Hošková, 'The economy of Slovakia', 35–36; Hošková, 'Investment on domestic industry', 32–36.

and their low level of reliance on domestic subsuppliers. After considering transfers between holding companies and their subsidiaries and deducting businesses with foreign investments we reach a better outcome. For instance for the year 2000 the share in imports would be 59.7% and exports 61.1%.[19] In the years 2000–2005 the new investors, as well as some of the older ones, turned to the creation of supplier capacities for their new factories directly in the Slovak region. This more favourable trend of the development was visible in the automotive industry. For example, the Korean maker of automobiles Hyundai – Kia came to Slovakia together with their sub-suppliers. However, a cheap workforce remains one of the key motivation elements of foreign-investment influx.

Foreign trade

The foreign business orientation of the transition countries underwent radical changes in the years 1989–1992. In the following period these changes were intensified. Qualitative changes of equal importance occurred in the commodity structure of imports and exports. In particular, this involved restrictions in the branches of heavy industry and strengthening of progressive departments with sophisticated production. The activities of foreign capital also contributed to structural changes by introducing new technologies. In spite of many difficulties, all the monitored countries achieved some movement in this direction. There was a positive phenomenon of willingness to continue long-term cooperation. The states did not repeat the mistakes of the post-1918 era, when, for ideological reasons, the successor states of the Habsburg monarchy refused to maintain free trade, at least for some time. As mentioned above, in 1992 the V4 economic bloc was formed with the aim of integrating central Europe. These goals were to be supported by a central European agreement about the creation of a free-trade zone and an agreement about a customs union amongst the successor states of Czechoslovakia. By the addition of Slovenia to this group of countries a bloc called the CEFTA 5 came into being. In the years 1992–1998 the amount of mutual trade between the CEFTA countries went up by 26%. On the other hand the share of the bloc in foreign trade of the member states went down while their share with the European Union increased. The analysis of trade exchange showed that in spite of the structural changes achieved the quality of several product categories remained below those traded in the European Union.[20] These concerns became of no account on May 1, 2004 when the CEFTA countries entered the EU and their mutual business relationships became part of the unified European market. The EU's share of Slovak foreign trade grew to more than 80% with the entrance of CEFTA countries and other transition countries to the unified European market, while total Slovak foreign trade at current prices grew by 62% in the years 2000–2004.[21]

Figure 5: Changes of territorial orientation of Czechoslovaks export in the years 1920–1937

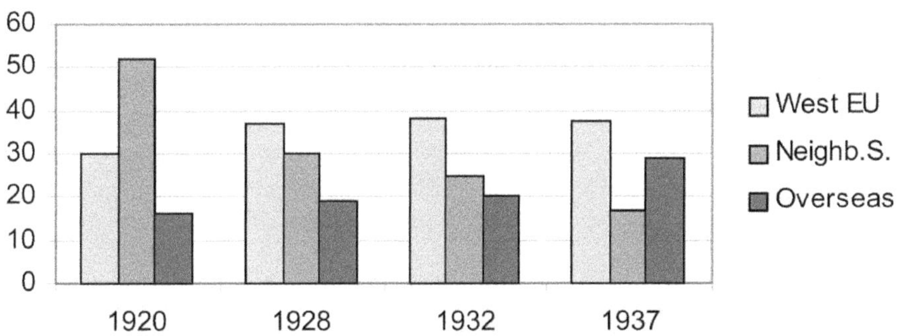

Source: Ivan Jakubec and Eduard Kubů, 'Veränderung der territorialen Orientierung des tschechoslowakischen Aussenhandels zwischen den Weltkriegen', in Alice Teichová, Alois Mosser and Jaroslav Pátek (eds.), *Der Markt im Mitteleuropa der Zwischenkriegszeit* (Prague: Vydavatelství Karolinum, 1997), pp. 292–293.

Note: West EU = western Europe, Neighb. S. = Neighbouring states, Overseas = Overseas states.

Figure 6: Share of selected territories on Slovakias exports in %

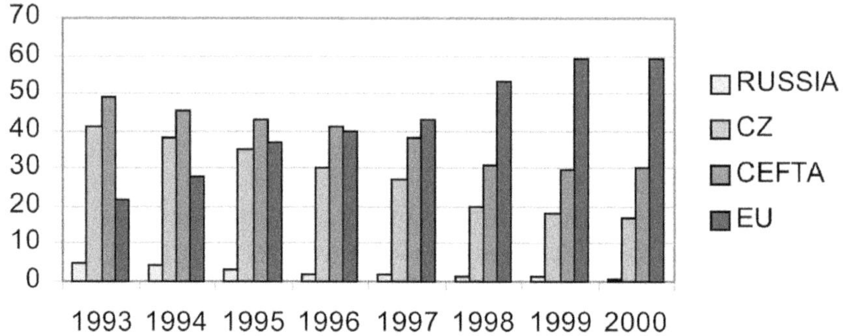

Source: *Foreign trade in Slovak Republic (FTSR)*, 12 (1993), 9; *FTSR* 12 (1994), 8; *FTSR* 12 (1995), 9; *FTSR* 12 (1996), 7; *FTSR* 12 (1997), 8; *FTSR* 12 (1998), 8; *FTSR* 12 (1999), 9; *FTSR* 12 (2000), 7; I. Okáli, H. Gabrielová, E. Hlavatý, K. Morvay and R. Outrata, 'Economic Development of Slovakia in 2000', *Ekonomický časopis* 2 (2001), 220; M. Jakoby, 'Zahraničný obchod', in A. Marcinčin and M. Beblavý (eds.), *Hospodárska politika na Slovensku 1990–1999* (Bratislava: Slovenská spoločnosť pre zahraničnú politiku 2000), pp. 157-158.

Figure 7: Share of selected territories on Slovakias imports in %

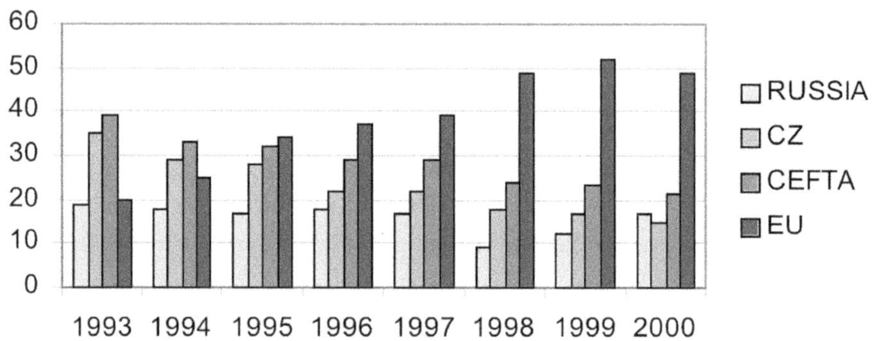

Sources: *Foreign trade in Slovak Republic (FTSR)*, 12 (1993), 9; *FTSR* 12 (1994), 8; *FTSR* 12 (1995), 9; *FTSR* 12 (1996), 7; *FTSR* 12 (1997), 8; *FTSR* 12 (1998), 8; *FTSR* 12 (1999), 9; *FTSR* 12 (2000), 7; Okáli, Gabrielová, Hlavatý, Morvay and Outrata, 'Slovakia in 2000', 220; Jakoby, 'Zahraničný obchod', pp. 157–158.

Figure 8: Slovakias export and import in billion Slovak Crowns

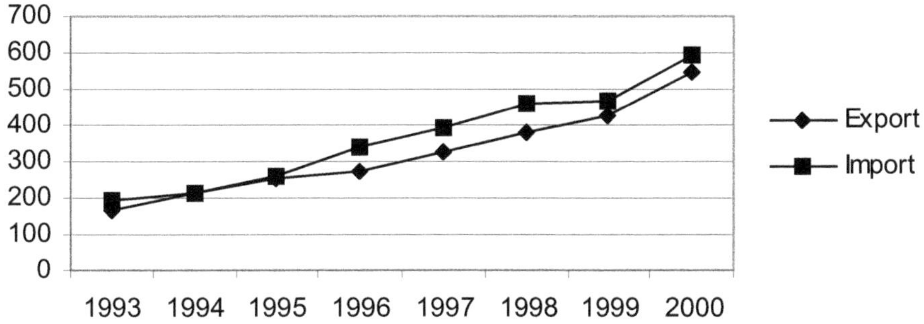

Sources: *Foreign trade in Slovak Republic (FTSR)*, 12 (1993), 9; *FTSR* 12 (1994), 8; *FTSR* 12 (1995), 9; *FTSR* 12 (1996), 7; *FTSR* 12 (1997), 8; *FTSR* 12 (1998), 8; *FTSR* 12 (1999), 9; *FTSR* 12 (2000), 7; Okáli, Gabrielová, Hlavatý, Morvay and Outrata, 'Slovakia in 2000', 220; Jakoby, 'Zahraničný obchod', pp. 157–158.

Figure 9: Trade balance to GDP ratio in Slovakia in %

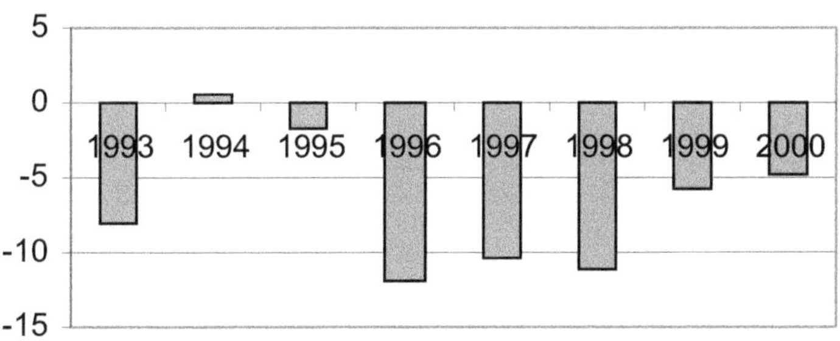

Sources: *Foreign trade in Slovak Republic (FTSR)*, 12 (1993), 9; *FTSR* 12 (1994), 8; *FTSR* 12 (1995), 9; *FTSR* 12 (1996), 7; *FTSR* 12 (1997), 8; *FTSR* 12 (1998), 8; *FTSR* 12 (1999), 9; *FTSR* 12 (2000), 7; Okáli, Gabrielová, Hlavatý, Morvay and Outrata, 'Slovakia in 2000', 220; Jakoby, 'Zahraničný obchod', pp. 157–158.

Figure 10: Structural qualitative changes of Czechoslovaks export in 1921/1923–1937/1938

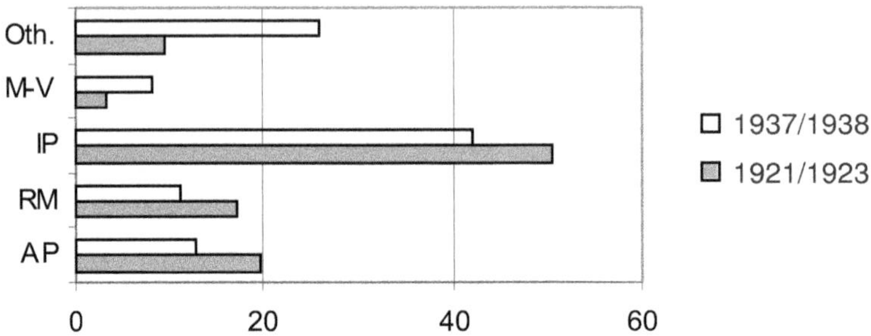

Source: M. C. Kaser and E. A. Radice, *The Economic History of Eastern Europe 1919–1975* (Oxford: 1985), p. 471.

Note: Oth. = others, M-V = machines and vehicles, IP = industrial products, RM = raw materials, AP = agricultural products.

Figure 11: Structural qualitative changes of exports of central european transition states (Share of branches with different degree of technological intensity in %)

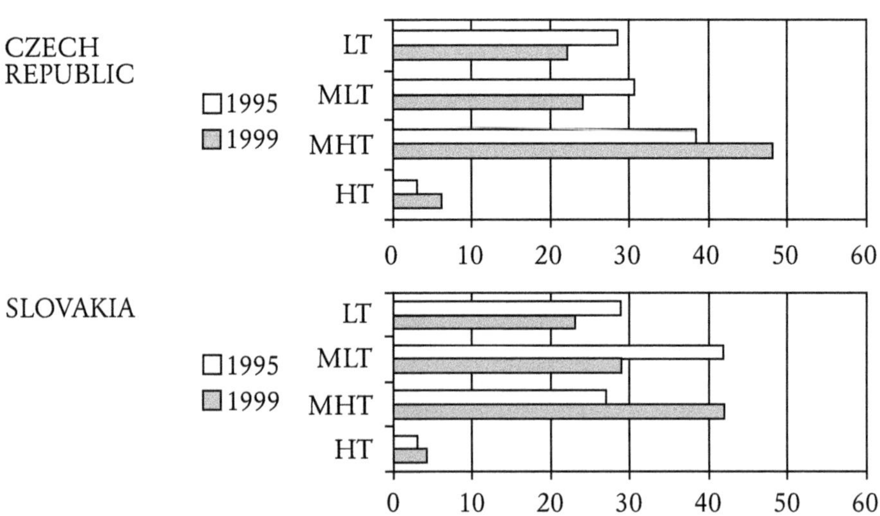

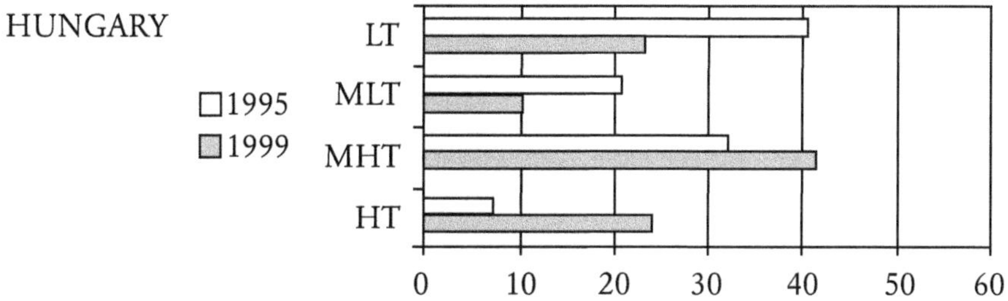

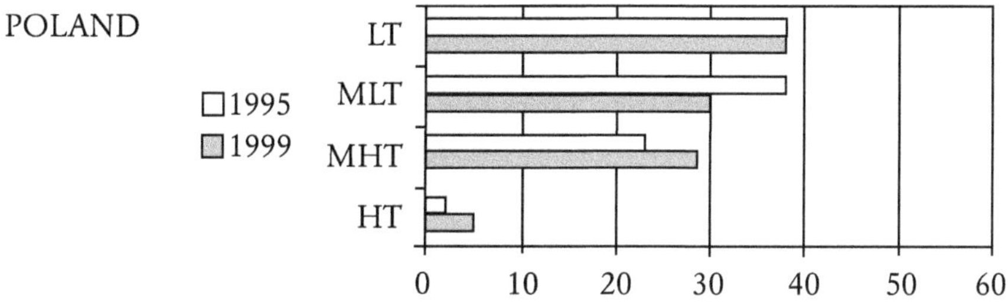

Source: A. Kadeřábková and M. Srholec,'Intenzita a kvalitativní charakteristika strukturálních změn v tranzitivních ekonomikách,' *Politická ekonomie* 4 (2001), 531.

Note: Degree of technological intesity: HT – high technological intensity, MHT- middle high technolog. intensity, MLT – middle low technological intensity, LT – low technological intensity

Slovakia's enterprise sector in the economic globalisation process

Industry

The entry of foreign firms and multinational corporations to Slovakia started shortly after 1989, while Czechoslovakia still existed. The interest of foreign investors was great but also cautious. This was enhanced by the complications of political development. Slovakia needed from foreign investors mainly compensation for the big losses resulting from the collapse of the armaments industry, by strengthening sectors producing finished goods. The clearest success in this respect was the development of the automobile industry, thanks mainly to one of the biggest automobile concerns in the world – Volkswagen. It succeeded in establishing itself in both parts of former Czechoslovakia, and this became the basis for the company's expansion into the markets of eastern Europe and Russia with potential capacity of 30 million automobiles a year. In Slovakia VW took over and modernised industrial companies, and by 2000 production had risen to 180,800 automobiles. The amount of investments grew to 1.4 billion DEM and investment of another 0.3 billion Euros was realised after 2000. The income in 2000 reached 4 billion DEM, while the share of exports on income was 99.6%. In this way VW became the biggest producer and exporter in Slovak industry with a 16% share of total Slovak exports, taking over the first position from the enterprises of heavy industry. The problem was high import demand and a focus on completion of imported parts. Since 1998 there has been a move towards more comprehensive mass production.[22] The activities of automobile companies and especially VW became one of the key phenomena of the transformation of most central European transition countries. In the Czech Republic VW bought the automobile department of Skoda from the state and in Hungary the offshoot of VW – Audi – built a new automobile enterprise. In 2000 the former German – now international – corporation VW produced a total of 689,000 automobiles in the Czech Republic, Slovakia and Hungary, and in all three countries it had become the most important exporter. In Poland an automobile subsidiary of the company Daewoo was established with an investment of 1.4 billion USD, and in Slovenia the French company Renault.[23] The automotive industry was the chief industrial branch in the central European transition states also after 2000. The older investors widened their investments and other leading automobile makers came – PSA, Peugeot – Citroen, Toyota, Hyundai, Kia Motors, MAN, Steyer – with tens of their sub-suppliers. New automobile factories were built by companies such as Peugeot – Citroen in the western Slovak town of Trnava and Kia Motors together with Hyundai Mobis in the northern Slovak town of •ilina with planned costs about 2.5 billion USD. PSA in Trnava started their production in 2005 in a factory with a future capacity of 300,000 automobiles a year, while PSA agreed to start a new factory building in Trnava with a capacity of 150,000 automobiles. After the new factory is finished in Trnava and Žilina the Slovak automotive industry together with the capacity of VW (which has grown to 280,000 automobiles), should by 2008 achieve a total annual production capacity of 1.2 million vehicles, and thereby become the greatest automobile producer per thousand inhabitants in the world followed by Belgium and the Czech Republic.[24]

Apart from Volkswagen a few more factories were built to produce components for the automobile industry. They are oriented to supplying VW or towards exports. These factories have been built mainly by subsidiaries of German companies, for example INA Wälzlager Schaffer Herzogenaurach and ZF Passau. Another German company, Sachs, invested 50 million DEM and also attracted the company Boge from the Siemens group. In 2001 Sachs merged with ZF Fridrichshafen. Together, they control firms in different countries with 55,000 employees and a turnover of 17 billion DEM. American companies also had their share in investments. The new investments of VW and particularly the construction of new automobile factories for PSA, Peugeot-Citroen and Hyundai-Kia have attracted many other sub-suppliers to come to Slovakia, such as Leoni (a German maker of electrical components for the automotive industry with four factories in Slovakia), the Belgian group Punch International, Jonson Controlos, Continental Teves, Osram, and also important southern Korean and other sub-suppliers. Foreign investment has also expanded the possibilities for domestic suppliers. The foreign investors contributed to the employment of 22,000–55,000 people in the automobile industry in 1993–2003.[25]

The investments in electrical engineering and electronics have great importance, especially for the progress of technology and restructuring. Mainly German, Japanese and American companies are engaged here. The German Siemens and subsidiaries of Japanese companies invested in the production of cable technology, which has a long tradition in Slovakia: the American firm Delphi built a factory for about a thousand employees. Two American corporations with companies in three continents – Emerson Electric Co. St. Louis and ON Semiconductor from the concern SCI LIC Phoenix, the member of the SCG Holding Corporation group – have already invested 145 million USD in two factories for semiconductors and other components: both factories have started their own technical development. The Belgian electronic company Punch International NV, with production in eight countries, built two factories with an investment of 21.5 million USD. The Sony company of Slovakia has started three operations to produce televisions and transformers, with investments reaching 85 million USD. Slovak Matshushita built factories in three towns to produce VCRs and other electronic equipment. The company Molex, the biggest independent producer of connectors in the world, is establishing its third factory with an investment of 75 million USD. It should become the largest of the company's 50 factories, which are distributed over 20 countries.[26] Other developments in foreign investment in electrical engineering since 2001 has been overwhelmingly influenced by sharp growth in the automotive industry and the sales of consumer electronics. The majority of new sub-suppliers are electro-engineering companies. In the field of consumer electronics new firms emerged, together with the expansion of such older investors as Sony and Matshushita: for example, the Dutch-Korean producer of monitors LG Philips Displays and the southern Korean Samsung. The Samsung company is building its largest European production, service, and developmental centre of electronics in the southern Slovak town of Galanta. The concentration not only on production but also on the development of new products is a positive factor because for that the company is planning to employ hundreds of workers. Especially because of foreign investments the volume of production in electrical engineering and electronics grew in the years 1999–2004 from about 1.1 billion to 2.8 billion Euros.[27]

Although all Slovak governments proclaimed the need for preferential development of technologically progressive industries, in practice they continued to support primarily the sectors based on imported raw materials: the metallurgy, petrochemical, gas and power industries. From 1998 the reforming government forced a transformation of these industries through privatisation by foreign strategic partners. The greatest event in the process of internationalisation of the Slovak economy in 2000 was the entry of the American strategic partner UC Steel Group into the biggest Slovak metallurgical works Východoslovenské Železiarne (East Slovakia Iron Works). The strategic partner bought the controlled package of shares and promised investments in the amount of 700 million USD. The huge aluminum works Závody SNP, which was refurbished in the mid 1990s with a loan of the World bank of 80 million USD, found a strategic partner in the Norwegian company Hydroaluminium Products and Systems. It took a majority share in the key subsidiary of the aluminum works Slovalco with basic capital of 150 million USD. The prominent petrochemical works Slovnaft entered a partnership with the leading Hungarian petrochemical company MOL and they are planning joint expansion into the refineries of central Europe and Russia. The only Slovak company extracting oil, Nafta Gbely, has sold 34% of its shares to the German gas company RWE Gas. Privatisation of the great gas transfer and processing company Slovenský Plynárenský Podnik was finished. Privatisation of the power industry has also been realised. Companies in these areas were the leading Slovak investors abroad.[28]

Foreign capital in a greater or smaller amount also penetrated other areas such as the wood and paper, cement, chemical and food processing industries. The international corporations Assi Domän, SCA Mölnycke and Austrian Neusiedler AG were successfully engaged in paper processing. The Italian family Zerbi built a new paper processing factory. In the area of wood processing, a subsidiary of Swedish Sweedwood Holding BV from the IKEA group built a complex of furniture factories, the biggest in Slovakia with a production value of 98 million USD. In the production of sawmill semi-finished products the most successful is the German family company Rettenmeier. In the textile and clothing industry a few foreign firms were taken over by other foreign firms. For example, the co-operative Dutch-Slovak company made strategic investments with credit from the Dutch government. The modernisation of traditional production of synthetic fibres was successful. Two international groups – Rhodia Industrial Yarns and Nylstar – invested 53 million USD and opened two factories. The first one became the biggest in the network of the Rhodia company with a 36% share in its turnover; and the factory of the group Nylstar achieved 50% in the overall turnover of the firm's 10 companies. The big investments into the development of fibres are also remarkable. In food processing the leading companies are RAJO and Coca-Cola, with investments of 67 million USD.[29] Foreign capital took over firms in the food industry, and much of the beer-brewing capacity too. Most breweries were taken over by Dutch Heineken and southern African giant South Africa Breweries Ltd., which also took over the

Czech breweries. One of the sectors where domestic Slovak capital was involved quite successfully in globalisation was the pharmaceutical industry. In 2005 the biggest Slovak and Czech pharmaceutical companies merged and formed the central European concern Zentiva, which then expanded into the Balkans.[30]

Banking, insurance industry, domestic trade, telecommunication

The process of privatisation and globalisation accelerated in the banking sector. In the period from June 1999 to June 2001 the shareholding of the state in banks was lowered from 59% to 13%. The branches of foreign banks and financial institutions with foreign investment represented the private sector until the year 1999. Austrian capital dominated this sphere. The government intervened in 1998 to recover key banks and offered them to foreign investors. The main privatisation events were the sale of the two biggest institutions, Všeobecná úverová banka (VÚB) and Slovenská Sporitel'ňa. The Italian group Intesta BCI, formed from Banca Intesa and Banca Commerciale Italiana, took control of the VÚB for 550 million Euros. The Italian group also took part in privatisation in Hungary and Croatia. Another Italian group, Unicredito Italiano with shareholdings in more transition countries, is also involved in Slovak banking. It established a subsidiary company, UniBank in Bratislava. The Austrian Erste Bank der Österreichischen Sparkassen acquired the Slovenská sporitel'ňa by buying 87% of its capital after taking over the Česká sporitelňa (Czech Savings Bank). The Belgian KBC became the strongest in the Czech Republic. It also took over the Československá obchodná banka which functions in both parts of the former Czechoslovakia. In Slovakia, Austrian capital has also prevailed in the privatisation of key banks. Apart from Erste Bank, it is represented by, for example, Volksbank and Bank Austria, which are found in different parts of central Europe. Austrian and Belgian capital gained a favourable position in the banking sector of the transition countries in spite of the fact that from the global point of view it played a minor role. Among the CEFTA countries privatisation of banks started in Hungary first, then in the Czech and Slovak Republics, while Poland and Slovenia have lagged

Figure 12: Share of domestic and foreign capital in Slovak banking (June 2001)

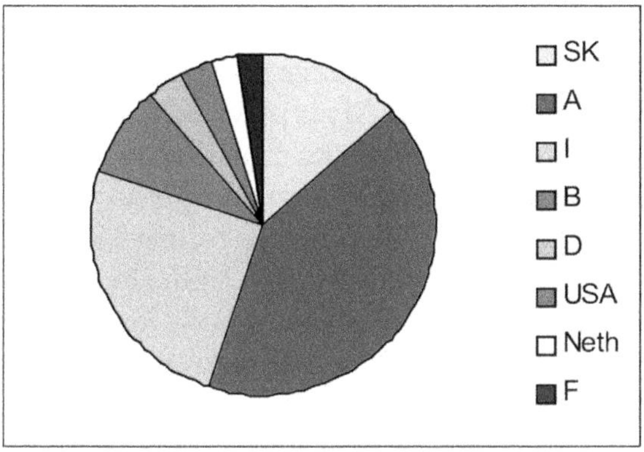

Figure 13: Share of domestic and foreign capital in Slovak insurance companies (September 2001)

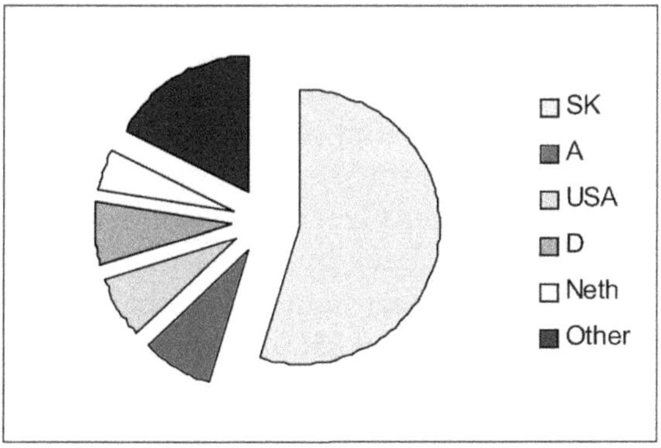

Sources Figure 12 and 13: 'Vývoj bankového sektora', *Trend* 39 (2001), 22; 'Privatizácia poisťovní', *Trend* 39 (2001), 23.

behind.[31] In the years 2001–2005 subsidiary companies were formed in Slovakia by the French Bank Dexia, the Hungarian OTP Bank and the German HVB Bank. In November 2005 after the amalgamation of the Italian group UniCredit and German HVB Bank into a common European concern UniCredit Group their bank subsidiaries in Slovakia UniBank and HVB Bank Slovakia also merged. Their common bank with assets of 2.25 billion Euros became the fifth greatest monetary institution of Slovakia amongst the ten independent banks. In the Slovak banking industry there are five branches of foreign banks. The last one to be established was the branch of Portuguese Banco Mais.[32]

Privatisation also progressed in the Slovak insurance industry. In the 1990s subsidiaries of several leading insurance companies of global character were established in Slovakia. After privatisation of the greatest Slovak insurance company Slovenská poist'ovňa by the German Allianz, foreign capital also gained almost complete control of this segment of the financial sphere. The pension reform, started by the reformist government in the years 2003–2006, split the retirement insurance into three so-called pillars. The second and third pillar were opened to domestic and foreign private insurance companies. A great share in the retirement insurance was gained by the Swiss bank Credit Suisse, merged with the insurance company Winterthur since 2006, German Allianz, Dutch ING and Aegon, as well as Italian Generali. Equity funds are a completely new phenomenon in the Slovak financial market, developing only in the last few years. The influence of foreign capital, especially Luxemburg, Belgian and American, in these funds was about 30% in autumn 2001.[33]

Dozens of global and smaller foreign retail companies have penetrated the network of the Slovak retail trade since 1989. The biggest department store chain in the former Czechoslovakia was taken over by the American K-Mart and later by the British Tesco. After the entrance of international department-store chains, the building of shopping centres with areas over 2500 m^2 started. Apart from Tesco the greatest activity in this direction has come from the French Carrefour, the German Kaufland, Lidl and Baumax, the Austrian Billa, the Dutch Hypernova and some other companies. On the other hand, the network of domestic cooperative stores has kept a dominant share of the market. Since 2000 the building of big shopping-entertainment centres by the Dutch group Rodam co. Europe, the Canadian-Hungarian group TriGránit, the Swedish Ikea, the Irish company Ballymore Properties and other investors has made great progress.[34]

After 1998 the area for the entrance of foreign capital into telecommunications has increased, especially with the privatisation process in the state company Slovenské telekomunikácie. A company Slovak Telekom was formed through privatisation. Subsidiaries of international corporations have played a pioneering role in the development of completely new communications media. Globtel, a member of the Orange Group, and Slovak Eurotel control the mobile-telephone net. In June 2005 Slovak Eurotel was taken over by another supranational company, T-Mobil.The cable TV network is controlled fully by the global group of Dutch origin United Pan-Europe Communications N.V. (UPC). This company bought the shares of all its competitors for 70 million USD in 1999. They included the company Slovenská káblová televízia. The mentioned companies gained control of about 90% of market volume in all fields of telecommunication and mobile networks, as well as in the sphere of providing Internet in Slovakia. Lately other companies have entered the market, for example the Norwegian Telenor Networks or the supranational central European group GTS Central Europe: a third mobile operator is also ready to enter.[35]

Conclusions

Dismantling of the long-established COMECON (RVHP) market was very important for the economic development of the post-communist countries in the 1990s and their subsequent integration into the economic relations of the developed market economies. Economic internationalisation of the transition countries after 1989 was achieved especially through reorientation of foreign trade relations and through the entrance of different forms of foreign capital. Internationalisation was essential to the further economic development of the post-Communist countries. This was valid especially for the small transition countries of central Europe with open economies and economic areas, which became even smaller on average after the break-up of Czechoslovakia, Yugoslavia and the Soviet Union. According to relevant indexes the country with the most open economy was the Slovak Republic. Unlike the processes of globalisation in other parts of the world, the economic internationalisation in central Europe was accompanied by great changes in the political systems and ownership relations. There was a complicated and often controversial privatisation of state-owned property. Its results had a determining influence on the circumstances for the entrance of foreign capital.

Another characteristic phenomenon of the situation in the transition countries after 1998 was a set of negative impacts of deglobalisation and internationalisation on their social-economic development. In particular, there were falls in the levels of economic development and GDP, together with the appearance of inflation, which was not known before, unemployment and deepening of social differences. As after the break of the Habsburg Monarchy, the central European countries had to go through restructuring and reconstruction of their economies as a result of the loss of their traditional markets and under the pressure of demanding competition in the markets of western countries. The movement to restructure the economy in all these countries included modernisation and new building as a result of the initiative of foreign capital. In both the 1920s and the 1990s the outward effect of the initial fall and following structural changes was stagnation of the overall indexes of economic development at the starting-point level, that is on the levels reached in 1913 and 1989. However, the position of the different central European countries has changed. While Poland had more dynamic development in the 1990s than in the 1920s, Slovakia and especially the Czech Republic were less successful in the 1990s. Hungary experienced similar development of its indexes in the two periods.

Table 8: Industrial output index in the Czech Lands, Hungary, Slovakia, Poland and Austria, the volumes of 1913, 1929 and 1938 compared (year 1913 = 100%)

Year	Czech Lands	Hungary	Slovakia	Poland	Austria
1929	141	112	108	91	98
1938	135	128	123	95	77

Sources: Z. Landau and J. Tomaszewski, *Zarys historii gospodarczej Polski 1918–1939* (Warszawa: 1971), pp. 59, 289–290; W. Fischer (ed.), *Handbuch der europäischen Wirtschafts-und sozialgeschichte* (Stuttgart: Klett-Cotta, 1987), vol. 6, pp. 543, 796; J. Faltus and V. Průcha, *Prehľad hospodárskeho vývoja Slovenska 1918–1945* (Bratislava: Vydavateľstvo politickej literatúry, 1969), pp. 14, 25, 43, 287; *Statistická ročenka Republiky československé* (1938), p. 61; V. Lacina, 'Dynamika průmyslového rozvoje v meziválečném Československu', *Český časopis historický* 2 (1996), p. 287.

Note: Values for individual countries are calculated on the basis of estimates.

Table 9: Development of industrial production in transition countries of central Europe (year 1989 = 100)

	1990	1991	1992	1993	1994	1995	1996	1997	1998	2000
CZ	96.3	72.8	67.0	63.4	64.9	68.7	71.9	76.2	80.0	84.8
H	95.5	78.0	70.4	73.2	79.9	80.7	83.3	91.7	100.8	112.9
PL	75.8	66.8	69.4	73.8	85.1	86.4	95.1	106.1	111.8	118.5
SK	95.5	78.7	67.6	60.4	64.3	67.8	68.7	70.8	68.0	69.1
SLO *	89.5	87.6	86.9	97.1	106.5	102.0	101.0	101.0	103.7	103.7

Sources: J. Borovský, 'Približuje transformačný proces slovenskú ekonomiku Európskej únii?', *Ekonomický časopis* 3 (2001), p. 450; I. Rendek, 'Slovinský export a nástroje na jeho podporu', *Ekonomický časopis* 6 (2000), p. 837.

Note: * previous year = 100.

We can say that from the many factors influencing the process of economic internationalisation of the central European transition countries after the year 1989 the following had a key role: the initial economic situation (structure and technical level of the economy, dependence on traditional markets, currency stability), the character and depth of changes in political systems, the pace and form of the transition from a centrally planned to a free-market economy, the strategy of economic policies especially in the currency area, foreign trade and privatisation, the concrete progress and results of privatisation, the progress and the depth of structural changes, overall economic stability, the level of stability in politics, the strategy of foreign policy in relation to western economic and military structures and the pace of the process of entry into the EU. We have documented the concrete results achieved in internationalisation of the economy in these countries at least on a few indexes – those of structural changes in foreign trade, the development of the main streams of foreign investments and the share of the stock of foreign direct investments in GDP.

The negative factors of globalisation, such as the exploitation of cheap labour by investors without greater investment in technologies, the elimination of competition and technical research and development in the country of capital entrance or 'brain drain' are seen also in the transition countries of central Europe. Since the end of the 1990s the character of investments started to change partially.

In Hungary and Czech Republic and later in Poland and Slovakia the share of top technologies grew, investments oriented not only to production but also to technical development appeared and centres of information technology started to be built. However, in comparison with countries such as Finland or Ireland the central European transition states still noticeably lag. The dependence on internationalisation and foreign investment is different in each CEFTA country. The greater part of the factories in Slovenia are being engaged in demanding markets through their own technologies. Although the Czech firm Skoda needed technological help from Volkswagen, it kept its identity. On the contrary, the majority of the industrial sectors of Slovakia, Hungary and Poland are penetrating world markets as part of international corporations. However, as a result of lack of sufficient domestic capital and technology, most of these countries are dependent on further deepening of integration, which is why the economic policy sphere supports it.

1 M. Godfrey, 'The struggle against unemployment: Medium- term policy option for transitional economies', *International Labour Review* 1 (1995), pp. 6–8; J. Borovský, 'Približuje transformačný proces slovenskú ekonomiku Európskej únii?', *Ekonomický časopis* 3 (2001), pp. 448–451.

2 J. Svejnar, 'CSFR: a solid foundation', in R. Porter (ed.), *Economic transformation in central Europe: A progress report* (London: 1993), pp. 29–33.

3 Ministry of Privatisation of Slovak Republic, 'Development of privatisation', State in December 1999: www.privatiz.gov.sk; Fund of National Property of Slovak Republic, State in December 1999: www.natfund.gov.sk.

4 Godfrey, 'Transitional economies', pp. 6–8.

5 Miroslav Beblavý, 'Monetárna politika', in Anton Marcinčin and Miroslav Beblavý (eds.), *Hospodárska politika na Slovensku 1990–1999* (Bratislava: Slovenská spoločnost' pre zahraničnú politiku, 2000), pp. 97, 109–111.

6 Top Trend 1997; M. Jacoby, 'Zahraničný obchod', in Marcinčin and Beblavý (eds.), *Politika na Slovensku 1990–1999*, pp. 145–146.

7 Ministry of Privatisation of Slovak Republic, 'Public Register of Privatised Property', State in June 1999; A. Marcinčin, 'Privatizácia', in Marcinčin and Beblavý (eds.), *Politika na Slovensku 1990–1999*, pp. 291–296.

8 J. Tóth, 'Exchange rate – is it really overvalued', *Slovak capital and money market report* 5 (1999), pp. 35–37.

9 T. Bucha, 'Eximbanka zefektivní pomoc podnikatel'om', *Národná obroda* 304 (1999), 5; M. Jacoby and I. Krautmannová, 'Zahraničný obchod', in *Sl'uby a realita – Slovenská ekonomika 1995–1998* (Bratislava: 1998), pp. 75–81.

10 Ministry of Privatisation of Slovak Republic, 'Development of privatisation', State in December 1999: www.privatiz.gov.sk; Ministry of Privatisation of Slovak Republic, 'Public Register of Privatised Property', State in June 1999; Anton Marcinčin, *Zákon o strategických podnikoch: Krok spät'?*, (Bratislava: Slovenská spoločnosť pre zahraničnú politiku, 1997), pp. 9–12.
11 Ivan Okáli, Herta Gabrielová, Egon Hlavatý, Karol Morvay and Richard Outrata, 'Economic Development of Slovakia in 2000', *Ekonomický časopis* 2 (2001), pp. 195–197.
12 Tóth, 'Is it really overvalued', pp. 35–37; 'Zahraničný obchod roku 2000', *Trend* 6 (2001), p. 8.
13 Vilma Juríčková, Jaroslav Vokoun and Mária Kačírková, 'Zmeny v správaní podnikovej sféry v priebehu transformácie ekonomiky Slovenskej republiky', *Ekonomický časopis* 1 (2005), pp. 57–61.
14 Ivan Okáli, Karol Frank and Herta Gabrielová, 'Hospodársky vývoj Slovenska v roku 2004', *Ekonomický časopis* 5 (2005), pp. 452–457; 'Vybrané ukazovatele hospodárskeho a menového vývoja Slovenskej republiky', *Biatec* 12 (2005), pp. 32–33.
15 Okáli, Frank and Gabrielová, 'Vývoj Slovenska v roku 2004', pp. 452–457; Soňa Ferenčíková and Marek Vážan, 'Nové trendy vo vývoji priamych zahraničných investícií v krajinách strednej a východnej Európy', *Hospodárske rozhl'ady* 4 (2005), pp. 523–524.
16 V. Baláž and A. M. Williams, 'Capital mobility in transition countries of central Europe', *Ekonomický časopis* 2 (2001), pp. 252–253.
17 Ibid., pp. 254–260; R. Češka, 'Privatisation in the Czech Rupublic', *Privatisation in the central and eastern Europe* 5 (1995), pp. 108–120; L. Csépi and E. Lukács, 'Privatisation in Hungary', *Privatisation in the central and eastern Europe* 5 (1995), pp. 180–197; I. Rendek, 'Slovinský export a nástroje na jeho podporu', *Ekonomický časopis* 6 (2000), pp. 836–839.
18 Kamel Djebari, 'Vplyv zahraničných investícií na tranzitívne ekonomiky nových členov Európskej únie', *Hospodárské rozhl'ady* 1 (2005), pp. 95–99.
19 A. Hošková, 'Impact of foreign direct investment on the economy of Slovakia', *Biatec* 9 (2001), pp. 35–36; Ferenčíková and Vážan, 'V krajinách strednej a východnej Európy', pp. 522–527.
20 R. Outrata, 'Foreign trade potential of central european countries and their strategic aiming at European Union integration', *Ekonomický časopis* 1 (2000), pp. 4–9.
21 Igor Melíšek, 'Vývoj a zmeny štruktúry zahraničného obchodu Slovenskej republiky', *Hospodárske rozhl'ady* 3 (2005), pp. 295–297.
22 'Volkswagen Slovakia a. s. Bratislava', *Trend* 18 (2001), 11; 'Top 2000', *Trend* 24 (2001), p. 4.
23 'Volkswagen Slovakia a. s. Bratislava', *Trend* 18 (2001), p. 11.
24 'Automobilový priemysel', *Trend* 49 (2005), p. 28.
25 *Trend* 4 (2001), p. 6; *Trend* 21 (2001), p. 11; *Trend* 24 (2001), p. 15; *Trend* 39 (2001), p. 8; 'Elektrotechnika pre automobily', *Trend* 44 (2005), p. 26; J. Uhrík, 'Slovenský automobilový priemysel v ére globalizácie', *Hospodárske rozhl'ady* 4 (2000), pp. 409–411.

26 *Trend* 16 (2001), p. 9; *Trend* 18 (2001), p. 6; *Trend* 21 (2001), p. 14; *Trend* 25 (2001), p. 18.
27 'Nové smery elektrotechnického priemyslu', *Trend* 50 (2005), p. 42.
28 *Trend* 1 (2001), p. 4; *Trend* 13 (2001), p. 11; *Trend* 24 (2001), p. 16.
29 *Trend* 18 (2001), p. 13; *Trend* 23 (2001), p. 2; *Trend* 24 (2001), p. 7; *Trend* 39 (2001), p. 8; 'Piliarsky priemysel', *Trend* 46 (2005), p. 33.
30 'Vývoz kapitálu', *Trend*, p. 44 (2005), p. 24.
31 'Bankové úvery', *Trend* 21 (2001), p. 2; 'Vývoj bankového sektora', *Trend* 39 (2001), p. 22; Baláž and Williams, 'Transition countries of central Europe', pp. 250–252.
32 'Fúzie bánk', *Trend* 46 (2005), p. 38.
33 'Privatizácia poist'ovní', *Trend* 39 (2001), p. 6; Martina Dubová, 'Pension funds in the central and eastern european coutries. Pension reform in the Slovak republic', *Hospodárske rozhl'ady* 2 (2005), pp. 160–164.
34 'Vnútorný obchod Slovenska', *Trend* 18 (2001), p. 12; 'Shoping centrá', *Trend* 50 (2005), p. 31.
35 *Trend* 4 (2001), p. 8; *Trend* 23 (2001), p. 6; 'Noví internetoví poskytovatelia', *Trend* 49 (2005), p. 36.

Contributors

ISABELLE CASSIERS is senior research fellow at the Belgian National Foundation for Scientific Research and professor of economics at the Catholic University of Louvain, Louvain-la-Neuve, Belgium.

THOMAS DAVID is assistant professor in economic and social history at the University of Lausanne, Switzerland.

HERMAN DE JONG is associate professor in economic history at the University of Groningen and director of the Dutch-Flemish Research School and Research Institute for Economic and Social History N.W. Posthumus Instituut, the Netherlands.

HANS OTTO FRØLAND is professor in contemporary European history at Norwegian University of Science and Technology, Trøndheim, Norway.

OLA HONNINGDAL GRYTTEN is professor in economic history at the Norwegian School of Economics and Business Administration in Bergen, Norway, and editor of the Scandinavian Economic History Review.

PATRICK HALBEISEN, Ph.D. in economic history at the University of Zurich, is the archivist of the Swiss National Bank in Zurich.

L'UDOVÍT HALLON is a researcher at the Department of History of Sciences and Technology of the Historical Institute of the Slovakian Academy of Sciences in Bratislava, Slovakia.

ANNE-LISE HEAD-KÖNIG is professor emerita in economic history at the Department of Economic History of the University of Geneva.

IVAN JAKUBEC is professor in economic and social history at the Charles University in Prague, Institute of Economic and Social History, Czech Republic.

GUDMUNDUR JONSSON is professor of history at the University of Iceland, Reykjavik, Iceland.

HEIN A.M. KLEMANN is professor at the History Department of Erasmus University Rotterdam, the Netherlands.

OLLE KRANTZ is professor emeritus of economic history at Umeå University, Sweden.

EVEN LANGE is professor of contemporary history at the University of Oslo, Norway.

PHILIPPE LEDENT is teaching assistant at the Catholic University of Louvain (IRES), Belgium.

ANDRÉ MACH is senior lecturer in comparative political economy at the Institute of Political and International Studies, University of Lausanne, Switzerland.

MARIA EUGÉNIA MATA is associate professor at the Faculdade de Economia, Universidade Nova de Lisboa, Portugal, and Alfred Chandler Jr. International Scholar 2007, at Harvard Business School.

MARGRIT MÜLLER is senior lecturer at the Institute for Empirical Research in Economics of the University of Zurich, Switzerland.

TIMO MYLLYNTAUS is professor of Finnish history at the University of Turku, Finland.

HELGE PHARO is professor of international history at the University of Oslo, Norway.

JAN PIETER SMITS is lecturer in economic history at the University of Groningen and research co-ordinator of the N.W. Posthumus Instituut, the Netherlands.

SIGURDUR SNAEVARR is Chief Economist of the City of Reykjavik, Iceland.

TOBIAS STRAUMANN is lecturer in economic history and research fellow at the Institute for Empirical Research in Economics of the University of Zurich, Switzerland.

LARS SVENSSON is associate professor in economic history at Lund University, Sweden.

KERSTI ULLENHAG is professor emerita of economic history at the Department of Economic History, Uppsala University, Sweden.

Jonathan Zeitlin / Philippe Pochet (eds.)
with Lars Magnusson

The Open Method of Co-ordination in Action

The European Employment and Social Inclusion Strategies
Second Printing

Bruxelles, Bern, Berlin, Frankfurt am Main, New York, Oxford, Wien, 2005.
511 pp., num. tables and graphs
Work and Society. Vol. 49
General Editor: Philippe Pochet, in collaboration with the National Institute of Working Life – SALTSA
ISBN 978-90-5201-280-3 / US-ISBN 978-0-8204-6645-3 pb.
sFr. 65.– / € 44.80 / €** 46.10 / € 41.90 / £ 29.30 / US-$ 49.95*

* includes VAT – valid for Germany ** includes VAT – valid for Austria

No development in European integration has aroused greater interest or greater controversy in recent years than the Open Method of Co-ordination (OMC), which has become an increasingly broadly applied instrument of EU governance since its invention as part of the «Lisbon Strategy» in 2000. Yet it is widely agreed that the debates surrounding the OMC suffer from a serious empirical deficit. This book, based on an international research network organised by the University of Wisconsin-Madison, the Observatoire social européen, and the SALTSA Programme, focuses on two highly developed OMC processes, the European Employment and Social Inclusion Strategies, concentrating on their operation and influence at national and subnational levels. It comprises a combination of national and comparative studies, covering eight countries (Denmark, France, Germany, Ireland, Italy, the Netherlands, Sweden, and the United Kingdom) and four transversal themes (hard and soft law, participation, gender equality, activation). These studies are framed by a historical overview of the OMC's place in the construction of Social Europe, and by a synthetic conclusion, which assesses the available evidence on the OMC in action, and proposes a reflexive reform strategy for realising its theoretical promise as a new mode of EU governance.

With contributions by: Lars Magnusson – Jonathan Zeitlin – Philippe Pochet – David M. Trubek – Louise G. Trubek – Kerstin Jacobsson – Maurizio Ferrera – Stefano Sacchi – Jelle Visser – Christine Erhel – Lou Mandin – Bruno Palier – Milena Büchs – Dawid Friedrich – Kenneth A. Armstrong – Rory O'Donnell – Brian Moss – Caroline de la Porte – Jill Rubery – Jean-Claude Barbier.

PETER LANG
Bern · Berlin · Bruxelles · Frankfurt am Main · New York · Oxford · Wien